■ Religion and Human Rights

Religion and Human Rights

An Introduction

EDITED BY

John Witte, Jr.

AND

M. Christian Green

UNIVERSITY PRESS

OXFORD
UNIVERSITY PRESS

Oxford University Press, Inc., publishes works that further
Oxford University's objective of excellence
in research, scholarship, and education.

Oxford New York
Auckland Cape Town Dar es Salaam Hong Kong Karachi
Kuala Lumpur Madrid Melbourne Mexico City Nairobi
New Delhi Shanghai Taipei Toronto

With offices in
Argentina Austria Brazil Chile Czech Republic France Greece
Guatemala Hungary Italy Japan Poland Portugal Singapore
South Korea Switzerland Thailand Turkey Ukraine Vietnam

Published by Oxford University Press, Inc.
198 Madison Avenue, New York, New York 10016
www.oup.com

Library of Congress Cataloging-in-Publication Data
Religion and human rights: an introduction/edited by
John Witte, Jr. and M. Christian Green.
p. cm.
Includes index.
ISBN 978-0-19-973344-6 (pbk.: alk. paper)—ISBN 978-0-19-973345-3
(hardcover: alk. paper) 1. Human rights—Religious aspects. 2. Religions.
3. Religion and politics. I. Witte, John, Jr. 1959– II. Green, M. Christian
(Martha Christian), 1968–
BL65.H78R43 2011
201.'723—dc22 2011007070

1 3 5 7 9 8 6 4 2
Printed in the United States of America
on acid-free paper

CONTENTS

Foreword — *vii*
MARTIN E. MARTY

Preface and Acknowledgements — *xiii*
Contributors — *xvii*

Introduction — 3
JOHN WITTE, JR. AND M. CHRISTIAN GREEN

PART ONE ■ Human Rights and Religious Traditions

1 A Jewish Theory of Human Rights — 27
DAVID NOVAK

2 Christianity and Human Rights — 42
NICHOLAS P. WOLTERSTORFF

3 Islam and Human Rights — 56
ABDULLAHI AHMED AN-NA'IM

4 Hinduism and Human Rights — 71
WERNER MENSKI

5 Confucianism and Human Rights — 87
JOSEPH C. W. CHAN

6 Buddhism and Human Rights — 103
SALLIE B. KING

7 Indigenous Religion and Human Rights — 119
RONALD NIEZEN

8 Religion, Human Rights, and Public Reason: The Role and Limits of a Secular Rationale — 135
DAVID LITTLE

PART TWO ■ Religion and Modern Human Rights Issues

9 The Phases and Functions of Freedom of Conscience — 155
STEVEN D. SMITH

10 Religion and Freedom of Choice 170
PAUL M. TAYLOR

11 Religion and Freedom of Expression 188
CAROLYN EVANS

12 Religion, Equality, and Non-Discrimination 204
NAZILA GHANEA

13 Religion and Freedom of Association 218
NATAN LERNER

14 The Right to Self-Determination of Religious Communities 236
JOHAN D. VAN DER VYVER

15 Permissible Limitations on the Freedom of Religion or Belief 254
T. JEREMY GUNN

16 The Right to Religious and Moral Freedom 269
MICHAEL J. PERRY

17 Keeping Faith: Reconciling Women's Human Rights and Religion 281
MADHAVI SUNDER

18 Religion and Children's Rights 299
BARBARA BENNETT WOODHOUSE

19 Religion and Economic, Social, and Cultural Rights 316
INGVILL THORSON PLESNER

20 Religion and Environmental Rights 330
WILLIS JENKINS

21 Religion, Violence, and the Right to Peace 346
R. SCOTT APPLEBY

22 Patterns of Religion State Relations 360
W. COLE DURHAM, JR.

Index 379

FOREWORD

For several years, in order to take part in a University of Minnesota Law School project, I accepted the invitation of Professor Robert Stein to spend a day annually with advanced participants. They were working with him on "The Rule of Law." Religion, not law, being my own scholarly field, I might have felt out of place. The first session convinced me that religion was very much in place, a conviction reinforced now by my reading of the essays which follow. The subfield I was to address had to do with my own project of some years earlier, a comparative study of the ways in which what we called "militant religious fundamentalisms" related to the rule of law in various polities and nations.

Finding cases for examination back then was easy, particularly because in the score of years after the Cold War ended, few subjects bade for attention more urgently than understanding such totalistic and belligerent uses of religion in international affairs. In my several meetings with the seminar, I would come armed with an outline of that season's topic and a sheaf of recent clippings or print-outs detailing the ways such religious movements or governments created problems for everyone who did not share the fundamentalists' views. Significantly, almost all these documentations, no matter what other topics they discussed—whether ritual, doctrine, strategy, or ways of life—revealed that the pinch point, finally, was the rule of law and challenges to it.

So radically did these problems and points increase in number and complexity that in 2008 I threw in the figurative towel, admitting in combined awe and resignation that I could not stay ahead or even keep up. Had this new book been available to me, I would have had much more to say and explore in the face of these most stressful and distressing set of questions. These revolved around one theme: What does religion or what do religions have to say about human rights, and, what do legal, political, and military conflicts over human rights have to do with and say about religion?

The "Rule of Law" seminars did not isolate and concentrate on this most profound theme, but instead set it into context. To prepare for that pursuit, I found significant resource in a book which anticipates this one: *Religious Human Rights in Global Perspective: Religious Perspectives* (John Witte, Jr., and Johan D. van der Vyver, eds. (The Hague: Martinus Nijhoff, 1996)). Some of the authors in that earlier book reappear in this one, having been given an opportunity to revisit, update, and advance their earlier research and essays. What is here now reinforces the case that the question of "Religious Human Rights" is at or near the center of multitudes of "rule of law" issues with which legal scholars, jurists, lawyers, religious leaders, and the public must deal. Were I to return to the scene of the seminars in Minnesota, this would be my first reference work and a volume I would commend to students and publics whose specialty is far from "Law and Religion." Nowhere can readers become familiar with the many dimensions of the subject as efficiently or confidently as they can if they are attentive to these essays by legal scholars who have long pursued the subject.

Readers who approach *Religion and Human Rights* with a highlighter or underliner in hand will likely end up with a colorful yellow and red manuscript if they simply accent the various subthemes which appear as bonuses in this book. Take one illustration, the question of "the secular"—or secularization as manifest in learning and law. For decades, most of higher education, intellectual, and professional life in European and American cultures have been structured in ways which admirers of the secularization thesis observe. It consists in a persistent and ever-increasing segregation or dismissal of religion from most serious inquiries. After the eighteenth century, it is noticed, various cultures, beginning in the West, have turned to rational, not revelational, texts and modes of approach to explore and settle controverted issues and chart practical ways of life. The phrase "separation of church and state," for instance, reduces almost to cliché an instance of the setting aside and boxing in of religious concerns in public life.

Whoever called attention to the signs suggesting that religion endured and even prospered in the century past was often dismissed as a victim of cultural lag, a special pleader for contending theologies or, some cynics would say, for the place of religious studies departments in universities and the placing of the Ten Commandments in public school rooms. Secularization pure and simply had "won." After that victory, it was said, the world might be less colorful, but it would be more peaceful, given the unsettlement which religion brings to so many sectors of life. However, the victory of "the secular" was not pure and it certainly was not simple. Numbers of authors in this collection comment that their essay deals with complexity. Readers will likely agree.

So the authors ask explicitly, or their cases demonstrate implicitly, that the ways in which "the secular" and "the religious" meet are anything but settled anywhere. Readers in the West who readily comment on how disturbing relations between the two are in other parts of the world will be reminded here, as elsewhere, that there are disturbances and challenges even in the United States. Its citizens may boast of the ways their nation has resolved many of the issues, but they are re-learning that few arguments which reach the United States Supreme Court or are on the agenda of local school boards are as disruptive of serenity and peace as are "church-state" contentions, which go to the heart of religion and human rights.

These contentions deal not only with doctrines, be they theological or judicial, but also and more vividly with practices. On these pages, we read of the ways a gold ring implanted in a nostril or a scarf covering the head of a school girl can lead to the pitting of citizen against citizen and religious citizen against law. Here we read of the ways religion is alive and well, or that because it is alive in some militant forms, it is *un*well, whether in controversies between men and women, parents and children, the old and the young, the clerical and the anti-clerical. However, the conflicts are first framed, they necessarily become legal problems which cannot be avoided or easily settled.

That highlighter or underliner of the scrupulous reader will be further put to work when several authors herein raise not easily addressed questions of definition. If we readers "knew" what secular and secularization meant after the eighteenth century Enlightenment in the West, we will be challenged as we find that several essayists call into question what was meant historically by the Enlightenment and then question the legacy itself. Defending the reasons which are traditionally associated with Enlightenment, "reason" has become a full-time job for many philosophers, historians, theologians, and jurists. They carry on, as do some writers here, asking for definitions of the grand themes of the "secular" and the "religious." It is important to have some concept of what religion is and does, all of the authors imply, but some of them are explicit: we no longer know, if we ever thought we did, exactly what a word in the title, "Religion," means. If so, they ask, how can such a term or concept be fairly used in courts?

If that is not enough on the definitional front, they would also add the question of how to define "rights." Each author frankly approaches that issue and throws light on it, but they tend to agree that what these mean makes the most sense when one sees the debates not generically or broadly but instead in separate and often competing cultures and societies. And if reading *that* has not done enough to disrupt the complacent, it is hard to bypass a theme that courses through the paragraphs in the pages which follow: how do the "separate and competing" cultures make demands on those who seek to synthesize "universals" with which one can generalize. Certainly, there must be something about "rights" in China, Chile, and Chicago which legal and religious people will find to be common to all? Certainly not, say most essayists here, though few of them use that emphatic form or response as a sign of defeat. Instead, it inspires them to find ways that their studies can make contributions toward understanding.

All these come to a head in the reflections which follow on the Universal Declaration of Human Rights (UDHR), the pioneer and most ambitious attempt to address the universal issue to which its title points. Admitting that that widely approved document represented an advance by setting off alarms, as well as bringing together the thoughts of people of great achievement and good will, they also reckon with the fact that its limits also have become more apparent as time passes. In this context, some readers may be ready to yawn when a subject they regard as over-addressed and almost reduced to truism or cliché has to be revisited: that is, many critics have seen the UDHR as "too Western," too bound by the Enlightenment heritage which both inspired and may have narrowed the worlds of its drafters and approvers of the UDHR back in 1948. Stifle the yawn, one pleads with those who have heard this complaint too often and been unsatisfied too long with attempts to find alternatives. Notice that there are fresh angles of vision in these essays, and they can serve as wake-up calls.

Those angles become most clear when the authors concentrate on voices and cultures not often heard or seen. One of the most informative and provocative treatments appears in Ronald Niezen's "Indigenous Religion and Human Rights," with its concerns for peoples and legal questions less familiar to most of us who might feel at home with issues posed by Islam and other "others" who are closer to home for those Western intellectuals who have concentrated on the "universal" topic since 1948. Significantly, many if not most of these indigenous peoples, inhabiting non-literate cultures through most modern times, have not left records of cases or arguments. They were not able to speak for themselves, but were spoken for, or against. Even a short essay such as the one by Niezen, can inspire, provoke, and inform themes of other cultures, closer by to most of them.

Singling out one essay and one author, as I have done, may seem to violate the "rights" or distort the "equality"—equality also being often addressed in this book—of the score of authors. Mentioning so few of them is an act congruent with my interpretation of the task of composing the Foreword: not to detail the separate chapters. Professors Witte and Green do some of that in their introduction which, as introductions should, is an anticipation of the main arguments of all the chapters and a brief comment on the structure and intention of the book as revealed through its many parts. Entering such comments at this point was certainly a temptation for me, because my manuscript copy is scribbled up with notes for further study and reaction.

Let me only say that in the chapters on the rights-issues of Jewish, Christian, Islamic, Hindu, Confucian, Buddhist, Indigenous, and Secular peoples and their diverse legal traditions—there are more which come to mind—readers, including specialists, are almost certain to make discoveries. The traditions are so ample and complex that no author will contend that he or she has dealt with all the main themes, but they have pointed to the central concerns and the highlights of histories and court cases. A Muslim reader may very well learn something new about Islam by learning how rights-issues in, say, Buddhism, have come to the fore, and vice versa. The potential for such learning is the fruit of conscientious and careful comparative scholarship. The authors may not all have found "universals" to match the assumptions of the UDHR, but their elaboration of the "particulars" which they find alluring and revealing can be helpful to all. The fact that some of the authors have been in formal conversation and conference with each other, or have long been familiar with the work of many of the others, makes it possible for their work as a whole to be seen as an invitation for the rest of us to join the conversation and enlarge it.

While the writers are all at home with comparative legal scholarship and are informed about the religions they discuss, some of them also show that their efforts do not lead to a weakening of religious conviction or a lapse into relativism of the sort of which interfaith discussants are often accused. They identify instead with the people of profound and enduring faith who bring faith-issues to court. Some of them can empathize and boldly state that if having to agree on some universal point about human rights which demonstrably wars against their faith tradition, then the universal must be eclipsed by the particular. People do not often give birth, raise children, live lives, worship, act ethically, or face death in the name of some abstract universal. They do these things in response to the stories, practices, and teachings which give clarity and purpose to their lives. That the universals and the particulars do not have to be in conflict and can often be seen as congruent is a hope and an understanding to which they are commonly committed. This book is an invitation to readers to deliberate these themes to better to understand what is at issue and, in broad outline, how we might do better on the "rights" front in this considered way than our legal, political, and religious cultures tend to do with these issues in these times of danger and crisis.

Martin E. Marty
The University of Chicago

PREFACE

Over the past two decades, the Center for the Study of Law and Religion at Emory University has had the privilege of directing fifteen major projects on law, religion, and human rights in interdisciplinary, interreligious, and international perspective. These projects have explored the contributions of various faith traditions to the cultivation—and abridgement—of human rights and democratic norms around the world. They have probed some of the hardest issues of religious persecution and bigotry, religious proselytism and discrimination, and rights for religious believers and communities. They have exposed the religious dimensions of rights for women and children, rights within marriages and families, rights to food, shelter, housing, work, education, and more. And they have provided a common table and an open lectern for deep dialogue and debate among scholars, advocates, and policy makers from multiple confessions and professions.

The obvious premise of these projects is that a legal regime of democracy and human rights is indispensable to the establishment of local and world order. Democracy is hardly a perfect system of government. But among current political forms, democracy holds the most promise for peace, justice, and a better life. It offers the best hope for those who suffer from persecution and penury, discrimination and deprivation. It affords the greatest opportunity for all to embrace and enjoy their faith, freedom, and family and to chart their own identity and agency as self-determining individuals and communities. Human rights norms, in turn, are not a complete map of the good life and the good society. But they have emerged today as one of the very few universal and cosmopolitan principles that are recognized around the world, even if sometimes honored in the breach. They provide normative ideals for persons and peoples, constitutional grounds for litigation and legislation, and diplomatic levers to press repressive regimes to reform themselves.

The less obvious premise of these projects is that religion and human rights need each other. On the one hand, human rights norms need the norms, narratives, and practices of the world's religions. There is, of course, some value in simply declaring human rights norms of "liberty, equality, and fraternity" or "life, liberty, and property"—if for no other reason than to pose an ideal against which a person or community might measure itself, to preserve a normative totem for later generations to make real. But, ultimately, these abstract human rights ideals of the good life and the good society depend on the visions and values of human communities and institutions to give them content and coherence—to provide what Catholic philosopher Jacques Maritain once called "the scale of values governing [their] exercise and concrete manifestation." It is here that religion must play a vital role. Religion is an ineradicable condition of human lives and human communities. Religions invariably provide many of the sources and "scales of values" by which many persons and communities govern themselves. Religions inevitably help to define the meanings and measures of shame and regret, restraint and respect, responsibility and restitution that a human rights regime presupposes. Religions must thus be seen as indispensable allies in the modern struggle for human rights. To exclude them from the struggle is impossible, indeed catastrophic. To include them, by enlisting their unique resources and protecting their unique rights, is vital to enhancing the regime of human rights and to easing some of the worst paradoxes that currently exist.

Conversely, religious narratives need human rights norms both to protect them and to challenge them. There is, of course, some merit in religious believers and groups quietly accepting the current protections of a modern human rights regime—the guarantees of liberty of conscience, freedom of exercise, rights to religious self-determination, and the like. But passive acquiescence in a secular scheme of human rights ultimately will not prove effective. And failure to press the unique rights claims of religious believers and communities will eventually leave many religious beliefs, practices, and communities too vulnerable. Religious communities must reclaim their own voices within the secular human rights dialogue, and reclaim the human rights voices within their own internal religious dialogues. Contrary to conventional wisdom, the theory and law of human rights are neither new nor secular in origin. Human rights are, in no small part, the modern political fruits of ancient religious beliefs and practices. Religious communities must be open to a new human rights hermeneutic—fresh methods of interpreting their sacred texts and traditions that will allow them to reclaim their essential roots and roles in the cultivation of human rights. Religious traditions cannot allow secular human rights norms to be imposed on them from without; they must (re)discover them from within.

This volume builds on these premises. The first cluster of chapters analyzes the contributions of the main world religions to modern understandings of human rights. These chapters show that the founding teachers and prophets, core texts and rituals, central traditions and practices of each of the world religions have much to offer to modern human rights talk—constructive and instructive, but also critical and reformist. A central question animating this first cluster of chapters is whether human rights are a universal good of human nature or a distinctly Western invention that has no easy resonance in other cultures with different founding beliefs and values. If human rights are truly universal, what other formulations besides those rooted in Western philosophy, theology, and culture need to be incorporated? If human rights are distinctly Western inventions, what other normative structures and systems do non-Western traditions offer to promote peace, justice, and an orderly society? A related question is whether human rights must now be cast in secular or neutral language in order to be legitimate and universal. Are Christian, Jewish, Islamic, Hindu, Buddhist, Confucian, Indigenous, and other such declarations of human rights by definition parochial, a defiance of the demand for universality of human rights, or are they appropriate religious translations and adaptations of a universal human good?

The second cluster of chapters analyzes a number of human rights issues that confront religious persons and communities today. These chapters focus not only on core issues of freedom of conscience, choice, and exercise of religion and beliefs, but also on freedoms of expression, association, morality, and self-determination on which religious parties essentially depend. Later chapters also highlight the role of religious ideas and institutions in the cultivation and abridgement of rights of women, children, and minorities, rights to education, healthcare, and labor, and rights to peace, orderly development, and protection of nature and the environment. A central question at work in this second section of the volume is whether freedom of religion or belief is something distinctive or simply the sum of all the other rights that other parties can claim, too. If religious freedom is distinctive, what special rights and liberties attach uniquely to religious parties that are not given to other non-religious parties? If religious freedom is not distinctive, how do core claims of conscience or central commandments of faith get protected when they run contrary to the cultural mainstream or to majoritarian rules?

The volume draws together a score of ranking experts to provide an authoritative but accessible treatment of these foundations and fundamentals of religion and human rights. The chapters are calibrated to reach educated but uninitiated readers. Each chapter is long enough to provide substantive analysis of the relevant issues and texts, but not so long that new readers get lost in the details. Readers who want to see more will find recommended readings at the end of each chapter, as well as cross references to other chapters in the book and other literature on point. This book is designed as a textbook for the college, law school, and divinity school classroom, and a handbook for scholars, advocates, NGOs, and religious and political officials looking for an up-to-date single volume on the human rights contributions and challenges of all the world's religions.

On behalf of our colleagues in the Center for the Study of Law and Religion, we would like to thank the authors of the chapters that follow for their superb contributions. We would like to thank Michael Gilligan, Terry Lautz, and Toby Volkman and their colleagues at The Henry Luce Foundation for their generous grant to our Center for the Study of Law and Religion for a project on "Law, Religion, and Human Rights in International Perspective" that allowed for this publication and a number of others. We wish to thank our Center colleagues April Bogle, Linda King, Anita Mann, and Amy Wheeler for their excellent work on this project—Amy Wheeler, in particular, for her work on this manuscript. We wish to thank our students, Silas Allard, Brian Green, Jennifer Heald Kidwell, and Jennifer Williams for their able and ample research assistance. And finally, we thank Theo Calderara and his colleagues for taking on this volume and for their expertise in bringing it to print.

John Witte, Jr. and M. Christian Green
Center for the Study of Law and Religion
Emory University

CONTRIBUTORS

Abdullahi Ahmed An-Na'im is the Charles Howard Candler Professor of Law, Director of the Center for International and Comparative Law, and Senior Fellow in the Center for the Study of Law and Religion at Emory University.

R. Scott Appleby is John M. Regan, Jr. Director and Professor of History in the Kroc Institute for International Peace Studies at the University of Notre Dame.

Joseph C.W. Chan is Professor of Political Science in the Department of Politics and Public Administration at the University of Hong Kong.

Carolyn Evans is Professor of Law and Dean of Melbourne Law School.

Nazila Ghanea is University Lecturer in International Human Rights Law and a fellow of Kellogg College at the University of Oxford.

M. Christian Green is Senior Fellow at the Center for the Study of Law and Religion at Emory University.

T. Jeremy Gunn is Associate Professor of International Studies at Al Akhawayn University in Morocco and Former Director of the American Civil Liberties Union Program on Freedom of Religion and Belief.

Sallie B. King is Professor of Philosophy and Religion at James Madison University.

Willis Jenkins is Margaret A. Farley Assistant Professor of Social Ethics at Yale Divinity School.

Natan Lerner is Professor of International Law at the Interdisciplinary Center, Herzlyia, in Israel.

David Little is T.J. Dermot Dunphy Professor of the Practice in Religion, Ethnicity, and International Conflict Emeritus at Harvard Divinity School.

Werner Menski is Professor of South Asian Laws at the School of Oriental and African Studies (SOAS) at the University of London.

Ronald Niezen holds the Canada Research Chair in the Comparative Study of Indigenous Rights and is Chair of the Department of Anthropology at McGill University.

David Novak is the Richard and Dorothy Schiff Chair of Jewish Studies, Professor of the Study of Religion, and Professor of Philosophy at the University of Toronto.

Michael J. Perry is Robert W. Woodruff Professor and Senior Fellow in the Center for the Study of Law and Religion at Emory University, as well as University Distinguished Visiting Professor in Law and Peace Studies in the Kroc School of Peace Studies, University of San Diego.

Ingvill Thorson Plesner is a Fellow in the Norwegian Centre for Human Rights in the Faculty of Law at the University of Oslo.

Steven D. Smith is the Warren Distinguished Professor of Law at the University of San Diego.

Madhavi Sunder is Professor of Law at the University of California at Davis.

Paul M. Taylor is a Fellow of Wolfson College, University of Cambridge and a Barrister-at-Law.

Johan D. van der Vyver is I.T. Cohen Professor of International Law and Human Rights and Extraordinary Professor in the Department of Private Law, University of Pretoria.

Senior Fellow in the Center for the Study of Law and Religion at Emory University.

John Witte, Jr. is Jonas Robitscher Professor of Law, Alonzo L. McDonald Distinguished Professor, and Director of the Center for the Study of Law and Religion at Emory University.

Nicholas P. Wolterstorff is Noah Porter Professor of Philosophical Theology Emeritus at Yale University.

Barbara Bennett Woodhouse is L.Q.C. Lamar Professor of Law and Co-Director of the Barton Child Law and Policy Center at Emory University.

Religion and Human Rights

■ Introduction

JOHN WITTE, JR. AND M. CHRISTIAN GREEN

In January 2008, news headlines and human rights websites around the world broadcast the story of a death sentence handed down by a local Afghan court to a 23-year-old journalism student, Sayed Perwiz Kambakhsh, for committing the crime of blasphemy. The student had downloaded and distributed an article from the Internet after annotating it with words deemed to be an insult to the prophet Mohammed. The article in question was critical of certain Islamic beliefs and practices that were seen as oppressive to women. Kambakhsh had allegedly added to the text some of his own criticisms of Mohammed's teachings on women. The death sentence drew criticism from journalists, human rights activists, and political leaders around the world, inspiring European Parliament President Hans-Gert Pöttering to protest to Afghan President Hamid Karzai: "The alleged 'crime' of this person would appear to be that he has distributed publications aimed at improving the situation of Afghan women."[1]

At the appeal court, Judge Abdul Salam Qazizada, a holdover from the Taliban era, was reportedly antagonistic toward Kambakhsh. In support of the blasphemy charge against Kambakhsh, the court considered as evidence anecdotal reports that that the young man was a socialist, was impolite, asked too many questions in class, and swapped off-color jokes and messages with friends. In October 2008, an Afghan appeals court overturned Kambakhsh's death sentence and sentenced him instead to twenty years in prison, presumably due to the considerable international attention to his case and international pressure on the Afghan government.[2] Kambakhsh began his prison term in March 2009, the same month in which Afghan President Hamid Karzai signed a law specifying circumstances in which Afghan women of the Shia Muslim tradition must have sex with their husbands under Muslim family law.[3] Interpretations of Islamic law as sanctioning marital rape were just the kinds of abuse of women's rights that the young journalist Kambakhsh was seeking to expose.

Such has been the state of religion and human rights in the fragile new democracy of Afghanistan purportedly liberated from the Taliban and other extremists. This kind of story recurs in endless variations in the Middle East, Africa, the Balkans, and various former Soviet nations and provinces in Eastern Europe, as well as in Central and Southeast Asia. Browse the daily news reports,[4] study the many briefings of human rights NGOs, pore over the annual reports from the United States Commission on International Religious Freedom[5] or the

United Nations Special Rapporteur on Religious Freedom and Belief,[6] and it becomes altogether too clear that religion and human rights do not yet coincide in many countries of the world, despite their rosy new constitutional provisions on religious freedom and human rights for all. Apostasy, Blasphemy, Conversion, Defamation, Evangelization—this is the new alphabet of offenses in a number of politically volatile nations around the world.

The alphabet goes on to include Fundamentalism, Genocide, Homicide, Injustice, and Jihad in many other nations. A recent comprehensive study of the 198 countries and self-administering territories in the world today show that more a third of these polities have "high" or "very high" levels of religious oppression, sometimes exacerbated by civil war, natural disasters, and foreign invasion that have sometimes caused massive humanitarian crises. The countries on this dishonor roll include Iran, Iraq, India, Pakistan, Bangladesh, Sri Lanka, Indonesia, Saudia Arabia, Somalia, Yemen, Sudan, Egypt, Israel, Burma, Rwanda, Burundi, the Congo, Chechnya, Uzbekistan, among others.[7]

Even in the more stable constitutional democracies of Western Europe and North America, religion and human rights are facing new changes and conflicts, although usually less violent. Ancient forms of Christian establishment and state favoritism in Scandanavia, England, Ireland, Spain, Italy, and Greece are giving way to new demands for religious pluralism and equal treatment for all. Many West European nations are now beset with urgent new constitutional struggles over the rights and freedoms of swelling populations of new Muslims and other immigrants. A number of European countries have recently passed firm new measures against "sects" and "cults" that set firm restrictions on religious dress, organization, and movement for various religious and cultural groups, including Muslims, Scientologists, and Römer. In Canada, traditional forms of church-state cooperation have given way to strong new equality norms, with particularly bitter contests emerging between same-sex parties and religious organizations. In the United States, the substantial weakening of the First Amendment has shifted many questions of religious liberty from the judiciary to the legislature, and from the federal to the state governments—often leaving religious liberty vulnerable to fleeting local politics and contingent upon a claimant's geographical location.

The tragic irony of all this is that these new sharp contests of religion and human rights have emerged at the same time that human rights norms respecting religion have have become increasingly refined. In part because of the new wave of democratization that has broken over the world since the 1970s, many countries have issued major new constitutional provisions, statutes, and cases on religion, replete with generous protections for liberty of conscience and freedom of religious exercise, guarantees of religious pluralism, equality, and non-discrimination on religious grounds. These national guarantees have been matched with a growing body of regional and international norms building upon foundational guarantees contained in the 1948 Universal Declaration of Human Rights and successor human rights instruments. Especially in the last 20 years, the international norms of religious freedom and human rights on the books have become remarkably comprehensive and sophisticated.

This underscores an elementary, but essential lesson—that human rights norms need a human rights culture to be effective. "[D]eclarations are not deeds," Judge John T. Noonan, Jr. reminds us. "A form of words by itself secures nothing. . . . [W]ords pregnant with meaning in one cultural context may be entirely barren in another."[8] Human rights norms have little salience in societies that lack constitutional processes that will give them meaning and measure. They have little value for parties who lack basic rights to security, succor, and sanctuary, or who are deprived of basic freedoms of speech, press, or association. They have little pertinence for victims who lack standing in courts and other basic procedural rights to pursue apt remedies. They have little cogency in communities that lack the ethos and ethic to render human rights violations a source of shame and regret, restraint and respect, confession and responsibility, reconciliation and restitution. As we have gradually moved from the first generations of human rights declarations following World War II to the current generation of more serious human rights implementation, this need for an effective human rights culture has become all the more pressing.

In the sections that follow, we first describe the place of religion in the modern human rights framework, and then analyze the kinds of intersecting roles of religion and human rights that are needed to build a more effective human rights culture. Along the way, we reference a number of the main themes that occupy the authors of the 22 chapters that follow.

■ RELIGION AND THE INTERNATIONAL HUMAN RIGHTS FRAMEWORK

The international rights and liberties recognized today have millennium-long roots in various religious, philosophical, and cultural traditions.[9] Their definitive modern formulation, however, came with the promulgation of the Universal Declaration of Human Rights (UDHR) in 1948. The UDHR was born out of desperation in the aftermath of World War II. The world had just stared in horror into Stalin's gulags and Hitler's death camps. It had just witnessed the terror of nuclear warfare in Hiroshima and Nagasaki. It had just endured the devastation of sixty million people killed in the bloodiest six years in the history of humankind. It was time to restate the basics of life, freedom, and community. It was time to take up Franklin Roosevelt's call to protect the "four freedoms" of everyone—"freedom of speech, freedom of religion, freedom from want, and freedom from fear."

The United Nations Commission on Human Rights, chaired by Eleanor Roosevelt, took up the task of drafting a definitive declaration on human rights. The drafting committee and the Commission as a whole were broadly inclusive in membership. The main drafters included René Cassin (a Jewish jurist from France and later Nobel Peace Prize winner), Peng-chun Chang (a distinguished Confucian scholar from China), John Peters Humphrey (a leading Canadian jurist who was then part of the UN Secretariat and prepared much of the first draft), Charles Malik (a Maronite Christian from Lebanon), and Jacques Maritain (a prominent French Catholic philosopher and France's ambassador to the Vatican). The Commission itself had representation from countries with majoritarian Atheist, Buddhist, Christian, Confucian, Hindu, and Muslim populations, including India, China, the Philippines, the U.S.S.R., Iran, Egypt, Lebanon, Austria, France, the United States, Panama, and Chile. The Commission further drew on bills of rights from around the world and drew from the expert opinions of sundry scholars, advocates, and NGOs of all manner of professions and confessions.

Jacques Maritain, a member of the drafting committee, was asked how such a diverse group of participants holding such divergent viewpoints could agree to a definitive list of fundamental rights. He replied: "Yes, we agree about the rights *but on condition no one asks us why*." The goal, he elaborated, was to agree "not on the basis of common speculative ideas, but on common practical ideas, not on the affirmation of one and the same conception of the world, of man, and of knowledge, but upon the affirmation of a single body of beliefs for guidance in action."[10] That "single body of beliefs" was set out in the Preamble and Article 1 of the UDHR, which affirmed that "the inherent dignity and the equal and inalienable rights of all members of the human family is the foundation of freedom, justice and peace in the world." Respect for human rights and human dignity is essential in all times and places, the UDHR insisted, and must be respected by and for all persons and peoples.

In thirty pithy articles, the UDHR set out the "universal rights" of all human beings: equality and freedom from discrimation; rights to life, liberty, privacy, and security of person; rights to national and cultural identity; freedom from slavery, servitude, and cruel and barbarous treatment; sundry criminal procedural protections; freedom of movement and asylum; rights to marriage and family life with special protections for mothers and children; rights to property; freedom of thought, conscience, religion, opinion, expression, and assembly; freedom to political representation and participation; rights to labor, employment, and social security; rights to healthcare, education, and cultural participation. In the decades after the UDHR, many of these discrete rights became subjects of more elaborate covenants, conventions, and declarations on rights. These international instruments, which fall largely under the vast auspices of the United Nations, were echoed and elaborated in both regional instruments like the 1950 European Charter of Human Rights and the 1969 American Convention on Human Rights. They were further elaborated in the numerous national constitutional provisions and cases passed during the political reconstruction of the world after World War II as well as in the many post-colonial democractic revolutions that followed in Africa, Latin America, and South Asia.

The UDHR and subsequent human rights instruments include both "freedom rights" (speech, press, religion, and the like) and "welfare rights" (education, labor, health care, and more). Later instruments also outline rights to peace, orderly development, and environmental protection.[11] As a number of chapters in this volume show, many of these rights have religious sources and dimensions, and religious parties often draw on these rights to protect their religious identities and practices. One of the hallmarks of the modern human rights movement is that human rights are "interrelated," "indivisible," and "interdependent."[12] Freedom rights are useful only if a party's basic welfare rights to food, shelter, health care, education, and security are adequately protected. The rights to worship, speech, or association mean little to someone starving in the street or dying from a treatable disease. Both freedom and welfare rights are often sacrificed in times of war, emergency, or force majeure.

While religious persons and communities often find refuge in sundry rights claims shared with non-religious claimants, a special category of religious rights and freedoms has also emerged to deal with some of the unique needs of religion. Articles 2 and 18 of the UDHR called these the rights of "thought, conscience, and belief" and the freedom from religious discrimination. Four international instruments, elaborating the UDHR, contain the most critical protections of religious rights and liberties: (1) the International Covenant on Civil and Political Rights (ICCPR),[13] (2) the United Nations Declaration on the Elimination of All Forms of Intolerance and Discrimination Based on Religion or Belief ("the Declaration on Religion"),[14] (3) the Concluding Document of the Vienna Follow-Up Meeting of Representatives of the Participating States of the Conference on Security and Cooperation in Europe (the "Vienna Concluding Document"),[15] and (4) the Declaration on the Rights of Persons Belonging to National or Ethnic, Religious, and Linguistic Minorities ("the Minorities Declaration").[16]

The ICCPR, a binding treaty accepted by 165 countries today, largely repeats the capacious guarantee of religious rights and liberties first announced in the UDHR. Article 18 of the 1966 Covenant reads:

1. Everyone shall have the right to freedom of thought, conscience, and religion. This right shall include freedom to have or to adopt a religion or belief of his choice, and freedom, either individually or in community with others and in public or private, to manifest his religion or belief in worship, observance, practice, and teaching.
2. No one shall be subject to coercion which would impair his freedom to have or to adopt a religion or belief of his choice.
3. Freedom to manifest one's religion or beliefs may be subject only to such limitations as are prescribed by law and are necessary to protect public safety, order, health, or morals. or the fundamental rights and freedoms of others.
4. The States Parties to the present Covenant undertake to have respect for the liberty of parents and, when applicable, legal guardians to ensure the religious and moral education of their children in conformity with their own convictions.

Article 18 thus distinguishes between the right to freedom of religion or belief and the freedom to manifest one's religion or belief—what American law labels as liberty of conscience and free exercise of religion, respectively. The right to freedom of religion (the freedom to have, to alter, or to adopt a religion of one's choice) is an absolute right from which no derogation may be made and which may not be restricted or impaired in any manner. Freedom to manifest or exercise one's religion (individually or collectively, publicly or privately) may be subject only to such limitations as are prescribed by law and are necessary to protect public safety, order, health, or morals or the fundamental rights and freedoms of others. The latter provision is an exhaustive list of the grounds allowed to limit the manifestation of religion. The requirement of necessity implies that any such limitation on the manifestation of religion must be proportionate to its aim to protect any of the listed state interests. Such limitations must not be applied in a manner that would vitiate the rights guaranteed in Article 18.[17] Article 20.2 of the 1966 Covenant calls for States Parties to prohibit "any advocacy of national, racial, or religious hatred that constitutes incitement to discrimination, hostility, or violence." Articles 2 and 26 further require equal treatment of all persons before the law and prohibit discrimination based, among other grounds, on religion.[18]

The 1981 Declaration on Religion or elaborates the religious liberty provisions that the ICCPR adumbrated. Like the ICCPR, the Declaration on Religion applies on its face to "everyone," whether "individually or in community," "in public or in private." Articles 1 and 6 set forth a lengthy illustrative catalogue of rights to "freedom of thought, conscience, and religion"—repeating but also illustrating more concretely the ICCPR's guarantees of liberty of conscience and free exercise of religion. Article 6 enumerates these rights as follows:

(a) To worship or assemble in connection with a religion or belief and to establish and maintain places for these purposes;
(b) To establish and maintain appropriate charitable or humanitarian institutions;
(c) To make, to acquire and use to an adequate extent the necessary articles and materials related to the rites or customs of a religion or belief;
(d) To write, issue, and disseminate relevant publications in these areas;
(e) To teach a religion or belief in places suitable for these purposes;
(f) To solicit and receive voluntary financial and other contributions from individuals and institutions;
(g) To train, to appoint, to elect, or to designate by succession appropriate leaders called for by the requirements and standards of any religion or belief;
(h) To observe days of rest and to celebrate holy days and ceremonies in accordance with the precepts of one's religion or belief; and
(i) To establish and maintain communications with individuals and communities in matters of religion and belief at the national and international levels.

Further guidance for the protection of a person's freedom of conscience would subsequently be provided in the 1990 Document of the Copenhagen Meeting of Representatives of the Participating States of the Conference on the Human Dimension of the Conference on Security and Co-operation in Europe (the "Copenhagen Document") which, glossing the earlier Declaration on Religion, recognizes "the right of everyone to have conscientious objection to military service" and calls for "various forms of alternative service . . . in combatant or civilian service" "which are compatible with the reasons for conscientious objections to military service."[19]

The Declaration on Religion, in Article 5, also dwells specifically on the religious rights of children and their parents. It guarantees the rights of parents (or guardians) to organize life within their household and to educate their children "in accordance with their religion or beliefs." Such parental responsibility within and beyond the household, however, must be discharged in accordance with the "best interests of the child." At minimum, the parents' religious upbringing or education of their child "must not be injurious to his physical or mental health or to his full development." Moreover, the Declaration provides more generically, "the child shall be protected from any form of discrimination on the ground of religion or belief. He shall be brought up in a spirit of understanding, tolerance, friendship among peoples, peace and universal brotherhood, respect for freedom of religion or belief of others, and in full conscience that his energy and talents should be devoted to the service of his fellow men." The Declaration leaves juxtaposed the parents' right to rear and educate their children in accordance with their own religion and beliefs and the State's power to protect the best interests of the child, including the lofty aspirations for the child's upbringing. Despite ample debate on point, the Declaration drafters offered no specific principles to resolve the disputes that would inevitably arise between the rights of parents and the powers of the State operating *in loco parentis*. Some further guidance on this subject is provided by the 1989 UN Convention on the Rights of the Child (CRC)—though the issue of parental rights over their child's religious upbringing and welfare remains highly contested.[20]

As these children's rights provisions illustrate, the Declaration on Religion, like the ICCPR, allows the "manifestation of religion" to be subjected to "appropriate" state regulation and adjudication. The Declaration on Religion permits states to enforce against religious individuals and institutions general regulations designed to protect public safety, order, health, or morals, or the fundamental rights and freedoms of others. It is assumed, however, that in all such instances, the grounds for such regulations are enumerated and explicit and that such regulations abide by the international legal principles of necessity and proportionality.

The Declaration on Religion includes more elaborate prohibitions than the ICCPR on religious discrimination and intolerance. Article 2 bars religious "discrimination by any State, institution, group of persons, or person." And it defines such discrimination as "any distinction, exclusion, restriction or preference based on religion or belief, and having as its purpose or as its effect nullification or impairment of the recognition, enjoyment or exercise of human rights or fundamental freedoms on an equal basis." All such discrimination based on religion or belief, the Declaration insists, is "an affront to human dignity" and a "disavowal" of the "fundamental freedoms" that form the cornerstone of national and international peace and cooperation. Accordingly, the Declaration calls on all States Parties "to take effective measures to prevent and eliminate" such discrimination "in all fields of civil, economic, political, social, and cultural life," including rescinding laws that foster discrimination and enacting laws that forbid it.[21]

The Declaration on Religion includes suggested principles of implementation and application of these guarantees. It urges states to take all "effective measures to prevent and eliminate discrimination on the grounds of religion or belief in the recognition, exercise and enjoyment of human rights and fundamental freedoms in all fields of civil, economic, political, social and cultural life." It urges states to remove local laws that perpetuate or allow religious discrimination and to enact local criminal and civil laws to combat religious discrimination and intolerance.

The 1989 Vienna Concluding Document extends the religious liberty norms of the Declaration on Religion, particularly for religious groups. Principle 16 rounds out the list of enumerated rights guarantees quoted above from the Declaration on Religion:

> (16) In order to ensure the freedom of the individual to profess and practice religion or belief the participating States will, *inter alia,*
>
> (16.1) take effective measures to prevent and eliminate discrimination against individuals or communities, on the grounds of religion or belief in the recognition, exercise and enjoyment of human rights and fundamental freedoms in all fields of civil, political, economic, social, and cultural life, and ensure the effective equality between believers and non-believers;
>
> (16.2) foster a climate of mutual tolerance and respect between believers of different communities as well as between believers and non-believers;
>
> (16.3) grant upon their request to communities of believers, practicing or prepared to practice their faith within the constitutional framework of their states, recognition of the status provided for them in their respective countries;
>
> (16.4) respect the right of religious communities to establish and maintain freely accessible places of worship or assembly, organize themselves according to their own hierarchical and institutional structure, select, appoint and replace their personnel in accordance with their respective requirements and standards as well as with any freely accepted arrangement between them and their State, solicit and receive voluntary financial and other contributions;
>
> (16.5) engage in consultations with religious faiths, institutions, and organizations in order to achieve a better understanding of the requirements of religious freedom;
>
> (16.6) respect the right of everyone to give and receive religious education in the language of his choice, individually or in association with others;

(16.7) in this context respect, *inter alia*, the liberty of parents to ensure the religious and moral education of their children in conformity with their own convictions;

(16.8) allow the training of religious personnel in appropriate institutions;

(16.9) respect the right of individual believers and communities of believers to acquire, possess, and use sacred books, religious publications in the language of their choice and other articles and materials related to the practice of religion or belief;

(16.10) allow religious faiths, institutions and organizations to produce and import and disseminate religious publications and materials;

(16.11) favorably consider the interest of religious communities in participating in public dialogue, *inter alia*, through mass media.

A number of these religious group rights provisions in the Vienna Concluding Document reflect the international right to self-determination of peoples. This right has long been recognized as a basic norm of international law, and is included, among other places, in the ICCPR, the Convention on the Rights of the Child, and the CSCE Copenhagen Document. It has its fullest expression in the Minorities Declaration. The right to self-determination belongs to "peoples" within plural societies. It affords a religious community the right to practice its religion, an ethnic community the right to promote its culture, and a linguistic community to speak its language without undue state interference or legal restrictions. Governments are required to secure the interests of distinct sections of the population that constitute a people in the above sense. The Minorities Declaration clearly spells out that obligation as entailing measures: to protect and encourage conditions for the promotion of the concerned group identities of minorities; to afford to minorities the special competence to participate effectively in decisions pertinent to the group to which they belong; to not discriminate in any way against any person on the basis of his or her group identity; and to take actions to secure their equal treatment at law. The Minorities Declaration further provides that: "States shall take measures to create favorable conditions to enable persons belonging to minorities to express their characteristics and to develop their culture, language, religion, traditions and customs, except where specific practices are in violation of national law and contrary to international standards."[22] So conceived, the right to religious self-determination provides religious groups some of the same strong protections afforded to religious individuals under the freedom of conscience guarantee.

The 2007 United Nations Declaration on the Rights of Indigenous Peoples gives specific elaboration of these rights of self-determination for indigenous, aboriginal, or first peoples. Article 12 provides that "Indigenous peoples have the right to manifest, practise, develop and teach their spiritual and religious traditions, customs and ceremonies; the right to maintain, protect, and have access in privacy to their religious and cultural sites; the right to the use and control of their ceremonial objects; and the right to the repatriation of their human remains." Article 25 provides further that "Indigenous peoples have the right to maintain and strengthen their distinctive spiritual relationship with their traditionally owned or otherwise occupied and used lands, territories, waters and coastal seas and other resources and to uphold their responsibilities to future generations in this regard."[23]

These are the basic international provisions on religious rights on the books. Various regional instruments, notably the European Charter on Human Rights (1950), the American Convention on Human Rights (1969), and the African Charter on Human and People's Rights (1981), elaborate some of these guarantees. Further amplification is provided in various religious declarations and treaties involving religious bodies, notably the recent concordats between the Vatican and Italy, Spain, and Israel, and other bilateral treaties between various nations.

A number of religious bodies have also issued important international declarations of human rights, including religious rights and liberties, that have helped to mobilize human rights reflection and activitism within these religious communities. Both the Roman Catholic Church and the Islamic world, each claiming well over a billion members worldwide, offer good examples. The Catholic declarations were issued during and after the Second Vatican Council (1962–1965), when the Church came to endorse many of the very same human rights and democratic principles that it had spurned a century before. "Every person," reads the famous Vatican decree *Dignitatis Humanae* (Of the Dignity of the Human Person) (1965), is created by God with "dignity, intelligence and free will . . . and has rights flowing directly and simultaneously from his very nature." Such rights include the right to life and adequate standards of living, to labor, education, and healthcare, to moral and cultural values, to religious activities, to assembly and association, to marriage and family life, and to various social, political, and economic benefits and opportunities. The Church emphasized the religious rights of conscience, worship, assembly, and education, calling them the "first rights" of any civic order. The church also stressed the need to balance individual and associational rights, particularly those involving the church, family, and school. Governments everywhere were encouraged to create conditions conducive to the realization and protection of these "inviolable rights" and encouraged to root out every type of discrimination, whether social or cultural, whether based on sex, race, color, social distinction, language, or religion. As a corollary, the Church advocated limited constitutional government, disestablishment of religion, and the separation of church and state. The vast pluralism of religions and cultures, and the inherent dangers in state endorsement of any religion, in the church's view, rendered mandatory such democratic forms of government. Armed with these new human rights teachings, the Catholic Church has become a critical force in the new democratic and human rights movements in Brazil, Chile, Central America, the Philippines, South Korea, Poland, Hungary, the Czech Republic, Ukraine, and elsewhere.[24]

The Universal Islamic Declaration of Human Rights (Islamic Declaration) of 1981 offers another compelling example of a religious community's new embrace of human rights. The foreword of this important document proclaims this instrument to be a "declaration for mankind," invoking a classic Quranic passage describing the creation of humanity "into nations and tribes, so that you might come to know one another."[25] The Islamic Declaration guarantees "freedom of belief, thought, and speech" and, more specifically, a person's "right to freedom of conscience and worship in accordance with his religious beliefs." It condemns actions that "hold in contempt or ridicule the religious beliefs of others or incite public hostility against them," and declares that "respect for the religious feelings of others is obligatory on all Muslims." Above all, it declares, that the "Quranic principle 'There is no compulsion in religion' shall govern the religious rights of non-Muslim minorities" and "[i]n a Muslim country religious minorities shall have the choice to be governed in respect of their civil and personal matters by Islamic Law, or by their own laws."[26]

The more recent 1990 Cairo Declaration on Human Rights (Cairo Declaration) contains no articles specifically devoted to religious freedom, but it does cite "race, color, language, sex, *religious belief*, political affiliation, [and] social status" as impermissible bases of discrimination.[27] Religious rights are mentioned in a provision on educational rights, as well as in the context of the believer's right "to live in security for himself, his *religion*, his dependents, his honor, and his property."[28] At the same time, a provision on free speech limits the applicability of free speech guarantees in cases where such speech would "arouse nationalistic or *doctrinal* hatred or do anything that may be an incitement to any form of racial discrimination."[29] In its linkage of religion to race and other categories of identity, the Cairo Declaration, is a precursor to the more recent connections made between religion, race, and ethnicity in the "combating defamation of religions" resolutions that have been introduced by the Muslim member states of the Organization of the Islamic Conference (OIC) at the United Nations in recent years.[30] The conflation of religion, race, and ethnicity in those resolutions suggests a potentially narrower ambit of religious freedom than the earlier Islamic Declaration. But it is equally important to recognize that the Cairo Declaration does affirm the fundamental nature of religious rights, even as it hints at the grounds for their restriction.

These international instruments on religion and human rights—and many others that can be adduced—highlight the hottest religion and human rights issues that now regularly confront national and international tribunals: How to protect religious and cultural minorities within a majoritarian religious culture—particularly controversial groups like Muslims, Mormons, Baha'ias, Jehovah's Witnesses, Scientologists, Unification Church members, and Indigenous peoples who often bring charges of religious and cultural discrimination. How to define limits on religious and anti-religious exercises and expressions that cause offense or harm to others or elicit charge of blasphemy, defamation, or sacrilege. How to adjudicate challenges that a state's proscriptions or prescriptions run directly counter to a party's core claims of conscience or cardinal commandments of the faith. How to balance private and public exercises of religion, including the liberty of conscience of one party to be left alone and the free exercise right of another to proselytize. How to balance conflicts between the rights of parents to bring up their children in the faith and the duties of the State to protect the best interest of the child. How to protect the distinct religious needs of prisoners, soldiers, refugees, and others who don't enjoy ready access to traditional forms and forums of religious worship and expression.

Many religion and human rights issues involve religious groups, for whom the right to organize as a legal entity with juridical personality is itself often a critical issue. How to negotiate the complex needs and norms of religious groups without according them too much sovereignty over their members or too little relief from secular courts in the event of fundamental rights violations by religious tribunals. How to balance the rights of religious groups to self-determination and self-governance and the guarantees of freedom from discrimination based on religion, gender, culture, and sexual orientation. How to balance competing religious groups who each claim access to a common holy site, or a single religious or cultural group whose sacred site is threatened with desecration, development, or disaster. How to protect the relations between local religious communities and their foreign co-religionists. How to adjudicate intra- or interreligious disputes that come before secular tribunals for resolution. How to determine the proper levels of state cooperation with and support of religious officials and institutions in the delivery of vital social services—child care, education, charity, medical services, and disaster relief, among others.

Each one of these issues of religion and human rights issues now commands a whole library of specialty literature, and a whole litany of human rights documents, cases, and field reports to consult. The chapters that follow, particularly in the second section of the volume, provide ample illustration of what is a stake and ample guidance on what more you might read.

■ THE PLACE OF RELIGION IN HUMAN RIGHTS

A number of distinguished commentators have argued that it is just because of all of these thorny problems that religion should have no place in a modern regime of human rights. Religious ideas may well have been the sources of human rights in earlier eras; some religious groups might even have helped to inspire the modern human rights revolution. But religion has now outlived its utility. Religion, by its nature, is too expansionistic and monopolistic, too patriarchal and hierarchical, too antithetical to the very ideals of pluralism, toleration, and equality inherent in a human rights regime. Religion is also too dangerous, divisive, and diverse in its demands to be accorded special protection. Religion is better viewed as just another category of private liberty, expression, and association and given no more preference than its secular counterparts. Indeed, to accord religion special human rights treatment is, in effect, to establish it and to discriminate against non-religious parties in the same position. Purge religion entirely, this argument concludes, and the human rights paradigm will thrive.[31]

This argument proves to be impractical. In the course of the twentieth century, religion defied the wistful assumptions of the Western academy that the spread of Enlightenment reason and science would slowly eclipse the sense of the sacred and the sensibility of the superstitious. Religion also defied the evil assumptions of Nazis, Fascists, and Communists that gulags and death camps, iconoclasm and book burnings, propaganda and mind controls would inevitably drive religion into extinction. Now, yet another great awakening of religion is upon us—global in its sweep and frightening in its power.[32]

It is undeniable that religion has been, and still is, a formidable force for both political good and political evil, that it has fostered both benevolence and belligerence, peace and pathos of untold dimensions. But the proper response to religious belligerence and pathos cannot be to deny that religion exists or to dismiss it to the private sphere and sanctuary. The proper response is to castigate the vices and to cultivate the virtues of religion, to confirm those religious teachings and practices that are most conducive to human rights, democracy, and rule of law.

Human rights ultimately needs religious ideas, institutions, and rights claims to survive and thrive. First, without religion, many rights are cut from their roots. The right to religion, Georg Jellinek once wrote, is "the mother of many other rights."[33] For the religious individual, the right to believe leads ineluctably to the rights to assemble, speak, worship, proselytize, educate, parent, travel, or to abstain from the same on the basis of one's beliefs. For the religious association, the right to exist invariably involves rights to corporate property, collective worship, organized charity, parochial education, freedom of press, and autonomy of governance. To ignore religious rights is to overlook the conceptual, if not historical, source of many other individual and associational rights.

Second, without religion, the regime of human rights becomes infinitely expandable. Many religious communities adopt and advocate human rights in order to protect religious duties. A religious individual or association has rights to exist and act not in the abstract but in order to discharge discrete religious duties. For many religions, freedoms and commandments, rights and duties belong together. To speak of one without the other is ultimately destructive. Rights without duties to guide them quickly become claims of self-indulgence. Duties without rights to exercise them quickly become sources of deep guilt.

Third, without religion, human rights become too captive to Western libertarian ideals. Many religious traditions cannot conceive of, nor accept, a system of rights that excludes, deprecates, or privatizes religion. Religion is for these traditions inextricably integrated into every facet of life. The rights of religion are, for them, an inherent part of rights of speech, press, assembly, and other individual rights, as well as ethnic, cultural, linguistic, and similar associational rights. No system of rights that ignores or deprecates this cardinal place of religion can be respected or adopted.

Fourth, without religion, the State is often given an exaggerated role to play as the guarantor of human rights. The simple state-versus-individual dialectic of many modern human rights theories leaves it to the State to protect and provide rights of all sorts. In reality, the State is not, and cannot be, so omnicompetent, as the fantastic failures of the twentieth-century Communist states made all too clear. Numerous "mediating structures" stand between the State and the individual, religious institutions prominently among them. Religious institutions, among others, play a vital role in the cultivation and realization of rights. They can create the conditions (sometimes the prototypes) for the realization of first generation civil and political rights. They can provide a critical (sometimes the principal) means to meet second generation rights of education, health care, child care, labor organizations, employment, artistic opportunities, among others. They can offer some of the deepest insights into norms of creation, stewardship, and servanthood that lie at the heart of third generation rights.

The challenge of this new century is to transform religious communities from midwives to mothers of human rights—from agents that assist in the birth of rights norms conceived elsewhere, to associations that give birth to and nurture their own unique contributions to human rights norms and practices. The ancient Abrahamic teachings and practices of Judaism, Christianity, and Islam have much to commend themselves to the human rights regime. As the chapters herein by David Novak, Nicholas Wolterstorff, and Abdullahi An-Na'im illustrate, each of these traditions is a religion of revelation, founded on the eternal command to love one God, oneself, and all neighbors. Each tradition recognizes a canonical text as its highest authority—the Torah, the Bible, and the Quran, respectively. Each tradition designates a class of officials to preserve and propagate its faith, and embraces an expanding body of authoritative interpretations and applications of its canons. Each tradition has a refined legal structure—*halakhah*, canon law, and Sharia, respectively—that has translated its enduring principles of faith into evolving precepts of works. Each tradition has sought to imbue its religious, ethical, and legal norms into the daily lives of individuals and communities. Each tradition has produced a number of the basic building blocks of a comprehensive theory and law of religious rights—conscience, dignity, reason, liberty, equality, tolerance, love, openness, responsibility, justice, mercy, righteousness, accountability, covenant, and community, among other cardinal concepts. Each tradition has developed its own internal system of legal procedures and structures for the protection of rights, which historically have and still can serve as both prototypes and complements for secular legal systems. Each tradition has its own advocates and prophets, ancient and modern, who have worked to achieve a closer approximation of human rights ideals.

Similarly, the ancient teachings of Buddhism, Confucianism, Hinduism, and Indigenous Religions have much to teach the world about human rights—particularly in their call to strike new balances between individual rights and social responsibilities, between the freedoms of humans and the needs of nature, between the legal order of the world and the cosmic order of the universe. As the chapters herein by Sallie King, Joseph Chan, Werner Menksi, and Ronald Niezen illustrate, Buddhist, Confucian, Hindu, and Indigenous defenses and declarations of rights are beginning to appear. And many members of these religious traditions now often eagerly embrace the freedom of religion and religious self-determination held out by modern human rights and constitutional instruments. But these Asian and Indigenous traditions have also maintained a healthy skepticism about modern formulations of human rights, and question whether human rights are truly universal or just the hegemonic creations of Western Christianity and Enlightenment liberalism.

■ THE PLACE OF HUMAN RIGHTS IN RELIGION

Human rights skeptics within the Asian religious world often found allies among Western religious believers as well. It is one thing, such religious skeptics argue, for religious believers and bodies to accept the freedom and autonomy that a human rights regime allows. This at least gives them unencumbered space to pursue their divine callings. It is quite another thing for religious communities to import human rights within their own polities and theologies. This exposes them to all manner of unseemly challenges.

Human rights norms, religious skeptics argue, challenge the structure of religious bodies. While human rights norms teach liberty and equality, most religious bodies teach authority and hierarchy. While human rights norms encourage pluralism and diversity, many religious bodies require orthodoxy and uniformity. While human rights norms teach freedoms of speech and petition, several religions teach duties of silence and submission. To draw human rights norms into the structures of religion would only seem to embolden members to demand greater access to religious governance, greater freedom from religious discipline, greater latitude in the definition of religious doctrine and liturgy. So why import them?

Moreover, human rights norms challenge the spirit of religious bodies. Human rights norms, religious skeptics argue, are the creed of a secular faith born of Enlightenment liberalism, humanism, and rationalism. Human rights advocates regularly describe these norms as our new "civic faith," "our new world religion," "our new global moral language." Influential French jurist Karel Vasak has pressed these sentiments into a full confession of the secular spirit of the modern human rights movement:

> The Universal Declaration of Human Rights [of 1948], like the French Declaration of the Rights of Man and Citizen in 1789, has had an immense impact throughout the world. It has been called a modern edition of the New Testament, and the Magna Carta of humanity, and has become a constant source of inspiration for governments,

> for judges, and for national and international legislators. . . . [B]y recognizing the Universal Declaration as a *living* document . . . one can proclaim one's faith in the future of mankind.[34]

In demonstration of this new faith, Vasak converted the "old trinity" of "*liberté, equalité, et fraternité*" taught by the French Revolution into a "new trinity" of "three generations of rights" for all humanity.[35] The first generation of civil and political rights elaborates the meaning of liberty. The second generation of social, cultural, and economic rights elaborates the meaning of equality. The third generation of solidarity rights to development, peace, health, the environment, and open communication elaborates the meaning of fraternity. Such language has become not only the *lingua franca* but also something of the *lingua sacra* of the modern human rights movement. In the face of such an overt confession of secular liberalism, religious skeptics conclude, a religious body would do well to resist the ideas and institutions of human rights.

Both these skeptical arguments, however, presuppose that human rights norms constitute a static belief system born of Enlightenment liberalism. But the human rights regime is not static. It is fluid, elastic, and open to challenge and change. The human rights regime is not a fundamental belief system. It is a relative system of ideas and ideals that presupposes the existence of fundamental beliefs and values that will constantly shape and reshape it. The human rights regime is not the child of Enlightenment liberalism, nor a ward under its exclusive guardianship. It is the *ius gentium* of our times, the common law of nations, which a variety of Hebrew, Greek, Roman, Christian, and Enlightenment movements have historically nurtured in the West and which today needs the constant nurture of multiple communities, in the West and well beyond. It is beyond doubt that many current formulations of human rights are suffused with fundamental libertarian beliefs and values, some of which run counter to the cardinal beliefs of various religious traditions. But libertarianism does not and should not have a monopoly on the nurture of human rights; indeed, a human rights regime cannot long survive under its exclusive patronage.

We use the antique term *ius gentium* advisedly—to signal the place of human rights as "middle axioms" in our moral and political discourse. Historically, Western writers spoke of a hierarchy of laws—from natural law (*ius naturale*), to common law (*ius gentium*), to civil law (*ius civile*). The natural law was the set of immutable principles of reason and conscience, which are supreme in authority and divinity and must always prevail in instances of dispute. The civil law was the set of enacted laws and procedures of local political communities, reflecting their immediate policies and procedures. Between these two sets of norms was the *ius gentium*, the set of principles and customs common to several communities and often the basis for treaties and other diplomatic conventions. The contents of the *ius gentium* did gradually change over time and across cultures as new interpretations of the natural law were offered, and as new formulations of the positive law became increasingly conventional. But the *ius gentium* was a relatively consistent body of principles by which a person and a people could govern themselves.[36]

This antique typology helps us to understand the intermediate place of human rights in our hierarchy of legal and cultural norms today. Human rights are the *ius gentium* of our time, the middle axioms of our discourse. They are derived from and dependent upon the transcendent principles that religious traditions (more than any other group) continue to cultivate. They also inform, and are informed by, shifts in the customs and conventions of sundry state law systems. These human rights norms do gradually change over time: just compare the international human rights instruments of 1948 with those of today. But human rights norms are a relatively stable set of ideals by which a person and community might be guided and judged.

This antique typology also helps us to understand the place of human rights within religion. Our argument that human rights must have a more prominent place within religions today is not an attempt to import libertarian ideals into their theologies and polities. It is not an attempt to herd Trojan horses into churches, synagogues, mosques, and temples to assail secretly their spirit and structure. Our argument is, rather, that religious bodies must again assume their traditional patronage and protection of human rights, bringing to this regime their full doctrinal vigor, liturgical healing, and moral suasion. Using our antique typology, religious bodies must again nurture and challenge the middle axioms of the *ius gentium* using the transcendent principles of the *ius naturale*. This must not be an effort to monopolize the discourse, nor to establish by positive law a particular religious construction of human rights. Such an effort must be part of a collective discourse of competing understandings of the *ius naturale*—of competing theological views of the divine and the human, of good and evil, of individuality and community—that will serve constantly to inform and reform, to develop and deepen, the human rights ideals now in place.

As the opening chapters in this volume illustrate, a number of religious traditions of late have begun the process of reengaging the regime of human rights, of returning to their traditional roots and routes of nurturing and challenging the human rights regime. This process has been incremental, clumsy, controversial, and at times even fatal for its proponents. But the process of religious engagement of human rights is now under way in Christian, Islamic, Judaic, Buddhist, Confucian, Hindu, and Indigenous communities alike. Something of a new "human rights hermeneutic" is slowly beginning to emerge among modern religions.[37]

This is, in part, a "hermeneutic of confession." Given their checkered human rights records over the centuries, religious bodies have begun to acknowledge their departures from the cardinal teachings of peace and love that are the heart of their sacred texts and traditions. They have begun to confess that their theologians and jurists have resisted the importation of human rights as much as they have helped in their cultivation, that their internal policies and external advocacy have helped to perpetuate bigotry, chauvinism, and violence as much as they have served to propagate equality, liberty, and fraternity. The blood of thousands is at the doors of our churches, synagogues, temples, and mosques. The bludgeons of pogroms, crusades, jihads, inquisitions, and ostracisms have been used to devastating effect within and among these faiths. Confession and restitution are essential first steps for any religious community to engage human rights fully.

This is, in part, a "hermeneutic of suspicion," in Paul Ricoeur's famous phrase. Given the pronounced libertarian tone of many recent human rights formulations, it is imperative that we not idolize or idealize these formulations. We need not be bound by current taxonomies of "three generations of rights" rooted in liberty, equality, and fraternity. Nor do we need to accept the seemingly infinite expansion of human rights discourse and demands. Rights bound by moral duties, by natural capacities, or by covenantal relationships might well provide better boundaries to the legitimate expression and extension of rights. We also need not be bound only to a centralized legal methodology of articulating and enforcing rights. We might also consider a more pluralistic model of interpretation that respects "the right of the [local] community to be the living frame of interpretation for [its] own religion and its normative regime."[38]

This is, in part, a "hermeneutic of history." While acknowledging the fundamental contributions of Enlightenment liberalism to the modern rights regime, we must also see the deeper genesis and genius of many modern rights norms in religious texts and traditions that antedate the Enlightenment by centuries, even by millennia. We must return to our religious sources. In part, this is a return to ancient sacred texts freed from the casuistic accretions of generations of jurists and freed from the cultural trappings of the communities in which these traditions were born. In part, this is a return to slender streams of theological jurisprudence that have not been part of the mainstream of the religious traditions, or have become diluted by too great a commingling with it. In part, this is a return to prophetic voices of dissent, long purged from traditional religious canons, but, in retrospect, prescient of some of the rights roles that the tradition might play today.

This is, in part, a "hermeneutic of law and religion." A century of legal positivism in the Western academy has trained us to think that law is an autonomous discipline, free from the influence of religion and belief. A century of firm laicization and strict separation of church and state has accustomed us to think that our law and politics must be hermetically and hermeneutically sealed from the corrosive influences of religious believers and bodies. An ample body of new scholarship has emerged, however, to show that law and religion need each sother, and that institutions like human rights have interlocking legal and religious dimensions.

The universality of human rights has held up "as long as no one asks why" in Maritain's famous phrase. The various covenants and conventions of international human rights law, as concerns religion, while not always unanimous in their acclamation or uniform in their application have generally been taken to be universal in their aspiration. What happens when increased globalization, communication, and internationalism in the legal sphere brings to light uncomfortable differences of opinion, orientation, and ontology in the religious sphere? Most religions have a stake in asserting the truth of their own beliefs against the apparent falsehood of the beliefs of others. At the level of normative interreligious engagement, refraining from asking the "why" questions may be difficult if not disingenuous, if one purports to want to truly understand and respect religious beliefs and religious diversity. How to have these conversations in a way that is both critical and constructive amid descriptive and doctrinal pluralism remains a crucial challenge for both religion and human rights.

■ NOTES

1 "EU Parliament President Calls for Life of Afghan Student to be Spared," theparliament.com, January 21, 2008. (www.eupolitix.com)

2 "No Death Sentence for Afghan Journalist," *The New York Times*, October 21, 2008.

3 Carlotta Gall and Sangar Rahimi, "Karzai Vows to Review Family Law," *The New York Times*, April 4, 2009.

4 For much of this part of the world, see the reports of Forum 18 (www.forum18.org)

5 See the collection of annual reports by the United States Commission on International Religious Freedom at (www.uscirf.gov); see also the recent manifesto by the Chicago Council of Global Affairs chaired by R. Scott Appleby and Richard Cizik: *Engaging Religious Communities Abroad: A New Imperative for U.S. Foreign Policy* (Chicago: Chicago Council of Global Affairs, 2010).

6 See the annual reports of the Special Rapporteur on Freedom of Religion or Belief collected at http://www2.ohchr.org/english/issues/religion/index.htm.

7 The Pew Forum on Religion and Public Life, "Global Restrictions on Religion," (December, 2009) (www.pewforum.org)

8 John T. Noonan, Jr., "The Tensions and the Ideals," *Religious Human Rights in Global Perspective: Legal Perspectives*, eds. Johan D. van der Vyver and John Witte, Jr. (The Hague: Martinus Nijhoff, 1996), 594.

9 See sources in John Witte, Jr., *The Reformation of Rights: Law, Religion, and Human Rights in Early Modern Calvinism* (Cambridge, NY: Cambridge University Press, 2008), 1–38.

10 Mary Ann Glendon, *A World Made New: Eleanor Roosevelt and the Universal Declaration of Human Rights* (New York: Random House, 2001), 77–78 (emphasis added).

11 On these latter rights, see the chapters by Ronald Niezen, Willis Jenkins, and Scott Appleby, herein.

12 See the chapter by Ingvill Thorson Plesner herein, citing the World Conference on Human Rights in Vienna, June 14-25, 1993.

13 International Covenant on Civil and Political Rights G.A. Res. 2200A (XXI), 21 U.N. GAOR Supp (No. 16) at 52, U.N. Doc. A/6316, 999 U.N.T.S. 171, *entered into force* March 23, 1976.

14 United Nations General Assembly, Declaration on the Elimination of All Forms of Intolerance and Discrimination Based on Religion or Belief, G.A. Res. 36/55, U.N. GAOR Supp. (no. 151), U.N. Doc. A/RES/36/55 (1981).

15 Concluding Document of the Third Follow-Up Meeting of Representatives of the Participating States of the Conference on Security and Cooperation in Europe (Vienna) 28 I.L.M. 527 (January 17, 1989).

16 United Nations General Assembly, Declaration on the Rights of Persons Belonging to National or Ethnic, Religious, and Linguistic Minorities, G.A. Res. 47/135, Annex, 47 U.N. GAOR Supp. (No. 49) at 210, U.N. Doc. A/47/49 (1993) (hereinafter "Minorities Declaration").

17 See the chapters by Paul Taylor and Jeremy Gunn, herein, and Symposium, "The Permissible Scope of Legal Limitations on the Freedom of Religion and Belief," *Emory International Law Review* 19 (2005): 465–1320.

18 See further the chapter by Steven Smith herein, on freedom of conscience.

19 Document of the Copenhagen Meeting of Representatives of the Participating States of the Conference on the Human Dimension of the Conference on Security and Co-operation in Europe,June 29, 1990, 29 I.L.M. 1305 (1990), Principle 18.

20 See further the chapter by Barbara Bennett Woodhouse herein, and Symposium, "What's Wrong with Rights for Children?" *Emory International Law Review* 20 (2006): 1–239.

21 See further the chapter by Nazila Ghanea, herein.

22 Minorities Declaration, Art. 4.2. See further the chapters by Natan Lerner and Johan van der Vyver, herein.

23 United Nations General Assembly, Declaration on the Rights of Indigenous Peoples, G.A. Res. 61/295, U.N. GAOR, A/61/L.67/Annex (2007). See further the chapter by Ronald Niezen, herein.

24 See the chapter by Nicholas Wolterstorff, herein; see also J. Bryan Hehir, "The Modern Catholic Church and Human Rights: The Impact of the Second Vatican Council," in *Christianity and Human Rights,* eds. John Witte, Jr. and Frank S. Alexander (Cambridge: Cambridge University Press, 2010), 113–134.

25 Universal Islamic Declaration of Human Rights (London: Islamic Council, 1981), Foreword (quoting Quran, Sura 49:13).

26 Ibid., Arts. 13, 12, 14, 10.

27 Cairo Declaration on Human Rights in Islam, Aug. 5, 1990, U.N. GAOR, World Conf. on Hum. Rts., 4th Sess., Agenda Item 5, U.N. Doc. A/CONF.157/PC/62/Add.18 (1993) [English translation], Art. 1 (emphasis added).

28 Ibid., Art. 22 (emphasis added).

29 Ibid., Art. 18 (emphasis added).

30 On this latter, see the chapter by Carolyn Evans, herein.

31 See the chapter by David Little, herein, weighing religious and secular justifications for human rights.

32 See the chapter by Scott Appleby, herein.

33 Georg Jellinek, *Die Erklärung der Menschen- und Bürgerrechte: ein Beitrag zur modernen Verfassungsgeschichte* (Leipzig: Duncker and Humblot, 1895), 42.

34 Karel Vasak, "A 30-Year Struggle," *UNESCO Courier*, November 1977, p. 29; see also Karel Vasak, "Foreword," in *The International Dimensions of Human Rights,* rev. ed., eds. Karel Vasak and Philip Alston (Westport, CT: Greenwood Press, 1982), xv; id., "*Pour une troisième génération des droits de l'homme,*" in *Études et Essais sur le Droit International Humanitaire et sur les Principes de la Croix-Rouge en l'Honneur de Jean Pictet*, ed. Christophe Swinarksi (The Hague: Martinus Nijhoff, 1984), 837–845.

35 Vasak, "Pour une troisième génération," 837.

36 See Brian Tierney, *The Idea of Natural Rights: Studies on Natural Rights, Natural Law, and Church Law, 1150–1625* (Grand Rapids, MI: Wm. B. Eerdmans Pub. Co., 1997).

37 Abdullahi Ahmed An-Na'im, "Towards an Islamic Hermeneutics for Human Rights," in *Human Rights and Religious Values: An Uneasy Relationship?* eds. Abdullahi Ahmed An-Na'im, et al. (Grand Rapids: Wm. B. Eerdmans, 1995), 229–242.

38 Abdullahi Ahmed An-Naim, *Toward an Islamic Reformation: Civil Liberties, Human Rights, and International Law* (Albany, NY: SUNY Press, 1990), 235.

■ RECOMMENDED READING

Ahdar, Rex and Ian Leigh. *Religious Freedom in the Liberal State* (Oxford: Oxford University Press, 2005)

An-Na'im, Abdullahi Ahmed, et al., eds. *Human Rights and Religious Values: An Uneasy Relationship* (Grand Rapids, MI: Wm. B. Eerdmans Pub. Co., 2005)

Appleby, R. Scott. *The Ambivalence of the Sacred: Religion, Violence, and Reconciliation* (Lanham, MD: Rowman & Littlefield, 2000)

Bauer, Joseph and Daniel Bell, eds. *The East Asian Challenge for Human Rights* (Cambridge: Cambridge University Press, 1999)

Bucar, Elizabeth M. and Barbra Barnett, eds. *Does Human Rights Need God?* (Grand Rapids, MI: Wm. B. Eerdmans Pub. Co., 2005)

Cane, Peter, Carolyn Evans, and Zoë Robinson, eds. *Law and Religion in Theoretical and Historical Context* (Cambridge: Cambridge University Press, 2008)

de Bary, William Theodore. *Asian Values and Human Rights* (Cambridge.: Harvard University Press, 1998)

Durham, W. Cole, Jr. and Brent G. Scharffs. *Law and Religion: National, International, and Comparative Perspectives* (New York: Aspen, 2010)

Evans, Carolyn. *Freedom of Religion Under the European Convention on Human Rights* (Oxford: Oxford University Press, 2001)

Evans, Malcolm D. *Religious Liberty and International Law in Europe* (Cambridge: Cambridge University Press, 1997)

Ghanea, Nazila, Alan Stephens, and, Raphael Walden, eds. *Does God Believe in Human Rights* (Leiden: Martinus Nijhoff Publishers, 2007)

Hackett, Rosalind I. J. ed. *Proselytization Revisited: Rights Talk, Free Markets and Culture Wars* (London: Equinox, 2008)

Lerner, Natan. *Religion, Secular Beliefs and Human Rights: 25 Years After the Human Rights Declaration* (Leiden: Martinus Nijhoff, 2006)

Lindholm, Tore, W. Cole Durham, Jr., and, Bahia G. Tahzib-Lie. *Facilitating Freedom of Religion or Belief: A Deskbook* (Leiden: Martinus Nijhoff Publishers, 2004)

Niezen, Ronald. *The Origins of Indigenism: Human Rights and the Politics of Identity* (Berkeley and London: University of California Press, 2003)

Novak, David. *Covenantal Rights: A Study in Jewish Political Theory* (Princeton: Princeton University Press, 2000)

Perry, Michael J. *Toward a Theory of Human Rights: Religion, Law, Courts* (Cambridge, NY: Cambridge University Press, 2007)

Runzo, Joseph, Nancy M. Martin, and, Arvind Sharma, eds. *Human Rights and Responsibilities in the World Religions* (Oxford: Oneworld, 2003)

Sharma, Arvind. *Hindu Narratives on Human Rights* (Santa Barbara, CA: Praeger/ABC-Clio, 2010)

Stahnke, Tad and J. Paul Martin, eds. *Religion and Human Rights: Basic Documents* (New York: Center for the Study of Human Rights, Columbia University, 1998)

Taylor, Paul M. *Freedom of Religion: UN and European Human Rights Law and Practice* (Cambridge: Cambridge University Press, 2005)

Van ver Ven, Johannes A., Jaco S. Dreyer, and, Hendrik J.C. Pieterse. *Is There a God in Human Rights? The Complex Relationship Between Human Rights and Religion* (Leiden: Brill, 2004)

Witte, John, Jr. and Johan D. van der Vyver, eds. *Religious Human Rights in Global Perspective*, 2 vols. (The Hague: Martinus Nijhoff, 1996)

Witte, John, Jr. and Joel A. Nichols. *Religion and the American Constitutional Experiment*, 3rd ed. (Boulder, CO: Westview Press, 2011)

Wolterstorff, Nicholas P. *Justice: Rights and Wrongs* (Princeton: Princeton University Press, 2008)

PART ONE

Human Rights and Religious Traditions

1 A Jewish Theory of Human Rights

DAVID NOVAK

JEWISH RIGHTS-TALK

Almost forty years ago, in his introduction to a collection of essays reflecting on rights-talk in the Jewish tradition, the Jewish political theorist Milton R. Konvitz noted, "There is no word or phrase for 'human rights' in the Hebrew Scriptures or in any other ancient Jewish text. . . . Yet the absence of these and related words and phrases does not mean the nonexistence of the ideals and values for which they stand or to which they point."[1] Konvitz seems to be suggesting that with some good historical research and some good philosophical reflection working with it, rights-talk could not only be found within the past Jewish tradition, but it could also be further developed in the present and preserved for the future by Jewish thinkers now engaged in rights-talk. And, in fact, the representation of Jewish rights-talk, bringing it up-to-date so to speak, could give it some influence in current discussions of human rights issues.

What we now need is a working definition of what is meant by the term "right." We should begin by raising the question of whether a "human" right can only be exercised by a human individual, or whether a human collective can exercise a right too. Certainly when dealing with the Jewish tradition, we should then consider whether humans (individually or collectively) can be claimed by a nonhuman person exercising his right. That is, we need to inquire whether God can be considered a rights-holder—indeed, *the* rights-holder—and if so, we need to enquire how a divine right is exercised. Furthermore, when dealing with the Jewish tradition, we should consider whether what look like human rights in that tradition are "natural" rights in the sense of being rights that could be exercised by any human being in any rational human society, or whether there are also what might be called "Torah" rights. (Generally, Jewish thinkers who are uninterested in the universal question of human rights are also uninterested in the more particular question of how rights might be seen to underlie specifically Jewish duties.) Are there rights (and not just duties) that only members of the covenant between God and Israel can exercise because they alone are the people obligated by the full Torah (Scripture and the Normative Jewish Tradition), which is the constitution of the Covenant (*ha-berit*)? Accordingly, we can speak of three kinds of rights: (1) divine rights that God justifiably claims for himself; (2) natural rights that all humans justifiably claim for themselves, individually or collectively; and (3) Torah rights that Jews justifiably claim for themselves, individually or collectively.

To be sure, how natural rights operate in the Jewish tradition will be of most interest to those engaged in the vibrant discussion of human rights being conducted today in secular societies. Yet for those whose primary communal commitment is to the Jewish community, their primary interest should be in divine rights and Torah rights. And they should then try to show how specifically human natural rights (where humans are both the subjects and the objects of the right) have been found and have been well nurtured in a culture where divine rights and Torah rights predominate, and that current rights theory can take much from culture and even build upon it.[2] As such, the affirmation of human natural rights in the modern sense need not be seen as having to overcome a "rightless" culture. Furthermore, for the sake of their own entrance into the current discussion of human rights, more traditionally committed Jewish legal and political theorists need to affirm the social necessity of natural human rights (especially in an era when they are so egregiously violated in so many places). They also need to remember that these rights are not sufficient for the constitution of a human community worthy of the transcendent thrust of human nature, which is the basic human need to be related to God. And that admission should become at least a question for the more secularly committed legal and political theorists. They need to ask or be asked: In the full existential sense, is the affirmation of human rights enough?

These are the questions that will guide this inquiry into the role human rights play in "Judaism," which is the religion of the Jews rooted in divine revelation, then transmitted and developed by the ongoing Jewish tradition, whose most immediately normative manifestation is "the Law" (*halakhah* in Hebrew).

■ RIGHTS AND DUTIES

To speak of a right is to speak of a justified claim made by a weaker party upon a stronger party to either do something *for* the claimant, or refrain from doing something *to* or *against* that claimant. Thus a right is a claim calling for an appropriate response *from* the person or persons so claimed.[3] A right is a *human* right when it is exercised by a human being for himself or herself (or for some other human being, like a child or an incapacitated human being), and when the reason or justification for the exercise of that right is the human *nature* or personhood of the human being making that claim upon an other. One's being human by nature, which means their membership in a species specifically characterized by the capacity to make justified claims, is the reason why that person's claim can be taken seriously by rational persons: they can be argued for. Human beings have certain inherent rights by virtue of their being members of humankind.

Humans make rights-claims in the interest of what they want for themselves or do not want for themselves. These "wants" are best justified when they are shown to stem from indispensable human needs, which are first uttered in the language of desire, and then argued for in the language of rights. So, it could be said that the most basic positive human right is the justified claim to be helped, and the most basic negative human right is the justified claim not to be harmed.

A rights-claim is only cogent when made in a society structured by law—what one could call a "constitutional polity"—where justice as "the rule of law" (best designated by the German term *Rechtstaat*) obtains. Jewish communities have always been such constitutional polities, even though they have not enjoyed the full range of national independence enjoyed by modern nation-states, that is, until the reestablishment of the State of Israel in 1948, though the relation of the State of Israel to the Torah as the traditional Jewish constitution is still undetermined.

The polity, originally in the name of its sovereign—who in Judaism is God—warrants the exercise of a right, by advocating the exercise of that right, enforcing that exercise, and punishing violators of that right. In interpersonal situations, individual persons have a twofold right: (1) their claim on an other individual person or persons to whom they are now directly related; and (2) their claim on the polity where they are now living to advocate that right, enforce it as much as possible, and punish violations of that right as much as possible. That right is a legal right when it can be enforced and violations of it punished by a human court. But when enforcement and punishment are beyond the scope of a human court and are in God's hands alone, that is a moral right.[4] Only in rare cases, when a moral right seems to be so much more justified than a competing legal right, is the moral right is to be enforced by a human court. In these rare cases, it is a matter of equity over positive law.[5]

All rights are essentially public matters (*res publica*). Even a so-called "private" right is only a *right to privacy*. That is, it is a right that certain individual actions be *deprived* of public scrutiny and are thus to be kept private. The public is therefore obliged to respect the privacy of these individuals, and these individuals are obliged to respect their own privacy by shielding certain actions from public scrutiny.[6] Since private acts are rarely if ever performed by an individual acting alone, private rights are actually *domestic* rights. They are the rights of families to conduct their familial relations—including but not confined to sexual relations between spouses—within the protective, opaque confines of their home. Nevertheless, these rights can and should be overridden when the abuse of individual rights like the right not to be physically or sexually abused are grossly violated within a home. In such cases, here is a social duty of public authorities to rescue an abused member of a family from their abuser.[7] And, of course in Judaism, nothing can be kept private from God's scrutiny and judgment, hence privacy is relative to inter-human relations. "Where can I go away from Your spirit, and where can I flee from Your presence?! If I ascend to heaven You are there; and if I make my bed in the netherworld, behold there You are!" (Psalms 139:7–8)

When a right is justified, it thereby entails an equally justified response or duty on the part of the person to whom the claim is made. This responsive person now has an obligation (*hovah* in Hebrew, coming from the verb "to owe") to the one claiming him or her. That is now his or her responsibility. Although it is disputed by those scholars who assume rights-talk is foreign to Judaism, I think it can be shown that even in the duty-laden normative Jewish tradition (where "commandment," in Hebrew *mitsvah*, is the most basic operative term) there is no duty without a prior right. Hence a right engenders a duty instead of a duty engendering a right. In this way, the priority of a right over a duty serves the rationality of the Law (what the ancient Rabbis called *ta'amei ha-mitsvot*, "the commandments' reasons") better than the obverse.[8] A right provides a justification or a reason for a duty, whereas to assert that the reason for a right is the fulfillment of a duty turns the duty into an arbitrary decree, which seems to be indiscreetly addressed to *whomever* rather than being a rational response to *someone's* justifiable claim. This is important to bear in mind in order to cogently counter the often-asserted opinion that the normative Jewish tradition only considers duties, not rights.

■ THREE SPHERES OF HUMAN RELATIONS

In the Jewish tradition, one can see that the rights-duties correlation operates in the three relational spheres in which humans are involved. They are: (1) God-human relations; (2) inter-human relations; and (3) community-individual relations.

In each of these relational spheres there are both natural rights-duties and Torah rights-duties. That combination shows how the Jewish tradition has incorporated the findings of secular wisdom into its own normative scheme, building upon them without superseding them. And divine rights are involved in all three relational schemes inasmuch as all of the commandments, embodying as they do rights-duties correlations, are either immediately or ultimately rooted in God's will. Nevertheless, the exercise of these divine rights by God is only immediately experienced within the covenanted community. There, God is both the direct source and the direct object of the commanded act. There, commandments are kept "for God's sake."[9] That cannot be cogently proposed in a secular society, which though not necessarily an atheistic society (officially or unofficially), is still a society that does not look to any historical event of divine revelation for its warrant. When such a society proposes *natural* rights, it is doing so because it looks to human nature rather than to revelation for its warrant. Moreover, each of these rights-duties correlations has both a positive and a negative manifestation. Let us now look at these three relational spheres and their respective normative correlations of rights and duties.

God-Human Relations

At the level of natural rights, pertaining as it does to human nature, the created nature of each and every human being is unique because "in the likeness of God [*be-demut elohim*] He made humankind [*ha'adam*]" (Genesis 5:1); and the human right to justice is "because in the image of God [*be-tselem elohim*] He made humankind."[10] For a number of exegetes, that means humans share with God the personal attributes of intellect and will. Now it is true that we certainly consider intellect and will to be indispensable human attributes, without which a human being could not exercise a right. In fact, even the right to life of those deprived of intellect and will has to be exercised on their behalf by another, more fully human person or persons. Moreover, that deprived human being has that right to life because he or she is usually the child of persons who do have sufficient intellect and will to have exercised their duty to "be fruitful and multiply" (Genesis 9:1). Nevertheless, that does not tell us *how* humans receive these attributes *from* God or *why* they receive them.

The answer to both of these questions is revealed when the Bible speaks of the first contact God makes with his human creatures: "The Lord God commanded [*va-yitsav*] humans" (Genesis 2:16). That contact is a commandment (*mitsvah*); and a commandment worthy of the response of a being who is capable of exercising intelligent choice could only come from someone who is himself a superior intelligent chooser. Indeed, to be capable of being addressed by God, and to have the capacity freely to accept or reject what God has commanded one to do, that is what makes humans unique.[11] Thus, one is known and chosen before one can know and choose, just as one must be the subject of a duty and the object of a right before he or she can exercise a right that claims someone else's duty. (Children only learn how to make intelligent rights-claims from having experienced intelligent rights-claims made upon them by their parents and teachers.) So, if God is to intelligently and freely claim the dutiful obedience of God's human creatures, then it would seem that God has to create them with his uniquely personal attributes of intellect and will in order to be able to respond in kind. And humans become aware of these attributes not so much when they exercise "dominion" (Genesis 1:28) over the non-human world beneath them in intellect and will but, rather, when as the subjects of a commandment they are called upon to respond. But, at the level of natural rights, what are humans being commanded to do? Are they commanded to respond *back* to God, or are they commanded to carry forth the divine command *away from* God *into* the world?

In rabbinic or talmudic thought, the predominant opinion is that God is commanding all humankind to do justice among themselves, specifically to set up courts of law (*dinim*) to rectify various injustices committed by one human person to another.[12] Like any social obligation, the obligation to establish a system of justice in a society can only be advocated by the individual members of that society who already believe themselves to be personally obligated to do justice, either for others or for themselves, even when a system of social justice is not operative or not yet in place in their society.[13] Moreover, responsible human dominion is to be primarily exercised among humans themselves. And it can only be exercised secondarily over the non-human creation which can be domesticated, namely, that part of creation humans are to "use and protect" (Genesis 2:15) and which they are required so to do when they recognize that they are only its stewards and not its creators or destroyers.[14] Thus, humans only have the right to use God's creation for their real needs, plus the duty not to wantonly destroy created beings, wanton destruction of which would be an unjustified over-extension of that original right.[15] When that human right is overextended, it thereby violates God's creator-right, which means that all other creatures having intellect and will (who seem to be humankind only) are duty-bound to treat the rest of God's creation with respect.[16] I don't see how, from a traditional Jewish perspective, one can speak of either "animal rights" or "environmental rights" inasmuch as neither animals nor any other creatures seem to have intellect and will, nor are they descended from creatures who do have intellect and will. Intellect and will are certainly necessary attributes of anyone who can be cogently called a "rights-holder" and "duty-bound."[17] And, in fact, a more persuasive case can be made for the protection of animals and the environment from wanton destruction by humans by emphasizing God's creator-right to have his creation respected, instead of the irrational presumption that these creatures are rights-holders themselves. Indeed, how can one presume they are rights-holders when no one could cogently propose they can act dutifully?

Getting back to human rights, it would seem that humans in their natural social state do not experience the claim upon themselves to do justice to be coming directly from God. Instead, they experience that claim to be coming directly from the cries of their fellow humans who are the victims of injustice.[18] Courts of law are essentially established to systematically respond to these cries in an appropriate fashion. Therefore, in this first "natural" commandment, humans in their natural social state do not experience the commandment as a direct divine right or claim made upon themselves. Instead, at this level, God is the One who ultimately *enables* or empowers the victims of injustice to make their claims upon their fellow citizens (that is, those humans who along with them are members of the same polity and subjects of the same positive law) *because* they are God's image. And God ultimately *authorizes* those capable of responding to these claims to do so *because* as God's image, their working or actualizing justice in the world is ultimately an imitation of the God who is "the Judge [*shofet*] of the whole world, who does justice [*mishpat*]" (Genesis 18:25).[19] Nevertheless, both the original enabling of the victims of injustice intelligently to seek justice and the ultimate authorization of those who are to adjudicate on their behalf, neither are claims God makes for himself. Accordingly, they are not claims in the usual human sense of claims as rights which claimants exercise for themselves. Instead, they are divine *entitlements* that enable victims of injustice to exercise their right to receive justice, and that authorize legal authorities to exercise their right to effect as much justice in the world as they can.[20]

It is within the covenanted community that God exercises his divine rights for himself which, as we have assumed, stems from God's desire for an ongoing intimate relationship with his elect people, a point made many times in the Bible and the rabbinic texts. That relationship is lived and celebrated when the people keep the commandments of the Torah, especially those commandments whose direct object is God himself. This can be seen in the beginning of the Decalogue: "I am the Lord your God who has taken you out of the land of Egypt, out of the house of bondage. You shall have no other gods in My presence" (Exodus 20:2–3). The recognition of God as the Liberator from slavery is not so much a claim on the people's gratitude as it is a divine assertion that just as God has graciously benefited the people by taking them out of Egypt, so God will continue to graciously benefit the people by giving them commandments that will enable them to survive in the wilderness and to survive and flourish in the Promised Land. Accordingly, the intention of these commandments is more prospective than retrospective. But that requires the total and ongoing commitment of the people to the One God with whom they are now involved in an unconditional and everlasting covenant. That relationship must not be diluted in any way by including in it any other objects of worship or devotion. Once the exclusivity of the covenantal relationship is determined, the people can accept in good faith the other commandments that primarily benefit them in this relationship and that function to give content to this relationship.

Despite all the universal implications of these commandments in the Decalogue, they are still only addressed to Israel. They are God's claim on his covenanted people alone. So it could be said that from the Bible's perspective, idolatry as the worship of "other" gods (who could be seen as the gods of "the others") is only proscribed to Israel.[21] For if idolatry is comparable to adultery, then just as a woman (to whom Israel is sometimes compared by the prophets and the rabbis) cannot be an adulteress unless she is already a party to a marital covenant, so gentiles who are not covenanted with the One God cannot be guilty of idolatrous unfaithfulness, since there is no covenant with them to which they could be unfaithful. Only her husband has a right to her faithfulness (and which is a right he may not waive).[22] Also, when it comes to the Sabbath, the rabbis assumed that because the Sabbath is the expression of covenantal intimacy "an everlasting token between Me and the children of Israel" (Exodus 31:17), it is exclusively for Israel as God's spouse as it were. No one else has a right to it.[23] Therefore, keeping the Sabbath is Israel's right to claim for herself, and it is her duty to do in the event she needs to be ordered to exercise that privilege.

However, Maimonides (d. 1204), building on the rabbinic teaching that idolatry is proscribed to all human beings everywhere, assumes that the prohibition of idolatry is the obverse of the positive commandment (indeed, for him, the most primary positive commandment) to affirm the being of God.[24] And this affirmation of the being of God is called for by the universal apprehension of the absolute and necessary being of God, hence a truth that itself commands as it were its own positive affirmation by everyone in the world intelligent enough to do so, and which entails the proscription of all idolatry that necessarily contradicts it.

Nevertheless, I would think modern advocates of human rights, especially the right of religious liberty, might be wary of Maimonides' approach for political reasons (let alone its metaphysical problems). For if the affirmation of God's being is a metaphysical necessity, doesn't that suggest that it should be a political necessity too?[25] Doesn't this at least suggest that the affirmation of God's existence, which inevitably takes on the character of the tradition of the persons so promoting it, will soon turn into the type of religious coercion which at times has been practiced by Christians and Muslims especially? As such, there might be very good political reasons for adopting the earlier, more "tolerant" view of the absence of universal divine rights, whether negative or positive.

Inter-Human Relations

To see how asserting a priority in the correlation of rights and duties does make a difference in the way the intentions of commandments (all of which involve this correlation) are understood, let us turn to the most famous biblical commandment, "you shall love your neighbor as yourself" (Leviticus 19:18). It is also the foundation of all Jewish moral law.[26] And, contrary to a prevalent misconception, the commandment of neighbor-love does not command us to feel good about our neighbor, though it is good or virtuous (*middah tovah* in Hebrew) to cultivate feelings of benevolence in order to be able to better intend the beneficence my neighbor deserves from me. In the Jewish tradition, the commandment prescribes specific acts of *beneficence*, such as comforting our neighbor when he or she is mourning the loss of a close relative.[27] Nevertheless, taking neighbor-love to be my neighbor's *right* to be loved by me can only claim that I *act* lovingly with him or her in a personally beneficial way. Feelings cannot be formally claimed; they can only be informally elicited by attraction.

About "the great commandment" we can ask: Are we commanded to love our neighbor *since* God has so designated our neighbor to be the object of our love, or are we commanded to love our neighbor *because* our neighbor is essentially loveable? In other words, is neighbor-love primarily the right of the object to claim from an other, or is it primarily the duty of the subject of that commandment to extend to an other? In the former interpretation of the neighbor-love commandment, there is no reason for us to love our neighbor other than the fact that God has commanded us to do so. Here we need only intend the *source* of the commandment, not its *end* (if, in fact, there is an end at all other than obedience alone). But in the first interpretation, our neighbor is essentially loveable. That is why our neighbor *is to be* loved. And, since this duty devolves on an individual, one should answer: my neighbor is to be loved because my neighbor has a *right* to my beneficence and I have a *duty* to provide that beneficence to him or her. But why is the neighbor essentially loveable? There are two answers.

The first answer is that the neighbor is loveable *insofar as* he or she is a human being created in the image of God. In other words, the neighbor is essentially lovable *inasmuch as* our being the image of God is the essence of our humanity; it is what makes us unique among all of God's creatures. That fact, by itself, commands our deepest recognition, which is love. We love those who claim us by their very *persona*, that is, by their very self-presentation to us. And, since every human being is to be the object of this commanded duty, that duty is the justified response to the exercise of a *natural* right, a natural right that is exercised by the very presence of one human person to an other.[28] Our neighbors are loveable, then, *because* God surely loves those whom God had made in his own image. They are surely the objects of God's loving concern. When we are aware of this value-laden fact, how could we not love them, for we now have good reason to love them? This is what creates the essential loveableness of our neighbors. It is the best, most sufficient reason why we are obligated to love them.

Neighbor-love is a natural right of its human object (the "beloved"), and it is a natural duty of its human subject (the "lover"). But, inasmuch as the right to receive neighbor-love cannot be enforced by human authorities, nor can one's refusal of the duty to give neighbor-love be penalized by human authorities, that right is a *moral* right as distinct from being a *legal* right. This approach is more conducive to the equation of the neighbor-love commandment with the famous maxim of Hillel the Elder (first century C.E.): "What is hateful to you, do not do to your fellow."[29] This seems to be the negative version of the positive commandment to love one's neighbor.[30]

The second answer is that our Jewish neighbor is essentially loveable *insofar as* he or she is a fellow member of the people elected by God for a covenantal relationship. That election could only be an act of love. As such, a Jew's fellow Jewish neighbors are loveable *because* they, like him or her, have been chosen by God to be part of God's covenanted people. This divine election is the essence of being Jewish; it is what makes a Jew a Jew indelibly. This comes out in the syntax of the neighbor-love commandment: "You shall love your neighbor as yourself [for] I am the Lord" (Leviticus 19:18). "The Lord" (YHWH) is the name of God used especially when discussing God's election of Israel. So, since for Judaism "Israel" is the Jewish people, in this view neighbor-love is the Torah right of its Jewish object, and it is the Torah duty of its Jewish subject.

Notwithstanding their differences, in both interpretations, the source of the commandment is God's will; in both interpretations, God's willing what is to be done has a discernable reason, and in both interpretations, there is no role for a human court to either enforce compliance with or punish violations of the exercise of that right. That is so whether one takes the commandment of neighbor-love to be based on a natural right or be based on a Torah right. In either interpretation of this right, it is a moral right, but not a legal right.[31] Only the Torah right of the poor of the covenanted community to receive definite, tangible, material, welfare benefits ("charity" or *tsedaqah* in Hebrew) is considered to be a legal right.[32] As such, that legal right can be enforced by human authorities, and human authorities can penalize non-response to this justifiable claim as dereliction of one's legal duty.

This approach is more conducive to the view that the maxim of Hillel the Elder: "What is hateful to you, do not do to your fellow" is a minimal universal norm, and that this maxim is hardly unique to Judaism.[33] Conversely, the commandment of neighbor-love is a maximal norm, and it can only be given to the Jewish people who have experienced the particular kind of divine love they are now supposed to extend to each other.[34] That belies the charge that those we are commanded to love we are, therefore, to hate. The positive right to be loved, though greater than the negative right not to be mistreated, does not imply mistreatment of those outside the range of covenantal love.[35]

It could be said, however, that the normative Jewish tradition has compromised between these two interpretations of the commandment of neighbor-love. For it clearly emphasizes that neighbor-love is a Torah right. It is something uniquely commanded to Jews and, therefore, something one Jew can claim from another. Nevertheless, it also teaches that any non-Jew—who could be any human being—could exercise that Torah right when that person is living within enough proximity to Jews to be able to be the object of the Jews' duty to provide neighbor-love to whomever they encounter.[36] In other words, *anybody* could benefit from the beneficence Jews are commanded to provide to *everybody* living in their midst, however temporarily or accidentally. As such, any non-Jew fortunate enough to be so located could enjoy being the object of a Torah duty that can be seen (at least *de facto*) as his or her exercise of a natural, *universal* right having a particular subject but a universal object. And that is why, in rabbinic thought, any non-Jew who publicly accepts what is considered to be basic moral law (called a "resident sojourner" or *ger toshav* in Hebrew) can be made into enough of a citizen of a Jewish polity to be able to enjoy the same civil rights and be obligated by the same duties as a full-fledged Jewish citizen of that polity.[37] Moreover, these non-Jewish citizens are not required to convert to Judaism, thus implying that they are able to retain a good deal of their right of religious liberty.

The only real difference between Jews and gentiles regarding the right and duty of neighbor-love is that Jews are commanded to seek out their fellow Jews to be benefited, which is not the case with gentiles.[38] Nevertheless, isn't that approach more consistent with the rights-based politics most modern people have come to accept and appreciate? After all, when one considers the fact that during most of history, when the members of one people reach out actively to benefit members of another people, there is often an agenda of political conquest or religious conquest behind that outreach, especially active proselytizing. However, doesn't the former type of conquest usually trample upon the right of others to their own political liberty, and doesn't the latter type of conquest usually trample upon the right of others to their own religious liberty? And haven't these two types of conquest often come together as two parts of one imperialist agenda? So, even though Jews may have lacked the political power to be able openly and aggressively to proselytize gentiles, and even though there is no explicit prohibition in the Jewish tradition preventing Jews from doing so, nevertheless, the long and painful experience of

Jews being the victims of various imperialist agendas, with the violations of their rights to political and religious liberty, have made most Jews wary of doing to others what they never wanted done to themselves.

Community-Individual Relations

It is in the sphere of the relation of an individual and his or her community, as dealt with by the Jewish tradition, that we find a predominance of the kind of legal rights with which modern people are most familiar. This is the relational sphere that is the concern of civil and criminal law. However, whereas modern secularists regard this relational sphere and its rights and correlative duties to be self-sufficient or autonomous, the Jewish tradition sees it to be only a part of a larger relational sphere that is the concern of moral law, and a still larger relational sphere that is the concern of religious law: the Law whose primary concern is the God-human relationship. This covenantal relationship is considered to be of cosmic significance.[39] Nevertheless, since civil and criminal laws are not deduced from moral law, their practical rulings can be formulated and applied as positive law and can even be considered "secular" law, since its concern is with exclusively inter-human matters.[40] These practical rulings need no direct and regular reference to the higher law that the positive law presupposes in theory. That is why so much of Jewish and civil law, dealing with such matters as contracts, torts, restitution, and penalties, does not look all that different from contemporary systems of civil and criminal law and their respective correlations of rights and duties.

In Jewish civil law, the most significant difference in the way Jews are treated and the way gentiles are treated is in the area of interest on loans. In the Bible and the rabbinic sources, Jews are forbidden to both take and pay interest on loans to one another, whereas they may pay interest on money borrowed from gentiles and charge interest on money lent to gentiles. Since Jews and gentiles have the same rights vis-à-vis each other, there is reciprocity here, even if not strict equality. That is no more unfair (and thus no violation of natural justice) than especially benefiting one's family members more than strangers, and not expecting any more special treatment from these strangers than one is to extend to them. However, this special Torah right and duty became an economic liability when, in an increasingly commercial economy, it became more profitable for Jews (and gentiles) that Jews be able to charge interest and pay interest to those who wouldn't lend to them otherwise. Therefore, to overcome this economic problem, a legal fiction was devised (*heter isqa*) that enabled would-be lenders and borrowers to become business partners in transactions that involved profit and loss rather than charging and paying interest. The end result of this legal maneuver was to make Jews and gentiles more strictly equals in terms of economic rights than they had been in the past.[41]

The discovery of facts like these has enabled the development of a modern discipline called "Hebrew jurisprudence" (*mishpat ivri*), which studies traditional

Jewish law (*halakhah*) as it would study any other comparable system of secular law. And this kind of comparative research has also shown how much Jewish civil law (Jewish criminal having been largely dormant much of the past two thousand years) has been influenced by the systems of law of the larger societies within which Jews have lived. And, even with the reestablishment of Jewish political independence in the State of Israel, Israeli law is far more influenced by the foreign systems of law with which Jews have had long contact than it is influenced by the more arcane Jewish civil and criminal law. This is especially so in the area of human rights, where Israeli law is most influenced by English common law and some of the systems of law operative in Western Europe (with closer ties to Roman law). That is the case despite the fact that the Israeli parliament (*keneset*) passed a law in 1980 that seemed to require current Israeli legislation and adjudication to look for precedents in traditional Jewish law as much as possible.[42]

The moral and religious presuppositions of Jewish law need only be considered, though, in more theoretical or philosophical reflections on the overall meaning of that system of positive law itself, which should be the issue of justice. This comes out, for example, when one becomes aware that people who do not consider themselves bound by a moral law not of their own making are unlikely to regard themselves as having a personal obligation to obey, let alone construct, a morally respectable system of civil and criminal law. Now a law "not of their own making" implies a God-made law, since who else could have possibly made it if it is not man-made? Thus it would seem that a metaphysically sufficient moral law implies a divine Lawgiver. But here again, that metaphysical issue, like the previous moral issue, need not be brought up in the practical discussions of positive law. That is why there seems to be a paucity of theological reflection, and even at times ethical reflection, in many of the discussions of Jewish civil and criminal law. Nevertheless, that ethical and metaphysical bracketing should not imply that these moral and metaphysical issues can be dismissed by Jewish legalists as issues that are irrelevant in Jewish law. In fact, these issues do arise when even practical discussions of positive law need to recognize the insufficiency of that law to legislate or deliver true justice. And the primary and ultimate business of law as justice is rights, especially when justice is viewed as a moral or religious phenomenon.

True justice, then, will only come about when the rights of God, the individual and collective rights of human beings, and the rights of the covenanted people of God, are all fulfilled and fully coordinated. Yet to make that idea an ideal, which is humanly impossible to ever fully realize, could well lead to a despairing rejection of Jewish concern with rights by taking it to be a fantastic diversion from the type of *Realpolitik* that is only concerned with historically contingent interests and powers. However, to take that idea to be a messianic desideratum, one that God alone can realize, enables the Jewish pursuit of justice—which can be conceived of as the full and final coordination of all rights—to be hopeful. It is a sober reminder to Jews that because they cannot really accomplish full justice does not mean they cannot contribute to its full realization by someone else. "Respite and deliverance will arise for the Jews from another place." (Esther 4:14)

NOTES

1 Milton R. Konvitz, "Introduction," *Judaism and Human Rights* ed. Milton R. Konvitz (New York: W.W. Norton, 1972), 13. For some key terms from classical Jewish sources that lend themselves to rights-talk, see David Novak, *In Defense of Religious Liberty* (Wilmington, DE: ISI Books, 2009), 194, n. 1. The term "rights-talk" is taken from Mary Ann Glendon's provocative book, *Rights Talk* (New York: Free Press, 1991).

2 See David Novak, *Natural Law in Judaism* (Cambridge: Cambridge University Press, 1998), 149–64.

3 See David Novak, *Covenantal Rights* (Princeton: Princeton University Press, 2000), 3–32. Parts of this essay are adaptations of parts of this book.

4 See e.g., *Mishnah* [hereafter "M."]: Baba Metsia 3.3 and *Babylonian Talmud* [hereafter "B."]: Baba Metsia 37a; also, M. Baba Metsia 4.2.

5 See B. Baba Metsia 83a re Prov. 2:20.

6 See M. Baba Batra 1.4; B. Baba Batra 59b–60a re Num. 24:2.

7 Thus, a wife has the right to petition a court to rescue her from a marriage to a man she finds repulsive (and probably abusive) by forcing her husband to divorce her. Here her right not to be her husband's "captive" (*shevuyah*) trumps his right to keep her in his domicile against her will. See Maimonides, *Mishneh Torah* [hereafter "MT"]: Marriage, 14.8 re B. Ketubot 63b.

8 See Novak, *Natural Law in Judaism*, 69–76.

9 See M. Avot 2.12; B. Nazir 23b.

10 See Novak, *Natural Law in Judaism*, 167–73.

11 See my late revered teacher, Abraham Joshua Heschel, *Who is Man?* (Stanford, CA: Stanford University Press, 1965), 97–106.

12 *Tosefta* 8.4–7; B. Sanhedrin 56a. See David Novak, *The Image of the Non-Jew in Judaism* (New York : Edwin Mellen Press, 1983), 53–83.

13 See B. Sanhedrin 73a re Lev. 19:16; B. Baba Kama 27a.

14 See Maimonides, *Guide of the Perplexed*, 3.17 re Deut. 12:20, and 3.48 re M. Berakhot 5.3

15 See David Novak, *Jewish Social Ethics* (New York: Oxford University Press, 1992), 118–32.

16 See e.g., B. Baba Metsia 85a re Ps. 145:9.

17 See Maimonides, MT: Repentance, 5.4.

18 This is seen in the priority given to answering human claims that justice be done for oneself or for others. See B. Berakhot 19b; B. Shabbat 127a re Gen. 18:3; B. Taanit 21a; B. Baba Kama 93a re Gen. 16:5. Also, see Emmanuel Levinas, *Totality and Infinity*, trans. A. Lingis (Pittsburgh: Duquesne University Press, 1969), 96–101; see also id., "The Rights of Man and the Rights of the Other," *Outside the Subject*, trans. M. B. Smith (Stanford, CA: Stanford University Press, 1994), 116–25.

19 See B. Sanhedrin 6b re 2 Chron. 19:6.

20 And when human authorities cannot effect justice, it is hoped that God will do so in this world or in the world-yet-to-come (*olam ha-ba*). See B. Baba 83b; B. Sanhedrin 37b; also, B. Kiddushin 39b.

21 See Novak, *The Image of the Non-Jew in Judaism*, 108–15.

22 Certain rights must be exercised, thus becoming in fact duties. See B. Sotah 25a; B. Kiddushin 32a. On the other hand, one is supposed to develop a desire to do the

commandments so that instead of them being done as duties (*hovot*) one must do, they are to become like rights (*zekhuyot*) one wants to do. See M. Makkot 3.16 re Isa. 42:21; M. Avot 2.4.

23 B. Sanhedrin 58a re Gen. 8:22; *Midrash Devarim Rabbah* 1.18.

24 *Guide of the Perplexed*, 2.33; also, *Book of Commandments*, pos. no. 1; MT: *Foundations*, 1.6 re Exod. 20:2–3.

25 See Maimonides, MT: Kings, 8.10.

26 *Palestinian Talmud* [hereafter "Y."]: Nedarim 9.3/14c; Maimonides, MT: Mourning, 14.1.

27 MT: Mourning, 14.1.

28 Y. Nedarim 9.3/14c re Gen. 5:1.

29 B. Shabbat 31a.

30 See Maimonides, MT: Character Traits (Deot), 6.3 and Mourning, 14.1, and *Book of Commandments*, pos. no. 206 re Lev. 19:18.

31 Courts can only enforce and punish violations of rights that have discernable limits as to how much they require be done. See M. Peah 1.1; Y. Peah 1.1/15a.

32 B. Baba Batra 8b.

33 See the chapter herein by Scott Appleby.

34 See Franz Rosenzweig, *The Star of Redemption*, trans. W. W. Hallo (New York: Holt, Rinehart and Winston, 1971), 239–40 ("The Neighbor and the Self").

35 See e.g., B. Baba Kama 113a–b; B. Hullin 94a; *Sefer Hasidim*, ed. Bolgna, no. 51.

36 *Tosefta*: Gittin 3.13–14; B. Gittin 61a.

37 B. Avodah Zarah 64b. See Hermann Cohen, *Religion of Reason Out of the Sources of Judaism*, trans. S. Kaplan (New York: Frederick Ungar, 1972), 124–28.

38 See Maimonides, MT: Gifts to the Poor, 8.10; 9.1;10.1–3.

39 B. Pesahim 68b re Jer. 33:25.

40 For the difference between the way Jewish civil law (*mamona*) and Jewish religious or "ritual" law (*isura*) are treated, see B. Berakhot 19b re Deut. 22:4; B. Baba Metsia 27b; B. Hullin 134a. For the greater rationality of Jewish civil law, see M. Baba Batra 10.8 and the comment of Rabbi Israel Lifshitz (*Tiferet Yisrael*) thereon.

41 See Novak, *Jewish Social Ethics*, 223–24.

42 For the complicated relations between *halakhah* and Israeli law, see Menachem Elon, *Jewish Law* 4 vols., trans. B. Auerbach and M. J. Sykes (Philadelphia: Jewish Publication Society, 1994), 1898–1946.

■ RECOMMENDED READING

Broyde, Michael J. and John Witte, Jr., eds. *Human Rights in Judaism* (Northvale, NJ: Jason Aronson, 1998)

Cohen, Hermann. *Religion of Reason Out of the Sources of Judaism*, trans. S. Kaplan (New York: Frederick Ungar, 1972)

Cohn, Haim H. *Human Rights in the Bible and the Talmud*, trans. S. Himelstein (Tel Aviv: MOD Books, 1989)

Elon, Menachem. *Jewish Law*, 4 vols., trans. B. Auerbach and M.J. Sykes (Philadelphia: Jewish Publication Society, 1994)

Goodman, Lenn E. *Judaism, Human Rights, and Human Values* (New York: Oxford University Press, 1998)

Heschel, Abraham Joshua. *Who is Man?* (Stanford, CA: Stanford University Press, 1965)

Konvitz, Milton R. *Judaism and Human Rights* (New York: W. W. Norton, 1972)

Levering, Matthew. *Biblical Natural Law* (New York: Oxford University Press, 2008)

Levinas, Emmanuel. *Totality and Infinity*, trans. A. Lingis (Pittsburgh, PA: Duquesne University Press, 1969)

_____. *Outside the Subject*, trans. M. B. Smith (Stanford, CA: Stanford University Press, 1994)

Novak, David. *The Image of the Non-Jew in Judaism* 2nd ed. (Oxford: Littman Library of Jewish Civilization, 2011)

_____. *Jewish Social Ethics* (New York: Oxford University Press, 1992)

_____. *Natural Law in Judaism* (Cambridge: Cambridge University Press, 1998)

_____. *Covenantal Rights* (Princeton: Princeton University Press, 2000)

_____. *In Defense of Religious Liberty* (Wilmington, DE: ISI Books, 2009)

Reed, Esther. *The Ethics of Human Rights* (Waco, TX: Baylor University Press, 2007)

Rosenzweig, Franz. *The Star of Redemption*, trans. W. W. Hallo (New York: Holt, Rinehart and Winston, 1971)

Sidorsky, D., ed. *Essays on Human Rights: Contemporary and Jewish Perspectives* (Philadelphia: Jewish Publication Society of America, 1979)

2 Christianity and Human Rights

NICHOLAS P. WOLTERSTORFF

The relation of Christians to human rights is a troubled relationship. It was not always so; it became so in the twentieth century. What I mean is that the relation of Christians to the claim that there are human rights became a troubled relationship. The relation was always troubled in that Christians, along with others, violated human rights. What happened in the twentieth century is that large numbers of Christians became hostile to the very idea of natural human rights. Though not absent among Catholics, this hostility was mainly to be found among Protestants. The entire argument in the "Declaration on Religious Liberty" of the Second Vatican Council in 1965 is based on the natural human right to religious liberty.

In his ground-breaking book, *The Idea of Natural Rights: Studies on Natural Rights, Natural Law and Church Law 1150–1625*, [1] Brian Tierney tells the story of the employment of rights-talk, including that of natural rights, by the canon lawyers of the twelfth century. Charles J. Reid, Jr., a student of Tierney, fleshes out the story in his *Power over the Body, Equality in the Family: Rights and Domestic Relations in Medieval Canon Law*.[2] In *The Reformation of Rights*,[3] John Witte, Jr. tells the story of the near-profligate appeal to natural rights by the early Calvinists. The story of appeals to natural rights in the late Middle Ages and early Renaissance has been told by Richard Tuck in *Natural Rights Theories: Their Origin and Development*.[4]

It was often said in the past, and is still said by many today, that the idea of natural rights was devised by the secular political philosophers of the Enlightenment, especially Hobbes and Locke. The studies mentioned above show decisively that this is false. The idea of natural rights emerged from the legal culture of the Christian West in the Early Middle Ages and has been employed by lawyers, theologians, philosophers, political theorists, and social and political activists ever since. The philosophers of the Enlightenment inherited the idea from their Christian forebears; they did not devise it.

The historical facts mentioned above are compatible with its being a matter of pure happenstance that the idea of natural human rights emerged from the legal culture of the Christian West and has been employed by Christian thinkers ever since. Some writers have argued exactly this, that Christian thought has no integral connection with the idea of natural human rights. Others have argued for the even stronger position that a deep understanding of the idea of natural rights shows it to be inimical to Christianity; the fact that Christians have embraced the idea reveals an almost inexplicable obtuseness on their part.[5] I will be getting to these claims later, after I have explained why many Christians in the twentieth century became skittish about natural human rights.

Of course the latter position, if not the former, is *a priori* implausible. It's one thing to hold that Hobbes and Locke were intellectually and spiritually obtuse—or as some would have it, evasive. It's quite another thing to hold that the Spanish theologians of the fifteenth and sixteenth centuries and the Reformed theologians of the sixteenth and seventeenth centuries were obtuse in failing to discern incompatibility between Christian doctrine and the idea of natural human rights. Possible, but not likely.

■ WHAT ARE NATURAL HUMAN RIGHTS?

First, though, I must present my understanding of what we are talking about, namely, natural human rights; a shared understanding cannot be assumed. Elsewhere I have expounded and defended my understanding at considerable length;[6] here I must confine myself to saying only enough for the purposes at hand—without, I hope, being obscure.

I understand a right to something as a legitimate claim to that "something." Or, to put the same idea in different terms: to have a right to something is for that to be *due* to an individual. Rights are not ontologically weird little entities to which we stand in the relation of having them. To have a right to something is just to bear a certain relationship to it, more specifically, a *normative* relationship.

That to which one bears the normative relationship of having a right is always *being treated a certain way* by others or, in the limiting case, by oneself. We do sometimes speak of a right to a share of the pie; and a share of the pie is not a way of being treated by others. But if we look more closely at the situation, we will see that the right in question is either the right to *being given* a share of the pie or the right *to be allowed to take* a share of the pie. And these, being given a share of the pie and being allowed to take a share of the pie, are ways of being treated by one's fellows. A right to something is thus not only a *normative relationship* but a normative *social* relationship. Rights have sociality built into them.

Rights are intimately connected to duties. I hold that we have duties to entities of certain sorts that do not themselves have rights—works of art, for example. So let's set aside entities of such a sort that they cannot have rights. Then the following *Principle of Correlatives* holds: A has a duty toward B to do X if and only if B has a right against A to A's doing X. For example: Mary has a duty toward Julius to do X if and only if Julius has a right against Mary to Mary's doing X.

This Principle of Correlatives has led some writers to conclude that rights-talk and duties-talk are just two ways of saying the same thing. To say that Mary has a duty toward Julius to do X, and to say that Julius has a right against Mary to Mary's doing X, is to say the same thing in different words. I cannot argue the point on this occasion; but this seems to me not correct. The Principle of Correlatives is what philosophers call a *synthetic* necessary truth, not an *analytic* necessary truth.

It's like the proposition that a triangle is equilateral if and only if it is equiangular. To say about a triangle that it is equilateral, and to say about it that it is equilateral, is not to say the same thing about it in different words.

Duty, as we all know, has a shadow side, namely, guilt. If I fail to do my duty, I am guilty. Rights also have a shadow side, namely, being wronged. If I am not treated by someone as I have a right to be treated, I am wronged by that person.

Rights have what some have called *peremptory* force; others, referring to the same characteristic, have said that rights are *trumps*, or that they have *trumping* force. (Given the Principle of Correlatives, if rights have peremptory or trumping force, then duties have such force as well.) What's meant is the following: If you have a right against me to my doing X, then, no matter how many goods I could bring about by not doing X, if nobody has a right to those goods, I should do X. Indeed, I ought to do X.

To understand this idea of the trumping force of rights, it's essential that one keep in mind the distinction between *prima facie* rights (rights that presumptively trump in most circumstances) and *ultima facie* rights (rights that are always binding all things considered). It's possible that you would have a *prima facie* right against me to my doing X and that, at the same time, Julius would have a *prima facie* right against me to my not doing X. I must then decide which of these *prima facie* rights is the weightier (and which of my correlative *prima facie* duties is the weightier). If it is *prima facie* rights that we are talking about, then it may well be the case that you have a *prima facie* right against me to my doing X but that it's quite okay if I do not do X because other people have more weighty *prima facie* rights. I might even be obligated (all things considered) not to do X. The trumping force of a right consists in the fact that if you have an *ultima facie* right against me to my doing X, then no matter how much good I could bring about by doing something else, I ought to do X.

If I have a right to being treated a certain way by others, then that way of being treated would be a *good* in my life; it would enhance my wellbeing, my flourishing. We don't have rights to being treated in harmful ways by others—unless those harmful ways are part of a package that, as a whole, enhances one's flourishing. Though the "something" to which one has a right is always the good of being treated a certain way, the converse is not the case; for each of us, there are many ways of being treated that would be a good in one's life but to which one does not have a right. I think it would be a good in my life were I to be awarded the Pulitzer Prize for one of my books. But I do not have a right to being awarded the Prize; I am not wronged should it never be awarded to me—as I am sure it never will be! Perhaps the greatest challenge facing any theory of rights is to explain what accounts for the fact that one has a right to certain ways of being treated that would be a good in one's life whereas, to other good ways of being treated, one does not have a right.

My own answer to this question is that rights are grounded in the worth, the excellence, the estimability, of the rights-bearer. To wrong a person is to treat her in a way that does not befit her worth—in a way that would only befit someone who did not have that worth. We could put it like this: rights are what respect for worth requires. If I am a professor, if you are a student in a course of mine, and if you have done top-notch work in the course, then you have a right to certain actions of approbation on my part—in particular, you have a right to an "A" on your record (in the American system of grading). If I give you a "D" and bad-mouth your work, I do not treat you as befits your worth. I treat you with disrespect.

Everything I have said thus far holds for rights in general. Now we have to say something about *natural* rights and about *human* rights. One's right to something is a *natural* right if nothing that any human being did generated that right in one or conferred it on one—or, for those that have been generated in one or conferred on one, if one would have it even had it not been generated or conferred. My right to a monthly Social Security check from the U.S. government is not a natural right; I have it only because it has been conferred on me by the Social Security legislation adopted by the Congress of the United States. By contrast, my right not to be tortured for the pleasure of the torturer is a natural right. I have that right whether or not it has been conferred on me by treaty or legislation.

The idea of a *human* right is a bit more complicated. One could elucidate the idea of a human right either by starting from the standard explanation of the idea or by starting from a standard list of such rights and trying to make sense of the list. These two approaches yield, or appear to yield, somewhat different results. If one follows the former approach and then looks at standard lists of human rights, one is puzzled by the appearance on the list of certain items; they don't seem to fit the concept as it is commonly explained. I propose elucidating the common explanation of the idea without, on this occasion, attempting to harmonize it with standard lists of human rights.

It's important to note, first of all, that human rights are not to be identified with *the rights that human beings have*. Human rights are a subset of the latter, a species. The core component in the idea of a human right is that a right that one has is a *human* right if the only status required for possessing the right is that one be a human being—not any particular kind of human being, just a human being.

The rights commonly cited as human rights have to be understood as *prima facie* rights; in a given case, one's *prima facie* human right to be treated a certain way may be outweighed by a conflicting *prima facie* right of someone else. Given the trumping force of rights, it can only be outweighed by other *prima facie* rights, however, not by goods to be brought about to which no one has a (*prime facie*) right. Of course, it may be that certain *prima facie* human rights are never outweighed by any other *prima facie* rights. I judge that one's right not to be tortured for the pleasure of the torturer is an example of such.

It is also worth pointing out that my right to be treated a certain way may be a human right even though I might find myself in a circumstance where I do not have the right—that is, in a circumstance where it is not even a *prima facie* right of mine. This would be the case if I found myself in a circumstance where it is impossible for others to treat me in the way specified. Human rights are not peculiar in this regard; in general, I don't have a right to be treated a certain way by others if it is impossible for them to treat me that way. Suppose that I have a right to fair access to adequate means of sustenance, and that this is a human right. Should my circumstance become that of extreme drought with no means of sustenance available to anyone, I would, in that circumstance, not have that right. Thus human rights are not to be equated with universal rights. Surely some are universal—once again, the right not to be tortured for the pleasure of the torturer.[7] But others are not.

The standard explanation of the idea of a human right has a second component. No doubt it's true that some of the ways of being treated by our fellow human beings to which we have a right by virtue of being human are such that certain animals also have a right to be treated that way by human beings. The standard account assumes, however, that this is not true for the whole package of human rights; the status of being human gives one some rights that no animal has.

Our focus in what follows will be on natural human rights. Whether there are some natural rights that are not human rights is an issue we need not get into.

■ THE AGAPIST OBJECTION TO THINKING IN TERMS OF RIGHTS

We are ready to address the question posed earlier: Why have a good many Christians in the twentieth century, mainly Protestants, been opposed to the idea of natural rights in general, and to natural *human* rights in particular? This opposition is surprising given that, ever since the twelfth century, rights-talk has been a standard part of Christian discourse. Why have Christians in the twentieth century rejected this part of their heritage?

Two quite different lines of thought have led to the same result. The more radical of the two is an interpretation of Christian ethics that became widespread among Protestant Christian theologians and ethicists in the twentieth century, an interpretation commonly called *agapism*, from the most common Greek word for *love* in the New Testament, "*agapê*." The classic text of the movement is Anders Nygren's *Agape and Eros*.[8] At the heart of the movement was an interpretation of what Jesus meant by "*agapê*" when he enjoined us to love our neighbors as ourselves. Jesus was not enjoining us to love our neighbors with one or another form of love, take your pick; and certainly he was not enjoining us to love our neighbors as justice requires. He was, so the agapists said, enjoining us to love our neighbors out of sheer gratuitous generosity, spontaneous benevolence.

Our love of the neighbor is to imitate God's forgiveness of the sinner. Justice does not require that God forgive the sinner; God's forgiveness has nothing to do with the requirements of justice. God forgives out of gratuitous generosity. We are to love the neighbor in that way, seeking out of gratuitous generosity to advance her wellbeing, paying no attention to what justice requires. Nygren recognized that justice was integral to the Old Testament. What he argued was that, in the New Testament, justice has been superseded by agapic love. Nygren made very few explicit references to rights. But if justice has been superseded in the New Testament, then obviously natural human rights have been superseded, too.

Anybody who talked about natural rights to a group of Protestants in the latter half of the twentieth century and the first decade of the twenty-first was likely to receive the rejoinder, "We should not be talking about rights; we should be talking about love." Agapism was in the air, partly because of the intellectual power of its major representatives—Karl Barth, Emil Brunner, Reinhold Niebuhr, Paul Ramsey, John Howard Yoder—but also, I judge, because the agapists were giving coherent expression to attitudes long present among Christians.

Elsewhere I have argued that the agapist position is internally incoherent.[9] Here let me confine myself to observing that it is implausible as an interpretation of the New Testament. The command to love one's neighbor that Jesus cited as one of the two greatest commandments in the Torah was quoted from Leviticus 19:18. When one looks at the context in which the command occurs, one discovers that it comes as the concluding summation of a large number of more specific commands, among those more specific commands being commands that explicitly enjoin the Israelites to treat their neighbors justly. Love is not presented as blind to justice, even less is it presented as in tension with justice; love incorporates justice. Treating the neighbor justly is an example of loving the neighbor. Given this as the original context of the command, surely anyone who holds that Jesus understood love as indifferent to justice, if not hostile, bears the burden of proof.

And the burden cannot be borne. No careful reader of the New Testament could conclude that justice has been superseded. The message of the New Testament is not that justice has been superseded but that the day when justice shall reign has been decisively inaugurated by Jesus. St. Luke reports that shortly after Jesus began preaching and teaching in public he attended the synagogue in Nazareth on a Sabbath and was invited to read from Scripture and comment on what he read. Luke reports him as reading a passage from Isaiah 61, with a line interpolated from Isaiah 58:

> The Spirit of the Lord is upon me,
> Because he has anointed me to bring good news to the poor.
> He has sent me to proclaim release to the captives
> and recovery of sight to the blind,
> to let the oppressed go free,
> to proclaim the year of the Lord's favor (Luke 4:18–19).

Bringing good news to the poor, proclaiming release to the captives, letting the oppressed go free—anybody schooled in the Hebrew Bible, as Jesus and his listeners were, would immediately have recognized these as standard examples of doing justice.

An additional piece of evidence is the following. In Matthew's telling of the story of Jesus, Jesus has already been teaching and healing for some time when

Matthew intrudes into the story and offers his own interpretation of the significance of the events he has been narrating. "This was to fulfill what had been spoken through the prophet Isaiah":

> Here is my servant, whom I have chosen,
> my beloved, with whom my soul is well pleased.
> I will put my Spirit upon him,
> and he will proclaim justice (*krisis*) to the Gentiles. . . .
> He will not break a bruised reed or quench a smoldering wick
> until he brings justice (*krisis*) to victory. (Matthew 12:17–21)

■ RIGHTS-TALK ACCUSED OF EXPRESSING AND ABETTING POSSESSIVE INDIVIDUALISM

I turn now to the second line of thought that has led a good many Christians in the twentieth century, in this case along with others, to be hostile to the idea of natural human rights. This line of thought, unlike the first, is not intrinsically hostile to justice. Many of its representatives affirm justice but deny that justice has anything to do with natural rights.

This second line of thought charges rights-talk in general, and natural rights-talk in particular, with expressing and abetting one of the worst aspects of our modern mentality, namely, possessive agonistic individualism. The language of rights, so it claims, is for each of us to assert our claims against the other. That's what it's for: claiming one's own entitlements. Thereby it feeds and waters self-aggrandizement. No need to argue that this is alien to the Christian gospel.

The reader may well be puzzled. In my discussion of rights I emphasized that rights are normative social relationships: a right is always to the good of being treated a certain way by one's fellows (or, in the limiting case, by oneself). I emphasized that rights and duties are corollaries of each other. I did not emphasize—it didn't seem necessary—that just as I have rights with regard to you, so also you have rights with regard to me. We come into each other's presence each bearing rights with regard to the other—and duties. Given all this, why would anybody hold that rights-talk is for claiming one's own entitlements against everybody else? Why would anybody think that rights-talk expresses and abets possessive agonistic individualism?

The answer to this question has both an historical component and what one might call a systematic component. Let me begin with the latter. As I mentioned earlier, there are different understandings of rights; I presented my own understanding without, on this occasion, contesting the others. A common understanding of rights, perhaps *the* most common, is that rights are safeguards to personal autonomy. We all have a right to personal autonomy; that right is fundamental. Our other rights are protectors of that fundamental right. If some way of being treated by one's fellows is necessary for exercising one's personal autonomy, then one has a right to being treated that way. Thus it is that we have a right to free speech, a right to assemble freely, a right to marry whom one wishes, a right to divorce, and so forth.

Those who follow the line of thought that we are presently exploring accept this understanding of rights. They do not develop their own understanding, as I have done; they accept this common understanding. And if this is how one thinks of rights, the charge that rights-talk expresses and abets possessive agonistic individualism is not implausible. Many writers who affirm rights and who think of them as protectors of autonomy would want to contest or qualify the charge. But if this is how one thinks of rights, then, whether or not the charge can be sustained, it is at least not implausible. On my understanding of rights, it is implausible.

The historical component offered in support of the charge is a narrative—or more precisely, two narratives—concerning the birth of the idea of natural rights, each of these narratives being strikingly different from that told in the writings mentioned at the beginning of this essay. Both narratives gained currency some decades before these writings appeared.

One narrative was apparently originated by Leo Strauss in his 1953 publication, *Natural Right and History*.[10] According to this narrative, thinkers in the West traditionally thought in terms of objective right, not in terms of subjective rights. That is to say, they thought in terms of an objective order specifying the right thing to do in various situations; they did not think in terms of rights that individuals have or possess. The change, Strauss said, occurred in Hobbes and Locke as part of their attempt to work out an individualistic, purely secular, account of political authority. It would not be a mistake to regard this change, from objective right to subjective rights, as a central component in the passage to modernity.

The alternative narrative was first told by the French legal historian, Michel Villey, in a number of publications in the 1950s.[11] Villey was a neo-Thomist who, like most neo-Thomists, viewed thirteenth-century Catholic philosopher Thomas Aquinas as the apogee of Western philosophy and regarded everything after Thomas as either a decline or an attempt to regain the heights. Villey argued that when it came to the idea of natural rights, the fall from grace came with the fourteenth-century nominalist philosopher, William of Ockham. In the course of defending his fellow Franciscans against attacks from the papacy, Ockham introduced the idea of natural rights. Just as Strauss saw the idea of natural subjective rights as born of individualist political philosophy, so Villey saw the idea as born of philosophical nominalism. The assumption, in both cases, was that the idea cannot be freed from the philosophical framework that gave it birth.

How shall we respond to this charge that rights-talk expresses and abets possessive agonistic individualism? Well, we now know that the Strauss-narrative and the Villey-narrative are both false; once again I refer to the publications mentioned at the beginning of this essay. It was possible for the Strauss and Villey narratives to gain popularity only because cultural amnesia had set in. Only if one has forgotten the role of the idea of natural rights in the thought of the sixteenth- and seventeenth-century Calvinist Reformers, and forgotten its role in the thought of the fifteenth and sixteenth century Spanish theologians, would the Strauss-narrative seem plausible; and only if one has forgotten the work of the canon lawyers of the twelfth century would the Villey-narrative seem plausible.

As to the assumption that natural rights are to be understood as protections for autonomy, I hold that this is a serious misunderstanding of rights. The underlying assumption, that we each have a right to autonomy, is false; there is no generalized right to autonomy. And a good many of our natural rights have nothing to do with autonomy. The Alzheimer's patient has rights. But she has no autonomy; she is incapable of autonomous action.

This leaves us with the charge itself, that rights-talk expresses and abets the evil of possessive agonistic individualism. The fact that the two arguments commonly cited in support of this charge, the systematic argument and the historical argument, both employ false premises, does not establish that the charge is false. Let's be clear on the nature of the charge: the charge is not that there are no natural rights; the charge is that we should not be talking about them, whether or not there are any. We should not be using such rights-talk.

It has to be conceded that, in our society, rights-talk does often express and abet an attitude of possessive agonistic individualism. That attitude is abroad in our society, and many use rights-talk to express it. Given this, is it perhaps best to avoid rights-talk and speak instead of responsibility, love, friendship, benevolence, and the like? Of course, the possessive individualist will abuse other parts of our moral vocabulary in the same way. He will talk long and loud about the duties of others to himself but fall silent when it comes to his own duties.

Would anything much be lost if we gave up rights-talk because of its abuse? My view is that something of great importance would be lost. The moral order has two fundamental dimensions, the agent-dimension, and the recipient-dimension (patient-dimension). With the language of duty, responsibility, love, benevolence, and the like we bring the agent-dimension to speech; with the language of rights we bring the recipient-dimension to speech. Guilt pertains to what I did; being wronged pertains to what was done to me. It's because rights-talk brings to speech the moral condition of the victims—they were wronged—that it has proved so powerful in protest movements. Yes, the wrongdoers did what they ought not to have done. But their guilt is not the only relevant moral condition; the victims have been wronged. And their being wronged is not the same thing in different words as the malefactors being guilty.

■ NATURAL HUMAN RIGHTS IMPLIED AND TAKEN FOR GRANTED BY THE CHURCH FATHERS

I come now to the important question that our discussion thus far leaves unanswered. Let's say we can agree that ever since the twelfth century, Christian activists and Christian thinkers—lawyers, philosophers, theologians, and political theorists—have spoken of natural rights in general and of natural human rights in particular. Let's say we can further agree that the hostility of many Christians in the twentieth century to the idea of natural rights is an aberration, presupposing both historical amnesia and a misunderstanding of what rights are. The question my argument thus far leaves unanswered, however, is whether the idea of natural rights is a mere addendum to Christian thought or whether the two have some integral connection to each other.

Though the twelfth-century canon lawyers seem to have been the first to employ the conceptuality of natural rights in any sustained way, the existence of such rights was taken for granted long before the twelfth century. Ambrose, the bishop of Milan in the late 300s, declared, "Not from your own do you bestow upon the poor man, but you make return from what is his." Basil of Caesarea made the same point more expansively: "That bread which you keep, belongs to the hungry; that coat which you preserve in your wardrobe, to the naked; those shoes which are rotting in your possession, to the shoeless; that gold which you have hidden in the ground, to the needy. Wherefore, as often as you were able to help others, and refused, so often did you do them wrong." And John Chrysostom makes the point more emphatically: The rich "hold the goods of the poor even if they have inherited them from their fathers or no matter how they have gathered their wealth. . . . Deprive not the poor of his living. To deprive is to take what belongs to another. . . . [T]he rich man is a kind of steward of the money which is owed for the distribution of the poor. . . . For his goods are not his own, but belong to his fellow servants. . . . I beg you to remember this without fail, that not to share our own wealth with the poor is theft from the poor and deprivation of their means of life; we do not possess our own wealth but theirs."[12]

The point is unmistakable: the poor are deprived of what *belongs to* them, deprived of what is *theirs*. They are wronged. Ambrose, Basil, and John would also have believed that the rich were failing in their duties. But that's not what they emphasize. What they emphasize is that those surplus shoes and that extra food *belong* to the poor. And nowhere do any of the three appeal to the laws of the land; their appeal is not to positive rights but to natural rights.

This is just an illustration of one prototypical right in the Church Fathers: the right to poor relief or social welfare. A full history of the recognition of natural human rights in the post-biblical Christian tradition would look first at the various natural rights that were taken for granted and implied in the writings of the Church Fathers; it would then look at how the canon lawyers of the twelfth century conceptualized what the Church Fathers took for granted and implied; and from there it would go on to study how the idea of natural rights, including natural *human* rights, was employed in the eight centuries following. We do not yet have such a history.

When one looks at the context of the three passages that I just quoted, one sees that in every case, the lines quoted occur in the context of biblical interpretation.

In saying what they did about the rights of the poor, Ambrose, Basil, and John saw themselves as elucidating what the Bible says. A study of the Church Fathers with the aim of finding out which natural rights they took for granted or implied would take note of the full panoply of biblical passages to which they appealed. Since that has not been done, we must address the question on our own: what are the components in biblical thought that might give rise to the assumption that there are natural human rights?

■ NATURAL HUMAN RIGHTS IMPLIED AND TAKEN FOR GRANTED IN SCRIPTURE

Begin with God. Running throughout Christian Scripture, Old and New Testament alike, is the assumption that God has rights with regard to us—a right to our obedience, a right to due acknowledgment of God's worth, both inherent worth and worth on account of what God has done. These rights are natural rights. Of course they are not natural *human* rights; they are rights that God has. But it is not by virtue of some human legislation or practice that God has these rights. Nor, indeed, by virtue of some divine legislation; God does not have a right to our obedience and praise on account of having conferred that right on himself by divine legislation. God's rights are grounded in what respect for God's worth requires.[13]

The assumption that God has a right to our praise and obedience underlies the assumption that God is acting justly when God punishes the wrongdoer; it also underlies the declaration that God forgives the penitent wrongdoer. To forgive someone for what he did to one presupposes that one has been wronged, deprived of something to which one had a right. If what was done to one amounts to no more than depriving one of something that one wished for, what's relevant is not forgiveness but regret.

What then about human beings and their natural rights? Does Christian Scripture also take for granted or imply that we human beings have natural rights? And in particular, does it take for granted or imply that we have natural *human* rights—rights just by virtue of being human?

It does indeed. Scripture assumes that we have natural obligations toward our fellows. Witness the Second Table of the Ten Commandments—with its injunctions to honor my father and mother, and not to murder, steal, commit adultery, give false testimony, or covet anything that is my neighbor's (Exodus 20). But if I have a natural obligation to my fellows, then, given the Principle of Correlatives, they have natural rights with regard to me. The sixth of the Ten Commandments (in one standard way of numbering) says, "You shall not murder." Given that you have the natural obligation toward me not to murder me, I have the natural right against you that you not murder me.

And this particular example of a natural right is a *human* right. Each human being has the natural right against each other human being that that other not murder him or her. One does not have to be a particular kind of human being to possess this right; all one has to be is a human being. It's true, of course, that the Ten Commandments were originally issued by God to Israel. But both the Jewish and Christian traditions have held that the Second Table, at least, applies to everyone.

We could draw our discussion to a close at this point. Our question was whether the idea of natural human rights is a mere addendum to Christian thought or whether the two have an integral connection. We have our answer. In its declaration that we have obligations to each other antecedent to any human legislation or practice, the Christian Scripture implies that we have natural rights with regard to each other, some of those being human rights. Nowhere in Scripture do we find natural human rights explicitly conceptualized. But as we saw with Ambrose, Basil, and John, one can take for granted or imply that there are natural human rights without explicitly conceptualizing them. The point is general: one does not have to conceptualize something in order to take its existence for granted or to imply it.

But rather than now dropping the discussion, let's ask why the Christian tradition has gone beyond affirming the existence of natural rights to the affirmation of natural *human* rights. Why has the tradition insisted, for example, that the obligation not to murder applies not just to Jews and Christians but to everybody? Why the pressure to universalize? Why the insistence that, just by virtue of being a human being—not a Jewish human being, not a Christian human being, just a human being—one has the right not to be murdered?

Two themes press toward universalizing, one shared with the Jewish tradition, the other unique to Christianity. The first is the declaration, found first in the opening chapter of Genesis, then again in Genesis 5 and 9, and thereafter assumed at various points in the Hebrew Bible/Old Testament (e.g., Psalm 8), that God created human beings in God's image or likeness. All human beings bear the *imago dei*. Not just certain kinds of human beings—all of them. In the Noachic blessing, as we find it in the opening verses of Genesis 9, the *imago dei* is explicitly connected with the evil of murder:

> Whoever sheds the blood of a human,
> by a human shall that person's blood be shed;
> for in his own image,
> God made humankind (Genesis 9:6).

Anybody who believes that all human beings bear the *imago dei* is bound to reflect on what is required by due respect for the worth that each human being possesses on that account. Due respect requires that no human being be murdered. What else does it require?

The second theme that presses toward universalizing is the theme that Paul emphasizes in his Letter to the Romans, as explanation and justification for his own missionary practice: God offers justification, and thereby fellowship, to Jews and Gentiles alike—that is, to everyone. In God there is no partiality.

Anybody who believes that to every human being God extends the offer of fellowship is bound to reflect on the implications of that conviction for how each and every human being is to be treated. To be offered justification by God is to be honored; to be so honored is to have worth bestowed on one. What does due respect for that worth require?

It must be said at once that Christians have often resisted the universalizing pressure of these two themes, sometimes by interpreting them in such a way that all pressure toward universalizing is removed. But the question we have been considering is not whether Christians have consistently honored the natural human rights of their fellow human beings; they have not. The question we have been considering is whether there is some integral connection between Christian thought and the idea of natural human rights. We have seen that there is. The concept of natural human rights and the declaration that there are such rights articulate what was implicit in the Old and New Testaments. The recognition of natural human rights is one of the great jewels bequeathed by Hebrew and Christian Scripture to humankind.

■ NOTES

1 Brian Tierney, *The Idea of Natural Rights: Studies on Natural Rights, Natural Law and Church Law*, 1150–1625 (Atlanta: Scholars Press, 1997).

2 Charles J. Reid, Jr. *Power over the Body, Equality in the Family: Rights and Domestic Relations in Medieval Canon Law* (Grand Rapids, MI: Wm. B. Eerdmans Pub. Co., 2004).

3 John Witte, Jr. *The Reformation of Rights: Law, Religion, and Human Rights in Early Modern Calvinism* (New York: Cambridge University Press, 2008).

4 Richard Tuck, *Natural Rights Theories: Their Origin and Development* (Cambridge: Cambridge University Press, 1979).

5 Joan Lockwood O'Donovan argues for this position in her essay, 'The Concept of Rights in Christian Moral Discourse,' in *A Preserving Grace: Protestants, Catholics, and Natural Law*, ed. Michael Cromartie (Grand Rapids, MI: Wm. B. Eerdmans Pub. Co., 1997).

6 In my *Justice: Rights and Wrongs* (New York: Cambridge University Press, 2008).

7 The distinction between *status* and *circumstance* that I employed in the text above is crucial for understanding rights in general, but especially human rights. A right that one has is a human right if the only *status* one needs to possess the right is that of being human; but there may be *circumstances* in which one does not possess the right, not even as a *prima facie* right, because in those circumstances one cannot be treated in accord with the right.

8 Anders Nygren, *Agape and Eros*, trans. Philip S. Watson (London: SPCK. 1953).

9 In my *Justice in Love* (Grand Rapids, MI: Wm. B, Eerdmans Pub. Co., 2011)

10 Leo Strauss, *Natural Right and History* (Chicago: University of Chicago Press, 1953).

11 Publication details can be found in Tierney, *The Idea of Natural Rights*.

12 The references for these three passages can be found in my *Justice: Rights and Wrongs*, 61–62.

13 See further the chapter by David Novak, herein.

RECOMMENDED READING

Kierkegaard, Sören. *Works of Love*, trans. and eds., Howard V. Hong and Edna H. Hong (Princeton: Princeton University Press, 1995)

Nygren, Anders. *Agape and Eros*, trans. Philip S. Watson (London: SPCK, 1953)

O'Donovan, Joan Lockwood. 'The Concept of Rights in Christian Moral Discourse,' in *A Preserving Grace: Protestants, Catholics, and Natural Law*, ed. Michael Cromartie, (Grand Rapids, MI: Wm. B. Eerdmans Pub. Co., 1997), 143–56

Ramsey, Paul. *Christian Ethics and the Sit-In* (New York: Association Press, 1961)

Reid, Charles J., Jr. *Power over the Body, Equality in the Family: Rights and Domestic Relations in Medieval Canon Law* (Grand Rapids, MI: Wm. B. Eerdmans Pub. Co., 2004)

Strauss, Leo. *Natural Right and History* (Chicago: University of Chicago Press, 1953)

Tierney, Brian. *The Idea of Natural Rights: Studies on Natural Rights, Natural Law and Church Law, 1150–1625* (Atlanta: Scholars Press, 1997)

Tuck, Richard. *Natural Rights Theories: Their Origin and Development* (Cambridge: Cambridge University Press, 1979)

Vatican Council II. 'Declaration on Religious Liberty (*Dignitatis Humanae*),' in *Vatican Council II: The Conciliar and Post Conciliar Documents*, vol. 1, ed. Austin Flannery (Northport, NY: Costello Publishing Co., 1975), 799–812

Witte, John, Jr. *The Reformation of Rights: Law, Religion, and Human Rights in Early Modern Calvinism* (New York: Cambridge University Press, 2008)

Wolterstorff, Nicholas P. *Justice: Rights and Wrongs* (Princeton: Princeton University Press, 2008)

_____. *Justice in Love* (Grand Rapids, MI: Wm. B. Eerdmans Pub. Co., 2011)

3 Islam and Human Rights

ABDULLAHI AHMED AN-NA'IM

Who is raising the question of religion/Islam and human rights, to whom, and to what end? Is the question raised for both sides of the equation, or only for the religion or the human rights side? There is a significant difference if the issue is raised by a religious believer who supports the universality of human rights, in contrast to a believer who opposes the universality of human rights, or an atheist who challenges the ability of religion (rather than religious believers) to support the universality of human rights. There is also a significant difference between raising the issue as a judgment about Islam or about human rights, as opposed to an inquiry about the implications of the universality of human rights for the integrity of a religious community.

Framing the question of whether Islam is inherently compatible or incompatible with human rights is problematic. The question assumes that there is a verifiably identifiable monolithic "Islam" to be contrasted with a definitively settled preconceived notion of "human rights." But who can definitively and exhaustively *know* what Islam is and what human rights are? No human being, whether self-identifying as a Muslim or not, can definitely and exhaustively "know" Islam, and no proposed human rights norms can qualify as universal standards unless and until they are accepted as such by their human subjects. The most anyone can legitimately speak of is his or her view of Islam, never Islam as such, and of human rights as they are already accepted by people around the world, including Muslims.

I also find it difficult to see how any conception of human rights can be "universal" by any definition of this term if it is inconsistent with the religious beliefs of Muslims at large. If universality is a normative claim that these rights *ought* to be universally accepted and applied, a believer will not voluntarily accept that claim if it is incompatible with her religious beliefs. To attempt to impose this notion on Muslims is not only imperialist, which is by definition a total negation of the concept of human rights itself, but also unsustainable in practice because it cannot be coercively enforced. Universality as an empirical assertion, that these human rights are actually accepted by the vast majority of people around the world, cannot be true if it is rejected by Muslims, an estimated quarter of humanity today.[1]

Framing the inquiry in terms of the inherent incompatibility between religion and human rights is also counterproductive. Speaking for myself as a

Muslim advocate of human rights, if I am faced with a choice between being Muslim or a commitment to human rights, I will choose being Muslim without any hesitation, and would in fact find the choice absurd. No conception of human rights can possibly compete with my religion as such, and should not be expected to do so. A more productive inquiry concerns how my understanding and practice of Islam influence and is influenced by my commitment to upholding the universality of human rights. On both sides of the issue, the inquiry would be about Islam as I know and believe in it, and human rights as I understand and uphold them. In other words, I am unable to see how one can speak of an "objective" or abstract experience of religion, apart from its believers, or a conception of human rights that is independent of the ethical sensibilities and material context of the human beings who claim to uphold that conception.

I am not suggesting that religion is the only way to justify or uphold human rights, but I am saying that a Muslim, or any other believer, is as entitled to found his or her commitment to these rights on a religious foundation as others are entitled to found their commitment on secular or atheistic beliefs. Moreover, I don't see the possibility of or need for any single foundation of human rights for all human beings everywhere, whatever that foundation may be. As I will explain later, self-determination, including the right to decide the foundation of human rights one finds acceptable, is integral to the "human" in human rights. The foundation of human rights we accept are specific to who we are, in our own context, which need not be, and is unlikely to be, accepted by all other human beings who share the same commitment to these rights.

It may be helpful here to clarify my position in relation to how David Little describes it in his contribution to this volume: "Nevertheless, he [An-Na'im] has in some of his writings explicitly opposed the idea of religious neutrality as a basis for human rights."[2] In fact, my objection to all claims of neutrality is not limited to religious neutrality. I made this point in the chapter cited by Little: "It is not possible, or desirable, in my view to identify a set of neutrally formulated human rights. Any normative regime, which justifies a set of rights and determines their content, must necessarily represent a commitment to a particular value system."[3] Since no foundation of human rights can be neutral, whether philosophically, ideologically, religiously, culturally or otherwise, none can or should be binding on all of us simply because some of us find that foundation acceptable. For instance, Dr. Little seems to favor a secular human rights language as the drafters of the Universal Declaration of the Human Rights understood them in relation to John Rawls' idea of public reason, subject to Little's own modification. While I am grateful to the drafters of the Declaration for their splendid work, and respect Little's and Rawls' view of the justification of human rights *to them*, I see no reason why that should necessarily be binding on me or any other person.

In light of these remarks, the appropriate framing of the general subject of Islam and human rights should be about how to promote the practical application of human rights among Muslims. In my view, this endeavor is more likely to succeed when human rights are presented to Muslims as consistent with their belief in Islam, rather than as a moral or political claim that is binding on them regardless of inconsistency with their religious beliefs. This is what I mean by the "framing" of the inquiry about Islam and human rights in the title of this chapter.

As I have suggested elsewhere, there are two aspects to this approach; one is an internal discourse among Muslims, the second is a cross-cultural dialogue between Muslims and non-Muslims.[4] The internal Islamic discourse, I believe, will include reinterpretation of certain aspects of Sharia (the normative system of Islam), especially issues of equality for women and freedom of religion.[5] Such reinterpretation is possible because any human conception of what Sharia means is necessarily a product of interpretation of its sacred sources (the Quran and Sunna of the Prophet) in the first place.[6]

The reference to "reframing" in the title is about transforming attitudes in social and religious life, and not about the application of the principles of Sharia as state law.[7] This reframing will not by itself resolve the problematic aspects of traditional interpretations of Sharia because of their social and personal consequences, but it will diminish the negative consequences of state enforcement of those aspects in practice, and facilitate resolution of the issues from an Islamic perspective. I am proposing a dual approach for promoting respect for human rights in Islamic societies and communities: challenging claims that Sharia can be enforced as state law, regardless of whether Muslims are the majority or minority of the population, while still striving to transform the social and personal understanding and practice of Sharia by Muslims outside the framework of state institutions.

The premise of both strategies is an appreciation that Islam is foundational for the commitment of Muslims to human rights, but that role is neither exclusive nor legal as such. The Universal Declaration of Human Rights (UDHR) of 1948 did not make any explicit reference to the foundations or sources of human rights to facilitate consensus over these rights. But this does not mean the issue of foundations is irrelevant or that human rights can only be founded on secular justifications. Believers have the right to found their commitment to human rights on their own religious beliefs, provided they are willing to concede the same right to others, each according to their own religious or philosophical convictions.

■ WHO IS THE "HUMAN" IN HUMAN RIGHTS?

By human rights, I mean moral and political entitlements that are due to all human beings equally by virtue of their humanity, and without any distinction on such grounds as race, sex, religion, or national origin. In other words, a human is entitled to these rights simply by being human, without any other requirement or qualification. The concept, normative content, and practice of human rights may perhaps be clarified by exploring the nature and implication of the mutual linking of the "human" and "human rights." This linkage, I suggest, helps us understand how perceptions of the human influence the scope, content, and methods of the protection of human rights, and the quality of being human is enabled and realized through the protection of human rights.

Human rights are by definition universal, but it may be helpful to consider what this means at three levels: the concept (idea), the content (norms or standards), and the context of defining and implementing these rights. First, as a *concept*, human rights are necessarily universal, because they are supposed to be the rights of every human being, yet the "human" in this concept of human rights is particular to her or his identity, beliefs, experiences, and context. Second, assuming acceptance of the concept, there is then the question of its *content*: what are these rights and what makes them universal in the reality of permanent and profound adversity among human beings, individually and collectively? How can people of different cultural, religious, or philosophical orientations, different social and economic classes, education, and so forth, agree on what is due to every human being by virtue of his or her humanity? Third, there is also the role of *context* in the definition as well as the implementation of human rights in the reality of deeply rooted and structural differences in power relations among and within societies.

Each of these three aspects raises a paradox that may be mediated through practice over time, but cannot be theoretically resolved conclusively and permanently. For instance, does the claim that human rights are universal imply or require the existence of a "universal human being," and if so, who is that person or how do we identify her or him? As I see it, the paradox is that it is problematic either to affirm or to deny the notion of a universal human. Regarding specific human rights norms, even if we concede the fiction that international human rights are binding on one generation because they were negotiated and adopted by their state representatives, why should subsequent generations remain bound by those same norms? Moreover, the rationale of taking context seriously itself means that there are bound to be disagreements about the nature and implications of that for different people and locations at different times. By mediation of paradox at each level of analysis I mean that it is better to "negotiate" consensus than to assume it exists or attempt to impose theoretical uniformity from one perspective or another.

There is paradox in the process of mediation itself. The human in human rights is a self-determining person who should have the right and ability to decide to accept or reject the concept of human rights itself, and contribute to defining its content and participate in the implementation of these rights. But how can any person be self-determining when the "self" is socially constructed, and all possibilities of "determination" are themselves pre-determined by factors and forces beyond the choice or control of the person? We have no choice regarding when or where we are born, which class, race, or sex we belong to, or which parents, families or communities we are raised in. We have no effective control over the psychological, social, economic, and other factors that influence our attitudes and behavior. Paradoxically, the conception, content, and implementation of human rights are all shaped by the same conditions they seek to challenge in the sense that it is difficult to imagine a right and how it can work in practice without imagining the violation of that right.

Moreover, the premise and rationale of self-determination is that the person should defend and protect her or his own rights, yet it is difficult to see how a victim of a human rights violation can have the ability and resources to protect her or his own rights. Whether it is arbitrary detention, suppression of freedom of speech and association, or denial of education, health care, or housing, the rights violation in fact hampers our ability to protect our rights. We need external resources and actors to protect our rights when we are actual victims of violations, yet reliance on external protection of rights is likely to perpetuate our dependency instead of enhancing our self-determination. Whoever provides the resources and acts to protect the rights of others will do so on his or her own terms which are, by definition, not those of the victims whose rights we purport to protect. When my rights are protected by others, they are the ones who decide what my rights mean and how they should be protected, and I become the "object" of their advocacy and charity, not the autonomous human subject who is protecting his own rights.

This paradox of "human rights dependency" can be mediated through the promotion of the cultural legitimacy of human rights in various societies in order to motivate and mobilize people to protect their own rights.[8] But the paradox continues, as dependency on external protection can only be diminished over time through the cooperation of internal and external actors. The difficulty here is not only that external actors are unlikely to appreciate the need to submit to internal initiative and leadership, but also that internal "beneficiaries" are unable to compel external actors to act against their view of which rights they wish to protect and how they wish to do that. Moreover, to require external actors to submit to internal leadership can be problematic when it means requiring external actors to accept attitudes and behavior within the community that they believe to be in violation of, for instance, the rights of women or children.[9] Yet, there is no alterative course of action to the constant mediation of these various levels and types of paradox within different cultural and political contexts.

Self-determination is primarily about an internal life, within each person, before it can be about interaction with external factors and actors, whether local or global. It is in that inner life that the people can find the moral courage to stand by their convictions about human rights, to be willing to endure hardship and risks to life and livelihood in protecting these rights for themselves. This inner moral resource will not only sustain victims of human rights violations when external help is not forthcoming, but also enable them to ensure that any external assistance that is forthcoming suits their own priorities and sensibilities. In other words, the moral courage from within enables people not only to resist oppression but also to negotiate on their own terms with those who claim to help them in doing so. A well-known example of what I mean is how Mahatma Gandhi's insight and ability to stand by his convictions and motivate other Indians to do the same launched a massive and sustained non-violent resistance movement that ultimately compelled the British Empire to leave India.

The purpose and rationale of the international human rights system (its norms, institutions, and processes) and movement (its non-governmental activities) are to protect all of us precisely because very few of us have the level and sustainability of moral courage that Gandhi was able to achieve in his own lifetime. But in my view, we all need to have a little of Gandhi within ourselves if we are to realize the true potential of the human rights system and movement. I would further argue that we all have that potential, which is what I mean by "the human in human rights," but that potential can be realized within each of us in terms of our own moral frame of reference. This is my understanding of the expression attributed to Gandhi: "be the change you want to see in the world,"[10] that we should realize the value of human rights within ourselves in order for it to be realized in the world around us. This is a causal relationship, whereby internal transformation within the person is the means for the desired external change, which is the practical protection of human rights in this case.

To relate this perspective to the subject of this chapter: for people to protect their own human rights, as the self-determining human in human rights, we must have the courage to uphold these rights, regardless of the apparent lack of prospects of relief. Paradoxically, the less chance of immediate relief, the more important it is that we are morally strong enough to stand up for our own human rights. If we fail to uphold human rights within ourselves and suffer the consequences, whatever others do to help us will not be "true" protection of our human rights, even if external intervention succeeds in stopping violations in the short term. Moreover, there is also the need to promote our convictions and moral courage to stand up for our own rights, rather than expecting that strength and that courage to suddenly materialize in times of crisis simply because we need them then. I am calling for the deliberate use of the "space" provided by short-term relief to strengthen our convictions and enhance our moral courage to stand by our human rights for ourselves.

The question I will now turn to is, where is this courage going to come from? With due respect and appreciation for the answer each of us may have for this question, for me, the source I can and should cultivate for this purpose is my religion. My belief in Islam as my own religion is the source and methodology of cultivating my inner life as a self-determining human being who is capable of upholding his human rights. I would accept assistance to avoid violations of my rights, but my religion is the source I draw on to uphold my human dignity and self-determination beyond that immediate relief. Islam for me is where my humanity comes into being, and where human rights are anchored. I am not saying that this must be the way all others, including other believers, must perceive the issue, but only that this is the way I feel. Being a member of a community of Muslim believers should enable me to bring the collective will and power of that community to support the cause of human rights in solidarity with others who share that commitment to human rights for their own reasons, too. But my ability to enlist the support of my community of believers to support and promote human rights depends on my ability to use arguments that are persuasive to them—in other words, through an Islamic discourse. To be able to make that argument, however, I need the protection of my human rights.

As suggested earlier, the appropriate *framing* of the subject of Islam and human rights is how to promote the practical application of human rights among Muslims as consistent with their belief in Islam. While this process calls for a variety of approaches, such as strategies of political and civil society mobilization and enhancement of institutional capacity, I will limit my remarks here to the role of Islamic discourse on human rights. The *reframing* I am proposing is that the question should relate to the religious and social realm and not in terms of enforcement of Sharia as state law. I will explain and support that side of the analysis in the next section of this chapter. For now I will focus on Islamic discourse on human rights.

■ CURRENT ISLAMIC DISCOURSE ON ISLAM AND HUMAN RIGHTS

In view of the history and current realities of Islamic societies around the world, we should expect a significant diversity of views about human rights, rather than uniformity or consistency of such views with preconceived notions of Islam and Muslims. Profound political and theological differences have divided Muslims from the beginning in the Arabia of the seventh century, leading to civil wars over issues of political power within a few decades of the Prophet's death. What came to be known as Sharia gradually evolved during the first three centuries of Islam through human interpretations of the Quran and Sunna of the Prophet.[11] That process was characterized by diversity of opinion among various schools of Islamic jurisprudence (*madhahib*) of the Sunni and Shia traditions, each according to its own methodology of *usul al-fiqh* (the science of sources or foundations of Islamic jurisprudence).[12] The established methodology of *usul al-fiqh* in that formative stage applied such techniques as reasoning by analogy (*qias*) and consensus (*ijma*) to develop a systematic corpus of Sharia principles out of the texts of the Quran and Sunna. When those textual sources were silent on a specific issue, the founding jurists of Sharia exercised their independent juridical reasoning (*ijtihad*).

Space does not permit explanation of the ways in which Sharia was implemented by communities, in contrast to the manner and extent it used to be applied or enforced by state institutions in the pre-modern era.[13] Whatever the situation may have been in various parts of the Muslim world through the centuries, Sharia principles were effectively displaced by European legislation and enforcement of positive state law during the colonial period in all fields except family law. Those colonial legal systems were generally continued by the new "nation states" with Muslim-majority populations after independence, with minor adjustments along similarly secular lines. There was certainly no general return to pre-colonial administration of justice anywhere in the post-colonial Muslim world in any field except in family law. Matters of marriage, divorce, custody of children, and inheritance remained governed by Sharia principles throughout the colonial and post-colonial era. Since the 1970s, however, there have been mounting demands for the enforcement of certain principles of Sharia as the official law of the State, commonly known as the rise of "political Islam." This tension between the reality of secular national legal systems, on the one hand, and popular demands for the enforcement of Sharia by the State, on the other, is the general background and context of current debates the relationship of Islam to state law, democratic governance, human rights, and related concepts. For our limited purposes here, I will now present a brief review of different perspectives on Islam and human rights in particular.

At one end of the spectrum, proponents of an Islamic state (hereinafter called Islamists) tend either to reject openly the idea of universal human rights as an imperial Western imposition, or to engage in an apologia for conflicts between Sharia and human rights. Some Islamists, like Abu al-Ala al-Mawdudi (d. 1979),[14] assert a competing notion of what he calls "human rights in Islam," which is neither consistent with the concept of human rights as such, nor accurately Islamic in the sense of conformity with Sharia. Mawdudi represents a clear and instructive example of this perspective not only as probably the most influential Islamist ideologue of the twentieth century, but also because he expressly addressed human rights and related issues in his work.[15] I will briefly discuss this particular aspect for our purposes here, but will try to quote him here as much as space permits to avoid the risk of distortion of his view, which I criticize as a dangerous combination of contradiction, intellectual dishonesty, and romantic naïveté.

Mawdudi criticized what he called Western human rights as limited in theory and hypocritical in practice, and asserted that Islam established human rights many centuries before the West and according to a much superior conception. In his view, "human rights in Islam" are conferred by God, and cannot be withdrawn, amended, or changed by any government or legislative assembly in the world. Such a romantic notion, however, was never true in the history of Islamic societies, up to and including the so-called Islamic states in Iran, Pakistan, and Saudi Arabia today. There is no practical or realistic way of forcing governments to uphold rights simply because some scholars say God has decreed those rights. If governments are made to do this out of fear of political opposition, then how is that different from the model of "Western democracy" that Mawdudi rejected?

Moreover, Mawdudi's claims about particular "human rights in Islam" are untenable not only for their excessive ambiguity and intellectual dishonesty, but also because they are not about human rights as the rights of human beings as such. For instance, according to Mawdudi, "Islam gives the right of freedom of thought and expression to all citizens of the Islamic State on the condition that it should be used for the propagation of virtue and truth and not for spreading evil and wickedness. … Under no circumstances would Islam allow evil and wickedness to be propagated."[16] But to speak of "Islam" at large is misleading in view of the permanent and profound diversity of opinions among Islamic schools of jurisprudence. Born and raised in India and then migrating to Pakistan after partition, Mawdudi must have been aware of that diversity at least among and between Sunni and Shia Muslims of the Indian sub-continent. Moreover, who is to determine what can be used "for the propagation of virtue and truth" and how and by whom can that issue be adjudicated and enforced in practice? Who is to decide what is "evil and wickedness" in order to disallow its propagation on behalf of Islam?

A striking illustration of Mawdudi's contradiction, intellectual dishonesty and romantic naïveté can be seen in his views on the status of non-Muslims in his ideal Islamic state. On the one hand, in his commentary on verse 2:29 of the Quran, which instructs Muslims to subdue non-Muslims, Mawdudi says:

> The purpose for which the Muslims are required to fight is not as one might think to compel the unbelievers into embracing Islam. Rather, their purpose is to put an end to the sovereignty and supremacy of the unbelievers so that the latter are unable to rule over men. The authority to rule should only be vested in those who follow the true faith; unbelievers who do not follow this true faith should live in a state of subordination. Unbelievers are required to pay *jizyah* (a poll tax) in lieu of the security provided to them as the *Dhimmis* ("Protected People") of an Islamic state.[17]

On the other hand, here is how he describes the status of non-Muslims in another publication:

> In an Islamic State, all non-Muslims will have the same freedom of conscience, of opinion, of expression (through words spoken and written) and of association as the one enjoyed by the Muslims themselves, subject to the same limitations as are imposed by law on the Muslims. Within those limitations they will be entitled to criticize the government and its officials, including the Head of the State.
>
> They will also enjoy the same rights of criticizing Islam as the Muslims will have to criticize their religion.
>
> They will likewise be fully entitled to propagate the good points of their religion, and if a non-Muslim is won over to another non-Islamic creed, there can be no objection to it. As regards Muslims, none of them will be allowed to change creed … and it will be perfectly within their constitutional rights if they refuse to act against their conscience or creed, so long as they do not violate the law of the land.[18]

The status of non-Muslims presented in the first statement is closer to the established status of non-Muslims under Sharia, but totally inconsistent with the rights granted to non-Muslims by Mawdudi in the second quotation. Contrary to what Mawdudi asserts, it is simply not true of any school of Islamic jurisprudence, Sunni or Shia, that "all non-Muslims have the same freedom of conscience … as the one enjoyed by the Muslims themselves." In fact this assertion is so obviously wrong according to Mawdudi's own interpretation of verse 2:29, quoted above, that it cannot be explained as a simple oversight. Moreover, the term "non-Muslims" is misleading in this context because it covers all unbelievers, whereas Sharia makes a clear distinction between People of the Book (mainly Christian and Jews) and those deemed by Sharia to be unbelievers, such as Buddhists, followers of native tribal religions, polytheists, and atheists. While People of the Book enjoy limited communal rights short of full citizenship, Sharia does not acknowledge any legal personality or security of person and property of an unbeliever in the second group.

At the other end of the spectrum from Islamist ideologues like Mawdudi we find Muslim advocates of international human rights standards who have recently attempted to develop Islamic support for human rights through a critical examination of Sharia and calls for *ijtihad* (independent juridical reasoning) and reinterpretation of the Quran and Sunna of the Prophet.[19] Since space does not permit a sufficiently detailed presentation of views for critique or evaluation, I will simply offer a few examples and cite their works for reference.

Well-known scholars publishing in English who have made significant contributions to the *ijtihad* re-interpretation approach include Abdolkarim Soroush,[20] Asghar Ali Engineer,[21] and Khaled Abou el-Fadl.[22] Muslim feminist scholars focusing on gender and the human rights of women and particular include Leila Ahmed,[23] Amina Wadud,[24] Kecia Ali,[25] Riffat Hassan,[26] and Shaheen Sardar Ali.[27] The call for a critical study of the Quran and a reevaluation of human rights from an Islamic perspective is made by several scholars under the banner of "progressive Islam." To Omid Safi, one of the founders of this approach, being a Muslim means affirming the humanity of all human beings, regardless of their religion, race, gender, and other factors. He calls for the practice and positive use of *ijtihad* (independent juridical reasoning) in order to promote a critical and progressive interpretation of Islam that enforces justice and equality throughout the world.[28] Safi's colleagues on the progressive path include Ulil Abshar-Abdallah, Farid Esack, and Amir Hussain.[29]

I am unable to offer specific comments or critique on pro-human rights scholars without first reviewing their work in accurate detail. In general, however, I see that the challenge is how to develop and apply a systematic and effective methodology of reinterpretation of Sharia, instead of arbitrarily selecting sources and historical evidence to support one view or another on an isolated issue or subject. It is easy to find verses of the Quran that apparently support various modern human rights principles, such as freedom of religion and equality for women. But one can equally quote verses that seem to support the opposing view. The real issue is to establish a consistent "framework of interpretation," and not simply the availability of texts of Quran that can be understood one way or another.

In my view, *Ustadh* Mahmoud Mohamed Taha has provided a consistent framework of interpretation that addresses a wide range of reform issues in a systematic manner on the basis of the historical contingency of revelations of the Quran and reversal of the process of abrogation (*naskh*) applied by early scholars of Sharia.[30]

Whether through Taha's methodology or another adequate approach, the need for systematic revision of the methodology of Sharia (*usal al-fiqh*) remains the primary theoretical challenge. There is also the practical challenge of how to promote such methodology among the Muslim public at large in the present national and global context of human rights debates everywhere.

Moreover, there is some urgency in this quest for an appropriate reform methodology and its practical propagation. In between the two poles of the spectrum outlined above, there is a wide range of civil society actors who seem to be either unaware of the human rights concerns with traditional interpretations of Sharia or hope to continue their work without having to confront that issue. Beyond all these active groups, the vast majority of the Muslim public is probably open to being persuaded one way or the other. In my experience, Muslims in general tend to have a vaguely favorable view of human rights, but that could change if confronted with a claim that human rights are inconsistent with Sharia, unless that negative view is effectively countered in favor of human rights. Though I am unaware of empirical evidence on the point, it seems reasonable to expect that civil society groups as well as the general Muslim public can be ambivalent in their human rights commitments when faced by a concerted assault from Mawdudi's type of argument, unless they are able to reply on an "Islamic defense."

■ CONCLUSIONS

I seem to have managed to end up caught in a paradox by insisting on the right of Muslims to assert a religious foundation or justification for human rights, without being able to establish the existence of such foundation in current Islamic discourse on human rights. In conclusion, I would still maintain that there is no alternative to accepting people's own foundations for human rights, whether religious or secular. In other words, whatever difficulty may arise in grounding human rights in religion for believers who wish to assert that foundation must be acknowledged and addressed. If we insist on a total frontal confrontation, the human rights side will lose among believers. In my view, however, such a zero-sum game is unnecessary. In the case of Islam in particular, I would recall my plea for a framing and reframing of the inquiry on Islam and human rights as a means for progressively mediating this apparent paradox, without necessarily totally resolving the tension between Islam and human rights.

As noted earlier, by "reframing" I mean focusing on transforming the attitudes of Muslims (and other believers) regarding the social and religious meaning and implications of human rights, and not in terms of the application of the principles of Sharia as state law. The fact that Sharia principles cannot by definition be enforced as state law,[31] even where Muslims are the predominant majority of the population, Sharia objections to human rights standards cannot affect the legal enforcement of those standards by the State. In other words, from a strictly legal point of view, Sharia as such should have no bearing on whether or not a

Muslim-majority state adopts and implements human rights treaties or not. However, the sociological and political challenge to such adoption and enforcement remains if Muslim public opinion is opposed in the belief that human rights norms are contrary to Sharia or Islam in general.

The premise of my argument is that, by its nature and purpose, Sharia can only be freely observed by believers, and its principles lose their religious authority and value when they are enforced by the State. This religious dimension requires free reflection and choice by believers among equally accessible competing interpretations and religious authorities, independently from the coercive authority of the State. This free reflection and observance is lost when the State enforces Sharia. Since effective governance requires the adoption of specific policies and the enactment of precise laws for systematic general application, the administrative and legislative organs of the State must select among competing views within the massive and complex corpus of Sharia principles. Whatever principle of Sharia is enacted by the State as positive law ceases to be truly Sharia by the very act of enacting it as the law to be coercively enforced by the State. The inherent subjectivity and diversity of Sharia principles mean that whatever is enacted and enforced by the State is the political will of the ruling elite, not the normative system of Islam as such. Yet, such legislation will be difficult for the general population to resist or even debate when state law is presented as divine command.

To mediate the delicate relationship between religious norms and state law, I am proposing that the rationale of all public policy and legislation should be based on what might be called "civic reason." Muslims and other believers should be able to propose policy and legislative initiatives emanating from their religious beliefs, *provided* they can support them in free and open debate by giving reasons that are accessible and convincing to the generality of citizens, regardless of their religion or other beliefs. But since such decisions will in practice be made by majority vote in accordance with democratic principles, all state action must also conform to basic constitutional and human rights safeguards to protect against the tyranny of the majority. Accordingly, the majority would not be able to implement any policy or legislation that violates the fundamental constitutional rights of all citizens, women and men, Muslims and non-Muslims alike.

In this way, both the adoption of human rights norms as well as opposition to them must be founded on civic reason, without reference to the religious beliefs of any community. At the same time, however, since Sharia principles will remain binding on all Muslims in individual and collective practice outside state institutions, the need for reform through internal debate about the interpretation of Sharia will continue.

In the final analysis, however, the realistic prospects of such constant mediation in the social and sociological realm, without affecting the legal obligations of the State to uphold human rights standards, will depend on the credibility and moral authority of the human rights themselves, as reflected in the practice of all states, especially the major powers. As I have argued elsewhere,[32] if the human rights project is to collapse, I believe, that would be as much the result of the failure of Western major powers to uphold these rights in their own domestic practice and international relations behavior, as the consequence of Islamic opposition to human rights.

■ NOTES

1 According to a study by the Pew Forum on Religion and Public Life, there are approximately 1.6 billion Muslims in the world today. 62.1%of the Muslims of the world live in Asia and the Pacific, 19.9% in the Middle East and North Africa, 15% in Sub-Saharan Africa, 2.7% in Europe, and 2.7% in the Americas. Europe is home to 44 million Muslims—around 6% of its population. More than half of the 5.2 million Muslims in the Americas live in the U.S.—however, they make up just 0.8%. of the population there. The data also showed that there were more Muslims in Germany than in Lebanon, and more in Russia than in Jordan and Libya together. See Pew Forum on Religion and Public Life, "The Future of the Global Muslim Population" (Washington, DC: Pew Research Center, 2011), accessible at: http://pewforum.org/The-Future-of-the-Global-Muslim-Population.aspx

2 See chapter by David Little herein in texts accompanying his notes 17 and 18.

3 Abdullahi Ahmed An-Na'im, "Toward an Islamic Hermeneutics for Human Rights," in *Human Rights and Religious Values: An Uneasy Relationship?* Abdullahi Ahmed An-Na'im, et al., eds. (Grand Rapids, MI: Wm. B. Eerdmans Pub. Co., 1995), 229.

4 Abdullahi Ahmed An-Na'im, ed., *Human Rights in Cross-Cultural Perspectives: Quest for Consensus* (Philadelphia: University of Pennsylvania Press, 1992).

5 See, for example, Abdullahi Ahmed An-Na'im, *Toward an Islamic Reformation: Civil Liberties, Human Rights and International Law* (Syracuse, NY: Syracuse University Press, 1990).

6 Abdullahi Ahmed An-Na'im, *Islam and the Secular State: Negotiating the Future of Sharia* (Cambridge: Harvard University Press, 2008), 12–15.

7 For a full statement and Islamic justification of this view see, generally, An-Na'im, *Islam and the Secular State.*

8 See, for example, An-Na'im, ed., *Human Rights in Cross-Cultural Perspectives.*

9 Abdullahi Ahmed An-Na'im, "Cultural Transformation and Normative Consensus on the Best Interest of the Child," *International Journal of Law and the Family* 8 (1994): 62–81.

10 Keri Smith, *The Guerilla Art Kit* (Princeton, NJ: Princeton Architectural Press, 2007), 15.

11 See, generally, Noel Coulson, *A History of Islamic Law* (Edinburgh: University of Edinburgh Press, 1964); Wael Hallaq, *The Origins and Evolution of Islamic Law* (Cambridge: Cambridge University Press, 2005).

12 Fazlur Rahman, *Islam* (Chicago: University of Chicago Press, 1979), 79–83.

13 See, for example, Knut Vikor, *Between God and Sultan: A History of Islamic* Law (Oxford: Oxford University Press, 2005).

14 On Mawdudi's life and work see, for example, jamaat.org, "A Short Biography of Syed Abul Ala Mawdudi" (2008) at http://www.abulala.com/about.aspx#ch2, viewed April 19, 2010; and *Encyclopedia of the Middle East* (MiddleEastWeb), "Abul Ala Maududi," http://www.mideastweb.org/Middle-East-Encyclopedia/abul-ala-maududi.htm, viewed April 18, 2010.

15 Mawdudi is reported to have written over 120 books, booklets and pamphlets and made over a 1000 speeches and press statements, of which about 700 are publicly

available now. His books have been translated into many major languages, including Arabic, English, Turkish, Persian, Hindi, French, German, Swahili, Tamil, and Bengali.

16 Abu al-Ala al-Mawdudi, *Human Rights in Islam*, 2nd ed. (Lahore: Islamic Publications Limited, 1995), 28.

17 Abu al-Ala al-Mawdudi, *Towards Understanding the Quran*, Vol. III, surahs 7–9 (Leicester: Islamic Foundation, 1990), 202.

18 Abu al-Ala al-Mawdudi, *Rights of Non Muslims in Islamic State*, 7th ed. (Lahore: Islamic Publications Limited, 1982), 29.

19 For discussion of the major Muslim scholars working on these and related issues see, for example, Shireen Hunter, *Reformist Voices of Islam: Mediating Islam and Modernity* (Armonk, NY: M.E. Sharpe, 2009).

20 In English see, *Reason, Freedom and Democracy in Islam: Essential Writing of Abdolkarim Soroush,* trans. and eds. Mahmoud Sadri and Ahmad Sadri (Oxford: Oxford University Press, 2000); Behrooz Ghamari-Tabrizi, *Islam & Dissent in Postrevolutionary Iran: Abdolkarim Soroush, Religious Politics and Democratic Reform* (New York: I. B. Tauris, 2008).

21 Asghar Ali Engineer, *The Rights of Women in Islam,*3rd rev. ed. (New Delhi: Sterling Publishers Pvt. Ltd., 2004).

22 Khaled Abou el-Fadl, *Speaking in God's Name: Islamic Law, Authority, and Women* (Oxford: Oneworld Press, 2005).

23 Leila Ahmed, *Women and Gender in Islam: Historical Roots of a Modern Debate* (New Haven: Yale University Press, 1992).

24 Amina Wadud, *Quran and Woman: Rereading the Sacred Text from a Woman's Perspective* (New York: Oxford University Press, 1999).

25 Kecia Ali, *Sexual Ethics and Islam: Feminist Reflections on Quran, Hadith, and Jurisprudence* (Oxford: Oneworld Publications, 2006).

26 See, for example, Leonard Grob, Riffat Hassan, and Haim Gordon, eds., *Women's and Men's Liberation: Testimonies of Spirit* (New York: Greenwood Press, 1991).

27 Shaheen Sardar Ali, *Gender and Human Rights in Islam and International Law: Equal Before Allah, Unequal Before Man* (The Hague: Kluwer Law International, 2000).

28 Omid Safi, "Introduction: The Times They Are A-Changin': A Muslim Quest for Justice, Gender Equality, and Pluralism," in *Progressive Muslims: On Justice, Gender, and Pluralism,* ed. Omid Safi (Oxford: Oneworld Publications, 2003), 3.

29 See their respective chapters in Safi, ed., *Progressive Muslims*. See also, for example, Farid Esack, *The Quran, Liberation and Pluralism* (Oxford: Oneworld Publications, 1997).

30 Mahmoud Mohamed Taha, *The Second Message of Islam* (Syracuse, NY: Syracuse University Press, 1987).

31 An-Na'im, *Islam and the Secular State*.

32 See, for example, Abdullahi Ahmed An-Na'im, "Why Should Muslims Abandon Jihad? Human Rights and the Future of International Law," *Third World Quarterly*, 27(5) (2006): 785–97.

■ RECOMMENDED READING

Abou el-Fadl, Khaled. *Speaking in God's Name: Islamic Law, Authority, and Women* (Oxford: Oneworld Publications, 2005)

Ahmed, Leila. *Women and Gender in Islam: Historical Roots of a Modern Debate* (New Haven: Yale University Press, 1992)

Ali, Shaheen Sardar. *Gender and Human Rights in Islam and International Law: Equal before Allah, Unequal Before Man?* (The Hague: Kluwer Law International, 2000)

An-Na'im, Abdullahi Ahmed. *Islam and Human Rights, Selected Essays of Abdullahi An-Na'im*, ed. Mashood A. Baderin (Surrey, UK: Ashgate Publishing Limited, 2010)

_____. *Muslims and Global Justice* (Philadelphia: University of Pennsylvania Press, 2011)

_____. *Toward an Islamic Reformation: Civil Liberties, Human Rights and International Law* (Syracuse, NY: Syracuse University Press, 1990)

Baderin, Mashood A. *International Human Rights and Islamic Law* (Oxford: Oxford University Press, 2003)

Dalacoura, Katerina. *Islam, Liberalism and Human Rights*, 3rd ed. (London and New York: I.B. Tauris, 2007)

Engineer, Asghar Ali. *The Rights of Women in Islam*, 3rd rev. ed. (New Delhi: Sterling Publishers Pvt. Ltd., 2004)

Mayer, Ann Elizabeth. *Islam and Human Rights: Tradition and Politics*, 4th ed. (Boulder, CO: Westview Press, 2007)

Oh, Irene. *The Rights of God: Islam, Human Rights and Comparative Ethics* (Washington, DC: Georgetown University Press, 2007)

Sachedina, Abdulaziz Abdulhussein. *Islam and the Challenge of Human Rights* (Oxford: Oxford University Press, 2009)

4 Hinduism and Human Rights

WERNER MENSKI

Both terms in the title—"Hinduism" and "human rights"—have many meanings and are internally plural concepts. As Abdullahi An-Na'im's chapter on Islam herein highlights, such labels catch us in a paradox, setting up ill-mannered shadowboxing contests between proponents of concepts that appear irreconcilable to many observers in ongoing discourses, marked by contradictions, intellectual dishonesty, and much romantic naïveté. Especially in comparison with Islam, scholarship on Hinduism and human rights has not yet progressed beyond levels of superficial engagement. Mutual demonizing prevails, and activist writers get away with twisting even basic facts. While Hinduism is under serious challenge, much evasive action from both sides seems to prevent serious intellectual engagement over what Hinduism and human rights mean and do for each other.

In this chapter, I use the methodology of legal pluralism to try to counter unproductive shadowboxing, and apply what An-Na'im calls "civic reason" to remove the dark shadows of mutual accusations of inferiority. For some human rights lawyers, however, especially those with universalist tendencies, legal pluralism itself remains a dirty word. For they often refuse to acknowledge difference and diversity, and are unwilling or unable to engage in plurality-conscious debate in today's global contexts. Efforts to silence specific voices or perspectives, while the realities of daily life and law remain deeply pluralistic are unconstructive in discourses about the relations of human rights to different cultures and religions. There is, after all, also a right to culture, and whatever God there may be has chosen not to create people of one kind and/or of one belief. Scholars, however, act as advocates of specific belief systems—including human rights—rather than as objective participants in ongoing global debates about the fundamental rules of human co-existence. At the root of such messiness lies thus unwillingness to respect and accept differences of all kinds and a concomitant desire to draw fixed boundaries where all we have is fuzzy categories, indeed multiple internal pluralities, which I now call "pops"—plurality of pluralities.[1]

Limited space allows little coverage of human rights generally, which are covered in the other chapters in this volume. Following two methodological sections on the difficulties posed by necessarily pluralist analysis, I seek to outline how even well-meaning human rights activism actually talks past Hindus and fails to involve them in respectful discussions about negotiating diversities and different perspectives. I then outline how different kinds of Hindus have cultivated their own understanding of human rights, demonstrating how in the process they may also fail—in various ways and with various agendas—to portray their respective religious and cultural perspectives adequately to a wider world. The chapter thus identifies significant breakdowns of intercultural communication, quite apart from deliberately misleading interjections and much outright rejection of "the other," designed to hurt and belittle, if not kill and silence. The field of human rights writing generates its own specific forms of violence and remains open to much abuse.

■ A SCENARIO OF CONFLICT IN CONDITIONS OF PLURALITY

Several contributors to this book identify that such problems are not unique to Hinduism. Faced with global deficiencies in cross-cultural communication and interdisciplinarity, it becomes imperative to link the debates about Hinduism and human rights into the wider framework of global discourses about legal pluralism, comparative law, and human rights protection. I start with that aspect to strengthen pluralist analytical methods. As scholars concerned to work on the practical applicability of contested concepts—and which concepts are not contested?—we need to protect at all times what Upendra Baxi calls "the most precious of all human rights—the constantly claimed *human right to interpret human rights*."[2]

To me, as a legal pluralist and specialist in South Asian laws, the terms "Hinduism" and "human rights" represent "pops," a plurality of pluralities, internally diverse concepts and constructs grown over time, commonly subsumed in popular parlance and scholarly discourse under a specific simple label. It has become critically important to acknowledge that such labels and the underlying pluralities are not at all new phenomena; they have existed for thousands of years and can still be excavated.[3] Such pluralities are marked by intense internal dynamisms, constantly developing new pluralities over time. We need to factor such dynamic diversities into current analyses to open our eyes to the diversities all around us instead of applying different blinders. Most urgently, we need to sensitize our perceptions towards acceptance of internal pluralities. Presently, verbal and visual signals associated with specific concepts are constantly rigidified in our minds and scholars waste much time criticizing each other for "essentializing."

Hearing words like "Hindu" or "Hinduism," for example, immediately invokes many negative mental images of religious domination, fortified by ancient fixed codes and powerful early law makers, leading to religiously sanctioned abuses of power such as today's gender-related and caste-based discriminations. Many people instantly associate multiple human rights violations with such a supposedly "religious" label of "Hinduism." These same people tend to associate "law" with rational, state-centric regulation and "human rights" with secular positive ideals, propounded by a global body.

It is then entirely unsurprising that in the virtual caldron of highly subjective perceptions and emotions dressed up as scholarly discourse, "Hinduism" is today widely perceived as "bad" because its presence counteracts various uniformizing ambitions. Hinduism is immediately linked to "tradition," "religion," and often now fascism. The Gujarat riots of 2002, as Scott Appleby's chapter herein and others confirm, have served as a signal event in the new millennium for many writers to identify Hindu nationalism and specifically *hindutva* ("Hinduness") as the main culprit, a sure sign that Hinduism and respect for human rights are seen as irreconcilable. Hinduism is often treated as irrational and morally questionable and dismissed as merely "constructed." Such argumentation conveniently forgets that Hinduism remains an important identity marker for at least 800 million people on this globe who could be identified as Hindus,[4] for thousands of communities and also for several states. To define it away by such caricatures resembles a human rights violation.

The term "human rights," by contrast, tends to trigger instant positive responses in the minds of many. This term effortlessly occupies the moral high ground and is widely perceived and portrayed as "modern," "rational," and simply "good." But human rights fundamentalism goes too far in demanding strict separation of "law," "religion," and "culture," indicating major methodological problems not only for the French model of laicization. When every aspect of human life is in fact interlinked, and law is part of culture, insisting on an academically or legally constructed separation of law, religion, and culture becomes fictitious and leads into intellectual cul-de-sacs, dark alleys in which shadowboxing has become an art form and a growth industry. But whose right is it to determine what drives people's identity constructions?

■ INSUFFICIENT METHODOLOGIES TO HANDLE PLURALISM

All over the world, we find many different religio-cultural and socio-legal normative systems that are deeply hybrid entities, grown over time and not fully separable by specialist academic analysis. Lawyers may endeavour to approach such phenomena from the perspective of comparative law,[5] or through applying global legal theory.[6] Other subject-specific approaches tackle the same predicaments from different angles, such as the self-regulatory power of religion,[7] only to face similar manifestations of plurality as a ubiquitous fact. Pluralism, this indicates, is not just a problem for lawyers, but seems to be blamed for recurrent human rights problems. Ongoing irritations over handling difference and diversity, as well as the much-noted rising salience of religion in politics seem to have led to a normative tussle and underpin new politics of tradition. International lawyers speak now of "political theology" but dismiss explicit recognition of religion as nostalgic chasing of some earlier and now irrelevant convictions. Such academic gymnastics lead to labored struggles, reflected in Arvind Sharma's observation that much current literature on human rights connects the secular outlook, individualism, and egalitarianism, bunching them together on the basis of their shared ideological orientations.[8] Such new and powerful anti-religious discourses about human nature and relationships continue to underpin worldwide conflicts of interpretation over constructions of "Hinduism" and other non-Western traditions in relation to human rights.

In common with "traditionalists" and most other non-Western people, many Hindus seem to "know" instinctively that the globally manifested "pop" phenomenon of virtually inevitable, visible and invisible macrocosmic and microcosmic forms of interlinkedness is a fact of human life and a matter of realism. My fieldwork indicates that formally uneducated South Asians are often much wiser about such issues than people with university degrees. Highly educated Indian modernists, who often reject the label "Hindu," generally and for themselves, dominate relevant public discourses, but do and can they speak for Hindus? Together with many persons from Western cultural contexts and certainly most human rights activists from all over the world, they seek to argue for individualized autonomy and the more or less strict divisions of competing elements of "law" and "religion," "church" and "state," rights and duties, and so on. This distinguishes what African people tend to call "spirituality" and what others refer to as "religiosity" from secularly constructed autonomous individualization and rationality of the post-Enlightenment, Protestant type. There will be many fuzzy boundaries of all those "pop" elements, with various broken lines and competing perspectives of the various religions, cultures, and human rights principles. One may treat the latter as new forms of natural law and some scholars have begun to see a new religion. A recent encyclopedia of law (with multiple entries on "human rights"[9]) indicates such underlying tensions:

> The term "human rights" contains a multitude of meanings that cross many academic disciplines. To the philosopher it is about the essential qualities of the human that lead us to an understanding of our duties towards others; to the specialist in international relations, it connotes a force in the management of relations between states; while to the political scientist, human rights are a tool in the construction of a liberal community. Law's approach to human rights is both simpler and more question-begging than any of these. . . . This is why human rights is an inherently interdisciplinary subject: law's grasp of the subject may be coherent but its reliance on authoritative documents renders its coverage inevitably incomplete.[10]

Unsurprisingly, both elements in the title of the present chapter are found in multiple tensions, more so since Hinduism is often wrongly perceived as entirely religious, while "law" and especially "human rights" are treated as secular. However, the entry in the same encyclopedia on "human rights scepticism"[11] immediately highlights more fuzzy boundaries:

> Human rights law is currently very popular, with human rights protected by a battery of international treaties and domestic laws. Some, however, see human rights as a secular religion with the same irrational impulses that inform even more spiritual faiths. Just as spiritual religion has attracted its sceptics, so there is also a sense of human rights delusion. . . . There is, however, no organized or co-ordinated movement of sceptics, and

> the ranks of those sceptical about this new form of theism include those sceptical of the very *idea* of human rights at one end of the spectrum, through to those who are sceptical about the *politics* of the human rights movement, to those who are sceptical about the *means* adopted to protect human rights at the other end. It is admittedly also the case, however, that although the human rights movement now enjoys a dominant voice in the law schools, it too does not speak with one voice, with its Evangelical, Fundamentalist, and Liberation wings.[12]

All this diversity is a wonderful playing field for academic grandstanding by Hindu scholars. Upendra Baxi, no stranger to claiming moral high ground and using verbal brilliance in human rights discourse, significantly remains coy about his own Hindu and Indian background and does not indicate that an atheist Hindu is not an oxymoron. Baxi states that "the originary authors of human rights are people in struggle and communities of resistance, which standard scholarship demotes to a lowly status." This raises the fundamental issue of whose voice needs to be heard and indicates considerable distrust of elitist discourses. In this context, Baxi continues, "Once claims to 'authorship' stand thus pluralized, it follows simply that 'human rights' are not the *gifts of the West to the Rest*; the dominant discourse is diversionary when it locates the origins of human rights in Euroamerican tradition and experience . . . and when it pursues endless debates over 'universality' and 'relativism' of human rights."[13]

Baxi acknowledges that writing about human rights "perforce, runs a thousand narrative risks!" He confirms that "[t]he non-Western traditions are usually considered bereft of notions of human rights," so that "[o]verall, human rights discursivity was and still remains, according to the narrative of origins, the patrimony of the West." While this also means that there are as many NGOs as there are human rights,[14] Baxi charts the emergence of new kinds of activism, maintaining, "A new kind of *normative politics* thus emerges, however riven with tensions and contradictions, concerning what it may mean to say 'human' and having 'rights,' and the contestation over the nature, number, limits, and scope of human rights amidst the rather endless and unproductive contention about their 'universality.'"[15] While Baxi clearly identifies that all this laboring with words "at best yields forms of *fragmented universality* of contemporary human rights," he makes the meaningful distinction between writing "on" human rights and "for" human rights. In his own typically sophisticated diction, he notes, "The context of this interrogation, I believe, paves the way for my translation of the category of production *of* politics into the notion of politics *for* human rights pitted against its other—the politics *of* human rights. It remains rather easy to describe the politics *for* human rights in the languages of 'transformative' or even as 'redemptive' politics."[16]

Such elaborate academic activism with words tells us nothing about Hinduism, however. Surely, one needs to warn that the "transformative" or "redemptive" politics of the state-sovereignty-oriented production of dominant and dominating truths stands constantly exposed as an expedient order of "cruel and wounding falsehoods."[17] In other words, we can neither trust states nor the increasingly ambitious international legal orders to act as effective guarantors of human rights.

But do such reservations need to involve denial or rejection of culture and religion? While activist vigilance remains important everywhere, India as the main abode of Hindus in the world pursues a much-misunderstood official policy of secularism. While this is not trusted to deliver effective human rights guarantees, the powerful Indian Constitution and its basic structural framework actually constitute effective protection mechanisms against the tyranny of the majority, so that India could never legitimately become a Hindu nation. That many Hindus are upset about this is an open secret. However, since these unique Indian "secular" arrangements are simply not trusted by human rights activists, insufficient analyses of Indian secularism just feed the rather sterile debates about the universality and relativity of human rights, which Baxi criticizes so ferociously, without himself telling us more about the culture-specific Indian methods of handling difference.[18]

One major reason for activist disquiet appears to be that India explicitly recognizes, through various structures of governance, the intrinsically linked nature of law and religion, which of course challenges "standard" definitions of secularism as separation of "law and religion." In the eyes of secular analysts, directly engaging with religion and administering it under the mantle of secularism (which, to make it absolutely clear, in India actually seems to mean equal treatment of all religions, not separation of law and religion) of course pollutes the entire system through the fatal infection of respect for religion per se. There is, however, a huge difference between recognizing the presence of "religion" and caving in to religious dictates, which seems to be the main, historically grounded fear among post-Enlightenment secularists. India would not even know which central authority to turn to for identifying alleged Hindu religious dictates, and indeed there is none,[19] while Muslims can at least try to fall back on Allah's words and then argue forever (and kill each other) over their interpretations.

Taking the helpful perspective of pluralist analysis, different strategies of handling and managing diversity and/or of harmonizing intrinsically conflicting and competing sources of legal norms can be skillfully combined, as the Indian model shows. From a mainstream secular perspective, however, because India recognizes a legitimate place for religion and because Hindus are a demographic majority, the Indian state is simply deemed to be religious, not secular. From this perspective, anything Hindu, indeed anything Indian, is without further analysis adjudged as inherently religious, and thus inimical to human rights. Shadowboxing is just so simple!

Analysts have rightly been asking what guarantee there is that the focus on rights is an appropriate strategy to achieve improvements in human rights protection, given that the various Asian value systems appear to focus more on duties, as Sallie King also highlights in her chapter herein on Buddhism. Baxi, too, pointedly asks for "[e]ndeavours at making and remaking contemporary human rights norms and standards,"[20] and indeed notes that "[t]he astonishing feature of the polymorphous production of contemporary human rights norms and standards, at all levels, . . . is its normative exuberance and excess."[21] Because leading human rights thinkers fail to employ methodologies of legal pluralism and avoid its rather plain and commonsensical language, hiding instead behind highly sophisticated constructs and verbal activism, it seems that even the most highly educated readers are not empowered to make the connections that supposedly uneducated humans can simply draw intuitively: human rights theorizing must be culture-specific, because everywhere law and culture are intrinsically linked, and law remains a culture-specific phenomenon in all its various manifestations.

Thus, the question remains whether human rights are just Western, and whether there is any scope for recognition of Hindu voices in global debates about human rights. The two following sections, necessarily briefly, address this issue, beginning with the negative approach, which is much more prominent in the literature.

■ HINDUISM AS A VIOLATION OF HUMAN RIGHTS

The ongoing strategy to dismiss Hindu religion and culture as a collection of backward normative systems, effectively violating even the most basic of human rights, is an ancient phenomenon. Well before the Christian era, Vedic Hindus, Buddhists, and Jains battled over the right way to lead a good life for all humans, and even other creatures.[22] It is here that the literate Brahmin elite of ancient India allegedly first began to assert its privileged position and built an elaborate empire of ritual precision, higher consciousness, and ultimately right knowledge and action, to claim privilege and power to the exclusion, potentially, of all other humans. This led many analysts to claim that the Brahmins did not develop human rights, but cultivated only their own caste-based interests.[23] For many critics, the Brahmins of India are the root cause of flagrant human rights denials to all other people, and of course especially the *dalits* (ex-untouchables) of India.[24]

For others, the term "Hindu" is associated with caste, gender-based discriminations, and unacceptable fascist tendencies that seem to have coagulated into the term *hindutva* ("Hinduness"). "*Hindutva*" is an ethnically colored and thus deeply polluted term for Hindu nationalism and the claims of Hindus to a place at the world table of cultural traditions. Significantly, over time the religious "others" for Hindus were first the Buddhists and the Jains, possibly also the Chinese, then early Jewish and Christian traders and later and prominently Muslims, followed in colonial times by various forms of Christianity and today, of course, simply "the West" and various globalizing pressures.

The Muslim invaders of early medieval India (from ca. 700 C.E. onwards) encountered highly developed civilizations in South Asia, so that South Asian Islam had to adjust to local conditions and developed differently from its Middle Eastern prototype. Indeed, there is growing evidence from detailed local studies that especially certain coastal areas of the Indian subcontinent were "cosmopolitan for millennia and that the social, architectural and religious fabric of the region has been constructed out of the exchange of population, trade goods and ideas."[25] Plurality, in other words, was normal, an accepted fact of life, and of course this led to multiple conflicts and a rich menu of individual choice-making that would then lead to many more conflicts. This is again simply the story of human life, confirming all the time not just the culture-specificity of all laws, but the enormous scope for violent clashes over disagreements when individuals, families, and whole communities make decisions that do not please or suit those around them.

Regarding specifically Muslim-Hindu relations, it can be generally said that the small ruling elite of medieval South Asian Muslims could not uproot Hindu culture and religion. Hence, new hybrids evolved in South Asia, with intense competition over everything from the ultimate "right truth" to access to women, space, and scarce resources. Edward Simpson shows how the memories of such earlier competitive scenarios have influenced more recent relations between local people belonging to different social and religious communities.[26] This leads more or less directly towards the grand narratives of recent communal violence in South Asia which made global news in 2002, by then strongly linked into ongoing human rights discourses.

The colonial period from 1600 onwards certainly put Hindu cultural concepts and Hinduism as a religion under new challenges. The rich literature on this demonstrates how missionary perceptions and constructions of Hinduism were themselves internally plural and dynamic. Geoffrey Oddie shows how intense struggles of competing belief systems and the constantly changing context of such competitive plurality led over time to new prominent challenges to Hindu culture and religion. Stereotypical views of Hinduism solidified during the colonial period but were never stagnant. Hinduism was imagined in certain ways before missionaries even set foot on Indian soil and was then constantly reimagined. Oddie offers intriguing evidence that Hinduism was perceived as primitive and pagan, even as a "monster tradition," but also that it remained a powerful reality. Many observable social evils and repugnant customs led to ethnicization of the colonized other, creating a deep sense of superiority in the minds of European colonizers.[27] Evidently, this approach reverberates strongly in current assessments of Hinduism, Hindu culture, and Hindu law by Western and non-Western scholars alike. Hindu tradition to this day seems forever tainted by these intense caricatures of missionaries and colonists. While Hinduism was widely portrayed as irrational, silent admiration for such an amazing system also grew, side by side with feelings of repugnancy and the formation of certain stereotypical views, which have proved persistent in the gradually forming global paradigms of Orientalism.[28]

Many missionaries and colonists were deeply impressed with the positive sides of Hinduism once they came to live among real Hindus. Oddie shows how sophisticated knowledge about Hinduism was much more widespread in the imperial center at that time than today,[29] strengthened by increasing family relationships through colonial and missionary personnel. Many missionaries focused eventually less on conversion as a mechanism to rescue lost Indian souls and turned themselves into social workers and virtual anthropologists. This led them to acknowledge a common humanity with Hindus, and even more positive attitudes towards Hinduism. They realized that the purported Brahmin domination of lower castes was a strongly engineered fiction and that Hinduism is more of a typically liquid natural religion than an Asian form of monotheistic construct, as Hindus themselves so often seek to claim.[30]

While missionaries eventually softened in their views on Hinduism, other scholars of political science and human rights continue vigorously to denigrate Hindu culture and Hinduism. Not unlike Western missionaries centuries ago, many so-called human rights activists today myopically treat anything Hindu as incapable of addressing human rights concerns. Hindu religion and customs are viewed as tainted by irrationality and adherence to backward customs such as *sati* (the burning of widows on the husband's funeral pyre),[31] forced marriages, dowry demands, frantic killings of non-believers in communal riots, and, of course, multiple caste-based discriminations.

Recent studies simply start from the presumption that equality is a value per se and that "the most plainly revealed system of inequality is associated with the Hindu order of castes." They conclude that the ancient principle of natural inequality, devised by Brahmans, "continues to define the system till today" and thus defies progress in terms of human rights protection.[32] Other authors complain that the proliferation of paradoxes in relation to postcolonial India, including adherence to the phenomenon of dynastic rule, keeps independent India in the shadows of the Empire and creates a political system very different from Western democracies.[33] Again, the assessment is negative, with otherness and plurality dismissed as problematic. One also finds much frantic activism and political correctness reflected in recent discussions concerning the projected inclusion of a question on caste in the Indian Census of 2011. This led to a hostile editorial in one of India's leading news magazines,[34] and rabid self-damning comments, including the observation that, "Our democracy is determined to show the world that whatever others can do, we can do worse. If in this process, individual initiatives are killed, standards lowered, and professional ethics compromised, there is no cause for worry. We can still sink a lot lower."[35]

Such negative approaches to anything remotely "Hindu" are also starkly evident in numerous critical assessments of modern India's performance as a secular nation-state. Sporadic outbreaks of ethno-religious conflicts and the way they have been handled have raised a noisy chorus of serious questions about India's claim to be a secular democracy. Many studies could be cited here, but it must be said, regrettably, that factual correctness often becomes a casualty, most commonly associated with scholarly myth-making about the Shah Bano saga and its aftermath in Indian law, which concerns the contested position of Muslim personal law in India.[36] A further blatant example of activist human rights sparring that did not shy away from blatant misrepresentation relates to the ongoing investigations of the Gujarat riots of 2002. In fact, currently, "more and more evidence is surfacing that the human rights lobby had, in many cases, spun macabre stories of rape and brutal killings by tutoring witnesses."[37]

Rich evidence of misuse of caste categories appears everywhere. The Indian scenario of superdiversity in relation to caste becomes ever more complex, now with terms like "*Mahadalit*" ("super-ex-untouchables"),[38] and never-ending debates about the merits of affirmative action for various disadvantaged classes of Indians. This confirms that while for understanding Hindu perceptions of difference, and Indian management strategies of competing diversities, the caste system is critical and eminently useful, it often serves as a focal point to pinpoint all that is wrong with Hinduism as a religious system, despite doubts whether "caste" is a "religious" category.

While a secular liberal democracy appears to be considered today a major requirement for human development and a virtual prerequisite for human rights protection, India's blood-stained history of communal riots and of violence in the name of culture and now increasingly "honor"—an evident spin-off from Western-led discourses—is perennially seen as living proof that Hindus simply have no respect for human rights.[39] The deliberate manipulations of well-known ancient and current fuzzy boundaries in ongoing assessments of various forms of violence in South Asia, as though that was the only place in the world in which such violence happens, indicate a rabid anti-Hindu stance in global academia, which probably also pleases various Muslim lobbies and allows the Chinese to hide behind such shadows.

■ HINDUISM AND HUMAN RIGHTS

It is evident that Hindus have become deeply upset about such manipulative denigrations of their traditions and have been learning to hit back in kind. Internet campaigns seeking bans of several Western studies on Hinduism, including Wendy Doniger's recent work, are signs of an unpleasant backlash. Some studies assert openly that the notion of human rights was prevalent also in ancient traditions,[40] but they face a wall of silence. Articulate defenders of Hindu tradition clearly recognize that Hinduism needs to change with the times, to avoid being "relegated to the status of a permanent delinquent in the race of modernity."[41] Examining the limits of the pluralistic nature of Hinduism and Hindu tolerance, Arvind Sharma argues that "Hinduism is conscious of its universalism because it considers consciousness to be the most universal dimension of existence."[42] Sharma does not claim, like some writers of the *hindutva* brigade, that all people are really Hindus, but skilfully explores the limits of tolerance, maintaining, "Hinduism's raison d'être should continue to be tolerance which, like Einsteinian space, should be unbounded but not infinite, and its mission in the world should remain what it has always been—the acceptance of all the religions of the world by all human beings as the inalienable religious heritage of every human being."[43]

Since there would have to be limits to recognition of legal pluralism, because infinite plurality risks ending up in total moral nihilism, Sharma suggests that there would also have to be limits to Hindu tolerance, particularly in terms of political realities:

> To conclude, *tolerance of tolerance* naturally appeals to Hinduism, but it has also unwisely displayed *tolerance of intolerance* by projecting its own internal ethos on other religions. Some of these have turned out to be *intolerant of tolerance* and have taken advantage of Hindu tolerance to undermine it. Hence I propose that, in the contemporary Indian setting, Hindus must develop *intolerance of intolerance*, and promote tolerance outside its own religious frontier by identifying and emphasizing the elements of tolerance in other religions. . . . Hinduism for our times therefore must aim at initiating an alliance among the liberal elements of all the religions of the world and in this way express its intolerance of intolerance and enhance tolerance of tolerance in a religiously plural world.[44]

Those seeking to argue that Hinduism and human rights can be harmonized and can co-exist with supposedly universal human rights principles are clearly given a tough time, as Sharma's advice to both sides is not being heeded. As a specialist on Hindu law, I am particularly aware that my own writing, until recently, was not perceived as relevant for human rights. Writing about traditional Hindu law, one becomes virtually polluted for life, indicating problems over the conceptualization of "liberal" in Sharma's advice. Probably more damaging for the cultivation of global tolerance is the refusal among secularity-focused human rights activists to perceive themselves as integral components of the religiously plural world. Putting itself on a pedestal, human rights jurisprudence as a new form of secular religion has turned out to be rabidly intolerant of religion and generates negative responses to its own intolerance. The shadowboxing contests have become ever more intricate.

In quiet moments, many Hindus admit it is difficult to convey to non-Hindus and to their own young people what Hinduism is really about.[45] Given a tendency to glorify ancient roots, since much ancient evidence contradicts current Hindu thoughts and practices, defensive confusions arise, blocking recognition that Hindu tradition, marked by intense plurality and dynamism, has never been static. A prominent flashpoint is the consumption of beef. Obviously an ancient Indic practice, it is today mainly restricted to poor Hindus in South India, for whom beef is an affordable delicacy, while "normal" Hindus react with horror. Since Muslims and many Christians also eat beef, and certainly do not worship the cow, conflicts are inevitably programmed into the superdiverse cultural stew of India. Some conflicts end up in court actions, and at times there are riots, which then take on communal colors and can be milked by all kinds of lobbies for further agitation.

Academic debates often lack sensitivity to the underlying tensions. Highlighting the difficulties of discussing Hinduism and human rights, Sharma imagines the subtlety of "calculation of the number of angels who can dance atop a pin" while stressing "the ambiguity which surrounds the terms themselves, to say nothing of the relationship."[46] Baxi further warns of "the uncertain futures of human rights in a hyperglobalizing world,"[47] which brings out that the current context of globalization increases recurrent worries about the adequacy of academic discourse and studies of human rights "to the tasks of resisting everyday human abuse and human, and human rights, violation."[48]

Arvind Sharma posits that Western human rights discourses are neither monolithic nor static.[49] Seeking to provide a Hindu-centric perspective, he advances the common explanation that Hindu approaches emphasize duties over rights, which is, however, generally laughed off as part of the "Asian values" debate. Perceptions of violations of individual rights depend, from a Hindu perspective, not only on what rights we grant to individuals, but more crucially perhaps what duties we expect them to honor for others. This becomes an integral aspect of tolerance, simply tolerance of the fact that the other is there and is an "other." Frequent Western-centric denials of individuality and individualism among Hindus are counteracted by the key concepts of *dharma* and *ācāra* or *sadācāra* (different terms for "doing the right thing") whose ultimate root and source is the satisfaction of the individual (*ātmanastushti*) that she or he has done what is appropriate. Sharma's discussion about intolerance of intolerance omits to mention that in certain situations, a Hindu may thus see reasons to kill in order to protect a higher order. Positivized interpretations of Hindu methods of ascertaining *dharma* fail to take this rather basic fact of life into account—choice-making is not primarily by rulers, but is a life-long challenge for every individual Hindu.

My own research suggests that since its early manifestations in Vedic times, Hinduism does not intrinsically privilege Hindus, let alone Brahmins, males or anyone. Every created being, including animals, living organisms, and plants (as many vegetarians believe) are interconnected in a giant cosmic spider web, called "Hindu" much later in time, but the net itself is ancient. This body of ancient perceptions also draws no clear boundaries between the religious and the secular. In Vedic Sanskrit there are two terms for Truth: *rita* as the invisible force, and *satya* as more tangible manifestations. These fuzzy boundaries between the religious and the secular, existing since the early beginnings of this complex cultural tradition, continue to cause ontological shadowboxing today, confusing Hindus as well as those outsiders who are intolerant of difference or struggle with accepting plural diversities.

■ CONCLUSIONS

We know that "law" as a phenomenon is everywhere culture-specific and internally plural. Taking a legal pluralism approach, this article demonstrates that arguments over the compatibility of Hinduism and human rights will not stop until we learn to be more tolerant of "others." Hindu traditions have clearly developed their own culture-specific forms of handling what today we perceive and describe as human rights concerns, subject to constant and enormous changes over time and space.

The *atman-Brahman* binary of individual and cosmos in Hinduism, particularly the notion of *karma* (action and reaction) as conceptual glue, undergird an inevitable pattern of interconnectedness, idealistic and altruistic in principle, which is remarkably akin to modern human rights concepts except that the latter privilege individual autonomy and secularity. In lived practice, the difficulty with both sets of idealized concepts appears to be that they both favor strong, powerful, and resourceful individuals who are aware of such connections and can manipulate them. Balance is thus always in danger, like justice, as Derrida clearly highlighted, because humans are selfish—another ancient truth that Hinduism is deeply aware of.

In response to aggressive human rights rhetoric from hegemonic or cosmopolitan and neo-colonial sources that treat Hinduism as primitive and inherently righticidal, defensive Hindu responses today again use exaggerated rhetoric to stake their claims and may resort to violence, leading to accusations of Hindu nationalism and fascism. The resulting politicized confusions and mental blockages are only partly explained by binary oppositions of age-old values versus modern post-Enlightenment thinking, religious versus secular methodology and predilections, or East versus West. The bigger issue is apparently that within an intensely pluralist scenario, fundamental global disagreements persist over the management of diversity or difference, the evaluation of the position of individuals, and—inevitably linked to all of this—the treatment of religion as a continuing factor in today's world. To blame either side for this struggle seems thoroughly unproductive.

■ NOTES

1 Werner Menski, "Sanskrit Law: Excavating Vedic Legal Pluralism." SOAS School of Law Research Paper No. 05-2010. [SSRN: http://ssrn.com/abstracts=1621384].

2 Upendra Baxi, *The Future of Human Rights* 3rd ed. (New Delhi: Oxford University Press, 2008): xv (emphasis in the original).

3 Menski, "Sanskrit Law."

4 Julius Lipner, *Hindus: Their Religious Beliefs and Practices*, 2nd ed. (London: Routledge, 2010).

5 Esin Örücü and David Nelken, eds., *Comparative Law: A Handbook.* (Oxford: Hart Publishing, 2007).

6 Werner Menski, *Comparative Law in a Global Context: The Legal Systems of Asia and Africa*, 2nd ed. (Cambridge: Cambridge University Press, 2006).

7 Michael E. McCullough and Brian L.B. Willoughby, "Religion, Self-Regulation, and Self-Control: Associations, Explanations, and Implications," *Psychological Bulletin* 135(1) (2009): 69–93.

8 Arvind Sharma, *Are Human Rights Western?; A Contribution to the Dialogue of Civilizations* (New Delhi: Oxford University Press, 2006): xvi.

9 Peter Cane and Joanna Conaghan, eds., *The New Oxford Companion to Law* (Oxford: Oxford University Press, 2008).

10 Ibid., 553–55.

11 Ibid., 561.

12 Emphases in the original.

13 Baxi, *The Future of Human Rights*, 2002: vi.

14 Ibid., ix, 24, 50.

15 Baxi, *The Future of Human Rights*, 2008: ix.

16 Ibid., xiv.

17 Ibid., xiv–xv.

18 Ibid., xii.

19 Werner Menski, *Hindu Law: Beyond Tradition and Modernity* (New Delhi: Oxford University Press, 2003).

20 Baxi, *The Future of Human Rights*, 2008: xii.

21 Ibid., xiv.

22 See Menski, "Sanskrit Law" with further references. On Buddhism in India and its challenges to Brahmanism and caste, see Gail Omvedt, *Buddhism in India: Challenging Brahmanism and Caste* (New Delhi: Sage, 2003), a study evidently propelled by the Indian communal carnages of 2002. On Jainism and its ancient and current global claims, see Aidan Rankin, *Many-Sided Wisdom: A New Politics of the Spirit* (Ropley: O Books, 2010).

23 Sharma, *Are Human Rights Western?*, 27.

24 Ibid., 30.

25 Edward Simpson, *Muslim Society and the Western Indian Ocean: The Seafarers of Kachchh* (London: Routledge, 2006), 1.

26 Ibid., 118.

27 Geoffrey A. Oddie, *Imagined Hinduism: British Protestant Missionary Constructions of Hinduism, 1793–1900* (New Delhi: Sage, 2006), 23, 26.

28 Ibid., 73, 348.

29 Ibid., 231–22.

30 Ibid., 243–45, 294.

31 It seems that this practice is more prominent in the literature than in social reality; it is evidently a favorite brush with which to tar all aspects of Hinduism. Wendy Doniger, *The Hindus: An Alternative History* (New Delhi: Penguin/Viking, 2009): 621 wryly notes that "suttee had PR value."

32 Kunal Chakrabarti, "Natural Inequality: Conceptualising Justice in Brahmanical Discourses" in *Justice: Political, Social, Juridical,* eds. Bhargava Rajeev, Michael Dusche, and Helmut Reifeld (New Delhi: Sage, 2008): 71. More aggressive still is Kancha Ilaiah, *Post-Hindu India: A Discourse on Dalid-Bahujan, Socio-Spiritual and Scientific Revolution* (New Delhi: Sage, 2009).

33 Mithi Mukherjee, *India in the Shadows of Empire: A Legal and Political History 1774–1950* (New Delhi: Oxford University Press, 2010).

34 See *India Today International*, May 24, 2010, 1.

35 Dipankar Gupta, "Caste Against Citizens," *India Today International*, May 24, 2010, 18.

36 See with further references Werner Menski, "The Uniform Civil Code Debate in Indian Law: New Developments and Changing Agenda," *German Law Journal* 9(3) (March 1,2008): 211–50

37 See Uday Mahurkar, "Inhuman Rights," *India Today International*, April 5, 2010:19–21, at 19–20.

38 Amitabh Srivastava, "Back to Basics," *India Today International*, May 17, 2010: 26–9.

39 Arvind Chhabra, "Honourable Justice," *India Today International*, April 12, 2010: 43–45.

40 Lal Deosa Rai, *Human Rights in the Hindu-Buddhist Tradition* (New Delhi: Nirala Publications, 1995).

41 Sharma, *Are Human Rights Western?*, 2.

42 Ibid., 62.

43 Ibid., 94.

44 Ibid., 69.

45 Efforts to convey essences have a remarkable tendency to be influenced by Western notions of religion. Ed Viswanathan, *Daddy, Am I a Hindu?* (Mumbai: Bharatiya Vidya Bhavan, 1992) invokes the blessings of Almighty when presenting the intense questioning by a 14-year-old American-born Indian teenager of his father.

46 Arvind Sharma, *Hinduism and Human Rights: A Conceptual Approach* (New Delhi: Oxford University Press, 2004): 1.

47 Baxi, *The Future of Human Rights*, ix.

48 Ibid., x.

49 Sharma, *Hinduism and Human Rights*, 30.

■ RECOMMENDED READING

Baxi, Upendra. *The Future of Human Rights*, 3rd ed. (New Delhi: Oxford University Press, 2008)

Bhargava, Rajeev, Michael Dusche, and, Helmut Reifeld, eds. *Justice: Political, Social, Juridical* (New Delhi: Sage, 2008)

Cane, Peter and Joanna Conaghan, eds. *The New Oxford Companion to Law* (Oxford: Oxford University Press, 2008)

Doniger, Wendy. *The Hindus. An Alternative History* (New Delhi: Penguin/Viking, 2009)

Ilaiah, Kancha. *Post-Hindu India: A Discourse on Dalid-Bahujan, Socio-Spiritual and Scientific Revolution* (New Delhi: Sage, 2009)

Lipner, Julius. *Hindus: Their Religious Beliefs and Practices*, 2nd ed. (London: Routledge, 2010)

McCullough, Michael E., and, Brian L.B. Willoughby. "Religion, Self-Regulation, and Self-Control: Associations, Explanations, and Implications." *Psychological Bulletin* 135(1) (2009): 69–93

Menski, Werner. *Comparative Law in a Global Context: The Legal Systems of Asia and Africa*, 2nd ed. (Cambridge: Cambridge University Press, 2006)

_____. *Hindu Law: Beyond Tradition and Modernity* (New Delhi: Oxford University Press, 2003)

_____. "Sanskrit Law: Excavating Vedic Legal Pluralism." SOAS School of Law Research Paper No. 05–2010. [SSRN: http://ssrn.com/abstracts=1621384]

_____. "The Uniform Civil Code Debate in Indian Law: New Developments and Changing Agenda." *German Law Journal* 9(3) (March 1, 2008): 211–50

Mukherjee, Mithi. *India in the Shadows of Empire: A Legal and Political History 1774–1950* (New Delhi: Oxford University Press, 2010)

Oddie, Geoffrey A. *Imagined Hinduism:. British Protestant Missionary Constructions of Hinduism, 1793—1900* (New Delhi: Sage, 2006)

Omvedt, Gail. *Buddhism in India: Challenging Brahmanism and Caste* (New Delhi: Sage, 2003)

Örücü, Esin and David Nelken, eds. *Comparative Law: A Handbook* (Oxford: Hart Publishing, 2007)

Rai, Lal Deosa. *Human Rights in the Hindu-Buddhist Tradition* (New Delhi: Nirala Publications, 1995)

Rankin, Aidan. *Many-Sided Wisdom: A New Politics of the Spirit* (Ropley, UK: O Books, 2010)

Sharma, Arvind. *Are Human Rights Western?: A Contribution to the Dialogue of Civilizations* (New Delhi: Oxford University Press, 2006)

_____. *Hinduism and Human Rights: A Conceptual Approach* (New Delhi: Oxford University Press, 2004)

Simpson, Edward. *Muslim Society and the Western Indian Ocean. The Seafarers of Kachchh* (London: Routledge, 2006)

Viswanathan, Ed. *Daddy, Am I a Hindu?* (Mumbai: Bharatiya Vidya Bhavan, 1992)

5 Confucianism and Human Rights

JOSEPH C.W. CHAN

The relation between Confucianism and human rights is a complex issue and raises a number of questions. Is Confucianism compatible with the idea of human rights? Is there a place for human rights in an ideal society as understood in Confucianism? Under what conditions would Confucianism accept human rights, if at all? Can it accept the specific human rights listed in the Universal Declaration of Human Rights? Different answers have been given to these questions, in part because they are based on different understandings or evaluations of both Confucianism and human rights. Some scholars who hold an incompatibilist position give Confucianism a rather positive portrayal and human rights a negative one, arguing that Confucianism as an ethics of benevolence and harmonious social relationships has no place for rights that are premised upon individualism and self-assertiveness. Others taking the same incompatibilist position give an opposite account, holding that Confucianism preaches an authoritarian morality and politics that has to be rejected and replaced by a political philosophy of human rights and democracy. The compatibilists, however, argue that while Confucianism may have no difficulty in accepting the idea of human rights, it may not accept a full-blown conception of human rights as expounded by certain liberal philosophies of rights or developed in international laws. Before examining these various controversies, let us start with a brief, and hopefully uncontroversial, description of the Confucian tradition and the idea of human rights.

As a tradition of thought, Confucianism began life in China more than 2500 years ago.[1] Although its core ideas can be traced back to the teachings of Confucius (551–479 B.C.E.), this tradition was never thought to be wholly created by Confucius himself. In fact, the original Chinese term of Confucianism, "*ru-jia*," makes no reference at all to Confucius. It rather refers to a school of *ru*, "a type of man who is cultural, moral, and responsible for religious rites, and hence religious."[2] Confucius himself stressed that he was not an inventor of any radically new vision of ethics or ideal society, but only a transmitter of the old tradition—the rites and social values developed in the Zhou dynasty (traditionally, mid-eleventh century to 256 B.C.E.) and even earlier. Nevertheless, it was Confucius who most creatively interpreted the tradition that he had inherited, gave it a new meaning at a time when it became stifling, and expounded it so effectively that his views have influenced a great number of generations of *ru* to come. *The Analects*, a record of his ideas and teaching compiled primarily by his disciples and later scholars, is the most fundamental text in the Confucian tradition. However, Confucius handed down no systematic philosophy—*The Analects* left a number of basic questions undeveloped, such as those about human nature, the metaphysical grounds of ethics, and the proper organization of the State. It was Mencius (ca. 379–289 B.C.E.) and Xunzi (ca. 340–245 B.C.E.) who filled in the details and more systematically developed the tradition into new, and different, directions. The thoughts of these three thinkers, together with the early classics upon which they drew, such as the *Book of History* and the *Book of Poetry*, constitute the classical tradition of Confucianism.

Confucianism has continued to evolve ever since its inception, in part as a response to the political needs of the time (as in Han Confucianism), and in part to the challenges of other schools of thought (as in Song-Ming Confucianism). Han Confucianism made Confucian ethics and politics rigid and hierarchical, placing the father and ruler at the center of absolute power in the family and polity, respectively. Song-Ming Confucianism, on the contrary, turned its inquiry inward into the human mind in order to meet the challenges of Buddhism and constructed robust theories of the inner life of human individuals. No matter what innovations were made in these later developments, however, classical Confucianism, especially the Mencius strand, has been recognized as the canon of the tradition, something which later thinkers claimed only to appreciate, vindicate, and enrich. This was exactly the kind of moderate claim made by Confucius himself regarding his attitude toward the tradition before him. In this sense, a deep respect for tradition—thinking that it was the sages in the past who had got things right—has always been a salient mark of Confucianism.

What are the core ideas in Confucianism? And how much influence has it had? Most simply put, Confucianism holds that people should cultivate their minds and virtues through life-long learning and participation in rituals and that they should treat their family members according to the norms of filial piety and fatherly love and show a graded concern and care for all outside of the family.[3] Political leaders should do their best to care for the ruled and serve as a moral exemplar for them. Learned intellectuals above all others should devote themselves in politics and education to promote the Way—the ideal ethical and political order—and help build the good society. More will be said concerning the content of Confucian ethics later in this chapter. But even this much characterization enables us to see that the Confucian vision of human life has fundamentally shaped the Chinese culture and the basic structure of society in the past two thousand years or so. Its vision, however, has extended far beyond the Chinese borders and has penetrated deeply into neighboring countries. Today, those East Asian societies that have been influenced by the Confucian culture, namely, mainland China, Hong Kong, Japan, Korea, Singapore, Taiwan, and Vietnam, have undergone modernization and been exposed to the powerful forces of global capitalism that have eroded their Confucian cultural traditions to a considerable extent. But Confucian values such as the importance of the family, the respect for learning and education, and the emphasis on order and harmony remain significant in these societies.

It is important to note that Confucianism has never been an established religion, although it has a strong religious dimension that stresses the harmony and unity of humanity and Heaven. The interest of Confucianism as a religious humanism lies in its concern for this world, with a clear mission to improve human life and society.[4] There was no official spokesperson for Heaven or revelation of Heaven's will in the form of a book or person. Confucius and other sages were not prophets, the *Analects* was not the Bible. The Way had to be embodied and expounded in human action, and the teachings in the classics were never meant to be timeless sacred creed handed down from Heaven. This fact about Confucianism has implications for its relation to human rights. Because Confucianism has always been an evolving tradition of thought, with many self-identified participants sharing only a cluster of values, beliefs, and practical concerns rather than a set of fixed creeds, the participants are at liberty to reinterpret, revise, and further develop the tradition of thought in a way they see fit. So the question about the compatibility of Confucianism and human rights is not a purely interpretive issue fixed by the canons, but a conscious normative choice to be made and defended by participants in the debate.

Similarly, with regard to the question of compatibility, we need to detach the idea of human rights from its associated doctrines or philosophies that have developed in recent centuries. Although Western natural law theories and various liberal thoughts have contributed much to the development of human rights, today the idea of human rights—minimally defined as rights that human beings have by virtue of their humanity—has gained currency in many different religions and cultures and has been supported by people appealing to different philosophical and religious traditions of thought. As will be seen later, some of the attacks on human rights made by Confucian-inspired scholars might better be seen as attacks on the kind of rights talk commonly found within certain strands of liberalism. Of course, the extent to which human rights as developed in international laws today can be separated from Western liberalism may be an open question, but it is a mistake to simply assume or assert an equivalence of the two.

■ REFUTING THE INCOMPATIBILITY VIEW

With these preliminary remarks in place, we may now consider some alleged Confucian arguments that reject human rights. The first is what we may call the argument of incompatibility, which holds that the idea of human rights carries some presuppositions that are either philosophically problematic or fundamentally at odds with Confucianism. This view is well represented in the work of Henry Rosemont, Jr., who points out that it is "a bedrock presupposition of [Western] moral, social, and political thinking that human beings have rights, solely by virtue of being human." However, every human being, he argues, "has a definite sex, a color, an age, an ethnic background, certain abilities; and we all live in a specific time and a specific place. From these facts some disturbing considerations follow. The first is that if rights are borne by human beings regardless of these differentiations, then those rights must obtain for human beings altogether independently of their culture. But then it becomes extremely difficult to imagine actual bearers of rights, because there are no culturally independent human beings."[5]

According to this view, the concept of human rights presupposes *acultural* (or *asocial*) beings, a view not only antithetical to the Confucian conception of personhood, but also philosophically untenable. But this argument misunderstands the nature of human rights. Rosemont is right in taking human rights as rights people have solely by virtue of being human, irrespective of their sex, ethnic, cultural, and historical background. He is mistaken, however, in arguing that the concept implies that human beings can be thought of as having none of these attributes. The concept asserts not a *descriptive* claim about human nature but a *moral* view about distribution of rights—one's sex, race, or culture is a morally irrelevant consideration insofar as one's entitlement to basic human rights is concerned.[6] Neither are international charters of human rights guilty of this charge. The International Covenant on Economic, Social, and Cultural Rights (ICESCR) protects people's interests in having a meaningful social and cultural life. The freedoms of expression and of religion in the International Covenant on Civil and Political Rights (ICCPR), which are taken by Rosement and others as individualistic rights, are to protect people's *social* interest in communication with others and joining religious associations, respectively. These rights presuppose the fact that people are social and cultural beings.

Even if the concept of human rights does not presuppose *acultural* or *asocial* beings, Rosemont continues, it is "closely related to our view of human beings as freely choosing autonomous individuals, a view which is at least as old as Descartes and which is reaffirmed in the 1948 United Nations Declaration of Human Rights." Indeed, "this concept is overwhelmingly drawn from the culture of the Western industrial democracies and is concerned to propose a particular moral and political perspective, an ideal, appropriate to that culture."[7] Other cultures or moral perspectives, in his view, do not affirm this idea of a free, autonomous self. In early Confucianism, according to Rosemont, "there can be no me in isolation, to be considered abstractly: I am the totality of roles I live in relation to specific others. I do not play or perform these roles; I am these roles. When they have all been specified I have been defined uniquely, fully and altogether, with no remainder with which to piece together a free, autonomous self."[8] In a similar vein, Roger Ames argues that "there is much in the Confucian tradition that might be a resource for rethinking our notion of autonomous individuality, especially that aspect of the individual which, given its priority over society and environment, effectively renders context a means to individual ends."[9]

This argument is problematic in both its understanding of the Universal Declaration of Human Rights (UDHR) and the Confucian conception of personhood. Nowhere in the UDHR can we find the concept of freely choosing autonomous individuals. Not only is this concept never mentioned, but none of the major ideas in the document can be easily construed as promoting a liberal-individualistic ideal of autonomy. In the UDHR, individual freedom is not an absolute value or license to do anything one pleases. The first article stipulates that "all human beings are born free and equal in dignity and rights," but what follows immediately is that "they are endowed with *reason* and *conscience* and should act towards one another in a spirit of *brotherhood*." The last article again insists that "everyone has duties to the community in which alone the free and full development of his personality is possible," and that the exercise of one's rights and freedoms must meet "the just requirements of morality, public order and the general welfare in a democratic society." In addition, the UDHR is silent on the grounding of civil rights, other than by associating it with "the dignity and worth of the human person." It certainly does not give an autonomy-based justification of those rights. In fact, even in the West, freedom of expression has often been justified on the grounds that it contributes to truth, arts, democracy, monitoring of government, and so forth, grounds that are not directly related to personal autonomy as such. Similarly, the rights not to be subjected to torture, arbitrary arrest, detention, or exile, the right to fair hearing, and the right to be presumed innocent until proved guilty are typically justified on the basis of our interests in a minimal notion of freedom, physical security, and fair treatment rather than any robust liberal idea of autonomy.

It is also problematic to describe the early Confucian conception of person as purely role-based. If by this, Rosemont means that Confucian individuals have no internal capacity to step back from social conventions to reflect upon, affirm, or reject their social roles and associated norms, then this is an incorrect interpretation of Confucian thought.[10] There is no shortage of discussion in the classical texts as to whether people should accept or continue to play their roles and how one should do so: whether a ruler should give up his throne, a gentleman should join the government, a son/minister should follow his father's/ruler's instruction, and so forth. All of this presupposes that Confucian individuals have the capacity to reflect critically upon their roles.

To be sure, Confucianism does place significant ethical constraints upon human action, and a good number of these have to do with social roles. But it would be a mistake to think that Confucianism sees all duties, or rights if any, as arising solely from social relationships, as Rosemont's description of the Confucian conception of personhood seems to imply. Although Confucianism does place great emphasis on particular social relationships, it is not a purely role-based or relation-based ethics. Confucian ethics of benevolence is ultimately based upon a common humanity rather than differentiated social roles—it carries ethical implications beyond these roles. For example, Mencius holds that people have compassion to help others in suffering even if they do not have any personal relationship with them. Confucius's golden rule—"do not impose on others what you yourself do not desire"—is also a moral principle applicable to everyone irrespective of social roles or status. Confucianism can accept non-role-based moral claims.[11]

Kwong-loi Shun argues that "while Confucian thinkers regard human beings as autonomous in having the capacity to reflect on, assess, and shape their lives without being determined by external influences, they also regard the exercise of this capacity as intimately linked to the social order." In particular, the basis of any claim individuals can make in such an order is "based on an understanding of the social dimensions of human life rather than on a conception of human beings as individuals who need protection in the pursuit of their individual ends."[12] I think it is fair to say that Confucianism does not give importance to the idea of individuals freely choosing their own ends, whatever these ends may be. The emphasis is more on acting rightly than freely, and to act rightly is to act in accordance with one's best understanding of the requirement of Confucian morality. But Confucianism never denounces or belittles individual interests understood as the needs and legitimate desires of individuals. One discourse in Confucianism that denounces "interests" refers to the self-interests (often selfish interests) of rulers, not those of the people; rulers are supposed to care for the people's basic interests first before caring their own. As Xunzi says, lordship is established for the people, not for the ruler.[13] For Confucianism, one of the important functions of a ruler is to "benefit" (*li*) the people, meaning to promote their interests (*li*). As the classical texts clearly show, the ruler's job is to protect people's interests in the subsistence and pursuit of material goods, in fair treatment in allocation of rewards and punishments, and in having proper familial and social relationships. Shun claims that "the focus of Confucian thinkers viewing the legitimate claims that an individual has on others is less on how the claims serve to protect that individual, but more on how they are part of a social setup that is to the communal good."[14] This seems an overdrawn conclusion, for he also notes, rightly in my view, that Confucian thought does not "downplay individual interests and subordinates it to the public good;" rather, "there is no genuine conflict between individual interest and the public good." I think one reason for the absence of genuine conflict is that the public or communal good is partially constituted by individual needs and entitlements. Peace and harmony are based on recognition of each other's due, or on fair treatment of individuals, as Xunzi puts it.

Xunzi fleshes out the idea of fairness in civil matters in exactly the same way as ancient Greek philosophers do—that justice or fairness consists in rendering to each person his due according to his personal characteristics, circumstances, or conduct.[15] "As a general principle, every rank and official responsibility, and each reward or punishment, was given as a recompense that accorded with the nature of the conduct involved" (*Xunzi* 18.3). The coming of honor or disgrace, therefore, is a reflection of one's inner virtue [*de*] (*Xunzi* 1.5), offices must be matched by appropriate ability, rewards must correspond to achievement, and penalties to offenses (*Xunzi* 8.3). It is important to note that for Xunzi, when it comes to justice, each person should be treated as an independent individual who is separate from other individuals, including family members. On this point, Xunzi maintains, "If rank fits the worth of the individual holding it, there is esteem, where it does not, there is contempt. In antiquity, penal sanctions did not exceed what was fitting to the crime, and rank did not go beyond the moral worth of the person. Thus although the father had been executed, his son could be employed in the government; although the elder brother had been killed, the younger could be employed. . . . Each was allotted what was his due according in every case to his true circumstances (*Xunzi* 24.3)."

Mencius and Xunzi also take justice as a moral imperative that trumps political goals such as the gaining of an empire. Mencius says that it is wrong to "kill an innocent man" or "take what one is not entitled to" in order to gain the empire, for doing so is contrary to rightness (*yi*) and benevolence (*ren*).[16] Xunzi is of the same view, namely that a gentleman (*ru*) "would not commit a single act contrary to the requirements of justice nor execute a single blameless man, even though he might thereby obtain the empire. Such a lord acts with justice (*yi*) and faithfulness (*xin*) toward the people" (*Xunzi* 8.2).

In light of this understanding, we may conclude not only that Confucian thought would not oppose basic individual interests as constituting the common good, but rather that it would take them as a basis for a legitimate social and political order. So Confucianism would not reject human rights on the ground that they protect fundamental individual interests. In fact, it would be hard to imagine Confucians rejecting such civil rights in the UDHR as the rights not to be tortured or subjected to arbitrary arrest and the right to a fair hearing, precisely because they protect the fundamental individual interests in physical security and fairness. The UDHR's notion of human rights does not presuppose or entail any notion of freely choosing autonomous individuals that ignores community responsibility or social relationship, nor does Confucian ethics see an opposition between the individual good and the common good. Social order and harmony can only be pursued by affirming and protecting people's interests in security, material goods, social relationships, and fair treatment. On these issues, at least, there is no incompatibility between Confucianism and the concept of human rights.

■ THE VALUE AND FUNCTION OF HUMAN RIGHTS

While there is no strict incompatibility between Confucianism and the idea of human rights, the tensions between the two lie in the more subtle issues about how Confucians understand the value of human rights and their proper function, and which of the many human rights in the international human rights treaties they accept as fundamental. There are two common approaches to understanding the value and function of fundamental human rights. One is an instrumental approach that takes human rights as an important device to protecting people's fundamental interests. The other approach does not deny the instrumental value of human rights, but insists that they also have non-instrumental value, in the sense that they are necessary expressions of human dignity or worth. In what follows, I shall argue that Confucianism would accept the first approach but not the second.

Joel Feinberg has made an influential argument for the expressive value of human rights.[17] He asks us to imagine "Nowheresville," a world in which "the virtues of moral sensibility" and "the sense of duty" flourish, and where it is filled with "as much benevolence, compassion, sympathy, and pity as it will conveniently hold without strain." What is lacking in this world is individual right—people have no right to make claims against each other. On Feinberg's view, having a right enables the right-holder to make certain claims against others, that is, to demand others to fulfill the duties they owe to her, to make a complaint and demand for compensation if she is wronged, and so forth. In Nowheresville, however, if people are treated inappropriately, they can do none of these things, and accordingly, they lack self-respect and human dignity. For having the capacity to assert rights claims is a necessary condition for self-respect and human dignity. Feinberg writes:

> Having rights enables us to "stand up like men," to look others in the eye, and to feel in some fundamental way the equal of anyone. To think of oneself as the holder of rights is not to be unduly but properly proud, to have that minimal self-respect that is necessary to be worthy of the love and esteem of others. Indeed, respect for persons (this is an intriguing idea) may simply be respect for their rights, so that there cannot be the one without the other; and what is called "human dignity" may simply be the recognizable capacity to assert claims. To respect a person then, or to think of him as possessed of human dignity, simply *is* to think of him as a potential maker of claims.[18]

Feinberg does not, however, give any argument for the claim that human dignity "may simply be the recognizable capacity to assert claims." In any case, Confucians would resist any view that tightly links human dignity with rights as the capacity to make rights claims. The concept of human dignity is broad and vague, and it allows different conceptions. If one minimally defines the concept as referring to the inner moral worth of human beings that entitles them a certain moral status and respect that no other living things or material objects possess,[19] then it seems clear that different cultural or philosophical perspectives have different views of the source of inner moral worth and hence different conceptions of human dignity. According to Mencius and Xunzi, the source of inner moral worth that makes human beings *gui* (translated as noble, honorable, or valuable) is the human capacity for benevolence and righteousness (*ren and yi*). Mencius says "every man has in him that which is exalted (*gui*)," which is his "benevolence and righteousness," (*ren yi*) although "this fact simply never dawned on him" (*Mencius* VIA.17). For Xunzi, among all living things only humans possess "a sense of righteousness" (*yi*), and for this reason they are "the noblest beings in the world" (*Xunzi,* 9.19). This inner worth of human beings allows Mencius to say that in politics "people are of supreme importance" (*Mencius* VIIB.12) and that not even an innocent life should be sacrificed in order to gain an empire (*Mencius* IIA.2). Confucians have no trouble seeing human beings as having an inner moral worth that gives them a special status and that the source for such worth lies in each person's potential capacity for benevolence and righteousness, not in the possession of rights.[20]

In an ideal situation, a Confucian society is one in which people are more or less virtuous and act in the spirit of benevolence—a graded care or love for each other, for one's family and friends, for all strangers as brothers in "the four seas." When things go wrong in this society, when people misbehave, Confucians would first appeal to each other's sense of benevolence and righteousness and reaffirm the norms and rituals that they are expected to follow, hoping that people who go astray would return to the path of benevolence and righteousness. If conflicts or inappropriate conduct persist, the parties involved should be brought to those who enjoy an exalted status and command respect from all parties (typically village elders) for mediation, in the hope of reconciling conflict and restoring social harmony.[21]

If mediation does not work, Confucians allows the issue to be litigated in court, though they prefer, if possible, to avoid litigation. Confucius says, "In hearing litigation, I am no different from any other man. But if you insist on a difference, it is, perhaps, that I try to get the parties not to resort to litigation in the first place."[22] But Confucius does not say that litigation should be avoided absolutely or at all costs. When people no longer act according to virtues or *rituals*—when they harm others, for example—there is a need to fallback on some institutional apparatus to protect the legitimate interests of those involved. More importantly, Confucius does *not* say that we should always yield to others at all times, particularly when we are unjustly harmed.[23] There is a passage that may correct this popular misunderstanding of Confucius, in which Confucius says, "Someone said. 'Repay an injury with a good turn. What do you think of this saying?' The Master said, 'What, then, do you repay a good man with? Repay an injury with straightness, but repay a good turn with a good turn.'" (*The Analects* XIV.34). When we are wronged, injured, or harmed by others, Confucius says that it would be appropriate to react by recourse to straightness—to seek justice and compensation through litigation.

Confucians would approach the value and function of human rights in the same way they approach litigation. Human rights are not necessary to the expression of human dignity, nor are they constitutive of virtues or virtuous relationships. In a non-ideal situation, however, they can serve as an important fallback apparatus to protect one's basic interests and needs.[24] In a modern society, human rights function as both normative principles and legal instruments, but what ultimately gives human rights their significance and impact is the latter. As legal instruments, they protect powerless individuals from harm by governments, corporations, or social groups. Human rights laws are no ordinary laws; they are higher laws that trump ordinary laws or policies made by governments. Human rights laws cannot be effective without rule of law and an independent court system with powers of judicial review. But when human rights laws are not yet in place or effective, human rights serve a powerful normative principle to critique the *status quo* and demand change, with the ultimate aim of turning human rights aspirations into effective positive laws.

We have seen that for Confucianism, when rituals and virtuous relationships break down, when local arbitration mechanisms fail, people may have recourse to litigation to protect their interests and to demand fair treatment. Confucians today, I believe, would also accept human rights as a fallback apparatus in the same spirit. Of course, as noted above, the human rights legal apparatus goes much further than the traditional Chinese penal and administrative law system in the following structural aspects (not to mention the difference in content): the distinction between higher and ordinary laws, judicial independence, judicial review, and the concept of a limited government. It would require another essay to examine in detail whether Confucianism can accept these structures and institutions. Suffice it to say that since Confucians regard people as being of supreme importance and put their interests before those of the State and rulers, Confucians today would embrace institutions that prove to be necessary to the protection of people's basic interests, even if in doing so they would have to revise or give up some of the traditional Confucian beliefs about political authority and institutions.

There is still a residual but important issue to address before Confucians can fully accept human rights as a fallback apparatus. In the Confucian view, the need to claim rights emerges only when virtues fail, rituals break down, and mediation becomes ineffective. But such actions, if frequently taken, can create a snowball effect that causes further social strain and encourages divisive ways of thinking and adversarial tactics. And the more readily people can access the rules and procedures of human rights, the more likely they are to use them in the first instance. In this scenario, rights would be brought from the background to the foreground, serving as the first resort rather than as fallback.[25]

We should be careful in understanding the problem. The first point to note is that a culture of litigation and adversarial actions may develop even without the introduction of human rights apparatus. When the level of general trust is low in a society and ordinary social norms and mechanisms are too weak to guide behavior, litigation might become the only lawful way to protect one's interests in case of conflicts, whether or not there are human rights laws. To prevent a culture of litigation from developing, we should try to rebuild social capital, revitalize social norms and mechanisms, and above all make sure the law is enforced in a fair and effective manner, before discouraging the use of litigation.

Second, whether, and how likely, the human rights apparatus will encourage rights talk and litigious behavior depends on a number of factors: how human rights are perceived, how wide-ranging the scope of these rights is, and whether there are alternative mechanisms to resolve conflicts or prevent abuses of power.

A culture of rights talk and litigious behavior will be more likely to develop in a society if human rights are given an exalted status and human rights protection covers a wide range of aspects of people's lives. In recent decades, the number of human rights international treaties and laws has significantly increased, expanding the "first generation" of rights from civil and political rights, to social and economic rights, and to minority and group rights and environmental rights. New bodies and mechanisms have been created to monitor compliance and implementation. These developments have encouraged rights movements and rights talk in international and national contexts. Many philosophers have challenged the long list of human rights that has been enumerated, raising questions about the coherence of the so-called "new generations" of rights. What is more worrying is that in public and academic discourse, rights talk seems to have eclipsed traditional moral vocabularies such as justice, common good, and duties and has become the main moral currency to tackle social problems. James Griffin, for example, has argued that "the fairly recent appearance of group rights is part of a widespread modern movement to make the discourse of rights do most of the important work in ethics, which it neither was designed to do nor . . . should now be made to do."[26] Coupled with the exalted status of human rights, this rights talk trend would have the effect of impoverishing people's moral vocabularies and encouraging a culture of rights-claims and litigation.

In my view, Confucianism should resist such a development. We have already seen that Confucians want to give human rights only a fallback-instrumental role, rather than construing them as an abstract ideal that expresses human dignity. To avoid the above problems, it seems obvious that Confucians would prefer a short list of human rights to a long one. The short list should consist of those rights (1) the violations of which are serious setbacks to social order as well as individual interests and often come from governments, and (2) which can be more easily implemented and protected by law than other kinds of rights. The first generation of rights—civil rights and political rights—appear to fit these two criteria better than social and economic rights and other kinds. Confucians certainly do not belittle the social and economic interests of people. Arguably they may be more basic than the interests in some civil liberties such as freedom of speech and association. But unlike civil rights, the protection of social and economic rights can hardly be done through litigation; they are to be realized in politics and policies, not the courtroom. What governments need to do is to make and enforce sound policies and institutions to promote economic growth and a fair distribution of resources. To appeal to the language of rights in these matters runs the risk of turning a complicated balancing of competing values such as social justice, basic needs, equal opportunity, efficiency, and general utility into a simplistic kind of legalistic reasoning. More importantly, the introduction of civil and political rights can help prevent violations of people's social and economic rights, for the latter are often a result of government corruption, maladministration, and mismanagement of economic policies. Amartya Sen has famously argued that famines are almost always associated with authoritarian political rule and that democracy plays an important instrumental role in preventing famines. "Famines are easy to prevent if there is a serious effort to do so, and a democratic government, facing elections and criticisms from opposition parties and independent newspapers, cannot help but make such an effort."[27] "The positive role of political and civil rights," Sen continues, "applies to the prevention of economic and social disasters in general."[28]

The nature of Confucianism also makes civil and political rights a priority. A long-standing feature in traditional Confucian thought (and in the Chinese political tradition) was the ruler's unchecked supreme status and authority. Although, theoretically, people were supposed to enjoy supreme importance, in reality they were not protected by legal institutions or empowered to protect themselves through political participation. The introduction of a human rights apparatus in the civil and political sphere would therefore help to redress the heavy imbalance of power between rulers and ruled. Relatively easy access to the legal apparatus to assert one's civil and political rights and legally challenge rights-violating laws and policies is actually something to be welcomed rather than deterred, for it provides powerless individuals a powerful means to defend themselves.[29]

On the contrary, rich cultural and ethical resources already exist within a Confucian society to deal with the sort of concerns raised by social and economic rights. There is no lack of emphasis on government's responsibility to cater to people's material needs, which is another long-standing feature in Confucian thought. A large part of the Confucian ideal of benevolent rule requires the setting up of social and economic policies to distribute land and economic opportunities for the ruled. Mencius's influential idea of a "well-field system" articulates what we may call today the sufficiency principle of social justice, which holds that government has a responsibility to provide for each household a certain amount of land to own and plough so that members of that household can live a decent material life and have spare time to learn and practice virtues in their dealings with family members and neighbors.[30] Mencius writes, "Hence when determining what means of support the people should have, a clear-sighted ruler ensures that these are *sufficient*, on the one hand, for the care of parents, and, on the other, for the support of wife and children, so that people always have sufficient food in good years and escape starvation in bad; only then does he drive them towards goodness (*Mencius* 1A.7, italics mine)."

It is interesting to note that like Sen, Mencius attributes poverty and famines to political factors rather than natural ones. Mencius is keenly aware of the seriousness of poverty and inequality of wealth in his times. He refers to the situation in which some people have "so plentiful good to be thrown to dogs and pigs," while "some drop dead from starvation by the wayside" (*Mencius* 1A.3). He also says, "nowadays, the means laid down for the people are sufficient neither for the care of parents nor for the support of wife and children. In good years life is always hard, while in bad years there is no way of escaping death" (*Mencius* 1A.7). The cause, for Mencius, is "despotic rulers and corrupt officials," of whom he observes, "Benevolent government must begin with land demarcation. When boundaries are not properly drawn (*ching*), the division of land according to the well-field system and the yield of grain for paying officials cannot be equitable (*jun*, *ping*). For this reason, despotic rulers and corrupt officials always neglect the boundaries. Once the boundaries are correctly fixed, there will be no difficulty in settling the distribution of land and the determination of emolument (*Mencius* 3A.3)."

In fact, Mencius goes so far as to claim that if people die of starvation under a ruler, then that ruler has not only failed in his obligation but has behaved no differently than if he had killed them, observing, "Now when food meant for human beings is so plentiful as to be thrown to dogs and pigs, you fail to realize that it is time for collection, and when men drop dead from starvation by the wayside, you fail to realize that it is time for distribution. When people die, you simply say, 'It is none of my doing. It is the fault of the harvest.' *In what way is that different from killing a man by running him through*, while saying all the time, 'It is none of my doing. It is the fault of the weapon.' Stop putting the blame on the harvest and the people of the whole Empire will come to you."[31]

■ CONCLUSIONS

In this chapter I have argued that there is no incompatibility between Confucianism and the idea of human rights. Confucians would regard human rights as a fallback apparatus to protect fundamental individual interests—they are important when virtuous relationships break down and mediation fails to reconcile conflicts. However, human rights are not necessary for human dignity or constitutive of human virtues. To avoid the rise of rights talk, Confucians would prefer to keep the list of human rights short. They would restrict it to civil and political rights, not because social and economic needs are less important, but because these rights are more suitable for legal implementation, while the promotion of economic rights requires sound economic institutions and policies that cannot be easily captured by legal human rights language. In addition, there are three reasons for giving civil and political rights a priority over social and economic rights in a Confucian-inspired society. First, the adoption of civil and political rights redresses a strong tendency within Confucianism to over-empower political leaders. Second, there are rich conceptual and ethical resources in a Confucian-inspired society to protect and promote people's material needs and social relationships, things that are the concerns of social and economic rights. Third, early Confucian thinkers such as Mencius recognize the contemporary argument that the chief cause of severe poverty and famine is political corruption and despotism and that a political solution is called for. This solution today is precisely a robust set of civil and political rights and legal apparatus, which protects not only people's physical security and freedom but also their fundamental material needs and interests.[32]

■ NOTES

1 This and the next two paragraphs are adapted from Joseph Chan, "Confucian Attitudes toward Ethical Pluralism," in *The Many and the One,* eds. Richard Madsen and Tracy B. Strong (Princeton: Princeton University Press, 2003), 154–58.

2 Tang Chun-I, *Essays on Chinese Philosophy and Culture* (Taipei: Students Book Co. Ltd, 1988), 362.

3 Which means particular levels of concern for different categories of people outside the family are hierarchically determined or preferenced by proximity to the family.

4 For a discussion on whether Confucianism is a religious tradition, see Xinzhong Yao, *An Introduction to Confucianism* (Cambridge: Cambridge University Press, 2000), 38–47.

5 Henry Rosemont, Jr., "Why Take Rights Seriously? A Confucian Critique," in *Human Rights and the World's Religions,* ed. Leroy Rouner (Notre Dame, IN: University of Notre Dame Press, 1988), 167.

6 See Joseph Chan, "A Confucian Perspective on Human Rights for Contemporary China," in *The East Asian Challenge for Human Rights,* eds. Joanne R. Bauer and Daniel A. Bell (Cambridge: Cambridge University Press, 1999), 216.

7 Rosemont, "Why Takes Rights Seriously," 168.

8 Ibid., 177.

9 Roger T. Ames, "Rites as Rights: The Confucian Alternative" in *Human Rights and the World's Religions*, 212.

10 See Kwong-loi Shun, "Conception of the Person in Early Confucian Thought," in *Confucian Ethics: A Comparative Study of Self, Autonomy, and Community*, eds. Kwong-loi Shun and David B. Wong (Cambridge: Cambridge University Press, 2004), 188–90.

11 For a more detailed discussion, see Chan, "A Confucian Perspective on Human Rights," 217–19.

12 Shun, "Conception of the Person," 194–95.

13 *Xunzi: A Translation and Study of the Complete Works*, 3 vols. , trans. John Knoblock, (Stanford, CA: Stanford University Press, 1988–1994), Chapter 27, section 68 (hereafter references will follow the format 27.68).

14 Shun, "Conception of the Person," 195.

15 For a fuller elaboration of this point, see Joseph Chan, "Is There a Confucian Perspective on Social Justice?" in *Western Political Thought in Dialogue with Asia*, ed. Takashi Shogimen and Cary J. Nederman (Lanham, MD: Rowman & Littlefield, 2008), 261–77.

16 *Mencius: A Bilingual Edition*, trans. D.C. Lau (Hong Kong: The Chinese University of Hong Kong, 2003), Book 2A, section 2 (hereafter 2A.2).

17 Joel Feinberg, "The Nature and Value of Rights," *The Journal of Value Inquiry* 4 (1970): 243–60.

18 Ibid., 252.

19 Rhoda E. Howard, "Dignity, Community, and Human Rights," in *Human Rights in Cross-Cultural Perspective: A Quest for Consensus,* ed. Abdullahi A. An-Na'im (Philadelphia: University of Pennsylvania Press, 1992), 83; Doron Schultziner, "Human Dignity: Functions and Meanings," in *Perspectives on Human Dignity: A Conversation,* eds. Jeff Malpas and Norelle Lickiss (Dordrecht, The Netherlands: Springer, 2007), 81.

20 For another critique of Feinberg's view from a Confucian perspective, see Craig K. Ihara, "Are Individual Rights Necessary? A Confucian Perspective," in *Confucian Ethics*, 11–30.

21 For a detailed discussion of the Confucian practice of mediation in traditional and modern China, see Albert Chen, "Mediation, Litigation, and Justice: Confucian Reflection

in a Modern Liberal Society," in *Confucianism for the Modern World*, eds. Daniel A. Bell and Hahm Chaibong (Cambridge: Cambridge University Press, 2003), 257–87.

22 *The Analects*, 2nd ed. , trans. D.C. Lau, (Hong Kong: The Chinese University of Hong Kong, 1992), Book XII, section 13 (hereafter XII.13).

23 And so, on the level of states, defensive wars can be morally legitimate, according to Mencius. For a detailed account of Mencius's view, see Daniel A. Bell, *Beyond Liberal Democracy: Political Thinking for an East Asian Context* (Princeton: Princeton University Press, 2006), 23–51.

24 See Chan, "A Confucian Perspective on Human Rights," 219–22.

25 For this argument, see Justin Tiwald, "Confucianism and Human Rights," in *Handbook of Human Rights,* ed.Thomas Cushman (New York: Routledge, 2011).

26 James Griffin, *On Human Rights* (Oxford: Oxford University Press, 2008), 256.

27 Amartya Sen, "Democracy as a Universal Value," *Journal of Democracy* 10(3) (1999): 8.

28 Ibid. This point goes some way to resist a common argument made by some Asian governments in the so-called "Asian Values" debate, which holds that civil and political liberties need to be sacrificed in order to meet more basic material needs. For a detailed discussion of the trade-offs argument and other points of contention in the "Asian Values" debate, see Bell, *Beyond Liberal Democracy,* 52–83. Bell, however, points out that while "the general claim that civil and political rights must be sacrificed in the name of economic development may not stand up to social scientific scrutiny, East Asian governments also present narrower justifications for curbing *particular* rights in *particular* contexts for *particular* economic or political purposes. These actions are said to be taken as a short-term measure to secure a more important right or more of that same right in the long term." Ibid., 56–57 (italics in original).

29 Space does not permit me to distinguish, and elaborate on, two kinds of civil freedom: One kind concerns political matters such as political speech, public demonstration, and association; the other has more to do with cultural and moral matters such as pornography, assisted suicide, homosexuality, and so forth. Elsewhere I have argued that Confucians would favor a more liberal approach to the first sort of freedom and a more conservative one to the second, which is another issue often discussed in the so-called "Asian Values" debate. For a detailed discussion of the issue about human rights and cultural and ideological differences, see my "Hong Kong, Singapore, and 'Asian Values': An Alternative View," *Journal of Democracy* 8(2) (1997): 35–48; "Thick and Thin Accounts of Human Rights: Lessons from the Asian Values Debate" in *Human Rights and Asian Values: Contesting National Identities and Cultural Representations in Asia,* eds. Michael Jacobsen and Ole Bruun (Surrey, U.K.: Curzon Press, 2000), 59–74; and "Moral Autonomy, Civil Liberties, and Confucianism," *Philosophy East and West* 52(3) (2002): 281–310.

30 For a detailed account of the early Confucian views on social justice, see my "Is There a Confucian Perspective on Social Justice?"

31 *Mencius* 1A.3 (italics mine); see also ibid., 1A.4.

32 My work on this essay was supported by a grant from the Research Grants Council of the Hong Kong Special Administrative Region, China (HKU 741508H).

■ RECOMMENDED READING

Ames, Roger T. "Rites as Rights: The Confucian Alternative," in *Human Rights and the World's Religions*, ed. Leroy Rouner (Notre Dame: University of Notre Dame Press, 1988), 199–216

Angle, Stephen C. *Human Rights and Chinese Thought* (Cambridge: Cambridge University Press, 2002)

The Analects, 2nd ed., trans. D.C. Lau (Hong Kong: The Chinese University of Hong Kong, 1992)

Bell, Daniel A. *Beyond Liberal Democracy: Political Thinking for an East Asian Context* (Princeton: Princeton University Press, 2006)

Chan, Joseph C. W. "Hong Kong, Singapore, and 'Asian Values': An Alternative View." *Journal of Democracy* 8(2) (1997): 35–48

______. "A Confucian Perspective on Human Rights for Contemporary China," in *The East Asian Challenge for Human Rights*, eds. Joanne R. Bauer and Daniel A. Bell, (Cambridge: Cambridge University Press, 1999), 212–37

______. "Thick and Thin Accounts of Human Rights: Lessons from the Asian Values Debate," in *Human Rights and Asian Values: Contesting National Identities and Cultural Representations in Asia*, eds. Michael Jacobsen and Ole Bruun, (Surrey, UK: Curzon Press, 2000), 59–74

______. "Moral Autonomy, Civil Liberties, and Confucianism." *Philosophy East and West* 52(3) (2002): 281–310

______. "Is There a Confucian Perspective on Social Justice?" in *Western Political Thought in Dialogue with Asia*, eds. Takashi Shogimen and Cary J. Nederman (Lanham, MD: Rowman & Littlefield, 2008), 261–77

Chen, Albert. "Mediation, Litigation, and Justice: Confucian Reflection in a Modern Liberal Society," in *Confucianism for the Modern World*, eds. Daniel A. Bell and Hahm Chaibong (Cambridge: Cambridge University Press, 2003), 257–87

Feinberg, Joel. "The Nature and Value of Rights." *The Journal of Value Inquiry* 4(4) (1970): 243–60

Ihara, Craig K. "Are Individual Rights Necessary? A Confucian Perspective," in *Confucian Ethics: A Comparative Study of Self, Autonomy, and Community*, eds. Kwong-loi Shun and David B. Wong (Cambridge: Cambridge University Press, 2004), 11–30

Mencius: A Bilingual Edition, trans. D. C. Lau (Hong Kong: The Chinese University of Hong Kong, 2003)

Rosemont, Henry, Jr. "Why Take Rights Seriously? A Confucian Critique," in *Human Rights and the World's Religions*, ed. Leroy Rouner (Notre Dame, IN: University of Notre Dame Press, 1988), 167–82

Shun, Kwong-loi. "Conception of the Person in Early Confucian Thought," in *Confucian Ethics: A Comparative Study of Self, Autonomy, and Community*, eds. Kwong-loi Shun and David B. Wong (Cambridge: Cambridge University Press, 2004), 183–202

Sim, May. "A Confucian Approach to Human Rights." *History of Philosophy Quarterly* 21(4) (2004): 337–356

Tiwald, Justin. "Confucianism and Human Rights," in *Handbook of Human Rights*, ed. Thomas Cushman (New York: Routledge, 2011)

Wong, David B. "Rights and Community in Confucianism," in *Confucian Ethics: A Comparative Study of Self, Autonomy, and Community*, eds. Kwong-loi Shun and David B. Wong (Cambridge: Cambridge University Press, 2004), 31–48

Xunzi: A Translation and Study of the Complete Works, 3 vols., trans. John Knoblock (Stanford, CA.: Stanford University Press, 1988–1994)

Yao, Xinzhong. *An Introduction to Confucianism* (Cambridge: Cambridge University Press, 2000)

6 Buddhism and Human Rights

SALLIE B. KING

In the early 1990s, a number of non-Buddhist Asian political leaders, prominently including Lee Kuan Yew of Singapore and Mahathir Mohamad of Malaysia, ignited the "Asian values" debate with their claim that human rights are a part of Western culture and therefore excessively individualistic; human rights, they claimed, did not suit Asian culture, which was inherently communitarian. These claims notwithstanding, already by that time a number of important contemporary Buddhist social and political activists, known as "Engaged Buddhists," had deeply incorporated the language of human rights into their campaigns to bring about fundamental political changes in their home countries. While there is debate among Buddhist intellectuals about the extent to which the concept of human rights is compatible with Buddhist culture, Buddhist activists continue to rely heavily upon the language of human rights as an integral part of their work.[1]

The most significant examples of Buddhist usage of human rights language can be found in Burma, Tibet, and Cambodia. Since the 1960s, Burma/Myanmar has been ruled by a brutal military dictatorship. Systemic human rights violations documented in Burma by Human Rights Watch include: summary executions; the killing of civilians by the military; forced labor; forced portage; predation of the military upon civilians; condoned military rape of women and children; destruction of the villages of ethnic minorities; the forcible recruitment of children into the military; and severe restrictions on movement, assembly, and speech. The struggle against this dictatorship is led by the National League for Democracy, which describes itself as a movement for democracy and human rights. This movement is led by Aung San Suu Kyi, students, and Buddhist monastics. In 1988, during the first popular uprising against the ruling junta, the Burmese people (who are almost all Buddhists) filled the streets, singing, "I am not among the rice-eating robots. . . . Everyone but everyone should be entitled to human rights."[2] In 2007, during the so-called "Saffron Revolution" (named after the color of Buddhist monastics' robes), the streets of Burma were again filled with Buddhist monks and nuns, calling upon the government to respect human rights or step down.

Since 1959, the Chinese annexation and occupation of Tibet has resulted in the deaths of an estimated one-million Tibetans, about one-sixth of the population, from both direct causes (executions, reprisals, torture, and harsh conditions in prisons and labor camps) and indirect causes (largely famine resulting from Chinese agricultural policies). The International Commission of Jurists announced in 1959 and 1960 that there was a prima facie case of genocide against China in Tibet. Since that time, frequent accusations of cultural genocide have been leveled against the Chinese in Tibet; that is to say that China is accused of threatening the continued existence of the Tibetans as a people. These are among the most serious accusations of human rights violations that could be made. Specific human rights frequently cited as violated by the Chinese government in Tibet include: the right to self-determination; the freedoms of religion, speech, assembly and movement; freedom of the press; and the right to peaceful protest. In response to all this, the Tibetan government in exile, led by the Dalai Lama, in addition to calling for Tibetan autonomy, has consistently called upon the Chinese government to respect the human rights of the Tibetan people. Not only the Tibetan government in exile, but also various ex-patriot Tibetan activist groups consistently make their case to the global community by naming and publicizing human rights abuses in Tibet.[3]

In Cambodia, between one and two million people (out of a population of seven million) were killed during the rule and auto-genocide of the Khmer Rouge. The legacy of the Khmer Rouge era has been a significant loss of traditional Buddhist-based morality. Even decades after the fall of the regime, Cambodia remains a country with a high degree of lawlessness and corruption, discredited legal institutions, de facto impunity, and little trust. In an effort to rebuild order and trust, the Buddhist community and secular Cambodian NGOs have combined their efforts to teach basic Buddhist morality together with international human rights. For example, the Cambodian Institute of Human Rights, a secular NGO, has developed their Human Rights Teaching Methodology project that has trained 25,000 teachers on "how best to convey messages about human rights, peace, democracy, and nonviolence." These teachers teach almost 3 million Cambodian school children every school year. They point out,

> Buddhism never vanished from the hearts of the Cambodian people during the dark years. There are parallels between modern ideas like democracy, human rights, and good governance and the ancient teachings of the Buddha—on treating other people with respect and kindness. The principle of non-violence (*avihimsa*), means less harm is done to others. Besides the initial five Buddhist precepts [the Five Lay Precepts—not to kill, steal, lie, commit sexual immorality or ingest intoxicants] . . ., four other Buddhist principles of interpersonal behavior are relevant [namely, loving-kindness, compassion, sympathetic joy and equanimity]. . . . These ideas, or Buddhism at least, is familiar and acceptable to all Cambodians, including leaders, so they [Buddhist teachings] are much more likely to be received favorably than if we simply talked about the International Covenant on Civil and Political Rights or other complicated documents considered Western and even alien.[4]

For their part, the Cambodian Buddhist leadership readily affirmed that human rights were consistent with Buddhist teachings. Maha Ghosananda, the late beloved Cambodian Buddhist monk called the "Gandhi of Cambodia," wrote that the "Cambodian people must obtain all basic human rights, including rights of self-determination and rights to freely pursue economic, social and cultural development."[5] Today Buddhist monks are trained in human rights as a part of their preparation to teach and are expected to include instruction in human rights as a regular part of their sermons. It is hoped that this will be a powerful approach, adding as it does an element of international cachet to the appeal to traditional authority and morality.

The above documentation of the embrace of the use of human rights language by Buddhist social and political activists is necessary because this language has been rather extensively debated by Buddhist intellectuals, some of whom challenge it and some of whom endorse it. It is significant that no prominent Buddhist activists have challenged this language. This suggests an endorsement in practice of the distinction drawn by ethicist Sumner Twiss, who urges us to recognize that when human rights are affirmed at the international, inter-cultural level, two kinds of justification are present: on the global level, an international "practical moral consensus" has formed that certain behaviors are necessary and some must be prohibited; on the level of individual traditions, each tradition, says Twiss, must look to "its own set of moral categories as appropriate to its particular philosophical or religious vision" in order to justify and articulate its participation in this consensus. The embrace of the "practical moral consensus" is a purely pragmatic agreement "grounded in shared historical experiences of what life can be like without these conditions."[6] The Burmese, Tibetan, and Cambodian people are acutely aware of what life *is* like without these conditions; it is little wonder that, in practice, they have eagerly embraced the rhetoric of human rights in the hope that it will help them to achieve their ends.

Aung San Suu Kyi of Burma speaks for many Buddhist activists in dismissing the "Asian values" argument against human rights, maintaining,

> Opponents of the movement for democracy in Burma have sought to undermine it by . . . condemning the basic tenets of democracy as un-Burmese. There is nothing new in Third World governments seeking to justify and perpetuate authoritarian rule by denouncing liberal democratic principles as alien. . . .
>
> It was predictable that as soon as the issue of human rights became an integral part of the movement for democracy the official media should start ridiculing and condemning the whole concept of human rights, dubbing it a western artefact [*sic*] alien to traditional values. It was also ironic—Buddhism, the foundation of traditional Burmese culture, places the greatest value on man, who alone of all beings can achieve the supreme state of Buddhahood. Each man has in him the potential to realize the truth through his own will and endeavour and to help others to realize it. Human life therefore is infinitely precious. "Easier it is for a needle dropped from the abode of Brahma to meet a needle stuck in the earth than to be born as a human being." . . .
>
> It is a puzzlement to the Burmese how concepts which recognize the inherent dignity and the equal and inalienable rights of human beings, which accept that all men

> are endowed with reason and conscience and which recommend a universal spirit of brotherhood, can be inimical to indigenous values. It is also difficult for them to understand how any of the rights contained in the thirty articles of the Universal Declaration of Human Rights can be seen as anything but wholesome and good. That the declaration was not drawn up in Burma by the Burmese seems an inadequate reason, to say the least, for rejecting it, especially as Burma was one of the nations which voted for its adoption in 1948. If ideas and beliefs are to be denied validity outside the geographical and cultural bounds of their origin, Buddhism would be confined to north India, Christianity to a narrow tract in the Middle East and Islam to Arabia.[7]

The Dalai Lama, another staunch Buddhist advocate of human rights, also refutes the "Asian values" argument:

> Recently some Asian governments have contended that the standards of human rights laid down in the Universal Declaration of Human Rights are those advocated by the West and cannot be applied to Asia and other parts of the Third World because of differences in culture and differences in social and economic development. I do not share this view and I am convinced that the majority of Asian people do not support this view either, for it is the inherent nature of all human beings to yearn for freedom, equality and dignity, and they have an equal [right] to achieve that. . . . Diversity and traditions can never justify the violations of human rights. Thus discrimination of persons from a different race, of women, and of weaker sections of society may be traditional in some regions, but if they are inconsistent with universally recognized human rights, these forms of behavior must change. The universal principles of equality of all human beings must take precedence.[8]

Here, the Dalai Lama makes it clear that the appeal to cultural diversity cannot override a universal right inherent in the nature of a human being. It is striking that the Dalai Lama, whose main responsibility is the protection of the diversity of culture—specifically, to protect Tibetan culture against Sinicization—does not hesitate to accede to the demand of universal human rights to supersede cultural particulars.

■ BUDDHIST JUSTIFICATIONS OF HUMAN RIGHTS

While Buddhist activists do not hesitate to embrace human rights, working out a properly Buddhist framework for understanding and justifying the use of human rights language is a complex business. Those Buddhist intellectuals who embrace the notion of human rights have given thoughtful explanations of how they are able to ground this embrace of human rights in properly Buddhist concepts, principles, and values. As we shall see, traditional Buddhism has no concept whatsoever of a "right." However, Buddhism does assign a high value to human beings, proclaims the inherent equality of human beings, and advocates for moral behavior, nonviolence, and human freedom. These traditional values form the foundation of Buddhist justifications for embracing human rights. Buddhist arguments for human rights fall into the following patterns.

The Preciousness of Human Birth and Human Enlightenability

The idea of human rights is premised in international documents upon recognition of the inherent dignity of human being. In Buddhism, this recognition is expressed in teachings of the preciousness of a human birth and teachings of human enlightenability. Buddhism teaches that sentient beings are born, die, and are reborn again and again and that this process has been going on for a vast amount of time and will continue on for a vast amount of time. Within these rounds of births, sentient beings may be born as animals, humans, gods, denizens of hell, and other sentient life forms. Of all of these births, however, a human birth is considered the "precious birth," even more precious than birth as a god, because it is only as a human that one can attain enlightenment. This birth, while precious, is very rare, as there are far more sentient beings born in other life forms than as humans. This enhances the preciousness of a human birth. This teaching is common to all forms of Buddhism. Mahayana forms of Buddhism add to this that all sentient beings possess within themselves the Buddha Nature, or fully developed Buddhahood, an immanent reality that, while it may be concealed at present, guarantees future realization (in a human birth) of that innate, but hidden, Buddhahood.

The Five Lay Precepts

As seen above in the Cambodian example, many Buddhist intellectuals immediately perceive considerable continuity between the Buddhist Five Lay Precepts and the moral content of international human rights. The Five Lay Precepts are the most basic of all the Buddhist moral codes. They instruct Buddhists not to kill, steal, lie, commit sexual misconduct, or ingest intoxicants. In some cases, these moral principles are examined one by one in order to link them with individual human rights. For example, L.P.N. Perera writes, "It is little realized that the second precept of the Buddhist *Panca-sila* [Five Lay Precepts]. . . dealing, as it does, with theft, becomes meaningful only if the property rights of every individual are fully recognized."[9] In other cases, an effort is made to look at the precepts as a whole and work out how it might be possible to move from the stance of the precepts, which are expressed in terms of responsibility, to the rights stance of human rights principles. Thus, Damien Keown writes, "In the context of the precepts . . . the right-holder is the one who suffers from the breach of Dharmic [moral] duty when the precepts are broken. In the case of the first precept, this would be the person who was unjustly killed. The right the victim has may therefore be defined as a negative claim-right upon the aggressor, namely the right not to be killed. In simple terms, we might say that the victim has a right to life which the aggressor has a duty to respect."[10]

Human Equality

Logically, the idea of human equality is a necessary, though not a sufficient, element in the development of human rights thinking. Traditional Buddhist sources for the recognition of intrinsic human equality include the following. Unlike other important teachers of his time, the Buddha was willing to teach all who would listen to him, without imposing restrictions based upon social class (caste), gender, education, or any other characteristics. That the Buddha did not simply step outside of the caste system but rejected it in principle is attested by the Buddha's critique of caste in the *Vasettha Sutta of the Majjhima Nikaya*. In this scriptural text, the Buddha states that unlike the differences between the classes of birds, fish, quadrupeds, and snakes, the differences among which are real and innate, class distinctions among humans—specifically the four great classes of the Hindu caste system—are based upon occupation and are not real but merely conventional. On many occasions recorded in the Buddhist scriptures, the Buddha states that a person's place in society should be determined by his actions, not by the class assigned him at birth. Moreover, persons of all classes, both genders and widely varying social backgrounds were, in fact, confirmed as having attained the fruits of liberation by the Buddha.

Nonviolence

In studying Buddhist writings, the philosopher Charles Taylor has come to the conclusion that human rights in Buddhism are best grounded in the fundamental Buddhist value of nonviolence. He sees nonviolence as calling for "a respect for the autonomy of each person, demanding in effect a minimal use of coercion in human affairs."[11] The first of the five lay precepts is non-harmfulness. If, as Keown suggests, we can read from precept to right, it does imply at least a right to life and a right not to be harmed.

Human Freedom

Saneh Chamarik writes that "there is no need at all to search for a place of human rights in the Buddhist tradition. Freedom is indeed the essence of Buddhism. . . ." He develops this notion by referring, first, to the Buddha's advice to the villagers of Kalama in which he urged them to make decisions on what spiritual path to follow by relying upon their own experiential knowledge, not upon anyone or anything external to themselves. Secondly, he refers to the dying words of the Buddha: "Be islands unto yourselves. . . . Be a refuge to yourselves; do not take any other refuge. . . . Work out your own salvation, with diligence." These ideas emphasize self-reliance in achieving the task of the human life: working towards enlightenment. "In the Buddhist view, then, the individual is not merely a means. One can sense a subtle meaning of equality here. Although men may not be born 'free,' they are equal in dignity and rights, that is to say, dignity and rights to their own salvation or freedom."[12]

The important monk Phra Payutto confirms and extends Chamarik's ideas. He writes: "Man is the best of trainable or educable beings. He has the potentiality of self-perfection by which a life of freedom and happiness can be realized. In order to attain this perfection, man has to develop himself physically, morally, psycho-spiritually and intellectually. . . . [T]he law of the Dharma [i.e., Buddhism] . . . entails that every individual should be left free, if not provided with the opportunity, to develop himself so that his potentiality can unfold itself and work its way toward perfection." To be left alone to pursue self-development, then, is a must and therefore a right. Ideally, Payutto continues, all conditions should be made to support the individual's effort at self-development. Thus, "freedom of self-development and the encouragement of opportunities for it" are a "foundation of . . . Buddhist ethics." "[E]very individual has the right to self-development. . . . [The Buddha] teaches the goal of freedom that is to be reached by means of freedom and a happy means that leads to a happy end."[13]

In his later work, as we shall see, Payutto tempers his support of human rights. However, here we see one of the most thoroughly Buddhist of all potential Buddhist justifications for human rights: the freedom to pursue Buddhahood, or self-perfection, is our innate right as human beings, based upon the deepest level of our identity as human beings. Certain internationally recognized rights are directly entailed in this end: freedom of thought, conscience, and religion. Other rights are essential to it: the rights to life, liberty, and personal security; the freedoms of speech, assembly, and movement. Potentially, one could develop a full list of human rights, including the right to self-determination, freedom from want, the collective rights of peoples to the protection of their culture, and more, on the basis of the recognition that they are important supports for the pursuit of spiritual self-development.

■ BUDDHIST CONCERNS ABOUT HUMAN RIGHTS

Buddhist intellectuals, Asian and Western, have raised a number of concerns about Buddhist cultures embracing human rights. The following is a review of these concerns, together with responses that have been made to them.

Individualism

One of the fundamental teachings of Buddhism is the doctrine of *anatman*, or "no self." According to this teaching, there is no soul or fixed self, no entity of any kind, constituting the core or foundation of human identity. Derek Jeffreys thus asks who, after all, it is that owns this alleged "right" since in light of the doctrine of *anatman* there is no self, no real person to own a human right. "The key difficulty for . . . a Buddhist human rights ethic is to define the rights-holder. Without a substance [substantial self], who claims a right?"[14]

This concern is a red herring. Buddhist ethics function adequately without a substantial self in other contexts. For instance, the first precept states, "I undertake the precept to abstain from the taking of life." Who is the one who undertakes the precepts? Whose life does one pledge not to take? A functional person, not a metaphysical entity, is all that is needed here and for human rights.

But there is a second concern regarding individualism. Craig Ihara points out that, "invoking rights has the inevitable effect of emphasizing individuals and their status, thereby strengthening the illusion of self."[15] Peter Junger also expresses a concern on this point, stating, "[I]t is undoubtedly true that the virtuous man—the Brahmin—will respect the rights of others that are recognized by the local laws. . . . On the other hand, the virtuous man—the Brahmin—is not going to cling to his own rights." In support of his view, he quotes the *Dhammapada*, "He is free from the very basics of desire for this world or for the next, he is the unfettered one, the desireless one—this one I call a Brahmin."[16] The concern here is with the consequences for the spiritual development of the person who takes the idea of his or her rights to heart. Does the embrace of human rights promote a kind of self-aggrandizement on the part of individuals who claim their "rights"? If this were the case (and many Buddhist intellectuals, seeing the hyper-individualism of Western culture, fear that it may be), it would be inimical to the fundamental values of Buddhism.

This concern is more serious for Buddhist use of human rights language. To respond briefly: human rights protect groups as well as individuals.[17] In fact, most Buddhist uses of human rights rhetoric (notably, in Tibet and Burma) are on behalf of groups—the Tibetan and Burmese people as a whole. It should also be recognized that the protection of the rights of a group (e.g., to free speech) may proceed on an individual-by-individual basis (e.g., in protecting a lone individual who dares to speak out) while protecting the rights of an individual also protects the rights of the group (that lone individual who is the first to speak out is the courageous one who pioneers the way for others and thus helps make the society as a whole more open).

This response, while important, does not entirely resolve the Buddhist concern regarding the aggrandizement of the individual self and the dread of a hyper-individualistic, contentious society that many Buddhists see as its product. We shall, therefore, continue the discussion of individualism below in connection with the fourth issue we shall discuss, the issue of the adversarial position implicit in human rights.

The Privileging of Humanity

In the Buddhist view, while human beings are special inasmuch as the human birth is the "precious birth" within which one can make progress towards

Buddhahood, it is still the case that humans are not rigidly separable from the larger category of sentient beings that includes the human alongside animals and a number of mythical beings such as gods, hungry ghosts, and denizens of the hells. This potential issue, however, was resolved by the Engaged Buddhists before it became a concern. Engaged Buddhist leaders, from the start, articulated a concept of human rights that is not in conflict with the rights of non-humans. Human rights in Engaged Buddhism are not conceived as separate from the rights of other beings. A.T. Ariyaratne of the Sri Lankan Engaged Buddhist movement Sarvodaya Shramadana writes that, "economic growth . . . has to take place with due acceptance of the rights of all forms of life to the resources of the planet, promoting equal and non-exploitative relationships between human beings and recognizing interdependence between human beings, the society and nature."[18] Endeavoring to guide Sri Lankan development along the lines of Buddhist values, Ariyaratne and his movement have conscientiously avoided sacrificing the interests of non-human beings for the sake of development that favors humans.

The Dalai Lama is also an ardent environmentalist who, due to the Buddhist emphasis upon the interdependence of all things, does not see the welfare of human and non-human life as belonging to separate categories.[19] "If an individual has a sense of responsibility for humanity, he or she will naturally take care of the environment." Caring for other species and the environment is also a natural expression of the fundamental Buddhist value of benevolence. "Compassion and altruism require not only that we respect human beings, but also that we respect, take care of, and refrain from interfering with other species and the environment."[20] The former Kalon Tripa (Prime Minister) of the Tibetan government in exile, Samdhong Rinpoche, has said, "a society's rights must be balanced against all humankind, all sentient beings, the entire planet."[21]

On this subject Ariyaratne and the Tibetans are representative of Engaged Buddhists as a whole. Coming out of a worldview stressing interdependence, compassion, and human membership in the larger category of sentient beings, Engaged Buddhists consistently advocate protections for the environment and other species. They simply do not see any reason why advocating human rights should entail any loss for the welfare of other species or the environment as a whole. This is, in fact, a contribution of Buddhism to global thinking about human rights.

Responsibility vs. Rights

The third issue, seen very frequently, is that Buddhist ethics are based upon the idea of responsibilities, not rights. Thai Engaged Buddhist leader Sulak Sivaraksa, who very much endorses the idea of human rights, raises this issue in noting, "[T]he classical Buddhist texts do not refer to rights, human or otherwise, but rather to duties or responsibilities. The duties of the *Sangha* [monastics] are outlined in the rule or *Vinaya*, those of rulers in the Dasarajadhamma, while guidelines for lay people are found at various places in the Buddhist canon such as the *Sigolavada Sutta*, the Five Precepts, the Noble Eightfold Path and the Jataka Tales."[22]

One sees this kind of remark frequently simply because it is correct; the language of the classical Buddhist texts on ethics is the language of responsibility. The question is whether this poses a problem for Buddhists adopting human rights ideas and language. In fact, Sulak raises this issue only to argue against it. He quotes Burmese Buddhist scholar and monk, Venerable U Rewata Dhamma, who points out, "In the early, organic, societies the Buddha was addressing, [these] responsibilities were assumed to be adequate guidelines for human behaviour, with no need to identify the corresponding rights. In modern, fragmented societies, however, where the fulfillment of responsibilities cannot be guaranteed by the immediate community, the corresponding rights are specified and protected by States and International Organisations."[23]

The Buddha lived in a state and society that allowed him to pursue religious seeking and teaching without hindrance and he had no reason to feel a need for protection from the State. Jack Donnelly claims that it was because modern states and capitalism first appeared in Europe that ideas of human rights first developed there. It follows, he says, that since "contemporary Asian individuals, families, and societies face the same threats from modern markets and states that Western societies do," they now "therefore need the same protections of human rights."[24]

Burma is a good example of a state in which, by virtue of a tremendous change in the nature of the State itself, Burmese people need human rights protections today that were not important, or even conceivable, before the advent of the colonial period. Venerable U Rewata Dhamma argues that in the modern state, human rights are needed. "The depiction of rights as simply a Western invention fails to understand the relationship of rights to responsibilities and ethical norms. . . . [T]he central values of all societies are very much the same. All ethical systems encourage people to love each other, and discourage killing, violence and so on. The universality and inseparability of human rights may therefore be understood as reflecting the universality and inseparability of inter-responsibility emerging from Dhamma [i.e., Buddhism]."[25]

Here Venerable U Rewata Dhamma's view seems to be that Buddhism points to a society of "inter-responsibility" in which I am responsible not to kill you, and you are responsible not to kill me. In this way, he sees the foundation for human rights in recognized responsibilities. Now, however, due to the fragmentation of society—colonialism and the unprecedented power of the modern state—in countries like Cambodia and Burma people need the explicit protections afforded by the recognition of rights.

The Dalai Lama, a consistent advocate of both human rights and what he calls "universal responsibility," provides the best reconciliation of rights and responsibilities. His support for human rights is always strong and unequivocal, justified by both philosophical and pragmatic considerations:

> No matter what country or continent we come from we are all basically the same human beings. We have the common human needs and concerns. We all seek happiness and try to avoid suffering regardless of our race, religion, sex or political status. Human beings, indeed all sentient beings, have the right to pursue happiness and live in peace and in freedom. As free human beings we can use our unique intelligence to try to understand ourselves and our world. But if we are prevented from using our creative potential, we are deprived of one of the basic characteristics of a human being. It is very often the most gifted, dedicated and creative members of our society who become victims of human rights abuses. Thus the political, social, cultural and economic developments of a society are obstructed by the violations of human rights. Therefore, the protection of these rights and freedoms are of immense importance both for the individuals affected and for the development of the society as a whole.[26]

Here we see human rights justified by an appeal to human sameness and the universal desire to live in happiness, together with an indirect reference to what Payutto named as the right to self-development (here, the freedom "to try to understand ourselves and our world . . . one of the basic characteristics of a human being"). The Dalai Lama then turns from this individualistic justification to a social justification: the need of society as a whole for individuals to be able to freely pursue their insights and creativity, incidentally undercutting the concern about the excessive individuality of human rights.

The Dalai Lama, however, is also a consistent advocate of "universal responsibility," one of the signature themes of his speeches. In some cases, this responsibility is actually derived from a prior recognition of rights:

> I am convinced that it is essential that we cultivate a sense of what I call universal responsibility. . . . When I say that on the basis of concern for others' well-being we can, and should, develop a sense of universal responsibility. . .[w]hat is entailed is… a reorientation of our heart and mind away from self and toward others. To develop a sense of universal responsibility—of the universal dimension of our every act and of the equal right of all others to happiness and not to suffer—is to develop an attitude of mind whereby, when we see an opportunity to benefit others, we will take it in preference to merely looking after our own narrow interests.[27]

In other words, in the Dalai Lama's view, the right to pursue happiness is a universal human right. Because we all equally share that right, given human sameness, objectively speaking there is no real justification for privileging one person above another. For the Dalai Lama, our task as human beings is to develop the wisdom that will allow us to see and accept this truth. When we do, it will be natural to us to want to take upon ourselves the responsibility of benefiting others, ultimately including all sentient beings.

Adversariality

Taitetsu Unno raises the most serious issue for Buddhists concerning human rights, the issue of adversariality, stating, "the concept of rights, as demanding one's due, arose as part of the adversarial legacy of the West. In East Asia, on the other hand, the consensual model of society prevailed, ruling out any assertions of self against recognized forms of authority, whether secular or religious."[28] Here the issue raised by the "Asian values" debate is further refined: not only are Asian societies fundamentally communitarian, where Western societies are individualistic, but in addition, Asian societies have no tradition of adversariality. It is an important virtue in these societies to fit harmoniously into the larger whole and to avoid conflict as much as possible. When conflict does arise, it is best to deal with it with a minimum of direct confrontation, using indirect means or third-party go-betweens.

Human rights, on the other hand, presuppose adversariality. Jack Donnelly writes, "If Anne has a right to *x* with respect to Bob, it is not simply desirable, good, or even merely right that Anne enjoy *x*. She is *entitled* to it. Should Bob fail to discharge his obligations, beyond acting improperly and harming Anne, he violates her rights. This makes him subject to special claims and sanctions that she controls."[29] In other words, human rights are fundamentally instruments of power. The formal enactment of rights transfers power from powerful elites and society at large to less powerful individuals and groups within a system of law recognized by all. Thus, human rights presuppose adversariality inasmuch as their effectiveness requires not only a general societal willingness to honor the protections afforded by human rights legislation, but also the readiness of individuals and groups to demand that their rights be respected, together with mechanisms to enforce such demands.

Some Buddhist leaders and societies recognize the way in which human rights have the potential of empowering them and are ready to embrace that empowerment, while others do not. The Tibetans, for example, have made the use of human rights rhetoric one of the cornerstones of their appeal to the world for the protection of Tibet from China. The Dalai Lama has articulated a detailed defense of human rights from the perspective of Buddhist principles; there is no doubt that it is sincere. At the same time, there can be no doubt that the Tibetan leadership also is trying to avail itself of the empowerment that the global embrace of human rights promises. The Dalai Lama has written, "It is natural and just for nations, people and individuals to demand respect for their rights and freedoms and to struggle to end repression, racism, economic exploitation, military occupation, and various forms of colonialism and alien domination. Governments should actively support such demands instead of only paying lip service to them."[30] The Tibetan people and their leadership have almost no power, especially when compared to the People's Republic of China. Since they utterly lack the power to oust the Chinese from Tibet by themselves, they must turn to the global community for support. There, the source of their suasion is the appeal of their cause, the charisma of the Dalai Lama, and the moral high ground that the Tibetans consistently occupy vis-à-vis the Chinese by means of their principled non-violent stance. The Tibetans' appeal to human rights is an invitation to powerful nations and their peoples to translate their sympathy for the Tibetans into action on their behalf. It is a use of the power implicit in the global endorsement of human rights.

As for the adversariality that seems explicit in the Dalai Lama's speaking of "demanding" human rights, it does not trouble the Tibetans. This is because to them it is clear that it is very bad for the Chinese, as well as the Tibetans, to so blatantly and extensively abuse the Tibetans' rights. In the Buddhist terms in which they think, the Tibetans believe that the Chinese perpetrators of crimes in Tibet are earning themselves very negative karmic retribution by their violent and harmful actions in Tibet. Those actions have initiated a karmic chain of events that will result in painful events and experiences to be suffered by the Chinese perpetrators in this or a future lifetime. It is therefore not adversarial at all, but for the good of all, both Tibetans and Chinese, that the Tibetans do everything non-violent in their power to try to stop the Chinese from violating the human rights of the Tibetans.

The case of the Cambodian embrace of human rights is very different. There is no evidence that the Cambodians recognize the way in which human rights are a form of empowerment. As we have seen, Cambodia is a society struggling with widespread amorality, corruption, and impunity. The teaching of human rights together in a package with the teaching of basic Buddhist moral principles demonstrates that the Cambodians recognize the compatibility of the moral content of Buddhist moral principles and the morality underlying international human rights. However, the fact that human rights are legal instruments that empower a group or individual to make demands upon another—demands that should be enforceable by law—is not taught. Nor could it be taught. Foreign observers note that the Cambodians' concept of moral behavior precludes adversariality. Their idea of morality comes in the traditional Cambodian form: "A harmonious relationship between a centralized and hierarchical government apparatus and Cambodian citizens, sharing a mutual respect and rightful conduct, is viewed as the appropriate goal. Frequently this goal is framed in terms of visions of an idealized past."[31] Moral behavior, in this view, is proper behavior, and proper behavior is harmonious. To behave in a confrontational, adversarial manner is to destroy the normative harmony of society and thus, by definition, morally wrong. Given this view of a good society in Cambodia, it is not possible at the same time to teach both the basic lessons of morality and tools to empower one individual or group when confronting another. Consequently, the latter is not taught.

Even the Thai monk, Phra Payutto, whom we saw above vigorously championing human rights on the basis of what he saw as our innate right to self-development, or to pursue Buddhahood, in later years came to express reservations about human rights due to their adversarial nature. In a 1993 speech, he spoke of "major flaws" in the concept of human rights, all related to adversariality, in that:

> Firstly, the concept itself is a result of division, struggle and contention. The idea of human rights has been established to ensure self-preservation and protection of mutual interests. Human rights are usually obtained by demand.

And again,

> [D]emands for human rights . . . are often based on or influenced by aversion, resentment or fear. As long as such feelings are there, it will be very difficult to obtain a truly good result from human rights activities, because the basic feeling behind them is not truly harmonious. When human rights activities are motivated by unskillful drives, the resulting behavior will be too aggressive to obtain the required result.[32]

Despite these concerns, however, Payutto remains a supporter of human rights, noting that it is precisely because we do live in "an age of contention," that human rights are "so important in this age. . . . Human rights are our guarantee of not destroying each other while we are still under the influence of such divisive thinking."[33]

■ CONCLUSIONS

Buddhist views on human rights may be summarized as follows. Buddhist social and political activists universally embrace human rights; some of them use human rights rhetoric as an important part of their work for change. Buddhist intellectuals are more varied in their positions on human rights. A number of leading monks have articulated Buddhist justifications for them. Others have raised concerns on the basis of Buddhist principles, the most important of which relate to Buddhist concerns over excessive individualism and adversariality. As we have seen in Phra Payutto, even those with concerns generally still endorse human rights, at least as an unfortunate necessity. Those who are oppressed endorse them with vigor.

■ NOTES

1 For a more extensive discussion of Buddhism and human rights, see Sallie B. King, *Being Benevolence: The Social Ethics of Engaged Buddhism* (Honolulu: University of Hawaii Press, 2005), Chapter 5, "Human Rights." I thank the University of Hawaii Press for permission to re-use excerpts from that text.

2 Quoted in Aung San Suu Kyi, *Freedom from Fear and Other Writings*, ed. Michael Aris (New York: Penguin, 1991), 174.

3 See, for example, Tibetan Centre for Human Rights and Democracy (http://www.tchrd.org/).

4 http://www.ned.org/grantees/cihr/civicorg.html, p. 4; accessed June 12, 2002.

5 Maha Ghosananda, *Step by Step: Meditations on Wisdom and Compassion* (Berkeley, CA: Parallax Press, 1992), 78.

6 Sumner B. Twiss, "A Constructive Framework for Discussing Confucianism and Human Rights," in *Confucianism and Human Rights,* eds. Wm. Theodore de Bary and Tu Weiming (New York: Columbia University Press, 1998), 35–36.

7 Aung San Suu Kyi, *Freedom from Fear,* 167, 174, 175.

8 His Holiness The XIV Dalai Lama of Tibet, "Human Rights and Universal Responsibility," in *Buddhism and Human Rights,* ed. Damien V. Keown, Charles S. Prebish, and Wayne R. Husted (Richmond, U.K.: Curzon Press, 1998), xviii–xix.

9 L. P. N. Perera, *Buddhism and Human Rights: A Buddhist Commentary on the Universal Declaration of Human Rights* (Colombo: Karunaratne and Sons, 1991), 50.

10 Damien Keown, "Are There Human Rights in Buddhism?" in *Buddhism and Human Rights,* 32.

11 Charles Taylor, "Conditions of an Unforced Consensus on Human Rights," in *The East Asian Challenge for Human Rights,* eds. Joanne R. Bauer and Daniel A. Bell (Cambridge: Cambridge University Press, 1999), p. 134.

12 Saneh Chamarik, "Buddhism and Human Rights." Preamble by Phra Rajavaramuni [P.A. Payutto]. Paper No. 12, ISBN 974-572-182-4. (Bangkok: Thai Khadi Research Institute, Thammasat University, 1982), 5, 22, 23.

13 Phra Payutto (Rajavaramuni) Preamble in ibid.

14 Derek S. Jeffreys, "Does Buddhism Need Human Rights?" in *Action Dharma: New Studies in Engaged Buddhism,* ed. Christopher Queen, Charles Prebish, and Damien Keown (London : RoutledgeCurzon, 2003), 276.

15 Craig K. Ihara, "Why There Are No Rights in Buddhism: A Reply to Damien Keown," in *Buddhism and Human Rights,* 51.

16 Peter D. Junger, "Why the Buddha Has No Rights," in *Buddhism and Human Rights,* 86.

17 See further the chapters by Johan van der Vyver and Natan Lerner herein.

18 A. T. Ariyaratne, "'The Non Violent Struggle for Economic and Social Justice,' printed copy of a presentation given to the 6th International Conference of the Society for Buddhist-Christian Studies, Tacoma, WA, August 5–12, 2000, Sarvodaya Shramadana, 2000, p. 26.

19 See further the chapter by Willis Jenkins herein.

20 Dalai Lama, *Worlds in Harmony* (Berkeley, CA: Parallax Press, 1992), 3–10; quoted in Arnold Kotler, ed., *Engaged Buddhist Reader* (Berkeley, CA: Parallax Press, 1996), 3–4.

21 Interview of the author with Samdhong Rinpoche, September 24, 2000, Cincinnati, Ohio.

22 Sulak Sivaraksa, "Buddhism and Human Rights in Siam," in *Socially Engaged Buddhism for the New Millennium: Essays in Honor of the Ven. Phra Dhammapitaka (Bhikkhu P.A. Payutto) on His 60th Birthday Anniversary,* ed. Sulak Sivaraksa (Bangkok: Sathirakoses-Nagapradipa Foundation and Foundation for Children, 1999), 196.

23 Venerable U Rewata Dhamma, "Dhamma, Ethics and Human Rights," discourse delivered to the Asian Leaders Conference, Seoul, December 1994, quoted in ibid.

24 Jack Donnelly, "Human Rights and Asian Values: A Defense of 'Western' Universalism," in *The East Asian Challenge for Human Rights,* eds. Joanne R. Bauer and Daniel A. Bell (Cambridge: Cambridge University Press, 1999), 69.

25 Venerable U Rewata Dhamma, "Dhamma, Ethics and Human Rights," 196.

26 His Holiness The XIV Dalai Lama of Tibet, "Human Rights and Universal Responsibility," in *Buddhism and Human Rights,* xvii.

27 Dalai Lama, *Ethics for the New Millennium* (New York: Riverhead Books, 1999), 4–5, 28.

28 Taitetsu Unno, "Personal Rights and Contemporary Buddhism," in *Human Rights and the World's Religions,* ed. Leroy S. Rouner (Notre Dame, IN: University of Notre Dame Press, 1988), 129.

29 Donnelly, "Human Rights and Asian Values," 61.

30 Dalai Lama, "Human Rights and Universal Responsibility," xx.

31 Caroline Hughes, "Human Rights in Cambodia: International Intervention and the National Response" (Ph.D. dissertation, University of Hull, 1998), 306.

32 P. A. Payutto, *Buddhist Solutions for the Twenty-First Century*, trans. Bruce Evans (Bangkok: Buddhadhamma Foundation, n.d.), 71.

33 Ibid., 70.

■ RECOMMENDED READING

Bauer, Joanne R., and Daniel A. Bell, eds. *The East Asian Challenge for Human Rights* (Cambridge: Cambridge University Press, 1999)

Chamarik, Saneh. "Buddhism and Human Rights." Preamble by Phra Rajavaramuni [P.A. Payutto]. Paper No. 12. (Bangkok: Thai Khadi Research Institute, Thammasat University, 1982)

Dalai Lama. *Ethics for the New Millennium* (New York: Riverhead Books, 1999)

Keown, Damien V., Charles S. Prebish, and, Wayne R. Husted, eds. *Buddhism and Human Rights* (Richmond, UK: Curzon Press, 1998)

King, Sallie B. "A Buddhist Perspective on a Global Ethic and Human Rights." *Journal of Dharma* 22(2) (April–June 1995): 122–36

______. *Being Benevolence: The Social Ethics of Engaged Buddhism* (Honolulu: University of Hawaii Press, 2005)

______. "Human Rights in Contemporary Engaged Buddhism," in *Buddhist Theology: Critical Reflections by Contemporary Buddhist Scholars,* eds. Roger Jackson and John Makransky (Richmond, UK: Curzon Press, 2000), 293–311

Payutto, P. A. *Buddhist Solutions for the Twenty-First Century,* trans. Bruce Evans (Bangkok: Buddhadhamma Foundation, n.d.)

Perera, L. P. N. *Buddhism and Human Rights: A Buddhist Commentary on the Universal Declaration of Human Rights* (Colombo: Karunaratne and Sons, 1991)

Sivaraksa, Sulak. "Buddhism and Human Rights in Siam," in *Socially Engaged Buddhism for the New Millennium: Essays in Honor of the Ven. Phra Dhammapitaka (Bhikkhu P.A. Payutto) on His 60th Birthday Anniversary,* ed. Sulak Sivaraksa (Bangkok: Sathirakoses-Nagapradipa Foundation and Foundation for Children, 1999), 195–212

Unno, Taitetsu. "Personal Rights and Contemporary Buddhism," in *Human Rights and the World's Religions,* ed. Leroy S. Rouner (Notre Dame, IN: University of Notre Dame Press, 1988), 129–47

7 Indigenous Religion and Human Rights

RONALD NIEZEN

"One is not born traditional; one chooses to become traditional by constant innovation."

—BRUNO LATOUR, *We Have Never Been Modern.*[1]

PARADOXES OF PRIMORDIALISM

The concept of "indigenous religion" refers to a global form of religiosity or (as some of its adepts prefer) spirituality associated with those defined in international law as "indigenous peoples." During the last several decades this term has been so thoroughly conventionalized that most Euro-American lay people presented with it would likely have some notion of what is meant by it, probably by drawing upon related ideas associated with such things as shamanism and forest spirituality. But given some thoughtful attention, indigenous religion as a reference point for human rights protections becomes fraught with ambiguity and paradox—so much so that the concept can be used not merely as a reference point for understanding some of the distinct human rights protections of indigenous peoples, but beyond this, as a starting point for considering a number of qualities and consequences of the human rights movement as a whole.

The first of these qualities I intend to discuss has to do with changes in the law itself: the emergence of human rights directed toward the rights of peoples, particularly the rights of religious freedom of indigenous peoples. The establishment of the legal foundations of the international movement of indigenous peoples is, in historical terms, a recent occurrence, only a few decades old. This includes the institutional space given to expressions of indigenous religion, which is even more recent and can be considered an emerging phenomenon, arising out of collaborative consolidations of indigenous identity.

From the point at which the legal space for expressions and protections of the religion of indigenous people has been secured in international law, it then becomes possible to consider the processes by which indigenous religion becomes formalized as a source of identity and of rights. I intend to show that these processes can result in disjuncture between conceptual ideals of indigenous spirituality and the consequences of law. For one thing, the very term "indigenous" is historically recent, but it has paradoxically become a starting point for claims of distinct identity and rights based upon the principles of original occupation of land and pursuit of traditional ways of life "from time immemorial." This paradox can be situated more generally in a tension consisting of ideals of indigenous permanence or "primordialism," which is fundamentally at odds with the marked tendency of law to fabricate persons and things through techniques of reification.[2] The propensity of the law to objectify and concretize the objects of its attention results in a disjuncture between indigenous statements of the significance of their spirituality, extending to generalized experience of life in forests, steppes, or savannahs, and the practical effect of law, which seeks to specify the foundations and applications of rights.

In human rights law there has emerged in recent decades a version of ethnic and indigenous politics of difference, sometimes associated with the concept of "third generation rights," that acts upon the rights of peoples with distinct identities on the margins of states. These are peoples that face special obstacles and are therefore in need of distinct protections, beyond those that are provided for other groups or minorities. Whereas most states and international state organizations prefer human rights protections to be "blind" to distinct collective rights and identities, various peoples are insisting upon an understanding of human worth and dignity situated within local cultures and the special, exclusive legal protection of cherished differences.

Ethnic groups are already familiar from a vast literature that began in the 1960s with questions surrounding the sources of ethnic differentiation in the context of mobility and cultural interaction, a literature that has been kept alive by concerns over the origins of nationalism, strident "ethno-nationalism" and inter-ethnic conflict. Another type of claimant to rights of self-determination, indigenous peoples, has made a more recent appearance on the international scene, only within the last several decades, with political objectives and strategies that differ in important ways from those of other minorities.

The most significant unique characteristic of the indigenous peoples' movement can be found in its transnational dynamics, not just in lobbying efforts, but in the almost global audience that is the target of persuasion and consumption of culture. The term "indigenous" and the rights that it entails in international and domestic law have been adopted by representatives of thousands of distinct indigenous peoples and organizations from six continents in processes of transnational networking and political activism. This transnational movement, as I intend to show, constitutes a global transformation in the foundations of political loyalty and collective self-representation of small-scale peoples and communities.

■ ASSIMILATION AND EMERGENCE

The emergence of the international movement of indigenous peoples has been of special significance for societies on the margins of states that have within living memory been subject to state-sponsored programs of assimilation, the goals of which have included the elimination of distinct spiritual practices. Assimilation policies were by definition oriented toward effacing groups and communities (not yet defined as peoples) by individualizing and absorbing them into the socio-political "mainstream" of colonial powers or emerging states. Such policies, which lasted well into the twentieth century, included the U.S. "Americanization" programs, principally involving boarding school education and urban relocation; the residential schools once run by churches in Canada, which are now recognized as having systemically fostered physical and sexual abuse, and which are currently the focus of a Truth and Reconciliation Commission; the formal prohibition of the Saami language in the northern Nordic countries of Norway, Sweden, and Finland, which followed upon centuries of Christianization and the suppression of shamanic practices; and a government-sponsored removal and fostering program in Australia targeted toward those with Australian aboriginal and Torres Strait Islander descent, which resulted in widespread trauma and loss of identity among those now collectively referred to as the "stolen generations." The common political goal of these assimilation efforts can be understood as that of eliminating the corporate status and hence the claims to territory and self-determination of distinct, non-dominant societies; but the public discourse and the motives they reveal were usually associated with improving and "uplifting" those living a disadvantaged economic, political and—above all—moral existence.

The wide distribution of such historical experience is striking. Almost every region in which a transition took place from colonial territory to statehood has its own history and legacy of efforts toward disrupting the transmission of knowledge between generations among those recognized today as indigenous—efforts that have since become widely shared reference points for both human rights protections and the restoration of tradition. It was the face-to-face discovery of this common experience in meetings that brought together indigenous delegates from around the world that has generated much of the transnational, common-cause energy behind indigenous activism.[3]

Although there is no formal definition of indigenous peoples in international law, no established set of criteria by which people and organizations are included in or excluded from UN meetings or human rights protections, the most simple and direct effort to provide guidance as to who they are can be found in Article 1 of International Labour Organization (ILO) Convention 169 Concerning Indigenous and Tribal Peoples in Independent Countries (1989): "[P]eoples in independent countries … are regarded as indigenous on account of their descent from the populations which inhabited the country, or a geographical region to which the country belongs, at the time of conquest or colonization or the establishment of present state boundaries and who, irrespective of their legal status, regain some or all of their own social, economic, cultural and political institutions."[4] While retaining those institutions and less tangible qualities that make them distinct, indigenous representatives have expressed their collective identity in terms of oppression and injustice at the hands of states and industries, as in a self-characterization that emerged from a 2010 UN meeting, "Indigenous Peoples:

Development with Culture and Identity," to the effect that, "Indigenous peoples suffer the consequences of historical injustices, including colonialism, the doctrine of discovery, dispossession from their lands and resources, oppression and discrimination. Today many indigenous peoples remain impoverished and marginalized and their right to development is denied. Development paradigms of modernization and industrialization have often resulted in the destruction of indigenous governance, economic, social, education, cultural, health, spiritual and knowledge systems and natural resources."[5]

The key feature, or historical "moment," that characterizes the origins of the indigenous peoples movement in international law can be found in a shift from the post World War I emphasis on the protection of the cultural integrity of "minorities," with its drive toward equal access to the benefits and protections of the State, to the postcolonial rejection of "minority" status in the late twentieth century by indigenous advocates who emphasized the rights of indigenous peoples within a particular regime of legal protections and entitlements.[6] Thus, articulating an essential aspect of the earlier post World War I regime, Article 22 of the Covenant of the League of Nations promotes a morally and practically unworkable ideal of "equality" within the mandate system, identifying as a "sacred trust" the "tutelage" by "advanced nations" of those "peoples not yet able to stand by themselves under the strenuous conditions of the modern world."[7] The emphasis on assimilation into states as a strategic response to human diversity did not come to an abrupt end with the post-World War II elaboration of human rights. It actively survived the period of decolonization and was only challenged in the last decades of the twentieth century with the increased recognition of the rights of peoples to self-determination and the emergence of the international movement of indigenous peoples (of which more below). The preamble of ILO Convention No. 107 (1957), for example, which outlines the right of all human beings "to pursue both their material well-being and their spiritual development in conditions of freedom and dignity," finds a challenge in the fact that "there exist in various independent countries indigenous and other tribal and semi-tribal populations which are not yet integrated into the national community and whose social, economic or cultural situation hinders them from benefiting fully from the rights and advantages enjoyed by other elements of the population."[8] Thus, the instrument that first formally identifies the distinct category of "indigenous peoples" is still oriented toward their assimilation into the body politic of states as a response to the imperatives of development (including "spiritual development") and equality.

This assimilationist orientation to the rights of indigenous peoples was challenged and set on a different course only in the last decades of the twentieth century when many of those who self-identified as indigenous established connections among themselves and made their presence felt in international forums. Paradoxically, this development can in part be attributed to earlier state-sponsored assimilation policies, which provided the requisite educational backgrounds and bureaucratic skills to a new transnational indigenous elite. It is no accident that the first indigenous leaders to make their presence known in international gatherings tended to originate from those states that had once actively pursued policies of compulsory education. A wide range of native organizations from the U.S., Canada, and Australia, as well as the Saami Council (representing the indigenous reindeer herders of northern Europe) were particularly active in the first international consultations on the rights of indigenous peoples in the 1970s and 1980s. A Latin American caucus of indigenous organizations that formed around the same time initially faced the obstacles of political repression, limited finances, and lack of familiarity with the language and processes of international agencies, and only later came into its own as an effective (if not dominant) source of influence. Indigenous peoples from the Russian Federation, many of which are today represented by the umbrella organization the Russian Association of Indigenous Peoples of the North (RAIPON), were able to organize and travel only after the breakup of the Soviet Union in the early 1990s. And indigenous organizations from Africa and Asia were also relative latecomers to the indigenous peoples' movement in the 1990s, bringing with them the controversies surrounding the definition of "indigenous" in the context of states no longer dominated by settler societies, which was subsequently offset by their contribution to a greater sense of the global distribution of indigenous peoples and the challenges they face in efforts to promote self-determination, cultural vitality, and prosperity.

The growing numbers and presence of individuals and organizations representing indigenous peoples in the UN system had a marked effect on human rights standards. This was first noticeable in the 1980s, marking a shift in emphasis from the immediate post-World War II goal of the assimilation of indigenous and tribal peoples into states (couched in terms of equal access to the benefits of the State), to the need for self-determination of those marginalized by states and the consequent need to protect those institutions and practices essential to a self-determining, self-developing people, based upon such things as culture, education, and religion. Indigenous religion is therefore legally situated in the recent elaboration of human rights instruments oriented toward the collective rights of indigenous peoples, understood to be a category of peoples determined to transmit their knowledge and customs, inherited from "time immemorial," to future generations.

A central reference point for the identity and activism of the indigenous peoples movement is Article 1 of the International Covenant on Civil and Political Rights (ICCPR), drafted in 1966 and entered into force in 1976, which unambiguously introduces the language of collective rights to the then-emerging international bill of human rights: "All peoples have the right of self-determination. By virtue of that right they freely determine their political status and freely pursue their economic, social and cultural development."[9] The wide ramifications of this "collective" human rights language can be seen, for example, in ILO Convention 169 (1989), which explicitly seeks to remove the "assimilationist orientation of the earlier standards" with an instrument that recognizes the aspirations of indigenous and tribal peoples "to exercise control over their own institutions, ways of life and economic development and to maintain and develop their identities, languages and religions, within the framework of the States in which they live."[10]

The contentions and consequent delays during the drafting of the UN Declaration on the Rights of Indigenous Peoples, ratified in 2007 after more than two decades in the making, is usually traced to assertions of indigenous peoples' rights of self-determination, which were resisted by assertions of the sovereignty and territorial integrity of states. The emergence of indigenous peoples' identity and the ultimate reason for their insistence on recognition of their rights of self-determination has more to do with the common global experiences of state-sponsored policies of assimilation that I just discussed—of strategic efforts to eliminate the political, cultural, and spiritual foundations of those who resisted or were excluded from the project of the State.

Efforts to prevent and counteract the worst effects of assimilation policies are reflected in several articles in the Declaration on the Rights of Indigenous Peoples oriented toward the protection of cultural and religious integrity. These include Article 8.1 ("Indigenous peoples and individuals have the right not to be subjected to forced assimilation or destruction of their culture"); Article 12.1 ("Indigenous peoples have the right to manifest, practise, develop, and teach their spiritual and religious traditions, customs and ceremonies; the right to maintain, protect, and have access in privacy to their religious and cultural sites; the right to the use and control of their ceremonial objects; and the right to the repatriation of their human remains"); Article 24.1 ("Indigenous peoples have the right to their traditional medicines and to maintain their health practices, including the conservation of their vital medicinal plants, animals and minerals"); and Article 25 ("Indigenous peoples have the right to maintain and strengthen their distinctive spiritual relationship with their traditionally owned or otherwise occupied and used lands, territories, waters and coastal seas, and other resources and to uphold their responsibilities to future generations in this regard").[11] A similar emphasis on cultural integrity and protection of religion is evident in Section 3 of the proposed American Declaration on the Rights of Indigenous Peoples. If anything, the American Declaration is moving more in the direction of such issues as the right to cultural integrity, philosophy, language, education, and spiritual and religious freedom as an alternative to the more contentious emphasis on self-determination that accompanied (and delayed) the drafting of the UN declaration.[12] The fact that there is a considerable amount of language in the Declaration on the Rights of Indigenous Peoples and the proposed American Declaration on the Rights of Indigenous Peoples oriented toward the protection of indigenous spiritual practice is an indication of the high value placed on these practices in the context of enduring legacies (and at times, ongoing realities) of state-sponsored assimilation policies.

Parallel to and inseparable from these human rights initiatives are UN efforts to preserve indigenous knowledge for future generations, following in part from the formative idea, expressed by Raphael Lemkin as early as the 1930s, that "[t]he contribution of any particular collectivity to international culture forms the wealth of all of humanity."[13] Such preservation efforts are also occasionally justified on the grounds that indigenous knowledge has the potential to make significant contributions to science, not as an embodiment of history so much as a potential source of practical information. Whatever its underlying motivations, there seems to be a new openness in a variety of UN agencies to projects of recording and preserving the phenomena referred to as Indigenous Knowledge (IK), Traditional Knowledge (TK), or Traditional Indigenous Knowledge (TIK). Traditional indigenous knowledge is the most recent expression of the urge to preserve ancient learning and lore, but in one of its iterations it is oriented toward an improvement or healing of the worst effects of modernity. Among those with a scientific bent, the rapidly extending reach of technology and Christianity brought with it the alarming prospect of an end to knowledge about ways of life that included unexplored pathways of human progress. Those whose knowledge and traditions lay beyond the destructive reach of civilization, or who had not yet entirely succumbed to it, embodied in their very existence the pre-history of humanity. Their knowledge was the knowledge of Europe's remote ancestors. Those who continue to hold this knowledge possess, in their alien languages, myths, ceremonies, and technologies, the earliest creation story of civilization.

Cultural preservation initiatives in the institutions of global governance (particularly UNESCO) are not entirely blind to the practical and moral complexities of their goals, but are pervaded by doubts concerning the creation of "museum cultures" through artificial forms of preservation, possibly promoting calls for political separatism or even "forms of apartheid."[14] Beyond this, there is a tension between the goals of recording such knowledge for its practical content, as in the pharmaceutical uses of plants, and the removal of knowledge from the control and benefit of those who originally possess it. The problem of "biopiracy," in turn, relates to the issue of ignorance toward the "non-practical," that is to say, spiritual or religious dimensions of indigenous or traditional knowledge. And this leads ultimately to the central task—revealing and problematic in itself—concerning the articulation of the essence of the indigenous worldview.

■ OBJECTIFICATION

Especially with regard to indigenous rights, law revolutionizes whenever it is used as an instrument of preservation, creating an entirely new foundation for the existence of the objects of its solicitude. For one thing, the identification of a distinct community in need of protection from a dominant society calls for a definition of that community, a more precise knowledge of its membership, of those who are identified (or identify themselves) as the beneficiaries of distinct rights. Even the open, collective self-definition and self-inclusionary nature of the indigenous peoples' movement involves a process by which public representations of human diversity, of non-state peoples, leads to sharper boundaries in the form of ethnonyms, constitutions, cadastres of territories, and citizenship registries, along with publicly sanctioned repertoires of cultural representation.

One practical tendency of laws oriented toward religious protection is to connect religious rights with particular sites and objects, which are identified as "sacred," while excluding from exercises of rights and recognition the intangibles of indigenous cosmologies and nature spirituality. Where legal protections of religion have their most evident effect is in defending ownership and control of places and things. Spiritual qualities and traditional practices unique to a specific location are sometimes invoked alongside subsistence practices in formulating claims to territory; and judiciaries proceed in their handling of religious claims by insisting on the specificity and identifiably of religious practice.

This is evident, for example, in the case of *Francis Hopu and Tepoaitu Bessert v. France,* in which the Human Rights Committee was called upon to determine whether the construction of a luxury hotel complex on ancient burial grounds in Tahiti, French Polynesia, involved a violation of the International Covenant on Civil and Political Rights, particularly Article 2, paragraph 1 concerning non-discrimination, and Article 27, concerning cultural protections. The Committee, finding little evidence of discrimination (the indigenous Polynesians were in fact being treated as any French citizens would be) and, faced with the difficulties of defining culture, turned instead to Article 17 of the Covenant and found that the authors had been subject to interference of their rights to family and privacy, stretching the definition of "family" to include the remains of unidentified ancestors.[15]

The *Hopu and Bessert v. France* case reveals two significant qualities of the human rights protections of indigenous religions. First, the focus on a burial ground as a cornerstone of the distinct way of life of the indigenous Polynesians (along with their fishing-based subsistence) points to the objectification that occurs when religious rights are defended through judicial process. Second, the case highlights the limited effectiveness of the major human rights instruments for the protection of culture and religion, oriented as these instruments are to individual rights and to the protection of individuals as citizens of states. The difficulty of bringing cases relating to religious protection to the Human Rights Committee goes some way toward vindicating the elaboration of specific instruments dedicated to articulating and extending the rights of indigenous peoples. More than this, it emphasizes the fact that human rights are in general not judicially enforceable, but rely for their effectiveness on processes of moral persuasion, popular indignation, or the "politics of embarrassment."

The influence of emerging human rights standards for indigenous peoples can perhaps be seen more readily in a recent claim pursued by the Saamis of northern Europe, which seeks to protect both subsistence and the sacred. The Saami grievance followed from plans unveiled by the Norwegian government and the North Atlantic Treaty Organization (NATO) in 2002 to expand bombing ranges in Halkavarre, a region in northern Norway important as a feeding and calving area for reindeer. It is also important for its ancient sacred sites, Sieidit, where gifts were laid and sacrifices performed, and the sacred hills Álda and Sáivu. The Norwegian Saami Parliament chose to pursue this grievance through the intercession of International Labor Organization and the UN High Commissioner on Human Rights.[16] The Saamis, however, even with UN support, were unable effectively to challenge Norway's assertion of the centrality of flight training in Halkavarre for NATO's defense operations.

In domestic law, too, there is a marked tendency to allow only those claims in which freedom of religion can be connected to a specific location or object of reverence. This tendency can partly be explained by the fact that states tend to act on indigenous rights only to the extent that they do not support claims to sovereignty or territory. At the same time, courts tend to support *any* claim only when it is readily identifiable and supported by demonstrable "facts." The objectification of indigenous religious claims follows from the very nature of state interest and juridical procedure.

One of the central reference points for defining the States obligations toward freedom of religion in the U.S., for example, is *Employment Division v. Smith*, a 1990 Supreme Court case in which the court determined that the State acted legally in denying unemployment benefits to a member of the Native American Church for his use of peyote in a religious ritual.[17] Here the essence of religious practice and the focal point of the contested intrusion of the State are as specific as possible: embodied in the (at the time) illegal "peyote buttons" in question. The state, the Court found in its consideration of this peyote, was entitled to accommodate otherwise illegal acts associated with religious practices, but had no obligation to do so.

A greater accommodation of native religious beliefs is evident in the 2007 U.S. Ninth Circuit Court of Appeals decision, *Navajo Nation v. U.S. Forest Service*, in which the Court found that the U.S. Forest Service had violated the religious rights of a coalition of tribal groups and organizations when it approved the use of recycled sewage effluent (euphemistically referred to as "reclaimed water") in the production of artificial snow on the San Francisco Peaks ski resorts, a mountain considered sacred by at least thirteen tribes of the region.[18] In this decision, the tangibility of the mountain as a sacred place is self-evident; and even its desecration takes precise form: in the traces of waste that remain in the treated sewage effluent to be used for producing snow. The central reference point for this decision is the 1993 Religious Freedom Restoration Act, which raises the standards for a compelling government interest to justify the federal government's infringement of religious beliefs. But the possibility cannot be excluded that human rights standards have gradually and indirectly promoted values of tolerance and religious pluralism, together with the corresponding trend toward reification or objectification, that have ultimately influenced the judiciaries of some states.

Given the overall primacy of state interests in the outcomes of such disputes, why do indigenous activists continue to pursue claims not just through courts but through the intercession of NGOs and UN agencies? What gives this kind of strategy the potential to succeed? The behavior of states is influenced by human rights largely to the extent that the reputational costs that follow from international recognition of patterns of rights violations threaten consequences for national identity and the State's influence in its international relations. In practice, this means that active lobbying is essential for those peoples and organizations that intend to make use of the mechanisms of "soft law" as a way to bring about the rights compliance of states. And this simple observation introduces more that is paradoxical to assertions of indigenous spirituality as unchangingly durable and humanly essential.

■ ESSENCE

One of the key features of the international movement of indigenous peoples is the discovery—through new media and epiphanies of encounter in international meetings—of unifying global experience, a vast array of independent histories and historical memories that are in fundamental respects shared, combined with a similarly shared commitment to legal reform and resistance. The foundation of indigenous rights and identities in global experience finds expression not only in common denominators of troubled relationships with states and dominant societies, but in positive expressions of global forms of indigenous spirituality, based on the idea expressed by the Global Indigenous Caucus in the 2009 meeting of the Permanent Forum on Indigenous Issues, that "Indigenous peoples of all over the world speak with one voice."[19]

A systematic effort to express this worldview was undertaken by the Native American Council of New York City, which concluded, "As the environment of the planet we all share, the source of life which many indigenous people call Mother Earth, continues to deteriorate after centuries of abuse, a philosophy that incorporates all living and nonliving things in its vision is being sought. Increasingly, people of all colors, cultures, and nations have been turning to the world's indigenous people: those of us who have lived on the lands of our ancestors since the beginning of history."[20] Indigenous peoples, as the Council characterizes them (from the perspective of being included among them), "are the caretakers of the earth; our philosophies, religions, and governments have been oriented towards that goal. Many native peoples of North America live under original laws given by the Creator, instructing us to care for the land upon which we live, the water that sustains us all, and our grandfather the sky."[21]

Similar expressions of indigenous peoples' reverence of the sacred in the natural world and its place in history are expressed by specific groups or caucuses, as in the following intervention by the Indigenous Women's Caucus to the 2008 meeting of the Permanent Forum on Indigenous Issues: "Since time immemorial, indigenous women bore the responsibility of looking after families. Stewards of

Mother Earth, we continue to bear the responsibility of ensuring its wellbeing and curing the wounds caused to it. We have traditional knowledge with regard to guardianship to Mother Earth. And possessing this knowledge, we wish to bring about a better world for following generations, not just for our children but all of humanity."[22] And in a speech delivered to the 2009 meeting of the Permanent Forum, Nicolas Lucas Tirum, a Mayan elder, outlined his people's world-view, centered on the cosmological change expected to take place on the 21st of December in the year 2012, the 13th B'aqtun (a period of 5,200 years, each year consisting of 360 days) of the Mayan calendar, in which a new era of self-respect and respect toward all beings in the universe will be realized, together with an end to hatred and bloodshed and a renewal of the values of love, solidarity, and brotherhood among humanity. Leading up to this world renewal, "it is urgent that universities and scientific institutes recognize the spiritual dimension of humanity, [and] the connection and interconnection of all the elements of the universe," transform their monocultural visions, and accept an approach to life that emphasizes the dignity, prosperity, and respect of all peoples of the world. "Let us all walk together toward the new B'aqtun," Tirum proclaimed. "May day dawn for the human race."[23]

These statements, taken together, point to a consistent refrain in descriptions of indigenous spirituality. They commonly emphasize the destructive nature of industrial modernity, along with the potential for indigenous spirituality to counteract it, given sufficient respect and recognition of its virtues. Indigenous knowledge can make a significant contribution to human welfare through a generalized heightened awareness of the connection with the sacred in the natural world, a sense of the removal of barriers between human and other-than-human, between life and beyond-life, and between the experience of memory, perception, and knowledge of the future, so that communication and interaction occurs in a vastly extended realm.

Despite the almost self-evident popular appeal of the spiritual messages of the indigenous peoples' movement, there are those who argue that such messages are paradoxically corrosive of those particular systems of knowledge that the recently elaborated rights of indigenous peoples are oriented to protect. Peter Brosius is arguably foremost among those who are skeptical toward the generalized (and to some extent generic) expressions of indigenous spirituality, in which the very idea of the sacred is, as he puts it, "part of the 'grammar of conquest.' "[24] Illustrating his conclusions through ethnographic research on the forest-based knowledge of the Penan of the East Malaysian state of Sarawak on the island of Borneo, Brosius finds that Penan knowledge of the supernatural does not, in the absence of destructive extractive industries and environmental lobbyists, incline toward generalized expressions of the sacred, but is built into a "rich, poetic vocabulary used in prayers and in the everyday use of avoidance terms intended to keep malevolent forces at bay."[25] This situated, language-based approach to supernatural forces changes dramatically when the Penan are drawn in to transnational struggles for forest preservation, in which they and their knowledge are represented by advocates and allies to remote audiences: "It is only when Penan arguments are incorporated into a broader circulation of images deployed by external agents—Malaysian and Euro-American activists alike—that we begin to see an appeal to the sacred or ineffable."[26]

This use of ethnography to highlight the disjuncture between generalized indigenous cosmology and the particular knowledge and practices of those living in forests, steppes, and savannahs takes us only so far toward understanding the consequences of human rights activism. Given the situation that Brosius describes, what could possibly motivate a transnational network of indigenous peoples and non-governmental organizations to take up the spiritual discourse of dominant societies as their own? It is not enough to emphasize the distortions and stereotyping that take place through articulating a distinct, global form of human existence; one should inquire further into the origins and shaping of those distortions. The social processes behind the formal protections and expressions of indigenous religion have the potential to tell us something significant about the way "soft law" works, the effect it has on (and the use it makes of) available repertoires of symbols and expressions of affect. This is to say, global transformations in the idioms and iterations of human worth and dignity result, from the fact that the most strategically resonant forms of spiritual expression are foregrounded, and thereby reshaped and (relative to claims made by indigenous spokespeople) distorted, by public mechanisms of human rights and humanitarian intervention.

■ PUBLIC MEDIATION

The rights of indigenous peoples were of course not exclusively elaborated in the abstract by bureaucrats, judges, or other "experts," but are an outcome of sustained activism through transnational networks, usually through entities that have come to be referred to as "indigenous peoples' organizations" (IPOs) or by those who less formally (but effectively, through their numbers) attend UN-sponsored meetings as delegates representing an indigenous people. Indigenous religion is therefore indissociable from the public claims and representations of those who (often strategically) identify as indigenous, and who articulate their claims in discourse and performance intended to stir the emotions, longings, and sympathies of their audiences. Once brought into being, underpinned by rights of self-determination, and strategically navigated as a source of rights and identity, the indigenous peoples concept has become a reference point by which common qualities have been sought out, articulated, performed, and ultimately protected in law. Indigenous religion, in other words, is not just the subject of specific human rights protections but is at the same time a conceptual and performative secondary elaboration of the indigenous peoples' concept.[27]

The central concepts that emerge from peoples' collective sense of belonging are not "natural," even when built upon claims of primordial origins, but rather, are elaborated in collaborative relationships oriented toward liberation, commonly articulated in terms of spiritual healing and political self-determination. Cultural claims are not only made by those who identify themselves as fully belonging to a distinct people or community but also those for whom particular strivings toward collective self-determination represent wider struggles to prevent global patterns of environmental destruction, social injustice, and shrinking of the human range of cultural possibility. The sympathies and interests of a wider, transnational public have bolstered those with previously unrecognized aspirations toward collective self-determination, both morally and organizationally.

One consequence of this is that, while human rights language is legal in character, there is at the same time a central popular impulse behind the religious protections of indigenous and traditional peoples. Those who find truth and comfort in representations of authentic indigenous knowledge tend to see the many forms of human diversity under the protective umbrella of law as a form of global betterment. The emergence of an indigenous worldview thus involves self-defining actors in processes or "projects" of collective self-definition mediated by culturally defining public outreach and collaborative activism.

Legal lobbying calls for a strategic, selective representation of justice claimants, for images or artefacts of testimony to be selected for their communicability, appeal, and potential to evoke strong emotions in others, above all for their ability to make an argument for their distinct worth and dignity, and hence the merits of the rights that protect them. It calls for collective rights claimants to ask themselves: "What is unique about our traditions? What aspects of our traditions are most likely to appeal to those who may be willing to share our cause and act on our behalf? What do we do collectively that can and should be given recognition and connected to our claims?"[28] The elaboration of legal protections of indigenous religion calls for the beneficiaries of these protections to formally identify those qualities of their collective knowledge and practice that can be considered to merit protection, above all those that can legitimately be seen by others as "spiritual" or "religious" in nature.

A central consequence of public lobbying is the increased formalism of those traditions associated with indigenous claims and identities. Alongside efforts to define and protect the collective claimants of rights, are parallel efforts to articulate those qualities that constitute the essence of a distinct people or category of peoples. From this has followed efforts to clothe rights claims with the details of human difference, including (perhaps above all) spiritual and religious practices.

The identification and special attention given to those practices that are more readily identified as qualifying for legal claims ultimately produces a new ordering of the universe, a cosmology based on the translatability and appeal of items (or knowledge that has become itemized) to those cultural outsiders who formally or informally pass judgment on the merits of a claim, usually based on subjective recognition of the practice as "spiritual" or "distinct-yet-universal," and with potential for their own inspiration and self-improvement.

NOTES

1 Bruno Latour, *We Have Never Been Modern*, trans. Catherine Porter (Cambridge: Harvard University Press, 1993), 76.

2 I am drawing here upon the vocabulary used by Alain Pottage in "Introduction: The Fabrication of Persons and Things," in *Law, Anthropology, and the Constitution of the Social: Making Persons and Things*, eds. Alain Pottage and Martha Mundy (Cambridge: Cambridge University Press, 2004) 1–39.

3 See Ronald Niezen, *The Origins of Indigenism: Human Rights and the Politics of Identity* (Berkeley: University of California Press, 2003), Ch. 3.

4 International Labor Organization, Convention Concerning Indigenous and Tribal Peoples in Independent Countries (C169), June 27, 1989, 72 ILO Official Bull. 59, 28 ILM 1382 (1989). An influential 1987 report by José Martinez Cobo, the "Study of the Problem of Discrimination against Indigenous Populations," defines indigenous communities, peoples and nations as "those which, having a historical continuity with pre-invasion and pre-colonial societies that developed on their territories, consider themselves distinct from other sectors of the societies now prevailing in those territories, or parts of them. They form at present nondominant sectors of society and are determined to preserve, develop and transmit to future generations their ancestral territories and their ethnic identity, as the basis of their continued existence as peoples, in accordance with their own cultural patterns, social institutions and legal systems." José Martinez Cobo, *Study of the Problem of Discrimination against Indigenous Populations,* vol. 5, U.N. Doc. E/CN.4/Sub.2/1986/7/Add.4; 48.

5 United Nations Permanent Forum on Indigenous Issues, Ninth Session, "Indigenous peoples: development with culture and identity: articles 3 and 32 of the United Nations Declaration on the Rights of Indigenous Peoples; Report of the international expert group meeting," New York, April 19–30 2010. U.N. Doc E/C.19/2010/14; par. 19 (February 5, 2010).

6 James Anaya, *Indigenous Peoples in International Law,* 2nd ed. (Oxford: Oxford University Press, 2004), 132–33.

7 Covenant of the League of Nations, Paris Peace Conference, signed June 28, 1919,*entered into force* January 10, 1920.

8 International Labor Organization, Convention Concerning the Protection and Integration of Indigenous and other Tribal and Semi-Tribal Populations in Independent Countries (C107) (Geneva, June 26, 1957) 328 U.N.T.S. 247(hereinafter ILO, C107 Indigenous and Tribal Populations Convention).

9 International Covenant on Civil and Political Rights G.A. Res. 2200A (XXI), 21 U.N. GAOR Supp (No. 16) at 52, UN Doc. A/6316, 999 U.N.T.S. (Dec. 16, 1966), 999 U.N.T.S. 171, *entered into force* March 23, 1976.

10 I.L.O, C107 Indigenous and Tribal Populations Convention.

11 United Nations General Assembly, Declaration on the Rights of Indigenous Peoples, U.N. GAOR, A/61/L.67/Annex (2007).

12 The comparison between the American Declaration and the UN Declaration is elaborated by Patrick Thornberry, *Indigenous Peoples and Human Rights* (Manchester, U.K.: Manchester University Press; New York: Juris Publishing, 2002), 401–4.

13 *L'apport de toute collectivité particulière dans la culture internationale rentre dans le trésor de l'humanité entière* (my translation). Raphaël Lemkin, "Les actes constituant un danger général (interétatique) considérés comme délites du droit des gens." http://www.preventgenocide.org/fr/lemkin/madrid1933.htm. Accessed October 16, 2009.

14 UNESCO Institute for Education, "CONFINTEA: Follow-up Report to the General Conference of UNESCO," Hamburg, November 1999, http://www.unesco.org/education/

uie/pdf/folloeng.pdf, para. 5.4. A somewhat more toned-down expression of this idea seeks merely to avoid the promotion of cultures that are "reified." UNESCO, "Diversity of Cultural Expressions; Intergovernmental Committee for the Protection and Promotion of the Diversity of Cultural Expressions," UNESCO Doc. CE/08/1.EXT.IGC/3 (April 3, 2008).

15 Human Rights Committee, *Francis Hopu and Tepoaitu Bessert v. France.* Communication No. 549/1993, U.N. Doc. CCPR/C/51/D/549/1993 (June 30, 1994).

16 Christian Nellemann and Ingunn Vistnes, "New Bombing Ranges and their Impact on Saami Traditions," *Polar Environment Times*, 3 (2003).

17 *Employment Division, Department of Human Resources of Oregon v. Smith*, 494 U.S. 872 (1990).

18 *Navajo Nation v. U.S. Forest Service*, 479 F.3d 1024 (9th Cir. 2007).

19 This from a verbatim transcription taken by me during the 2008 meeting of the Permanent Forum on Indigenous Issues at the UN headquarters in New York.

20 The Native American Council of New York City, "Introduction," in *Voice of Indigenous Peoples: Native People Address the United Nations* (Santa Fe, NM: Clear Light Publishers, 1994), 19.

21 Ibid., 20.

22 This is a close paraphrasing of the intervention, based on my notes taken during the 2008 meeting of the Permanent Forum at the UN headquarters in New York.

23 *Es urgente que las universidades y los centros de investigación científica reconozcan la dimensión espiritual del ser humano, [y] la conexión e interconexión de todos los elementos del universo.* My translation. Nicolas Lucas Tirum, "Mensaje de los Mayas de Ayer y de Hoy para el Futuro de la Humanidad: Un Compromiso Imperativo de los Estados y Gobiernos en el Marco del Trece B'aqtun." Unpublished presentation to the 8th meeting of the Permanent UN Forum on Indigenous Issues, New York, May 27, 2009, 2.

24 Peter Brosius, "Local Knowledges, Global Claims: On the Significance of Indigenous Ecologies in Sarawak, East Malaysia," in *Indigenous Traditions and Ecology*, ed. John Grim (Cambridge: Center for the Study of World Religions, Harvard Divinity School/Harvard University Press, 2001), 126.

25 Ibid., 141.

26 Ibid., 150.

27 See analogous discussions of the understanding of how to construct the understanding of "human" in "human rights" in the chapter by Abdullahi Ahmed An-Na'im herein.

28 I elaborate on the influence of publics (very much in the plural) in human rights claims in my *Public Justice and the Anthropology of Law* (Cambridge: Cambridge University Press, 2010), especially in Chapters 2 and 3.

■ RECOMMENDED READING

Anaya, James. *Indigenous Peoples in International Law,* 2nd ed. (Oxford: Oxford University Press, 2004)

Brosius, Peter. "Local Knowledges, Global Claims: On the Significance of Indigenous Ecologies in Sarawak, East Malaysia," in *Indigenous Traditions and Ecology,* ed. John Grim (Cambridge: Center for the Study of World Religions, Harvard Divinity School/ Harvard University Press, 2001), 125–57

Cobo, José Martinez. *Study of the Problem of Discrimination Against Indigenous Populations*, vol. 5, U.N. Doc. E/CN.4/Sub.2/1986/7/Add.4, 48

Niezen, Ronald. *The Origins of Indigenism: Human Rights and the Politics of Identity* (Berkeley: University of California Press, 2003)

_____. *Public Justice and the Anthropology of Law* (Cambridge: Cambridge University Press, 2010)

Pottage, Alain. "Introduction: The Fabrication of Persons and Things," in *Law, Anthropology, and the Constitution of the Social: Making Persons and Things*, eds. Alain Pottage and Martha Mundy (Cambridge: Cambridge University Press, 2004)

The Native American Council of New York City. "Introduction," in *Voice of Indigenous Peoples: Native People Address the United Nations* (Santa Fe, NM: Clear Light Publishers, 1994), 19–27

Thornberry, Patrick. *Indigenous Peoples and Human Rights* (Manchester, UK: Manchester University Press; New York: Juris Publishing, 2002)

United Nations. Permanent Forum on Indigenous Issues. "Indigenous peoples: development with culture and identity: articles 3 and 32 of the United Nations Declaration on the Rights of Indigenous Peoples; Report of the international expert group meeting." (Ninth Session, New York, April 19–30, 2010). U.N. Doc E/C.19/2010/14 (February 5, 2010)

8 Religion, Human Rights, and Public Reason

The Role and Limits of a Secular Rationale

DAVID LITTLE

The claim that human rights language is "secular" has aroused a strong reaction in scholarly, philosophical, and theological circles. In particular, the fact that the 1948 Universal Declaration of Human Rights (UDHR) and subsequent human rights documents exclude religious warrants as a basis for justification is thought to raise at least three serious problems.

One problem is whether it is even possible to justify human rights apart from religious belief. The positions of four authors represented in this book illustrate the conviction that secular warrants for human rights finally fail, and that religious justifications are required. In *Justice: Rights and Wrongs*,[1] Nicholas Wolterstorff supports the moral potency of rights language in general, and human rights language in particular, by advancing a theological argument as the only satisfactory basis for "inherent rights," as he calls them. He contends that rights language, including human rights, assures vital protection against arbitrary abuse, resting on a conviction of the irreducible, equal worth of every human being. Secular theories, like those of Ronald Dworkin, Alan Gewirth, or John Rawls, do not succeed in supporting a notion of equal inherent human worth, nor is there much likelihood that other such theories can ever do so. The only plausible alternative, in his view, is a theistic conviction, namely, that the God of Hebrew and Christian Scriptures "bestows worth" on all human beings "equally and permanently."

Michael Perry provides another version of a religious justification of human rights.[2] His claim is that key human rights terms like "the inherent dignity" of "all members of the human family" necessarily presuppose a religious or sacred ground, and therefore that "the idea of human rights is ineliminably religious." While Perry does not share Wolterstorff's belief in one preferred theological position, he does agree that "there is, finally, no intelligible secular version of . . . human rights." Consequently, determining the grounds of human rights "is, finally [and unavoidably], a theological project."

David Novak takes a comparable position from the perspective of Judaism.[3] Concentrating on "the question of the religious foundation of human rights," Novak argues that "the task of the religious believer—Jewish, Christian, or Muslim—is to provide a better foundation for the [human rights] claims of the secular realm where the vast majority of . . . citizens profess religious belief and, indeed, see their very allegiance to that secular realm as itself being religious."

He defends this assertion by arguing that for Judaism religion can only be seen "as the source of *all* other rights," whether understood as the rights among human beings or between human beings and God. The major problem with secularist views of human rights, such as the social contract theory, is that society "must be seen as an artificial construct" created by a collection of self-interested, unattached individuals. Such a view makes, for Novak, the offensive assumption "that the human individual is sovereign rather than God."

The Muslim scholar, Abdullahi An-Na'im, is more ambivalent about the adequacy of a secular defense of human rights than the preceding figures. Nevertheless, he has in some of his writings explicitly opposed the idea of religious neutrality as a basis for human rights,[4] and he argued in a major 2008 publication that human rights should not be thought of "as the standard by which Islam [or, presumably, any religion] should be judged." Indeed, An-Na'im recently declared in public that, in the end, human rights are justified because they make it possible for him to be a good Muslim, apparently reaffirming an earlier claim that "any normative regime . . . which justifies a set of rights . . . must necessarily represent a commitment to a specific [non-neutrally formulated] value system."

A second problem concerns a deep suspicion about what it means to embrace human rights as "a secular system." Talal Asad[5] contends that human rights language, as an expression of "the secular," is not a neutral, generally beneficial means of addressing conflict and injustice around the world. If anything, it makes matters worse. That is because human rights ideas, taken to be religiously neutral and universally applicable, in fact disguise the ominous character and implications of those ideas. In Asad's opinion, human rights language is embedded in and inseparable from modern secular nationalism, with its notions of a "centralizing," totalizing state oriented toward this-worldly, self-serving purposes and possessing ultimate, exclusive, and all-determining authority over politics and economic life, as well as over the moral and religious convictions of its citizens.

Accordingly, human rights are "floating signifiers that can be attached or detached from various subjects and classes constituted by the market principle and by the most powerful nation-states." For instance, they are the "secular language of redemption" at the heart of the "universalizing moral project of the American nation-state—the project of humanizing the world" in America's image. In a word, human rights ideas are a grand mystification masking the "secular" or this-worldly and self-serving interests of the modern nation-state.

A third problem is that human rights are seen as set over against and superior to religious beliefs, thereby encouraging a secularist form of intolerance and, consequently, creating the risk that the very system designed to protect persecuted religious believers might itself become their oppressor. This is the position of human rights scholar Malcolm Evans.[6] According to him, statements by UN officials concerning the need for everyone, including religious people, to avoid "categorical, inflexible attitudes," "blind obstinacy," and "gratuitous accusations" implies "that freedom of religion does not include the right of others to adhere to a religion which is intolerant of the beliefs of others." In his view, protecting the freedom of thought, conscience, and religion "does not mean that the relationship between a secularist concept of human rights and religious perspectives of the rights and duties of the individual can, or should, be determined exclusively from and through [secularist] perspectives."

The difficulty with all these objections and reservations developed in reaction to describing human rights language as secular is that they ignore a consistent, if carefully circumscribed, rationale on the part of the drafters for deliberately excluding all confessional or religious references from the UDHR. Understanding, expanding on, and tracing the practical effects of that rationale go a long way toward defusing and dispelling these objections and reservations.

■ HUMAN RIGHTS AND PUBLIC REASON

A helpful way to make sense of human rights language as the drafters understood it is to see it in relation to John Rawls's idea of public reason.[7] The fit is by no means perfect, and some important adjustments must be made. Still, when viewed that way, it is possible to appreciate the basic strengths of the language, including the way it both accommodates and delimits references to the secular.

Five parallels are worth noting. First, Rawls describes the notion of public reason as the appropriate idiom of communication among the citizens of a democratic order, "of those sharing the status of equal citizenship," who, "as a collective body, exercise final political and coercive power over one another in enacting laws and amending their constitution." "The subject of their reason," he says, "is the good of the public," of what is required of "society's basic structure of institutions, and of the purposes and ends they are to serve." That refers, primarily, to "constitutional essentials," namely, the character and ranking of "certain basic rights, liberties, and opportunities (of the kind familiar from constitutional democratic regimes)."[8]

Second, public reason, Rawls emphasizes, has a distinctly limited reach. It provides common terms of discourse in a society assumed to be made up of citizens espousing a variety of divergent "general and comprehensive doctrines." These are religious or philosophical systems of belief intended to apply to a large, possibly unlimited, number of adherents, and that include "conceptions of what is of value in human life, and ideals of human character, as well as ideals of friendship and associational relationships, and much else that is to inform our conduct," and, potentially, to life as a whole. In the face of an array of such doctrines that invariably compete with each other, public reason "is framed solely to apply to the basic structure of society, its main political, social, and economic institutions," and "it is presented independently of any wider comprehensive religious or philosophical doctrine," and is, as such, considered to be a "freestanding view." There is presumed to be, he goes on, "no reason why any citizen, or association of citizens, should have the right to use state power to decide constitutional essentials as that person's, or that association's, comprehensive doctrine directs. When equally represented, no citizen could grant to another person or association that political authority. Any such authority, therefore, is without grounds in public reason. . . ." In short, public reason provides a common, religiously neutral language of last resort in regard to the regulation of force.[9]

The fact that public reason is conceived of as freestanding by being independent of any comprehensive religious or other doctrine implies that the idea is *secular in a limited sense*. Officially, it neither authorizes nor is authorized by any religious position, yet it espouses a notion of "reasonable pluralism" and a commitment to tolerance of diverse religious and other convictions so long as adherents to those convictions agree to live in accord with the constitutional essentials presupposed by the idea of public reason.[10]

Third, Rawls mentions that "reasonable comprehensive doctrines recognize [these values]," leading to his notion of "overlapping consensus." For reasons based on an interpretation of their own respective traditions, proponents of "reasonable comprehensive doctrines" consensually embrace as freestanding the values associated with public reason. As such, the values accepted by the overlapping consensus imply their own independent, non-comprehensive grounding, arrived at, for Rawls, on the basis of what he calls "political constructivism."[11]

Rawls makes very clear that, in his view, an overlapping consensus is not the same as a "*modus vivendi*" based upon a coincidental and temporary convergence of convictions and interests. It is, rather, a "moral conception" based on "moral grounds." It supports a notion of public reason involving a deliberate and self-conscious commitment to a "principle of legitimacy," according to which each citizen accepts a *moral duty*—"the duty of civility"—"to be able to explain to one another on those fundamental questions how the principles and policies they advocate and vote for can be supported by the political values of public reason." In other words, public reason is a common framework of communication based on values each citizen can reasonably expect others to endorse.[12]

Fourth, Rawls considers public reason to apply in general to the conduct of official forums, such as the proceedings of the legislature and the official communications and actions of the executive, but, interestingly, it applies especially to the judiciary, and, above all, to the highest court in a constitutional democracy with judicial review. "This is because the justices have to explain and justify their decisions as based on their understanding of the constitution and relevant statutes and precedents." Because that is sometimes not the orientation of legislators and executives, "the court's special role makes it the exemplar of public reason."[13]

Fifth, Rawls stresses that the idea of public reason is *an ideal*, consisting of an understanding and a set of rational norms to be aspired to, and not something that is necessarily operational in complete form in the real world.[14]

In comparison, human rights language reveals significant similarities at all five points. First, it is a language fitted to the ideal of democratic citizenship where the "good of the public" or "general welfare" is understood to encompass a "society's basic structure of institutions," and particularly its "constitutional essentials," including "certain basic rights, liberties, and opportunities," as well as specific public goods. In the words of UDHR, Article 29.2: "Everyone shall be subject only to such limitations as are determined by law solely for the purpose of securing due recognition and respect for the rights and freedoms of others and of meeting the requirements of morality, public order, and the general welfare in a democratic society."[15]

Similarly, rights to freedom of expression, peaceful assembly, and freedom of association may be limited only where "the rights and freedoms of others," or public, safety, order, health, or morals, or national security must be protected.[16] The same is largely true for the right to the freedom of religion or belief,[17] except that states are explicitly required to punish, among other things, expressions of "religious hatred" "that constitute . . . incitement to discrimination . . . or violence."[18] Presumably, by violating basic protections against discrimination and violence, such incitements are seen as a direct threat to "the good of the public."

As to the grounds on which the State protects public goods, it has been authoritatively determined that they must be truly public or broadly inclusive. They must, that is, "be based on principles not deriving exclusively from a single tradition," but "from many social, philosophical and religious traditions."[19] Beyond these provisions, Articles 3 through 21 of the UDHR and Articles 6–27 of the ICCPR further enumerate the basic rights of "equal citizenship" under the rule of law.[20]

Second, human rights language is designed to provide guidance in the face of a large array of divergent and competing comprehensive views. As a way of finding minimal common ground in the face of many different belief systems, it is a language "presented independently of any wider comprehensive religious or philosophical doctrine," and is, as such, presupposed to be the language of last resort in regard to the regulation of force. No individual or group, as Rawls says, "should have the right to use state power to decide constitutional essentials as the comprehensive doctrine of that individual or group dictates." This orientation explains why, after a series of contentious deliberations over proposals—eventually rejected—to include in the Preamble references to "divine origin" and "immortal destiny," the drafters reached consensus that "the Universal Declaration is a secular document by intent." "Secular" is meant here to include, in the spirit of Rawls, a notion of public good that is assumed to be held in common by all citizens and that does not directly depend on any religious or other comprehensive view. This orientation also explains why the drafters ultimately concluded that the document should take no position "on the nature of man and of society," and that all "metaphysical controversies, notably conflicting doctrines of spiritualists, rationalists, and materialists regarding the origins" human rights should be avoided. Rather, these matters should be left to individual conscientious deliberation under the protection of the freedom of religion or belief.[21]

That means that religious (and, equally, nonreligious) beliefs are fully respected by being provided for and protected by the State, subject of course to the limitations mentioned. There is also no prohibition against offering religious (or other) justifications for human rights as enumerated in the documents, or against discussing and advocating them in public. It is simply that no provision exists for legally requiring or enforcing such beliefs.[22]

Furthermore, it explains why the document adopts a "thin approach" to the government's role in dealing with comprehensive views. In contrast to a "thick approach," in which a government takes "responsibility for the delivery and maintenance of a special cultural, religious, or linguistic tradition," in a thin approach, the government sets up "a fair (legal) framework within which its people can, singly or in groups, pursue their own notions of . . . human good, as long as [the rights, freedoms, and public goods] mentioned in Article 29 are not violated."[23]

Third, the authoritative ruling that the grounds on which the State protects public goods must be "be based on principles not deriving exclusively from a single tradition," but "from many social, philosophical and religious traditions" hints at Rawls's idea of an overlapping consensus, though more must be said. As we saw, an overlapping consensus on Rawls's understanding is not simply the acceptance of a set of values resulting from a coincidental and temporary convergence of convictions and interests. It is rather a common consensual commitment on the part of the adherents of many different comprehensive doctrines to values associated with public reason regarded as freestanding or as having their own independent, non-comprehensive grounding.

The drafters held such a view, even though the particular grounds they came to embrace are by no means the same as Rawls's. They were not "political constructivists," as we shall see later. For now, we may highlight the points of similarity between Rawls's position and theirs. In particular, a careful review of the legislative history of the UDHR confirms the conclusion that it was the result of serious and extensive interaction among a large number of people from around the world, many of whom were representatives of what Rawls calls "reasonable comprehensive doctrines." For reasons based on an interpretation of their own respective traditions, they eventually reached consensus on the provisions of the UDHR, such that, "Before the whole two-year process from drafting and deliberation to adoption reached its end, literally hundreds of individuals from diverse backgrounds had participated. Thus [Charles] Malik, [a Lebanese Christian Thomist, and one of the principal drafters] could fairly say, 'The genesis of each article, and each part of each article, was a dynamic process in which many minds, interests, backgrounds, legal systems and ideological persuasions played their respective determining roles'."[24]

Moreover, as with Rawls, the values embodied in the UDHR and subsequent documents involve "moral conceptions" and assumed "moral grounds," illustrated by the following passage from the Preamble to the UDHR: "Disregard and contempt for human rights have resulted in barbarous acts which have outraged the conscience of mankind." The underlying moral convictions include a "principle of legitimacy," according to which each citizen accepts a *moral duty*—along the lines of Rawls's "duty of civility"—to operate in accord with the system, as well as to extend and promote it. The Preamble goes on to declare that the UDHR is, "a common standard of achievement for all peoples and nations, to the end that every individual and every organ of society, keeping this Declaration in mind, shall strive by teaching and education to promote respect for these rights and freedoms and by progressive measures, national and international, to secure their universal and effective recognition and observance, both among the peoples of the Member States and among peoples and territories under their jurisdiction."

Above all, the values agreed to as the result of an overlapping consensus are considered freestanding. To have included in the Preamble references to the central ideas of religious or other comprehensive doctrines, as was proposed, would have contradicted the principle of non-discrimination, according to which human rights are attributed "without distinction of any kind, such as . . . religion . . . or other opinion."[25] In addition, the values are non-comprehensive in the sense that they apply only to the rights, freedoms, and public goods enumerated in the UDHR and other documents, and leave the elaboration and defense of comprehensive doctrines to individual conscience.

Fourth, human rights language is legal in character, which means it is intended to be submitted to the interpretation and administration of judicial and quasi-judicial bodies like the European Court of Human Rights, the ICCPR Human Rights Committee, and the UN Special Rapporteur on Freedom of Religion or Belief. These bodies and officials, in line with Rawls's comments about the highest court of a well-ordered democracy, may be understood to be special "exemplars of public reason," meaning that their judgments and patterns of reasoning, together with reactions to them, should be the particular focus of efforts to understand and apply public reason in its human rights form.

Fifth, concerning the UDHR "as a common standard of achievement for all peoples and all nations," human rights language is "ideal" in Rawls's sense. That means that human rights language enshrines values to be aspired to, and that they are not necessarily operational in complete form in the real world. But it also means that the language is ideal in that it stands as a proposal or exhortation offered for conscientious consideration. The language may punish only violations in practice of the enumerated rights, freedoms, and public goods; it may not regulate beliefs as such, presumably, even beliefs that support or criticize existing human rights. In other words, human rights language constitutes "outer limits" on matters of conscientious belief by authorizing the legal inhibition of actions deduced from particular theological or philosophical comprehensive doctrines that in practice violate the human rights code. It does not prohibit deliberation and debate over the contents of the code or over efforts to amend the code according to due process.

Despite these five instructive parallels between Rawls's idea of public reason and human rights language, there is, as we have hinted along the way, one critical point of divergence. That concerns the way in which the "constitutional essentials," namely, "certain basic rights, liberties, and opportunities," are justified. As a "political constructivist," Rawls regards basic rights as derivative, as the result of a political agreement, not the precondition for one, whether the agreement is arrived at among nations or among members of a single state. Internationally, Rawls's approach is tailored for established, sovereign nation-states that already understand themselves to be constitutional democracies. He starts with the idea of "sovereign peoples" and their representatives, rather than with individuals, and a reasonable international agreement concerning basic rights would, on Rawls's account, permit significant deviations from fundamental human rights norms.[26]

Similarly, provisions for basic rights in any well-ordered constitutional democracy only *come after* the founding agreements of the society have been accepted. Strictly speaking, basic rights are the result of a "political construction." Moreover, the founding agreements, the fundamental "fair terms of cooperation," are determined by the "reciprocal advantage" they represent to contracting parties, a notion that explicitly does not rest on any prior "moral authority" or "order of moral values."[27] The contractors' reason for entering into the social contract in the first place is that "they are prudential seekers of their own advantage . . . imagined as concerned to advance their own conception of the good . . . [with] no stipulation that such a conception need include any altruistic elements."[28] It is only after the contractors have agreed to cooperate on the basis of mutual advantage that the terms of Rawls's famous image of the Veil of Ignorance apply, according to which they accept as reasonable the principles of justice, including the "constitutional essentials."

The assumptions underlying human rights language are very different. According to the words of the Preamble to the UDHR, "All human beings are born free and equal in dignity and rights." Basic rights are, *to begin with*, "inalienable" and the property of "all members of the human family," and "should be protected by the rule of law." Some rights, such as protections against racial, religious, gender, and other forms of discrimination, as well as extra-judicial killing, torture, and cruel, inhuman or degrading treatment or punishment, involuntary medical or scientific experimentation, or violations of the freedom of religion or belief, are under no circumstances to be subject to political or legal abridgement. In the terms of international law, such basic rights comprise a set of obligations that transcend statutory or treaty agreements and are grounded in universal peremptory principles, at once legal and moral in character. Certainly, genocide, and other "crimes against humanity" enumerated in the Rome Statute, must be understood in the same way.

Accordingly, human rights are understood to *precede* or *predate* all international agreements and covenants, including human rights covenants, as well as all national constitutions, rather than to derive from or depend upon them. The UDHR was taken to represent, in the words of the Preamble, a prior "common standard of achievement for all peoples and nations, to the end that every individual and every organ of society, keeping this Declaration in mind, shall strive by teaching and education to promote respect for these rights and freedoms." Human rights are also believed to rest upon preexisting moral foundations that are universalistic in character. Rene Cassin, a French Jew and another principal drafter of the UDHR, is reported to have written that the title "Universal" "meant that the Declaration was morally binding on everyone, not only on the governments that voted for its adoption. The UDHR, in other words, was not an 'international' or 'intergovernmental' document; it was addressed to all humanity and founded on a unified conception of the human being."[29] Mary Ann Glendon expands on that theme: The drafters "were not homogenizers, but . . . universalists in the sense that they believed that human nature was everywhere the same and that the processes of experiencing, understanding, and judging were capable of leading everyone to certain basic [moral] truths."[30]

These observations fill out the ways in which the drafters regarded human rights to be freestanding and secular. As a result of the worldwide catastrophe they had witnessed, the drafters believed the basis for affirming and promoting human rights was immediate, direct, and indubitable. The words of the Preamble, "disregard and contempt for human rights have resulted in barbarous acts which have outraged the conscience of mankind," presupposed a common conviction concerning "obvious and self-evident moral facts about inherent [and inalienable] rights." Since, as the drafters saw it, the rights enumerated in the UDHR are "morally self-justifying," human rights for that reason do not need special religious justification, and to that extent are secular. Regardless of differences of culture, ethnic, or national identity, religion "or other opinion," etc., all human beings—simply as human—are entitled to appeal to certain fundamental human rights and are legitimately held accountable to them.

As Morsink shows, the idea of human rights is grounded in a feeling of "shared moral revulsion" toward "the absolutely crucial factor of the Holocaust," encompassing as it did the array of atrocities perpetrated so widely in the 1920s, '30s, and '40s. Without that shared revulsion, "the Declaration would never have been written." "The drafters . . . generalized their own feelings over the rest of humanity." Revolted by Hitler and all his works, "they believed that any morally healthy human being would have been similarly outraged when placed in similar circumstances. [Moreover,] this shared outrage explains why the Declaration has found such widespread support." The assumption here is that expressing moral outrage in response to Hitler's atrocities is itself a critical, if minimal, defining characteristic of what it means to be a "morally healthy human being."[31]

It is this particular moral understanding that provides the all-important basis for universal accountability, including legitimate legal enforceability, that is an intrinsic feature of human rights language. Without some such grounding, people are only hypothetically accountable, depending on whether they happen in one way or another to have committed themselves to human rights standards. Lacking such a commitment, an exercise of enforcement is illegitimate. So long as there is no binding basis for accountability, individuals or governments who consistently refrain, as did Hitler, from accepting such standards are morally and legally exempt from their jurisdiction.

■ THE PLAUSIBILITY OF THE DRAFTERS' RATIONALE[32]

The drafters' rationale would appear to rest on four firmly held propositions that underlie their diagnosis of the Holocaust and of their prescription for a cure and for preventing similar events in the future. First, the use of force, defined as the infliction of death, impairment, disablement, deprivation, destruction, severe pain, and/or involuntary confinement, begs strong moral justification wherever it occurs, both because of the obvious adverse consequences that result from using force and of the powerful temptation in human affairs to use force arbitrarily (i.e., without "strong moral justification"). Second, no human being could reasonably doubt that Hitler's grounds for the kind and amount of force used at his command were grossly self-serving and manifestly unfounded, and led to forms of arbitrary abuse that *must* be labeled "atrocities" (i.e., strongly condemnable). That should be plain to everyone; those who fail to recognize it are themselves under moral suspicion. Third, Hitler's atrocities rested on a belief in total domination, namely, the right of a government to treat citizens in any way it sees fit, including the relentless enforcement of a particular comprehensive doctrine. Fourth, an indispensable means of inhibiting the recurrence of such practices, and of preventing "as a last resort" "rebellion against tyranny and oppression,"[33] is the affirmation and enforcement of human rights as enumerated in the UDHR and subsequent documents.

As the drafters perceived, the effects of the fascist experiment of the mid-twentieth century made transparently clear the deep conceptual divide between force and morality. Wherever it occurs, force, as defined, inflicts highly unfavorable and unwanted consequences that obviously demand strong justification of a special kind. Giving as a reason *only* the self-interest of the one using force, thereby utterly disregarding the interests of others,[34] or giving reasons that are unfounded, especially when done knowingly and avoidably, simply cannot count as valid justifications for actions with those consequences. In fact, using force for such "reasons" defines the basic meaning of "arbitrary force."

It follows that the idea of morality, understood as the practice of justifying provisions for fundamental human welfare, "self-evidently" excludes arbitrary "reasons" for the use of force, namely exclusive references to the self-interest of the user or knowing and avoidable references to mistaken evidence and argument offered in defense. This was all so transparent because Hitler was so paradigmatically an exemplar of arbitrary force. According to a classic biography of him,

> [Hitler's] twelve years' dictatorship was barren of all ideas save one—the further extension of his own power and that of the nation with which he had identified himself. . . . [T]he sole theme of the Nazi revolution was domination, dressed up as the doctrine of race. . . . [The Nazi Constitution was] "the will of the Fuehrer." This was in fact literally true. The Weimar Constitution was never replaced, it was simply suspended by the Enabling Law, which was renewed periodically and placed all power in Hitler's hands. . . . What Hitler aimed at was arbitrary power.[35]

In addition, the evidence mustered in defense of the invasion of Belgium, the Netherlands, and Luxembourg "was entirely without justification. It was carried out in pursuance of policies long considered and prepared, and was plainly an act of aggressive war. The resolve to invade was made without any other consideration than the advancement of the aggressive policies of Germany."[36] The same may be said of his invasion of Poland, Denmark, and Norway.

Most damaging of all was Hitler's self-confessed duplicity in defending his use of force. As revealed in *Mein Kampf*, he felt little need to worry about justifications since the "broad masses" are so easily hoodwinked by propaganda. They readily remain "unaware of the shameless spiritual terrorization and the hideous abuse of their human freedom, for they absolutely fail to suspect *the inner insanity of the whole doctrine*. All they see is the ruthless force and brutality of its calculated manifestations, to which they always submit in the end."[37]

In carrying out his campaign for total and centralized domination, Hitler "enjoyed a more complete measure of power than Napoleon or Stalin or Mussolini, since he had been careful not to allow the growth of any institution which might . . . be used to check him."[38] This point is dramatically symbolized by the systematic repression of all religious beliefs and institutions, along with all other "deviant" beliefs and institutions, in the name of imposing by force the Nazi comprehensive doctrine. Judaism, as well as all expressions of Roman Catholicism and Protestantism inconsistent with Nazi ideology, were outlawed and adherents officially harassed and punished even for avowing, let alone for acting on, unauthorized beliefs.

Against this background, it is hardly surprising that the drafters drew the conclusions they did about the indispensability of the "constitutional essentials"—the set of rights, freedoms, and public goods—enshrined in the UDHR and subsequent documents that were designed to prevent the recurrence of fascism, or anything approximating it, anywhere in the world.

■ IMPLICATIONS

This human rights-based version of public reason suggests some responses to the three problems raised in the Introduction to this volume. As to the conviction that human rights as such require a religious foundation, we now have a plausible basis, at least, for disagreeing. The drafters' shared belief in moral grounds for human rights that are freestanding and non-comprehensive, and in that sense secular, shows why religious warrants are not necessary. According to the drafters' rationale, there are good reasons for thinking that certain attempts to justify the use of force—appeals exclusively to self-interest, as well as knowing and avoidable appeals to mistaken evidence and argument—are self-evidently invalid and immoral. So far as devising a set of constitutional essentials worthy of condemning and inhibiting arbitrary force goes, there is no need to appeal to a comprehensive doctrine, religious or otherwise. There are quite adequate secular grounds for doing it, namely, the common "natural" aversion to being subjected to arbitrary force.

The Hitler experience suggests an additional reason why confusing force and comprehensive doctrines is profoundly ill-advised. The relentless effort to enforce a Nazi comprehensive doctrine on the beliefs and practices on Germans and other conquered peoples leaves little doubt that the proper limits of force were massively exceeded. In the light of that experience, it is not hard to understand the impetus for rights to "freedom of conscience, religion, or belief," as well as the rights of free speech, press, assembly, and participation in government, or for provisions for public order, safety, health, and morals that are specifically circumscribed by the protection of rights. These and more are all essential safeguards against the form of collective domination that characterized the fascist experiment.

As a matter of fact, a belief in a set of basic rights, freedoms, and public goods that are taken to be freestanding and non-comprehensive, and that can be identified with the reconstructed version of public reason we have outlined, has strong support in a significant segment of Western Christianity, and, it appears, some developing support in parts of Judaism and Islam as well.[39] So far as Western Christianity goes, it is to the natural rights tradition that we refer. As convincingly demonstrated by recent scholarship, the idea of natural rights by no means originated as an anti-religious doctrine inspired by the eighteenth-century Enlightenment(s), but as a doctrine complementary to Christian revelation, and first developed by medieval monastic theologians and canon lawyers. Furthermore, it was extensively refined and promoted by the Calvinist wing of the Protestant Reformation, and especially by figures associated with Anglo-American Calvinism, like Roger Williams and John Locke.

What is essential is that "from the beginning, the subjective idea of natural rights was not derived specifically from Christian revelation . . . but from an understanding of human nature itself as rational, self-aware, and morally responsible."[40] Natural rights were thus understood as pre-political entitlements available to and binding upon all human beings regardless of religious, ethnic, or other forms of identity. They established standards of political legitimacy according to which well-ordered states would protect equally a set of basic rights, freedoms, and public goods based on the common "natural" interests of all members of the political community, and implying a set of appeals and modes of discourse reminiscent of the idea of public reason we have sketched. Along with rights to freedom of speech, press, assembly, and participation in government, the tradition eventually elevated the rights of the freedom of conscience and religion, thereby endorsing the ideals of tolerance and religious pluralism. Of the greatest importance, natural rights came to be seen as constituting strict limits on a state's exercise of force. In the words of Francisco Suarez, the influential Spanish Jesuit, "the greatest of rights" was the right of self-defense, a right that "inhered in individuals and communities," and that "could be exercised by subjects against a tyrannical ruler."[41]

The second problem raised in the Introduction—the worry expressed by Talal Asad that human rights language represents a grand mystification masking the "secular" or this-worldly and self-serving interests of the modern nation-state—can now rather readily be disposed of. Although Asad notes in passing that German fascism and the record of Nazi atrocities committed during World War II was the basis for drafting and adopting the UDHR, he does not grasp the full significance of those experiences, nor does he understand the true character and implications of the human rights system that was inaugurated in 1948. Above all, human rights were formulated in direct and self-conscious response to a highly exceptional example of "modern secular nationalism," one that had, in fact, gone radically pathological. Fascist Germany is the paradigm case of Asad's image of the modern secular state. Under Hitler, the State arrogated to itself the supreme authority both to define the "true interests" and the "true ideals" of all citizens, including what is an acceptable understanding of religion and morality, and to impose that comprehensive doctrine by means of a thoroughly arbitrary use of force at home and abroad.

Human rights instruments were designed precisely to withstand and prevent the kind of tyrannical nationalism that fascism represented. That would amount to a constitutional democracy enshrining the basic rights, freedoms, and public goods enumerated in the UDHR and subsequent documents. Their fundamental purpose is to prevent within a state the sort of arbitrary force exercised by Hitler, and when supplemented by international humanitarian law and transnational human rights institutions such as the European Court of Human Rights and other agencies, to prevent it internationally as well. While Asad doubts the efficacy of transnational human rights institutions, their record, along with that of other international and national governmental and non-governmental organizations, including the media, is by no means without effect.[42]

Finally, the third problem—Malcolm Evans's claim that a secular approach to human rights leads to a domineering, intolerant, and repressive attitude toward religious belief and practice—is, on the evidence, overstated, if not without some support. Considering the activities of transnational human rights legal and quasi-legal institutions, such as the European Court of Human Rights, the Human Rights Committee mandated by the ICCPR, and the Office of the UN Special Rapporteur, the accomplishments are mixed, though here and there they are moving to overcome the domineering, intolerant, and repressive "secularist" attitudes that Evans fears.

Until recently, the European Court has, it is true, been consistently reticent to protect minority religious beliefs and practices that are regarded as peculiar or unfamiliar. There has been a strong inclination to extend to the State a very large "margin of appreciation" to decide as it sees fit what constitutes an unacceptable "manifestation of conscience" or a threat to public order, safety, health or morals. That results in the allocation of special, often unfair, advantages to the adherents of those comprehensive doctrines that are well-established and widely identified with. In the words of one author, "the European Court [has been] more willing to accommodate State interference with religious freedom than affirm and uphold the measures of protection that have been entrusted to it." Moreover, the "European institutions have undoubtedly accommodated clear instances of State intolerance (particularly against minority religions)."[43]

However, new scholarship demonstrates that the recent practice of the European Court, along with the Human Rights Committee and the Office of the Special Rapporteur, has been given to restricting the discretion of the State, and has extended greater equal freedom to minority religious expression, particularly in regard to matters like taxation, conscientious objection to military service, proselytism, and the right of autonomy for religious groups. The effect is to limit the opportunity for the arbitrary exercise of state authority.

The Human Rights Committee "appears to have been far more consistent than the European institutions" "when applying Article 9 [the right to freedom of religion or belief] of the European Convention and, in particular, has not shown equivalent respect for State restrictions on religious freedom." It has "made a number of critical advances in standards affecting religious freedom in the face of substantial obstacles posed by the demands of the States," which, it appears, can provide constructive guidance. This appears to be true also of the work of the Special Rapporteur whose reports have effectively singled out areas of urgent concern and "could be of invaluable help in enabling the European Court to apprehend more fully the right to [freedom of] religion or belief in the global context and in the light of recurring threats to such practices."[44]

Insofar as more minority religious beliefs and practices are being considered, and, in a growing number of cases, permitted by the transnational legal and quasi-legal human rights institutions, it appears that religious or other fundamental forms of expression are not being abolished from the "public square," nor is a domineering, intolerant, and repressive attitude being encouraged, which are the usual complaints against the idea of public reason. On the contrary, with the expansion of sustained and serious public consideration of religious and other forms of expression, there is reason to hope that a new spirit of tolerance and pluralism will also expand.

NOTES

1 Nicholas Wolterstorff, *Justice: Rights and Wrongs* (Princeton: Princeton University Press, 2008). See Chaps. 13, 14, and 15. In particular, see pp. 15–17, 333–334, 335–340, and 360.

2 Michael J. Perry, *The Idea of Human Rights: Four Inquiries* (New York: Oxford University Press, 1998), esp. 35, 39.

3 David Novak, "Religious Human Rights in Judaic Texts," in *Religious Human Rights in Global Perspective: Religious Perspectives,* ed. John Witte, Jr. and Johan D. van der Vyver (The Hague: Martinus Nijhoff Publishers, 1996), 175–201. In particular, see 177 (original italics), 179, 180, and 200–201.

4 Abdullahi Ahmed An-Na'im, "Toward an Islamic Hermeneutics for Human Rights" in, *Human Rights and Religious Values: An Uneasy Relationship?* eds. Abdullahi Ahmed An-Na'im, et al. (Grand Rapids, MI: Wm. B. Eerdmans Publishers, 1995), 229. Also Abdullahi Ahmed An-Na'im, *Islam and the Secular State: Negotiating the Future of Sharia* (Cambridge: Harvard University Press, 2008), 112.

5 Talal Asad, *Formations of the Secular: Christianity, Islam, and* Modernity (Stanford, CA: Stanford University Press, 2003), 6, 129, 227, 256.

6 Malcolm Evans, *Religious Liberty and International Law in Europe* (Cambridge: Cambridge University Press, 1997), 260–61. See also ibid. 375–76.

7 The effort here to build on and modify Rawls's notion of public reason and human rights has been prompted by discussions with Christian Rice, a doctoral candidate at Harvard University, who, in developing his dissertation on rights and the common good, takes up Rawls in a most insightful way.

8 John Rawls, *Political Liberalism.* (New York: Columbia University Press, 1996), 213, 214, 217.

9 Ibid., 13, 223, 144, 226.

10 Ibid., 170, 194–95.

11 Ibid., 133–172. "Political constructivism," as contrasted with moral realism or "moral constructivism," *à la* Kant, consists of four features that supply the basis upon which political values for citizens of a liberal society are agreed upon: an *impartial procedure*; an emphasis on *practical reason*—thinking about subjects like a just constitutional regime as the object of political endeavor; a *complex conception of person and society,* according to which persons belong "to a political society understood as a fair system of social cooperation from one generation to the next; and a commitment to *the idea of the reasonable*, rather than the idea of truth (Ibid., 91–95, and, generally, Lecture III).

12 Ibid., 147, 216–17.

13 Ibid., 216.

14 Ibid., 213.

15 International Covenant on Civil and Political Rights G.A. Res. 2200A (XXI), 21 U.N. GAOR Supp (No. 16) at 52, U.N. Doc. A/6316, 999 U.N.T.S. 171, *entered into force* March 23, 1976 (hereinafter "ICCPR"), Art. 18 (3) does not mention democracy as such, though Article 25 prescribes several of the conditions of democratic participation in government. Cf. European Convention for the Protection of Human Rights and Fundamental Freedoms, (ETS No. 5), 213 U.N.T.S. 222, *adopted* in Rome, November 4, 1950, *entered into force* September 3, 1953, art. 9(2): "Freedom to manifest one's religion or beliefs shall be subject only to such limitations as are prescribed by law and are necessary in a democratic society in the interests of public safety, for the protection of public order, health or morals, or for the protection of the rights and freedoms of others."

16 ICCPR, Arts. 19, 21, and 22.

17 Unlike ICCPR, Arts. 19, 21, and 22, Article 18 does not include "national security" as a basis for imposing limitations, since the right to freedom of religion or belief is considered non-derogable (Art. 4). See further the chapter by T. Jeremy Gunn herein on permissible limitations on human rights.

18 ICCPR, Art. 20, par. 2.

19 UN Human Rights Committee, "General Comment No. 22: Article 18" (Forty-eighth session, 1993), U.N. Doc. CCPR/C/21/Rev.1/Add.4 (1993). Though the General Comment applies specifically to the term "public morals" in Article 18 (3), it may be assumed to apply similarly to "public order, safety, and health" wherever the terms appear in the covenant.

20 According to the Preamble of the Universal Declaration of Human Rights, "human rights should be protected by the rule of law." See, Universal Declaration of Human Rights, G.A. res. 217A (III), U.N. Doc A/810 at 71 (1948) (hereinafter "UDHR"), Preamble.

21 Johannes Morsink, *The Universal Declaration of Human Rights: Origins, Drafting, and Intent* (Philadelphia: University of Pennsylvania Press, 1999), 287, 289.

22 The point here is that any reference to religious warrants in the UDHR was intentionally eliminated by the drafters. It is true that the Human Rights Committee, an eighteen-member supervisory agency mandated by the ICCPR (Pt. IV) for the purpose of monitoring State Party compliance and issuing General Comments on the meaning of the covenant, has held that Article 18 of the ICCPR does not prohibit the recognition of a "state religion" or one that is "established as official or traditional." However, the committee concomitantly imposed rigorous conditions that in effect challenge the standard prerogatives of a state or established religion; it declares that under a state or established religion there shall be no "impairment of the enjoyment of any of the rights under the Covenant . . . nor any discrimination against adherents of other religions or non-believers." The demand that the understanding of public goods be based on several traditions imposes another condition on standard prerogatives of state or established religion.

23 Morsink, *The Universal Declaration of Human Rights*, 259.

24 Cited in Mary Ann Glendon, *A World Made New: Eleanor Roosevelt and the Universal Declaration of Human Rights* (New York: Random House, 2001), 225.

25 UDHR, Art. 2.

26 In his *The Law of Peoples* (Cambridge: Harvard University Press, 2001), 30ff., Rawls envisions his famous notion of the "original position" as applying in two stages: the first stage relates to individuals faced with the task of agreeing to a system of common benefit where, it is understood, no one's comprehensive doctrine may take precedence over others. The second stage relates to a set of "sovereign peoples" faced with the task of agreeing to an international arrangement between liberal and less liberal peoples ("decent hierarchical peoples" (ibid., 59ff.). In the second stage the critical actors are not individual citizens but the representatives of the national interests of the various peoples concerned. On Rawls's description, the agreement allows substantial deviations from international human rights norms, especially discrimination based on religion or belief (65, fn. 2). According to the ICCPR, Art. 4.1, the right of non-discrimination may under no circumstances be abridged.

27 Rawls, *Political Liberalism*, 97.

28 Martha Nussbaum, *Frontiers of Justice: Disability, Nationality, and Species Membership* (Cambridge: Harvard University Press, 2006), 56.

29 Glendon, *A World Made New*, 161, 230, 232 (where she says that all the framers could do "was to state the truths they believed to be self-evident.").

30 Ibid.

31 Morsink, *The Universal Declaration of Human Rights*, xiii–xiv, 91.

32 Providing considerations in favor of the plausibility of the rationale is all we can attempt here. I have made a fuller attempt to substantiate such an approach in "Ground to Stand On: A Philosophical Reappraisal of Human Rights Language" (forthcoming).

33 UDHR, Preamble.

34 A case of "necessity," where an innocent party must be killed for the sake of the survival of another, is not an exception to this statement since the reasons excusing an act of necessity *must also include proof* that there was no alternative course of action. Such a defense is not "only" a reference to the self-interest of the one using force since it does not utterly disregard the interests of others.

35 Alan Bullock, *Hitler: A Study in Tyranny* (New York: Harper & Row, 1962), 806, 403, and 266.

36 Judgment of the International Military Tribunal for the Trial of German Major War Criminals.

London: His Majesty's Stationery Office, 1951. Shofar FTP Archive File: imt/tgmwc/judgment/j-invasion-belgiumLast-Modified: 1997/09/12.

37 Adolf Hitler, "The Bigger the Lie, the Better," in *Man and the State: Modern Political Ideas*, William Ebenstein, ed. (New York: Rinehart and Co., 1947), 302 (emphasis added).

38 Bullock, *Hitler,* 380

39 See David Little, "Religion, Human Rights, and Secularism: Preliminary Clarifications and Some Islamic, Jewish, and Christian Responses," in *Humanity Before God: Contemporary Faces of Jewish, Christian, and Islamic Ethics,* eds. William Schweiker, Michael Johnson, and Kevin Jung (Philadelphia: Fortress Press, 2006), 256–85.

40 Brian Tierney, *Idea of Natural* Rights (Atlanta: Scholars Press, 1997), 76, 314.

41 Ibid.

42 See, for example, Samantha Power and Graham Allison, eds., *Realizing Human Rights: Moving from Inspiration to Impact* (New York: St. Martin's Press, 2000). See, also, below for a discussion of the contribution of transnational human rights institutions like the European Court of Human Rights to advancing the rights to freedom of religion or belief.

43 Ibid., 351.

44 Ibid., 344, 350–51.

■ RECOMMENDED READINGS

An-Na'im, Abdullahi. *Islam and the Secular State: Negotiating the Future of Sharia* (Cambridge: Harvard University Press, 2009)

Bucar, Elizabeth M. and Barbara Barnett, eds. *Does Human Rights Need God?* (Grand Rapids, MI: Eerdmans, 2005)

Evans, Carolyn *Freedom of Religion Under the European Convention on Human Rights* (New York: Oxford University Press, 2001)

Evans, Malcolm D. *Religious Liberty and International Law in Europe* (Cambridge: Cambridge University Press, 1997)

Krishnaswami, Arcot. "Study of Discrimination in the Matter of Religious Rights and Practices," in *Religion and Human Rights: Basic Documents*, eds. Tad Stahnke and J. Paul Martin (New York: Center for the Study of Human Rights, Columbia University, 1998), 2–55

Lerner, Natan. *Religion, Beliefs, and International Human Rights* (New York: Orbis Books, 2000)

Lindholm, Tore, W. Cole Durham, Jr., and, Bahia G. Tahzib-Lie, eds. *Facilitating Freedom of Religion or Belief: A Deskbook* (Leiden: Martinus Nijhoff, 2004)

Little, David. "A Christian Perspective on Human Rights," in *Human Rights in Africa*, eds. Abdullahi Ahmed An-Na'im and Francis M. Deng (Washington, DC: Brookings Institution, 1990), 51–76

———. "Culture, Religion, and National Identity in a Postmodern World." *Anuario del Derecho Eclesiastico del Estado* 22 (2006): 19–35

———. "Religion, Human Rights, and Secularism: Preliminary Clarifications and Some Islamic, Jewish, and Christian Responses," in *Humanity Before God: Contemporary Faces of Jewish, Christian, and Islamic Ethics*, eds. William Schweiker, Michael Johnson, and Kevin Jung (Philadelphia: Fortress Press, 2006), 256–85

———. "Religious Minorities and Religious Freedom," in *Protecting the Human Rights of Religious Minorities in Eastern Europe*, eds. Peter Danchin and Elizabeth Cole (New York: Columbia University Press, 2002), 33–57

———. "Rethinking Religious Tolerance: A Human Rights Approach," in *Religion and Human Rights: Toward and Understanding of Tolerance and Reconciliation*, eds. David Little and David Chidester (Atlanta: Emory Humanities Lectures, Academic Exchange, 2001)

Perry, Michael J. *The Idea of Human Rights* (New York: Oxford University Press, 1998)

Rawls, John. *Political Liberalism* (New York: Columbia University Press, 1996)

———. *The Law of Peoples* (Cambridge: Harvard University Press, 2001)

Runzo, Joseph, Nancy M. Martin, and, Arvind Sharma, eds. *Human Rights and Responsibilities in the World Religions* (Oxford: Oneworld, 2003)

Sachedina, Abdulaziz. *Islam and the Challenge of Human Rights* (New York: Oxford University Press, 2009)

Stahnke, Tad and J. Paul Martin, eds. *Religion and Human Rights: Basic Documents* (New York: Center for the Study of Human Rights, Columbia University, 1998)

Symposium. "The Permissible Scope of Legal Limitations on the Freedom of Religion or Belief." *Emory International Law Review* 19 (2005): 465–1320

Taylor, Paul M. *Freedom of Religion: UN and European Human Rights Law and Practice* (Cambridge: Cambridge University Press, 2004)

Traer, Robert. *Faith in Human Rights* (Washington, DC: Georgetown University Press, 1991)

Wolterstorff, Nicholas P. *Justice: Rights and Wrongs* (Princeton: Princeton University Press, 2008)

PART TWO

Religion and Modern Human Rights Issues

9 The Phases and Functions of Freedom of Conscience

STEVEN D. SMITH

Conscience, or an inner capacity for judging some actions to be right and others wrong, seems to be virtually coextensive with—and essential to—humanity. Mark Twain observed that "[m]an is the only animal that blushes. Or needs to." And blushing and even more so the need to blush are often enough the painful products of conscience. To put the point more positively, the attribute of conscience is understood by many to be central to what gives human beings a special "dignity."[1]

If conscience is found wherever human beings are, the moral duty to follow conscience is widely accepted as well. Indeed, the duty may be a sort of practical tautology, reducing down (given human fallibility) to something like the proposition that "a person should do what *he believes* to be right"—which in turn seems pretty much equivalent to saying that "a person should do what he believes he should do."

But the subject of this chapter is not simply *conscience*, but rather *freedom of conscience*. And from the observation that people have consciences and the (perhaps tautological) proposition that people should follow their consciences, nothing automatically follows with respect to freedom of conscience. Take it as established: You should do as your conscience admonishes. In itself, this proposition in no way entails that anyone else—the government, for example, or the church—owes any special deference to your (perhaps misguided) exercise of conscience. Thus, medieval authorities such as Thomas Aquinas and the canon law were not balking at logic when they taught that a person should follow conscience, even if its dictates contradicted church teachings, but did not go on to endorse anything like freedom of conscience.[2]

That idea appears to be a more modern phenomenon. This chapter will discuss that phenomenon in three sections, which correspond to three phases in the career of freedom of conscience. Section I will discuss the connection between freedom of conscience and religious toleration. Section II will consider what is often called the problem of free exercise exemptions. Section III will address the travails of freedom of conscience, and the partial but problematic convergence of conscience and autonomy, in an age of secular equality.

■ FREEDOM OF CONSCIENCE AS RELIGIOUS TOLERATION

Freedom of conscience is sometimes traced back to unlikely (and mutually denunciatory) sources—to the stirring statements and defiant deeds of sixteenth-century Protestant reformer Martin Luther in his stand against Church and Empire ("My conscience is captive to the Word of God. … Here I stand; I can do no other. … God help me."[3]) and of English Catholic Thomas More in his fatal refusal to swear acceptance of Henry VIII's divorce and takeover of the English church ("I … leave every man to his own conscience. And methinketh in good faith that so were it good reason that every man should leave me to mine."[4]). Neither Luther nor More supported freedom of conscience in any very fulsome sense; as Lord Chancellor, More vigorously persecuted and sometimes executed Protestants. Nonetheless, in the next century the incipient commitment to freedom of conscience was seized upon, developed, and defended by Roger Williams, Pierre Bayle, Baruch Spinoza, John Locke, William Penn, and a host of less-remembered preachers, politicians, and pamphleteers.[5]

In this first stage of its development, freedom of conscience was virtually synonymous with religious toleration. And far from having the bland and almost platitudinous character that it sometimes carries today, religious toleration was then a suspect and even radical notion. The prevailing assumption, inherited from medieval Christendom, held that religious unity was essential to political community and that governments had the responsibility to suppress heresy and to maintain the one true faith. Even as the Protestant Reformation led to the disintegration of Christendom, these assumptions persisted, often generating official and unofficial violence, international and domestic, among Christians of different theological persuasions. The execution of Michael Servetus for his anti-Trinitarian views in Calvin's Geneva was one vivid expression of this position; the so-called "wars of religion" that convulsed Europe in the sixteenth and seventeenth centuries were another.

Through all this turmoil, the dominant model was that of the "confessional state." That model was ratified in the Peace of Westphalia (1648) under the slogan of *cuius regio, eius religio*: each prince would determine the religion of his own realm. Proponents of toleration, or freedom of conscience, resisted this program of enforced uniformity, and they developed a variety of arguments in support of their position. Three recurring rationales in particular should be noticed: We can call these the incompetence rationale, the voluntariness/futility rationale, and the dual jurisdiction rationale.

The *incompetence rationale* maintained that secular rulers should not enforce religious orthodoxy because they lack competence to judge between truth and error in religious matters. "The one only narrow way which leads to heaven is not better known to the magistrate than to private persons," seventeenth-century English philosopher John Locke declared, "and therefore I cannot safely take him for my guide, who may probably be as ignorant of the way as myself, and who is certainly less concerned for my salvation than I am."[6]

The *voluntariness/futility rationale* argued that the only kind of religion that pleases God and conduces to salvation is a sincere, freely chosen faith—hence the futility of enforced religious conformity. "[T]rue and saving religion consists in the inward persuasion of the mind," Locke insisted, "without which nothing can be acceptable to God. And such is the nature of the understanding that it cannot be compelled to the belief of anything by outward force."[7]

The *dual jurisdiction rationale* reflected the longstanding Christian view that understood God's universe as divided into spiritual and temporal domains, each governed by designated authorities to whom proper respect is due. We must "render unto Caesar the things that be Caesar's," as Jesus had taught, "and unto God the things that be God's."[8] In the Middle Ages, the struggle to liberate God's domain from Caesar's domination had given rise to a papal campaign for *libertas ecclesiae*—freedom of the church. Later, in Protestant realms, some of the spiritual authority formerly vested in the church came to be assigned to the individual conscience. Protestant thinking held, as John Witte explains, that "[e]ach individual stands directly before God, seeks God's gracious forgiveness of sin, and conducts life in accordance with the Bible and Christian conscience."[9] Consequently, the medieval argument that government had no jurisdiction over the affairs of *the church* evolved into the argument that government lacked jurisdiction over *the conscience.*

The eighteenth-century Connecticut legislator and Yale rector Elisha Williams made the point vividly: "[I]f CHRIST be the *Lord* of *Conscience*, the sole King in his own Kingdom; then it will follow, that *all such* as in any Manner or Degree *assume* the Power of directing and governing the Consciences of Men, are justly chargeable with *invading* his rightful Dominion; He alone having the Right they claim."[10]

In the United States, all three of these classical rationales were embraced by advocates of religious toleration and, later, religious equality. James Madison's celebrated *Memorial and Remonstrance* of 1785 condemned the notion that "the Civil Magistrate is a competent Judge of Religious truth" as "an arrogant pretension falsified by the contradictory opinions of Rulers in all ages, and throughout the world" (the *incompetence rationale*). Madison asserted that religious coercion is futile because "the duty which we owe to our Creator and the Manner of discharging it, can be directed only by reason and conviction, not by force or violence" (the *voluntariness/futility rationale*). Explicitly distinguishing the duties owed to "the Universal Sovereign" from obligations owed to "Civil Society," Madison proceeded to draw the jurisdictional conclusion that "Religion is wholly exempt from [Society's] cognizance"(the *dual jurisdiction rationale*).[11]

As we will see, the last of these classical rationales has largely dropped out of modern academic and legal discussions; that is because the Christian worldview informing the "dual jurisdiction" rationale has come to seem implausible or inadmissible in a self-consciously secular discourse. Conversely, the incompetence and voluntariness/futility rationales by now seem so axiomatic to most people in Western societies that many might wonder how Christians could have failed to grasp these obvious truths during the centuries separating Constantine from Madison. But in fact earlier Christian thinkers had not been oblivious to such rationales; they simply found the arguments unconvincing, or overridden by contrary considerations. A closer examination (for which this is not the occasion) just might show that the pre-modern proponents of enforced religious uniformity were not so perversely obtuse, and that the more modern arguments are not so compelling, as we sometimes complacently suppose.[12]

Over time, in any case, the rationales for toleration came to prevail. They prevailed in part on their merits, perhaps, but also because they were reinforced by powerful prudential considerations. The simple fact, to which the various wars and civil wars based on religion gave bloody testimony, was that the religious differences let loose by the Reformation could not be either argued away or forcibly suppressed. Peoples in Europe and America desperately needed to find ways to live together in pluralistic peace. And religious toleration came to seem the most promising response to this challenge.

By later standards, the early enactments of toleration were seriously incomplete. The Edict of Nantes, issued by Henry IV in France in 1598 (and revoked in 1685), granted limited toleration to Protestants but subjected them to significant legal and political restrictions, and it did not extend to Jews or Muslims. In 1689, the English Parliament adopted an Act of Toleration that granted freedom of worship to some dissenting Protestants, but it did not cover Catholics, Quakers, Jews, or Unitarians, and it left even tolerated Protestant dissenters subject to severe political disabilities. A good deal of toleration came to flourish under less formalized arrangements.[13] Officials would turn a blind eye to private worship conducted in dissenters' homes, or would permit dissenters to congregate and worship beyond city walls—in fields or in neighboring jurisdictions. These arrangements allowed for religious toleration and freedom of conscience but relegated religious dissenters to "outsider" status.

In the founding era of the eighteenth-century United States, most state constitutions explicitly affirmed freedom of conscience or freedom of religion, and the First Amendment to the United States Constitution likewise protected the free exercise of religion. But political leaders like Madison argued that protecting conscience under the heading of *toleration* was not enough: American constitutions ought to embrace religious *equality*. If a particular religion is the State's established church, it is hard to say that all religions are being treated equally. Thus, the ideal of religious equality eventually led Americans to adopt non-establishment of religion as a constitutional commitment.[14] Virginia led the way with the enactment in 1786 of Thomas Jefferson's famous Act for Establishing Religious Freedom. Half a decade later, the First Amendment forbade established religion at the national level, and the last states (Connecticut and Massachusetts) had fallen into line by the 1830s.

Although some European nations retained (and still retain) their established churches, by the mid-twentieth century the basic commitment to religious toleration was well entrenched in international human rights documents such as the Universal Declaration of Human Rights. Indeed, before its demise, even the Soviet Union officially recognized a right to freedom of conscience providing that "each citizen independently decides his own attitude towards religion and enjoys the right of confessing any religion either alone or jointly with others, or not to confess any religion, and to express and spread convictions."[15]

■ THE PROBLEM OF FREE EXERCISE EXEMPTIONS

In some parts of the world, the kinds of views and conflicts that troubled early modern Europe remain very much alive: Clashes between Christians and Muslims, for example, or between Muslims and Hindus continue to provoke political turmoil and violence. Christians and other religionists are reportedly regulated or suppressed in China. In these regions, freedom of conscience in the classical sense of religious toleration is an ideal yet to be realized.

In societies that have generally accepted religious toleration, by contrast, freedom of conscience might seem to have completed its work. But in these societies freedom of conscience came to be implicated in a new kind of controversy—the controversy over so-called "free exercise exemptions."

Suppose a government enacts legislation or regulates conduct on the basis of legitimate secular aims, but the regulations have the effect of burdening some people's exercise of their religion. A law commands these believers to do things their religion forbids (such as serving in the army), perhaps, or forbids them to do things their religion requires (such as using particular hallucinogenic drugs as part of their worship). In any large and religiously diverse nation, it is probably inevitable that general laws will sometimes conflict with some citizens' religious commitments. Such conflicts arose early on in American history in connection with Quakers and others who objected on religious grounds to supporting war or to taking oaths in court,[16] and these controversies foreshadowed decades of similar controversies.

These laws are not like the measures against which freedom of conscience was originally deployed; they are not enacted for religious purposes or with the aim of enforcing a religious orthodoxy. Indeed, they are usually based on entirely secular rationales and directed to secular ends. So, does the fact that such laws happen to frustrate some people's exercise of religion present a legal problem? Should believers whose religion would be burdened be presumptively excused from obeying such laws?

The classical rationales for freedom of conscience as *religious toleration* provide only ambiguous support for free exercise *exemptions* from general laws.

Thus, as we have seen, Locke and others argued that governments lack competence to make religious judgments. That rationale seemed pertinent when governments were overtly acting on religious grounds to enforce a religious orthodoxy. But the sorts of laws that are the subject of current controversies—military conscription laws, anti-drug laws, anti-discrimination laws—are not based on religious grounds or animated by religious objectives. Instead, such laws attempt to serve presumptively legitimate secular purposes. Modern secular governments claim no religious competence, in short, so their lack thereof has no obvious relevance to the issue of exemptions.

The same is true of the voluntariness/futility rationale. Locke, Madison, and others argued forcefully that governments could not coercively secure anyone's salvation. But modern governments do not aim at (or, probably, do not even give any thought to) salvation; they seek to secure wholly secular objectives.

The classical rationale that might in theory provide some support for free exercise exemptions is the dual jurisdiction argument. If, as Madison argued, "it is the duty of every man to render to the Creator such homage, and such only, as he believes to be acceptable to him," and if governmental obstruction of the performance of such duties interferes with prior obligations to "the Governor of the Universe," then it would seem that earthly rulers have a powerful reason to avoid burdening the exercise of religion, even for secular ends. In this vein, in offering a contemporary version of Madison's justification, John Garvey argues that religious rationales provide the only plausible justification for giving special legal protection to free exercise of religion.[17]

But these rationales provoke a familiar objection: at least in academic and legal discourse, religious justifications are widely viewed as implausible or inadmissible. Public discourse and public justifications, it is widely assumed, are supposed to be secular. Ironically, the mandate of public secularism is often derived from the very commitment to religious freedom, or non-establishment of religion, that the classical religious rationales helped to secure. In a sense, it seems, religious arguments like the dual jurisdiction rationale have operated to cancel themselves out.[18]

In sum, the classical rationales may support freedom of conscience in its classical sense—namely, religious toleration—and the resulting commitment to "freedom of conscience," secured through an outpouring of ink and sometimes blood, can then be invoked in support of conscience-based exemptions from general, secular laws. But it is arguable that an equivocation is at work here: the meaning of "freedom of conscience" is being subtly altered in the course of the argument.

In the United States, the question of free exercise exemptions has typically been adjudicated under the First Amendment's free exercise clause. Scholars have disagreed about whether the enactors of that clause intended to require such exemptions: some, like Michael McConnell, say yes, while others, like Philip Hamburger, say no.[19] The Supreme Court's answers to the question have fallen roughly into three stages. In the late nineteenth century, when the issue first came before it, the Court ruled that the free exercise clause protects only religious *belief*, not *conduct*. Hence, members of the Church of Jesus Christ of Latter-Day Saints (Mormons) had no free exercise right to practice polygamy, even if they believed the failure to do so would lead to damnation.[20]

In the mid-twentieth century, however, the Court began to suggest that the free exercise clause offered some protection for religious conduct, and eventually, in a 1963 case called *Sherbert v. Verner*,[21] this suggestion was elaborated in the form of a "compelling interest" test. If a law burdens a person's exercise of religion, the Court said, then the person should be exempted from complying unless the government has a compelling or overriding reason and cannot achieve its objective in any less burdensome way.

The "compelling interest" test appeared to provide strong protection for the free exercise of religion—but appearances can be deceiving. In reality, courts struggled with (and against) the *Sherbert* test for almost three decades, most often rejecting claims for free exercise exemptions with the explanation that the believers' practice of religion was not "burdened" in the requisite way, or that the *Sherbert* test did not apply in contexts such as the military or prisons, or that the government's interest in uniform taxation or regulation was sufficient to outweigh a believer's interest in the practice of religion.

In 1990, in *Employment Division v. Smith* (the so-called "Peyote Case"),[22] the Supreme Court largely abandoned the compelling interest test, ruling that so long as a law is "neutral" toward religion and "generally applicable," free exercise exemptions are not constitutionally required. The Court's decision seemed to leave a couple of exceptions open, however, so that later courts have found some room to protect the exercise of religion. In one case,[23] for example, Judge (now Justice) Samuel Alito ruled in favor of Muslim police officers who objected on religious grounds to a police department's "no beards" regulation: If the department exempted officers who had medical reasons for having beards, Alito reasoned, it must likewise exempt officers who have religious obligations to have beards. In addition, the Peyote decision was resoundingly unpopular, and Congress and a number of state legislatures have sought to reestablish a compelling interest test protecting religious exercise as a matter of statutory law.

In international law, freedom of conscience is protected in such statements and conventions as the Universal Declaration on Human Rights (UDHR) and the International Covenant on Civil and Political Rights (ICCPR).[24] At least on paper, these instruments provide significant protection for the exercise of religion and conscience. For example, Article 18 of the ICCPR declares that "[e]veryone shall have the right to freedom of thought, conscience and religion," that this right includes the right "to manifest his religion or belief in worship, observance, practice and teaching," and that "[f]reedom to manifest one's religion or beliefs may be subject only to such limitations as are prescribed by law and are necessary to protect public safety, order, health, or morality or the fundamental freedoms of others."

The appearance of strong protection for religion and conscience may be deceptive, however, just as the ostensible protection offered under the *Sherbert v. Verner* "compelling interest" doctrine was misleading. International law provisions recognizing rights of free exercise and conscience are subject to "limitations clauses" that can give governments considerable latitude to restrict these rights in deference to other public interests. One scholar's study of the work of the Human Rights Committee, charged with implementing and interpreting the International Covenant, led him to conclude that although the Committee's language is often expansive and affirming, in practice the Committee gives little protection to religious freedom. "Perhaps the most abiding impression of an examination of the work of the [Committee] ... is that freedom of religion is, either expressly or by implication, viewed as more of a problem than as an ambition—something which, although doubtless a good thing in principle, is to be viewed with caution."[25]

The issue of conscientious exemption continues to be controversial, in the United States and globally. In the United States, the issue has arisen recently with respect to laws that permit doctors who are religiously opposed to abortion to decline to participate in the procedure, or pharmacists who morally disapprove of contraceptives to refuse to provide them.[26] Similarly, the movement for legalizing same-sex marriage has generated debate about whether and how religious people or churches should be exempted from performing or recognizing such unions.[27] In 2009, such conflicts led a group of Christian leaders and scholars in the United States to issue what they called "The Manhattan Declaration," subtitled "A Call for Christian Conscience."[28] The signatories criticized, "a growing body of case law [that] has paralleled the decline in respect for religious values in the media, the academy and political leadership, resulting in restrictions on the free exercise of religion. We view this as an ominous development, not only because of its threat to the individual liberty guaranteed to every person, regardless of his or her faith, but because the trend also threatens the common welfare and the culture of freedom on which our system of republican government is founded." The Declaration ended on a defiant note: "We will fully and ungrudgingly render to Caesar what is Caesar's. But under no circumstances will we render to Caesar what is God's."

In European nations and Canada, conflict has arisen from the application of laws prohibiting "hate speech" to religious condemnation of homosexual conduct. Another current subject of contention involves religious proselytizing. Some religions, especially Christian denominations, teach the duty of spreading the faith to nonbelievers and persons of other religions; but the targets of such proselytizing may view it as an attack on their own beliefs. If governments respond by attempting to forbid some forms of proselytizing, the potential conflict between law and conscience is apparent.[29]

■ THE DISSOLUTION OF FREEDOM OF CONSCIENCE?

The ultimate outcome of such conflicts is difficult to predict. The uncertainty in part reflects the recently tenuous status of freedom of conscience: even as it has become entrenched in Western law and political thought, freedom of conscience has in a different way come to seem increasingly alien in the modern world. That is because it fits awkwardly with two of the most central modern political commitments—to secular public discourse and to equality.

As noted, it is widely supposed in Western societies that governments ought to be secular in character, and that important political decisions ought to be debated and made on secular grounds. Within this secular framework, the classical rationales for freedom of conscience—and in particular the dual jurisdiction rationale—can come to seem implausible or inadmissible. Proponents of freedom of conscience may accordingly try to replace the classical rationales with more acceptable secular ones. But even if these secular rationales are persuasive—a large *if*—they may have the effect of denaturing freedom of conscience even as they try to maintain it.

One strategy, for example, is to link freedom of conscience to the widespread modern commitment to personal autonomy as a central constitutional value. A partnership between conscience and autonomy can seem natural enough; indeed, the connection can seem virtually irresistible. Go back to the "conscience tautology" noted in the introduction—the tautology in which the duty to follow conscience is understood to mean, basically, that a person should do what *he believes to be right*, which in turn seems equivalent to saying that a person should do what *he believes he should do*. This practical truism can morph into a commitment to personal autonomy as a sort of overriding ideal.

Thus, suppose you start by asserting, "A person should do what she believes to be *right*." How can anyone disagree? Does anyone think people should do what they do *not* believe to be right? Then you change your intonation: "A person should do what *she* believes to be right." Now your initially irresistible admonition has subtly mutated into a Kantian-style injunction to be Enlightened, to "think for yourself," to make your own judgments without reliance on external authorities like tradition or churches or books of scripture.

To be sure, a *non sequitur* seems to be at work here. Why couldn't a person's conscientious judgment—the sensible conclusion of "thinking for herself"—be that what is right is precisely to follow the counsel of some wiser authority? Still, the slippage is subtle and prone to pass without detection, and in this way the conscience tautology may easily merge with the familiar elevation of "personal autonomy" to the status of a sort of master value for modern man.

But attaching freedom of conscience to autonomy may have the effect of both transforming and trivializing the commitment. In its formative period, after all, the commitment to freedom of conscience rested precisely on a belief that people are *not* autonomous, but rather are dependent on—and obligated by—a higher and personal Power, called God. That belief was what justified special respect for people who were acting not just from the normal mundane motives, and certainly not as autonomous agents, but from conscience. Luther, after all, did not declare, "Here I *choose* to stand," but rather "I can do no other." Dissolving conscience into autonomy turns conscience on its head and deprives it of this justification for special respect.

Thus, Marie Failinger remarks that freedom of conscience "began as an argument that government must ensure a free response by the individual called distinctively by the Divine within" but by now "has come to mean very little beyond the notion of personal existential decision-making."[30] In a similar vein, Ronald Beiner suggests that a book on the subject by David Richards demeans the concept of conscience: "The spuriousness of this recurrent appeal to the sacredness of conscience is very clearly displayed in the discussion of pornography. How can this possibly be a matter of *conscience*? What is at issue here, surely, is the sacredness of consumer preferences."

And Beiner goes on to scoff that "[b]y [Richards's] contorted reasoning, the decision to snort cocaine constitutes an act of conscience."[31]

The challenge to freedom of conscience posed by public secularism is compounded by the commitment to equality, which has become perhaps the most powerful theme in contemporary political and constitutional thought. Opponents of free exercise exemptions underscore the apparent inconsistency. If a nonreligious objector to, say, a military conscription law would not be exempted, why should a religious objector receive special treatment? If a single mother who cannot find day care is ineligible for unemployment compensation because she refuses to accept Saturday work, why should a Seventh-Day Adventist be deemed eligible?

The objection is no less powerful for being the effect more of the *rhetorical* than the *analytical* force of equality. Analytically, as Peter Westen has famously argued, equality means that *like* cases should be treated alike, or that *similarly situated* people should be treated similarly.[32] If there is good justification for treating the exercise of religion as a special constitutional commitment, then it would seem to follow that people who act from religious conviction are *not* "similarly situated" to people who act from other motives of different constitutional status. Hence, the argument that exempting religious but not secular pacifists offends equality begs the central question. As a rhetorical matter, nonetheless, question-begging arguments can be immensely powerful. And the substantive questions associated with equality are questions that many people—including legal scholars, and judges—often seem disposed to beg.[33]

The interactions of equality (or, what seems in this context the flip side of the same coin, religious *neutrality*) with freedom of conscience can be complex. Where a regulation contains exceptions calculated to avoid burdening some people on secular grounds, equality can support the argument that religious objections must be equally accommodated: we have already noticed such an instance in the Newark police department case (the "beard" case).[34] Or the logic can run the other way: A commitment to equality may have the effect, at least initially, of *expanding* freedom of conscience to encompass secular as well as religious manifestations of conscience. But whichever way it runs, the expansion may render the enlarged commitment conceptually awkward or even incoherent, and it may also make the commitment to freedom of conscience untenable as a practical matter.

These possibilities were already discernible in the Vietnam War era, as the United States Supreme Court, driven by concerns of equality or neutrality, indulged in some good-hearted hermeneutical violence to construe the draft law's exemption for theistic pacifists to cover sincere secular objectors as well.[35] In essence, the Court expanded the exemption to encompass anyone with a sincere, reflective moral objection to war in general. At the same time, the Court purported to respect the statutory language *which denied* exemptions to men whose objection rested on "essentially political, sociological, or philosophical views, or a merely personal moral code." That denial no doubt reflected the inconvenient reality that in many contexts it would simply not be feasible to excuse anyone who has a "political, sociological, … philosophical … or personal moral" disagreement from complying with general legal obligations. To do that, as the Court has observed elsewhere, would be "courting anarchy."[36] In the draft cases, though, having effectively repudiated Congress's decision to limit the exemption to theistic pacifists, the Supreme Court could give no intelligible account of the difference between the category of objectors who *qualified* for exemptions and the category of objectors who were explicitly *denied* exemptions.

In sum, aspirations to religious equality or neutrality induced the Court to significantly expand the domain of protected conscience but also, in doing so, to render the law less coherent and more vulnerable. If the war and the draft had continued, and if the Court had persisted in exempting all sincere moral objectors, the enlarged exemption might have become practically and politically unsustainable. In this way, the expansion of freedom of conscience in the draft cases may have foreshadowed the eventual diminution of free exercise rights in the Peyote Case.

Moved by similar egalitarian influences, many academic theorists and some jurists have increasingly come to reject free exercise exemptions, or to dissolve such commitments into other more currently respectable commitments such as equality or freedom of speech.[37] Noah Feldman has argued that in religion clause jurisprudence the historical commitment to freedom of conscience has been largely displaced by a commitment to equality.[38] Feldman laments this development, however, and it may be that the displacement is not irreversible. At least in American society, it seems, the ideas of freedom of conscience and free exercise exemptions continue to enjoy considerable popular support; Congressional attempts to overturn the Peyote Case reflect as much. In part this support may be a manifestation of the long-standing nature of the commitment to freedom of conscience and religion: that commitment has arguably become a central part of the American political tradition and self-conception. In part the support may show that classical religious rationales for religious freedom are still influential, even if those rationales are now deemed suspect or inadmissible in more official settings.

In sum, freedom of conscience seems increasingly beleaguered, and perhaps befuddled. But it has hardly retired. Its ultimate fate and shape remain in doubt.

■ CONCLUSION

It is possible that the commitment to freedom of conscience will dwindle in importance. The commitment has surely played a central role in the development of modern understandings of liberalism and human rights. But perhaps that idea has done its work and served its purpose (at least in liberal Western societies). If the rationales that historically supported freedom of conscience are no longer viable, and if its currently justifiable functions can be served by other legal commitments such as equality or freedom of speech, perhaps the sensible course would be to bid freedom of conscience an appreciative, affectionate farewell.

Maybe. But it is also arguable, as I suggested at the outset, that conscience is central to human dignity, and that figures like Locke and Madison who celebrated freedom of conscience were not merely promoting a passing phase in the development of political and constitutional thought; they may have been expounding something vital and eternal about the human species and the human enterprise. If so, then the phasing out of freedom of conscience would represent a tragic loss.[39]

In addition, it may be that freedom of conscience (and perhaps even the classical rationales for freedom of conscience) even yet have valuable work to do in something like their original sense—even in tolerant and "liberal" societies. To be sure, the modern liberal state, as opposed to the old confessional state, no longer purports to impose an orthodoxy laid down by a higher Power or authority. The liberal state not only *is* tolerant (at least in its own estimation); it *defines itself* in terms of toleration, equality, and religious neutrality. But modern states still sometimes reach into people's minds and hearts, or attempt to, to instill what are deemed to be correct beliefs and attitudes. Public school curricula and rituals are an instance; programs in colleges and elsewhere for promoting diversity and multiculturalism (and corollary attitudes) are another; proliferating anti-discrimination policies and laws regulating "hate speech" and "hate crimes"—"hate" designating a category of accordion-like scope—are yet another.

To be sure, the fact that contemporary correctness is not justified by reference to any higher Power or eternal Truth may reduce the risk of old-fashioned oppression. Or perhaps not—because there is no longer any acknowledged higher Truth by means of which a state's policies can be assessed or criticized. And a state that defines itself as tolerant, like a person whose very self-concept includes tolerance and broad-mindedness, may thereby be rendered oblivious to its own parochialism and officiousness.

Against these persistent possibilities, freedom of conscience may continue to provide a potentially valuable base of vigilance and, if necessary, resistance: the Manhattan Declaration is perhaps an instance.[40] And even the classical rationales may continue to resonate, reminding us that government and "Civil Society" are eminently fallible (even, or especially, when they are serenely sure of themselves), that good character and genuine virtue cannot be coercively imposed, and that there is something—a domain within, or above—that transcends the State's or society's legitimate jurisdiction.

■ NOTES

1 For example, the magisterium of the Roman Catholic Church expressed this view in *Dignitatis Humanae* (Of theDignity of the Human Person) December 7, 1965. See further the chapters by Nicholas P. Wolterstorff and Michael J. Perry herein.

2 See Michael J. White, "The First Amendment's Religion Clauses: 'Freedom of Conscience' versus Institutional Accommodation, *University of San Diego Law Review* 47(4) (2010): 1075–1106; Brian Tierney, "Religious Rights: A Historical Perspective," in *Religious Liberty in Western Thought,* eds. Noel B. Reynolds & W. Cole Durham, Jr. (Atlanta: Scholars Press 1996), 29, 37.

3 Noah Feldman argues that Luther's stance was one of the foundations of modern freedom of conscience. Noah Feldman, "The Intellectual Origins of the Establishment Clause," *New York University Law Review* 77 (2002): 346, 357–59.

4 For a discussion of More's views and actions regarding conscience, see Steven D. Smith, "Interrogating Thomas More: The Conundrums of Conscience," *St. Thomas Law Journal* 1 (2003): 580.

5 For an excellent account of these developments, see Andrew R. Murphy, *Conscience and Community: Revisiting Toleration and Religious Dissent in Early Modern England and America* (University Park: Pennsylvania State University Press, 2001).

6 John Locke, *A Letter Concerning Toleration* [1689], in John Locke, *The Second Treatise of Government and A Letter Concerning Toleration* (Mineola, NY: Dover Publications, 2002), 113, 130.

7 Ibid., 119.

8 Luke 20:25 (KJV).

9 John Witte, Jr., *God's Joust, God's Justice: Law and Religion in the Western Tradition* (Grand Rapids, MI: Wm. B. Eerdmans Pub. Co., 2006), 16.

10 Elisha Williams, *The Essential Rights and Liberties of Protestants: A Seasonable Plea for the Liberty of Conscience, and the Right of Private Judgment, In Matters of Religion, Without any Controul from Human Authority* (Boston: S. Kneeland and T. Green, 1744), 12.

11 Ibid.

12 For helpful presentations of the perspectives and rationales that supported intolerance, see Tierney, "Religious Rights"; Benjamin J. Kaplan, *Divided by Faith: Religious Conflict and the Practice of Toleration in Early Modern Europe* (Cambridge: Belknap Press of Harvard University, 2007), 15–72.

13 Ibid., 144–234.

14 Exactly what the constitutional commitment to non-establishment entails is of course a subject of continuing debate.

15 Reprinted in MacClear, *Church and State,* 501.

16 See Michael W. McConnell, "The Origins and Historical Understanding of Free Exercise of Religion," *Harvard Law Review* 103 (1990): 1409, 1467–69.

17 John H. Garvey, *What Are Freedoms For?* (Cambridge: Harvard University Press, 1996), 42–57.

18 For more detailed discussion, see Steven D. Smith, "The Rise and Fall of Religious Freedom in Constitutional Discourse," *University of Pennsylvania Law Review* 140 (1991): 1419.

19 Compare McConnell, "The Origins," with Philip A. Hamburger, "A Constitutional Right of Religious Exemption: An Historical Perspective," *George Washington Law Review* 60 (1992): 915.

20 *Reynolds v. United States,* 98 U.S. 145 (1879).

21 374 U.S. 398 (1963).

22 494 U.S. 872 (1990).

23 *Fraternal Order of Police v. Newark,* 170 F.3d 359 (3d Cir. 1999).

24 See Michael J. Perry's chapter herein.

25 Malcolm D. Evans, "The United Nations and Freedom of Religion: The Work of the Human Rights Committee," in *Law and Religion,* Rex J. Ahdar ed. (Aldershot, U.K.: Ashgate, 2000), 35, 52. See further the chapters by Paul Taylor and Jeremy Gunn herein.

26 See Robert K. Vischer, *Conscience and the Common Good: Reclaiming the Space Between Person and State* (Cambridge: Cambridge University Press, 2010), 155–78.

27 For essays discussing such conflicts, see Douglas Laycock, et al., eds., *Same-Sex Marriage and Religious Liberty: Emerging Conflicts* (Lanham, MD: Rowman and Littlefield, 2008).

28 The Declaration can be found at http://manhattandeclaration.org/the-declaration/read.aspx.

29 For a critical discussion of some of these conflicts, see Rex Ahdar and Ian Leigh, *Religious Freedom in the Liberal State* (Oxford: Oxford University Press, 2005), 374–96. On the problem of proselytizing under international law, see Peter G. Danchin, "Of Prophets and Proselytes: Freedom of Religion and the Conflict of Rights in International Law," *Harvard International Law Journal* 49 (2008): 249.

30 Marie Failinger, "Wondering After Babel," in *Law and Religion,* 94.

31 Ronald Beiner, *Philosophy in a Time of Lost Spirit* (Toronto: University of Toronto Press, 1997), 30.

32 See Peter Westen, "The Empty Idea of Equality?" *Harvard Law Review* 95 (1982): 357.

33 See Steven D. Smith, *The Disenchantment of Secular Discourse* (Cambridge: Harvard University Press, 2010), 26–33.

34 See *Fraternal Order of Police v. Newark.*

35 *United States v. Welsh,* 398 U.S. 333 (1970); *United States v. Seeger,* 380 U.S. 163 (1965).

36 *Employment Division v. Smith,* 494 U.S. 872, 888 (1990).

37 See, e.g., Christopher L. Eisgruber and Lawrence G. Sager, *Religious Freedom and the Constitution* (Cambridge: Harvard niversity Press, 2007); Anthony Ellis, "What is Special about Religion?" *Law & Philosophy* 25 (2006): 219; James W. Nickel, "Who Needs Freedom of Religion?" *Colorado Law Review* 76 (2005): 941, 943.

38 Noah Feldman, "From Liberty to Equality: The Transformation of the Establishment Clause," *California Law Review* 90 (2002): 673.

39 For elaboration of these suggestions, see Steven D. Smith, "Religious Freedom and Its Enemies, or Why the *Smith* Decision May Be a Greater Loss Now Than It Was Then," *Cardozo Law Review* 32(5) (2011): 2033–2054.

40 See note 28 above and accompanying text.

■ RECOMMENDED READING

Dreisbach, Daniel and Kermit Hall, eds. *The Sacred Rights of Conscience: Selected Readings on Religious Liberty and Church-State Relations in the American Founding* (Indianapolis: Liberty Fund, 2009)

Feldman, Noah. "From Liberty to Equality: The Transformation of the Establishment Clause." *California Law Review* 90 (2002): 673

_____."The Intellectual Origins of the Establishment Clause."*New York University Law Review* 77 (2002): 346

Greenawalt, Kent. *Religion and the Constitution: Volume I, Free Exercise and Fairness* (Princeton: Princeton University Press, 2006)

Kaplan, Benjamin J. *Divided by Faith: Religious Conflict and the Practice of Toleration in Early Modern Europe* (Cambridge: Belknap Press of Harvard University, 2007)

McConnell, Michael W. "The Origins and Historical Understanding of Free Exercise of Religion." *Harvard Law Review* 103 (1990): 1409

Murphy, Andrew R. *Conscience and Community: Revisiting Toleration and Religious Dissent in Early Modern England and America* (University Park: Pennsylvania State University Press, 2001)

Smith, Steven D. *The Disenchantment of Secular Discourse* (Cambridge: Harvard University Press, 2010)

_____. "The Tenuous Case for Conscience." *Roger Williams Law Review* 10 (2005): 325

Tierney, Brian. "Religious Rights: A Historical Perspective." in *Religious Liberty in Western Thought*, eds. Noel B. Reynolds and W. Cole Durham, Jr. (Grand Rapids, MI: Wm. B. Eerdmans Pub. Co, 1996), 29

Vischer, Robert K. *Conscience and the Common Good: Reclaiming the Space Between Person and State* (Cambridge: Cambridge University Press, 2010)

Witte, John Jr., *God's Joust, God's Justice: Law and Religion in the Western Tradition* (Grand Rapids, MI: Wm. B. Eerdmans Pub. Co., 2006)

10 Religion and Freedom of Choice

PAUL M. TAYLOR

The key texts in the United Nations instruments which most directly concern religious choice, and which are the primary focus of this chapter, are Article 18 of the 1948 Universal Declaration of Human Rights (UDHR), Article 18 of the 1966 International Covenant on Civil and Political Rights (ICCPR), and Article 1 of the 1981 Declaration on the Elimination of all Forms of Intolerance and of Discrimination based on Religion or Belief (Declaration on Religion). The freedoms which they embody were much in contention in the development of these texts, none more so than on the question of religious choice. This chapter aims to chart both the historical developments within the UN and some contemporary challenges facing the freedom of choice in religious matters. It also aims to demonstrate the numerous facets of religious choice that are not obvious from the face of those texts.

DISTINCTIVE FEATURES OF THE FREEDOM

To put this discussion in context, at least three distinctive features of the freedom of religion as expressed in Article 18 of the ICCPR deserve comment at the outset since they all bear directly on religious choice and operate to enhance the protection afforded by Article 18 in the scheme of related rights.

First, certain constituent rights within the freedom of religion cannot be restricted under any circumstances. These are the right of every individual to have complete free choice in religion (including the right to choose a particular religion for the first time, to change from one religion to another, to become an agnostic or an atheist) and the right not to be subject to coercion which would impair that choice. Only the right of "manifestation" can be restricted, i.e., the freedom of each person "either individually or in community with others and in public or private, to manifest his religion or belief in worship, observance, practice and teaching." Even then it is also clear that the freedom of outward manifestation of religion may only be restricted in tightly prescribed circumstances and subject to strict preconditions, that is, those that "are prescribed by law and are necessary to protect public safety, order, health, or morals or the fundamental rights and freedoms of others."[1]

Secondly, Article 18.3 is unique among so-called limitation provisions for its inclusion of the word "fundamental" when identifying the grounds on which manifestation of religion may be restricted. If the "rights and freedoms of others" are to be the legitimate basis of State restrictions on the manifestation of religion, they must be "fundamental." Among the most conspicuous forms of religious manifestation, and central to religious choice, is the promulgation of belief by various means and by assorted names including proselytism, evangelism, and teaching. These are protected activities under Article 18.3, under the rubric of "worship, observance, practice and teaching" (see discussion in this chapter below under the heading *Manifestation of Religious Choice*) and clearly should not be restricted on the basis of rights that are not characterized as "fundamental."

Thirdly, Article 18 is distinctive in that it is among very few rights that are non-derogable. This is explained by Article 4, which permits contracting states to take measures derogating from their obligations under the Covenant in times of officially proclaimed public emergency which threatens the life of the nation, to the extent strictly required by the exigencies of the situation. What is particularly interesting about the treatment of Article 18 among the non-derogable rights is that the whole of Article 18 is non-derogable, not just those parts that, according to the terms of Article 18, may not be restricted (on grounds of "public safety, order, health, or morals or the fundamental rights and freedoms of others"). This, coupled with the fact that public emergency situations must be so extreme in order to be a basis of derogation from other freedoms under Article 4, at least may suggest that the permissible limitations in Article 18.3 should not be lightly invoked.

These distinctive features are central to the nature of the freedom and are important to keep in mind when considering the elements of religious choice, how they were developed, and the variety of ways they are under challenge in practice.

■ THE ELEMENTS OF RELIGIOUS CHOICE: KEY TEXTS, CORE RIGHTS

The Right to Change Religion

The development of Article 18 of the UDHR, Article 18 of the ICCPR, and much of the Declaration on Religion was not without its struggles, especially on the question of the right to change religion. Article 18 of the UDHR states, in the clearest possible way, that "[e]veryone has the right to freedom of thought, conscience and religion; this right includes freedom to change his religion or belief." However, this formula could not later be repeated in the drafting of Article 18 of the ICCPR as a result of concerns from certain countries (Saudi Arabia in particular) that the text should also emphasize freedom to maintain a religion. In order to avoid any religious choice becoming final and permanent, which would in effect restrict further choice, the text was ultimately settled to read: "This right shall include freedom to have or to adopt a religion or belief of his choice."

The text of the Declaration on Religion is couched in terms of "*freedom to have a religion or whatever belief of his choice*" as a result of continuing concerns (by Egypt, Iraq, Kuwait, and Saudi Arabia) that even the ICCPR's phrase "*or to adopt*" still placed too much emphasis on a right to change religion. Those concerns were met in the final text, even though it clearly imports the right to change from any one religion to another or to adopt a religion for the first time. In the interests of progressing the draft, those who favored the ICCPR's more explicit formula conceded, but only on the basis that the text of the Declaration on Religion was understood to entitle everyone to have or adopt their religion of choice as Article 18 of the ICCPR provided.

The debates in the context of the Declaration on Religion serve to emphasize the already clear interpretation of Article 18 of the ICCPR so as to include a right to change religion. At the same time there was no dilution of standards, given the adoption in the Declaration of Article 8, which states that "*[n]othing in the present Declaration shall be construed as restricting or derogating from any right defined in the Universal Declaration of Human Rights and the International Covenants on Human Rights.*" Partsch commented on the UDHR and ICCPR debates that "[i]n the extended discussions, one element stands out as of utmost importance. No one who favored deleting the express mention of the right to change one's religion denied that right."[2] It is also worth observing that no country entered any reservation to Article 18 of the ICCPR even though it would have been possible to do so. The Human Rights Committee's interpretation of Article 18 is clear from paragraph 5 of General Comment No. 22, which states that: "the freedom to 'have or to adopt' a religion or belief necessarily entails the freedom to choose a religion or belief, including, *inter alia*, the right to replace one's current religion or belief with another or to adopt atheistic views, as well as the right to retain one's religion or belief."[3] The effect is to remove any ambiguity that may have resulted from the reformulation of the freedom in the ICCPR.

Freedom from Coercion in Religious Choice

Added to this, of course, is the fact that both the ICCPR and Declaration on Religion each include an express freedom from coercion that would impede religious choice. Article 18.2 of the ICCPR reads: "No one shall be subject to coercion which would impair his freedom to have or to adopt a religion or belief of his choice." It was originally proposed by Egypt to alleviate the concerns of those countries which wanted to dampen the emphasis on an explicit right to change religion and which also considered a simple right to change religion to be too one-sided and to favor missionaries and proselytizers. The amendment was accepted as simply making explicit something that was already implied and provided that it was not restrictive of the freedom of teaching, worship, practice, and observance, that it did not prevent persuasion or appeals to conscience, or preaching and seeking to influence a person either to maintain or to change his religion, and that it did not restrict argument and discussion (in other words, these activities of themselves were not to constitute coercion).

The Human Rights Committee's interpretation of Article 18.2 is provided in paragraph 5 of General Comment No. 22 and puts clear emphasis on coercive force, in contrast to appeals to conscience and exposure to the teachings of other religions, missionary activity, and so on, in specifying that:

> Article 18.2 bars coercions that would impair the right to have or adopt a religion or belief, including the use or threat of physical force or penal sanctions to compel believers or non-believers to adhere to their religious beliefs and congregations, to recant their religion or belief or to convert. Policies or practices having the same intention or effect, such as for example those restricting access to education, medical care, employment or the rights guaranteed by article 25 and other provisions of the Covenant are similarly inconsistent with article 18.2. The same protection is enjoyed by holders of all beliefs of a non-religious nature.

Contemporary examples of such coercion take extreme, as well as more subtle, forms. Recent illustrations of more extreme forms of coercion from the mandate of the Special Rapporteur on Freedom of Religion or Belief (in examining incidents and governmental action incompatible with the Declaration on Religion) include reports of alleged death threats made by local authorities in the Lao People's Democratic Republic against Christians if they did not give up their faith; allegations that members of a banned church in Eritrea were arrested for taking part in Christian worship in a private home, two of whom later died in a nearby army camp as a result of torture to impel them to abandon their faith; allegations that the Indonesian Office of Religious Affairs attempted to force members of the local Baha'i community to recant their faith by threatening to burn their houses and suggesting that their safety could not be guaranteed; allegations that prison guards in the U.S. attempted to force four Muslim detainees in Rikers Island jail in Queens, NY, to become Christians; and allegations that in the Lao People's Democratic Republic a pastor and two church members were held in wooden stocks with handcuffs and leg restraints as a consequence of not signing documents to renounce their faith after three opportunities to do so.[4]

Examples of allegations of coercion in relation to economic, social, and cultural rights include allegations that in the Lao People's Democratic Republic the police prevented Christians from tending their rice fields—they burned those rice fields and took citizenship papers in a climate of persecution that was so intense that it allegedly succeeded in forcing the believers to officially renounce their Christian faith; that the Ministry of Defense in Eritrea put pressure on a prominent Christian singer to sign a statement renouncing her faith and promising to cease her participation in any Christian activities in Eritrea; that in Iran, universities were instructed to expel any student who was discovered to be a Baha'i, whether at the time of enrollment or in the course of their study; and the marginalization of Muslim children wearing traditional dress in the French public school system as a result of recent French legislation banning religious signs in public schools.[5] The Human Rights Committee, in *Raihon Hudoyberganova v. Uzbekistan*, recently examined a similar complaint that all students wearing the *hijab* at the Tashkent State Institute for Eastern Languages were "invited" to leave their courses and to study at the Tashkent Islamic Institute instead. The Committee considered that "to prevent a person from wearing religious clothing in public or private may constitute a violation of article 18, paragraph 2, which prohibits any coercion that would impair the individual's freedom to have or adopt a religion. As reflected in the Committee's General Comment No. 22 (para. 5), policies or practices that have the same intention or effect as direct coercion, such as those restricting access to education, are inconsistent with article 18, paragraph 2."[6]

This is to be contrasted with the European Court's unusual approach of permitting wide discretion to states (including through the doctrine of "margin of appreciation") so that, for example, in *Şahin v. Turkey* the European Court upheld restrictions on the wearing of the *hijab* at a secular university on the grounds of "public order" and "the rights and freedoms of others" of the same faith who might feel pressure to conform.[7]

In practice, it may be difficult to determine whether a particular violation falls under Article 18.1 or 18.2. As a rule of thumb, however, Article 18.1 typically entails restrictions on the freedom to change (or maintain) religion or adverse consequences for those that do; Article 18.2 violations typically are marked by the element of coercion. Issues of apostasy may fall under either Article and (amid concerns at prohibitions on a change of religion) have been raised by both by the Human Rights Committee when considering state reports in relation to Morocco, Yemen, and Sudan,[8] and by the Special Rapporteur in communications addressed to Malaysia, Afghanistan, Iran, and Jordan.[9]

On occasion, a violation of Article 18.2 might also be a violation of the right to manifest religion under Article 18.3, as illustrated by the *hijab* cases noted above and the European Court case of *Ivanova v. Bulgaria*. In *Ivanova*, the applicant was dismissed from her position as a swimming pool manager in a school because of her religious beliefs and membership of "Word of Life," an organization that had been the subject of an aggressive media campaign calling for the dismissal of particular followers, including the applicant. The applicant claimed that official school inspectors had threatened that if she did not resign of her own accord or did not renounce her faith, she would be dismissed on disciplinary grounds. In finding a violation of Article 9, the European Court emphasized the primary importance of the right to freedom of thought, conscience, and religion and the fact that a state cannot dictate what a person believes or take coercive steps to make him change his beliefs.[10]

Manifestation of Religious Choice and the Rights and Freedoms of Others

The forms of manifestation commonly and most closely associated with religious choice are those which involve conveying the elements of one's faith with a view to convincing others of the truth or value of that faith. For present purposes, this may be termed "proselytism." Missionary work may involve proselytism but is perhaps more typically characterized by the provision of humanitarian or other services motivated by religious belief and by which the expression of that belief is conspicuous in its practical application.

Two questions that immediately arise are, first, whether both activities are legitimate and protected forms of religious manifestation and, secondly, whether and in what circumstances may these activities conflict with the freedom of religious choice (or indeed different rights) of others?

In response to the first question, it would appear that proselytism has been long recognized as a legitimate form of religious manifestation, evident throughout the Special Rapporteur's mandate but including among recent communications those addressed to Turkmenistan over the arrests of Jehovah's Witnesses for discussing their faith with others, Bhutan where those screening the film "Jesus" were arrested because proselytism of any religion is prohibited in order to maintain and preserve society's harmony, and Uzbekistan, where recently introduced legal amendments restricted the right to promote the Bible outside prayer houses and the "pastor" of the church to which a person who does that belongs can be fined or punished.[11] Furthermore, the Special Rapporteur recently gave supportive acknowledgment to actions aimed at persuading others to believe in a certain religion and noted that "[t]he question of missionary activities and other forms of propagating religion has been at the centre of the mandate on freedom of religion since the beginning."[12]

The Human Rights Committee has also indicated its support for missionary work, for example, in *Joseph* et al. *v. Sri Lanka*, when a group of Catholic nuns engaged in teaching and other charity and community work claimed that the refusal to allow the incorporation of their Order constituted a breach of Article 18 of the ICCPR. The Committee observed that "for numerous religions, including according to the authors, their own, it is a central tenet to spread knowledge, to propagate their beliefs to others and to provide assistance to others. These aspects are part of an individual's manifestation of religion and free expression, and are thus protected by article 18, paragraph 1, to the extent not appropriately restricted by measures consistent with paragraph 3."[13]

Similarly, the jurisprudence of the European Court under Article 9 of the European Convention is unambiguously supportive of proselytism by any religion that equates with "true evangelism . . . an essential mission and a responsibility of every Christian and every Church."[14]

In response to the second question, however, one limit which must be observed at all times (not just in the case of proselytism) is that defined by the need to observe the right of others to be free from coercion in religious choice. This is a point taken up by the European Court in *Kokkinakis v. Greece* which distinguished "true evangelism" from so-called "improper proselytism." The latter represented a corruption or deformation of it, which may "take the form of activities offering material or social advantages with a view to gaining new members for a Church or exerting improper pressure on people in distress or in need; it may even entail the use of violence or brainwashing; more generally, it is not compatible with respect for the freedom of thought, conscience and religion of others." In short it recognizes the limits of proselytism in the rights and freedoms of others.

This particular statement has been much criticized for its uncertainty, especially since it was invoked in *Kokkinakis* merely to construct a rationale for a finding of violation on the narrowest possible grounds. This was in keeping with a practice, for which the European Court has more generally been reprehended in academic literature, of developing principles which allow wide discretion to states in the use of limitation provisions, both through permitting a wide margin of appreciation, or range of discretion, to states, and in its almost automatic acceptance of claims by states to be pursuing a "legitimate aim." For example, in *Kokkinakis*, the Court accepted that the aim of laws might be designed to punish extreme or "improper" proselytism when that sort of proselytism was never at issue. The distinctively European approach in permitting states broad latitude represents a marked departure from UN jurisprudence, even though it is clear that conventional proselytism is unequivocally treated as a legitimate form of manifestation.

The dissenting judges in *Kokkinakis*, unhappy with the way in which the European Court dealt so narrowly with this issue, grappled in more detail than the majority did with the interaction between the right to proselytize and its appropriate limits. A valuable description of the balance between the right of manifestation through proselytism and the corresponding rights and freedoms of others is that provided by Judge Pettiti in his partly concurring opinion in *Kokkinakis*, when he observes that, "[b]elievers and agnostic philosophers have a right to expound their beliefs, to try to get other people to share them and even to try to convert those whom they are addressing. The only limits on the exercise of this right are those dictated by respect for the rights of others where there is an attempt to coerce the person into consenting or to use manipulative techniques."

Judge Martens (partly dissenting in *Kokkinakis*) was rather more skeptical about the supposed coercive effects of proselytism when commenting that, "[c]oercion in the present context does not refer to conversion by coercion, for people who truly believe do not change their beliefs as a result of coercion; what we are really contemplating is coercion in order to make somebody join a denomination and its counterpart, coercion to prevent somebody from leaving a denomination. Even in such a case of 'coercion for religious purposes' it is in principle for those concerned to help themselves."

From a UN perspective, Natan Lerner usefully observed as follows, when commenting on the newly settled text of the Declaration on Religion after some hard fought debates on the subject of coercion:

> Coercion in religious matters is always a grave violation of human rights. The use of coercion to induce others to adopt a religion which is not theirs or to abandon their own beliefs has played a particularly horrible role in the history of mankind. The condemnation of coercion in the field of religious rights is thus beyond controversy. . . . The question of freedom of propagation of one's religion and the legitimacy of attempts to convince others of one's religious truth is different. In modern human rights law, the right to change one's religion, in the absence of coercion and as a result of free will is considered a recognized freedom. [15]

The particular conditions in which certain proselytizing or mission activities occur are important, since these activities may enliven the rights of others in one context but not in another. For example, the European Court in *Larissis and other v. Greece* upheld restrictions on proselytism by members of the armed forces directed at lower-ranking colleagues, on the basis that "what would in the civilian world be seen as an innocuous exchange of ideas which the recipient is free to accept or reject, may, within the confines of military life, be viewed as a form of harassment or the application of undue pressure in abuse of power."[16] Yet restrictions on the same form of proselytism directed at civilians constituted a violation. Clearly the military context in this case was decisive for the European Court.

Nevertheless, the special circumstances in which proselytism sensitizes the rights and freedoms of others represent the exception and are relatively confined. The Special Rapporteur was recently prompted to examine the impact of missionary work in her report on a visit to Sri Lanka following a number of complaints after the 2004 Indian Ocean tsunami about "unethical conversions" by those offering material benefits such as food and medicine to the most poor and vulnerable.

> 43. The description of the behavior complained of is not clear, but has mainly to do with a feeling that the religious groups that are the objects of complaint deceive people because they are not totally transparent about their motivations. It is claimed, in particular, that some groups promise material benefits such as food and medicine, bicycles or even housing. In some cases, assistance was promised with getting a job or an authorization to build a house.
>
> 44. It is claimed that those who are the most sensitive to these appeals are the poorest sections of the population. Therefore, it is felt by many that those actions are a form of manipulation and abuse of the most vulnerable.
>
> 45. After the tsunami, it was reported that in the east of the country many have converted for health reasons because medical assistance and supplies were brought in by Christian non-governmental organizations and groups. However, a significant number converted back to their original religions later, which sometimes provoked negative reactions from the community.

> 46. Even members of those Christian communities whose beliefs are relatively close to those being complained of told the Special Rapporteur that it was true that some Evangelical Churches were conducting a rather aggressive form of proselytism with which Sri Lankans were not familiar and which disturbed them. Many, including Christians themselves, emphasized that the Buddhists and Hindus have a far less proactive attitude in propagating their religion.
>
> 47. Members of the communities blamed for aggressive proselytism have categorically denied using any coercive methods. Most have also denied using unethical methods, but a few have argued that inducement is central to all beliefs, like the promise of reward for being pious and adhering to the tenets of one's belief. They claimed that there was inducement in all conversions like there was inducement in all political campaigns before elections, but ultimately the choice lies with every individual."[17]

In assessing these complaints, the Special Rapporteur commented that incidents of conversion and proselytizing were usually vaguely described and unclear with regard to the circumstances. She did not meet any person who had changed their religion because of allurement or other form of inducement and was not aware of any substantiated cases that would constitute a violation of the right to freedom of religion or belief, such as forced conversions. At worst, it would seem, that the conduct was very disrespectful and dishonest towards the local population they were addressing, and culturally insensitive and lacking respect for the beliefs of Sri Lankans.[18] Nevertheless, in her view this did not constitute violation of the freedom of religion of others. She described the reaction to this activity as "sharp and alarmist"; by contrast, the resulting acts of violence and threats against the Christian community were characterized as clearly in violation of their freedom of religion or belief.

Nevertheless, the Special Rapporteur did make recommendations that religious groups should separate their religious work from their humanitarian efforts, and where necessary, to avoid disturbing religious harmony, they should respect other religious beliefs in their missionary activities and not use aggressive forms of proselytizing.[19] This does not imply that failure to do so would constitute a violation, since it is clear that the underlying concern (as noted in the Rapporteur's general report on her mandate) is for the broader interests of tolerance, such that, "apart from forcible and other conversions that are improper in the sense of human rights law, there are many cases which, while not constituting a human rights violation, nevertheless raise serious concern because they disturb a culture of religious tolerance or contribute to the deterioration of situations where religious tolerance is already being challenged."[20]

This visit also gave the Special Rapporteur opportunity to examine Sri Lankan's legislative proposals to criminalize certain acts leading to "unethical" conversions. These proposals had been mooted for years and were not an immediate reaction to events following the tsunami. Support for them was drawn from Article 9 of the Constitution which states that "The Republic of Sri Lanka shall give to Buddhism the foremost place and accordingly it shall be the duty of the State to protect and foster the Buddha *Sasana*, while assuring to all religions the rights granted by Articles 10 and 14(1)(e) [freedom of religion in terms similar to the International Covenant]." In the case of one of the proposals the Supreme Court of Sri Lanka ruled as unconstitutional only one or two non-central aspects (such as the requirement that a person who is converting and any person performing or involved in a conversion ceremony must report to the authorities) but otherwise let it pass to the next legislative phase.

The Special Rapporteur concluded that the Supreme Court decisions supporting the proposals were "in the realm of conjecture or speculation that the disadvantaged or vulnerable would be subject to improper conversion." She remained doubtful about claims of violation resulting from inducements (in the absence of any convincing proof). Her emphasis then shifted to concern for a different dimension of the element of choice of the person proselytized, namely their right to convert even in response to an inducement and she pointed out that impairment in that choice would be a violation, since "[w]hile some maintain that freedom of religion, and in particular the right to choose a religion, may be violated in cases where, for example, a person in need has converted after having received presents and inducements that may significantly improve his or her life, the enjoyment of that right by the same person may equally be impaired if he or she does not have the possibility to freely decide to convert to another religion, even after having received a gift."[21]

The Sri Lankan proposals agitate many of the issues raised in *Kokkinakis* but dealt with inadequately by the European Court's judgment. Judge Martens, in his partly dissenting opinion in *Kokkinakis*, questioned the propriety of any legislation directed even against "improper proselytism." "Admittedly, the freedom to proselytise may be abused, but the crucial question is whether that justifies enacting a criminal-law provision generally making punishable what the State considers improper proselytism." He answered this in the negative: "the State, being bound to strict neutrality in religious matters, lacks the necessary touchstone and therefore should not set itself up as the arbiter for assessing whether particular religious behaviour is 'proper' or 'improper.'" The Human Rights Committee has similarly expressed concerns about anti-proselytism laws, for example in relation to Uzbekistan when noting de facto limitations on the right to freedom of religion or belief, including the fact that proselytizing constitutes a criminal offence.[22]

In an overview of violations and other issues associated with a change of religion the Special Rapporteur emphasized one further aspect of the coexistence of, as she put it, "the right to freedom of religion of those who take the decision to convert (freedom of conscience and the right to change one's religion) and the right to freedom of religion of persons who perform acts leading to the conversion of others (missionary activities and the propagation of one's religion)." It is that the right to change religion is absolute and is not subject to any limitation whatsoever, and that any legislation that would prohibit or limit the right to change one's religion would be contrary to international human rights standards.[23] The Special Rapporteur has also repeatedly contrasted the breadth of the freedom to propagate one's religion with the narrowness with which certain limitations may be imposed in accordance with article 18.3 of the ICCPR, by stressing

> that this article allows for restrictions only in very exceptional cases. In particular the fact that it mentions the protection of "*fundamental* rights and freedoms" (emphasis added) of others as a ground for restriction indicates a stronger protection than for some other rights whose limitation clauses refer simply to the "rights and freedoms of others" (e.g. article 12, 21 and 22). It could indeed be argued that the freedom of religion or belief of others can be regarded as such a fundamental right and freedom and would justify limitations to missionary activities, but the freedom of religion and belief of adults basically is a question of individual choice, so any generalized State limitation (e.g. by law) conceived to protect "others'" freedom of religion and belief by limiting the right of individuals to conduct missionary activities should be avoided. . . . The test of legality of a prohibition of any act motivated by belief or religion is therefore extremely strict.[24]

These comments were deliberately confined to questions of individual choice affecting adults. Quite different principles apply in relation to children in so far as it is necessary to respect the rights of parents and guardians in the education of children.

Parental Choice in the Education of Children

The State's obligations under Article 18.4 of the ICCPR "to have respect for the liberty of parents and, when applicable, legal guardians to ensure the religious and moral education of their children in conformity with their own convictions," according General Comment No. 22.6, "is related to the guarantees of the freedom to teach a religion or belief stated in Article 18.1." Even though "related" to the freedom to teach a religion or belief, the right is far from equivalent to it since it is clear from paragraph 8 that "the liberty of the parents and guardians to ensure religious and moral education cannot be restricted." Teaching, as a form of manifestation, by contrast, is capable of limitation (in strictly prescribed circumstances).

Violations might take the form of an entrenched state tradition in public education, such as in Norway where the constitution stipulated that individuals professing the Evangelical-Lutheran religion were bound to bring up their children in the same faith.[25] Violations might also include practices or trends in religious education that result in limited access to secular education. Such was the case in Ireland where the Human Rights Committee was concerned that the vast majority of Ireland's primary schools were privately run denominational schools that adopted a religiously integrated curriculum that afforded insufficient access to secular primary education for those who wanted it.[26]

This right is quite unlike other rights within Article 18 and is more commonly linked to issues of discrimination, largely because one of the issues that is closest to the surface in education, especially in the public sector, is that of curriculum-based religious instruction, which frequently conflicts with parental convictions. General Comment No. 22.6 resolves this by requiring that non-discriminatory exemptions or alternatives be made available in public schools, so that children may avoid receiving the conflicting teaching, since "article 18(4) permits public school instruction in subjects such as the general history of religions and ethics if it is given in a neutral and objective way. . . . The Committee notes that public education that includes instruction in a particular religion or belief is inconsistent with article 18(4) unless provision is made for non-discriminatory exemptions or alternatives that would accommodate the wishes of parents and guardians."

Compulsory instruction of religious subjects should respect the convictions of parents and guardians who do not believe in any religion.[27] Moreover, any scheme of exemption from instruction in a particular religion must be practicable (without unduly burdening the parents) and ensure that exempt pupils are not required to perform religious observance such as the learning by heart of prayers, singing hymns, and attendance at religious services.[28] The same principles do not apply in the private sector, particularly in the context of faith-based schooling.

Article 18.4 also interacts with the requirements of non-discrimination in the terms on which state funding is provided, if it is provided at all. A claim was successfully made before the Human Rights Committee in *Arieh Hollis Waldman v. Canada* [29] under Article 26 (non-discrimination) of the ICCPR because full state funding was available for Roman Catholic schools in Ontario but not for Jewish private schools. Article 18.4 does not impose any obligation on the State to support non-secular schools but if financial support is available for private faith-based schools, for example to recognize the fact that the State is spared the burden and cost of education for those taken out of the public system, support must be available without discrimination.[30]

Discrimination and Religious Choice

The interaction between principles of non-discrimination and religious choice in Article 18 is extremely important. Non-discrimination, even on grounds of religion, has the potential to vitiate Article 18 rights. For example, an over-simplistic approach to non-discrimination in the employment context would admit no distinctions on grounds of religion. Yet it would be perfectly absurd to imagine that, for example, leadership of churches, mosques, synagogues, and temples must be open to candidates of any religion (or none). Distinctions of a religious kind are obviously necessary based on the requirements of the position. The same may be true of appointments within religious organizations formed in exercise of any of the following forms of religious manifestation in Article 6 of the Declaration on Religion:

(a) To worship or assemble in connection with a religion or belief, and to establish and maintain places for these purposes;

(b) To establish and maintain appropriate charitable or humanitarian institutions; . . .
(e) To teach a religion or belief in places suitable for these purposes; . . .
(g) To train, appoint, elect or designate by succession appropriate leaders called for by the requirements and standards of any religion or belief.

All of these activities are immediately relevant to religious choice in that, in the absence of the ability of religious groups to function through these means, the collective expression of the religion in question is not available in any form, group participation in the religion is not feasible, nor is meaningful membership of the religious community. Collective forms of manifestation are what create religious communities. The need for places of worship is undeniable but they would be stripped of all value if not supported by the freedom to teach according to the doctrines of the faith in question coupled with the freedom to appoint leaders who are best equipped to discern and expound those doctrines. Similarly with other religious organizations: leaders, teachers, and others in significant roles are often selected on the basis of the values espoused by the community in order to give expression to the community's religious wishes and beliefs. This is fundamental to religious choice on a collective level. Distinctions based on religion are not only inevitable but to one degree or other are integral to the right to manifest religion and to basic choice in religion.

The freedom of manifestation has much in common with the freedom in Article 18.4 in the context of religious schools established to give effect to parental wishes to ensure the religious and moral education of their children in conformity with their own convictions. In the case of faith-based private schools, there may be an expectation that staff with a teaching function or position of influence would be members of the founding religion of the school, if not also be able to demonstrate positive commitment to that religion, as a condition of employment. Much depends on the character of the school or other institution, in particular the extent to which it is established for religious purposes. But there comes a point at which the essential character and purpose of the institution may be entirely lost by an impaired ability to make distinctions based on religion in pupil selection or in employment by virtue, for example, of the need to avoid conflict with the religious susceptibilities of pupils or parents, the inherent requirements of the work or to maintain the mission-oriented focus of the institution.

The principles of non-discrimination in Articles 2.1, 3 and 26 of the ICCPR are reconcilable with the sort of distinctions that are unavoidable in such matters as the appointment of religious leaders, the teaching of religion, and in establishing and maintaining religious institutions. Those principles do not mandate a total ban on differentiation on religious grounds. General Comment No. 18 (on non-discrimination)[31] provides the Human Rights Committee's interpretation of the term "discrimination." It does not require the avoidance of all distinction on any recognized ground (such as race, color, sex, language, or religion) but *only where* a distinction has the purpose or effect of impairing the recognition, enjoyment, or exercise by all persons, on an equal footing, of all rights and freedoms. The Committee also pointed out that the enjoyment of rights and freedoms on an equal footing does not mean identical treatment in every instance, observing that "not every differentiation of treatment will constitute discrimination, if the criteria for such differentiation are reasonable and objective and if the aim is to achieve a purpose which is legitimate under the Covenant."[32]

Both General Comment No. 22 and the Human Rights Committee decisions themselves answer the Article 18.4 requirements in the school curriculum by differentiation. Thus, schools provide exemptions or alternatives to those who need to avoid the conflicting teaching, and provide state aid for all faith-based schools, not just selected religious schools. The Committee used a similar principle of differentiation in cases of conscientious objection to military service (which the Committee considers is derived from Article 18), by allowing conscientious objectors alternative forms of non-combat service. The thrust of the Committee's approach is to embrace the need for differentiation, but in such a way that the practical operation of any scheme of differentiation is not discriminatory. In the same way that limitation provisions "must not be applied in a manner that would vitiate the rights guaranteed in Article 18," it would be nonsensical to suggest that principles of non-discrimination may do so.

As Western societies increasingly shift towards secular state models and are shaped by and give expression to secularist viewpoints and culture, greater will be the need for differentiation to ensure that Article 18 freedoms are not stifled. Examples abound of discrimination on the basis of religion that is sufficient to vitiate religious choice. They may take overt or subtle forms, they may be direct or indirect, and they may take the form of discrimination in relation to any number of rights but all are important to apprehend as violations of the fundamental right to free choice in religion. Discrimination is perhaps most pervasive when it takes the form of systematically undermining particular faiths as a deterrent to joining or continued participation in those faiths. Adherents are often held in public contempt or find it virtually impossible to exhibit any evidence of their religious choice without recrimination, with the inevitable result that only the most convinced believers remain in their chosen faith. Illustrations that most explicitly involve such discrimination affecting religious choice include the incessant accounts of repression, torture, and imprisonment of Falun Gong members in China in attempts to force them to renounce their belief; allegations of the detention of Christians in Eritrea solely because of their faith and aimed at forcing them to abandon their beliefs; and reports from refugees from the Democratic People's Republic of Korea that parents were afraid to pass on their faith to their children and that churches lead an entirely underground existence under constant threat of punishment.[33]

Registration requirements for religious communities can similarly have a powerful effect in eradicating particular groups from the religious landscape, notably the smaller or more recently founded minorities, with corresponding impacts on religious choice. Basic citizenship rights are commonly the basis of discrimination against particular religious groups. In Saudi Arabia and in provisions for a draft Constitution in the Maldives, for example, it is allegedly not possible for non-Muslims to obtain citizenship. In Malaysia, a change of religious identity would be denied because ethnic Malays are defined as Muslims under the Constitution.[34] In some countries, key official documents (identity cards, passports, and birth certificates) cannot be obtained by members of certain religious groups or not easily, with the consequence that, among other things, they experience difficulties in gaining access to higher education, health care, and public sector employment, they cannot open bank accounts, or easily run a business, and in the case of passport requirements are denied freedom of movement.[35] Marriages by those of certain religions are not registered in some countries, nor are inter-religious marriages (so that in Malaysia, for example, a Muslim designation on an identity card would prevent marriage to a Christian), with consequences both for marriage and succession rights. In Costa Rica, only Catholic marriages have civil effect.[36] Religious affiliation is required on official documents in many countries, which is against the right not to manifest one's religion, and the rights under Article 17.1 of the ICCPR to be free from arbitrary or unlawful interference with privacy. In some countries, only limited preselected options of religious affiliation are available, such as in Egypt where only Islam, Christianity, and Judaism are mentioned, with the added consequence that those not falling within those categories are forced to lie about their religious affiliation in order to obtain a card, which is a criminal offence. Changes to official documents to reflect a change of religion may also result in other adverse consequences. In all of these instances, the discriminatory denial of basic rights on the ground of religion is the consequence of the choice to remain affiliated to that religion, and the consequence also for anyone who makes the choice to change to such a religion.

■ CONCLUSIONS

Freedom of religious choice, as a fundamental guaranteed right, has many more facets than the text of the key articles of international human rights instruments would suggest. It is not enough to enact in perfect constitutional, statutory, or codified terms a simple right to freedom of choice without also rendering it free of any ambiguity that it includes freedom to change religion in any circumstances and freedom from coercion that would restrict that choice. Religious manifestation is also central to religious choice, particularly in the area of proselytism, both from the perspective of the exponent and the absolute right of others to take the decision to convert in response. Among the most insidious forms of coercion or pressure in religious choice is the pervasive effect of discrimination against a chosen religion. Thus freedom of religious choice, if it is to have any value, must also be underpinned by guarantees against non-discrimination among other things on the ground of religion. Even that guarantee is insufficient without suitable recognition that certain forms of discrimination should more properly be considered as restrictions on religious choice and altogether impermissible. At the same time, principles of non-discrimination should not be applied in such a way as to vitiate Article 18 rights, particularly those based on religious choice.

■ NOTES

1 See Jeremy Gunn's chapter herein for further commentary.

2 K.J. Partsch, "Freedom of Conscience and Expression, and Political Freedoms," in *The International Bill of Rights: The Covenant on Civil and Political Rights,* ed. Louis Henkin (New York: Columbia University Press 1981), 211.

3 United Nations Human Rights Committee, "General Comment No. 22: Article 18," Article 18 (Forty-eighth session, 1993), U.N. Doc. CCPR/C/21/Rev.1/Add.4 (1993), par. 5.

4 Descriptions of these incidents are provided in the reports of the UN Special Rapporteur on Freedom of Religion or Belief at: U.N. Docs: E/CN. 4/2005/61/Add. 1 (2005), par. 162; A/HRC/4/21/Add. 1 (2007), par. 132; A/HRC/7/10/Add. 1 (2008), par. 112; A/HRC/7/10/Add. 1 (2008), par. 280; A/HRC/10/8/Add. 1 (2009), par. 129.

5 Descriptions of these incidents are provided in the reports of the UN Special Rapporteur on Freedom of Religion at: U.N. Docs: E/CN. 4/2005/61/Add. 1 (2005), par. 163; A/HRC/4/21/Add. 1 (2007), par. 129; A/HRC/10/8/Add. 1 (2009), par. 91; E/CN. 4/2005/61 (2004), par. 68.

6 *Raihon Hudoyberganova v. Uzbekistan,* Communication No. 931/2000, U.N. Doc. A/60/40 (Vol. II) (2005), par. 6.2.

7 *Şahin v Turkey,* 44 EHRR 5 (2007) (EctHR, 2005-XI, 175, November 10, 2005) (Grand Chamber Judgment), pars. 108–09. See further the chapter by Carolyn Evans herein.

8 See the following reports of the United Nations Human Rights Committee. U.N.Docs: HRC A/60/40 (Vol. I) (2005) par. 84(21); HRC A/60/40 (Vol. I) (2005) par. 91(18); HRC A/62/40 (Vol. I) (2007) par. 88(26).

9 See following reports of the UN Special Rapporteur on Freedom of Religion or Belief at: U.N. Docs. : E/CN. 4/2006/5/Add. 1 (2006), par. 246; A/HRC/4/21/Add. 1 (2007), pars. 4–6; A/HRC/10/8/Add. 1 (2009), par. 95; E/CN. 4/2006/5/Add. 1 (2006), par. 216 & A/HRC/10/8/Add. 1 (2009), par. 113.

10 *Ivanova v. Bulgaria* (ECtHR, April 12, 2007), par. 79.

11 See the following reports of the UN Special Rapporteur on Freedom of Religion or Belief, U.N. Docs: E/CN. 4/2005/61/Add. 1 (2005), par. 273; A/HRC/4/21/Add. 1 (2007), par. 69–73; A/HRC/4/21/Add. 1 (2007), par. 335.

12 See the report of the UN Special Rapporteur on Freedom of Religion or Belief at U.N.Doc. A/60/399 (2005).

13 *Immaculate Joseph* et al. *v. Sri Lanka,* Communication No. 1249/2004, U.N. Doc. A/61/40 (Vol. II) (2006), p. 347, par. 7.2. See also *Kang v. Republic of Korea,* Communication No. 878/1999, U.N.Doc. A/58/40, Vol. II (2003), 152 where the distribution of communist leaflets was recognized by the Human Rights Committee as the manifestation of a belief.

14 *Kokkinakis v. Greece,* 17 EHRR 397 (1994) (ECtHR 260-A, May 25, 1993), par. 48.

15 N. Lerner, "The Final Text of the UN Declaration against Intolerance and Discrimination Based on Religion or Belief," *Israel Yearbook on Human Rights* 12 (1982): 185, 188.

16 *Larissis and Others v. Greece*27 EHRR 329(1998) (ECtHR, 1998-I, no. 65, Feburary 24, 1998), par. 51.

17 Report of the UN Special Rapporteur on Freedom of Religion or Belief, U.N. Doc. E/CN. 4/2006/5/Add. 3 (2005).

18 Ibid., par. 50.

19 Ibid., par. 120.

20 Report of the UN Special Rapporteur on Freedom of Religion or Belief, U.N. Doc. A/60/399 (2005), par. 66.

21 Report of the UN Special Rapporteur on Freedom of Religion or Belief, U.N. Doc. E/CN. 4/2006/5/Add. 3 (2005), par. 73.

22 Report of the UN Human Rights Committee, U.N. Doc. HRC A/60/40 (Vol. I) (2005) par. 89(22).

23 Report of the UN Special Rapporteur on Freedom of Religion or Belief, U.N. Doc. A/60/399 (2005), pars. 57 and 58.

24 Report of the UN Special Rapporteur on Freedom of Religion or Belief, U.N. Doc. A/60/399 (2005), paras. 62–63, repeated in numerous later reports eg concerning India and Uzbekistan.

25 Report of the UN Human Rights Committee, U.N. Doc. HRC A/61/40 (Vol. I) (2006), par. 81(15).

26 Report of the UN Human Rights Committee, U.N. Doc. HRC A/63/40 (Vol. I) (2009), par. 84(22).

27 *Folgerø and Others v. Norway,* 46 EHRR 47 (2008) (ECtHR, June 29, 2007).

28 *Leirvåg et al. v. Norway*, Communication No. 1155/2003, U.N. Doc. A/60/40 (Vol. II) (2005), 203.

29 *Arieh Hollis Waldman v. Canada*, Communication No. 694/1996, 7(2) I.H.R.R. (2000), p. 368.

30 For an interesting English finding of unlawful discrimination in the oversubscription policy of a voluntarily aided Jewish school, which gave priority to children recognized as Jewish according to matrilineal descent or conversion in accordance with the tenets of Orthodox Judaism (but not the claimant's non-Orthodox conversion), see *R (on the application of the E) v JFS Governing Body* [2009] UK SC 15. See further the chapter by Natan Lerner herein.

31 UN Human Rights Committee, "General Comment No. 18: Non-discrimination," (Thirty-seventh session, 1989), Compilation of General Comments and General Recommendations Adopted by Human Rights Treaty Bodies, U.N. Doc. HRI/GEN/1/Rev.6 at 146 (2003).

See also recent comments of the Special Rapporteur when individuals or groups in the same situation are treated differently as well as when individuals or groups are treated in the same way although their situation is different at U.N. Doc. HRC. 10/8 (2009), at par. 31.

32 Ibid., pars. 8, 13. For further discussion on the subject of discrimination, see Nazila Ghanea's chapter herein.

33 Report of the UN Special Rapporteur on Freedom of Religion or Belief, U.N. Docs. : E/CN. 4/2005/61/Add. 1 (2005), par. 64; A/HRC/4/21/Add. 1 (2007), par. 132; E/CN. 4/2005/61/Add. 1 (2005), par. 74.

34 Report of the UN Special Rapporteur on Freedom of Religion or Belief, U.N. Docs. A/63/161 (2008), par. 29; A/HRC/10/8/Add. 1 (2009), par. 146; A/HRC/10/8/Add. 1 (2009), par. 136.

35 Report of the UN Special Rapporteur on Freedom of Religion or Belief, U.N. Doc. A/63/161 (2008), pars. 31–36.

36 Report of the UN Human Rights Committee, U.N. Doc. HRC A/63/40, Vol. I (2009), par. 75(10).

RECOMMENDED READING

Amor, Abdelfattah. "The Role of Religious Education in the Pursuit of Tolerance and Non-discrimination," and the "Final Document of the International Consultative Conference on School Education in Relation to Freedom of Religion or Belief, Tolerance and Non-Discrimination," U.N. Doc. E/CN. 4/2002/73, Appendix (November 23–25, 2001)

Baer, Richard A., Jr. and James C. Carper. " 'To the Advantage of Infidelity' or How Not To Deal With Religion in America's Public Schools." *Educational Policy* 14(5) (2000): 600

Dickson, B. "The United Nations and Freedom of Religion." *International and Comparative Law Quarterly* 44 (1995): 327

Jack, H. A. *The UN Declaration for Religious Freedom: The Result of Two Decades of Drafting* (New York: W.C.R.P., 1981)

Lerner, Natan. "The Final Text of the UN Declaration against Intolerance and Discrimination Based on Religion or Belief." *Israel Yearbook of Human Rights* 12 (1982): 185

_____. "Proselytism, Change of Religion, and International Human Rights." *Emory International Law Review* 12 (1998): 477

_____. *Religion, Beliefs and International Human Rights* (Maryknoll, NY: Orbis Books, 2000)

Liskofsky, Sidney. "The UN Declaration on the Elimination of Religious Intolerance and Discrimination: Historical and Legal Perspectives," in *Religion and the State: Essays in Honor of Leo Pfeffer* ed. James E. Wood, (Waco, TX: Baylor University Press 1985), 441

Ramcharan, B. G. "Religious Witness and Practice in Political and Social Life as an Element of Religious Liberty," in *The Right to Religious Liberty: The Basic ACLU Guide to Religious Rights,* eds. Barry W. Lynn, Mark D. Stern, and, Oliver S. Thomas (Carbondale, IL: Southern Illinois University Press 1995)

Sears, J. T. and J. C. Carper, eds. *Curriculum, Religion and Public Education: Conversations for an Enlarging Public Square* (New York: Teachers' College Press, 1998)

Sullivan, D. J. "Advancing the Freedom of Religion or Belief through the UN Declaration of the Elimination of Religious Intolerance and Discrimination." *American Journal of International Law* 82 (1988): 487

ODIHR Advisory Council of Experts on Freedom of Religion or Belief "Toledo Guiding Principles on Teaching about Religions and Beliefs in Public Schools." (Warsaw: OSCE Office for Democratic Institutions and Human Rights, 2007), accessible online at: www.osce.org/odihr/29154

Walkate, J. A. "The Right of Everyone to Change His Religion or Belief—Some Observations." *Netherlands International Law Review* 30 (1983): 146

_____. "The UN Declaration on the Elimination of All Forms of Intolerance and Discrimination Based on Religion or Belief (1981)–An Historical Overview." *Conscience and Liberty* 1(2) (1989): 21

11 Religion and Freedom of Expression

CAROLYN EVANS*

If freedom of religion were to disappear overnight from the various treaties, constitutions, and statutory bills of rights in which it is currently found, much that is currently protected as religion could equally be covered as a manifestation of freedom of expression. While religion certainly has its contemplative internal dimension, most religions are also communicative in a variety of ways. Religious individuals may pray together, sing or chant, read from holy works, teach their children, write religious works of various kinds, preach, protest, and proselytize—all examples of free speech as well as the free exercise of religion. Additionally, religions make use of the realm of symbolic expression in a variety of ways: in religious dress, the display of religious symbols, the performance of religious rituals, and the wearing of religious items and particular hairstyles. These too are covered by the notion of freedom of expression in many jurisdictions.

While some forms of religious expression have remained beyond the realm of legitimate State intervention in democracies, others have proved much more contentious. One area of contention is proselytism or missionary activity: religious speech and associated activities that aim to convert others to the religion of the speaker. This is covered in the chapter herein by Paul Taylor. The current chapter explores several other areas of particular contention with respect to the overlap between freedom of expression and religion, in particular, the wearing of religious dress or symbols, hate speech and religious defamation, prayer or religious education in public schools, and religious symbols in public institutions.

WEARING RELIGIOUS CLOTHING OR SYMBOLS

Many religious believers feel either obligated by their religion or have a strong religiously motivated desire to wear clothing or religious symbols that express their adherence to a particular religion. Practices that some members of a religion may adopt include the wearing of a turban and *kirpan* (religious knife) by Sikh men, wearing a headcovering for Muslim and Jewish women, Rastafarians wearing their hair in dreadlocks, Jewish men wearing a yarmulke, and Christians wearing a cross.[1] Individuals within the same religion may have different conceptions of what is required by their religion in this respect. For example, the English case of *SB v. Denbigh High*[2] involved a Muslim student who wished to wear the stricter *jilbab* rather than the *shalwar kameeze* school uniform for Muslim girls that had been developed in consultation with the school's Muslim community. The case revealed some of the different opinions of Muslims within the school, and within the local and the national community, about what form of religious dress was appropriate or required for an adolescent Muslim girl. In addition to garb adopted by ordinary religious believers, some religious offices may involve the wearing of particular robes, vestments, or symbols of office in a manner that differentiates them from lay members of the same religion. The United Nations Human Rights Committee has recognized that displaying religious symbols or "the wearing of distinctive clothing or headcoverings" is a manifestation of religion and thus protected in international law.[3]

Decisions about whether a form of religious dress or symbolism will be worn should essentially be individual ones. Naturally, various religious organizations and leaders will have particular views about these issues and may seek to convince adherents of their merits (and may even refuse to allow membership of the community to those who do not adhere to them). The state, however, does not have a role in instantiating one form of religious orthodoxy as state law. In some countries, such imposition of orthodoxy is quite overt. Women are forced to veil themselves in countries including Iran and Saudi Arabia regardless of whether or not they believe that this is required of their religion and indeed regardless of their religion. According to the report of the United Nations Special Rapporteur on Freedom of Religion or Belief, for example, the Iranian Chief of Police claimed that "in 2006 more than one million women were stopped relating to the way they wear the *hijab* (Islamic veil) and 10,000 charged for violating the dress code."[4] Such coercion limits both the religious and expressive freedom of the individuals involved, as well as posing a serious intrusion into liberty and gender rights.

The converse situation is beginning to arise in several countries, particularly in Europe, where Muslim women who wish to wear the headscarf are increasingly being denied the right to do so.[5] The space for women wearing the headscarf appears to be diminishing in some European countries, and there have also been moves against wearing the headscarf in schools in countries such as Singapore.[6] In one of the first cases in the European Court of Human Rights to consider the issue, the Court found that it was reasonable to require a primary school teacher to remove her headcovering, in part because of the vulnerability of her young students to proselytism.[7] However, in less than ten years, the Court also approved a Turkish law that prevented a medical student from studying at university with her head covered and a French law that prevented a French secondary school student from attending a public school with her head covered, despite the fact that there was no issue of vulnerable students in those cases.[8] Those cases were notable for the desire to prohibit the headscarf being linked to the messages that it was said to communicate—messages of proselytism, fundamentalism, and gender inequality—and little thought appeared to be given by the Court as to whether (even if the significant assumption that such controversial linkages were justified is accepted) there was sufficient justification for banning the expression of such views. The cases instead focused solely on the religious dimension of wearing the head covered.

There have recently been moves towards even more comprehensive limitations that would effectively preclude a woman with wearing a veil that covers her face from entering many public spaces in countries including France, Belgium, and Italy. Political proponents of such laws in some of these countries have also fallen into the error of assuming that they can determine what is required by a religion. For example, the Italian Equal Opportunities Minister Mara Carfagna claimed the prohibition on the wearing of *burqas* was not a restriction on religious freedom because they were not religious symbols. She referred to pronouncements by Muslim clerics to validate this claim, saying that "that is not us saying it, but the top religious authorities of the Islamic world, like the imams of Cairo and Paris."[9] This claim, however, misses the point. There is certainly a school of thought that says that veiling is not required by Islam, but there are other schools of thought that claim that it is. This is an important internal debate within Islam, but it is not for the Italian government to determine the outcome of this religious debate and impose this on Italian Muslims, any more than it is the place of the Iranian government to enforce the opposite religious viewpoint.

However, a range of other reasons have been given to justify restrictions on religious clothing and symbolism. While they cannot be examined in detail here, several of the more significant are worth noting.[10] One is public security or safety. Sometimes such limitations are quite specific and justified. For example, a Sikh man who was charged with a violent crime was prohibited from wearing his *kirpan* to court because of the risk that he might use it in a manner that endangered others; this decision was upheld on appeal. By contrast, a Sikh schoolboy who was prohibited from wearing his *kirpan* to school under a general prohibition on knives in school (and despite his willingness to take steps to limit the danger caused by the *kirpan*) was held by the Canadian courts to have had his rights violated.[11] The Canadian experience demonstrates the feasibility of a nuanced approach to the wearing of religious symbols and matters of safety, rather than blanket claims that any or no restrictions are possible. At other times, broader claims are made about the danger that religious clothing poses to national security, particularly about Islamic veils that cover the face. Such veils are sometimes claimed to be associated with fundamentalism or to allow for breaches of national security (generally in an unspecified manner). The French Conseil d'Etat recently warned that French proposals to ban such clothing generally on the basis of national security were not proportionate or targeted to a demonstrable threat to public safety and would thus be likely to be in breach of religious freedom as protected under the European Convention on Human Rights (ECHR).[12]

Another common reason given for banning the Islamic headscarf is that wearing it is inconsistent with women's rights. This question is itself a source of debate within the Muslim community, with some Muslim women's groups supportive of banning some or all forms of veiling in order to promote women's rights and others opposed. In one of the leading European Court of Human Rights cases on the right of a student to wear a headscarf at university, the majority of the Court held that one of the reasons that justified the law forbidding the wearing of head-scarves in certain Turkish public institutions was the importance of the equal rights of men and women. However, the Court gave little by way of explanation of whether and how the wearing of a headscarf perpetuated gender inequality. In her dissenting opinion, Judge Tulkens wrote:

> [The] wearing [of] the headscarf is considered synonymous with the alienation of women. The ban on wearing the headscarf is therefore seen as promoting equality between men and women. However, what, in fact, is the connection between the ban and sexual equality? The judgment does not say. Indeed, what is the signification of wearing the headscarf? As the German Constitutional Court noted in its judgment of September 24, 2003, wearing the headscarf has no single meaning; it is a practise that is engaged in for a variety of reasons. It does not necessarily symbolise the submission of women to men and there are those who maintain that, in certain cases, it can even be a means of emancipating women. What is lacking in this debate is the opinion of women, both those who wear the headscarf and those who choose not to.[13]

In some cases, a related concern is that the religious clothing is not being worn voluntarily but because of pressure, possibly even threats of violence, by family or community members. This is particularly relevant in cases involving school girls, and there is evidence that some Muslim girls in some schools are supportive of limits or bans on religious clothing because otherwise they may come under pressure or criticism for failing to comply with stricter religious cloth-ing codes.[14] The relationship between religious freedom and gender rights is a complex and contested one that is given more detailed consideration in the chapter herein by Madhavi Sunder. For present purposes, it is sufficient to note that the promotion of the equal rights of men and women is a permissible ground for limiting religious freedom under international law. But care should be taken to ensure that there is a rational connection between the promotion of women's rights and the protective measures selected and that these measures are propor-tionate to the harm suffered. Women from minority religious communities, in particular, can suffer from state paternalism and from ignorance or stereotypes that lead to more legal intervention in their lives and greater regulation of their religious expression than occurs for women from majority communities.

■ RELIGIOUS HATE SPEECH AND DEFAMATION OF RELIGION

Another complex intersection between religion and expression has been the debate about whether (and, if so, how) the State should deal with forms of expression that subject religions, or religious individuals, to hate, contempt, ridicule or negative stereotyping. Article 20(2) of the International Covenant on Civil and Political

Rights (ICCPR) requires that: "Any advocacy of national, racial or religious hatred that constitutes incitement to discrimination, hostility or violence shall be prohibited by law."[15] States parties are thus obligated to implement laws that prohibit what is sometimes known as religious hate speech or religious vilification.

Such laws have a complicated relationship with both freedom of religion and freedom of expression. On the one hand, the advocacy of hatred against minority religions can play a significant role in creating conditions in which discrimination, hostility, or even genocide can thrive. These dangers are particularly acute in deeply divided communities, where religious groups exist in a state of tension with one another, or where religious persecution has been present in the past. When a minority religious community feels threatened and under attack, the capacity of individuals to exercise their religion freely and without fear is undermined. Threats, intimidation, and religious hate speech may also make it difficult for members of minority groups to speak out on issues of importance to them, even limiting their capacity to use speech to stem the hate speech, if they fear that doing so will make them the target of abuse or even violence.

However, overly broad enactments of prohibitions of religious hatred may also be problematic from the point of view of both religious freedom and free speech.[16] Religious speech may well itself constitute religious hatred of a very dangerous kind—it has certainly been known for religious leaders to be among those who have whipped up hatred against other religious groups, advocated violence and legitimized discrimination. However, there are forms of religious speech that may well be caught up in religious hatred laws that create concerns for freedom of religion. Within some religious traditions, for example, the denunciation of the errors of other religions and the proclamation of the sole truth of the speaker's religion is an important manifestation of religious conviction. Yet, particularly if religious hatred laws are drafted in wide terms, such speech could be construed as religious hatred. In a controversial case in Australia, for example, two Christian pastors from a small evangelical church had a civil complaint brought against them under the Racial and Religious Tolerance Act 2001 for a variety of statements made at a seminar on Islam and in some publications. The statements made were extensive and wide-ranging. They included the suggestions that in Islam "there is not much value of woman" and that the people we call terrorists "actually they are true Muslim [*sic*] because they have read the Qur'an . . . and now they are practising it," and they implied that money is derived from drug sales to sponsor Muslim proselytism and that Muslims in Australia had doubled their population in seven years because they control the Immigration Department.[17] The cumulative effect of these statements was held at first instance to amount to religious vilification. The decision was appealed to the Victorian Court of Appeal which overturned it, but did not determine whether the speech was vilifying or not.[18] A particularly problematic feature of the decision at first instance was the reliance by the tribunal on controversial aspects of Islamic law, such as whether Islam was "really" a religion of peace or "really" encouraged discrimination against women. While some of the wilder claims made by the pastors (such as the doubling of the population and taking over of the Immigration Department) were factually untrue and inflammatory, other claims were intemperate but still a matter for debate and discussion rather than a determination by the tribunal as to their "truth." The case illustrates the problems that can arise with such legislation when judges may be asked to make some difficult decisions as to what is acceptable, robust (maybe even offensive or hurtful) debate on controversial matters, and what crosses the line into creating hate of a kind that may lead to violence or other forms of harm.[19]

Religious hate laws also run the risk of cutting short passionate but publicly important debates, including debates that would not be caught by the legislation, for fear of breaching it. (This is sometimes known as the "chilling effect" of legislation that restricts freedom of expression; people may self-censor because they fear the possibility of litigation.) When speakers, including both those supportive of a particular religion and those deeply critical of religion in general or a specific religion, are fearful about the consequences of speaking their minds, an important public debate on an important social phenomenon is stifled.

An even more problematic approach to protecting religions from offensive expression has been the development of the notion of the "defamation of religion." This concept, which appears to build on human rights notions such as the prohibitions of hate speech, racism, and xenophobia, was first put forward in the Commission on Human Rights at its 62nd meeting in April 1999 by Pakistan on behalf of the Organization of the Islamic Conference,[20] and in the General Assembly at its 81st plenary meeting in December 2006 by Azerbaijan on behalf of the Organization of the Islamic Conference.[21] Since that time, non-binding resolutions condemning defamation of religion have been passed many times by the Commission of Human Rights and its successor, the Human Rights Council. It has, however, been controversial since its inception. The March 25, 2010 resolution, for example, passed by only 20 votes to 17 with 8 abstentions[22] and a resolution on the freedom of religion adopted on March 24, 2011, contained no reference to the defamation of religion at all.[23] Defamation of religion is an amorphous concept and the resolutions relating to it encompass a number of issues on which there is a high degree of international consensus and strong support in international human rights law, for example, the need to combat discrimination, violence, or intimidation of people on the basis of their religion and to protect religious sites from attacks. While the resolutions focus on the protection of individuals or groups from violations of their human rights, they fall within the human rights mainstream. Where they become more controversial is when they recommend that legal measures be taken to protect the reputation of a religion itself. For example, the first resolution on defamation passed by the Human Rights Council expressed concern that the media was inciting "intolerance and discrimination towards Islam and any other religions." It also expressed deep concern at the "negative stereotyping of religions" and that "Islam is frequently and wrongly associated with human rights violations and terrorism."[24] While such stereotyping of religions certainly can lead to hostility against followers of a religion, there is a danger that such protection of religion as such can protect religions from legitimate criticism, questioning, debate, or internal dissent. A joint statement by three of the United Nations Special Rapporteurs with responsibilities in the area of religion, racism, and speech set out the concern as having to do with "the difficulties in providing an objective definition of the term 'defamation of religions' at the international level make the whole concept open to abuse. At the national level, domestic blasphemy laws can prove counterproductive, since this could result in de facto censure of inter-religious and intra-religious criticism. Many of these laws provide different levels of protection to different religions and have often proved to be used in a discriminatory manner."[25]

The concept of the defamation of religion has been the subject of considerable political and scholarly criticism, particularly the concern that it can be seen as a justification for blasphemy and apostasy laws. It has been used in practice to justify punishments by Muslim states for effectively religious crimes such as blasphemy, heresy, and apostasy and to protest about Islamaphobia (but not other forms of religious hate) in non-Muslim countries.[26] Indeed, the first draft resolution on defamation of religions, which was introduced by Pakistan, only condemned "new manifestations of intolerance and misunderstanding, not to say hatred, of Islam and Muslims," and there was some debate and resistance to reframing it in more religiously neutral terms.[27] The most recent resolution from the Human Rights Council singles out the need to protect Muslims many times but makes no mention of other forms of common religious persecution including that suffered by religious minorities in Muslim states.[28] Religious hate laws are intended (even if they do not always succeed) to protect vulnerable religious minorities from the personal consequences of vilification. The extension beyond hate laws to the concept of defamation of religions, however, may be used to shore up the power and authority of the religious majority and its political and religious hierarchy. By adopting the institutions of international human rights and aligning some of the language in the defamation of religion resolutions with the language of human rights, those states that have supported the development of the concept of the defamation of religion have sought to legitimize actions that would otherwise be breaches of freedom of religion and expression.

The danger posed by the argument that religious orthodoxy requires state protection is far from hypothetical. In recent reports, the United Nations Special Rapporteur on Freedom of Religion or Belief has noted the widespread use of domestic laws to enforce particular religious viewpoints and to punish those who are seen to deviate from them. Recent reports have described the prosecution of the Ahmadiyya communities in countries including Pakistan and Indonesia for "deviant" teachings of Islam; the widespread use of blasphemy laws in Pakistan against religious minorities and Muslims who question accepted orthodoxy; the introduction of the death penalty in Iran for apostasy; the prohibition on private religious education in Kazakhstan; and the forcing of Christians to destroy their own churches and religious symbols in Myanmar.[29] The language of defamation or hurt feelings of religious majorities is increasingly being used in such countries to justify and legitimate these repressive actions.

■ PRAYER AND RELIGIOUS EDUCATION IN SCHOOL

Freedom of religion and expression both take on a different complexion when placed in the context of a public institution, particularly institutions such as schools, prisons, or the armed forces where there may be little freedom for some participants to remove themselves from forms of religious speech or other expression that they find offensive. Schools have proved a particularly controversial battleground for issues of expression and religion. Religious teachers and students who spend a large proportion of their time in schools may wish to express their religion in various ways in school hours. This may include wearing religious clothing or symbols (as discussed above), praying, or participating in other forms of religious expression, such as Bible reading or religious meditation. In addition, parents, or sometimes children themselves, may wish the school to teach religious values or doctrine or to exclude from the curriculum subjects that they feel undermine religious teachings (for example, sexual education or evolution)? However, other parents, teachers, or students may be hostile to these forms of religious expression or feel oppressed by them or pressured to participate in them.

International law provides some guidance on this issue. Article 18(4) of the ICCPR states: "The States Parties to the present Covenant undertake to have respect for the liberty of parents and, when applicable, legal guardians to ensure the religious and moral education of their children in conformity with their own convictions." This provision clearly gives parents the primary right to determine the religious and moral education of children and was developed in response to the odious practices of totalitarian regimes that used the education system to turn children against their parents' values.

However, the precise way in which this protection plays out in practice, particularly in public schools where children of a range of religions or beliefs must co-exist, is far from straightforward. Courts and tribunals in different jurisdictions have taken a variety of approaches to resolving these tensions. Generally, it is accepted that it is a breach of human rights to force students to participate in overtly religious practices or to impose compulsory participation in sectarian religious education or other forms of religious expression.[30] Some countries that have a very strict separation of church and state, such as the United States, put more serious limits on the capacity of public schools to engage with religion, even if that engagement is not compulsory.[31] For example, in the *McCollum* case, the Supreme Court held that an "opt in" school scheme that allowed parents to enroll their children in religious classes, taught by representatives of various religions on school property, was a breach of the Establishment Clause of the U.S. Constitution. This was because the teaching used tax-supported property and required the "close cooperation" of the school and religious authorities.[32] The fact that children who did not wish to attend religious education classes could continue other secular studies classes during the time for religious studies was irrelevant to the constitutional issue.[33] Similarly, schools were prohibited from endorsing religion through the use of prayers, even when participation was voluntary. The Supreme Court held that: "School sponsorship of a religious message is impermissible because it sends the ancillary message to members of the audience who are non-adherents 'that they are outsiders, not full members of the political community, and an accompanying message to adherents that they are insiders, favored members of the political community.'"[34]

Courts in some other jurisdictions and the United Nations Human Rights Committee have not been quite so prescriptive, probably in part because their focus has been on religious freedom without the complicating factor of a non-establishment clause. They have been prepared to allow for religious education as long as parents or students have a genuine and not unduly onerous way of opting out of those classes. In addition, the subject matter that is taught (including material on religion) does not have to be excluded simply because some parents or students may have religious or philosophical objections to its inclusion. In a challenge to a course in religion and belief conducted in Norwegian public schools, the European Court of Human Rights summarized its case law from the preceding decades.[35] The Court noted that religious education classes are not a special case: the religion or belief of parents must be respected "throughout the entire State education programme. That duty is broad in its extent as it applies not only to the content of education and the manner of its provision but also to the performance of all the 'functions' assumed by the State."[36] Minority interests cannot simply be subordinated to those of the majority: "a balance must be achieved which ensures the fair and proper treatment of minorities and avoids any abuse of a dominant position,"[37] but parents do not have a "right that their child be kept ignorant about religion or philosophy in their education."[38] The European Court has also been more open to the notion that allowing students to opt out of religion classes is sufficient to protect their rights without seeming to take the pressures and social difficulties that this may cause for children with much seriousness.[39]

■ RELIGIOUS SYMBOLS IN PUBLIC SPACES

A similar tension to that which arises in schools is caused by the question of whether religious symbols have a place in public spaces or institutions. Cases that have raised this issue include those dealing with crucifixes in Italian classrooms[40] displays of the Ten Commandments in a U.S. courthouse[41] and on the grounds of a State Capitol,[42] refusals to erect monuments to competing religions,[43] displays of nativity scenes by local councils,[44] and the erection of *succahs* to celebrate the autumn Jewish festival of Sukkot.[45] Particularly in countries where there is a strong, historical dominance of a particular religious group, there can be a sense from some that the symbols of that group are part of the broader culture, rather than simply religious, and are entitled to be displayed as a recognition of the important role of the particular religion within the culture. However, others find this a breach of the appropriate degree of separation of church and state and are concerned that religious symbols make public institutions hostile or alienating to those from religious minorities and those who are not religious.

Religious clothing may also cause concerns when worn by individuals in public sector employment with respect to whether it inappropriately proselytizes or implies that the State adopts or approves of the religion of the wearer. This tends to be the case with employees whose roles bring them into contact with the public and is particularly acute when the wearer has a position of authority such as a teacher or a judge.[46] Even when worn on the body of a private individual, clothing worn by public sector employees can raise questions as to whether the clothing is itself an inappropriate imposition of religious symbolism in public spaces.

The passion with which these issues are debated can be seen in the public reaction to the European Court of Human Rights judgment in *Lautsi v. Italy*, the "Italian crucifixes case."[47] The case was brought by the mother of two children who were taught in a state school that displayed crucifixes on the walls. The mother objected that this interfered with her freedom of religion and also her right to educate her children according to her own beliefs and values. She also challenged a Ministry of Education directive that recommended that school classrooms have a crucifix on display. The applicant argued that the display of crucifixes "led to pressure being undeniably exerted on minors and the impression given that the State was estranged from those who did not share Christian beliefs. The concept of secularism required the State to be neutral and keep an equal distance from all religions, as it should not be perceived as being closer to some citizens than to others." By contrast, the government argued that the display of a cross was not a "sign of preference for one religion, since it was a reminder of a cultural tradition and humanist values shared by persons other than Christians." The state acknowledged that it had a duty of neutrality and impartiality, but argued that it has not been breached in this case. While the European Court of Human Rights accepted that the crucifix had multiple meanings, it held that its predominant meaning was religious. It concluded that the presence of the crucifixes breached the right of the parent to have her child educated in conformity with her beliefs (Article 2 of Protocol 1) in combination with the right to freedom of religion or belief (Article 9)[48] The Court reasoned thus:

> The presence of the crucifix may easily be interpreted by pupils of all ages as a religious sign, and they will feel that they have been brought up in a school environment marked by a particular religion. What may be encouraging for some religious pupils may be emotionally disturbing for pupils of other religions or those who profess no religion.

> That risk is particularly strong among pupils belonging to religious minorities. Negative freedom of religion is not restricted to the absence of religious services or religious education. It extends to practices and symbols expressing, in particular or in general, a belief, a religion or atheism. That negative right deserves special protection if it is the State which expresses a belief and dissenters are placed in a situation from which they cannot extract themselves if not by making disproportionate efforts and acts of sacrifice.[49]

The decision of the Court (which has been appealed to the Grand Chamber) was greeted with strong condemnation from Italian politicians, the Vatican, and many members of the Italian public. The heightened rhetoric around the place of religious symbols in public life, and the way in which the issues can be perceived to have significant cultural implications can be seen in the response of the Italian education minister, Maria Stella Gelmini, who was quoted as saying: "No one, not even some ideologically motivated European court, will succeed in rubbing out our identity." Another government minister added that: "The European court has trodden on our rights, our culture, our history, our traditions and our values."[50] Such statements reflect the high cultural stakes that become attached to religious symbols in some contexts; such passions can make a negotiated settlement of differences over such issues difficult to achieve.

▪ CONCLUSIONS

The relationship between religious freedom and freedom of expression is a complex one. Religious believers express their beliefs in both explicit statements and also in a range of important symbolic ways. Without a robust protection of freedom of expression, many religious practices are threatened. To that extent, the two freedoms have an important, complementary relationship. Yet, some forms of expression are threatening to religious people or to religious freedom. Hate speech, vilification, blasphemy, and other forms of speech directed against religious beliefs can be challenging to some religious believers and lead to calls for restrictions on expression in order to protect religious believers from harm, offense, or hurt. Displays of religious symbols by public institutions or the teaching of religion in public schools may appear to some to be an important acknowledgement of the cultural importance of a particular religion in a society, but to others such expressions can appear oppressive and alienating; associating the State with a particular religious viewpoint at the expense of other forms of religion or belief. The wearing of religious clothing has important religious and expressive dimensions, but may raise complicated issues about women's rights or national security.

There is no simple or formulaic way to resolve such tensions. Neither freedom of religion or belief nor freedom of expression is given absolute protection in international law or most domestic bills of rights, which acknowledge that these rights must sometimes give way to other important considerations. When it comes to the practical resolution of particular issues in specific countries, cultural and political factors may be as important as legal and human rights considerations. The issues discussed in this chapter, however, are only likely to become more acute in coming years. Certain forms of religiosity have become intolerant of forms of expression that do not comply strictly with orthodox religious viewpoints and at the same time a divide is growing between those who wish to see more expression of religiosity in the public sphere and those who wish to see less religious symbolism. Globalization means that a dispute about crosses in Italy or cartoons in Denmark can spread across the world in a matter of days and cause serious social disruption in countries far from the origin of the dispute. In such circumstances, societies and courts are likely to have to deal with a wider range of complicated issues at the intersection of religion and expression with the political and social consequences of such resolutions being increasingly significant.

■ NOTES

* This chapter is based in part on research undertaken as part of an Australian Research Council-funded project on freedom of religion and non-discrimination law. My thanks to Duncan Kauffman for his research assistance with this chapter.

1 See, for example, Homa Hoodfar, "The Veil In Their Minds and On Our Heads: Veiling Practices and Muslim Women," in *Women, Gender, Religion: A Reader*, ed. Elizabeth Castelli (New York: Palgrave, 2001) 420–46; Wasif Shadid and Pieter Sjoerd van Koningsveld, "Muslim Dress in Europe: Debates on the Headscarf," *Journal of Islamic Studies* 16 (2005): 35; Susan Michelman, "Changing Old Habits: Dress of Women Religious and Its Relationship to Personal and Social Identity," *Sociological Inquiry* 67 (1997): 350; Janet Mayo, *A History of Ecclesiastical Dress* (London: BT Batsford, 1984). A number of these sources note the ambivalence towards, and multi-layered meaning attributed to, religious clothing by some of those who wear it.

2 *R (SB) v Governors of Denbigh High School* [2007] 1 AC 100.

3 United Nations Human Rights Committee, "General Comment No. 22: Article 18 (Forty-eighth session, 1993), U.N. Doc. CCPR/C/21/Rev.1/Add.4 (1993) (hereinafter "General Comment No. 22").

4 Asma Jahangir, Special Rapporteur on Freedom of Religion or Belief, "Report of the Special Rapporteur on Freedom of Religion or Belief–Addendum–Summary of Cases Transmitted to Governments and Replies Received," U.N. Doc A/HRC/7/10/Add.1 (February 28, 2008) 125.

5 Gareth Davies, "Banning the Jilbab: Reflections on Restricting Religious Clothing in the Light of the Court of Appeal in *SB v Denbigh High School*, Decision of March 2, 2005," *European Constitutional Law Review* 1 (2005): 511 (noting that "A wave of bans and restrictions on religious clothing is sweeping Europe").

6 See, e.g., BBC News Online, "Singapore Headscarf Ban Faces Lawsuit," April 22, 2002.

7 *Dahlab v. Switzerland* (ECtHR 2001-V, 449, Feburary 15, 2001).

8 *Şahin v Turkey*, 44 EHRR 5 (2007) (EctHR, 2005-XI, 175, November 10, 2005) (Grand Chamber Judgment); *Dogru v. France*, 49 EHRR 8 (2009) (ECtHR, 1579, December 4, 2008).

9 David Charter, "Belgium Poised to be First in EU to Ban the Burqa," *The Times* (London), April 1, 2010. For an explanation of moves in Egypt that have been referred to in justifying the banning by a number of European countries, see "Niqab banned at al-Azhar University," DAWN.com, October 9, 2009.

10 For a more detailed analysis, see Bahia G. Tahzib-Lie, "Dissenting Women, Religion or Belief and the State: Contemporary Challenges that Require Attention," in *Facilitating Freedom of Religion or Belief: A Deskbook*, eds. Tore Lindholm, W. Cole Durham, Jr. and Bahia G. Tahzib-Lie (The Hague: Martinus Nijhoff, 2004), 455.

11 See *Multani v Commission Scolaire Marguerite-Bourgeoys* [2006] 1 SCR 256 (school boy case); *Hothi v The Queen* [1985] 33 Man R (2d) 180 (criminal trial case).

12 Assemblée Générale Plénière du Conseil d'Etat "Étude Relative Aux Possibilités Juridiques d'Interdiction du Port du Voile Intégral," (March 25, 2010); Henry Samuel, "French Burka Ban 'Unconstitutional,'" *The Daily Telegraph* (London), March 31, 2010.

13 *Şahin v Turkey*, dissenting judgment of Judge Tulkens, par 11.

14 Davies, "Banning the Jilbab," 518–19.

15 International Covenant on Civil and Political Rights G.A. Res. 2200A (XXI), 21 U.N. GAOR Supp (No. 16) at 52, U.N. Doc. A/6316, 999 U.N.T.S. 171, *entered into force* March 23, 1976.

16 On the complex issues of hate speech generally, see Ivan Hare and James Weinstein, *Extreme Speech and Democracy* (Oxford: Oxford University Press 2008).

17 *Catch the Fire Ministries Inc and Others and Islamic Council of Victoria Inc* (2006) 15 VR 207 [41], [47], [60], [62]. In this section of the judgment, Nettle, J.A. is critical of the way in which Higgins. J. paraphrased the claims by the pastors and he sets them out in more detail and with more context, which is not possible to reproduce in this chapter.

18 The Court of Appeal held that the decision of the tribunal contained errors, but because it was an administrative law review the role of the Court was not to make a final determination on the merits of the claim. Rather the Court sent the matter back to the Tribunal to be determined by another member. The parties then came to a settlement of the complaint, so that no final determination was made as to whether the conduct engaged in was in breach of the *Act* or not.

19 See, e.g., Rex Ahdar, "Religious Vilification: Confused Policy, Unsound Principle and Unfortunate Law," *University of Queensland Law Journal* 26 (2007): 293; Dermot Feenan, "Religious Vilification Laws: Quelling Fires of Hatred?" *Alternative Law Journal* 31 (2006): 153; Lawrence McNamara, "Salvation and the State: Religious Vilification Laws and Religious Speech," in Katharine Gelber and Adrienne Stone, eds., *Hate Speech and Freedom of Speech in Australia* (Sydney: Federation Press, 2007), 145–68; Dan Meagher, "The Protection of Political Communication under the Australian Constitution," *University of New South Wales Law Journal* 28 (2004): 30.

20 United Nations Commission on Human Rights, "Defamation of Religions", CHR Res 1999/82, 55th sess, 62nd mtg, U.N. Doc E/CN.4/1999/L.40/Rev.1 (April 30, 1999).

21 United Nations General Assembly, "Combating Defamation of Religions," GA Res 13/16, U.N. GAOR, 61st sess, 81st plen mtg, Agenda Item 67(b), U.N. Doc A/RES/61/164 (December 19, 2006).

22 United Nations Human Rights Council, "Combating Defamation of Religions," HRC Res 13/16, 13th sess, 42nd mtg, Agenda Item 9, U.N. Doc A/HRC/RES/13/16 (March 25, 2010).

23 United Nations Human Rights Council, "Freedom of Religion or Belief," HRC Res 16/13, 16th sess, 46th mtg, Agenda Item 3, U.N. Doc A/HRC/RES/16/13 (March 24, 2011).

24 United Nations Commission on Human Rights, "Defamation of Religions", CHR Res 1999/82, 55th sess, 62nd mtg, U.N. Doc E/CN.4/1999/L.40/Rev.1 (April 30, 1999).

25 Githu Muigai, Asma Jahangir, and Frank La Rue, "Joint Statement on Freedom of Expression and Incitement to Racial or Religious Hatred by UN Special Rapporteurs on Contemporary Forms of Racism, Racial Discrimination, Xenophobia and Related Intolerance, Freedom of Religion or Belief, and the Promotion and Protection of the Right to Freedom of Opinion and Expression," Office of the High Commission for Human Rights, Side Event at Durban Review Conference, Geneva, April 22, 2009, http://www2.ohchr.org/english/issues/ opinion/docs/SRJointstatement22April09New.pdf.

26 Rebecca J. Dobras, "Is the United Nations Endorsing Human Rights Violations? An Analysis of the United Nations Combating Defamation of Religions Resolutions and Pakistan's Blasphemy Law," *Georgia Journal of International and Comparative Law* 37 (2009): 339; Julian Rivers, "The Question of Freedom of Religion or Belief and Defamation of Religion." *Religion and Human Rights: An International Journal* 2 (2007): 113.

27 See Lorenz Langer, "The Rise (and Fall?) of Defamation of Religion," *Yale Journal of International Law* 35 (2010): 258.

28 United Nations Human Rights Council, "Combating Defamation of Religions," HRC Res 13/16, 13th sess, 42nd mtg, Agenda Item 9, U.N. Doc A/HRC/RES/13/16 (March 25, 2010).

29 Asma Jahangir, Special Rapporteur on Freedom of Religion or Belief, "Report[s] of the Special Rapporteur on Freedom of Religion or Belief–Addendum–Summary of Cases Transmitted to Governments and Replies Received," U.N. Doc. A/HRC/7/10/Add.1 (February 28, 2008), 178–182 (treatment of Christians in Myanmar); U.N. Doc A/HRC/10/8/Add.1 (February 16, 2009), 55–60 (treatment of the Ahmadiyya community in Indonesia), 95–100 (death penalty for apostasy in Iran), 117–121 (prohibition on private religious education in Kazakhstan), and 158–161 (treatment of the Ahmadiyyah community in Pakistan); U.N. Doc A/HRC/13/40/Add.1 (February 16, 2010), 194 (treatment of the Ahmadiyyah community in Pakistan).

30 General Comment No. 22.6: "The Committee notes that public education that includes instruction in a particular religion or belief is inconsistent with article 18.4 unless provision is made for non-discriminatory exemptions or alternatives that would accommodate the wishes of parents and guardians."

31 See, e.g., *Illinois ex rel McCollum v. Board of Education*, 333 US 203 (1948); *School District of Abingdon Township v. Schempp*, 374 US 203 (1963); *Wallace v. Jaffree*, 472 US 38 (1985); *Edwards v. Aguillard*, 482 US 578 (1987); *Kitzmiller v. Dover Area School District*, 400 F.Supp. 2d 707 (2005).

32 *McCollum v. Board of Education*, 464 (Black J., for the Court).

33 Ibid., 472–75 (Frankfurter J., concurring).

34 *Santa Fe Independent School District v. Doe*, 530 US 290 at 309 (2000) (Stevens J, for the Court) quoting *Lynch v. Donnelly*, 465 US 668 at 688 (1984) (O'Connor J, concurring).

35 *Folgerø and Others v. Norway*, 46 EHRR47 (2008) (ECtHR, June 29, 2007), par. 1186–7. Some of the key earlier judgments of the Court on this topic include: *Kjeldsen, Busk Madsen, and Pedersen v. Denmark*, 1 EHRR 711 (1979-1980) (ECtHR 23, series A, December 7, 1976); *Campbell and Cosans v. United Kingdom*, 4 EHRR 293 (ECtHR 48, series A, March 22, 1983).

36 *Folgerø v. Norway*, par. 1186. This does not commit the school to respecting any passing whim or preference of parents, but only those "views that attain a certain level of cogency, seriousness, cohesion and importance." Ibid.

37 Ibid., par. 1187.

38 Ibid., 1188–9. See also the ODIHR Advisory Council of Experts on Freedom of Religion or Belief, "Toledo Guiding Principles on Teaching about Religions and Beliefs in

Public Schools," (Warsaw: OSCE, Office for Democratic Institutions and Human Rights, 2007).

39 Although the Court gave a little more serious consideration to the problems of opting out in *Folgerø v. Norway*.

40 *Lautsi v. Italy*, 50 E.H.R.R. 42 (2010) (ECtHR, November 3, 2009) (Second Section Judgment).

41 *McCreary County, Kentucky v. ACLU of Kentucky*, 545 US 844 (2005).

42 *Van Orden v. Perry*, 545 US 677 (2005).

43 *Pleasant Grove City, Utah v. Summum*, 129 S.Ct. 1125 (2009).

44 *County of Allegheny v. ACLU of Greater Pittsburgh*, 492 US 573 (1989); *Lynch v. Donnelly*, 465 US 668 (1984).

45 *Syndicat Northcrest v. Amselem* (2004) SCC 47.

46 Holly Bastian, "Religious Garb Statutes and Title VII: An Uneasy Coexistence," *Georgetown Law Journal* 80 (1991–1992) 211; Derek Davis, "Reacting to France's Ban: Headscarves and Other Religious Attire in American Public Schools," *Journal of Church and State* 46 (2004): 221; Human Rights Watch, *Discrimination in the Name of Neutrality: Headscarf Bans for Teachers and Civil Servants in Germany* (2009); Karl Klare, "Power/Dressing: Regulation of Employee Appearance," *New England Law Review* 26 (1991–1992): 1395; Sylvie Langlaude, "Indoctrination, Secularism, Religious Liberty and the ECHR," *International and Comparative Law Quarterly* 55 (2006): 929; Hindy Lauer Schachter, "Public School Teachers and Religiously Distinctive Dress: A Diversity-Centred Approach," *Journal of Law and Education* 22 (1993): 61.

47 *Lautsi v. Italy* (Second Section Judgment).

48 Ibid., par. 32 (argument of applicant), par. 40 (argument of respondent government), pars. 51, 57–58 (decision of Court).

49 Ibid., par. 55.

50 John Hooper, "Human Rights Ruling Against Classroom Crucifixes Angers Italy," *The Guardian* (London), November 3, 2009. See also Richard Owen, "Italy challenges ruling that crucifix in class violates religious freedom," *The Times* (London), November 3, 2009. See further on this case the chapter by Barbara Bennett Woodhouse herein.

■ RECOMMENDED READING

Cumper, Peter. "Inciting Religious Hatred: Balancing Free Speech and Religious Sensibilities in a Multi-Faith Society," in *Does God Believe in Human Rights*, eds. Nazila Ghanea, Alan Stephens, and, Raphael Walden (Leiden: Martinus Nijhoff, 2007), 233–258

Evans, Carolyn. "Religious Education in Public Schools: An International Human Rights Perspective." *Human Rights Law Review* 8 (2008): 449–473

Evans, Malcolm D. *Manual on the Wearing of Religious Symbols in Public Areas* (Strasbourg: Council of Europe Publishing, 2009)

Hare, Ivan and James Weinstein. *Extreme Speech and Democracy* (Oxford: Oxford University Press, 2009)

Hoodfar, Homa. "The Veil In Their Minds and On Our Heads: Veiling Practices and Muslim Women," in *Women, Gender, Religion: A Reader*, ed. Elizabeth Castelli (New York: Palgrave, 2001), 420–446

Langer, Lorenz. "The Rise (and Fall?) of Defamation of Religion." *Yale Journal of International Law* 35 (2010): 257–263

Langlaude, Sylvie. "Indoctrination, Secularism, Religious Liberty and the ECHR." *International and Comparative Law Quarterly* 55 (2006): 929–944

Laycock, Douglas. "High-Value Speech and the Basic Educational Mission of a Public School: Some Preliminary Thoughts." *Lewis & Clark Law Review* 12 (2008): 111–30

Lerner, Natan. *Religion, Secular Beliefs and Human Rights: 25 Years After the 1981 Declaration* (Leiden: Martinus Nijhoff, 2006), esp. Chaps. 7 and 10

Rivers, Julian. "The Question of Freedom of Religion or Belief and Defamation of Religion." *Religion and Human Rights: An International Journal* 2 (2007): 113–118

Sunder, Madhavi. "Piercing the Veil." *Yale Law Journal* 112 (2003): 1399–1472

Tahzib-Lie, Bahia G. "Dissenting Women, Religion or Belief and the State: Contemporary Challenges that Require Attention." in *Facilitating Freedom of Religion or Belief: A Deskbook*, eds. Tore Lindholm, W. Cole Durham, Jr., and, Bahia G. Tahzib-Lie (The Hague: Martinus Nijhoff, 2004), 455–496

12 Religion, Equality, and Non-Discrimination

NAZILA GHANEA

The rights of non-discrimination and equality have long engaged political and legal philosophers, thinkers, and practitioners alike. They serve social, economic, political, and symbolic purposes and are used as a description of facts or prescription of ideals. Though many have assumed non-discrimination and equality to reflect two sides of the same coin, closer attention suggests that the principles apply differently and sometimes even diverge. They are also construed and applied differently in different jurisdictions. Their bearing on freedom of religion or belief gives rise to particular implications. With a recent legislative and policy shift from non-discrimination to equality in a number of jurisdictions, it is timely to examine the implications of these two principles for freedom of religion or belief. Furthermore since equality and non-discrimination often provide the framework within which religion or belief exemptions are sought, and may be rejected, it is appropriate to revisit the question of religion or belief claims in this context. That is the subject matter of this chapter.

NON-DISCRIMINATION, EQUALITY, AND INTERNATIONAL HUMAN RIGHTS

While the ideals of non-discrimination and equality have literary, philosophical, political, legal and other implications, this chapter focuses on the legal sphere. Within international human rights law one can, in turn, conceive of equality and non-discrimination as rights, as principles, and as cross-cutting norms. In the former capacity, they both constitute rights in themselves and they inform other rights in a cross-cutting manner. This chapter will limit itself to equality and non-discrimination as legal rights within international human rights law, providing beneficiaries with specific legal claims.

Provisions on non-discrimination and equality have long been the *sine qua non* of all international human rights instruments, beginning with the initial articulation of non-discrimination in the 1948 Universal Declaration of Human Rights (UDHR) and the 1966 International Covenants on Civil and Political Rights and on Economic, Social and Cultural Rights (ICCPR and ICESCR). The 1969 International Convention on the Elimination of All Forms of Racial Discrimination (CERD) added a recognition that discrimination may be non-formal and thus harder to detect and eliminate. The 1979 Convention on the Elimination of All Forms of Discrimination against Women (CEDAW) articulated the understanding that discrimination often arises in the private sphere and is regularly perpetuated in the name of tradition. The 1990 International Convention on the Protection of the Rights of All Migrant Workers and Their Families added that rights to non-discrimination are sometimes extinguished because of the illegal status of the bearer of rights. The right to non-discrimination has traversed a rich investigative journey, leading to a growing discovery and appreciation of where it may still linger and how to counteract it. Through this journey, equality has been a regular and somewhat silent companion. It is only in recent years that the impact of its distinctive role is coming to be emphasized and better appreciated.

The definition of discrimination is understandably nuanced in relation to the area being addressed. For example, the 2008 Convention on the Rights of Persons with Disabilities includes within the definition of discrimination the denial of reasonable accommodation that is "necessary and appropriate modification and adjustments not imposing a disproportionate or undue burden, where needed in a particular case, to ensure to persons with disabilities the enjoyment or exercise on an equal basis with others of all human rights and fundamental freedoms" (Article 2). The CEDAW emphasizes the positive role of states not only to condemn discrimination, but to "pursue by all appropriate means and without delay" a policy of eliminating discrimination against women through legal and extra legal measures, in the public sphere and beyond, to the extent of undertaking to "modify or abolish existing laws, regulations, customs and practices which constitute discrimination against women" (Article 2).

The 1981 UN Declaration on the Elimination of All Forms of Intolerance and of Discrimination Based on Religion or Belief (Declaration on Religion), as its very title suggests, emphasizes non-discrimination on the basis of religion or belief rather than equality. In fact, equality is only mentioned twice in the preamble—in recalling the inherent equality of human beings and the principle of equality before the law established in the International Bill of Rights. Intolerance and discrimination based on religion or belief is defined as "any distinction, exclusion, restriction or preference based on religion or belief and having as its purpose or as its effect nullification or impairment of the recognition, enjoyment or exercise of human rights and fundamental freedoms on an equal basis." The same article recognizes that this discrimination may stem from a "State, institution, group of persons, or person" (Article 2).

This nuanced understanding of discrimination in instruments dealing with different areas of human rights concern suggests that the notion of equality needs to be similarly nuanced in relation to the areas being addressed. After all, these human rights concerns raise different contextual considerations that need to be borne in mind. *Not* taking them on board can undermine the objectives being sought and lead to unintended consequences.

THE INADEQUACY OF NON-DISCRIMINATION: THE GENDER IMPACT

Despite this strong foundational pillar of non-discrimination in international human rights instruments, with time this reliance shifted to anticipation for the norm of equality to deliver where non-discrimination apparently failed, or at least for equality to fill the gaps. This has not only allowed the norms of non-discrimination to permeate further into society, but has also enriched the very notion of equality as well.

Feminist critiques played a formative role here, though the fight against racial discrimination also helped. Feminist critics persuasively argued that non-discrimination would always prove insufficient for the advancement of women, since that policy relied on the mere absence of discrimination as the basis for allowing women to become equal with men. The presumption behind non-discrimination on the basis of sex was that if women were not discriminated against, they could enjoy a level playing field with men. This, however, ignored the systemic stereotyping and institutionalized prejudice that had long sustained a woman's inferior legal status. What such a myopic position failed to observe was that in this way international human rights law would still have *not* systematically taken on board the interests of the discriminated target—in this case women. The international law of human rights itself, feminist critics pointed out, had been "developed in a gendered way" that privileged men and subordinated women.[1] "If people start off on a different footing then they will not end up on an equal footing if they are merely treated equally."[2]

Feminist critics thus pressed for more holistic and interrogative human rights values and policies that offered a more sustained appreciation of the perspectives of discriminated targets like women. This has helped to foster a new understanding of the norm of equality that goes beyond merely tinkering with numbers and instead addresses the burden of history, the structures ensuring the persistence of discrimination on the grounds of sex, and the fact that "sex is a central organizing category in society."[3] A new focus on norms of sexual equality alongside non-discrimination on the basis of sex aims to address "the underlying structures and power relations that contribute to the oppression of women," to "transform these structures,"[4] and contribute "to a world transformed by the interests of women."[5]

Although there is something unique about the persistence and structural basis of sex as an organizing category in society, there are societies where religious discrimination similarly manifests itself in a structural manner. For example, UN expert Arcot Krishnaswami wrote in 1960: "Underlying most discriminatory practices are prejudices which have crystallized into *mores* of a society. In the particular case of attitudes towards religions or beliefs, perhaps more than in any other field, *mores* are slow to change since they stem from deeply held convictions."[6] In many societies over the past five decades, that crystallization has set in more deeply.

Once such an understanding of the need to combine norms of equality and non-discrimination permeated laws and policies relating to gender, it had a spill-over effect in other target populations that had historically suffered discrimination. So much so, that in 2001 one observer referred to "the start of a new era for equality law."[7] In the European Union, for example, equality legislation has been developed with the objective of addressing gender, sexuality, age, and religion or belief, but not national status or citizenship. The United Kingdom has gone further than the required European legislation and instigated a unified equalities legislation to cater to all areas of discrimination. All in all, since the 1990s, international fora have come to an appreciation of the limitations of non-discrimination and this has led to a consequent push towards equality.

This push has, in turn, broadened the boundaries of former understandings of equality and increased attention to the fact that it is a "multi-faceted and complex, contextually bound concept."[8] As Sandra Fredman explains: "Equality as a civil and political right has been primarily concerned with duties of restraint. This manifests as an injunction that the State be restrained from treating similarly situated individuals differently."[9] She critiques such a position in the following, when arguing that socio-economic inequality should be addressed as human rights duties:

> The stress on duties of restraint arises from the assumption that agents are only responsible for inequalities which they have deliberately caused. . . . Yet it is now well established that inequality and discrimination are not necessarily caused by any one individual. This assumption also confines remedial action to a complaints-based model of enforcement through litigation. Because the duty is no more than one of restraining deliberate action, an individual rights-holder must find a perpetrator and prove breach before her inequality can be addressed. Not only does this fault-based orientation impose a heavy burden on the individual rights-holder. In addition, the many forms of structural discrimination which cannot be traced to individual action go unremedied.[10]

■ RELATIONSHIPS BETWEEN, AND DEFINITIONS OF, NON-DISCRIMINATION AND EQUALITY

This broadened understanding of both non-discrimination and equality, and their necessary interrelationship has moved human rights discussions from "formal" equality (a claim for equal treatment in relation to another individual or group) to "substantive" equality (a recognition that where the starting point is unequal, then merely levelling the playing field cannot deliver equality). Formal equality, "while important, is often radically inadequate to achieve equal enjoyment . . . because of significant historically determined differences."[11] O'Donovan and Szyszczak address this head on when commenting that "this conception of equality is limited, for it abstracts persons from their unequal situations and puts them in a competition in which their prior inequality and its effects are ignored."[12] These unequal situations may stem from history, background, social conditions, and other factors. The same holds for groups of individuals. "To equal up opportunity . . . to even up life chances, our notion of equality of opportunity is imperfect."[13]

The idea of substantive equality addresses this imperfection. As Fredman observes: "Substantive equality transcends equal treatment, recognizing that treating people alike despite pre-existing disadvantage or discrimination can simply perpetuate inequality. . . . [S]ubstantive equality must include some positive duties" on behalf of the State and other social institutions.[14] Substantive equality focuses on facilitating enjoyment on an equal basis with others. It recognizes that positive measures—for example preferential treatment, positive discrimination, or affirmative action—may be required for "racial and ethnic minorities, women, persons from scheduled and lower castes, and persons with disabilities—to combat the constraining effects of socially construed circumstances."[15] These interventions towards substantive equality need consideration in relation to religion or belief, especially in informing decisions regarding claims for exemptions, accommodations, or immunities from general laws in order to uphold claims of conscience.[16]

Gillian MacNaughton argues against collapsing status-based non-discrimination and positive equality precisely because the former is often used to reject and extinguish claims towards the latter. She notes that most discussions are indeed restricted to a consideration of status-based non-discrimination, otherwise known as bloc equality,[17] rather than a full exploration of positive equality, since, "[P]ositive and negative forms of equality are very different. When positive equality is the norm, any inequality must be justified. When negative equality is the norm, most inequalities are accepted; only inequalities based upon one of the prohibited grounds, for example, race, sex, language or religion, must be justified. . . . By [international law] equating the two forms of equality in international human rights law and calling them 'non-discrimination,' the positive right to equality has disappeared."[18]

Accepting an "active" and "positive" understanding of equality is the starting point for embracing its complexity. Christopher McCrudden gives four meanings to equality in European Community Law, clarifications which are in fact of wider application and will be used in our discussion. He distinguishes between: (1) equality as "rationality"; (2) equality as "rights protecting"; (3) equality as preventing "status harms" arising from discrimination on particular grounds; and (4) equality as proactive promotion of equality of opportunity between particular groups.[19] McCrudden defines this first meaning of equality as "rationality" as being essentially rationality-based and limited in scope to non-discrimination as "a self-standing principle of general application, without specific limitation on the circumstances in which it is applicable." This limited principle is that "likes should be treated alike, unless there is an adequate justification for not applying this principle."

Equality as "rights protecting" links the non-discrimination principle to access to "public goods" and focuses on the "distribution of the public good, rather than the characteristics of the recipient, except for the purpose of justifying different treatment." "The principle is essentially that in the distribution of the 'public good,' equals should be treated equally, except where differences can be justified." "Equality as preventing 'status harms' arising from discrimination on particular grounds" shifts the focus of attention from the "public good" to the discrimination suffered by people holding, or perceived as holding, particular characteristics such as race or gender. Here, "the meaning of discrimination expands beyond the principle that likes should be treated alike to embrace also the principle that unlikes should not be treated alike. This meaning is essentially aimed at preventing status-harms arising from discrimination on particular grounds." Here, "positive/affirmative action is permitted, but not required." McCrudden declares this as the new meaning of equality.

"Equality as proactive promotion of equality of opportunity between particular groups," McCrudden argues, constitutes a further development of the status-based approach above. Here, equality of opportunity is understood to require "not just a duty on the public authority to eliminate discrimination from its activities. . . . Under this fourth approach, a public authority to which this duty applies is under a duty to do more than ensure the absence of discrimination from its employment, educational, and other specified functions, but also to act positively to promote equality of opportunity and good relations between different groups throughout all its policy-making and in carrying out all its activities." This duty is an "active" one.

■ McCRUDDEN'S FOUR EQUALITIES: IMPACTS ON RELIGION OR BELIEF

McCrudden calls us to move *from* concepts of equality that (1) likes should be treated alike unless differences can be adequately justified, and that (2) equals should be treated equally in the distribution of public goods, unless differences can be justified; *to* concepts that (3) unlikes should not be treated alike in order to prevent status-harms and positive action is permitted, and that (4) public authorities have an active duty to act positively to promote equality of opportunity and good relations between groups. In making this move, the engagement of government actors in assessing *inter alia* the implications of equality on grounds of religion or belief becomes more and more crucial.

As the focus shifts from a negative stance to a positive one, there is a concurrent shift to a calling on public goods and resources. Here, close attention needs to be given to the distinction between a *discriminatory* and appropriately *discriminating* approach. Indeed, different (or "differential" or non-identical) treatment may be legally prohibited, legally permitted, or even legally mandated, depending on the situation.[20] Different treatment is legitimate if it is based on reasonable and objective criteria and designed to achieve a legitimate purpose. Indeed, many groups of individuals call precisely for such "a recognition of difference."[21] In the religion or belief realm, such claims for differential treatment take on a number of guises. We should take on board Fredman's rejection of a fault-based orientation and McCrudden's emphasis on active and positive action towards equality, and see where that will take us in relation to our consideration of this realm.

With that understanding of equality, we move to the question of *equality for whom?* In the context of religion or belief, are we to assess such a freedom for the individual alone or also for groups of individuals? Within the limitations of this chapter, we will not be able to get into the rich and contested discussions regarding individual versus collective rights, hence we will use the more cumbersome term "groups of individuals or 'communities of religion or belief.'"[22]

MacNaughton's distinction between the "one-to-one conception" of equality and the "bloc conception" of equality is informative in this regard. One-to-one equality is defined as the equal application of general rules and laws, such as education and no-parking, to everyone. The bloc conception of equality, meanwhile, focuses on equality between blocs.[23] This addresses "various forms of inequality between groups, including direct and indirect discrimination, intentional and disparate impact discrimination, and de facto and de jure discrimination."[24] MacNaughton uses Article 2 of the International Covenant on Civil and Political Rights to identify these blocs: race, color, sex, language, religion, political or other option, national or social origin, property, birth or other status" and notes that bloc equality is regularly known as non-discrimination.[25] In the context of religion or belief, one-to-one equality alerts us to non-discrimination against individuals on the basis of their religion or belief and also intra-religious discrimination. Bloc equality alerts us to non-discrimination against particular groups on the basis of their religion or belief affiliation. It should be noted that in this equality strand, like others, "it is not always true that inequality within a group matters less than between groups."[26]

The application of standard equality approaches to religion or belief requires closer attention, in order to ensure that the particular complexities which arise in this context are not masked and the important bearings on outcomes not neglected.

■ EQUALITY AND RELIGION OR BELIEF

Examining equality in relation to freedom of religion or belief requires us to take into account a number of factors. Such contextualization is crucial not only in distinguishing between "likes" and "unlikes" for the purposes of McCrudden's four equalities but, more crucially, in assessing a state's duty to act positively to promote equality of opportunity throughout all its activities. I would like to suggest three main areas where contextual factors can substantively impact the parameters of action towards equality regarding religion or belief. These three levels of concern relate to the need to distinguish between: (1) religion as formal set truth claims; (2) religion as practiced by individuals; and (3) religious as practiced by groups of individuals.[27] My purpose is not to claim that there is no overlap between these levels; to the contrary, many instances in fact call upon more than one level. Clarifying the levels will aid us in addressing equality claims that stem from this arena.

Truth Claims

The first level is that of the formal truth claims of religion or belief. Questions that arise include whether the State identifies itself with a particular religion or belief and, if so, what is the impact of this formal identification on other religions or beliefs? When a state declares a formal position with regard to a particular religion or belief, demands of it to ensure the rights of the others merits sharper consideration. But is the State obliged to address those areas of discrimination against individuals and groups, or is it obliged to widen its formal affiliation with a particular religion or belief to all others?

Sophie Van Bijsterveld summarizes the range of relationships between states and religions or beliefs into three categories: "[1] systems of established churches, [2] systems of co-operation and [3] systems of separation of church and state." She recognizes this multi-tiered and differentiated range of relationships between states and religions in Europe as being inevitable, stating that "historical, social-demographical and religious realities make them unavoidable." In fact, she recognizes such differential positions as often being indicative of "a system that is beneficial to the manifestation of religion in its various facets." They may not be a priori made problematic, she argues, nevertheless the system should be tolerant and open.[28]

Van Bijsterveld, in addressing the European rather than global picture, may be overstating the case by celebrating differentiated relationships between religions and states as *often* being indicative of a favorable climate to manifestation of religion. One can think of many examples when sharp differentials of relationships are designed to suppress the very existence of communities of (minority) religions and beliefs, let alone their public manifestation. But her claim does remind us that one cannot establish a Rawlsian "veil of ignorance moment" of absolute equality of relationships between all religions or beliefs and a particular state either. The underlying asymmetries of history, culture, tradition, and community make this impossible. The only solution would be to destroy all such traces in order to achieve an absurd lowest-common-denominator of equality for all religions or beliefs. However, even then such an ahistorical "equalization" project would be impossible to deliver at the cultural level unless the State took radical steps to obliterate such traces. It is perhaps for this very reason that the UN Human Rights Committee has not condemned state religions per se,[29] but reiterated a strong reminder that such constitutional systems do not give legitimate grounds for discrimination against other religions.

Of course, the complicating factor here is that many state-religion relationships do not only have historical and symbolic impacts, they also sometimes end up establishing religion wholesale. This is a huge topic that cannot be addressed fully here. Suffice it to say that any difficulties that may flow from this—for example with regards to freedom of expression or family law—should be addressed directly, rather than under the guise of needing to extend that state-religion relationship to all religions and beliefs.[30]

It is worth noting that in human rights instruments, all *persons* are entitled to equality before the law and equal protection of the law; but religions or beliefs as such are not persons. In such instruments they are entitled to equality *before* the law rather than *in* the law. In sum, the right to equality in human rights law does not support claims to equality for the truth claims of religions and beliefs as such. The promotion of equality, pluralism, and tolerance requires respect for the human rights of individuals or groups of individuals believing in those belief systems. That does not rest on "respect for the beliefs themselves."[31] The claim for equal treatment should relate to an individual or group of individuals not to a religious or other belief system.[32]

We have observed that in human rights law it is not the truth claims that are protected but the freedom of an individual or groups of individuals to hold those ideas and claims. Put more generally, in upholding status-based equality it is not the status that needs protection but the rights of individual(s) who (choose to continue to) hold and to assert that status. Therefore, it is not ultimately at this formal level that the need for equality can or should be delivered, but at the level of the enjoyment of particular rights by individual(s). This requires attention to numerous areas of law and not just to the formal state-religion relationship.

The Individual and Freedom of Religion or Belief

The second level of analysis of equality concerns the freedom of religion or belief of the individual. I argued above that formal equality for all religions or beliefs is not feasible and, in any case, would not be required by human rights law by reason of religions or beliefs not constituting "persons." But individuals should not suffer disadvantages in their enjoyment of religion or belief rights or of other rights such as those to child custody, inheritance, expression, or association.

As Van Bijsterveld has argued, there are a number of reasons why equality and religion or belief is often addressed at this individual level alone. She argues that individualism, litigation, and other societal developments have contributed to what she terms a "narrowing of perspectives" to this level.[33] States are also most comfortable with individual claimants rather than acknowledging the continuity of the group upon which full enjoyment of a number of rights may be predicated. But ensuring equality on the basis of the individual's religion or belief has both external and internal, horizontal and vertical dimensions. One dimension is that of ensuring that the individual is not discriminated against and enjoys equality on the basis of her or his religion or belief in wider society and in relation to a wide range of human rights. These rights include those to political or other leadership, marriage, participation in public life, work (career choice), custody, inheritance, expression, enjoyment of economic, social and cultural life, and so on. Another dimension is that the individual is not discriminated against and enjoys equality on the basis of his or her status as a group member of the community of religion or belief both in relation to others and within that group. This has been called intra-religious discrimination.

The very articulation of freedom of religion or belief, however, makes construing inequality on the basis of religion or belief as being purely an individual consideration nonsensical.

The Group and Freedom of Religion or Belief

Article 18 of the ICCPR recognizes freedom to manifest "alone or in association with others" so we need to factor in enjoyment of equality by a community of religion or belief as well. Communities of religion or belief should enjoy both equal treatment at law, and appropriate external and internal protections. Externally, they should not face discrimination and should enjoy equality with others in relation to public life and services—most readily with other communities of religion or belief. Internally, they should enjoy equality with other communities of religion or belief in managing their internal affairs.

Unlike other social groups, communities of religion and beliefs do not always treat their members equally. They sometimes privilege men over women, or full members over members under discipline in making employment or ordination decisions. In the field of freedom of religion or belief, it is crucial to avoid an unjustifiable narrowing of the right of formal equality to apparently neutral criteria that create a disparate impact on manifestation of religion or belief. Apparently neutral criteria can lead to severe restrictions on the manifestation of freedom of religion or belief by individuals and groups, and the claim of neutrality should not be exploited to mask such violations or fail to address them. At the same time, states and communities with a strongly predominant religion or belief affiliation must be careful to avoid using religiously grounded discrimination as a pretext for trampling on the rights of others. An important first step is to accept the rich scope and diversity of the life of freedom of religion or belief in international human rights. Equality and non-discrimination within a human rights framework after all

> incorporates a human rights framework within its conceptual core. . . the approach creates the potential for a more purposeful and workable application of law and policy, through correlating the equalities and the human rights agenda and removing any artificial conceptual distinction among them. In addition, the human rights based approach presents a tenable and workable framework to the equality and non-discrimination

> agenda which has the potential to avoid the political rhetoric which surrounds so much current equality and non-discrimination discourse. . . . [E]quality and non-discrimination are. . . inherent, fundamental and indivisible to human rights.[34]

The richest capturing of manifestation of religion or belief in international human rights law was probably that offered by Arcot Krishnaswami. It is worth considering him at some length, as a major difficulty in relation to equality and religion or belief is the very denial that certain areas of life have religious or belief connotations. In this way there can be a dramatic shrinking of the scope of freedom of religion or belief at the outset rather than, what I would argue that the international human rights system necessitates, the legal justification of necessary limitations on manifestation of religion or belief. Considering this expert's detailed observations, it becomes clear that a human rights understanding of freedom of religion or belief should firstly give pronounced attention to rights to have, adopt, or change religion or belief without coercion experienced by an individual or groups of individuals in relation to these rights. Secondly, we should not neglect the rights to manifest religion or belief in association with others in worship, observance, practice, and teaching. There is a tendency to impoverish these four areas to suit the jurisdiction under concern in order not to inconvenience a secular majority or the machinations of a particular state-religion relationship. However, Krishnaswami alerts us to the rich diversity and scope of such religious manifestations in worship, practice and observance, teaching and dissemination of religion or belief; and the management of religious affairs. State protections of the rights of equality and non-discrimination for communities of religion or beliefs must give separate attention to "whether there are disabilities or discrimination imposed by law, statutory or customary, which lead to a curtailment of the right of an individual to maintain or manifest his belief or philosophy by imposing upon him disabilities or subjecting him to discrimination in the enjoyment of rights other than the right to religious freedom."[35]

Of course, individuals and communities of religion or belief do not only assert particular manifestations, at times they also claim special exemptions, accommodations, and immunities from general laws in order to avoid violations of their core claims of conscience and central commandments of faith. Principles of equality and non-discrimination sometimes appear to conflict when addressing such claims for exemptions. This chapter has been unable to address, let alone resolve, such tensions. However, it asserts that a strong reason for such apparent conflict is the failure to adopt the expanded understandings of both non-discrimination and equality in international human rights law; and due to assessing claims of or flowing from freedom of religion or belief at the wrong level.

We have said that that religion or belief communities should (externally) enjoy equality with others in relation to public life and services and (internally) they should enjoy equality with other communities of religion or belief in managing their internal affairs or initiating requests for exemptions. The fact that the beliefs of the religion or belief community in question do not enjoy formal status in the jurisdiction concerned (level 1) should be irrelevant to the application of equality to the enjoyment of individuals of such rights (level 2). Any claims to special exemptions, accommodations, and immunities from general laws that are granted should be considered with due respect to equality with other religion or belief communities (level 3), regardless of their formal status or otherwise (level 1). They should be considered out of our growing understandings from equality legislation over the decades that there can be an inordinate impact from apparently neutral positions on particular status-based claims. They should also be considered in parallel with any concerns regarding the rights of particular individual(s) (level 2). If religion or belief communities claim the need to discriminate against certain other individual and groups on religious grounds—in decisions regarding their leadership, membership or employment, for example—these claims need to be analyzed at both levels 2 and 3. They should not be pursued as claims of equality for truth claims (level 1), as we have argued that such requests are mute in international human rights terms. The point is not to pursue formal recognition for particular religious truth claims, the point is to analyze equality in relation to particular individuals or groups of individuals.

■ CONCLUSIONS

The modest observations offered here suggest that identifying claims at inappropriate levels confuses the human rights context of such claims. These can, on the one hand, have the effect of amplifying the claims beyond the human rights framework and, on the other, can hide legitimate group claims (level 3) on grounds of the impossibility of equalising the formal truth claim affiliation or state-religion or belief status to all (level 1). Misconstrued comparators for freedom of religion or belief communities (level 3) also run the risk of extinguishing legitimate human rights granted such groups of individuals within human rights law, albeit subject to possible limitations. These observations are somewhat indicative of the impact of equality patterns on religion or belief communities. Though "human rights law does not magically resolve debates,"[36] good faith requires that, at a minimum, the full spectrum of its standards should be utilized to inform human rights claims.

■ NOTES

1 Hilary Charlesworth and Christine Chinkin, *The Boundaries of International Law: A Feminist Analysis* (Manchester: Juris Publishing, 2000), 231.

2 Noelle Higgins, "The Right to Equality and Non-Discrimination with Regard to Language," *Murdoch University Electronic Journal of Law* 10 (1) (2003), available at http://www.murdoch.edu.au/elaw/issues/v10n1/higgins101nf.html (last accessed May 2010).

3 Katherine O'Donovan and Erika Szyszczak, *Equality and Sex Discrimination Law* (Oxford: Basil Blackwell, 1988), 2.

4 Charlesworth and Chinkin, *The Boundaries of International Law*, 231.

5 Ibid., 248.

6 Arcot Krishnaswami, Special Rapporteur on the Prevention of Discrimination and Protection of Minorities "Study of Discrimination in the Matter of Religious Rights and Practices," U.N. Doc. E/CN. 4/Sub. 2/200/Rev. 1, UN Sales No. 60. XIV. 2 (1960), 63.

7 Sandra Fredman, "Equality: A New Generation?" *Industrial Law Journal* 30(2) (June 2, 2001): 145.

8 Alicia Ely Yamin, "Shades of Dignity: Exploring the Demands of Equality in Applying Human Rights Frameworks to Health," *Health and Human Rights* 11(2) (2009): 13, available at http://hhrjournal.org/index.php/hhr/article/view/169/268 (last accessed May 2010).

9 Sandra Fredman, *Human Rights Transformed: Positive Rights and Positive Duties* (Oxford: Oxford University Press, 2008), 176.

10 Ibid.

11 Yamin, "Shades of Dignity," 6.

12 O'Donovan and Szyszczak, *Equality and Sex Discrimination Law*, 4.

13 Ibid., 5.

14 Fredman, *Human Rights Transformed*, 178

15 Yamin, "Shades of Dignity," 6.

16 See further discussion of this in the chapters by Steven D. Smith and Paul Taylor, herein.

17 Gillian MacNaughton, "Untangling Equality and Non-discrimination to Promote the Right to Health Care for All," *Health and Human Rights* 11(2) (2009): 52, available at http://hhrjournal.org/index.php/hhr/article/view/181/262 (last accessed May 2010).

18 Ibid., 48.

19 The paragraphs that follow are from Christopher McCrudden, "The New Concept of Equality," *ERA-Forum* 3 (2003): 16–21.

20 Alexander H. E. Morawa, "The Concept of Non-Discrimination: An Introductory Comment," *Journal on Ethnopolitics and Minority Issues in Europe* 3 (2002): 10, available at http://www.ecmi.de/jemie/download/Focus3–2002_Morawa.pdf (last accessed May 2010).

21 Bal Sokhi-Bulley, "Non-Discrimination and Difference: The (Non-) Essence of Human Rights Law," *Human Rights Law Commentary* 1 (2005): 12, available at http://www.nottingham.ac.uk/hrlc/documents/publications/hrlcommentary2005/nondiscriminationanddifference.pdf (last accessed May 2010).

22 See Peter Jones, "Human Rights, Group Rights, and Peoples' Rights" *Human Rights Quarterly* 21 (1999): 80–107.

23 Ibid., 48.

24 Ibid., 51.

25 MacNaughton, "Untangling Equality and Non-discrimination," 49.

26 Yamin, "Shades of Dignity," 4.

27 It is interesting to note here Jeremy Gunn's depiction of religion as: belief, identity and way of life. T. Jeremy Gunn, "The Complexity of Religion and the Definition of 'Religion' in International Law," *Harvard Human Rights Journal* 16 (2003): 189. Yamin refers to the non-formal positions i.e., the religion as practiced as "human status (group based) and human treatment (individual)." Yamin, "Shades of Dignity," 4.

28 Sophie van Bijsterveld, "Equal Treatment of Religions? An International and Comparative Perspective," in *Religious Pluralism and Human Rights in Europe: Where to Draw the Line?*, eds. M.L.P. Loenen and J.E. Goldschmidt (Antwerp: Intersentia, 2007), 106–17.

29 United Nations Human Rights Committee, General Comment No. 22: Article 18 (Forty-eighth session, 1993), U.N. Doc. CCPR/C/21/Rev.1/Add.4 (1993), par. 9.

30 See further discussion of the rights and limits of religious groups and state enforcement of religious legal systems in the chapters by Johan van der Vyver and Natan Lerner, herein.

31 Paola Uccellari, "Banning Religious Harassment: Promoting Mutual Tolerance or Encouraging Mutual Ignorance?" *The Equal Rights Review* 2 (2008): 7.

32 I would, however, add a word of caution here. This distinction can become nonsensical in very extreme circumstances. Arguably, if one is brainwashed from a young age to consider particular others as evil or worthy of destruction, within a state framework that overtly fuels that hatred, and communicates that such killing would not be punishable by law, particularly where there has been a history of such destruction, then this should be examined within the remit of the protections offered within the exacting criteria of Article 20 of the ICCPR regarding the prohibition of the incitement of hatred or within CERD's 2005 indicators of patterns of systematic and massive racial discrimination. It should not automatically be assumed that this is absolved from consideration because it falls within this level. See Nazila Ghanea, "Minorities and Hatred: Protections and Implications," *International Journal on Minority and Group Rights* 17(3) (2010): 423–46.

33 van Bijsterveld, "'Equal Treatment of Religions?,'' 105.

34 The Equal Rights Trust, "The Ideas of Equality and Non-Discrimination: Formal and Substantive Equality," 6–7, available at http://www.equalrightstrust.org (last accessed May 2010).

35 Krishnaswami, *Study of Discrimination*, 76.

36 Yamin, "Shades of Dignity," 14.

■ RECOMMENDED READING

van Bijsterveld, Sophie. "Equal Treatment of Religions? An International and Comparative Perspective," in *Religious Pluralism and Human Rights in Europe: Where to Draw the Line?*, eds. M.L.P. Loenen and J.E. Goldschmidt (Antwerp: Intersentia, 2007), 103–17

Fredman, Sandra. *Human Rights Transformed: Positive Rights and Positive Duties* (Oxford: Oxford University Press, 2008)

Ghanea, Nazila. "Minorities and Hatred: Protections and Implications." *International Journal on Minority and Group Rights* 17(3) (2010): 423–46

Gunn, T. Jeremy. "The Complexity of Religion and the Definition of 'Religion' in International Law." *Harvard Human Rights Journal* 16 (2003): 189–215

Jones, Peter. "Human Rights, Group Rights, and Peoples' Rights." *Human Rights Quarterly* 21(1) (1999): 80–107

Krishnaswami, Arcot. Special Rapporteur on the Prevention of Discrimination and Protection of Minorities "Study of Discrimination in the Matter of Religious Rights and Practices," U.N. Doc. E/CN. 4/Sub. 2/200/Rev. 1, U.N. Sales No. 60. XIV. 2 (1960), 63.

MacNaughton, Gillian. "Untangling Equality and Non-discrimination to Promote the Right to Health Care for All." *Health and Human Rights* 11(2) (2009): 47–63

McCrudden, Christopher. "The New Concept of Equality." *ERA-Forum* 3 (2003): 9

The Equal Rights Trust, "The Ideas of Equality and Non-Discrimination: Formal and Substantive Equality," (November 8, 2007), available at http://www.equalrightstrust.org

Yamin, Alicia Ely, "Shades of Dignity: Exploring the Demands of Equality in Applying HumanRights Frameworks to Health." *Health and Human Rights* 11(2) (2009): 1–18

13 Religion and Freedom of Association

NATAN LERNER*

The quest for religious freedom preceded the general struggle for human rights. Presently, freedom of association, a fundamental human right, is a prerequisite for the exercise of freedom of religion, and both rights are closely related. Most attempts to curtail freedom of religion and worship start with restrictions upon freedom of association. Since religion is not only an individual phenomenon but can hardly express itself in society without collective behavior and institutions, and since some forms of legitimate religious worship require a quorum or group, the right to associate and create institutions, permanently or for a discrete purpose, becomes an essential element to ensure freedom of religion.[1]

Freedom of association implies, of course, the right not be coerced to join an association. Similarly, freedom of religion means freedom to reject religion, to change one's religious beliefs, to opt out from a group defined by religion or belief and join another one, or to remain without any affiliation of a religious character.[2] A distinction is necessary, however, between membership in a religious community or group—whether a majority or a minority in a given state—and membership in a religious association that may or may not have juridical personality. In principle, freedom of association does not require membership in a group or community, except in some states where membership in a recognized community is a legal fact or status that is hard to escape. Such was (and still is in some cases) the situation in states that were part of the Ottoman Empire: the law regarded individuals born into a Muslim, Jewish, Christian or other community to be automatic members of that community. Today, it is when a number of individuals together decide to join in a formal structure, an association or an organization, that the matter of freedom of association becomes relevant and sometimes crucial.

While the protection of human rights in general started with the protection of freedom of religion, it was only after World War II that international legislation concerning human rights developed in an impressive way. Paradoxically, in this new period human rights directly related to religion made rather slow progress. The theoretical but crucial question whether human rights originated in religious thought or were based on a secular approach that developed after 1948, and to what extent the lessons of the genocide and the Holocaust in World War II influenced the post war evolution concerning human rights, may be relevant to this question.[3] But in the decades after the promulgation of the 1948 Universal Declaration of Human Rights, the human rights community has come to appreciate the interaction between freedom of religion or belief and freedom of association and the reciprocal influences between them.

In some cases it may be legal, and necessary, to restrict the right to associate because of social dangers involved in the activities of certain associations, even if they have a stated purpose of exercising a legitimate right of religious liberty. This is quite obvious, for instance, in the work of sects or cults that have illegal or anti-social aims, or in some other situations where an existing faith group engages in practices that cannot be tolerated by the surrounding society—whether performing human sacrifices, harming the body or the mind of their members or supporters, or advocating or inciting suicide or violence against others. Recent general social and political developments also have a strong impact on the issue of full respect for freedom of association on religious grounds—concerns about the waves of new immigrants in some countries, the rising fear of violence, frequently, but not exclusively, originating in Islamic fundamentalist groups, and suspicions of the *bona fides* of new religions, sects, or cults. All these factors have to be kept in mind when assessing the difficulties and problems affecting freedom of association.

Human rights are, in general, not absolute, although some human rights may never be derogated, such as those listed in Article 4 of the 1966 International Covenant on Civil and Political Rights (ICCPR).[4] Among them is Article 18 of the ICCPR, dealing with freedom of religion. But freedom of association does not belong to that category and can be subjected to restrictions or limitations necessary in a democratic society to protect social values or the fundamental rights and freedoms of others.

This can increase tensions between freedom of association and freedom of religion. Article 18 of the ICCPR—and similar provisions in regional texts—states explicitly that the exercise of the freedom to manifest one's religion or belief may be limited as prescribed by law and necessary to protect public safety, order, health, morals, or the fundamental rights of others.[5] This raises several complex issues to be discussed in this chapter. Among them: mandatory registration for associations with religious aims; the claim of some states to reserve for themselves the exclusive right to decide which religious groups will be entitled freely to associate and which will be restricted in that right; the obligation of an individual to belong to a religious framework or association, independent of his or her will; the scope of rights and duties pertaining to members of a religious organization vis-à-vis the organization; the freedom to join an association or to opt out from it; the extent of the legal personality of religious associations, namely, what they can do and what is prohibited to them; and the degree to which the general society may interfere in issues belonging to the internal life of churches and religious communities, namely the autonomy of religious associations.

THE APPLICABLE INTERNATIONAL LAW

Article 20.1 of the Universal Declaration of Human Rights (UDHR) proclaims the right of everyone "to freedom of peaceful assembly and association."[6] Article 20.2 adds that no one may be "compelled to belong to an association." The ICCPR deals in more detail with the two rights of assembly in Article 21. It addresses rights of association in Article 22, which reads:

1. Everyone shall have the right to freedom of association with others. . . .
2. No restrictions may be placed on the exercise of this right other than those which are prescribed by law and which are necessary in a democratic society in the interests of national security or public safety, public order (*ordre public*), the protection of public health or morals or the protection of the rights and freedoms of others. . . .

Article 18 of the UDHR grants to *everyone* the right to freedom of thought, conscience, and religion. This right includes freedom to change one's religion or belief, and freedom, either alone or in community with others and in public or private, to manifest his religion or belief in teaching, practice, worship, and observance. Article 18 of the UDHR influenced all the subsequent texts concerning freedom of religion or belief, such as the 1966 covenants on human rights (the ICCPR and ICESCR), the 1981 United Nations Declaration on the Elimination of All Forms of Intolerance and Discrimination Based on Religion or Belief (Declaration on Religion), and the main regional instruments. Despite the time elapsed between the proclamation of the UDHR and the adoption of the covenants and the Declaration on Religion, these instruments reflect the spirit of the UDHR, which was critical in the development of the legal and political philosophy prevailing since its adoption and considered one of the most important documents of our time.

The differences between a declaration, even a solemn one adopted without dissent, and a treaty are obvious, and so are those between general human rights texts and specific documents devoted to a single though broad subject such as the Declaration on Religion. Despite those differences, it may be said that in regard to freedom of religion or belief, the UDHR, as expanded by later legal instruments, provides the conceptual and positive basis for the approach of international law, at the global and regional levels, to the issues of freedom of association and of religion or belief and their interaction.[7]

Article 18 of the ICCPR developed the provisions of Article 18 of the UDHR. It made no substantial changes, save some changes in wording that, mainly because of the issue of proselytism and conversion, were considered necessary to facilitate its adoption.[8] Article 18 should be read in conjunction with Articles 20, 26, and 27 for purposes of understanding the topic of this chapter. The Human Rights Committee, in charge of implementing the Covenant, issued in 1993 its General Comment No. 22 on Article 18, which has also been very useful for the interpretation of the provisions on freedom of religion or belief.

The Declaration on Religion, though not a mandatory instrument, created a system of control and implementation through the work of its United Nations Special Rapporteur. Of particular relevance to the present remarks are its Articles 1 and 6, containing a catalog of rights that reflects an almost universally agreed minimum standard in the area of human rights related to religion or belief.[9] Article 1 of the Declaration on Religion follows in general the pattern of Article 18 of the ICCPR. In its first paragraph it refers to the freedom to manifest religion or belief, individually or in community with others and in public or private, in worship, observance, practice and teaching. "In community with others" implies the rights to association and assembly. In Article 6, a series of specific freedoms in this connection are listed:

a) to assemble in connection with a religion or belief, and to establish and maintain places for those purposes;
b) to establish and maintain appropriate institutions;
c) to teach a religion or belief in places suitable for these purposes;
d) to receive voluntary financial contributions;
e) to train and appoint leaders;
f) to observe days of rest and holidays and ceremonies as prescribed by the respective religion or belief;
g) to communicate with individuals and communities in matters of religion and belief, at the national and international levels.

The exercise of all these rights requires freedom of association and, for some of those purposes, the association requires a legal personality or juridical status at law.

Regional instruments follow the UDHR and the ICCPR quite closely with regard to the issues of freedom of religion and association. Particularly notable are the 1989 Concluding Document of the Vienna Follow-Up Meeting of Representatives of the Participating States of the Conference on Security and Cooperation in Europe (Vienna Concluding Document)[10] and the 1990 Document of the Copenhagen Meeting of Representatives of the Participating States of the Conference on the Human Dimension of the Conference on Security and Co-operation in Europe (CSCE) (Copenhagen Document).[11] Of direct and detailed relevance to the present article is Article 16.3 of the Vienna Concluding Document,[12] which urges participating States, *inter alia*, to grant to communities of believers "recognition of the status provided for them in their respective countries". Principle 16.4 calls for respect of the right of religious communities to establish and maintain freely accessible places of worship or assembly; to organize themselves "according to their own hierarchical and institutional structure"; to appoint personnel "in accordance with their respective requirements and standards"; and to receive voluntary financial and other contributions. Principle 16.5 deals with the right to engage in consultations with religions, institutions, and organizations. Principle 16.6 refers to the right to give and receive religious education, individually or in association with others. According to Principle 16.8, participating states must allow the training of religious personnel in appropriate institutions. Articles 16.9 and 16.10 deal with the rights to acquire, produce, import, and disseminate religious publications and materials.

Also relevant is Principle 19 of the Vienna Concluding Document, which calls states to protect and create conditions "for the promotion of the ethnic, cultural, linguistic and religious identity of national minorities on their territory." Following the resistance to acknowledge collective rights, Principle 19 refers to the exercise of rights by "persons belonging" to minorities, and has explicit references to "believers, religious faiths . . . in groups or on an individual basis" and the right "to maintain contacts and communications, in their own and other countries."

The 1990 Copenhagen Document refers in Principle 30 to national minorities and religious groups. Principle 32 deals with the right of "persons belonging to national minorities" to maintain institutions, organizations, or associations and to exercise other rights involving the rights to associate and maintain "unimpeded contacts" within their country and across frontiers. The rights of persons belonging to national minorities can be exercised individually as well as in community with other members of their group. Here, too, the collective dimension is acknowledged, albeit in muted form.

The main regional treaties refer specifically to the rights of assembly and association. The 1950 European Convention on Human Rights deals in Article 9 with freedom of religion or belief and in Article 11 with the freedom of assembly and association.[13] The 1969 American Convention on Human Rights proclaims in Article 12 the freedom of conscience and religion and to profess or disseminate one's religion or belief, either individually or together with others.[14] The 1981 African (Banjul) Charter on Human and Peoples' Rights deals similarly with the issue in Article 10.1.[15]

■ REACH AND LIMITS OF FREEDOM OF ASSOCIATION

Freedom of association is a basic right, the observance of which is essential for the free exercise of many fundamental freedoms.[16] From this viewpoint, it has a double function. It is a fundamental right in itself, the protection of which is of great importance for a democratic society. It also plays an instrumental role in the sense that, when it is ignored or restricted illegally, it jeopardizes the enjoyment of other human rights that depend on it. This is the case with freedom of association, which may be endangered when the State imposes abusive limitations of the right to associate and establish and maintain a religious organization.

The individualistic orientation of early human rights instruments underplayed the right to freedom of association. The trend after World War II was to deal with individual rights and not attach sufficient weight to group rights. The UDHR and the ICCPR both refer to the rights of "everyone" to freedom of association.

The UDHR adds that "no one" may be compelled to belong to an association. But the drafters of these early international human rights instruments were reluctant to go beyond individual rights and pay attention to the needs and tasks of groups, including religious groups, whatever their structure and form of organization may be. While, of necessity the 1948 Convention on the Prevention and Punishment of the Crime of Genocide contains a clear group ingredient, it was only at a later stage that the rights of religious groups as such were also dealt with.

Today, however, it is clear that the right to organize and associate in a religious entity is a basic individual right but also a right of the group, the community, the congregation, or the church, as such, and it must be protected equally. Today, the right of the group or association is no less important than the right of every individual to create or join that group or association. The new emphasis on the group dimension of human rights can be seen in recent texts dealing specifically with religion, such as the 1981 Declaration on Religion, the 1992 United Nations Declaration on the Rights of Persons Belonging to Minorities, and the 2007 Declaration on the Rights of Indigenous Peoples.[17] Article 12 of the Indigenous Peoples Declaration refers specifically to a series of rights related to religion to be enjoyed by indigenous peoples.[18]

Recent developments on the international scene testify to the fact that gross violations of the freedom of religion or belief, in fact, often affect less the rights of individuals than those of religious groups, communities, associations, or churches. This is due to the fact that limitations are imposed on religious groups or collectivities more than on individuals, especially when dealing with freedom or association.

The strength of the freedom of association for religious purposes is influenced by the system regulating the relationship between the State and religion. In general terms the constitutional models concerning that relationship are (1) separation of religion and state (seldom an absolute "wall of separation"); (2) the absence of an established state church; (3) neutrality or impartiality of the State in its dealings with different religious communities; (4) autonomy of religious groups; and (5) collaboration on a consensual or pragmatic basis between the State and certain religious groups with strong roots in the country—*notorio arraigo*, to use the terminology of the Law on Religious Liberty of Spain. It is difficult to identify any of those models in pure form; frequently they are combined. Even when secularism or *laicité* are proclaimed in fundamental laws, as in France, Turkey, or Russia, or when the State declares itself as neutral with regard to the various religions, practice shows the impact of concessions, compromise, or inapplicability of "pure" systems. For that reason, as Silvio Ferrari points out, "the Constitutions of the post-Communist countries have preferred a pragmatic orientation, avoiding identifying themselves with God or with *laicité*, with one specific religion or with a program of secularization of the public institutions."[19] This development coincides with what the same author describes as a crisis of the state church-model.[20]

A consequence of this pragmatic approach is that there are today no major differences in the formal law governing basic freedoms between the former communist regimes and the legal systems prevailing in the West. In both areas some basic principles have become common—respect for individual religious freedom; a reasonable degree of autonomy and self-administration recognized to some religious groups; collaboration, on a selective basis, between the State and some communities. But, in practice, in various post-communist countries a regressive trend can be noted, expressing itself in the need for religious groups to officially register with the State, which is granted, restricted, conditioned, or denied, sometimes in an arbitrary way. For example, Latvia recognizes only seven religious denominations, while Hungary and Poland recognize 136 and 158 respectively.[21]

General norms concerning freedom of association are, of course, applicable to religious associations and their establishment. There are, however, differences emanating from the nature of the rights involved. For instance, rules governing trade unions would differ in many countries from the principles valid in general for other associations. The right to associate for religious purposes and establish a congregation or a church is subject in many countries to special regulations, different from those dealing with commercial or cultural non-profit associations. The ways to achieve juridical personality are not the same for an economic entity and a religious group. Obviously, freedom of association for political purposes also requires special treatment. But, on the whole, as Christian Tomuschat points out, freedom of association "can be considered to constitute the very foundations of a democratic society, where concertation and interaction between different societal groups is necessary in order to allow the different viewpoints held by citizens to crystallize and to be articulated."[22] The same author indicates that religious communities may enjoy a special protection in addition to general principles on freedom of association, certainly in the European framework.

In principle, the general rules on freedom of association should apply equally to religious groups. These rules include norms concerning certain forms of nondiscrimination (for instance, on grounds of nationality), the requirement of a minimum number of persons to form an association, the right to choose the group's name, to set conditions for membership, to impose obligations of membership, and to preserve exit rights, the right to elect or appoint religious leadership, to enjoy autonomy of internal governance, financial management, and more.

These norms may, however, in practice, differ in the case of religious associations. The reasons for that are not always the same but, in general, they reflect the legal relation of the State and religion prevailing in the respective countries. They also reflect to what extent religion is a phenomenon with regard to which no state can remain indifferent. Besides ideology, politics, and the frequent interaction between politics and religion, sometimes engendering violence and terrorism, play a major role in inducing governments to try to exercise a rigorous control of religious associations. One of the results of that interaction may lead a state to grant favorable treatment or conditions to some belief groups, notwithstanding the rule of impartiality and neutrality that the authorities have to observe when exercising their regulatory power.[23] Also the opposite is possible, when a state discriminates against, or singles out a given belief group for stricter regulatory measures than others.

■ REGISTRATION AND LEGAL PERSONALITY

In principle, freedom of association means that everyone and every group of persons are entitled to come together and join efforts in order to exercise their fundamental right to freedom of religion and worship. It is not an absolute right, and it can be regulated when the State considers that a public interest is involved. In practice, when such a group exists or is created, its activities will usually produce the need to go beyond mere togetherness, to get organized, and to achieve the legal status that will permit the group to act publicly—to buy, sell, or rent property, to employ people, to publish, administer, or open bank accounts, to submit formal petitions or requests to the authorities, to receive funds from the State, when pertinent, to communicate with other people of similar ideas, and to undertake many other actions that necessarily relate to public interests. In other words, the group needs and is entitled to legal or juridical personality.

When this develops, and usually it does develop, the State and the law have a role to perform. Human rights norms provide guidelines on the proper role of the State, as can be seen in the useful set of "Guidelines for the Review of Legislation Pertaining to Religion or Belief" published by the Office for Democratic Institutions and Human Rights of the Oganization for Security and Cooperation in Europe.[24] While individuals and groups "should be free to practice their religion without registration if they so desire," and registration should not be mandatory, the Guidelines provide, it may be "appropriate to require registration for the purposes of obtaining legal personality and similar benefits." High minimum membership requirements should not be allowed, and it is not appropriate to require lengthy existence before registration is permitted, nor other excessively "burdensome constraints or time delays." "Excessive government discretion" in giving approvals also should not be allowed. Official discretion in this respect should be "carefully limited." Provisions that operate retroactively or require re-registration of religious entities "under new criteria" should be questioned.[25] The document also deals with matters related to the principles of autonomy and intervention in internal religious affairs, to be discussed below.

The Guidelines are a careful document recommending states how to deal with the often sensitive issues surrounding registration of religious groups. Religious groups should be submitted to rules similar to those that govern other associations for any other legitimate purpose, such as political parties, economic corporations, and cultural or social non-profit entities. They should not enjoy special privileges, but should also not be exposed to excessive suspicion nor requested to fulfill more requirements than others. The problem is that, in practice, particularly in some countries, religious associations applying for registration are submitted to multiple procedural and/or bureaucratic obstacles resulting from prejudice, pressure on the part of dominant churches, or political interests. In this respect, it is pertinent to quote an authoritative source, the former Special Rapporteur on Freedom of Religion or Belief, Asma Jahangir, who, in her 2009 report to the UN General Assembly, included, among issues of concern in relation to her mandate, "some domestic registration procedures for religious communities . . . applied in a discriminatory manner by the authorities, often curbing the freedom of religion or belief of minority communities such as new religious movements or indigenous peoples."[26]

Another authoritative report, the *International Religious Freedom Report 2009*, an official document published yearly by the United States State Department,[27] lists the questioning of loyalty to the State, hostility towards minorities, failure to address societal intolerance, and institutionalized bias and presumption of illegitimacy among the reasons or pretexts for restrictive registration policies that have led to abuses and discrimination against some religious groups. Azerbaijan, China, Egypt, Eritrea, Iran, Laos, North Korea, Russia, Saudi Arabia, Tajikistan, Turkey, Turkmenistan, Uzbekistan, and Vietnam are mentioned as countries where registration practices are used against some minority faiths.

A detailed analysis of issues that arise in connection with religious association laws was made by W. Cole Durham, Jr. in 2004.[28] Durham points out that most regimes now recognize that the right to freedom of religion or belief precludes laws that make registration a mandatory precondition. But he finds several problems in this respect: the obligation of registration or other forms of state approval or license; the high minimum number of members needed to register (in Slovakia, for example, 20,000 members are required); the condition of a minimum, sometimes extended period of time (25 years in Russia) before an association can be registered; other "burdensome requirements" for acquiring entity status, such as providing foreign certificates of proper behavior, proof of an "historically canonized scripture," or personal information on founding members; excessive governmental discretion and vague standards are all frequent in emerging legislation. While frequently the difficulties raised by the authorities in the process of registration are a consequence of prejudice or of local political or church interests, the request of registration in itself may be seen as correct if it does not exceed the norms concerning registration of other entities. The interest of the State in the action of religious groups is justified as long as regulation is done in good faith, which is not always the case.

As to legal personality, religious associations, if they wish to be able to act as a juridical person, should not be required to go through procedures more burdensome than those applicable to civil non-profit or commercial entities. In practice, governments that do not see in a favorable way the creation of religious associations because of prejudice or suspicion will most probably raise obstacles to their legal personality. Such difficulties may certainly deprive the association of the right to exercise its freedom of religion. It would be unable to perform essential collective activities, even if each of the members of the group will still enjoy freedom of religion or belief.

This has a powerful impact on the exercise of freedom of religion. Religious associations may thus deserve "more sensitive, although not absolute" protection, writes an American scholar commenting on American law.[29] Similarly, the Strasbourg Court, in a frequently cited decision, *Metropolitan Church of Bessarabia v. Moldova*, declared that "the autonomous existence of religious communities is indispensable for pluralism in a democratic society," that denial of recognition would be an interference with freedom of religion, that judicial protection of the community, its members, and its assets is necessary, and that lacking legal personality a church could not operate.[30]

■ AUTONOMY OF RELIGIOUS ASSOCIATIONS AND COMMUNITIES

Any discussion of religion and freedom of association would be incomplete without reference to the complex issue of the extent of autonomy that religious associations and communities should enjoy. The matter is frequently influenced by political considerations and intentions and is likely to engender controversy. On the whole, it seems fair to point out that there has been progress in this matter and presently the trend is to facilitate the aims of religious association by allowing a wide spectrum of autonomy at least to the major religious groups, as long as no essential public interest is endangered.[31] Autonomy for religious associations or communities means that the State should abstain from interfering in matters concerning the religious beliefs and peaceable practices of the entity. This is different from the right, and duty, of the State to exercise control, within the limits of the law, of the activities of collective entities in the political, economic, or social fields of life. In addition to purely theological issues beyond the competence of the State, the State should also limit its intervention in some organizational matters that are difficult to separate from theological or ideological subjects. Such would be, for instance, the appointment of religious functionaries, priests, teachers of doctrine, and similar staff members, an area in which a religious entity may discriminate, on grounds that would be unacceptable with regard to a professional or commercial entity. While a business corporation may not exclude a qualified person from its board of directors just because he is a Christian or a Jew, a synagogue may deny a rabbinate to a person just because he is a Christian.[32]

In a case concerning the application of Articles 9 and 11 of the European Convention on Human Rights to a religious community, the Strasbourg Court declared that a believer's right to freedom of religion "encompasses the expectation that the community will be allowed to function peacefully free from arbitrary State intervention. Indeed, the autonomous existence of religious communities is indispensable for pluralism in a democratic society."[33] "Autonomous existence" means that the religious association has an exclusive right to interpret its dogma, as well as the right freely to conduct its activities within the limits of public order in a democratic society. State bodies should carefully avoid interfering in theological or dogmatic questions; regarding organizational or administrative matters state interference may be necessary, provided there is no clash with the basic doctrine of the respective community.

This may involve difficulties, and it is up to the reason, good will, and objective assessment of the limitations of freedom of religious activities in a pluralist and democratic society to determine the extent of state involvement in the non-theological actions and dimensions of religious associations. In this respect, different democratic societies may adopt different criteria, with the level of state intervention affected by the constitutional form of religion-state relations: the greater the constitutional separation of religion and state, the wider the zone of religious autonomy needs to be. International practice provides a variety of models in this respect, and domestic and regional jurisprudence is helpful to design the limits of religious autonomy in matters that do not belong strictly to dogma. In some cases, agreements between the State and individual churches are useful to avoid conflicts in doubtful situations.[34]

A judgment of the British House of Lords, which caused significant controversy and criticism, is a good illustration of the difficulties sometimes surrounding the ambit and exercise of religious autonomy. On December 16, 2009, the House of Lords decided, by a divided majority vote, that the Jewish Free School (JFS), an "outstanding" school in the words of Lord Phillips, President of the Court, had engaged in racial discrimination violating the Race Relations Act 1976 by refusing to admit a twelve-year-old boy whose father was Jewish and whose mother, though born an Italian Catholic, had converted to the Jewish faith by a non-Orthodox rabbinic tribunal.[35] The JFS, founded in 1732 and state-funded, considers itself an Orthodox Jewish institution and recognizes the authority of the Chief Rabbi of Great Britain. It does not accept therefore a conversion that is not performed according to *halakhah*, the Jewish religious law. President Phillips stated that "nothing in the judgment should be read as giving rise to criticism on moral grounds of the admissions policy of JFS in particular or the policies of Jewish faith schools in general, let alone as suggesting that these policies are 'racist' as that word is generally understood." He also admitted that "there may well be a defect in our law of discrimination."[36] But, he concluded that, although giving preference to the special needs of a minority racial group will be justified, a policy "which directly favors one racial group will be held to constitute racial discrimination."

A secular, non-observant, or non-religious Jew may not accept the Orthodox rule concerning descent, and may also object to the Orthodox monopoly concerning conversion. He will still find this judgment contrary to the principle of religious autonomy, since it denies Jewish Orthodox self-definition and understanding. There is no claim that the school is racist and that its admission policy may be seen as violating fundamental human rights principles or norms of *jus cogens*. Every religious school in Britain or elsewhere gives preference to students belonging to its founding religion. And the self-understanding of what that religion is should be respected, as long as it does not involve acts or expressions clashing with fundamental norms of the public order in the respective state. This is, in essence, the meaning of religious autonomy.[37]

A special problem may arise when dissident or splinter groups wish to get the same recognition from the State that the original group enjoys. Such a situation developed in France with the Jewish liturgical association, Cha'are Shalom ve Tsedek, an ultra-orthodox (*haredi*) group that split away from the Jewish Central Consistory of Paris, and claims to have about forty thousand adherents. This group alleged a violation of the religious freedom provisions of Article 9 of the European Convention on Human Rights on account of the French authorities' refusal to grant it the approval necessary for access to slaughterhouses with a view to performing ritual slaughter in accordance with its own practices. It also alleged violation of the religious discrimination provisions of Article 14 in that only the Jewish Central Consistory, created by a decree of Napoleon I in 1808, to which the large majority of Jews in France belong, has received the approval in question, thus enjoying a monopoly. The French authorities adhered to its own legislation and Cha'are Shalom ve Tsedek, after exhausting all the local remedies, appealed to the European Court. In its decision,[38] the European Court reiterated its consistent respect for the margin of appreciation of the State and avoided granting a remedy to the applicant association. A minority of seven judges dissented, however, following the more flexible approach in *Manoussakis and Others v. Greece*, where the Court underscored the need to ensure true religious pluralism.[39]

On the whole, the catalog of rights enunciated in Article 6 of the Declaration on Religion may be useful to clarify the extent of activities permitted by the principle of autonomy of religious associations. As we saw, it includes the rights to assemble, to establish and maintain places for this purpose, to maintain appropriate charitable or humanitarian institutions, to make, acquire, or use the necessary articles related to their rites or customs, to produce and disseminate relevant publications, to teach their religion in suitable places, to solicit and receive contributions, to train and appoint their leaders,[40] to observe days of rest and celebrate holidays and ceremonies, to establish and maintain communications with individuals and communities in matters of religion or belief. The obvious right to delineate the fundamental principles of each religious group is not mentioned in Article 6, but this provision deals with activities and not with doctrine. Religious doctrine or dogma belongs to the essential nature of religion or belief and remains certainly beyond the interference of the State, unless its manifestations justify limitations as foreseen in Article 1 of the Declaration. Problems may also arise in situations where taxation is imposed by the State on members of religious communities, or when such communities refuse to provide services to persons belonging to the same religion because of organizational matters, or rules of the association which may clash with general human rights.

■ SECTS, CULTS, NEW RELIGIONS

This brings us to the issue of sects, cults, or new religions that in some cases may be subjected to restrictions or even to being outlawed. Although "sects," "cults," and "new religions" are not identical notions, they have in common elements that justify their joint discussion in an article on religion and freedom of association. "Sect" and "cult" are similarly defined in dictionaries, but the term "sect" has acquired a negative and pejorative meaning, as a consequence of tragic events in which such groups have been involved. Such events took place in countries with different legal systems, and in several of them special legislation was drafted. In France, a law dealing with sects was adopted in 2001. In Belgium, in 2006, a parliamentary enquiry committee formulated recommendations. Austria enacted legislation in 1997, distinguishing between traditional, recognized religions, and "confessional communities" that have to satisfy numerical criteria and exist for a number of years. In Germany, the Church of Scientology was singled out as a sect and not considered a legitimate religious group. European case law contains decisions showing confusion between legitimate religions and dubious religious groups, loosely described as sects or cults.

"New religions" is a more objective and neutral notion, putting more emphasis on the religious character of a developing group, as opposed to the words "sect" or "cult" in which emphasis is on dissidence or action and sometimes on secrecy and illegality that may be present. Human rights instruments do not define religion, and this may have created confusion concerning the concepts of sects, cults, and new religious movements. Former UN Special Rapporteur on Freedom of Religion or Belief, Abdelfattah Amor, who dealt with this issue, wrote that, despite the original neutral meaning of the word "sect," "it often has now a pejorative connotation so that it is frequently regarded as synonymous with danger, and sometimes a non-religious dimension when it is identified with a commercial enterprise."[41]

An intense and often emotional public debate concerning sects and new religions has developed. It has been pointed out that "many new religious movements are never able to mount the momentum to graduate from dangerous sect to legitimate religion."[42] Several countries have adopted new legislation intended to prevent abuses and criminal activities of some fringe associations whose actions have caused public alarm.[43] Other countries have established governmental and parliamentary commissions to investigate the activities of sects. In 1999, the Council of Europe adopted a Recommendation stressing the difficulties involved in regulation of the matter and stating that "major legislation on sects was undesirable" and "might interfere with the freedom of conscience and religion" and "harm traditional religions."[44]

The issue is delicate and requires careful legal treatment. Different legal systems and scholars take different approaches to the issue. This may be a good reason to renew the discussion of devising a universally agreed-upon legal definition of religion and belief, difficult as it may be. But without an international covenant or treaty on religious freedom that would include such a definition, it is up to domestic legislation to provide answers to this complex issue, distinguishing between legitimate old and new religions, on the one hand, and adventurous or even illegal activities, sometimes of a psychotic or commercial character, on the other.

■ CONCLUSIONS

A short article cannot provide an exhaustive analysis or the many issues involved in the interaction between the two basic liberties of freedom of religion and freedom of association. Many ideological, philosophical, and emotional reasons influence the subject, in addition to less charged political and economic considerations. Profound changes in political structures and regimes around the world over the past half century, particularly the fall of communism, have also contributed to the complexities of the mentioned interaction. Some of these post-communist countries have faced the greatest difficulties concerning the freedom of association, particularly in their often discriminatory methods of registration, re-registration, and state control of religious groups.

Some other issues, such as autonomy of religious associations, the differences between legitimate, normative religions associations, old and new, on the one hand, and sects or cults constituting threats to public order and individual rights, on the other, also deserve special examination, and are presently a controversial issue in several places. Thousands of young faith organizations and groups, some of them serious and well intentioned, others with hidden and suspect purposes, are struggling for recognition and respect in various nation-states around the world. The impact of the general constitutional relationship between the State and religion on the organizational dimension has a bearing on how freedom of association for religious groups is treated, and it requires careful attention not only from legal scholars but also from political and religious officials.

■ NOTES

* Many thanks to my research assistant, Stav Cohen, for her most valuable help in the preparation of this chapter.

1 Manfred Nowak, in his *Commentary* on the ICCPR writes that, while freedom of association is an individual right, "it also covers the collective right of an existing association to perform activities in pursuit of the common interests of its members." States are "under a *positive duty* to provide the legal framework for founding juridical persons." See his *U.N. Covenant on Civil and Political Rights, CCPR Commentary* (Kehl, Germany: N.P. Engel, 1993), 386–400, at 387. See also, on freedom of association generally, Karl Josef Partsch, "Freedom of Conscience and Expression, and Political Freedoms," in *The International Bill of Rights*, ed. Louis Henkin (New York: Columbia University Press, 1981), 209–45; Martin Scheinin, "Article 20," in *The Universal Declaration of Human Rights*, eds. Gudmundur Alfredsson & Asbjorn Eide (The Hague: Martinus Nijhoff, 1999), 417–29; Christian Tomuschat, "Freedom of Association," in *The European System for the Protection of Human*

Rights, eds. R.J. St. Macdonald, F. Matscher, H. Petzold (The Hague: Martinus Nijhoff, 1993); W. Cole Durham, Jr., "Facilitating Freedom of Religion or Belief Through Religious Association Laws," in *Facilitating Freedom of Religion or Belief, A Deskbook,* eds. Tore Lindholm, W. Cole Durham, Jr., Bahia G. Tahzib-Lie (Leiden: Martinus Nijhoff, 2004), 321–495.

2 See further the chapter by Paul Taylor, herein.

3 See further the chapter by David Little, herein.

4 General Comment No. 22 of the Human Rights Committee states that Article 18.3, permitting limitations, should be "strictly interpreted." United Nations Human Rights Committee, General Comment 22: Article 18 (Forty-eighth session, 1993) U.N. Doc. HRI/GEN/1/Rev.1 (1994), 35.

5 See further the chapters by Paul Taylor and Jeremy Gunn, herein.

6 Many authors deal with both rights, of assembly and of association, together. This article is devoted only to freedom of association. Although freedom of assembly is also relevant to religious rights, problems arise mainly with regard to permanent associations.

7 On the subject see, generally, Natan Lerner, *Religion, Secular Beliefs and Human Rights* (Leiden: Martinus Nijhoff, 2006), and relevant sources therein on the UDHR ICCPR, and ICESCR.

8 See further the chapter by Paul Taylor, herein.

9 Lerner, *Religion, Secular Beliefs and Human Rights.*

10 Concluding Document of the Third Follow-Up Meeting of Representatives of the Participating States of the Conference on Security and Cooperation in Europe (Vienna) 28 I.L.M. 527 (January 17, 1989).

11 Document of the Copenhagen Meeting of Representatives of the Participating States of the Conference on the Human Dimension of the Conference on Security and Co-operation in Europe, June 29, 1990, 29 I.L.M. 1305 (1990).

12 The character and extension of the present article precludes a detailed reference to the existing instruments. For the relevant texts, see Organization for Security and Cooperation in Europe and Office for Democratic Institutions and Human Rights, Advisory Panel of Experts on Freedom of Religion or Belief, "Guidelines for the Review of Legislation Pertaining to Religion or Belief," adopted at the Venice Commission, 59th Plen. Sess., June 18–19, 2004 and welcomed at the annual session of the OSCE Parliamentary Assembly, Edinburgh, 2004, Appendix I, 31–51 (www.osce.org/odihr/13993).

13 European Convention for the Protection of Human Rights and Fundamental Freedoms, (ETS No. 5), 213 U.N.T.S. 222, *adopted* in Rome, November 4, 1950, *entered into force* September 3, 1953.

14 American Convention on Human Rights, O.A.S.Treaty Series No. 36, 1144 U.N.T.S. 123, *entered into force* July 18, 1978, *reprinted in* Basic Documents Pertaining to Human Rights in the Inter-American System, OEA/Ser.L.V/II.82 doc.6 rev.1 at 25 (1992).

15 African [Banjul] Charter on Human and Peoples' Rights, adopted June 27, 1981, OAU Doc. CAB/LEG/67/3 rev. 5, 21 I.L.M. 58 (1982), *entered into force* October 21, 1986.

16 Nowak, *U.N. Covenant on Civil and Political Rights,* 385 points out that freedom of association lies in the overlapping zone between civil and political rights, and is "indispensable for the existence and functioning of democracy."

17 For its text, Blackstone's Statutes, *International Human Rights Documents,* 6th ed. (Oxford: Oxford University Press, 2008). See further the chapters by Ronald Niezen and Johan van der Vyver, herein.

18 For its text, see ibid., 233.

19 See Silvio Ferrari, "Conclusion–Church and State in Post-Communist Europe," 416–17.

20 Ibid.

21 W. Cole Durham, Jr. rightly stresses that the law governing the creation, recognition, and registration of legal entities "is vital for the life of most religious communities in a modern legal setting." Durham, "Facilitating Freedom of Religion or Belief," 321.

22 Christian Tomuschat, "Freedom of Association," 493.

23 As expressed by the Strasbourg Court in a leading case on freedom of religious association, *Metropolitan Church of Bessarabia v. Moldova* (ECtHR, 2001-XII, 860, December 13, 2001), par. 116.

24 See, OSCEODIHR, "Guidelines,"

25 Ibid., 17.

26 See Asma Jahangir, Special Rapporteur on Freedom of Religion or Belief "Report of the Special Rapporteur on Freedom of Religion or Belief," U.N. Doc. A/HRC/13/40, December 21, 2009, par. 37.

27 Under Secretary for Democratic and Global Affairs, Bureau of Democracy, Human Rights, and Labour, October 26, 2009.

28 Durham, "Facilitating Freedom of Religion or Belief," 321–405.

29 Aviam Soifer, *Law and the Company We Keep* (Cambridge: Harvard University Press, 1995), 51, commenting on U.S. Supreme Court decision in *Widmar v. Vincent* 454 U.S. 263, 269 (1981) which granted religious worship additional protection as forms of speech and association covered by the First Amendment. On religion in the United States, generally, see, *inter alia*, Michael S. Ariens and Robert A. Destro, *Religious Liberty in a Pluralistic Society*, 2nd ed. (Durham, NC: Carolina Academic Press, 2002), 358–65 (on freedom of religious association); Ronald B. Flowers, Melissa Rogers, and Steven K. Green, *Religious Freedom and the Supreme Court* (Waco, TX: Baylor University Press, 2008).

30 See *Metropolitan Church of Bessarabia v. Moldova.* On case law of the Court, see, Malcolm D. Evans, *Religious Liberty and International Law in Europe* (Cambridge: Cambridge University Press, 1997); Javier Martinez-Torron, "Freedom of Expression versus Freedom of Religion in the European Court of Human Rights," in *Censorial Sensitivities: Free Speech and Religion in a Fundamentalist World* (Utrecht: Eleven International Publishing, 2007), 233–69.

31 On autonomy of religious associations, see Roland Minnerath, "The Right to Autonomy in Religious Affairs," in *Facilitating Freedom of Religion or Belief*, 292–319. See also Johan van der Vyver, "Self-Determination and the Right of Secession of Religious Minorities under International Law," in Peter G. Danchin and Elizabeth A. Cole, eds., *Protecting the Human Rights of Religious Minorities in Eastern Europe* (New York: Columbia University Press, 2002), 251–93, where the notion of "sphere sovereignty" is discussed. See also van der Vyver's chapter in this volume.

32 See further the chapter by Nazila Ghanea, herein.

33 *Hasan and Chaush v. Bulgaria*, 34 EHRR 55 (2002) (ECtHR, October 26, 2000), par. 56.

34 Minnerath, "The Right to Autonomy in Religious Affairs," 317–18 mentions particularly the concordats between the Holy See and States with a "Catholic background" and others without such a background, like Israel, or where Catholics are a small minority, like Estonia. Special agreements signed in Germany, Italy, and Spain with entities representing religious minorities are also relevant.

35 For the Judgment, *R v Governing Body of JFS and the Admissions Appeal Panel of JFS and others*, [2009] UKSC 15, December 16, 2009. For criticism, see H. H. H. Weiler,

"Discrimination and Identity in London: The Jewish Free School Case," in *Jewish Review of Books* 1 (Spring 2010).

36 Ibid., par. 9.

37 Weiler, "Discrimination and Identity in London," writes that what is troubling "is the sheer incomprehension and consequent intolerance of a religion whose self-understanding is different than that of Christianity." We do not want, he adds, "the legislature or the courts to be in the business of setting religious criteria for Jewishness."

38 See *Cha'are Shalom Ve Tsedek v. France*, 350 EctHr 233 (ECtHR, 2000-VII, 84, June 27, 2000).

39 *Manoussakis and Others v. Greece*, 23 EHRR 387 (1996) (ECtHR1996-IV, 1376, September 26, 1996).

40 The United States Supreme Court, in *Kedroff v. St. Nicholas Cathedral,* 344 U.S. 94 (1952) decided that the Moscow patriarchate enjoyed the right to appoint the clergy of the Russian Orthodox Church in North America and declared unconstitutional legislation intended to accord that right to the local Church. Justice Frankfurter stated that what was at stake was "the power to exercise religious authority." "St. Nicholas Cathedral is not just a piece of real estate... A cathedral is the seat and center of ecclesiastical authority." See, Flowers et al., *Religious Freedom and the Supreme Court,* 307.

41 See Abdelfattah Amor, Special Rapporteur on Freedom of Religion or Belief "Implementation of the Declaration on the Elimination of All Forms of Intolerance and of Discrimination Based on Religion or Belief," U.N. Doc. E/CN.4/1998/6 (January 22, 1998), par. 116.

42 See Lance S. Lehnhof, "Freedom of Religious Association: The Right of Religious Organizations to Obtain Legal Entity Status Under the European Convention," *Brigham Young University Law Review* (2002): 561–609, at 561.

43 On sects and new religions, see *inter alia,* Paul M. Taylor, *Freedom of Religion: UN and European Human Rights Law and Practice* (Cambridge; Cambridge University Press, 2005), esp. 292ff.; James R. Lewis, *Cults,* 2nd ed. (ABC CLIO, 2005); David G. Bromley and J. Gordon Melton, eds., *Cults, Religion and Violence* (Cambridge: Cambridge University Press, 2002).

44 Parliamentary Assembly, Council of Europe, "Recommendation 1412 (1999), Illegal Activities of Sects," *adopted* June 22, 1999.

■ RECOMMENDED READING

Durham, W. Cole, Jr. "Facilitating Freedom of Religion or Belief Through Religious Association Laws," in *Facilitating Freedom of Religion or Belief: A Deskbook,* eds. Tore Lindholm, W. Cole Durham, Jr., and, Bahia G. Tahzib-Lie (Leiden: Martinus Nijhoff, 2004), 321–495

Evans, Malcolm D. *Religious Liberty and International Law in Europe* (Cambridge: Cambridge University Press, 1997)

Ferrari, Silvio. "Conclusion–Church and State in Post-Communist Europe," in *Law and Religion in Post-Communist Europe,* eds. Silvio Ferrari, W. Cole Durham, Jr., and, Elizabeth A. Sewell (Leuven: Peeters, 2003), 411–427

Flowers, Ronald D., Melissa Rogers, and, Stephen K. Green. *Religious Freedom and the Supreme Court* (Waco, TX: Baylor University Press, 2008)

Lerner, Natan. *Religion, Secular Beliefs and Human Rights* (Leiden: Martinus Nijhoff, 2006)

Minerath, Roland. "The Right to Autonomy in Religious Affairs," in *Facilitating Freedom of Religion or Belief: A Deskbook,* eds. Tore Lindholm, W. Cole Durham, Jr., and, Bahia G. Tahzib-Lie, 291–319

Nowak, Manfred. *U.N. Covenant on Civil and Political Rights, CCPR Commentary* (Kehl, Germany: N.P. Engel, 1993)

Organization for Security and Cooperation in Europe and Office for Democratic Institutions and Human Rights (OSCE-ODIHR). Advisory Panel of Experts on Freedom of Religion or Belief, "Guidelines for the Review of Legislation Pertaining to Religion or Belief," adopted at the Venice Commission, 59th Plen. Sess., June 18–19, 2004 and welcomed at the annual session of the OSCE Parliamentary Assembly, Edinburgh, 2004 (www.osce.org/odihr/13993)

Partsch, Karl Josef. "Freedom of Conscience and Expression, and Political Freedoms," in *The International Bill of Rights,* ed. Louis Henkin (New York: Columbia University Press, 1981), 209–245

Scheinin, Martin. "Article 20," in. *The Universal Declaration of Human Rights,* eds. Gudmundur Alfredsson and Asbjorn Eide (The Hague: Martinus Nijhoff, 1999), 417–429

Taylor, Paul M. *Freedom of Religion: UN and European Human Rights Law and Practice* (Cambridge: Cambridge University Press, 2005)

Tomuschat, Christian. "Freedom of Association," in *The European System for the Protection of Human Rights*, eds. R. St. J. Macdonald, F. Matscher, and H. Petzold (Dordrecht: Martinus Nijhoff, 1993), 93–513

Witte, John, Jr. and Johan D. van der Vyver, eds. *Religious Human Rights in Global Perspective*, 2 vols. (The Hague: Martinus Nijhoff, 1996)

14 The Right to Self-Determination of Religious Communities

JOHAN D. VAN DER VYVER

Sunali Pillay was a teenage South African girl of Hindu extraction. She gained entry into the Durban Girls' High School—one of the most prestigious state schools in South Africa—where she received an excellent education. When she reached a certain stage of maturity, a golden stud was inserted in her nose, which is a custom in the Hindu community indicating that a girl has become eligible for marriage. This brought her into conflict with the school authorities. The school's code of conduct, signed by her parents as a condition for Sunali's admission to Girls' High, prohibited the wearing of any jewelry, except earrings and then only under meticulous conditions specified in the code of conduct. Sunali's mother explained to the school authorities that her daughter did not wear the nose stud as a token of fashion, but in deference to an age-old tradition of the Hindu community. The school management refused to grant Sunali an exemption from its dress code. A complaint was thereupon filed by Mrs. Pillay in the equality court, based on discrimination. The equality court ruled in favor of the school,[1] and the matter eventually came before the Constitutional Court of South Africa. The Constitutional Court decided that refusal by the school authorities to grant Sunali an exemption from the jewelry provision in the school's code of conduct amounted to unreasonable discrimination and was therefore unlawful.[2]

Leyla Şahin was a Muslim student at Istanbul University in Turkey. She was excluded from classes because she wore a headscarf. A Turkish law banned the wearing of headscarves in all universities and official government buildings, basing the proscription on the fact that Turkey is a secular state. In 1998, Leyla filed a complaint under the European system for the protection of human rights and fundamental freedoms.[3] The Grand Chamber of the European Court of Human Rights—the court of final instance in the European system of human rights protection—gave judgment in favor of Turkey. It decided that the headscarf ban is based on the constitutional principles of secularism and equality and consequently did not constitute a violation of the European Convention for the Protection of Human Rights and Fundamental Freedoms—nor did her suspension from the university for refusing to remove the headscarf amount to a violation of the Convention.[4] Ms. Şahin subsequently left Turkey and is now living in Vienna.

The judgment of the South African Constitutional Court was based on the nondiscrimination provisions in the Promotion of Equality and Prevention of Unfair Discrimination Act of 2000,[5] and was more precisely based on the proscription of discrimination based on religion and on culture.[6] Basing its decision on the proscription of discrimination was perhaps dictated by the fact that the case came to the Constitutional Court via the equality court and therefore under the Promotion of Equality and Prevention of Unfair Discrimination Act. By referring to discrimination based on religion and culture, the Court avoided the dilemma of deciding whether the wearing of a nose stud was a matter of religion or merely a Hindu custom. Had the matter been raised along a different route, the Court might have been constrained to deal with it under the religion prong of the right of everyone to "freedom of conscience, religion, thought, belief and opinion."[7] It is somewhat surprising that, while noting that prohibiting Sunali to wear a nose stud "affects other constitutional rights as well" (besides human dignity), the Court mentioned freedom of expression only, and not freedom of religion.[8] This omission was perhaps prompted by the Court's declining to decide definitively whether the wearing of a nose stud by Hindu women was a matter of religion or one of culture. This seems to be an easy case of the right to self-determination of cultural, religious, and linguistic communities, which, under the South African Constitution, includes the entitlement of such communities "to enjoy their culture, practice their religion and use their language."[9]

The case of Sunali Pillay thus illustrates the entanglement of different religion-specific principles: the proscription of discrimination based on religion or belief, freedom of religion, and the right to self-determination of religious communities. Although these principles overlap quite considerably, their application involves in each instance quite unique elements and, consequently, must be clearly distinguished.

The case of Leyla Şahin illustrates that several countries of the world, including Turkey, do not subscribe to the right to self-determination of distinct communities within their borders, basing their negative attitude on a general denial of, or unwillingness to afford relevance to ethnic, religious, or linguistic varieties among their respective citizens and residents. Other countries siding with Turkey in this regard include Greece and France. Greece is particularly unaccommodating of the claim to a distinct identity of people of Macedonian extraction in Florina (Northern Greece). As far as France is concerned, President Jacques Chirac on March 15, 2004, signed into law an amendment to the French Code of Education that now prohibits, as a principle of the separation of church and state, "the wearing of symbols or garb which shows religious affiliation in public primary and secondary schools."[10] And let it also not pass unnoticed that four countries with a prominent indigenous population voted against the adoption of the United Nations Declaration on the Rights of Indigenous Peoples of October 2, 2007, those countries being Australia, Canada, New Zealand, and the United States of America. These countries based their objections in part on (drafting of) the right to self-determination afforded to indigenous peoples.[11]

The right to self-determination has come to be an important principle of international law. It is mentioned in the Charter of the United Nations (Arts. 1.2;

see also Art. 73) and has been afforded a special place of prominence in the Covenant on Economic, Social and Cultural Rights (Art. 1) and in the Covenant on Civil and Political Rights (Art. 1). It is included in the Convention on the Rights of the Child (Art. 30) and features prominently in the UN Declaration on the Granting of Independence to Colonial Countries and Peoples of 1960 (Art. 2) and the Declaration on Principles of International Law concerning Friendly Relations and Co-Operation among States in accordance with the Charter of the United Nations of 1970. On the regional level, it has been endorsed by no less than the Helsinki Final Act of 1975 (par. VIII).

■ HISTORICAL PERSPECTIVES

The concept of self-determination owes its origin to economic socialism. In 1913, Joseph Stalin composed a detailed pamphlet on *Marxism and the National Question* in which he denoted the disposition of political communities within the over-arching and universal economic structures of communism as a matter of "self-determination." In March 1916, V.I. Lenin published a more elaborate exposition of the same theme in his seminal work, *Thesis on the Socialist Revolution and the Right of Nations to Self-Determination*—described by one analyst as "the first compelling enunciation of the principle" of self-determination of peoples.[12] Self-determination of nation-states within a non-negotiable economic world order was not where it all ended.

The prominence of the right to self-determination in international law has mostly been attributed to American President Woodrow Wilson. Robert Friedlander thus credited President Wilson's Fourteen Points Address of January 8, 1918 as "transforming self-determination into a universal right"[13]—though the president never really used the word "self-determination." He included in those Fourteen Points one that proclaimed "[a] free, open-minded, and absolutely impartial adjustment of all colonial claims, based upon a strict observance of the principle that in determining all such questions of sovereignty the interests of the population concerned must have equal weight with the equitable claims of government whose title is to be determined."[14] This statement has come to be regarded as the basis of the League of Nations policy for dealing with the future dispensation of nation-states that were part of the world empires defeated and dissolved through World War I.[15] But this, too, was not where it all would end.

Leaving aside the connotation attributed to that concept within socialist political thought, the right to self-determination, over time, acquired at least four quite distinct meanings, depending in each instance on the nature and disposition of the peoples claiming that right.[16] First, the post-World War I nuance of the term denoted the right to eventual political independence, within the confines of the mandate system of the League of Nations, of nation-states that had been part of the Ottoman, German, Russian, and Austro-Hungarian empires. In this context, self-determination vested in "ethnic communities, nations, or nationalities primarily defined by language or culture,"[17] and thus denoted the right of "peoples" in the sense of (territorially defined) nations to political independence. Second, following World War II, the emphasis shifted to the principle "of bringing all colonial situations to a speedy end,"[18] and here the right to self-determination vested in colonized peoples, while the substance of their right again denoted political independence.[19] The United Nations Millennium Declaration extended the principle of decolonization to include "the right to self-determination of peoples which remain under . . . foreign occupation."[20]

Third, in the 1960s, yet another category of "peoples" with a right to self-determination came to be identified, namely those subject to a racist regime. Here, the concept substantively signified the right of such peoples to participate in the structures of government within the countries to which they belonged.[21] The "self" in self-determination was no longer perceived to be territorially defined sections of the population in multinational empires or colonial dominions, but also came to be identified with the entire population of a territory where the social, economic, and constitutional system was structured on institutionally sanctioned racial discrimination.[22]

Fourth, and finally, in contemporary international law, the right to self-determination has been extended to national or ethnic, religious, and linguistic communities within a political society whose particular entitlements are centered upon a right to live according to the traditions and customs of the concerned group. The right to self-determination of such "peoples" has been defined in compelling terms in the 1966 International Covenant on Civil and Political Rights (ICCPR), such that: "In those States in which ethnic, religious or linguistic minorities exist, persons belonging to such minorities shall not be denied the right, in community with the other members of their group, to enjoy their own culture, to profess and practice their own religion, or to use their own language."[23] The 1992 Declaration on the Rights of Persons Belonging to National or Ethnic, Religious and Linguistic Minorities similarly speaks of "the right [of national or ethnic, religious and linguistic minorities] to enjoy their own culture, to profess and practice their own religion, and to use their own language, in private and in public, freely and without interference or any form of discrimination."[24] This, then, is where the right to self-determination or religious communities comes in.

■ SPHERE SOVEREIGNTY AND SELF-DETERMINATION

The right to self-determination is closely related to, but must be distinguished from, the principle of sphere sovereignty; that is the right of religious institutions to regulate and to administer their internal affairs without interference from external sources. The distinction is closely related to the difference between a religious community and a religious institution.[25] A religious institution, such as the Episcopal, Baptist, Roman Catholic, or Greek Orthodox Church, is a formally structured or organized group entity, has an identity separate from that of its members, and qualifies for legal personality. A legal institution also has its own internal structures, organization, and activities. A religious institution, as a legal person, can own property, sue and be sued, and exercise other competencies within the legal sphere in its own name. A religious institution has sovereign powers within its own internal sphere in virtue of which it may conduct its internal affairs without undue outside (including state) interference.

A very special problem that has been debated at some length is whether a religious institution can also be the beneficiary of rights and freedoms protected through a constitutional bill of rights. The South African Constitution expressly affords to legal persons, including churches and other religious institutions, the rights protected under its Bill of Rights "to the extent required by the nature of the right and the nature of the juristic person,"[26] and also makes the Bill of Rights binding on legal persons, including churches and other religious institutions, "taking into account the nature of the right and the nature of the duty imposed."[27] Ironically, the question whether or not a religious institution as a juristic person has the right to freedom of religion, belief and opinion[28] is controversial in modern day South Africa. According to Stuart Woolman, "[c]orporations have neither conscience nor religion" within the meaning of the constitutional protection of freedom of religion, belief and opinion.[29] Gerrit Pienaar likewise argues that faith and conscience are highly personal and cannot vest in a church or other religious body.[30] E.F.J. Malherbe, on the other hand, maintains that a church institution does have a right to freedom of religion.[31] It is respectfully submitted that a doctrinal confession is an essential component of a religious community and, when under threat, can at least be vindicated by the institutional structures serving that community.

The power of a religious institution to regulate its own internal affairs without external interference, including interference through the laws and administrative action of the State, is commonly referred to as sovereignty of the religious institution within its own domestic sphere. This, too, is part and parcel of the South African constitutional dispensation and includes the principle that "in ecclesiastical matters, it was salutary that disputes, as and when they arose, should ideally be resolved through internal mechanisms."[32] In a recent judgment, the equality court decided that the dismissal of an organ teacher at the arts academy of a congregation of the Dutch Reformed Church in Pretoria on account of his involvement in a same-sex relationship amounted to unfair discrimination based on sexual orientation.[33] The equality court based its decision in part on the fact that the organ teacher's employment responsibilities was in no way linked to the spiritual mission of the church, and stated expressly that if that had not been the case, and given the doctrinal objections of the church to homosexuality, the court would not have overruled the decision of the church authorities to terminate the plaintiff's employment. The judge cited, with approval, the following passage from a leading analyst of the religion clauses in the South African Constitution:

> Few exercises are more central to religious freedom than the right of a church to choose its own spiritual leaders. If a court were to hold that churches could not deem sexual orientation, or any of the other enumerated grounds in the equality clause, a disqualifying factor for the priesthood, the effect on many churches could be devastating. Consequently, although the value of equality is foundational to the new constitutional dispensation, it is unlikely that equality considerations could outweigh the enormous impact of failing to give churches an exemption in relation to their spiritual leaders. Where the appointment, dismissal and employment conditions of religious leaders (such as priests, imams, rabbis, and so forth) are concerned, religious bodies are likely to be exempted from compliance with legislation prohibiting unfair discrimination.[34]

As far as the United States is concerned, recent analyses of First Amendment jurisprudence conducted by Paul Horwitz looked beyond the legal norms that may or may not be enacted by Congress under the constraints imposed by the Constitution to uncover the role of institutions functioning within the protected enclave of the First Amendment, such as universities, the press, and religious associations.[35] Based on the doctrine of sphere sovereignty of the Dutch political philosopher, Abraham Kuyper, Horwitz argued convincingly that such "First Amendment institutions" should be afforded the right to operate on a largely self-regulating basis and beyond the supervision of external legal regimes.

The constitutions of several countries contain provisions that signify what in essence amount to sphere sovereignty of religious institutions. The Constitution of Singapore confines the internal sovereignty of religious groups "to managing their own religious affairs" (Art. 15.3); the Romanian Constitution permits the organization of religious sects "in accordance with their own statutes" but "under the terms defined by the law" (Art. 29.3). The Italian Constitution affords independence and sovereignty, "each within its own order," to the State and the (Roman) Catholic Church only (Art. 7). The Irish Constitution more generously proclaims the right of every religious denomination "to manage its own affairs" (Art. 44.2, 44.5). In its Charter of Fundamental Rights and Basic Freedoms, the Czech Republic proclaims that "Churches and religious societies govern their own affairs," "establish their own bodies and appoint their clergy," and "found religious orders and other church institutions, independent of state authorities" (Art. 16.2). Poland defines the relationship between the State and churches and other religious organizations on basis of "the principle of respect for their autonomy and the mutual independence of each in its own sphere, as well as . . . the principle of cooperation for the good of the individual and for the common good" (Art. 25.3).

In the United States, the case of *Kedroff v. St. Nicholas Cathedral* (1952) makes clear that the church has a constitutional right to freedom of religion.[36] To place this judgment in its proper historical perspective, in 1925, New York adopted a new law for the purpose of acquiring a cathedral for the Russian Orthodox Church in North America as a place of worship "in accordance with the doctrine, discipline and worship of the Holy Apostolic Catholic Church of Eastern Confession as taught by the holy scriptures, holy tradition, seven ecumenical councils and holy fathers of the Church." In consequence of strong anti-Soviet sentiments that prevailed in the United States at the time, Article 5-C was added to the Religious Corporation Law of New York in 1945 (with clarifying amendments being added in 1948) with a view to transferring the control of the New York churches of the Russian Orthodox religion from the central Patriarchate in Moscow to the governing authorities of the Church in America. The Archbishop of New York was subsequently elected in that capacity by a *sobor* of American churches to serve as head of the Metropolitan of All America and Canada. A dispute erupted as to his competence, in virtue of Article 5-C, to occupy the church property in New York. In *Kedroff*, the matter was decided in favor of the Moscow Patriarchate, the Court holding that Article 5-C violated the constitutional right to "the free exercise of an ecclesiastical right, the Church's choice of its hierarchy." Justice Reed, speaking for the majority, referred to "a spirit of freedom for religious organizations" embracing "power to decide for themselves free from state interference, matters of church government as well as those of faith and doctrine," which freedom includes the right to select the clergy of the Church.[37] An American analyst of *Kedroff* defined the substance of the institutional group rights vesting in the church as a matter of sphere sovereignty such that, "The heart of the pluralistic thesis is the conviction that government must recognize that it is not the sole possessor of sovereignty, and that private groups within the community are entitled to lead their own free lives and exercise within the area of their competence an authority so effective as to justify labeling it a sovereign authority."[38]

How, then, does the institutional sphere sovereignty of a religious institution differ from the right to self-determination of a religious community? A religious community is made up of people sharing the same confession of faith. The group comprising a religious community is not structured or organized in any formal way but its members are bound together by a common religious commitment or belief. In the Greco-Bulgarian Communities Case of 1930, the Permanent Court of International Justice defined as follows the "general traditional conception" of a community, which in contemporary usage would be called a people, such that "the 'community' is a group of persons living in a given country or locality, having a race, religion, language and tradition of their own and united by this identity of race, religion, language and tradition in a sentiment of solidarity, with a view to preserving their traditions, maintaining their form of worship, ensuring the instruction and upbringing of their children in accordance with the spirit and traditions of their race and rendering mutual assistance to each other."[39]

International law denotes communities with a right to self-determination in the contemporary sense as "peoples." According to Yoram Dinstein, peoplehood comprises two elements: an objective component, designated by the factual contingencies upon which the unity of the group depends; and a subjective component, constituted by a certain state of mind—the consciousness of belonging, and perhaps the will to be associated with the group.[40] The right to self-determination belonging to a people, including a religious community, is therefore a group right of a special kind, namely a *collective group right*. A collective group right must be distinguished from an *institutional group right*.

A collective group right is afforded to individual persons belonging to a certain category, such as children, women, or ethnic, religious, and cultural community. The right of national minorities to peaceful assembly, freedom of association, freedom of expression, and freedom of thought, conscience, and religion,[41] thus belongs to every member of the group and can be exercised separately or jointly with any other member(s) of the group. An institutional group right, on the other hand, vests in a social institution as such and can only be exercised by that collective entity through the agency of its authorized representative organs.

The religious community has a right to self-determination. Members of the group are entitled to profess and practice their religion without undue constraints imposed on that entitlement by the political powers that be. A collective group right of religious communities to self-determination has been recognized in the United States on various fronts, for example to substantiate the payment of unemployment benefits to Sabbatarians who refused to work on their day of rest,[42] or to a Jehovah's Witness who refused, on religious grounds, to accept employment in a factory which produced parts that would be used in military armament.[43] This rights of religious communities to self-determination has also been applied or to exempt members of the Old Order Amish religion and of the Conservative Amish Mennonite Church, on religious grounds, from the statutory obligation to send their children to high school until they were sixteen years old.[44]

The right to self-determination, as a collective group right, involves more than merely an accommodating disposition toward particular sectional beliefs and practices. In virtue of the right to self-determination, governments are required to secure, through their respective constitutional and legal systems, the interests of distinct sections of the population that constitute a people in the above sense. The Declaration on the Rights of Persons Belonging to National or Ethnic, Religious, and Linguistic Minorities clearly spells out that obligation: protect, and encourage conditions for the promotion of, the concerned group identities of minorities under the jurisdiction of the duty-bound state (Arts. 1.1 and 4.2); afford to minorities the special competence to participate effectively in decisions pertinent to the group to which they belong (Art. 2.3); do not discriminate in any way against any person on basis of his or her group identity (Art. 3), and in fact take action to secure their equal treatment by and before the law (Art. 4.1). The Declaration further provides that "States shall take measures to create favorable conditions to enable persons belonging to minorities to express their characteristics and to develop their culture, language, religion, traditions and customs, except where specific practices are in violation of national law and contrary to international standards."[45]

The Council of Europe's Framework Convention for the Protection of National Minorities specified minority rights in much the same vein. It guarantees equality before the law and equal protection of the laws (Art. 4.1). States Parties promise to provide "the conditions necessary for persons belonging to national minorities to maintain and develop their culture, and to preserve the essential elements of their identity, namely their religion, language, traditions and cultural heritage" (Art. 5.1). States Parties further recognize the right of a person belonging to a national minority "to manifest his or her religion or belief and to establish religious institutions, organizations and associations" (Art. 8).

■ LIMITATIONS OF THE RIGHT TO SELF-DETERMINATION

People are involved in all kinds of group affiliations, some deriving from biological attributes (such as sex, race, and family ties) and others founded on an historical base (such as a shared national, cultural, religious, or linguistic alliance). The group affiliation of persons tends to provoke any degree of commitment to traditional beliefs and practices perceived by their constituents as a *sine qua non* for maintaining the identity and interests of the group. Those beliefs and practices may include ones that have come to be discredited in view of contemporary notions of human rights and fundamental freedoms. Such beliefs and practices have brought onto the agenda of sociologists, lawyers, and political scientists how best to accommodate the group identities represented in a political community within the laws and/or structures of the State—where to draw the line, for example, between practices of—religious communities that ought to be protected under the rubric of a right to self-determination and those that can no longer be tolerated in this day and age of humane governance. There are two quite distinct aspects to the problem posed: (1) to what extent to accommodate group formations in the political structures of the State; and (2) how to respond through legal interventions to religiously-based practices that have come to be identified as a threat to life or limb of vulnerable members of the group.

It must at the outset be emphasized that the right to self-determination recognizes in broad outline the existence of ethnic, cultural, religious, and linguistic diversities within a political society (pluralism) as a salient fact that ought to be accommodated in the political structures and legal arrangements of the State. However, it is equally important that group alliances based on a common ethnic extraction, cultural heritage, religious conviction, or linguistic identity ought not to be afforded a role within the body politic beyond the distinctive attribute that constitutes the bond between members of the group. That is to say, it is of the essence of the right to self-determination that the relevance of group interests are to be cut down, to size, to be dictated by the nature of the group. The protected interests of a cultural group are to be confined to cultural affairs, of a religious group to matters of religion, and so on. To afford *political* representation in the structures of government to a *cultural* or a *religious* group, would amount to affording to those latter modalities that qualify the group a pertinence beyond the confines of their true (and useful) destination in the aggregate of human society.

As to the second question mentioned above, it is important to note that the right to self-determination is not absolute. Self-determination is generally said not to legitimize violations of human rights that might be part and parcel of an ethnic tradition or religious usage. This assessment is somewhat superficial. International law seems to tolerate discrimination against women as a manifestation of a cultural tradition or religious dogma, but is quite vocal in its condemnation of, for example, female genital mutilation—a practice which at least in some communities is founded on religious considerations. The principle applied seems to be that political authorities will not use the long arm of the law to prohibit religious practices that merely amount to (gender-based) discrimination, but will not tolerate, under pretences of a right to self-determination, religious or cultural practices which constitute violations of the right to life or physical integrity.

Withholding life-sustaining medication or therapeutic treatment from a child upon instructions of the parents based on religious conviction presents a very special problem in this regard. In the United States, dealing with this problem has had a checkered history.[46] There are, on the one hand, state laws in place that exempt parents who prefer spiritual treatment or faith healing from statutory requirements to furnish health care to a child in their care,[47] but this concession to freedom of religion will not absolve a parent from criminal liability for involuntary manslaughter if the child should die in consequence of being denied conventional medical treatment.[48] Parents will therefore be prosecuted for providing spiritual treatment for their children in lieu of traditional medical care, but only if such treatment turned out to be ineffective and resulted in death of the child.[49] In South Africa, on the other hand, the High Court as upper guardian of all children can intervene by sanctioning feasible medical procedures while the life of the child can still be saved. It can consequently overrule the decision of parents who, for religious reasons, would not give their consent for a child to receive a blood transfusion (or other therapeutic treatment) considered by a pediatrician to be necessary for the survival of the child.[50] In South Africa, the constitutionally protected right to life of a child will in all circumstances trump the claim to the exercise of religious liberty of the parent.

As noted in the introductory paragraphs of this essay, the South African Constitutional Court and the European Court of Human Rights, both applying the principle of equal treatment and non-discrimination, came to opposite conclusions as to the legality of laws prohibiting distinctive symbols or clothing based on religious practices. Applying the principle of equality from the perspective of constitutional secularism in Turkey, the European Court of Human Rights was precluded from accommodating the truism that equal treatment actually demands differentiations for legal purposes based on distinct group formations in cases where the differentiations are truly relevant to the criterion which distinguishes the one group from the other. Mindful of the plural composition of the South African population and the concomitant constitutional right to self-determination of religious communities, the South African Constitutional Court, by contrast, decided that not upholding the distinct practices of the Hindu community would amount to unbecoming discrimination.

Failure of national systems to provide such protection to sectional interests of peoples within their area of jurisdiction, or merely the perception of being marginalized, must be seen as an important contributing cause of the tireless aspirations toward the establishment of homogenous states for sections of the political community with a strong group consciousness: the Muslim community of Kashmir, the Basques in Northern Spain, the Hindu factions in Sri Lanka, the Catholic minority in Northern Ireland, the Christian community in Southern Sudan, the Kurds in Iraq and Turkey, people of Macedonian extraction in Florina (Northern Greece), and many others.

■ THE RIGHT TO SELF-DETERMINATION AND SECESSION

The right to self-determination vesting in ethnic, religious, or linguistic communities does not include a right to secession or political independence—even in cases where a government, in breach of international law, does not uphold the right to self-determination of sections of its subordinates. International law is quite explicit in proclaiming that self-determination of ethnic, religious, and linguistic communities must co-exist with "the territorial integrity of states"—a phrase denoting the sanctity of existing national borders. The right to self-determination, furthermore, vests in a people while a new state created through secession is essentially territorially defined (it is a defined territory that secedes from an existing state and not a people).

General definitions of the right to self-determination, such as the one contained in the Declaration on the Granting of Independence to Colonial Countries and Peoples proclaiming the right of peoples to "freely determine their political status" and the right to "freely pursue their economic, social, and cultural development" should therefore not be seen as a general sanction of a right to political independence but must be limited and understood in the context of the subject-matter of the document from which they derive: peoples subject to colonial rule or foreign domination do have a right to political independence; national or ethnic, religious and linguistic communities in an existing state do not. It is unfortunate that the substance of the right as applied to colonial countries and peoples is sometimes cited in instruments dealing with the right to self-determination of national or ethnic, religious, or linguistic peoples. The 2007 United Nations Declaration on the Rights of Indigenous Peoples thus proclaims that, by virtue of their right to self-determination, indigenous peoples are entitled to "freely determine their political status and freely pursue their economic, social and cultural development."[51] But lest this provision be interpreted to denote political independence, the Declaration stipulates that "[n]othing in this Declaration may be . . . construed as authorizing or encouraging any action which would dismember or impair, totally or in part, the territorial integrity or political unity of sovereign and independent States."[52] The United Nations' 1993 World Conference on Human Rights similarly said it all when the right of peoples to "freely determine their political status, and freely pursue their economic, social and cultural development" was expressly made conditional upon the following proviso: "This [definition of self-determination] shall not be construed as authorizing or encouraging any action which would dismember or impair, totally or in part, the territorial integrity or political unity of sovereign and independent States conducting themselves in compliance with the principles of equal rights and self-determination of peoples and thus possessed of a Government representing the whole people belonging to the territory without distinction of any kind."[53]

In 1996, the Supreme Court of Canada was instructed to consider, among other things, whether there is a right to self-determination under international law that would give the National Assembly or the government of Quebec the right to effect secession of Quebec from Canada unilaterally. The Canadian Supreme Court for several reasons answered the question in the negative.[54] It should be evident to everyone that the inhabitants of Quebec, being composed of a variety of ethnic or cultural, religious, and linguistic population groups, do not constitute a people as defined in international law, and for that reason alone cannot claim a right to self-determination. Sections of the population of Quebec, united by a common ethnic extraction, cultural heritage, religious affiliation, or linguistic preference could of course lament the denial of their right to self-determination on the grounds that they are not permitted to accede to a lifestyle dictated by their national or ethnic, religious or linguistic identities. But that is *de facto* not the case—at least not as far as (Francophone) Quebecois are concerned.

There are many compelling reasons why the destruction of existing political communities harboring a plural society should be avoided at all costs. First, a multiplicity of economically non-viable states will further contribute to a decline of the living standards in the world community. Second, the perception that people sharing a common language, culture, or religion would necessarily also be politically compatible is clearly a myth, and disillusionment after the event might provoke profound resentment and further conflict. Third, movement of people within plural societies across territorial divides has greatly destroyed ethnic, cultural, or religious homogeneity in regions where it might have existed in earlier times, and consequently, demarcation of borders that would be inclusive of the sectional demography which secessionists seek to establish is in most cases quite impossible. Fourth, affording political relevance to ethnic, cultural, or religious affiliation not only carries within itself the potential of repression of minority groups within the nation, but also affords no political standing whatsoever to persons who, on account of mixed parentage or marriage, cannot be identified with any particular faction of the group-conscious community, or to those who—for whatever reason—do not wish to be identified under any particular ethnic, religious, or cultural label. And, fifth, in consequence of the above, an ethnically, culturally, or religiously defined state will more often than not create its own "minorities problem." Because of the ethnic, cultural, or religious incentive for the establishment of the secession state, such a development will almost invariably result in profound discrimination against those who do not belong, or worse still, a strategy of "ethnic cleansing."

■ CONCLUSIONS

Scholarly endeavors to find a feasible answer to the question of group alliances within the body politic has thus far rendered a rich variety of socio-political theories and practices, ranging from strict individualism to any number of totalitarian designs. The most extreme manifestations of individualism deny the relevance—if not the very existence as part of empirical reality—of institutional group entities and tend to devaluate the community interests of the persons who make up a distinct community to a subordinate and insignificant part of the human make-up. Totalitarianism, on the other hand, attributes to a particular group—whether the State or a racial, ethnic, or religious community—an inflated significance and dominant disposition over individuals within, and often beyond the constituency of, the concerned group. It aspires toward homogeneity or, alternatively, subordination, repression and/or persecution of the other. It cultivates a sense of group-defined superiority and domination, exploits a sense of xenophobia within its number, and might on the fringes culminate in genocide or lesser forms of "ethnic cleansing."

The right to self-determination, on the contrary, appreciates and seeks to accommodate the group identities of sections of a political community. It promotes pride in one's cultural extraction and religious affiliation. It is patron to a political dispensation comprising, in the celebrated words of Archbishop Desmond Tutu, "a rainbow people." Accommodating, and indeed protecting, the right to self-determination of religious communities within the political structures of the body politic is after all also in the interest of the State.

The South African Constitutional Court has on several occasions emphasized the vital importance of religion as a component of South Africa's constitutional democracy. In *Christian Education, South Africa v. Minister of Education*, Justice Albie Sachs had this to say:

> There can be no doubt that the right to freedom of religion, belief and opinion in an open and democratic society contemplated by the Constitution is important. The right to believe or not to believe, and to act or not to act according to his or her beliefs

> or non-beliefs, is one of the key ingredients of any person's dignity. Yet freedom of religion goes beyond protecting the inviolability of the individual conscience. For many believers, their relationship with God or creation is central to all their activities. It concerns their capacity to relate in an intensely meaningful fashion to their sense of themselves, their community and their universe. For millions in all walks of life, religion provides support and nurture and a framework for individual and social stability and growth. Religious belief has the capacity to awake concepts of self-worth and human dignity which form the cornerstone of human rights. It affects the believer's view of society and founds the distinction between right and wrong. It expresses itself in the affirmation and continuity of powerful traditions that frequently have an ancient character transcending historical epochs and national boundaries.[55]

In a case that afforded legality to same-sex marriages, Justice Sachs, delivering the unanimous decision of the Court, emphasized the importance of religion for the State:

> Religious bodies play a large and important part in public life, through schools, hospitals and poverty relief programmes. They command ethical behaviour from their members and bear witness to the exercise of power by State and private agencies; they promote music, art and theatre; they provide halls for community activities, and conduct a great variety of social activities for their members and the general public. They are part of the fabric of public life, and constitute active elements of the diverse and pluralistic nation contemplated by the Constitution. Religion is not just a question of belief or doctrine. It is part of the people's temper and culture, and for many believers a significant part of their way of life. Religious organizations constitute important sectors of national life and accordingly have a right to express themselves to government and the courts on the great issues of the day. They are active participants in public affairs fully entitled to have their say with regard to the way law is made and applied.[56]

He went on to say that the Court must recognize the distinctive spheres which the secular and the sacred occupies and not force the one into the sphere of the other; it must "accommodate and manage [the] difference of intensely held worldviews and lifestyles in a reasonable and fair manner" and not impose the religious views of one section of the population on the other, and it must in particular protect minorities against discrimination through majority opinions.

This, then, is what upholding of the right to self-determination of religious communities within the social, political and legal structures of a nation is in the final analysis all about.

■ NOTES

1 *Pillay v. MEC for Education: KwaZulu-Natal & Others*, 2006 (6) SA 363 (EqC) (S. Afr.).

2 *MEC for Education: KwaZulu-Natal & Others v. Pillay & Others*, 2008 (1) SA 474 (CC) (S. Afr.).

3 *Şahin v. Turkey,* 44 EHRR 5 (2007) (EctHR November 10, 2005) (Grand Chamber Judgment).

4 Ibid. See also *Kurtulmuş v. Turkey* (ECtHR, 2006-II, January 23, 2001); *Köse and 93 Others v. Turkey* (ECtHR, 2006-II, January 24, 2006). See further the chapter by Carolyn Evans, herein.

5 The Promotion of Equality and Prevention of Unfair Discrimination Act 4 of 2000 was enacted under Section 9(4) of the Constitution of the Republic of South Africa, Act 108 of 1996 [hereafter "South African Constitution"] to prohibit unfair discrimination by persons or institutions other than the State.

6 *MEC for Education: KwaZulu-Natal & Others,* at par. 68, with reference to "The Promotion of Equality and Prevention of Unfair Discrimination Act," Art. 6.

7 South African Constitution, sec. 15(1).

8 *MEC for Education: KwaZulu-Natal & Others,* at par. 93.

9 South African Constitution, sec. 15(1).

10 Loi no. 2004–228 du 15 mars 2004 encadrant, en application du principe de laïcité, le port de signes ou de tenues manifestant une appurtenance religieuse dans les écoles, colleges et lycées publics.

11 See S. James, Anaya, *International Human Rights and Indigenous Peoples* (Leiden: Wolters Kluwer, 2009), 71–75 (U.S.A.), 83–84 (Australia), 84–86 (Canada), 86–87 (New Zealand) (2009). See further the chapter by Ronald Niezen, herein.

12 Antonio Cassese, *Self-Determination of Peoples: A Legal Reappraisal* (Cambridge: Cambridge University Press, 1995), 15.

13 Robert Friedlander, "Self-Determination: A Legal-Political Inquiry," *Detroit College of Law Review* 1 (1975): 71, 73.

14 "Fourteen Points Address delivered on January 8, 1918 to a Joint Session of Congress by President Woodrow Wilson, Point 5" in *Public Papers of Woodrow Wilson: War and Peace,* eds. R.S. Baker & W.E. Dodd (New York : Harper and Bros., 1927), 1: 155–59.

15 Vernon van Dyke, *Human Rights, the United States, and World Community* (New York: Oxford University Press, 1970), 86.

16 See Johan D. van der Vyver, "Sovereignty and Human Rights in Constitutional and International Law," *Emory International Law Review* 5 (1991): 321, 395–416; Johan D. Van der Vyver, "Self-Determination and the Peoples of Quebec," *Journal of Transnational Law & Policy* 10 (2000): 1, 14–19; Johan van der Vyver, "Self-Determination and the Right to Secession of Religious Minorities under International Law," in *Protection the Human Rights of Religious Minorities in Eastern Europe,* eds. Peter G. Dachin & Elizabeth A. Cole (New York: Columbia University Press, 2002), 251, 258–61; Johan D. van der Vyver, "Cultural Identity as a Constitutional Right in South Africa," *Stellenbosch Law Review* 14 (2003): 51.

17 N. Berman, "Sovereignty in Abeyance: Self-Determination and International Law," *Wisconsin International Law Journal* 7 (1988): 51, 53–56, 58, 86–87.

18 *Western Sahara* (Advisory Opinion), 1975 I.C.J. 1, 31 (May 25, 1975); and see also *Legal Consequences for States of the Continued Presence of South Africa in Namibia* (South West Africa) *Notwithstanding Security Council Resolution* 276 (1970) (Advisory Opinion), 1971 I.C.J. 16, 31 (June 21, 1971) (the Court holding that the right to self-determination was applicable to "territories under colonial rule" and that it "embraces all peoples and territories which 'have not yet attained independence'").

19 Berman, "Sovereignty in Abeyance," 54; see also Cassese, *Self-Determination of Peoples,* 76; van Dyke, *Human Rights, the United States,* 87; R. Emerson, "Self-Determination,"

American Journal of International Law 66 (1971): 459, 463; O. Schachter, "The United Nations and Internal Conflict," in *Law and Civil War in the Modern World,* ed. J.N. Moore (Baltimore, MD: Johns Hopkins University Press, 1974), 401, 406–07; G. Tesfagiorgis, "Self-Determination: Its Evolution and Practice by the United Nations and its Application in the Case of Eritrea," *Wisconsin International Law Journal* 6 (1987): 75, 78–80.

20 United Nations Millennium Declaration, G.A. Res. 55/2, U.N. GAOR, 55th Sess., Supp. No. 49, at 4, U.N. Doc. A/55/49 (2000), par. 4.

21 The linkage within the confines of the right to self-determination of systems of institutionalized racism and colonialism or foreign domination may be traced to the United Nations General Assembly's Declaration on the Inadmissibility of Intervention in the Domestic Affairs of States and the Protection of Their Independence and Sovereignty of 1965, in which the United Nations demanded of all States to respect "the right to self-determination and independence of peoples and nations, to be freely exercised without any foreign pressure, and with absolute respect for human rights and fundamental freedoms," and to this end proclaimed that "all States shall contribute to the complete elimination of racial discrimination and colonialism in all its forms and manifestations." Declaration on the Inadmissibility of Intervention in the Domestic Affairs of States and the Protection of Their Independence and Sovereignty, G.A. Res. 2131, 20 U.N. GAOR Supp. (No. 14) at 11, U.N. Doc. A/6014, (1965) par. 6.

22 This development was probably prompted by the claim of South Africa that the establishment of independent tribal homelands as part of the policy of separate development (apartheid) constituted a manifestation of the right to self-determination of the different ethnic groups within the country's African population. Not so, responded the international community. The tribal homelands were a creation of the minority (white) regime and did not emerge from the wishes, or political self-determination, of the denationalized peoples themselves.

23 International Covenant on Civil and Political Rights, G.A. res. 2200A (XXI), 21 U.N. GAOR Supp. (No. 16) at 52, U.N. Doc. A/6316 (1966), 999 U.N.T.S. 171, *entered into force* Mar. 23, 1976; and see in general Felix Ermacora, "The Protection of Minorities Before the United Nations," in (1983-IV) *Recueil des Cours,* 246.

24 Declaration on the Rights of Persons Belonging to National or Ethnic, Religious and Linguistic Minorities, Art. 2.1, G.A. Res. 47/136, 47 U.N. GAOR Supp. (No. 49), at 210, U.N. Doc. A/Res/47/135 (1992) (hereinafter "Minorities Declaration").

25 See Johan D. van der Vyver, *Leuven Lectures on Religious Institutions, Religious Communities and Rights* (Leuven: Uitgeverij Peeters, 2004), 3–5. See further the chapter by Natan Lerner, herein.

26 South African Constitution sec. 8(4).

27 Id., sec. 8(2).

28 Id., sec. 15.

29 Stuart Woolman, "Application," in Matthew Chaskalson et al., *Constitutional Law of South Africa*, 10.2(d). (Revised Service 5, 1999).

30 Gerrit Pienaar, "Konstitutsionele Voorskrifte Rakende Regspersone," *Tydskrif vir Hedendaagse Romeins-Hollandse Reg* 60 (1997); 564, 581; Gerrit Pienaar, *Legal Subjectivity and the Juristic Person* (Potchefstroom: Potchefstroom University for Christian Higher Education, 1999), 100, n. 2.

31 E.F.J. Malherbe, "Die Grondwetlike Beskerming van Godsdiensvryheid," *Tydskrif vir die Suid-Afrikaanse Reg* (1998): 673, 679.

32 *Methodist Church of Southern Africa v. Mtongana,* 2008 (6) SA 69, par. 10 (TkHC) (S. Afr.).

33 *Strydom v. Nederduitse Gereformeerde Gemeente, Moreleta Park*, 2009 (4) SA 510 (Equality ourt, TPA) (S. Afr.), applying the prohibition, in virtue of the Promotion of Equality and Prevention of Discrimination Act 4 of 2000, of discrimination by the state and by non-state institutions based on sexual orientation.

34 Ibid. par. 15, with reference to Paul Farlam, "Freedom of Religion" in *Constitutional Law of South Africa*, 2nd amended ed., vol. 3., eds. Stuart Woolman, Theunis Roux, and Michael Bishop (St. Paul, MN: Thomson/West, 2009), chs. 41. 47.

35 See Paul Horwitz, "Universities as First Amendment Institutions: Some Easy Answers and Hard Questions," *U.C.L.A. Law Review* 54 (2007): 1497; Paul Horwitz, "Churches as First Amendment Institutions: Of Sovereignty and Spheres," *Harvard Civil Rights and Civil Liberties Law Review* 35 (2009): 79.

36 *Kedroff v. St. Nicholas Cathedral*, 344 U.S. 94 (1952); see John H. Garvey, "Churches and the Free Exercise of Religion," *Notre Dame Journal of Law, Ethics & Public Policy* 4 (1990): 567, 578–84 (concluding with reference to *Kedroff* (at 584) that "churches as groups may also claim a right to the free exercise of religion").

37 Ibid., 116, 119.

38 Mark DeWolfe Howe, "Foreword: Political Theory and the Nature of Liberty," *Harvard Law Review* 67 (1953): 91.

39 The Greco-Bulgarian "Communities," P.C.I.J., Series B, Advisory Opinions, vol. 2, No. 17, 21 (July 31, 1930).

40 Yoram Dinstein, "Collective Human Rights of Peoples and Minorities," *International Law Quarterly* 25 (1976): 102, 103.

41 See European Framework Convention for the Protection of National Minorities, Art. 7, E.T.S 157, reprinted in 34 I.L.M. 351 (1995).

42 *Sherbert v. Verner*, 373 U.S. 398 (1963); see also *Hobbie v. Unemployment Appeals Commission of Florida*, 480 U.S. 136 (1987); *Frazee v. Illinois Department of Employment Security*, 489 U.S. 829 (1989).

43 *Thomas v. Review Board, Indiana Employment Security Division*, 450 U.S. 707 (1981).

44 *Wisconsin v. Yoder*, 406 U.S. 205 (1972).

45 Minorities Declaration, Art. 4(2).

46 See Edward Egan Smith, "The Criminalization of Belief: When Free Exercise Isn't," *Hastings Law Journal* 42 (1991): 1491.

47 *Walker v. Superior Court*, 763 P. 2d 852, 858 (1988) (referencing sec. 270 of the California Penal Code).

48 Ibid., 878.

49 See John Dwight Ingram, "State Interference with Religiously Motivated Decisions on Medical Treatment," *Dickinson Law Review* 93 (1988): 41, 59.

50 *Hay v. B*, 2003 (3) SA 492 (W) (S. Afr.).

51 Declaration on the Rights of Indigenous Peoples, Art. 3, G. A. Res. 61/295, U.N. Doc. A/RES/62/295 (2007).

52 Ibid., Art. 46(1).

53 Vienna Declaration, World Conference on Human Rights , Vienna, 14–25 June 1993, U.N. Doc. A/CONF.157/24 (Part I) at 20 (1993).

54 *Reference Re Secession of Quebec* [1998] 2 S.C.R. 217.

55 *Christian Education South Africa v. Minister of Education*, 2000 (4) SA 757; 2000 (10) BCLR 1051 (CC) par. 36 (S. Afr.).

56 *Minister of Home Affairs v. Fourie; Lesbian and Gay Equality Project v. Minister of Home Affairs*, 2006 (1) SA 524; 2006 (3) BCLR 355, par. 93 (CC) (S. Afr.). Subsequent quotes are in ibid. par. 94–95.

■ RECOMMENDED READING

Anaya, S. James. *International Human Rights and Indigenous Peoples* (Leiden: Wolters Kluwer, 2009)

Cassese, Antonio. *Self-Determination of Peoples: A Legal Reappraisal* (Cambridge: Cambridge University Press, 1995)

Berman, N. "Sovereignty in Abeyance: Self-Determination and International Law." *Wisconsin International Law Journal* 7 (1988): 51–105

Dinstein, Yoram. "Collective Human Rights of Peoples and Minorities." *International Law Quarterly* 25 (1976): 102–120

Emerson, R. "Self-Determination." *American Journal of International Law* 66 (1971): 459–475

Friedlander, Robert. "Self-Determination: A Legal-Political Inquiry." *Detroit College of Law Review* 1 (1975): 71–92

Garvey, John H. "Churches and the Free Exercise of Religion." *Notre Dame Journal of Law, Ethics & Public Policy* 4 (1990): 567–590

Horwitz, Paul. "Churches as First Amendment Institutions: Of Sovereignty and Spheres." *Harvard Civil Rights and Civil Liberties Law Review* 35 (2009): 79–131

Tesfagiorgis, G. "Self-Determination: Its Evolution and Practice by the United Nations and Its Application in the Case of Eritre." *Wisconsin International Law Journal* 6 (1987): 75–128

Van der Vyver, Johan D. "Cultural Identity as a Constitutional Right in South Africa." *Stellenbosch Law Review* 14 (2003): 51–67

_____. *Leuven Lectures on Religious Institutions, Religious Communities and Rights* (Leuven: Uitgeverij Peeters, 2004)

_____. "Self-Determination and the Peoples of Quebec." *Journal of Transnational Law & Policy* 10 (2000): 1–37

_____. "Self-Determination and the Right to Secession of Religious Minorities under International Law," in *Protecting the Human Rights of Religious Minorities in Eastern Europe*, eds. Peter G. Dachin and Elizabeth A. Cole (New York: Columbia University Press, 2002), 251–293

_____. "Sovereignty and Human Rights in Constitutional and International Law." *Emory International Law Review* 5 (1991): 321–443

van Dyke, Vernon. *Human Rights, the United States, and World Community* (New York: Oxford University Press, 1970)

15 Permissible Limitations on the Freedom of Religion or Belief

T. JEREMY GUNN

The most important international conventions, treaties, and instruments promoting human rights emerged following the adoption of the Universal Declaration of Human Rights (UDHR) in 1948. During the phase of the human rights movement following the UDHR, the principal focus of public attention was on the language in human rights texts that identified the rights of people. These included, for example, the freedom of expression, the freedom of association, and the freedom of religion and belief. Over time, attention has increasingly shifted from the description of rights to the language in conventions that identifies the restrictions that states may impose on the exercise of rights. These portions of human rights conventions that set out the circumstances under which a state may justifiably restrict the exercise of rights are commonly referred to as "limitations clauses." This chapter provides an overview of the principal issues that arise under the limitations clauses related to the freedom of religion and belief.

THE MEANING OF "LIMITATIONS CLAUSES"

Granting Clauses

International human rights conventions and constitutions of countries of the world often include protections for the freedom of religion and belief. Such rights are identified in what may be called "granting clauses," which identify the scope and breadth of the right.[1] The granting clause for freedom of religion in Article 18 of the 1948 UDHR provides, for example, that: "Everyone has the right to freedom of thought, conscience and religion; this right includes freedom to change his religion or belief, and freedom, either alone or in community with others and in public or private, to manifest his religion or belief in teaching, practice, worship and observance."

The relevant granting clause of the 1966 International Covenant on Civil and Political Rights (ICCPR) similarly provides in Article 18 that:

1. Everyone shall have the right to freedom of thought, conscience and religion. This right shall include freedom to have or to adopt a religion or belief of his choice, and freedom, either individually or in community with others and in public or private, to manifest his religion or belief in worship, observance, practice and teaching.

2. No one shall be subject to coercion, which would impair his freedom to have or to adopt a religion or belief of his choice. . . .[2]

Constitutions of countries of the world typically contain granting clauses for freedom of religion as well. The German *Grundgesetz* of 1949 provides in Article 4 that: "(1) Freedom of creed, of conscience, and freedom to profess a religious or non-religious faith are inviolable. (2) The undisturbed practice of religion is guaranteed." The First Amendment to the Constitution of the United States, drafted a century and a half earlier in 1787, provides that "Congress shall make no law respecting an establishment of religion or prohibiting the free exercise thereof." Most constitutions of countries of the world will include some type of granting clause related to the freedom of religion. These clauses typically use broad language that speaks of the inviolability of the freedom to hold religious beliefs or of the right of a person to manifest religion through worship and practice. It is likely that most people, when they think of rights of religion (or of any other right for that matter), focus on granting clauses as the principal articulation of the freedom.

Limitations Clauses

Although granting clauses are a fundamental component of human rights texts, they are only half of the story. Human rights conventions and constitutions contain not only granting clauses, as explained above, but also "limitations clauses" that identify the circumstances under which a state or a government legitimately may restrict the exercise of the right. One example of a limitations clause is found in one of the oldest and most famous documents identifying the right to freedom of conscience, the French Declaration of the Rights of Man and Citizen of 1789, which has subsequently been incorporated into the current French constitution. Article 10 of the Declaration of the Rights of Man provides that: "No one may be disturbed on account of his opinions, even religious ones, *as long as the manifestation of such opinions does not interfere with the public order established by law.*"[3] The italicized portion of the text is a "limitations clause" that explains that the manifestation of religious and other opinions, which otherwise should not be infringed, may be restricted by the State in order to guarantee the public order. Although what is meant by "public order" is not explained in the Declaration, the text presumes that the greater interests of society may in some circumstances be grounds for restricting religious expression.

While human rights activists and religious believers are likely to focus on the freedoms that they wish to exercise, states and public authorities are more likely to be concerned with what they see as potential harms to the public order that are caused by religious actors, particularly when those actors engage in what may be seen as extreme or excessive manifestations of religion. State officials are likely to be concerned about the political dangers of religious radicalism (or violence) or the destabilizing effects that religious activists might provoke in society.

Some of the more dramatic examples of states attempting to suppress the activities of religious (or quasi-religious) actors include the United States government's attack on the Branch Davidians in 1993 at the Mount Carmel Center near Waco, Texas, Central Asian states' efforts to suppress the literature of the radical *Hizb-ut-Tahrir*, or French authorities attempting to ban the wearing of the Muslim headscarf (*hijab*) in French public schools. Even when there are no real dangers of political extremism, state officials may nevertheless focus on the possible harm that religion might inflict on the young, the vulnerable, or those who are susceptible to undue influence by charismatic religious leaders. States may thus use limitations clauses to restrict religions that rely on faith-healing, or that isolate believers from the larger society, or that promote excessive loyalty to religious leaders.[4]

Explicit and Implicit Limitations

Limitations clauses may be inextricably connected to a particular granting clause, or may be inserted in an entirely separate section of the instrument that applies generally to all granting clauses, or it may even be implicit and not be found anywhere in the written text. The conscience provision of the French Declaration of the Rights of Man, quoted above, is an example where the granting clause and limitations clause are tied inextricably together. The ICCPR offers another version of the first type, and now represents the most typical approach to inserting limitations clauses. The first two sections of Article 18 of the ICCPR, quoted above, are granting clauses. The immediately following section, Article 18.3, however, is the limitations clause that identifies the circumstances where a state legitimately may restrict the rights explained in the first two clauses: "Freedom to manifest one's religion or beliefs may be subject only to such limitations as are prescribed by law and are necessary to protect public safety, order, health, or morals or the fundamental rights and freedoms of others." Although the third clause of the ICCPR's article provides greater detail than the French Declaration, it similarly provides little clear guidance.

The UDHR, also referenced above, provides an example of the second type of placement of a limitations clause. Rather than being connected directly to a particular granting clause, as in the French Declaration and the ICCPR, the UDHR contains a limitations clause at its end that applies generally to all of the preceding granting clauses of the text. It is located at the end in Article 29.2 and specifies: "In the exercise of his rights and freedoms, everyone shall be subject only to such limitations as are determined by law solely for the purpose of securing due recognition and respect for the rights and freedoms of others and of meeting the just requirements of morality, public order and the general welfare in a democratic society."

Similar to the ICCPR, the UDHR contains language that is somewhat more detailed than the French Declaration, though it, too, provides relatively little guidance on how the limitations clause should be interpreted.

Finally, a limitations clause may be implicit rather than explicit. The Constitution of the United States offers a case in point. According to the text of the First Amendment itself, the United States Congress had no power to enact *any* law whatsoever that would interfere with the free exercise of religion. When the U.S. Congress enacted a statute in the 1870s prohibiting the practice of polygamy in federal territories, members of the Church of Jesus Christ of Latter-day Saints (Mormons) challenged the law as an infringement on their religious practice of engaging in plural marriage. The law was indeed a legislative attempt by Congress that targeted the Mormon practice of polygamy. Although the text of the First Amendment itself would have appeared to support the Mormon position, the Supreme Court found an implicit but unwritten "limitations clause" in the first amendment to explain that the right of free exercise of religion was not absolute. Thus, almost a century after the absolutist language of the First Amendment was first adopted, the Supreme Court interpreted it to provide that while the Congress "was deprived of all legislative power over mere *opinion*" or belief, it nevertheless was legitimate to restrict "*actions* which were *in violation of social duties or subversive of good order*."[5] Another sixty years later, in 1940, the Supreme Court reaffirmed this same basic belief/action distinction in more contemporary language when it held that the free exercise of religion "embraces two concepts—freedom to believe and freedom to act. The first is absolute, but in the nature of things, the second cannot be. Conduct remains subject to regulation for the protection of society."[6] Thus the First Amendment has been interpreted to be less absolutist than its language suggests, and it permits the State to limit manifestations of religion that are believed to be harmful to society.

While granting clauses in human rights conventions and constitutions may contain broad and even absolutist language protecting manifestations of religion or other human rights, limitations clauses—whether explicitly or implicitly—allow the State to restrict manifestations of those rights that are interpreted as being harmful to "public order" or to other important values of the State. Whereas human rights activists and religious actors may seek to promote an expansive interpretation of granting clauses, states and public authorities are more likely to emphasize an expansive reading of limitations clauses and their responsibility limit manifestations of religion that they believe are not in the interest of the State or the public.

■ THE DISTINCTION BETWEEN THE "*ABSOLUTE* FREEDOM OF BELIEF" AND THE "*LIMITED* FREEDOM TO MANIFEST BELIEFS"

The U.S. Supreme Court has held that there is a difference in constitutional protections for beliefs as opposed to constitutional protections for actions as described in the nineteenth- and twentieth-century cases described above. There should be an *absolute* protection for the freedom of belief, but only a *qualified* protection for the free exercise of religion, even though the text of the United States Constitution itself does not itself offer any basis for the distinction. This belief/action distinction explained by the United States Supreme Court has, under different terminology, been broadly accepted in international human rights jurisprudence.

The limitations clause Article 18.3 of the ICCPR, quoted above, provides that the freedom to manifest one's religion or beliefs may be subject to limitations under certain specified conditions (to be discussed more fully in the next part below). The text can be read as implicitly providing that the right to hold beliefs is not subject to any control by the State. The absolute freedom to hold beliefs without limitation has been explicitly stated by the United Nations Human Rights Committee, the body created for the purpose of interpreting and applying the ICCPR. In its General Comment 22.3, the Human Rights Committee made this clear in noting that "Article 18 distinguishes the freedom of thought, conscience, religion or belief from the freedom to manifest religion or belief. *It does not permit any limitations whatsoever on the freedom of thought and conscience or on the freedom to have or adopt a religion or belief of one's choice.* These freedoms are protected unconditionally, as is the right of everyone to hold opinions without interference. . . . No one can be compelled to reveal his thoughts or adherence to a religion or belief."

The 1950 European Convention on Human Rights (ECHR),[7] the human rights treaty that has been the subject of the most detailed judicial interpretation due to the extensive jurisprudence of the European Court of Human Rights, makes an identical distinction. Article 9 of the European Convention is divided into two clauses, the first of which is the granting clause and the second is the limitations clause.

1. Everyone has the right to freedom of thought, conscience, and religion; this right includes freedom to change his religion or belief, and freedom, either alone or in community with others and in public or private, to manifest his religion or belief, in worship, teaching, practice and observance.
2. Freedom to manifest one's religion or beliefs shall be subject only to such limitations as are prescribed by law and are necessary in a democratic society in the interests of public safety, for the protection of public order, health, or morals, or the protection of the rights and freedoms of others.[8]

The limitations clause, Article 9.2, explains that there may be limitations on the manifestations of religion although, like the ICCPR, it implicitly suggests that there may be no limitation on beliefs. The European Court of Human Rights, in agreement with the United Nations Human Rights Committee, has made explicit what is implicit in the text of the European Convention: "the freedoms of thought, conscience and religion . . . are absolute. The Convention leaves no room whatsoever for interference by the State."[9] The Law Lords in Great Britain have made a similar distinction.[10] The term that is widely used in international law to identify the "internal" realm of beliefs that are absolutely protected from state interference is the "*forum internum*," while the external realm of manifesting beliefs, which may be restricted by states, is identified as the "*forum externum*."

The obvious question that arises once the "internal/external" or "belief/action" distinction is made is what exactly is included within the scope of "beliefs" (the *forum internum*) that lies beyond the authority of the State to restrict? It is broadly accepted that "beliefs" include the right to have or not to have beliefs. Thus the State may not interfere with a person's right to believe in a monotheistic God or a polytheistic universe, or to be an atheist. All of these beliefs should be free from any state interference. Most international human rights bodies, including the European Court and the United Nations Human Rights Committee, similarly argue that "belief" includes the right of individuals to change their beliefs. An individual may convert to Islam, to Christianity, or to Sikhism—all without being confronted by state intervention.[11] A widely accepted additional aspect of this absolute right to hold beliefs is the right of individuals not to be forced to disclose their beliefs to others. Thus, there is understood to be the right to privacy in beliefs. The state also should not be able to coerce a change in beliefs.[12]

■ THE STANDARD THREE-STEP ANALYSIS OF LIMITATIONS CLAUSES

In a proper limitations clause analysis, the threshold question is whether the proposed state limitation purports to restrict beliefs, in which case it is necessarily illegitimate. If the restriction targets manifestations only, the next step is to subject the limitation to a three-step analysis. This three-step analysis is specifically identified in two of the most influential human rights instruments: the ICCPR and the ECHR. Both conventions require that a state satisfy each of the three requirements in order for the limitation to be legitimate. If a state is able to satisfy only one or two, its restriction on the manifestation of a religion is impermissible.

The limitations clause of Article 9.2 of the ECHR, which closely resembles the ICCPR, provides that the State may restrict manifestations of religious activity only when each of three specified conditions is met. First, the limitation must be "prescribed by law." Second, the limitation must be in furtherance of at least one of five specifically identified interests: public safety, public order, health, morals, or the protection of the rights of others. Finally, the limitation on the manifestation must be "*necessary* in a democratic society." These three conditions will be considered in turn.

First, the limitation must be "prescribed by law"

The "prescribed by law" condition under international law generally, and the ECHR specifically, contains three requirements. First, the restriction must be based upon a *law* and not simply on a practice or an act of state authorities. Actions by authorities that restrict manifestations must be based upon a law and not on their own discretion. Second, the law that restricts the manifestation of religion or belief must be *accessible*, meaning that the law containing the restriction must have been published and be available for the public to consult. This means that secret laws or unpublished administrative regulations, for example, cannot be used as the basis for interfering with the right to manifest religion. The third and final "prescribed by law" requirement is that the law limiting religious activity must be written in such a way as to be sufficiently understandable so that a person reading it could know whether or not the actions in questions are prohibited by the law. Another way of saying this that is often used is that a person consulting the laws must be able to "foresee" that an action is a violation of the law. Thus laws restricting manifestations of religion may not be vague, unclear, arbitrary, or give unfettered discretion to state authorities.[13]

Second, the limitation must be in furtherance of a legitimate state interest

The next condition that must be satisfied to limit a manifestation of religion is that the limitation must be in furtherance of at least one of five identified legitimate state interests. The ECHR like the ICCPR, identifies the five legitimate grounds upon which a state may restrict manifestations of religion: the protection of (1) public safety, (2) public order, (3) public health, (4) public morals, or (5) the rights and freedoms of others. Other grounds, such as "national security" or "protecting traditional religions" do not satisfy the condition.[14] Examples of state interests that would satisfy the requirements could possibly include preventing a provocative demonstration that sought to denounce another religion in a place where the event might provoke violence. A "religious" cemetery could be obligated to comply with sanitary rules involving disposal of bodies. A state might prohibit parents from relying on "faith healing" for sick children, either on the grounds of health or protection of the rights and freedoms of others.

A problem that necessarily arises in trying to identify the scope of any of these "legitimate state interests" is that states may readily argue that almost any restriction they wish to impose could be justified on at least one of the five grounds. Based upon this element alone, a state could undertake very extreme measures with a plausible justification that it was consistent with the "legitimate state interest." An extreme example would be a state prohibiting all religious gatherings whatsoever on the grounds that it seeks to protect the public health against communicable diseases.[15] Because international tribunals have been sufficiently deferential to states with regard to this second condition, it ultimately has played almost no role in limitations clause adjudication. Of course if tribunals were to look at this condition more critically and to require states to provide a solid justification rather than make a mere appeal to "public order," the condition could play a much more substantial role than it has thus far. For all practical purposes, however, the European Court of Human Rights and the UN Human Rights

Committee have been highly deferential and accepting of the rationales offered by states to justify limitations on religious practices.[16] To the extent that limitations clauses impose practical limits on states actions, the "legitimate purpose" requirement is the weakest prong.

Third, the limitation must be "necessary" (or "proportional")

The third limitations clause condition according to the ICCPR is that legitimate restrictions on a manifestation of religion must be "*necessary*." The ECHR requires further that the limitation be "necessary in a democratic society." While it generally has not been difficult for a state to satisfy the first two conditions described above ("prescribed by law" and "in furtherance of a legitimate state interest"), satisfying the third condition—"necessity"—typically has been much more challenging. While there are some examples of a state not satisfying one of the first two conditions when pressed by international tribunals, it is the third that is taken most seriously and is the condition that states are most likely to fail. When the European Court of Human Rights finds that a state's action is not consistent with the requirements of the limitations clause of Article 9, it has almost always done so under the "necessary in a democratic society" prong.

Unfortunately, the meaning of "necessary" is not explained in the texts of the ECHR and the ICCPR. The word "necessary" itself suggests something absolute, a *sine qua non*, or something that is essential or required. The plain meaning of "necessary in a democratic society" would seem to be that the restriction on manifesting religion would either be something that must be imposed in order to preserve democracy or that a democratic society concludes is necessary to protect itself. The sense of the term is something much stronger than being merely a "good idea" or "beneficial" or "helpful" or "appropriate" or "reasonable" or "desirable" or "advantageous" or "having a long-term positive effect." "Necessary" is a strong term suggesting that no other option is possible or that the consequences will be dire if the restriction is not imposed. Although international tribunals do not emphasize the word "necessary," they do state as a general principal that limitations should be seen as the exception to the rule and that limitations clauses should not be employed in a way that undermines the basic right. The UN Human Rights Committee has stated that limitations pursuant to ICCPR Article 18.3 should "be strictly interpreted."[17] A symposium convened by the International Commission of Jurists developed what are called the "Siracusa Principles" for interpreting limitations clauses and derogations clauses. The Siracusa Principles state that limitations may not be undertaken in such a way as "to jeopardize the essence of the right concerned" and that "[a]ll limitation clauses shall be interpreted strictly and in favor of the rights at issue."[18]

However absolutist the term "necessary" might seem to be in the language of the conventions, neither the European Court nor other tribunals have interpreted it in such a strong or uncompromising manner. In order to avoid the consequences of giving "necessary" an overly robust interpretation that would lead to striking down state restrictions that were somewhat less than absolutely necessary, international tribunals have substituted an entirely different term that does not appear anywhere in the text: "*proportional*." Thus, rather than asking whether a state restriction was in fact "necessary," the European Court asks instead whether the restriction is "proportional" to the harm that the State seeks to avoid. The following section probes the meaning of "proportionality" in limitations clause analysis.

PROPORTIONALITY IN LIMITATIONS CLAUSE ANALYSIS

In many ways, the most important element for adjudicating limitations clauses is not provided in the texts of limitations clauses themselves: the appropriate standard of review. The language of the limitations clauses does not explain, for example: (1) how deferential courts should be to state authorities; (2) how important the right to manifest religion should be in comparison to state interests; (3) what evidence should be considered in resolving competing claims; (4) which party has the responsibility for providing what evidence; and (5) which party bears the "burden of proof." The answers to these basic "standard of review" questions are not arcane or academic; the answers are likely to determine the outcome of the case. In the European Court case evaluating Turkey's prohibition of women students wearing the headscarf (*hijab*), for example, the Court deferred to the Turkish state's assertions that the wearing of the headscarf would harm the State's secularist principles without requiring any evidence that this was so.[19] Nor did the European Court take seriously the religious claims of the university student, Leyla Şahin, who was prohibited from wearing the headscarf. With exactly the same evidence presented before the Court, the decision could have been in favor of Ms. Şahin rather than the Turkish state if the Court had assumed the fundamental right to wear religious attire and had demanded proof (rather than the mere assertion) from Turkey that headscarves are disruptive. Although we cannot know the personal attitudes of the European Court judges towards the wearing of the *hijab*, it is quite clear that the Court majority deferred to the Turkish state and accepted at face value the State's unproven claims. Thus it may be imagined that the standard of review applied in a particular case may not only influence the outcome, it may indeed be outcome determinative.

Although the meaning of "proportionality" in law has ancient origins, its introduction into modern law has been most influenced by German jurists.[20] The concept of proportionality is best known in the common law of England and the United States in relationship to punishments for crimes. It is now generally accepted that a punishment should be proportional to the crime that was committed. Perhaps the most common example used to illustrate the point is that the death penalty is now easily understood as being a disproportionately severe punishment for the crime of pick-pocketing.

Moving beyond the "punishment should fit the crime" explanation of proportionality, a metaphor that is frequently used to describe it is that "a sledge hammer should not be used to crack a nut." While no doubt employing such a heavy tool would be effective in breaking even the hardest of walnut shells, it would be at the cost of crushing the meat inside. The force is sufficient to accomplish the necessary task of breaking the shell but with the unacceptable consequence of making the nut worthless. The hypothetical example offered above of a state permanently forbidding all religious meetings in order to slow the spread of communicable diseases would be an example of the unacceptable and disproportionately severe sledgehammer approach.[21]

Proportionality analysis in limitations clause jurisprudence assumes that there should be a proportionate correlation between the seriousness of the harm that the State seeks to prevent when imposing the restriction on the manifestation of religion and the severity of the infringement on the liberty that the restriction imposes. To the extent that a state restriction prevents a great harm and the infringement on the liberty is slight, the restriction presumably is justifiable. For example, the State might delay the opening of a new building for religious worship for a few days until after a fire inspection is complete. On the other hand, if the State's interest is low and the infringement on liberty is high, the State action presumably is not justifiable. For example, the State's refusal to allow religious groups to meet without prior authorization of the State presumably is not justifiable, particularly when the State imposes long delays on registration.

The proportionality cases identified in the preceding paragraph are relatively easy to analyze. The more difficult cases are those where there are strongly competing interests of the State and of people seeking to manifest their religion. Should pacifists be permitted to distribute anti-war literature at the entrance to a military base when a country is at war? Should a state official be permitted to proselytize his employees during non-working hours? Should Hindus be permitted to hold a religious celebration in the city of Ayodhya, India, near the site where Hindu nationalists had earlier destroyed the Babri mosque if the celebration might provoke a communal clash? Should the State be able to force children to receive medical treatment that will save their lives if both the children and their parents do not want the treatment? Should state prison authorities in the United States and Canada be required to allow the building of ritual sweat lodges inside prisons for Native Americans? Should women wearing the face-covering *burqa* be required to remove it for state identification photos? May women wearing the *burqa* be prohibited from driving automobiles or testifying in court in against a criminal or before a jury? May Sikh motorcyclists be required to wear helmets that would force them to remove their turbans? Courts and legislators have been required to answer each of these questions, with the inevitable result that either a legitimate state interest or a form of legitimate religious manifestation has been compromised.

Proportionality analysis has now become the principal method judges employ for evaluating whether state restrictions on particular manifestations of religion are permissible under the ICCPR and the ECHR. Unfortunately, proportionality has been applied by the European Court of Human Rights in a relatively ad hoc way with judges evaluating the criteria in somewhat different ways in each case. The fact that the underlying factors have been given such varying weights in different cases has led to the inevitable criticism that proportionality "analysis" is, in reality, a results-oriented exercise that uses the language of proportionality simply to justify the preferred outcome. Although it is not be possible to eliminate all discretion and all vagaries in proportionality analysis, it would be valuable to standardize and clarify as many of the steps as possible rather than leave it as open ended as it has become. The following elements are inherent to proportionality analysis, regardless of whether they are actually or consciously identified during the evaluation process. It would be helpful if courts could be clearer, more consistent, and more transparent with regard to the following four important and interrelated issues when making their proportionality analyses.[22] These issues will be illustrated with reference to the decision of the European Court of Human Rights in the *Şahin v. Turkey* case, in which the Court upheld the decision of the Turkish state to prohibit women from wearing the *hijab* headcover at state universities.[23]

First, the tribunal should identify its role clearly

In some cases, international human rights tribunals identify themselves as institutions created for the purpose of ensuring that rights are fully protected. On other occasions, they suggest that their responsibility is to defer to the judgments of state authorities. In the *Şahin v. Turkey* case, for example, the European Court of Human Rights gave no serious analysis to the felt religious needs of Muslim women who wear the *hijab*, nor to the consequences of prohibiting intelligent, veiled women from obtaining a university education. The Court deferred completely to the unproven assertions of the Turkish state that "secularism" demanded that the wearing of the *hijab* be prohibited at state universities. The Court showed much greater interest in defending the ideology of "secularism"—a term which appears nowhere in the ECHR—rather than in defending the right to manifest a religion, which is a core element of freedom of religion.

Second, the tribunal should identify the "burden of proof" of each of the parties

Parties coming before a tribunal offer various assertions and evidence to support their claims. It is important that consistent and coherent rules be applied to each party and that the rules clarify the evidentiary obligations and the types of evidence that will be admitted in proof of the claims. In a general way, it presumably should be the burden of the applicants in religious freedom cases to prove that the actions limited by the State were manifestations of their religious beliefs and, depending on the significance of the State's need to restrict the manifestations, that the manifestations were important, central, or critical to their religious beliefs rather than merely incidental. The State, on the other hand, should be obligated to prove that the threats to the public order, public health, and the like are real and measurable rather than merely speculative or ideological, as well as that the proposed restrictions would actually reduce the danger. Leyla Şahin, for example, should have been required to prove that wearing the *hijab* was mandated by her religious beliefs and that she believed it to be a religious obligation.[24] The Turkish state should have been required to prove that the *hijab* itself is inherently dangerous or that it was being used for the purpose of disrupting university education.[25]

Third, the tribunal should consider less restrictive alternatives, with appropriate evidentiary obligations being placed on both parties

It may be the case that the State can prove that there is a harm associated with a particular manifestation of religion that it wishes to restrict and that the procedures it employs are effective in reducing or eliminating the harm. The question remains, however, whether there is a less restrictive alternative action that the State could have employed that similarly would have eliminated the real harm but would also have imposed less of an infringement on the human right in question. If an alternative is available that satisfies the State's legitimate interests but poses less of a burden on the human right in question, the doctrine of proportionality would suggest that the less burdensome alternative should be employed. But this creates an evidentiary problem: Whose obligation is it to prove that no less restrictive alternative is available? While this might at first glance seem to be the obligation of the State, it nevertheless would be unfair to place the burden on the State of proving that no other alternative was available, as it may be impossible to prove a negative (i.e., in this case to prove that there was no less restrictive alternative available).

There is a reasonably practical solution to this problem that could be made by shifting the burden of proof at strategic points. To illustrate this, we can return to the walnut-cracking example as if it were a case before a tribunal. In such this case the State could of course present compelling evidence (as required by the second point above) that the shell of the nut is hard and that the sledgehammer will effectively be able to break it. The applicant to the court would then counter by arguing that there is a less harmful alternative: the nutcracker. Once evidence of a less restrictive alternative has been provided, the burden of proof should then shift back to the State to prove that the nutcracker will not work for one reason or another. By establishing a rule something like outlined here, it would allow tribunals to be more precise and careful in making their proportionality judgments.[26]

Fourth, the tribunal should identify the relevant degree of scrutiny (or clarify the relevant standards of proof)

It was explained above that the term "necessary" in limitations clauses as well as the statements that limitations should be the "exception rather than the rule" suggest that states should resort to limiting human rights only in the most compelling and pressing cases. This is not, however, how tribunals have applied limitations clauses in the two leading human rights conventions, the ICCPR and the ECHR. The tribunals have shown themselves to be much more deferential to states than the strong language of the conventions would imply, and frequently the tribunals defer to states without pressing them to provide compelling evidence or to consider seriously less restrictive alternatives.

It would be appropriate, particularly given the high standards that in theory should apply to state limitations on manifestations of religion and belief, for international tribunals to identify clearly the standards to which they hold states accountable by outlining exactly the evidentiary standards that states should satisfy and to explain directly the degree of scrutiny that they believe should be applied to state assertions. Under the current regime, the tribunals largely let such questions go without comment. Appropriate standards should be set, articulated, and applied consistently.

■ NOTES

1 Although called here a "granting clause," this does not necessarily mean that the clause itself creates the right. Depending on the theory of rights reflected in the document, it may be that the granting clause merely identifies a natural right that exists regardless of whether it is included in the document. The Ninth Amendment of the United States Constitution, for example, specifically assumes that the people possess other rights not identified in the constitution.

2 International Covenant on Civil and Political Rights, G.A. res. 2200A (XXI), 21 U.N. GAOR Supp. (No. 16) at 59, U.N. Doc. A/6316 (1966), 999 U.N.T.S. 302, *entered into force* March 23, 1976 (hereinafter "ICCPR").

3 "Nul ne doit être inquiété pour ses opinions, même religieuses, pourvu que leur manifestation ne trouble pas l'ordre public établi par la Loi."

4 A legal issue that is closely related to, but is different from "limitations clauses," is that of "derogation clauses." Derogations pertain to the rare emergency circumstances when a state may ignore certain human rights obligations in order to protect the life of the nation. Examples of derogation clauses may be found in Article 4 of the International Covenant for Civil and Political Rights and Article 15 of the European Convention for Human Rights. Notably, the ICCPR does not allow a derogation for freedom of religion or belief, although the ECHR does. For interpretations of derogations clauses see United Nations Economic and Social Council, Commission on Human Rights, Sub-Commission on Prevention of Discrimination and Protection of Minorities, "The Siracusa Principles on the Limitation and Derogation Provisions in the International Covenant on Civil and Political Rights," U.N. Doc. E/CN.4/1985/4, Annex (1984) (hereinafter "Siracusa Principles") and United

Nations Human Rights Committee, "General Comment No. 29: States of Emergency (Article 4)" U.N. Doc. CCPR/C/21/Rev.1/Add.11 (2001).

5 *Reynolds v. United States,* 98 U.S. 145, 164 (1879) (emphasis added).

6 *Cantwell v. State of Connecticut,* 310 U.S. 296, 303–304 (1940).

7 European Convention for the Protection of Human Rights and Fundamental Freedoms, (ETS No. 5), 213 U.N.T.S. 222, *adopted* in Rome, November 4, 1950, *entered into force* September 3, 1953 (hereinafter "ECHR").

8 In the ECHR, the limitations clause for freedom of religion or belief, Article 9.2, is quite similar to limitations clauses for other freedoms, including Article 8 (rights of private family life), Article 10 (freedom of expression), and Article 11 (right of peaceful assembly).

9 *Kokkinakis v. Greece,* 17 EHRR 397 (1994) (ECtHR 260-A, May 25, 1993), par. 14.

10 The Law Lords have similarly accepted absolute freedom with regard to belief, and limited freedom with regard to manifestations. *Regina v. Secretary of State for Education and Employment and others (Respondents) ex parte Williamson (Appellant) and others,* [2005] UKHL 15.

11 It is of course well known that many Muslim countries deny the right of Muslims to convert to a religion different from Islam. Muslim-majority countries often have laws and practices that impose penalties—sometimes including death—on Muslims who convert to other religions, although they welcome Christian converts to Islam. See further the chapter by Paul Taylor, herein.

12 *Kjeldsen, Busk Madsen, and Pedersen v. Denmark,* 1 EHRR 711 (1979-1980) (ECtHR 23, series A, December 7, 1976) (Chamber Judgment); *Buscarini and Others v. San Marino,* 30(2) EHRR 208 (2000) (ECtHR, 1999-I, February 18, 1999) (Grand Chamber Judgment).

13 *Hasan and Chaush v. Bulgaria,* 34 EHRR 55 (2002) (ECtHR, October 26, 2000).

14 It should be noted that the grounds of "national security" is *not* included as one of the grounds for restricting manifestations of religion, even though both the European Convention and the ICCPR provide that national security may be a legitimate ground for limiting other freedoms. (ICCPR, Art. 19; ECHR, Art. 10) This of course creates the anomaly that if "religious speech" were re-categorized as "expression," which is not a difficult task, it could be restricted on national security grounds.

15 Even though "national security" is explicitly excluded as one of the grounds for limiting manifestations, it would not be difficult for a state simply to characterize a national security grounds as "public order" or "public safety."

16 For a criticism of the excessive deference to states, see Paul M. Taylor, *Freedom of Religion: UN and European Human Rights Law and Practice* (Cambridge, UK: Cambridge University Press, 2005), 301–05.

17 UN Human Rights Committee, "General Comment 22," par. 8. Human Rights Committee, General Comment 22: Article 18 (Forty-eighth session, 1993) U.N. Doc. HRI/GEN/1/Rev.1 (1994), par. 8.

18 "Siracusa Principles," I.A.2, 3.

19 *Şahin v Turkey,* 44 EHRR 5 (2007) (EctHR, 2005-XI, 175, November 10, 2005) (Grand Chamber Judgment).

20 I have discussed elsewhere some of the origins of the judge-created term "proportional" in jurisprudence. For most practical purposes, it generally comes from the civil law rather than the common law and specifically from German jurisprudence. *See* T. Jeremy Gunn, "Deconstructing Proportionality in Limitations Analysis," *Emory International Law Review* 19 (Summer 2005): 465–98.

21 Of course there might be certain circumstances, as in the case of an influenza pandemic, where the State might reasonably impose such limitations during the course of the pandemic.

22 The following four points are among the most important. For a much more detailed discussion of these issues, see Gunn, "Deconstructing Proportionality," 476–94.

23 *Şahin v Turkey.* See further the chapter by Carolyn Evans, herein.

24 Of course many Muslim women and men believe that wearing the *hijab* is not a religious obligation. It is not the proper function of the tribunal to interpret Islamic law and reach a judgment on this issue—but to inquire as to whether the applicant seriously and sincerely believed that it is an obligation.

25 The fact that secular students or faculty might be offended by the *hijab* or that they might cause a disturbance in reaction to its being worn should be irrelevant. In this case the disruption is due not to those who wear the *hijab*, but by others, and it is they who should be restrained by the State.

26 There are, of course, important refinements that ultimately should be made to this basic rule. The most obvious case is where one of the parties, and probably most frequently the State, has access to information and evidence that the applicant does not have. In such cases, the State should perhaps either be required to make the data available or be required to prove the negative for at least some specified alternatives.

■ RECOMMENDED READING

Evans, Carolyn. *Religious Freedom Under the European Court of Human Rights* (Oxford: Oxford University Press, 2001)

Evans, Malcolm D. *Religious Liberty and International Law in Europe* (Cambridge: Cambridge University Press, 1997)

Gunn, T. Jeremy. "Deconstructing Proportionality in Limitations Analysis." *Emory International Law Review* 19 (Summer 2005): 465–98

Martinez-Torrón, Javier. "Limitations on Religious Freedom in the Case Law of the European Court of Human Rights." *Emory International Law Review* 19 (Summer 2005): 587–636

Symposium. "The Permissible Scope of Legal Limitations on the Freedom of Religion or Belief." *Emory International Law Review* 19 (Summer 2005): 465–1320

Taylor, Paul M. *Freedom of Religion: UN and European Human Rights Law and Practice* (Cambridge: Cambridge University Press, 2005)

United Nations, Economic and Social Council, Sub-Commission on Prevention of Discrimination and Protection of Minorities, "The Siracusa Principles on the Limitation and Derogation of Provisions in the International Covenant on Civil and Political Rights." U.N. Doc E/CN.4/1985/4, Annex (1984)

United Nations Human Rights Committee, "General Comment No. 22: Article 18" (Forty-eighth session, 1993), U.N. Doc. CCPR/C/21/Rev.1/Add.4 (1993).

United Nations Human Rights Committee, "General Comment No. 29: States of Emergency (article 4), U.N. Doc. CCPR/C/21/Rev.1/Add.11 (2001).

van der Vyver, Johan D. "Limitations of Freedom of Religion or Belief: International Law Perspectives." *Emory International Law Review* 19 (Summer 2005): 499–537

16 The Right to Religious and Moral Freedom

MICHAEL J. PERRY

The articulation of the right to religious and moral freedom that is set forth in the International Covenant on Civil and Political Rights (ICCPR) is canonical in the sense that the great majority of the nations of the world—over 85 percent—are parties to the ICCPR: As of April 2011, 167 of the 195 countries that are members of the United Nations were parties to the ICCPR, including, as of 1992, the United States.

Article 18 of the ICCPR declares:[1]

1. Everyone shall have the right to freedom of thought, conscience and religion. This right shall include freedom to have or to adopt a religion or belief of his choice, and freedom, either individually or in community with others and in public or private, to manifest his religion or belief in worship, observance, practice and teaching.
2. No one shall be subject to coercion which would impair his freedom to have or to adopt a religion or belief of his choice.
3. Freedom to manifest one's religion or beliefs may be subject only to such limitations as are prescribed by law and are necessary to protect public safety, order, health, or morals or the fundamental rights and freedoms of others.
4. The States Parties to the present Covenant undertake to have respect for the liberty of parents and, when applicable, legal guardians to ensure the religious and moral education of their children in conformity with their own convictions.[2]

Note the breadth of the right that according to Article 18 "[e]veryone shall have": the right not just to freedom of *religion* but also to freedom of *conscience*. The Article 18 "right shall include freedom to have or adopt a religion *or belief* of his choice, and freedom, either individually or in community with others and in public or private, to manifest his religion *or belief* in worship, observance, practice and teaching" (emphasis added). Moreover, Article 18 explicitly affirms that it is about moral as well as religious freedom when it states that "[t]he State parties to the [ICCPR] undertake to have respect for the liberty of parents and, when applicable, legal guardians to assure the religious *and moral* education of their children in conformity with their own convictions" (emphasis added). So, the Article 18 right protects freedom to practice one's morality without regard to whether one's morality is religiously-based. Article 18 protects not only freedom to practice one's religion, including one's religiously-based morality; it also protects freedom to practice one's non-religiously-based morality. The Article 18 right protects freedom "to manifest his . . . belief in . . . practice" *even if the belief is embedded not in a transcendent worldview but in a worldview that is not transcendent.* By a "transcendent" worldview, I mean a worldview that affirms, rather than denies or is agnostic about, the existence of a "transcendent" reality, as distinct from the reality that is the object of natural-scientific inquiry.[3]

Given the breadth of the right of which Article 18 is the canonical articulation, we can fairly call it the right to religious *and moral* freedom. The Canadian Supreme Court has emphasized that the right protects freedom to practice one's morality without regard to whether one's morality is religiously-based. Referring to Canada's constitutional version of the right—section 2(a) of the Canadian Charter of Rights and Freedoms, which states that "[e]veryone has . . . freedom of conscience and religion"—the Court explained: "The purpose of s. 2(a) is to ensure that society does not interfere with profoundly personal beliefs that govern one's perception of oneself, humankind, nature, and, in some cases, a higher or different order of being. These beliefs, in turn, govern one's practices."[4] According to the Canadian Supreme Court, s. 2(a) "means that, subject to [certain limitations], no one is to be forced to act in a way contrary to his beliefs or his conscience."[5]

Religious and moral freedom is, as the Canadian Supreme Court explained, the freedom to live one's life in harmony with one's most fundamental convictions and commitments: specifically, those that are the yield of one's response to what are sometimes called "ultimate" questions, such as: Who are we? Where did we come from; what is our origin, our beginning? Where are we going; what is our destiny, our end?[6] What is the meaning of suffering? Of evil? Of death? And there is the cardinal question, the question that comprises many of the others: Is human life ultimately meaningful or, instead, ultimately bereft of meaning, meaning-less, absurd?[7] If any questions are fundamental, these questions—what Catholic theologian David Tracy has memorably called "religious or limit questions"[8]—are fundamental. Such questions—"naive" questions, "questions with no answers", "barriers that cannot be breached"[9]—are "the most serious and difficult . . . that any human being or society must face . . ."[10] And one's answers to such questions obviously bear strongly on this fundamental question: What sort of life is constitutive of, or conducive to, one's religious (or, if you prefer, "spiritual") and/or moral well-being? (Religious and/or moral well-being, that is, as distinct from physical and psychological well-being.) Historically extended communities—"traditions"—are principal matrices of answers to all such "religious or limit" questions.[11]

Recall Bertrand Russell's worldview:

> That man is the product of causes which had no prevision of the end they were achieving; that his origin, his growth, his hopes and fears, his loves and his beliefs, are but the outcome of accidental collocations of atoms; that no fire, no heroism, no intensity of thought and feeling, can preserve an individual life beyond the grave; that all the labor

of the ages, all the emotion, all the inspiration, all the noonday brightness of human genius, are destined to extinction in the vast death of the solar system, and that the whole temple of man's achievement must inevitably be buried beneath the debris of a universe in ruins—all these things, if not quite beyond dispute, are yet so certain that no philosophy which rejects them can hope to stand. Only within the scaffolding of these truths, only on the firm foundation of unyielding despair, can the soul's habitation henceforth be safely built.[12]

Russell's statement, and many others like it,[13] are salutary reminders and powerful illustrations that those who struggle with "religious or limit" questions—such as the question "Does God exist?"—do not invariably end up giving answers that are embedded in a transcendent worldview. To the contrary, many end up giving answers that reject any transcendent worldview. Nonetheless, John Paul II was surely right in his encyclical *Fides et Ratio* that such questions "have their common source in the quest for meaning which has always compelled the human heart" and that "the answer given to these questions decides the direction which people seek to give to their lives."[14]

This point bears emphasis: The practices protected by the right to religious and moral freedom include not just practices one believes oneself religiously and/or morally obligated to engage in. After all, a practice one believes oneself obligated to engage in (*e.g.*, forsaking meat on Lenten Fridays) may be relatively inconsequential next to a practice one does not believe oneself obligated to engage in *but that one nonetheless has strong religious/moral reason to engage in*: *e.g.*, receiving communion wine. As the Supreme Court of Canada put the point:

[T]o frame the right either in terms of objective religious "obligation" or even as the sincere subjective belief that an obligation exists and that the practice is required . . . would disregard the value of non-obligatory religious experiences by excluding those experience from protection. Jewish women, for example, strictly speaking, do not have a biblically mandated "obligation" to dwell in a succah during the Succot holiday. If a woman, however, nonetheless sincerely believes that sitting and eating in a succah brings her closer to her Maker, is that somehow less deserving of recognition simply because she has no strict "obligation" to do so? Is the Jewish yarmulke or Sikh turban worthy of less recognition simply because it may be borne out of religious custom, not obligation? Should an individual Jew, who may personally deny the modern relevance of literal biblical "obligation" or "commandment", be precluded from making a freedom of religion argument despite the fact that for some reason he or she sincerely derives a closeness to his or her God by sitting in a succah? Surely not.[15]

Some ICCPR rights—such as the Article 7 right not to "be subjected to torture or to cruel, inhuman or degrading treatment or punishment"—are unconditional (absolute): they forbid (or require) government to do something, *period.*[16] Some other ICCPR rights, by contrast, are conditional: they forbid (or require) government to do something *unless certain conditions are satisfied.* As Article 18 makes clear, under the right to religious and moral freedom, government may not ban or otherwise impede a practice protected by the right, unless three conditions are satisfied:[17]

- ***The legitimacy condition:*** The ban or other policy serves a legitimate government interest.
- ***The least burdensome alternative condition:*** If the policy serves a legitimate government interest, it is necessary to serve that interest, in the sense that it serves that interest significantly better than would any less burdensome (to the protected practice) policy.
- ***The proportionality condition:*** What the policy achieves in serving that interest (i.e., the "benefit" of the policy) is sufficiently weighty to be proportionate to (commensurate with) the disadvantage the ban/policy visits on those subject to the policy (i.e., the "cost" of the policy).

The right to religious and moral freedom obviously would provide no meaningful protection for practices covered by the right if the consistency of a ban or other policy with the right was to be determined without regard to whether the benefit of the policy was proportionate to the cost of the policy. And, indeed, Article 18 is authoritatively understood to require that the benefit of the policy be proportionate to the cost of the policy.[18]

The Universal Declaration of Human Rights (UDHR) states, in Article 1, that "[a]ll members of the human family . . . should act towards one another in a spirit of brotherhood." The relationship between the imperative to "act towards one another in a spirit of brotherhood" and the right not to "be subjected to . . . cruel, inhuman or degrading treatment or punishment" is clear: to subject someone "to cruel, inhuman or degrading punishment" is obviously not to treat him "in a spirit of brotherhood". What is the relationship between the "in a spirit of brotherhood" imperative and the right to religious and moral freedom?

To prevent someone from living his life in harmony with his most fundamental convictions and commitments, or to make it significantly more difficult for him to do so, is hurtful to him, sometimes greatly hurtful. The countries of the world—the great majority of them—agree that for a government to cause anyone such hurt is not for it to treat him "in a spirit of brotherhood" . . . *unless* the law or other policy that is the source of such hurt satisfies the three conditions: legitimacy, least burdensome alternative, and proportionality. Again, the right to religious and moral freedom is not unconditional.

■ WHAT GOVERNMENT INTERESTS ARE NOT LEGITIMATE UNDER THE RIGHT TO RELIGIOUS AND MORAL FREEDOM?

The Siracusa Principles state that "[t]he scope of a limitation referred to in the Covenant shall not be interpreted so as to jeopardize the essence of the right concerned."[19] Article 18 does not call into question the legitimacy of government's acting to protect—to list the most obvious examples—the lives, health, safety, liberty, property, or socio-economic well-being of the citizenry and other human beings; human rights; the orderly functioning of society, including the orderly functioning of democratic and judicial processes; or non-human animals, other sentient life, or the environment. However, because government's pursuit of certain interests is fundamentally inconsistent with the right to religious and moral freedom, to affirm the right to religious and moral freedom is necessarily to hold that government may not pursue those interests—that those interests are not legitimate government interests. What government interests are not legitimate under the right to religious and moral freedom?

In determining whether a law or other policy is consistent with the right to religious and moral freedom, no interest is a legitimate government interest if in pursuing that interest, government is acting as an arbiter of "religious or limit" questions, such as: Is Jesus Lord? Is same-sex sexual conduct contrary to the will of God? Under the right to religious and moral freedom, therefore, neither of the two following imaginable government interests is legitimate:

1. Protecting (what the political powers-that-be believe to be) true answers to "religious or limit" questions

We can easily imagine the political powers-that-be declaring: "Certain teachings are true—for example, the teaching that one who embraces Christianity has a much better chance of being saved[20]—and no government should lack authority to ban practices that may lead some people to reject those teachings." We can also easily imagine a different political powers-that-be declaring: "Certain teachings are true—for example, the teaching that 'religion is unscientific, superstitious, and an enemy of progress'[21]—and no government should lack authority to ban practices that may lead some people to reject those teachings."

Both declarations (and whatever laws or other policies are based thereon) are jarring to those of us who, after reflecting on historical experience, concur in the Lockean judgment that "[n]either the right nor the art of ruling does necessarily carry along with it the certain knowledge of other things, and least of all true religion."[22] (To Locke's "does necessarily carry" we may add "or has ever carried".) "The one only narrow way which leads to Heaven," said Locke, "is not better known to the Magistrate than to private persons, and therefore I cannot safely take him for my Guide, who may probably be as ignorant of the way as my self, and who certainly is less concerned for my Salvation than I my self am."[23] In our Lockean judgment, government is not to be trusted as an arbiter of true answers to "religious or limit" questions. Or, because we here in conversation are citizens of a democracy, we may say that a political majority is not to be trusted as an arbiter of true answers to such questions. Moreover, there is no need for government to act—it is utterly unnecessary for government to act—as such an arbiter, if, as Locke put it, "the business of laws is not to provide for the truth of opinions, but for the safety and security of the commonwealth, and of every particular man's goods and persons."[24]

One can imagine the Roman Catholic Church of an earlier time replying that "so long as the State accepts the Catholic Church as the arbiter of religious truth, there is no problem, because the Catholic Church has 'certain knowledge' of religious, including moral, truth."[25] By the time of the Second Vatican Council (1962–65), however, the cardinals and bishops of the Catholic Church—a large majority of them—had come to accept that the era had ended in which the Church could realistically expect ever again to wield the kind of influence over a state—any state—it had once wielded over some states, and that the Church too, therefore, should not trust any government, including (especially?) any political majority in a democracy, as an arbiter of true answers to ultimate questions.[26]

The second imaginable-but-illegitimate government interest, unlike the first, does not presuppose that government can be trusted as an arbiter of true answers to "religious or limit" questions. The subtext of the second interest is that it can be better for a community to settle on one answer to *some* such questions—even if the answer may not be true, or may not be the only plausible answer—than to live amidst a centrifugal cacophony of competing answers:

2. Protecting the unity—and thereby the strength—of the community

We can easily imagine the political powers-that-be declaring: "In the long run, unity in our answers to some 'religious or limit' questions, understood as a kind of 'glue', enhances the strength of a nation; united in our answers to some such questions, we stand, divided in our answers to those questions, we fall; therefore, no government should lack authority to ban practice that over time may diminish the nation's unity and thereby weaken the nation." [27] (In 1931, the fascist dictator of Italy, Benito Mussolini, proclaimed that "religious unity is one of the great strengths of a people."[28]) But that position too is belied by historical experience—not least, the historical experience of the United States. Indeed, given the suffering it causes and the divisiveness it precipitates, the coercive imposition of answers to ultimate questions is more likely to corrode than to nurture the strength of any democracy that is, as democracies typically and increasingly are, religiously and morally pluralistic.[29]

■ CONCLUSIONS

This, then, is the heart of the fundamental warrant for the right to religious and moral freedom: Governments, including political majorities, should not be trusted as arbiters of true answers to "religious or limit" questions; moreover, given the suffering it causes and the divisiveness it precipitates, the coercive imposition of answers to such questions is more likely to corrode than to nurture the strength of a democracy.[30] The warrant—rooted not in philosophical abstractions but in concrete, extended historical experience—is fundamental in the sense that it is ecumenical: All citizens—believers of every stripe and nonbelievers—have the same basic reason to insist that government not ban or otherwise impede a practice protected by the right to religious and moral freedom unless the legitimacy, least burdensome alternative, and proportionality conditions are each satisfied.

■ NOTES

1 Article 9 of the European Convention for the Protection of Human Rights (ECHR) and Fundamental Freedoms and Article 12 of the American Convention on Human Rights (ACHR) are substantially identical. See European Convention for the Protection of Human Rights and Fundamental Freedoms, 213 U.N.T.S. 222, *adopted* in Rome, November 4, 1950, *entered into force* Sept. 3, 1953; American Convention on Human Rights, O.A.S.Treaty Series No. 36, 1144 U.N.T.S. 123, *adopted* in San José, Costa Rica, November 22, 1969, *entered into force* July 18, 1978.

2 Article 18 of the ICCPR is an elaboration of Article 18 of the UDHR s: "Everyone has the right to freedom of thought, conscience and religion; this right includes freedom to change his religion or belief, and freedom, either alone or in community with others and in public or private, to manifest his religion or belief in teaching, practice, worship and observance." See International Covenant on Civil and Political Rights G.A. res. 2200A (XXI), 21 U.N. GAOR Supp. (No. 16) at 52, U.N. Doc. A/6316 (1966), 999 U.N.T.S. 171, *entered into force* March 23, 1976; Universal Declaration of Human Rights, G.A. res. 217A (III), U.N. Doc A/810 at 71 (1948).
Another international document merits mention here: United Nations General Assembly, Declaration on the Elimination of All Forms of Intolerance and of Discrimination Based on Religion or Belief, G.A. Res. 36/55, 36 U.N. GAOR Supp. (No. 51) at 171, U.N. Doc. A/36/684 (1981). See Symposium, "The Foundations and Frontiers of Religious Liberty: A 25th Anniversary Celebration of the 1981 U.N. Declaration on Religious Tolerance," *Emory International Law Review* 21 (2007): 1–275.

3 On the idea of the "transcendent", see Charles Taylor, *A Secular Age* (Cambridge: Belknap Press of Harvard University Press, 2007); Michael Warner, Jonathan VanAntwerpen, & Craig Calhoun, eds., *Varieties of Secularism in a Secular Age* (Cambridge: Harvard University Press, 2010).

4 *R. v. Edwards Books and Art Ltd.*, [1986] 2 S.C.R. 713, 759.

5 *R. v. Big M Drug Mart Ltd.*, [1985] 1 S.C.R. 295, 337.

6 "In an old rabbinic text three other questions are suggested: 'Whence did you come?' 'Whither are you going?' 'Before whom are you destined to give account?'" Abraham J. Heschel, *Who Is Man?* (Stanford, CA: Stanford University Press, 1965), 28. "All people by nature desire to know the mystery from which they come and to which they go." Denise Lardner Carmody & John Tully Carmody, *Western Ways to the Center: An Introduction to Religions of the West* (Belmont, CA: Wadsworth Publishing Co., 1983), 198–99. "The questions Tolstoy asked, and Gauguin in, say, his great Tahiti triptych, completed just before he died ("Where Do We Come From? What Are We? Where Are We Going?"), are the eternal questions children ask more intensely, unremittingly, and subtly than we sometimes imagine." Robert Coles, *The Spiritual Life of Children* (Boston: Houghton Mifflin, 1990), 37.

7 For the person deep in the grip of, the person claimed by, the problem of meaning, "[t]he cry for meaning is a cry for ultimate relationship, for ultimate belonging", wrote Heschel. "It is a cry in which all pretensions are abandoned. Are we alone in the wilderness

of time, alone in the dreadfully marvelous universe, of which we are a part and where we feel forever like strangers? Is there a Presence to live by? A Presence worth living for, worth dying for? Is there a way of living in the Presence? Is there a way of living compatible with the Presence?" Heschel, *Who Is Man?*, 75. Cf. W.D. Joske, "Philosophy and the Meaning of Life," in E.D. Klemke, ed., *The Meaning of Life* (New York: Oxford University Press, 1981), 248, 250. ("If, as Kurt Vonnegut speculates in *The Sirens of Titan,* the ultimate end of human activity is the delivery of a small piece of steel to a wrecked space ship wanting to continue a journey of no importance whatsoever, the end would be too trivial to justify the means."); Robert Nozick, *Philosophical Explanations* (Cambridge: Belknap Press of Harvard University Press, 1981), 586. ("If the cosmic role of human beings was to provide a negative lesson to some others ('don't act like them') or to provide needed food to passing intergalactic travelers who were important, this would not suit our aspirations—not even if afterwards the intergalactic travelers smacked their lips and said that we tasted good.").

8 David Tracy, *Plurality and Ambiguity: Religion, Hermeneutics, Hope* (New York: Harper & Row, 1987), 86.

9 In Milan Kundera's *The Unbearable Lightness of Being,* the narrator, referring to "the questions that had been going through Tereza's head since she was a child", says that "the only truly serious questions are ones that even a child can formulate. Only the most naive of questions are truly serious. They are the questions with no answers. A question with no answer is a barrier than cannot be breached. In other words, it is questions with no answers that set the limits of human possibilities, describe the boundaries of human existence." Milan Kundera, *The Unbearable Lightness of Being* (New York: HarperCollins, 1984), 139.

10 David Tracy, *The Analogical Imagination* (Chestnut Ridge, NY: Crossroad Publishing Co., 1981), 4. Tracy adds: "To formulate such questions honestly and well, to respond to them with passion and rigor, is the work of all theology. . . . Religions ask and respond to such fundamental questions . . . Theologians, by definition, risk an intellectual life on the wager that religious traditions can be studied as authentic responses to just such questions." Ibid.

11 "Not the individual man nor a single generation by its own power, can erect the bridge that leads to God. Faith is the achievement of many generations, an effort accumulated over centuries. Many of its ideas are as the light of the star that left its source a long time ago. Many enigmatic songs, unfathomable today, are the resonance of voices of bygone times. There is a collective memory of God in the human spirit, and it is this memory which is the main source of our faith." From Abraham Heschel's two-part essay "Faith", first published in volume 10 of *The Reconstructionist*, November 3 & 17, 1944. For a later statement on faith, incorporating some of the original essay, see Abraham J. Heschel, *Man is Not Alone* (New York: Farrar, Straus & Young: 1951), 159–76.

12 Bertrand Russell, *Mysticism and Logic* (New York: Longmans, Green & Co., 1917), 47–48.

13 Consider, for example, Clarence Darrow's bleak vision (as recounted by Paul Edwards):

> Darrow, one of the most compassionate men who ever lived, . . . concluded that life was an "awful joke." . . . Darrow offered as one of his reasons the apparent aimlessness of all that happens. "This weary old world goes on, begetting, with birth and with living and with death," he remarked in his moving plea for the boy-murderers Loeb and Leopold, "and all of it is blind from the beginning to the end." Elsewhere he wrote: "Life is like a ship on the sea, tossed by every wave and by every wind; a ship headed for no port and no harbor, with no rudder, no compass, no pilot; simply floating for a

> time, then lost in the waves." In addition to the aimlessness of life and the universe, there is the fact of death. "I love my friends," wrote Darrow, "but they all must come to a tragic end." Death is more terrible the more one is attached to things in the world. Life, he concludes, is "not worthwhile," and he adds . . . that "it is an unpleasant interruption of nothing, and the best thing you can say of it is that it does not last long."

Paul Edwards, "Life, Meaning and Value of," *Encyclopedia of Philosophy*, Paul Edwards, ed., 4 (New York: Macmillan, 1967), 467, 470. Whether Clarence Darrow was in fact "one of the most compassionate men who ever lived" is open to question. For a revisionist view of Darrow, see Gary Wills, *Under God: Religion and American Politics,* (1990), chaps. 8–9 Listen, too, to another lawyer, Bruce Ackerman: "There is no moral meaning hidden in the bowels of the universe." Bruce A. Ackerman, *Social Justice in the Liberal State* (New Haven: Yale University Press, 1980), 368.

14 John Paul II, *Fides et Ratio* (On the Relation Between Faith and Reason) September 14, 1998, In the introduction to *Fides et Ratio,* John Paul II wrote:

> Moreover, a cursory glance at ancient history shows clearly how in different parts of the world, with their different cultures, there arise at the same time the fundamental questions which pervade human life: Who am I? Where have I come from and where am I going? Why is there evil? What is there after this life? These are the questions which we find in the sacred writings of Israel and also in the Veda and the Avesta; we find them in the writings of Confucius and Lao-Tze, and in the preaching of Tirthankara and Buddha; they appear in the poetry of Homer and in the tragedies of Euripides and Sophocles as they do in the philosophical writings of Plato and Aristotle. They are questions which have their common source in the quest for meaning which has always compelled the human heart. In fact, the answer given to these questions decides the direction which people seek to give to their lives.

Ibid., Introduction, pt. 1. See also Ibid., chapter 3, pt. 26. (*Fides et Ratio* would more accurately be named *Fides et Philosophia.*) We find a similar statement in the opening part of the Second Vatican Council's declaration *Nostra Aetate* (On the Relation of the Church to Non-Christian Religions) October 28, 1965:

> Men expect from the various religions answers to the unsolved riddles of the human condition, which today, even as in former times, deeply stir the hearts of men: What is man? What is the meaning, the aim of our life? What is moral good, what sin? Whence suffering and what purpose does it serve? Which is the road to true happiness? What are death, judgment and retribution after death? What, finally, is that ultimate inexpressible mystery which encompasses our existence: whence do we come, and where are we going?

15 *Syndicat Northcrest v. Amselem,* [2004] 2 S.C.R. 551, 588.

16 Article 7 states: "No one shall be subjected to torture or to cruel, inhuman or degrading treatment or punishment. In particular, no one shall be subjected without his free consent to medical or scientific experimentation."

17 The right to the free exercise of religion protected by the constitutional law of the United States is not unconditional; it permits government to prohibit some religious practices. See, e.g., *Reynolds v. United States,* 98 U.S. 145, 166 (1879) (upholding the constitutionality of a law banning polygamy):

> Laws are made for the government of actions, and while they cannot interfere with mere religious belief and opinions, they may with practices. Suppose one believed

> that human sacrifices were a necessary part of religious worship, would it be seriously contended that the civil government under which he lived could not interfere to prevent a sacrifice? Or if a wife religiously believed it was her duty to burn herself upon the funeral pile of her dead husband, would it be beyond the power of the civil government to prevent her carrying her belief into practice?

By its very terms the free exercise right forbids government to prohibit, not the exercise of religion, but the "free" exercise of religion—that is, the freedom of religious exercise. Just as government may not abridge "the freedom of speech" or "the freedom of the press", so too it may not prohibit the freedom of religious exercise. The right to freedom of religious exercise is not an unconditional right to do, on the basis of religious belief or for religious reasons, whatever one wants. One need not concoct outdated hypotheticals about human sacrifice to dramatize the point. One need only point, for example, to the refusal of some Christian Science parents to seek readily available lifesaving medical care for their gravely ill child. See, e.g., *Lundman v. McKown*, 530 N.W.2d 807 (Minnesota 1995). See also Caroline Frasier, "Suffering Children and the Christian Science Church," *The Atlantic Monthly* (April 1995): 105. Just as the right to freedom of speech does not privilege one to say, and right to the freedom of the press does not privilege one to publish, whatever one wants wherever one wants whenever one wants, the right to freedom of religious exercise does not—because it cannot—privilege one to do, on the basis of religious belief or for religious reasons, whatever one wants wherever one wants whenever one wants.

18 United Nations Economic and Social Council, Commission on Human Rights, Sub-Commission on Prevention of Discrimination and Protection of Minorities,"The Siracusa Principles on the Limitation and Derogation Provisions in the International Covenant on Civil and Political Rights," U.N. Doc. E/CN.4/1985/4, Annex (September 28, 1984), I.A.10.

Of course, proportionality inquiry is fraught with difficulty. See, in this volume, Jeremy Gunn, "Permissible Limitations on Religion".

19 "Siracusa Principles," I.A.2.

20 See "Other Faiths Are Deficient, Pope Says," *The Tablet* [London], February 5, 2000, 157: "The revelation of Christ is 'definitive and complete', Pope John Paul affirmed to the Congregation for the Doctrine of the Faith, on January 28. He repeated the phrase twice in an address which went on to say that non-Christians live in 'a deficient situation, compared to those who have the fullness of salvific means in the Church.'" Nonetheless, "[John Paul II] recognised, following the Second Vatican Council, that non-Christians can reach eternal life if they seek God with a sincere heart. But in that 'sincere search' they are in fact 'ordered' towards Christ and his Church." Ibid.

21 See Lawrie Breen, "A Chinese Puzzle," *The Tablet* [London], March 5, 2005 (reporting that "new regulations confirm that Beijing perceives religion as unscientific, superstitious and an enemy of progress"). "Last year a secret document, issued by the Central Committee's Propaganda Department, called for a new drive to promote Marxist atheism." Ibid.

22 John Locke, *Letter Concerning Toleration* (1689), in *On Politics and Education* (New York, NY: Walter J. Black, 1947), 39.

23 Ibid. See James Madison, *Memorial and Remonstrance against Religious Assessments* (1785) (explaining why "We the subscribers, citizens of the said Commonwealth [Virginia]," reject the proposed "Bill establishing a provision for Teachers of the Christian Religion"):

> 5. Because the Bill implies either that the Civil Magistrate is a competent judge of Religious Truth; or that he may employ Religion as an engine of Civil policy. The first is an arrogant pretension falsified by the contradictory Rulers in all ages, and throughout the world; the second an unhallowed perversion of the means of salvation.

24 Locke, *Letter Concerning Toleration.*

25 Pope Pius IX, in his *Syllabus of Errors,* December 8, 1864, condemned as an error—Error # No. 55—this proposition: "The Church ought to be separated from the State, and the State from the Church."

26 I have discussed the post-Vatican II Church's embrace of the right to religious freedom elsewhere: Michael J. Perry, *The Political Morality of Liberal Democracy* (Cambridge: Cambridge University Press, 2010), 80–86; Michael J. Perry, "Liberal Democracy and the Right to Religious Freedom," *Review of Politics* 71 (2009): 621–635.

27 See Michael W. McConnell, "Establishment and Disestablishment at the Founding, Part I: Establishment of Religion," *William & Mary Law Review* 44 (2003): 2105, 2182. "Machiavelli, who called religion 'the instrument necessary above all others for the maintenance of a civilized state,' urged rulers to 'foster and encourage' religion 'even though they be convinced that is it quite fallacious.' Truth and social utility may, but need not, coincide." (Quoting Niccolo Machiavelli, *The Discourses* (1520), ed. Bernard R. Crick, trans. Leslie J. Walker, rev. trans. Brian Richardson (London: Penguin 1970), 139, 143). Cf. "Atheist Defends Belief in God," *The Tablet* [London], March 24, 2007, 33:

> A senior German ex-Communist has praised the Pope and defended belief in God as necessary for society . . . "I'm convinced only the Churches are in a state to propagate moral norms and values," said Gregor Gysi, parliamentary chairman of Die Linke, a grouping of Germany's Democratic Left Party (PDS) and other left-wing groups. "I don't believe in God, but I accept that a society without God would be a society without values. This is why I don't oppose religious attitudes and convictions."

28 Quoted in John T. Noonan, Jr., *A Church That Can and Cannot Change* (Notre Dame, IN: University of Notre Dame Press, 2005), 155–56.

29 Cf. Paul Cruickshank, "Covered Faces, Open Rebellion," *The New York Times,* October 21, 2006. The Declaration on the Elimination of All Forms of Intolerance and of Discrimination Based on Religion or Belief states: "[T]he disregard and infringement of . . . the right to freedom of thought, conscience, religion or whatever belief, have brought, directly or indirectly, wars and great suffering to mankind . . ."

30 Some citizens may have a different or stronger reason for embracing the right to religious and moral freedom. In particular, some citizens may have a religion-specific reason. See E. Gregory Wallace, "Justifying Religious Freedom: The Western Tradition," *Penn State Law Review,* 114 (2009): 485, 488. "[T]he original reasons for singling out religion and placing it beyond government's power were mostly religious." Wallace then states, in a footnote: "I am indebted to Michael McConnell for first calling my attention to this fact and stirring my curiosity to investigate it further. Judge McConnell has made the point in several writings. . . . Steven Smith's seminal article discussing the underlying justifications for religious freedom also helped shape my early thinking on this matter." Ibid., n. 11 (citing Steven D. Smith, "The Rise and Fall of Freedom in Constitutional Discourse," *University of Pennsylvania Law Review,* 140 (1991): 149).

■ RECOMMENDED READING

Gunn, Jeremy, "Permissible Limitations on Religion," in this volume

Kalscheur, Gregory A., SJ. "Moral Limits on Morals Legislation: Lessons for U.S. Constitutional Law from the Declaration on Religious Freedom." *Southern California Interdisciplinary Law Journal* 16 (2006): 1

Locke, John. *A Letter Concerning Toleration* (1689), trans. William Popple (New York: MacMillan Publishing Co., 1989)

Murray, John Courtney, SJ. *We Hold These Truths: Catholic Reflections on the American Proposition* (New York: Sheed and Ward, 1960)

Novak, William J. *The People's Welfare: Law and Regulation in Nineteenth-Century America* (Chapel Hill: University of North Carolina Press, 1996)

Perry, Michael J. "Liberal Democracy and the Right to Religious Freedom." *Review of Politics* 71 (2009): 621

_______. *The Political Morality of Liberal Democracy* (Cambridge: Cambridge University Press, 2010)

Pope Paul VI, *Dignitatis Humanae* (On the Dignity of the Human Person December 7, 1965, also known as the Second Vatican Council's Declaration on Religious Freedom. Symposium. "Freedom of Conscience: Stranger in a Strange Land." *University of San Diego Law Review* 47 (2010): 993

Urban Morgan Institute. "The Siracusa Principles on the Limitation and Derogation Provisions in the International Covenant on Civil and Political Rights." *Human Rights Quarterly* 7 (1985): 3

Vischer, Robert K. *Conscience and the Common Good: Reclaiming the Space Between Person and State* (Cambridge: Cambridge University Press, 2010)

17 Keeping Faith: Reconciling Women's Human Rights and Religion

MADHAVI SUNDER*

The Indian Constitution recognizes sex equality yet confers jurisdiction over civil matters such as marriage and divorce to religious "personal laws," which make no similar guarantee. In the United States, courts have created a "ministerial exception," granting religious institutions an exemption from Title VII of the Civil Rights Act of 1964, which prohibits sex discrimination in the workplace. More than 180 countries are signatories to the international Convention on the Elimination of All Forms of Discrimination Against Women (CEDAW) of 1979—often referred to as the "international bill of rights for women"—and yet ratifying countries have conditioned their ascent to instances where there is no conflict between CEDAW and religious law.

Since Hillary Rodham Clinton famously articulated the idea that "women's rights are human rights" at the United Nations Fourth World Conference on Women in Beijing in 1995, women's equality has been considered a fundamental part of the human rights fabric. Women's rights as human rights imply universality, and indeed, today women's rights are widely recognized in both international and national laws. In addition to CEDAW, the constitutions of countries from Afghanistan to Bangladesh, India, Indonesia, Iraq, Morocco, and Nigeria (to name just a few) include provisions recognizing sex equality. Despite these provisions in formal law, however, women's rights in fact are often culturally relative. As the examples above indicate, law itself often formally yields to claims by religious groups that seek to discriminate against women in the name of religious or cultural freedom. Notably, women's rights stand alone among the rights sacrificed in the name of religious freedom today.[1] The end result is that for women, at least, in a postmodern world in which eighteenth- and nineteenth-century notions of unmediated *national sovereignty* have been properly put to rest, religion and culture represent the New Sovereignty. Human rights abuses that since World War II are no longer acceptable when committed by states are paradoxically tolerated when justified in the name of religion or culture.

For some time, scholars and human rights practitioners have posited the conflict between women's equality and religious liberty as inherent. As the late feminist theorist Susan Moller Okin starkly put it, religion and culture are "bad" for women.[2] Okin and other similarly minded feminists argued that women must set themselves free of the shackles of religion and culture if they truly want to be free. Contemporary legal theory takes a similar approach. Under current law, women must choose either religion (on discriminatory terms) or freedom (in the public sphere). Discrimination in the religious sphere is not only accepted, it is expected. So long as women may exit their religious or cultural groups and seek equality in the public sphere, law tolerates gender discrimination in the name of religion.

But increasingly, women in the modern world reject this binary—*religious liberty versus gender equality*—as a false and unacceptable choice in the twenty-first century. To be sure, religious freedom has long been considered a fundamental freedom. John Rawls described it as "one of the fixed points of our considered judgments of justice."[3] As Martha Nussbaum, among others, have described the resulting "liberal dilemma," the primacy of this right has led liberals to restrain from judging sex discrimination justified in religious terms.[4] But the current approach appears wanting in many ways. First, offering women a life of dignity and human rights only in the public sphere denies women's equal right to enjoy religious community, which they must exit for the sake of freedom. At the same time, women today increasingly reject that their participation in religion requires that they accept patriarchal religion. Contrary to formal law, which time and again defers to religious leaders who seek to justify gender discrimination, women today are piercing the veil of religious sovereignty, asking whether discriminatory practices are essential to the faith. Put simply, today more and more women want religion, but on their own terms. Increasingly, they seek to modernize and harmonize religion with global and local norms of gender equality. Notably, their avenue for pursuing equality and justice is not a purely secular one, seeking freedom and equality outside of religious community. Rather, reformers demand justice and equality *within* religious community, as well as outside of it.

This chapter explores the specific challenges posed to traditional legal understandings of religion and culture by women reformers who, rather than choosing liberty *or* equality, demand both. Call it the New Enlightenment. As my case studies from the frontlines of women's reform efforts in the Muslim world demonstrate, increasingly today, women reformers reject the traditional liberal/legal approach of deference to religious leaders' claims to discriminate. New Enlightenment reformers, as I call them, refuse to be passive victims—either of religious patriarchs or of a liberalism that would deny them their religion on terms of equality with men. Instead, these women are on the frontlines of religious and human rights reform movements around the world, calling on states to recognize the plural traditions and values within their religious communities that support norms of sex equality and human rights, rather than to simply rubber-stamp fundamentalist claims about Islam and Muslim law. Significantly, reformers' efforts to mine their religious and cultural traditions for laws and values that reinforce sex equality are more than merely strategic. Reformers today are making the bold, new normative claim that for women to have an equal right to enjoy religious community, they must be guaranteed freedom from discrimination within these communities. Furthermore, reformers recognize the historical connection between women's equality in the public sphere and discriminatory norms, customs, and religious laws that govern the private sphere. Discriminatory religious norms about women's place in society limit women's actual capabilities for flourishing in the public sphere. This is one of the central insights of CEDAW. New Enlightenment reformers recognize that meaningful gender equality in all spheres requires critically assessing and debating traditional ideas about women, culture, and religion.[5]

The New Enlightenment and the New Sovereignty go hand in hand. As religious leaders witness more internal debate and dissent within religious communities—often about women's roles—they turn to traditional legal concepts such as the "freedom of religion" and the "right to culture" to buttress their power and squelch dissent. Paradoxically, fundamentalists take advantage of the legal tradition of deference to religion, obtaining exceptions from gender equality norms in the name of religious liberty. Women fight back in turn, questioning previously accepted religious dogma and insisting on the compatibility of religion and rights, faith and freedom.

Notably, these reformers question not only religion, but law's view of religion, as well. A crucial distinction between the New Sovereignty and the New Enlightenment is their underlying conception of religion itself. The New Sovereignty is premised on a vision that understands religion as the "other" of law. Religious communities are homogeneous, irrational, hierarchal, and patriarchal. Gender discrimination in religious communities is not only accepted, it is expected. Ironically, this liberal/legal view of religious community is in line with the fundamentalist/religious view. Both approaches view religion as incompatible with human rights and with sex equality in particular.

The New Enlightenment, in contrast, exposes religious communities as dynamic and heterogeneous with plural traditions and interpretations, many of which support human rights and women's rights. In this sense, the New Enlightenment offers a blueprint out of the liberal dilemma. As my examples that follow show, women reformers in the Muslim world are seeking change and equality for women not through the traditional path of rejecting religion and religious law, but by debating and reforming religious law to be compatible with twenty-first century human rights norms and lifestyles. But it is law, stuck in an outmoded old Enlightenment view of religion as a space of unfreedom, that often stands in the way. In short, human rights law, not religion, is the problem. Let us first take a closer look at some examples that illustrate the phenomenon of the New Sovereignty, and then we will turn to women's response—what I call the New Enlightenment.

THE NEW SOVEREIGNTY

Personal Religious Laws (India)

In 1975 in Madhya Pradesh, India, a 62-year old Muslim woman named Shah Bano was thrown out of her home by her husband after 43 years of marriage and five children. Her husband, a wealthy lawyer, returned her *mahr*, or the marriage settlement that had been given by her family in 1932 (which forty years later amounted to about $3,000), and paid Shah Bano maintenance of about Rs. 179/per month (roughly $18) during the period of *iddat* (approximately three months after a divorce). This, he argued, was the entirety of his financial obligation to Shah Bano under Muslim personal law, which governs all Indian Muslims in matters of marriage and divorce in India. India has no uniform civil code to govern matters such as marriage and divorce; individuals are identified by a particular religion at birth and are governed by the personal laws of that religion in civil matters. Thus, Indian Christians, Hindus, and Muslims are all governed by their respective religious personal laws. The settlement was inadequate for Shah Bano's survival and she sued.

Shah Bano sought relief under Section 125 of the Indian Criminal Procedure Code, which "requires a person of adequate means to protect relations from destitution." This law had been enacted in 1973 to require men from all religious groups to pay permanent alimony. Between the years 1973 and 1985, most state high courts in India applied the law to require Muslim men to pay permanent alimony. This was the result in Shah Bano's case. Her ex-husband earned a healthy Rs. 5000/per month and could easily afford to continue minimal payments to his ex-wife, who was elderly and ill. The Madhya Pradesh High Court directed the ex-husband to continue to pay Rs. 179/per month to his ex-wife. Shah Bano's husband appealed to the apex Indian court, arguing that this provision of the criminal code was inapplicable to Muslims and that Muslim men's maintenance obligations were limited to payments for just three months after divorce.[6]

In 1985, the Indian Supreme Court rendered a judgment in Shah Bano's favor, affirming that the criminal law provision applied to all Indians, regardless of religious affiliation. Seeking a middle ground between recognizing Muslim personal law and women's rights to permanent maintenance, the Court found that while Muslim personal law does limit a husband's liability to provide maintenance for his divorced wife to the period of *iddat*, the Court argued that the Muslim personal law did not contemplate a situation in which a divorced Muslim wife would not be able to maintain herself after the *iddat* period—the precise case covered by Section 125 of the Criminal Code. The Court in *Shah Bano* thus concluded that where a Muslim wife could support herself after the *iddat* period, Muslim personal law governed. But where a divorced wife could not do so, she could appeal to the criminal law for continued maintenance from her ex-husband. Notably, rather than simply holding that Indian criminal law preempted Muslim personal law, the Court quoted progressive Muslim commentators who argued that Muslim law itself supported a right of divorced women to receive permanent alimony.

But the Court's reference to the Quran to support its position, along with some unfortunate statements by the Hindu justice writing for the Court, provoked conservative Muslims in India and led to one of the largest mobilizations of Muslims for legal change in Indian history. The political maelstrom ended in then Prime Minister Rajiv Gandhi signing into law the Muslim Women Protection of Rights Upon Divorce Act (MWPRDA) in 1986. The Act, which largely catered to the outcries of conservative Muslims, effectively nullified the Supreme Court's holding in *Shah Bano* and deprived divorced Muslim women of their right of maintenance under the criminal code, thus putting them at a disadvantage under the law vis-à-vis Christian and Hindu women. Particularly galling to Muslim women in India was that they were scarcely consulted before the passage of the Act; the government bowed to the pressure of religious conservatives as the arbiters of Islamic law and failed to engage the broader Muslim community's sentiments about maintenance for destitute women. As we shall see later in this chapter, however, this actual plurality of values and sentiments within the Muslim Indian community could not be so easily contained or disregarded.

The Ministerial Exception (U.S.)

While the United States does not expressly delegate the governance of private matters to various communities through personal or customary laws, deference to religious or other private communities arises nonetheless in a number of contexts. The freedoms of religion, speech, and association guaranteed by the First Amendment offer one principal mechanism for halting public intervention on behalf of women within religious organizations. In particular, a judicially created "ministerial exception" or "ecclesiastical exception" in U.S. law insulates religious organizations' employment decisions from judicial scrutiny under Title VII when the decision involves an employee whose duties are important to the spiritual mission of the church. The exception, first articulated by the U.S. Court of Appeals for the 5th Circuit in 1972,[7] has been widely adopted and extended to exclude claims under the Americans with Disabilities Act, the Age Discrimination in Employment Act, and the Fair Labor Standards Act. The purpose of the exception is to protect religious organizations' free exercise of religion and to prevent an establishment of religion as required by the Free Exercise and Establishment Clauses of the First Amendment of the Constitution. The Establishment Clause forbids excessive government entanglement with religion, which courts argue would result if the State inquired too closely into the gender-related beliefs of a church. The Free Exercise Clause guarantees a church's freedom to decide how it will govern itself.[8]

In practice, the ministerial exception leads courts to dismiss Title VII gender discrimination complaints brought by women employees of religious institutions, on the ground that reviewing such claims would require an unacceptable encroachment of the State into an area of religious freedom that is Constitutionally forbidden. In 1996, in the case of *E.E.O.C. v. Catholic University of America*,[9] for example, Sister McDonough was the first woman appointed to the canon law faculty at Catholic University. After McDonough was denied tenure, she filed sex discrimination charges alleging that the university violated Title VII of the Civil Rights Act of 1964. But the Court of Appeals for the District of Columbia Circuit dismissed the claim on the ground that its adjudication on the merits would violate the "the constitutional right of a church to manage its own affairs free from governmental interference."[10] The ministerial exception has been applied to dismiss the claims of discrimination brought by a dismissed music teacher in a religious elementary school,[11] a Catholic schoolteacher fired for signing a pro-choice statement,[12] and a professor fired from a religious seminary,[13] among other cases.

In short, the First Amendment freedom of religion bars women's claims of gender discrimination under Title VII, except when the employee had no position that affected the organization's spiritual message. Every one of the federal circuit courts of appeals to consider the issue has concluded that application of Title VII of the Civil Rights Act of 1964 to a minister-church relationship would violate—or would risk violating—the First Amendment and, accordingly, has recognized some version of the ministerial exception. To the extent that a claim involves a church's selection of clergy—in other words, its choice as to who will perform particular spiritual functions—most of the circuits have held that the exception bars any inquiry into a religious organization's underlying motivation for the contested employment decision.

Reproductive Freedom (U.S.)

In the United States, 45 states have "conscience laws" which enable individuals to refuse to provide birth control options that are contrary to their religious or moral beliefs. Further, the Weldon Amendment of 2005 prohibits federal funding to any state that discriminates against an institution that follows the "conscience laws" and refuses to provide birth control services. However, a number of states have decided that the "conscience laws" do not apply to emergency contraception; only abortions, sterilization, and artificial insemination are covered under "conscience laws." There is controversy as to a pharmacist's right to refuse to fill prescriptions for birth control, specifically, the "morning after pill." In accord with the view of the American Pharmacist Association, four states have laws allowing pharmacists to refuse to fill prescriptions for religious or cultural reasons while seven states require pharmacists to fill prescriptions or give a timely referral of where the prescription can be filled. Approximately 20 states are considering legislation allowing pharmacists to not fill prescriptions that are against their religious or moral beliefs.

CEDAW (International)

Adopted by the United Nations in 1979, CEDAW is the only major human rights treaty to address women's rights exclusively. It is a wide-ranging, comprehensive treaty that seeks to promote women's rights in all walks of life, including not only civil and political rights but also social, cultural, and economic rights.[14] CEDAW is a milestone achievement for international women's rights in that is seeks to end gender discrimination not only in the public sphere but also in the private spheres of family, culture, and religion. Article 2 of CEDAW calls for states to "eliminate discrimination against women by any person, organization, or enterprise" [15] and to "take all appropriate measures, including legislation, to modify or abolish existing laws, regulations, customs and practices which constitute discrimination against women." [16]

But CEDAW's ambition of eradicating private as well as public discrimination has also been its downfall. CEDAW has the dubious distinction of being both one of the most ratified conventions in international law (as of April 2010, 186 countries had ratified CEDAW), while also having the highest number of states expressing "reservations" to the agreement. Some of the most damning of the reservations are those that reject CEDAW's obligations where they would interfere with religious or customary law. Multiple Islamic countries such as Bahrain, Bangladesh, Iraq, Malaysia, Oman, Saudi Arabia, and Syria, for example, do not consider Article 2 binding if its requirements conflict with Sharia laws based on the Quran. Nearly a dozen Muslim countries have objected to Article 16, which requires state parties to "eliminate discrimination against women in all matters relating to marriage and family relations." [17] Thus, despite CEDAW's call to recognize women and men as equals in marriage, with "the same right to enter into marriage," the "same right freely to choose a spouse and to enter into marriage only with their free and full consent," and "the 'same rights and responsibilities during marriage and its dissolution,'[18] states have avoided meeting these obligations, arguing that they conflict with Sharia law.

The CEDAW Committee has stated that Articles 2 and 16 are core provisions of the Convention, and the committee has expressed concern about the wide number of reservations to these provisions.[19] But complaints by some CEDAW member states that these reservations are illegal under international law because they undermine the "object and purpose" of the treaty have been met with accusations of cultural imperialism and religious intolerance. The upshot has been that countries have successfully resisted having to fully operationalize CEDAW on the grounds of religious and cultural exceptionalism. Thus, although very few countries have yet to ratify CEDAW—including the United States, Iran, Qatar, Nauru, Palau, Tonga, Somalia, and Sudan[20]—and there is steady pressure on these holdout nations to do so,[21] the continuation of reservations by states claiming exceptions from the norm of gender equality on religious and cultural grounds continue to undermine the goal of universal gender equality.[22] The upshot? Despite its claims to universalism, the international human rights community has, in practice, ascribed to a theory of religious exceptionalism and cultural relativism in the case of women's rights.

As I shall show in the next section, however, there is much more contest on the ground in member states about whether Islamic law is, in fact, incompatible with the norms of gender equality affirmed in CEDAW. More than a decade of robust debates in Moroccan civil society, for example, have led to a number of reforms in that country's laws, most notably a new Family Law Code adopted in 2004 that affirms women and men as equals in marriage and with equal rights to divorce. I examine this reform effort in the next section. I note that the Moroccan reforms did not arise from a rejection of Islamic law in favor of international human rights norms, but rather, were the result of more than a decade of internal Muslim debate and renovation which notably involved a reinterpretation of Moroccan Islamic law to be consistent with modern ways of life and evolving norms.

■ THE NEW ENLIGHTENMENT

In 2004, Moroccan feminists working with a broad civil society coalition succeeded in upending a decades-old discriminatory and oppressive Muslim family law. The old law enshrined husbands' authority over their wives in marriage, prescribed unequal minimum marriage age for women and men (15 for women and 18 for men), and gave only men the right to initiate divorce. Rather than rejecting Islamic law in favor of international human rights norms, however, Moroccan activists pioneered a holistic approach to law reform, contesting the old measures on four levels: as violating (1) Islamic principles, (2) principles of equality enshrined in the national constitutions, (3) CEDAW and international human rights law, and (4) finally, as conflicting with the lived realities of Moroccan women in the twenty-first century. The result was a reformed Moudawana, or family code, which is still expressly "Muslim" but now recognizes husbands and wives as equals, sets an equal minimum marriage age for women and men at 18, and provides equal rights to divorce, among other things. In developing an Islamic reformist approach, women activists sought to return to Morocco's own progressive Muslim traditions; indeed, they identified regressive, patriarchal policies with "foreign" Muslim traditions. At the same time, reformers compared Moroccan Muslim law with other "Muslim" family laws elsewhere, which were both progressive on women's rights and expressly "Islamic." Ultimately, the Moroccan people were convinced that Muslim law can and must recognize the norm of gender equality.

The new Moroccan family law, or Moudawana, has become a model law for Muslim women reformers worldwide. In 2009, more than 250 Muslim women reformers from 47 countries gathered in Kuala Lumpur, Malaysia, to launch a "global movement for equality and justice in Muslim family laws." The movement, called "Musawah," which means equality in Arabic, seeks to enable Muslim feminists from around the world to share ideas and arguments that can be used to pursue reform at home. They see the Moroccan law—and the holistic reform strategy that led to it—as a blueprint for seeking change in their own countries. What is notable is that the women gathered there, including journalists, scholars, and grassroots community organizers, used *Islamic* feminist reformist arguments to counter discriminatory laws and practices at home. The women, from Afghanistan, Gambia, Indonesia, Iran, Morocco, Nigeria, Pakistan, and even Saudi Arabia, to name just a few of the countries represented, came to learn and share the best arguments to use as ammunition against religious *mullahs* or conservatives who argue for the status quo in their home countries.[23]

The reformers' approach to religion and religious communities varies sharply from the traditional legal approach of deference to religious elites. Human rights law typically presumes religious communities to be homogeneous, hierarchical, patriarchal, and irrational. Religious meaning is presumed to flow from traditional authorities and is imposed on members of the community from the top down. Women reformers in the Muslim world, in contrast, claim their right to contest and create religious meaning themselves. Increasingly, for example, Muslim women claim their right to read and interpret Islam for themselves. As the founding director of Sisters in Islam and a founder of the Musawah effort, Zainah Anwar, declared at the opening of the conference, "we are all experts here" with the authority "to think, to feel, to question what it means to be Muslim in the twenty-first century."

This approach of opening up religious discourse to democratic participation, critical thinking, and human rights norms, is itself a powerful means for helping individuals and communities to question patriarchal policies that some seek to justify in the name of religion. Upon closer, critical examination of such claims, we may find that in fact egalitarian, religious options exist—or, that the contested practice is in fact not religiously prescribed at all. A particularly moving moment during the Musawah meeting in 2009 came when Dr. Isatou Touray, a reformer from Gambia who was circumcised at the age of 11 without ever asking questions, shared her shock upon first reading the Quran as an adult and discovering that "there is no mention in the Quran of" any such requirement. The revelation led Touray to found the Gambia Committee on Traditional Practices Affecting the Health of Women and Children (GAMCOTRAP). She says that some 75% of girls in Gambia, between birth and age 12, are subjected to female genital mutilation (FGM) in the name of Islam. But reformers' protests are beginning to penetrate, she says. When they raise the fact that the Quran is silent on this practice, religious leaders have no reply and in fact have stopped making religious arguments for the practice, she says. That opening makes it easier to counter FGM with arguments about girls' and women's health and sexual freedom. In 2007, several communities in Gambia publicly condemned FGM.

To be sure, this strategy of reform *within* Islam remains controversial, especially among many avowedly "secular" feminists, many of whom are a part of the Musawah movement. At the same time, women reformers cannot give up the terrain of religion and culture to fundamentalists. First, as a practical matter, women must directly confront the arguments used to suppress their rights—and many of these arguments today are presented in religious and cultural terms. As the UN Special Rapporteur on Violence Against Women, Yakin Ertürk, has argued, there is a pressing need for women to deconstruct culture and religion in order to fight violence against them.[24]

Reformers use of religion is more than strategic, however. By claiming their rights to debate and reform religious community to recognize women's equality, women reformers affirm their own religious freedom. Increasingly, today, these women find the choice between religion and rights wanting. Today women demand equality and freedom in all the spheres of life that are most dear to them.

Islamic fundamentalism is a global phenomenon. So, too, is this movement to counter the hegemonic discourse on what it means to be Muslim. This movement, too, has grand ambitions: reformers hope that in the next decade "25 more Muslim countries in the world will join Morocco in recognizing marriage as a partnership of equals, where we will have the equal right to marry, to divorce, and to the custody of our children." [25]

Equality Without Reservations

On December 10, 2008, the 60th Anniversary of the Universal Declaration of Human Rights, Morocco's King Mohammed VI announced the withdrawal of Moroccan reservations to CEDAW—all of them.[26] The move was hailed as a victory for Muslim women's groups, which spearheaded a regional "Equality Without Reservations" campaign in 2006 along with feminists from the Middle East, North Africa, and the Gulf regions. The campaign pressed for the lifting of all reservations to CEDAW by Muslim countries and for their ratification of the CEDAW Optional Protocol, which allows individuals to bring claims of discrimination directly to the CEDAW Committee.

Declarations notwithstanding, however, to date the Moroccan government has not yet taken the formal steps necessary to withdraw its CEDAW reservations. According to Article 23 of the Vienna Convention, "The withdrawal of a reservation or of an objection to a reservation must be formulated in writing" [27] and to date, the Secretary General of the UN has yet to receive any such writing from the Royal government of Morocco.[28]

Still, the Equality Without Reservations campaign, like Musawah, seems a productive alternative to the New Sovereignty. Rather than simply accepting the claims of traditional religious leaders lying down, ordinary women are asking questions about Muslim laws, exposing plural Muslim traditions, and ultimately forcing authorities to justify their choices in light of multiple options that exist—all in the name of Islam. That women are discovering and developing religious interpretations that are consistent with global norms of human rights and gender equality should not be surprising. Contrary to the bad rap when it comes to women's rights, the world's religions, including Islam, teem with norms and values that affirm human rights, from equality to the dignity of all persons. As the name "Musawah" illustrates, no one tradition can lay claim to these core human values.

Muslim Alimony Law in India Revisited

Indian Muslim family law, too, has seen recent changes that affirm the plural values in Islamic law and its potential compatibility with Indian Constitutional guarantees of equality and dignity. As I have already described, Indian law hit a low point with the hasty and regressive legislative adoption of the Muslim Women Protection of Rights Upon Divorce Act in 1986, which had as its aim the appeasement of conservative Muslims upset by the Indian Supreme Court's decision in *Shah Bano* a year earlier affirming Muslim women's right to permanent alimony. It is telling, however, that even this new Act could not contain the plural demands for justice within Indian Muslim families. After its passage, state high courts again seized upon ambiguous language in the new law which, although it clearly limited Muslim men's payment obligation to the three months after divorce, nonetheless required that Muslim men make a "fair and reasonable provision" for the ex-wife. Lawyers for divorced Muslim women argued that this provision of the Act meant that Muslim men must pay a reasonable alimony to provide for the ex-wife until her remarriage or death—but that this payment must be made within the three months following the divorce. Many state high courts agreed, and thus the debate over Muslim men's alimony obligations continued well beyond *Shah Bano* and the new Act.

In 2001, the Indian Supreme Court was again asked to consider the issue—this time through a challenge to the constitutionality of the Muslim Women Protection of Rights Upon Divorce Act. Activists argued that the Act denied Muslim women's Constitutional rights to equal protection under laws (Article 14), their right to religious freedom (Article 15), and the right to live in dignity (Article 21). In *Danial Latifi v. Union of India*, the Court offered a landmark decision that affirmed an egalitarian interpretation of the Act's provision that "a reasonable and fair provision and maintenance" is "to be made and paid to [the ex-wife] within the *iddat* period by her former husband." Where conservative Muslims argued that this meant Muslim husbands could dispose of their duty to their wives by paying her maintenance for approximately three months after a divorce, progressive interpreters argued that Muslim men's obligation under the Act was to pay the ex-wife a reasonable maintenance that would sustain her for the remainder of her life or until remarriage—but that this amount needed to be paid within the *iddat* period just following the divorce. Guided by the principle that the Court should uphold the statute so long as a constitutionally valid understanding of it was possible, the Court upheld the validity of the law on the basis of the latter interpretation. According to the Court, the calculation of the reasonable maintenance due the ex-wife extends for the entire life of the divorced wife until she remarries. Only such an interpretation of the Act would not offend the Constitution of India.[29] Any reading to the contrary, the Court argued, would mean "a divorced Muslim woman has obviously been unreasonably discriminated" against.[30] In short, the Court found that multiple readings of Muslim law were possible, and upheld the Act's constitutionality by choosing an interpretation that affirmed the rights of Muslim women to equality, religious liberty, and human dignity. Unfortunately, even after this ruling, there is pressure on Muslim women not to pursue claims for maintenance beyond the *iddat* period, an option which is presented by conservative Muslim leaders as un-Islamic.[31] But increased discussion within the religious community and outside of it about interpretations of men's obligations under Muslim law that promote equality and dignity, as the Supreme Court itself offered, show that Muslim law can, indeed, be compatible with human rights.

■ RELIGION IN THE PUBLIC SPHERE

Thus far I have discussed the importance of recognizing the Enlightenment values of freedom, equality, and dissent within the religious sphere. But what about the reverse phenomenon—the recognition of religion in the public sphere? In recent years, this issue has focused specifically on women and girls, with the flashpoint debate centering on Muslims wearing religious headscarves (*hijab*) or the more conspicuous full-body covering *burqa* in public. Approaches to the issue are as wide-ranging as traditions of secularism. In the United States, where the free exercise of religion is guaranteed in the Constitution, there has been a wide latitude given to the wearing of religious garments, including headpieces and jewelry, in the public sphere. In Europe and elsewhere, there has been much greater furor over and objection to such practices. Partly this derives from strong traditions of *laïcité* in countries like France and Turkey, which understand secularism as the absence of religion in the public sphere. In both of these countries, however, concerns about gender equality also drive the debates about Muslim women's dress, which is seen as a symbol of inferior status and incompatible with women's equality guaranteed by secular law.

France and Turkey: Banning Headscarves from Schools

In 2004, the French parliament passed The "Headscarf Law," which made it illegal to wear large and conspicuous articles of religious dress in public schools. France has a large Muslim population, estimated at five million. Under this law, Muslim headscarves, large Christian crosses, turbans for Sikhs, and Jewish yarmulkes are all prohibited. Although the law covers all religious garments, including large crosses, the impetus for the law was Muslim girls wearing a religious headcovering—a headscarf—to school. France invoked *laïcité*, a commitment to gender equality, and the failure of the Muslim population to integrate as justifications for the law. The French tradition of secularism, known as *laïcité*, envisions a strict absence of religion from the public sphere. Moreover, public debate presumed that the girls wearing headscarves had no choice in the matter, and that they were coerced by their parents into doing so. Finally, public discussions and politicians spoke of girls wearing headscarves as a sign of "aggression"[32]—that is, as Muslim defiance against traditional French culture and the norm of assimilation.

Turkey has long had a similar ban on religious headscarves in the public sphere, including public secondary schools and even universities. Since the founding of the modern secular Turkish republic by Mustafa Kemal Atatürk in 1923, Turkey has established a staunchly secular state with a strong policy of *laïcité* similar to France. The veil, in particular, was banned from the public sphere since the Republic's founding because Ataturk and other founders saw it is a symbol of backwardness and women's oppression. In more recent years, as the continuation of the policy has been debated, many fear that reversing the ban and allowing women to wear a veil in public will put pressure on women who choose not to veil. Upholding the religious freedom of women who choose not to veil and protecting them from so-called "street pressure" is an important argument against lifting the Turkish ban. In the meantime, the European Court of Human Rights has upheld Turkey's ban, holding that it does not violate the religious liberty of those who want to veil. The petitioner in the case, Leyla Şahin, was a medical student at the University of Istanbul who was denied access to lectures, courses and two written exams because she was wearing an Islamic headscarf. Şahin claimed the headscarf ban forced students to choose between education and religion and violated her right to freedom of religion.[33] But the European Court of Justice upheld the Turkish law by a vote of 16 to 1. The court observed that freedom of religion could "not be equated with a right to wear any particular religious attire." The court justified its decision, arguing that "once outside the private sphere, freedom to manifest one's religion could be restricted on public-order grounds to defend the principle of secularism." The court further opined that "granting legal recognition to a religious symbol of that type in institutions of higher education was not compatible with the principle that State education must be neutral, as it would be liable to generate conflicts between students with differing religious convictions or beliefs."[34]

In recent years, however, a popular and political movement to reverse the Turkish ban has grown, and in 2008 the Turkish legislature voted overwhelmingly to overturn the nearly century-old ban on the veil. The main argument for overturning the ban was that it prohibited religious women from having equal access to higher education and violated other human rights, such as the freedom of religion and movement. Supporters of overturning the ban also argued that the strict prohibition on dress was not in conformity with European and human rights norms of liberty. A few months later, however, Turkey's highest court invalidated the law, arguing that allowing headscarves in the public sphere violated the State's Constitutional commitment to secularism.

Burqa Ban

More recently, public debate in a number of European countries has erupted around the issue of banning women from wearing the *burqa* in public places. The *burqa* is an enveloping garment covering a woman from head to toe when she leaves her home and enters the public sphere. The dress is intended to preserve women's modesty when outside the home. In spring 2010, French President Nicolas Sarkozy made headlines by calling for legislation that would ban women from wearing a *burqa* in public. Sarkozy denounced the garment as oppressive to women and not welcome in France. The proposed law states that no one in France will be permitted to wear anything designed to hide the face in public places like shops, hospitals, schools, and on public transportation. Other European countries, from Belgium to Germany, the Netherlands, and Spain have followed France with legislative debates of their own considering a similar ban. Opponents of the *burqa* cite concerns about national security, gender equality, and argue that face coverings are not conducive to the social relations required in a liberal democracy. In Britain, politicians such as former Prime Minister Tony Blair and former foreign secretary Jack Straw have pronounced that "they do not want Muslim women to cover their faces, because this threatens social harmony." In an interview with the BBC, Jack straw stated, "communities are bound together partly by informal chance relations between strangers, people being able to acknowledge each other in the street or being able to pass the time of the day." In Holland, a bill making a Muslim *burqa* illegal was introduced into law. The bill was justified by the argument that "society will work well only if people can see one another's faces as they pass one another in the street." Violators of the new law risk a fine of 15 to 25 Euros or a prison sentence of one to seven days.

The conflicts over Muslim women's dress illustrate well the insufficiencies of the conventional "liberty versus equality" approach to women's human rights and religion. To begin with, the parties claiming religious freedom in these cases are women and girls. But here, rather than defer to religious discrimination, the State intervenes in the name of gender equality, seeking at least to eradicate the veil as a marker of inequality from the public sphere. It may be tempting to see Muslim dress regulations as a victory for the New Enlightenment—in these instances, at least in rhetoric, the norm of gender equality trumps religious freedom. Religious attire is banned in public for fear that women are coerced into wearing it, or because the dress symbolizes a rejection of secularism and human rights. But this is too simple an analysis. In many instances, women's human rights are actually denied by banning religious garments from schools and the public sphere. Girls with strong convictions to the veil are prohibited from attending public school, ironically forced to attend religious Islamic schools instead. Indeed, the CEDAW Committee has expressed concern over the negative repercussions of the ban on women's access to education. Furthermore, the laws severely compromise women's freedom of conscience. In 2008, the Human Rights Commission expressed concern that such laws violate Article 18 of the International Convention on Civil and Political Rights (ICCPR), which protects "freedom of conscience and religion."

On closer look, the regulations of Muslim women's dress appear consistent with the New Sovereignty, not the New Enlightenment. The prohibitions similarly presume religion to be incompatible with gender equality, and assert a stark separation between religion and the liberal value of equality.

There is another problem with the traditional "liberty versus equality" approach: women's and girls' donning of a headscarf may not even be religious. Muslim immigrant girls in France, for example, testify that they choose to wear the veil more as a political statement than a religious one—to show, for example, that despite an official policy of "equality of all" in the public sphere, Muslim immigrants are not equal citizens. Finally, there is a live debate over whether the veil is a religious requirement of Islam at all. Leila Ahmed, for example, has written that the veil predates Islam and is more a cultural artifact of the time of Mohammed's revelation than a specific religious requirement. Ahmed contends that a strict reading of the Quran reveals that the instruction to veil was only intended for Muhammad's wives, and not all women.[35]

Perhaps the veil and *burqa* debates best illustrate the extent to which we cannot make simplistic claims about the incompatibility of religion—or any specific religion, such as Islam—and women's rights. In truth, secular laws may be just as guilty of limiting women's basic human rights (here to education and religious freedom). Moreover, we must recognize that states acting under the rhetoric of upholding norms of "gender equality" are often motivated by animus toward religion—indeed, this is precisely the concern underlying the liberal/legal tradition of non-interference with religious communities. Today in the United States, for example, there is growing opposition to the public presence of mosques. Where in the past, opposition was voiced in the neutral terms of concerns about traffic and noise, today opponents simply voice a rejection of Islam itself, which is equated with fundamentalism, discrimination, and terrorism.[36] Similar public outcry has attended decisions such as Harvard University's to prescribe special sex-segregated pool hours to accommodate the requests of Muslim students. We must always be wary of the extent to which criticisms of such accommodations are fueled by religious animosity. On the other hand, we must also be vigilant against presuming that every criticism of religion is inappropriate.

■ CONCLUSIONS

So how, then, do we keep faith with both religion and human rights? The first answer to this complex question (and the limited answer offered in this chapter) is to deconstruct staid and outmoded understandings of religion itself as inherently discriminatory and oppressive. As I have sought to show in this chapter, our conception of religion matters. If we imagine religion as a sphere of unfreedom, our laws will simply defer to claims of self-proclaimed religious guardians to discriminate. If we recognize religions as plural and potentially compatible with human rights, however, we will allow for greater internal deliberation about women's roles and will see that outright discrimination against women becomes much harder to justify. Second, those who care about gender equality must remember that religious freedom is a fundamental part of women's human rights, as is the right to equality. Increasingly, today, women find the traditional liberal/legal choice between freedom and faith, or equal rights and religion, wanting. The challenge for law in the twenty-first century is to actualize plural rights and values in all spheres of women's lives.

■ NOTES

* I would like to thank Roya Ladan, Rabia Paracha, Dominick Severance, and Erin Murphy for excellent research assistance.

1 See, for example, Ann Elizabeth Mayer, "A 'Benign' Apartheid: How Gender Apartheid Has Been Rationalized," *UCLA Journal of International Law & Affairs* 5 (2001): 237 (comparing the treatment of racial and gender apartheid in international human rights law).

2 Susan Moller Okin, "Is Multiculturalism Bad for Women?" in Joshua Cohen, et al. eds., *Is Multiculturalism Bad for Women?* (Princeton: Princeton University Press, 1999), 7.

3 Martha Nussbaum, *Women and Human Development* (Cambridge: Cambridge University Press, 2000), 84 (quoting Rawls).

4 Ibid., 81–87.

5 See further the chapter by Nazila Ghanea, herein.

6 For a detailed overview of recent changes to Muslim family law in India, see Narendra Subramanian, "Legal Change and Gender Equality: Changes in Muslim Family Law in India," *Law & Social Inquiry*, 33 (Summer 2008): 631–72.

7 *McClure v. Salvation Army*, 460 F.2d 553 (1972).

8 See generally George Blum, "Application of First Amendment's 'Ministerial Exception' or 'Ecclesiastical Exception' to Federal Civil Rights Claims," 41 A.L.R. Fed. 2d 445 (2010).

9 83 F.3d 455, 458 (D.C. Cir. 1996).

10 Ibid., 460.

11 *E.E.O.C. v. Roman Catholic Diocese of Raleigh, N.C.*, 213 F.3d 795 (4th Cir. 2000).

12 *Curray-Cramer v. Ursuline Academy of Wilmington*, 450 F.3d 130 (3rd Cir. 2006).

13 *Klouda v. Southwestern Baptist Theological Seminary*, 543 F.Supp.2d 594 (N.D. Tex. 2008).

14 Convention for the Elimination of Discrimination Against Women, G.A. res. 34/180, 34 U.N. GAOR Supp. (No. 46) at 193, U.N. Doc. A/34/46, *entered into force* September 3, 1981.

15 Ibid., Article 2(e).

16 Ibid., Article 2(f).

17 Ibid., Article 16.1. The reserving countries are Algeria, Bangladesh, Egypt, Iraq, Jordan, Kuwait, Lebanon, Libya, Morocco, and Tunisia. Some refer directly to the Sharia

laws and others refer to domestic legislation as their reason for making the reservation. See Eva Brems, *Human Rights: Universality and Diversity* (The Hague: Martinus Nijhoff Publishers, 2001), 275.

18 Ibid.

19 The list of reserving nations and reservations is available at http://www.un.org/womenwatch/daw/cedaw/reservations.htm

20 The transcript of the convention, including debates over reservations, is available at: http://www.un.org/womenwatch/daw/cedaw/text/econvention.htm.

21 The Vatican has also refused to sign CEDAW, concerned about CEDAW's commitment to women's reproductive freedom. See *Rights by Stealth: The Role of UN Human Rights Treaty Bodies in the Campaign for an International Right to Abortion*, white paper by Douglas Sylva and Susan Yoshihara of the International Organizations Research Group (July 18, 2007). Predominantly Catholic countries, however, have not made consistent and express reservations to CEDAW as have predominantly Muslim countries.

22 Sarah R. Hamilton, "The Status of Women in Chile: Violations of Human Rights and Recourse Under International Law," *Women's Rights Law Reporter L. Rep.* 25 (2004): 111–123.

23 See generally Sabrina Travernise, "In Quest for Equal Rights, Muslim Women's Meeting Turns to Islam's Tenets," *The New York Times*, February 15, 2009, A8.

24 Yakin Ertürk, Special Rapporteur on Violence Against Women, "Report of the Special Rapporteur on Violence Against Women, Its Causes and Consequences: Intersections Between Culture and Violence Against Women," U.N. Doc. A/HRC/4/34 (January 17, 2007).

25 Opening Statement of Zainah Anwar, Musawah Launch Event, Kuala Lumpur, February 14, 2009.

26 "The Moroccan Report on the Implementation of the Convention to the CEDAW Committee," January 2008, available at http://www.unifem.org/cedaw30/success_stories/#morocco.

27 Vienna Convention on theLaw of Treaties available at http://untreaty.un.org/ilc/texts/instruments/english/conventions/1_1_1969.pdf. 1155 U.N.T.S. 331, 8 I.L.M. 679, *entered into force* January 27, 1980.

28 In April 2010, Liesl Gerntholtz, the director of the Women's Right Division of the Human Rights Watch sent a letter to King Mohammed VI expressing concern about his delay in lifting the reservations. See http://www.hrw.org/fr/news/2010/04/14/letter-king-morocco-his-commitment-withdraw-reservations-cedaw.

> As a result of the pressure from Moroccan women's groups, the Moroccan government has announced its intention to withdraw its reservations to CEDAW. See http://www.learningpartnership.org/lib/press-release-withdrawal-reservations-cedaw-morocco.

29 *Danial Latifi & Anr. v. Union of India* MANU/SC/0595/2001.

30 Ibid.

31 *See* Saumya Uma, "Muslim Women's Rights to Maintenance in India," *The Daily Star.* January 30, 2005, 1.

32 Then-President Jacques Chirac openly asserted in 2003 that "wearing a veil is a kind of aggression."

33 *Şahin v Turkey*, 44 EHRR 5 (2007) (EctHR, 2005-XI, 175, November 10, 2005) (Grand Chamber Judgment).

34 Ibid., 12. See further the chapter by Carolyn Evans, herein.

35 Leila Ahmed, *Women and Gender in Islam* (New Haven: Yale University Press, 1993), 54.

36 *See* Laurie Goodstein, "Around Country, Mosque Projects Meet Opposition: Foes See Islam as Issue," The *New York Times*, August 8, 2010, A1.

RECOMMENDED READING

Ahmed, Leila. *Women and Gender in Islam* (New Haven: Yale University Press, 1993)

Afkhami, Mahnaz, ed. *Faith and Freedom: Women's Human Rights in the Muslim World* (Syracuse, NY: Syracuse University Press, 2000)

An-Na'im, Abdullahi Ahmed. *Islam and the Secular State* (Cambridge: Harvard University Press, 2008)

Benhabib, Seyla. *The Claims of Culture: Equality and Diversity in the Global Era* (Princeton: Princeton University Press, 2002)

Bowen, John Richard. *Why the French Don't Like Headscarves: Islam, the State and Public Space* (Princeton: Princeton University Press, 2007)

Coomaraswamy, Radhika. "Different but Free: Cultural Relativism and Women's Rights as Human Rights," in *Religious Fundamentalisms and the Human Rights of Women*, ed. Courtney W. Howland (New York: St. Martin's Press, 1999), 79–90

Abou El Fadl, Kahled. *Speaking in God's Name: Islamic Law, Authority and Women* (Oxford: Oneworld, 2001)

Ertürk, Yakin. Special Rapporteur on Violence Against Women, "Report of the Special Rapporteur on Violence Against Women, Its Causes and Consequences: Intersections Between Culture and Violence Against Women," U.N. Doc A/HRC/4, January 34, 17, 2007

MacKinnon, Catherine A. *Are Women Human? And Other International Dialogues* (Cambridge: Harvard University Press, 2006)

Mahmoud, Saba. *Politics of Piety: The Islamic Revival and the Feminist Subject* (Princeton: Princeton University Press, 2005)

Mir-Hosseini, Ziba. *Islam and Gender* (Princeton: Princeton University Press, 1999)

Nussbaum, Martha. *Liberty of Conscience* (New York: Basic Books, 2008)

______. *Women and Human Development* (Cambridge: Cambridge University Press, 2000)

______. *Sex and Social Justice* (Oxford: Oxford University Press, 1998)

Sunder, Madhavi. "Piercing the Veil." *Yale Law Journal* 112 (2003): 1399–1472

18 Religion and Children's Rights

BARBARA BENNETT WOODHOUSE

Maria Urso entered first grade when she was barely five, around the time of her first communion. She had to stand on a desk to reach the blackboard. An exceptionally intelligent child, she was promoted rapidly from grade to grade. Maria was impressionable, soaking up information and ideas from her surroundings. She believed in God and attended mass with her mother. She prayed with her family around the dinner table. Her secular education and religious education were intermixed. Attending a free public school operated by Catholic nuns, she would gaze at the symbols on the schoolroom wall—a large crucifix depicting Jesus on the cross, flanked by portraits of Victor Emmanuel, King of Italy, and his beautiful consort, Elena of Montenegro. Maria worshipped her teacher, also called Elena, and thought of her as the Queen incarnate. Indoctrination in fascism was also a part of the mix. Her family was apolitical. But fascism was everywhere—all the children belonged to fascist youth groups and Maria was proud of her Girls of the Fascia uniform of a white blouse and black skirt. Children reciting the alphabet were taught to say "A is for Albero (tree)" and "M is for Mussolini." Maria saw and felt sorry for children she saw in her village who had to work instead of attending school. But, far removed from the persecution engulfing Jewish children in other parts of Italy and Europe and growing up in a comfortable farmhouse surrounded by olive trees and almond trees, with a large family and many farm animals for companions, and with fields for running and the ocean for swimming, Maria experienced her childhood as a "paradise."

Then came the Allied invasion—the beach where she had played was black with ships. The airplanes and bombs, the amphibian tanks, the alien soldiers, the destruction and terror would mark her forever. "A child is never the same," is how she puts it. But amid this chaos, she also experienced the solace of prayer and the power of her own agency. Ten-year-old Maria prayed for deliverance when a huge airplane came down the street strafing it with gunfire and all the doors she pounded on were barricaded. She escaped the bullets and was able to reach safety. Later, she stopped her family from leaving their sanctuary; terrified of the bombers, she refused when her father tried to move the family back to their farmhouse. That night, a huge bomb destroyed the farmhouse including the very room where Maria and her family would have been sleeping. It was her force of will that saved her family.

Maria's belief in God and in herself survived the war and the many horrors she witnessed, but her faith in the omnipotence of Mussolini and Queen Elena did not. At age 79, Maria Urso looks back at her childhood from the perspective of a retired teacher with over fifty years of experience in the public schools of Florence, where she and her family moved after the war. When I interviewed her in 2010, she was skeptical about a recent case from the European Court of Human Rights that bans the crucifix in Italian schools—for her, it is hard to imagine schoolrooms without the cross. But she was aware and sensitive to the role religious and political symbols played in her own education and indoctrination. When asked to explain her philosophy of children's education she replied: "The most important thing is the opportunity to express oneself."[1]

As this story graphically illustrates, children's experiences of family, education, religion, and the State are complex and evolving, and always embedded in a larger social and historical context. Relationships and environments are of cardinal importance. Many people in the Western liberal tradition tend instead to see rights in isolation from relationships, as a facet of human autonomy. They imagine a zero sum game, with rights for one individual pitted against rights of another individual. From this perspective, parents' and children's religious rights might seem to be antagonistic. Maria's parents had a right to decide where to send her to school and what to teach her. Grownups controlled the curriculum, and would inevitably include "false" truth claims (Mussolini's omnipotence) along with "true" faith claims (God's grace). According religious rights to children would defeat the interests of states and the rights of parents. Attributing competing rights to Maria would destroy both the social and the familial harmony. In order to protect children, it almost seems we must reduce the child to a mere vessel for the adult's beliefs and ideologies, denying the child's own agency and her own rights of thought, conscience, and religion.[2]

But the process of Maria's religious education, as this description shows, was far more complex and interactive than such a zero sum account of rights implies. It occurred in relationship to family, the natural world, the village, the school, state authority, symbolic images, and personal experiences of faith. The child's and the parents' religious rights were integrally related. As one wise observer commented, "it is not coercive or indoctrinating in itself to bring a child into a religious community."[3] Without protection for the process of transmitting religious beliefs to the next generation—a process that is reflected to some degree in virtually every world religion—there might soon be no more believers. However, no individual, especially a vulnerable young person who has acquired and cherishes a religious faith, should be coerced into denying her beliefs or abandoning her faith—even if the coercion comes from her parents.

The traditional approach in Western liberal thought to reconciling parental rights to inculcate religion in the young with children's rights to religious freedom has been to delay legal recognition of children's religious autonomy until they reach the age of majority and are legally free from adult control. Unlike age requirements for driving a car or viewing pornography, this approach is not based on a belief that children have no place in the religious sphere. Children have always been central to religious practice. Infants are baptized or circumcised and pledged to their parents' faith; young children attend religious training and holy days and dietary rules are observed by adults and children alike. Muslim children pray so frequently throughout the day that prayer becomes a part of the child's natural rhythm. When Hindu children eat their vegetarian meals they are practicing their Hindu identity.[4]

Research in child development tells us that children form deeply held beliefs and acquire a religious identity long before they reach adulthood. This reality is reflected in rites of passage common to many religious traditions in which the pre-adolescent or adolescent child is called upon to make a knowing and personal commitment to her faith.[5] These practices recognize a religious "coming of age" for children and youth often far younger than the age of legal majority.

These religious landmarks of maturation are steps along a path traveled in the company of family, peers, and religious communities; no individual is ever fully autonomous or ever fully mature in acquiring a religion. Religious development, like development of ethics and morals, is achieved in dialogue with parents and with the secular and religious communities. It begins long before the individual is ready to make conscious and conscientious choices and continues until and, in some religions, past the end of this life.[6] Religious tolerance is fundamental to democratic societies.

Applying the free exercise and anti-establishment clauses of the United States Constitution's First Amendment, the Supreme Court of the United States has decided many cases involving parents and children allied against a coercive state or seeking protection from discrimination. The Court has grounded its holdings on parents' freedom to practice their own religion and raise their children in the religion of their fathers, and on parents' fundamental rights to control the education and upbringing of their children. Rarely does it rest its holding on children's religious rights alone because cases involving children in conflict with parents and religious communities are relatively rare.[7] Such cases rarely arise and usually involve adolescents.[8] As the Court stated in *In re Gault*: "the Bill of Rights is not for adults alone." Cases involving children's religious rights push us to think more deeply about what it means to be religious, how we acquire a religious identity, and what role parents and community play in nurturing and vindicating children's religious rights.

■ THE EMERGENCE OF CHILDREN'S RIGHTS AS HUMAN RIGHTS

Rights were once perceived in the Western legal tradition as something to be exercised by autonomous adults on behalf of themselves and their dependents. Children's rights were viewed as a by-product of adults' responsibilities—adults' legal responsibility to support their children created a right in the child to receive parental support and a duty in the child to obey. In the past century, the legal landscape has shifted radically as new constitutions and treaties explicitly incorporate references to children's human rights and old constitutions are expanded to include doctrines borrowed from emerging human rights principles.[9]

Children's suffering and persecution during wartime has speeded the development of children's human rights.[10] In 1924, the League of Nations adopted the Geneva Declarations of the Rights of the Child and the United Nations built on this foundation with the 1959 Declaration of the Rights of the Child. These nonbinding declarations were followed in 1966 by two UN covenants. The International Covenant on Civil and Political Rights (ICCPR) speaks of a child's right to "measures of protection."[11] The International Covenant on Economic, Social and Cultural Rights (ICESCR) provides for "special measures of protection and assistance without discrimination."[12] Regional treaties such as the African Charter of Rights and Welfare of the Child and the European Convention on the Exercise of Children's Rights provide rules for regional bodies.[13]

Most comprehensive of the treaties is the United Nations Convention on the Rights of the Child (CRC), opened for signature in 1989.[14] The CRC is the most rapidly and widely accepted human rights document in history. Sixty-one nations signed it on the first day and it entered into force in record time, only seven months later. By July 1997, all nations but the U.S. and Somalia had ratified the CRC.[15]

The CRC is composed of fifty-four Articles and two Optional Protocols. It requires states parties to respect and ensure the rights enshrined in the document, and bans discrimination because of "the child's or the parent's race, colour, sex, language, religion, political or other opinion, national, ethnic or social origin, property, disability, birth or other status."[16] Various articles address children's rights to family, identity, education, participation, healthcare, rest, and play; many articles reinforce the importance of parents' rights in assuring children's well-being. Children's rights to protection from harm play a more prominent role in the CRC than in documents focusing on adults. In addition to protections against abuse and exploitation, the CRC articulates special protections for children who are more vulnerable because of their status or situation, including refugee children, children separated from their families, children with disabilities, and children in the justice system.

The CRC requires that States Parties do more than merely refrain from harming or discriminating against children. In addition to recognizing various economic rights to parental and government support, it requires the State to make the child's best interest a primary consideration in all actions concerning children. While confirming the centrality of family and the notion that parents have the primary responsibility for the upbringing and development of the child, it binds states parties to render appropriate assistance to parents in the performance of their responsibilities and to ensure the development of facilities and services for care of children.[17] In essence, States Parties commit to partnering with families in assuring children's well-being.

The CRC contains no enforcement mechanism. Instead, States Parties agree to submit periodic reports to the Committee on the Rights of the Child. The reporting process engages government, citizens, and NGOs in evaluation of where the State is succeeding and where it is falling short of its CRC commitments. In addition, the CRC provides the guiding principles when national representatives and NGOs gather for regional or global events such as the 2002 UN Special Session on Children. These events spark discussion of children's rights, engage children in dialogue, and result in issuance of reports and calls for action. The CRC also fosters participation by children and youth in public and political life. In the past ten years, the principle of youth participation, once dismissed as symbolic and lacking in practicality, has blossomed into active youth engagement around the world on issues of policy that are important to children.[18] The CRC has become the global starting point for discussion of children's issues and children's rights.

The United States remains largely outside this discussion because it is the only nation, with the exception of Somalia, that has failed to ratify the CRC. In December of 2006, the UN General Assembly passed a resolution urging "States that have not yet done so" to become parties to the CRC. The resolution passed 185–1, with the United States casting the only "no" vote. Opponents in the U.S. are a diverse group, including, the Religious Right, libertarians, homeschoolers, some feminists and advocates for the poor and minorities who have been voicing concerns that strengthening children's rights will provide a wedge for government to intervene in poor, minority, and female-headed households. Despite wide support among mainstream U.S. groups, and despite growing pressure from the international community, powerful opposition from the Religious Right and conservative Republicans prevents any progress toward ratification. The election in 2008 of President Barack Obama, who has expressed support for considering ratification of the CRC, seems to have inflamed rather than calmed opposition, and prospects for ratification by the U.S. remain uncertain.[19]

■ CHILDREN'S RELIGIOUS RIGHTS UNDER THE CRC

Children's religious rights under the CRC are most explicitly addressed in Articles 14 and 30. They read as follows:

> Article 14: 1. States Parties shall respect the right of the child to freedom of thought, conscience and religion. 2. States Parties shall respect the rights and duties of the parents and, when applicable, legal guardians, to provide direction to the child in the exercise of his or her right in a manner consistent with the evolving capacities of the child. 3. Freedom to manifest one's religion or beliefs may be subject only to such limitations as

> are prescribed by law and are necessary to protect public safety, order, health, or morals or the fundamental rights and freedoms of others....
>
> Article 30. In those States in which ethnic, religious, or linguistic minorities or persons of indigenous origin exist, a child belonging to such a minority or who is indigenous shall not be denied the right, in community with other members of his or her group, to enjoy his or her own culture, to profess and practice his or her own religion, or to use his or her own language.

These provisions make clear that children have freedoms of thought, conscience, and religion, as well as rights to enjoy, practice, and profess their own language, culture, and religion, but it is no accident that they are presented in the context of family and community. The CRC views children as embedded in family and community. It is the parent's right, as well as responsibility, to raise the child and guide the exercise of the child's own rights, but "in a manner consistent with the evolving capacities of the child." This key phrase reflects a developmental theme that is common to many faiths as well as to modern psychology—the child's increasing capacity to engage independently in religious exercise.

Article 14 has been the most controversial of the CRC rights, and many states have called for a narrow reading or have lodged reservations to Article 14. States Parties that entered various reservations and declarations have struggled to fit their domestic and religious laws into the CRC frame. In certain states, religious choice by adults, not to mention children, conflicts with law as well as tradition. Working out the tensions between domestic law, state religions, and the CRC has been a delicate process. Saudi Arabia, for example, entered reservations to Article 14 arguing that its provisions might offend Islamic law and the teachings of the Qu'ran. Following meetings between the UN Committee and Saudi Arabian officials, a compromise was reached in which the CRC would be read as a secondary authority on children's freedoms and would not be deemed incompatible with the Quran.[20]

Sylvie Langlaude has examined in detail the current state of children's religious rights in international law—not only the treaty documents but cases, comments, and decisions involving the ICCPR, the CRC, the Special Rapporteur for the Commission on Human Rights, and the European Court of Human Rights. In the closing chapter of her book on the rights of the child, Langlaude concludes that human rights principles require respect for children's religious beliefs, and that children may assert this freedom against both the State and if necessary their parents.[21] This interpretation is reinforced by Article 18.1 of the International Covenant on Civil and Political Rights, which states: "No one shall be subject to coercion which would impair his [or her] freedom to have or to adopt a religion or belief of his choice."[22] However, as many scholars, including Langlaude, have noted, children's rights to choose a religion are only one part of the human rights scheme that also incorporates respect for parents' rights and the concept that exercise of such rights is linked to the child's evolving capacities.[23]

The Committee on the Rights of the Child has interpreted Article 14 rather aggressively as calling for examination of potential conflicts between existing laws and children's religious autonomy. In the Committee's view, both the parent and the State must respect the decisions of the child and should limit their guidance and instruction to that which is necessary to support the child in his or her religious and moral development.[24] Parents are entitled to provide direction but not to coerce children into a certain belief system if it goes against the "evolving capacities of the child." The Committee's approach has drawn criticism for overemphasizing the child's autonomy without due respect for the child's relationships to family and community.

Langlaude asserts that the Committee "has a tendency to treat the child as an autonomous religious believer, with only tenuous links to family and religious community. This is translated by far too much intervention within the family, and the Committee presumes far too quickly that the family is not always acting in the best interest of the child in family matters."[25] However, as in cases involving the United States Constitution, very few human rights cases invoking children's religious rights involve actual conflicts between parents and children.

The near universal adoption of the CRC has not miraculously transformed the lives of the world's children. Many nations lack the resources or the will to achieve the goals the CRC articulates or to provide the protections the CRC requires. Many States Parties have made reservations and declarations undercutting the CRC's coherent application. Yet the CRC represents a major step in bringing children's rights from the margins to center stage. Twenty years of experience with the CRC and other children's rights documents suggests that children's human rights to freedom of thought, conscience, and religion, rather than endangering parental rights, as some critics of children's rights had feared, have reinforced parental rights. They have also opened the way to a more nuanced understanding of what it means to all human beings to inherit and embrace a religion and to be free to follow one's conscience without coercion from the State.[26]

■ HOW AND WHEN DO CHILDREN DEVELOP RELIGIOUS BELIEFS?

The emphasis in the CRC on the child's evolving capacities illustrates the crucial role played by the science of child development in thinking about children's rights. Modern Western scholars of child development have been heavily influenced by the stage theories of Jean Piaget, a Swiss developmental psychologist. Stage theorists describe the development of religious thought in children as a process that begins with attributing human-like qualities to non-human entities and ends in a more theoretical conception of God as an abstract being. Piaget believed that children under the age of seven understood adults and parents to be omnipotent and omniscient and that the world had been created by the humans around them. When children matured out of this stage and realized the fallibility of adults, they no longer had an entity to whom they could attribute the creation of the world, nor could they rely on the idealized qualities of omnipotence and omniscience of humans. Instead, they transferred these concepts to the conception of God, which was then enhanced by religious instruction. According to this theory, the concept of God maintains the anthropomorphisms of early childhood stages, but these human characteristics begin to blend with the more abstract until the child "passes out of the stage of concrete operations, sometime in early adulthood."[27] For a pre-adolescent child, an omniscient and omnipotent God exists as a man in the sky with human-like physical features. Under Piaget's understanding of children's cognitive development, a child of seven and a mature adult would have strikingly different concepts of God.

Children who are involved in research studies have been teaching us more and more about their inner religious lives—a testament to the importance of children's participation and listening to children's voices. Recent research with children shows that children develop the basic concept of religious thought at a very early age. In addition, it is clear that the cultural and religious identity of the child help to shape the way children perceive not only the role of religion but also the contours of essential human rights. Thus, children's development can only be understood in an ecological context.[28]

Researchers still believe that childhood anthropomorphism develops into a more abstract understanding of God, but it is clear that this occurs around age seven, which is much earlier than Piaget supposed.[29] Older children attribute more anthropomorphic qualities to God in tests and research studies because they are asked questions that steer them to such answers. In actuality, children's beliefs about the metaphysical resemble those of adults.[30] When a child is asked to write a letter to God or draw a picture of God, the child will attribute human characteristics to the deity, in much the same way that adults will recite religious teachings ingrained in them over time, when asked questions about miracles or God's physical presence, even if they harbor a very different inner God concept.[31] In order to determine better whether children's and adults concepts differ, researchers suggest we must take a closer look at the particular "theory of being" of the individual human being we are observing. When we do so, we may find that common intuitions about children's religious life are overly simplistic. Boyer and Walker, reviewing many different studies that ask whether children have religious beliefs and how they are different from those of adults, conclude: "There are definite continuities between children's and adults' religious concepts. To see them, however, one needs to abandon the narrow view of religious concepts in which they reduce to explicit statements about matters officially labeled 'religious.'" In both children and adults, religious concepts share certain traits: they involve "socially transmitted, attention grabbing, counterintuitive elements," such as the idea of a God who can be everywhere at one time or a statue, icon, or other material object that can hear and answer prayers. These concepts are viewed as "real" although miraculous, but are integrated into a background understanding which develops very early in life of a world where people and things cannot be everywhere and inanimate objects do not speak and hear. "Children's explicit statements about gods or spirits differ from adults' for two main reasons: A six year old simply lacks some of the relevant cultural knowledge. Only gradually can one learn that God's being "eternal" means that he was around before cars were invented or that God probably does not have to brush his teeth. . . . Many of the alleged discontinuities [between adults and children] might be due to our failure to detect "theological correctness." That is, children's and adults' concepts may be continuous, not just because the child already uses most of the tacit principles of adult ontology, but also because the adult's religious concepts are much more governed by early developed principles than adults themselves (or their religious teachers) would like to think."[32] The essential elements necessary to acquire a God concept are present in children from a very young age. Children aged three or four can distinguish between the sensible, the possible, and the silly, and integrate matters of faith into this scheme. As children acquire a greater knowledge base they are better able to hone their concept of God. This refining does not signify however, that the principles underlying children's concept of God change with maturity; the basic foundation seems to remain quite similar throughout life.

While the basic cognitive foundation for religious thought is similar in early childhood and adulthood, the amount and nature of exposure to religion affects a child's continued religious development. In a study of children educated at inter-religious schools as opposed to Christian schools, the children from inter-religious schools were more understanding and tolerant of diverse beliefs, while maintaining their families' religious identity. Yet children in this school who experienced God on a daily basis, through prayer and ritual, considered God a friend and protector, while those who encountered God in stories as opposed to practices did not see religion as a formative factor in their lives.[33]

It is important to remember the limitations of scientific method, the incompleteness of our understanding of religious belief and the impossibility of truly capturing in words or images what religion means to children or, for that matter, to adults. But what we are learning about children's spiritual lives suggests God is no less significant to the child than to the adult. A children's rights perspective would respect the authenticity and meaningfulness of children's religious beliefs. Absent a serious and imminent danger to the child's well-being, a child-centered theory would also avoid any intervention that risks destabilizing the ecology of the child's family and faith community. Even when risks to children seem clear, experience tells us that aggressive interventions can turn deadly or be far more damaging than leaving children in place. Examples from my own country include the 1993 government assault on the Branch Davidian compound in Waco, Texas, in which many children died, and the forcible removal by Texas authorities of 465 children from the compound of the Fundamentalist Church of Jesus Christ of the Latter-day Saints, later found by the Texas Supreme Court to be damaging and unwarranted.[34]

APPLYING PRINCIPLES OF CHILDREN'S RELIGIOUS RIGHTS TO A SPECIFIC CASE

Courts addressing children's religious rights, whether applying the CRC, the European Convention on Human Rights (ECHR), or some other human rights document, must strike a delicate balance between children's rights, parents' rights, state interests, and the child's evolving capacities while also taking account of history, tradition, and culture. Cases invoking human rights conventions are increasingly common in courts of national or regional bodies.[35] Many of the authors in this volume explore recent religious rights cases involving children and youth.[36] Rather than covering ground already covered by others, I will focus on the case of *Lautsi v. Italy*.[37] Returning to Italy, where this chapter began, offers insights into the interplay and evolution of historical, developmental, human rights, and cultural factors in thinking about children and religion.

In the years since World War II, with globalization and its membership in the European Union, Italy has become far more diverse. After the war, the monarchy was replaced by a new constitutional republic which adopted a policy of neutrality toward religion. Another factor in the *Lautsi* case was a recent backlash against immigration and fears that Italian culture will lose its distinctive qualities. When Soile Lautsi, an Italian citizen born in Finland and residing in Padua, objected to the presence of crucifixes in public schools, many Italians reacted negatively. Lautsi wished to raise her sons, Dataico and Sami, then 10 and 14, as secularists. Acting on her own and her sons' behalf, she asked for removal of the crucifix from the Italian public school her sons attended. She claimed this practice promoted the Catholic religion, violated her children's freedom to believe or not to believe, and infringed her right to raise her children in accordance with her own secularist beliefs. The Lautsi family invoked Italian law (which includes the CRC) and the ECHR and pointed to judgments of the Italian Constitutional Court holding that the Italian Constitution mandated impartiality and equality of treatment among religions and between religious believers and atheists. The Italian Tribunale Amministrativa Regionale per Veneto and the Consiglio di Stato rejected the Lautsi family's claims, accepting the arguments of the Ministry of Education that the crucifix had become a secular symbol of Italian constitutional democracy and religious tolerance and was no longer a symbol of the Catholic religion.[38]

The Lautsi family took their case to the European Court of Human Rights. In 2009, applying the ECHR a seven-judge panel of the Second Section of the European Court held that the State must refrain from imposing religious beliefs on its citizens, especially on young children who are extremely vulnerable to coercion.[39] While education about religious thought could play a valid role in schools, it must be conveyed in an "objective, critical, and pluralistic way." Since the crucifix has a predominantly religious meaning and since the child might feel pressured into believing the message of the crucifix, the Court held that the display of the crucifix violated the children's right to choose what to believe and whether to believe. The European Court panel gave significant attention to the history of display of the crucifix in Italian schoolrooms. Mandating the crucifix in schools was an integral part of the fascist campaign. The regulations imposing the requirement dated to circular no. 68 from the Ministry of Education, issued on November 22, 1922, only a month after Mussolini's march on Rome precipitated the fascist takeover. The circular states: "In recent years the image of Christ and the King's portrait have been removed from many of the Kingdom's primary schools. That is a manifest and intolerable breach of the regulations and above all an attack on the dominant religion of the State and on the unity of the nation. . . . We therefore order [restitution of these] two sacred symbols of faith and national consciousness" to all primary schools.[40] While the European Court panel did not rest its decision on this history, the history is illuminating. It also sheds light on the experiences of Maria Urso, attending a school where a Fascist dictatorship mobilized lessons about Italian history and Christianity as tools for indoctrinating children into its political ideology.

Looking at the contemporary significance of the crucifix in Italy, the European Court panel rejected the argument that the message of the crucifix has become a humanistic message that could be read independently of its religious dimensions and held that it still carried an explicitly religious meaning. "The schooling of children is a particularly sensitive area in which the compelling power of the state is on minds which still lack (depending on the child's level of maturity) the critical capacity which would enable them to keep their distance from the message derived from a preference manifested by the state in religious matters."[41] Issues of child development, including children's vulnerability to coercion and fear of retaliation played a leading role in the European Court panel's analysis. Interestingly, the panel judges never questioned the rights or the capacity of the Lautsi boys, at eleven and thirteen, to embrace a secularist belief system or to feel intimidated by the display of religious that marked them as outsiders. By the time the European Court panel's decision was handed down, the Lautsi children had "come of age" legally and in developmental terms. While some have criticized the European Court in past cases for failing to highlight the rights of the child, in the *Lautsi* case the Second Section panel treated children's beliefs as valid and examined the meaning of the crucifix through preadolescent children's eyes.

Rulings of courts seldom change deeply rooted traditions. Reaction in Italy was intense and largely negative. The Vatican commented: "It is astonishing that the European Court would intervene so heavy-handedly in a matter so profoundly connected with the historical, cultural, and spiritual identity of the Italian people." Prime Minister Silvio Berlusconi angrily accused the Court of trying to "deny Europe's Christian roots." Pier Casini, leader of the Unione Di Centro, a democratic Christian party, fumed, "This is the consequence of the pusillanimity of the European politicians who balked at referring to Christian roots in the European Constitution. The crucifix is the identifying symbol of Christian Italy and

Christian Europe." Perhaps the most common view was one of bafflement. "How could an ancient tradition like the crucifix be offensive to anyone?" The president of the Muslim Union of Italy disagreed, arguing, "A State that defines itself as secular may not oppress all the other faiths by displaying the symbol of a chosen faith."[42]

In April and May of 2010, a year after the decision was announced, when I was doing field work in Italy on the ecology of childhood, crucifixes still adorned the walls of every classroom I visited. All the teachers I asked, including Maria Urso, expressed the belief that the crucifix will never come down because it is such an integral part of Italian culture. A court decision, they explained, could not change this reality. School children would continue to study in classrooms with crosses, continue to go on school trips to visit the cathedrals of Rome and Florence and continue to study Italy's great works of art because these religious symbols, places, and images are integral to the nation's history and tradition.

Maria Urso and the other teachers were proved right. The Italian government, with support from many other states and non-governmental organizations (NGOs), sought review of the *Lautsi* decision by the ECHR sitting as a Grand Chamber and review was granted. On March 18, 2011, a panel of 17 judges sitting as the Grand Chamber issued a decision reversing the Second Section panel and upholding the display of the crucifix in Italian schools.[43] The Grand Chamber rejected several of the arguments offered by Italy and other intervening governments and NGOs—e.g., that the crucifix is not a religious symbol and that display of a passive symbol does not implicate religious freedom in schooling because it is not part of the didactic program. However, the Grand Chamber found that no consensus existed in the many countries that are states parties to the European Convention on Human Rights as to whether display of religious symbols transgressed Article 2, Protocol No. 1 of the ECHR.[44] In the absence of consensus, States must be given a greater margin of appreciation in deciding the role of such symbols in the school setting. While States must practice religious tolerance and respect religious pluralism, the law did not impose a requirement of secularism or of absolute neutrality with respect to religion and, indeed, certain contracting States retained official state religions. Each case must be judged within the context of the history and tradition of the country. The Grand Chamber held that the display of the crucifix in Italian schools, taken in historical and cultural context, did not constitute a form of indoctrination that failed to respect parents' or children's religious and philosophical convictions. The decision emphasized that no evidence had been offered to substantiate the coercive effects on the Lautsi children or any other children of the display of the crucifix. In addition, the government had offered evidence that Italy had adopted a strong pluralistic policy, protecting the display by students of religious symbols of all different religions, permitting the wearing of headscarves and protecting the observance in schools of minority religious holidays. In this larger context, it could not be said that the display of the crucifix and relative predominance of Christian symbols and traditions in the Italian school environment crossed the line into indoctrination.

Two judges dissented and several others offered concurring opinions, illustrating the high seriousness and strong passions evoked by questions of religion and its place in education. Judge Bonello issued a passionate defense of tradition.

> "A European court should not be called upon to bankrupt centuries of European tradition. No court, certainly not this Court, should rob the Italians of part of their cultural personality. I believe that before joining any crusade to demonize the crucifix, we should start by placing the presence of that emblem in Italian schools in its rightful historical perspective. For many centuries, virtually the only education in Italy was provided by the Church, its religious orders and organizations—and very few besides. Many, if not most schools, colleges, universities and other institutes of learning in Italy had been founded, funded, or run by the Church, its members or its offshoots. The milestones of history turned education and Christianity into almost interchangeable notions, and because of this, the age-old presence of the crucifix in Italian schools should come as no shock or surprise. In fact, its absence would have come as a surprise and a shock. . . . Now, a court in a glass box a thousand kilometers away has been engaged to veto overnight what has survived countless generations. The Court has been asked to be an accomplice in a major act of cultural vandalism. I believe William Faulkner went to the core of the issue: The past is never dead. In fact it is not even past.[2] Like it or not, the perfumes and the stench of history will always be with you."

In spite of its nuanced attention to context, unfortunately, the majority opinion of the Grand Chamber downplays and virtually dismisses the experiences of pupils. In my view, this should be at the center of our analysis. While evidence was not offered in the *Lautsi* case of the actual impact of display of the crucifix, future challengers and defenders of such laws will have to offer empirical evidence on this issue. Does children's actual experience reflect the traditions of tolerance and pluralism that Judge Bonello celebrates? Do children perceive that all religions are respected? A time may come when the context will change so radically that the *Lautsi* decision becomes an historical artifact. I can imagine that increasing pluralism and tolerance may neutralize objection to the display of the crucifix because real educational pluralism is so firmly entrenched. I can also imagine a situation in which increasing divisions between competing religious sects and ethnic groups sharpens the controversy over display of religious symbols in Italian schools. In preparing for the future, we should begin by asking the children of Italy what they think about when they see the crucifix—Muslim and Hindu children as well as Buddhist, Jewish and Christian children—since they are the ones who will inherit and need to resolve these tensions between human rights and religious tradition. Only time, and the evolving meanings of human rights, will tell where the rights of children to believe or not to believe will take us.

■ NOTES

1 Interview by Barbara Bennett Woodhouse with Maria Urso, Florence, Italy, May 24, 2010.

2 Martha Fineman, "Taking Children's Interest Seriously," in *What Is Right for Children?: The Competing Paradigms of Religion and Human Rights,* eds. Martha Fineman and Karen Worthington (Hampshire, U.K.: Ashgate Publishing, 2009), 230; Barbara Bennett Woodhouse, "Speaking Truth to Power: Challenging 'The Power of Parents to Control the Education of Their Own,'" *Cornell Journal of Law and Public Policy* 11 (2002): 481.

3 Sylvie Langlaude, *The Right of the Child to Religious Freedom in International Law* (Amsterdam: Hotei Publishing, 2007), 252.

4 Ibid., 13–29.

5 Gustav K. K. Yeung and Wai-yin Chow, "'To take up your own responsibility': the religiosity of Buddhist adolescents in Hong Kong," *International Journal of Children's Spirituality* 15(1) (2010): 8. Langlaude, *The Right of the Child,* 13–35 discusses how children are brought into Christianity, Islam, Hinduism, and many other faiths and belief systems.

6 See chapter herein by Sallie King.

7 Barbara Bennett Woodhouse, "'Who Owns the Child'? *Meyer* and *Pierce* and the Child as Property," *William and Mary Law Review* 33 (1992): 995–98; Margaret F. Brinig, "Children's Beliefs and Family Law," *Emory Law Journal* 58 (2008): 67–68; Emily Buss, "What Does Frieda Yoder Believe?" *University of Pennsylvania Journal of Constitutional Law* 2 (2009): 53–61.

8 Buss, "What Does Frieda Yoder Believe," 61–63.

9 Barbara Bennett Woodhouse, "Recognizing Children's Rights: Lessons from South Africa," *Human Rights* 26 (1999): 15–17; Barbara Bennett Woodhouse, "The Constitutionalization of Children's Rights: Incorporating Emerging Human Rights into Constitutional Doctrine," *University of Pennsylvania Journal of Constitutional Law* 2 (1999):1–11; John Wall, "Human Rights in Light of Childhood," *International Journal of Children's Rights* 16 (2008): 522.

10 Barbara Bennett Woodhouse, *Hidden in Plain Sight: the Tragedy of Children's Rights from Ben Franklin to Lionel Tate* (Princeton : Princeton University Press, 2008), 29–47.

11 International Covenant on Civil and Political Rights, GA Res. 2200A (XXI), 21 U.N. GAOR, (No. 16) at 52, U.N. Doc. A/6316 (1966), 999 U.N.T.S. 171, *entered into force* March 23, 1976.

12 International Covenant on Economic, Social, and Cultural Rights, GA Res. 2200A (XXI), 21 U.N. GAOR Supp. (No. 16) at 49, U.N. Doc. A/6316 (1966), 993 U.N.T.S. 3, *entered into force* January 3, 1976.

13 Woodhouse, *Hidden in Plain Sight,* 32.

14 Convention on the Rights of the Child, GA Res 44/25, annex, 44 U.N. GAOR Supp. (No. 49) at 167, U.N. Doc. A/44/49 (1989), *entered into force* September 2, 1990. (hereinafter "CRC").

15 Cris R. Revaz, "An Introduction to the UN Convention on the Rights of the Child," in *The UN Convention on the Rights of the Child: An Analysis of Treaty Provisions And Implications of U.S. Ratification,* eds. Jonathan Todres et al. (Amsterdam: Hotei Publishing, 2006), 9.

16 CRC, art. 2. See Barbara Woodhouse and Kathryn Johnson, "The United Nations Convention on the Rights of the Child: Empowering Parents to Protect Their Children's Rights," in *What Is Right for Children?,* 10; David M. Smolin, "Overcoming Objections to the Convention on the Rights of the Child," *Emory International Law Review* 20 (2006): 81–110.

17 CRC, art. 18.

18 Laura Lundy, "Children, Education, and Rights in a Society Divided by Religion: The Perspectives of Children and Young People," in *What Is Right for Children*, 311–328. Barbara Bennett Woodhouse, "Enhancing Children's Participation in Policy-Making," *Arizona Law Review* 45 (2003): 751; Barbara Bennett Woodhouse, "The Courage of Innocence: Children as Heroes in the Struggle for Justice," *University of Illinois Law Review* (2009): 101.

19 United Nations General Assembly, Resolution 61/146 Rights of the Child, A/RES/61/146, *adopted* December 19, 2006, 8, par. 31(a); Martin Guggenheim, *What's Wrong with Children's Rights* (Cambridge: Harvard University Press, 2005).

20 Rachel Hodgkin and Peter Newell, "Child's Right to Freedom of Thought, Conscience, and Religion," in *Implementation Handbook for the Convention on the Rights of the Child*, 3rd ed. (Geneva: United Nations Pubns, 2008), 185–88; Kathleen Marshall and Paul Parvis, "The UN Convention on the Rights of the Child," in *Honouring Children: The Human Rights of the Child in Christian Perspectives* (Edinburgh: Saint Andrew Press, 2004), 25–29. See further the chapter by Paul Taylor herein.

21 Langlaude, *The Right of the Child*, 103.

22 Hodgkin and Newell, "Child's Right to Freedom," 186.

23 Woodhouse, *Hidden in Plain Sight*, 27; Langlaude, *The Right of the Child*, 61. See further the chapters herein by Johan van der Vyver and Natan Lerner on group rights.

24 United Nations Committee on the Rights of the Child, "Summary Record of the 701st meeting: Turkey," U.N. Doc. CRC/C/SR.701, at 25 (2001). Langlaude, 108–09.

25 Langlaude, *The Right of the Child*, 117.

26 Woodhouse, *Hidden in Plain Sight*, 304–313.

27 Justin L. Barrett, "Do Children Experience God as Adults Do?" in *Religion in Mind: Cognitive Perspectives on Religious Belief, Ritual, and Experience*. ed. Jensine Andresen (New York: Cambridge University Press, 2001), 174; Woodhouse, *Hidden in Plain Sight*, 18–19 (describing Piaget's theories).

28 Barbara Bennett Woodhouse, "A World Fit for Children is a World Fit for Everyone: Ecogenerism, Feminism, and Vulnerability," *Houston Law Review* 46 (2009): 818–24.

29 Barrett, "Do Children Experience God," 176; Nicola Knight et al., "Children's Attributions of Beliefs to Humans and God: Cross-Cultural Evidence," *Cognitive Science* 28 (2004): 121; Note, "Minors' Free Exercise Rights and the Psychology of Religious Development," *Harvard Law Review* 115 (2002): 2205–2226.

30 Carl N. Johnson, "Putting Different Things Together," in *Imagining the Impossible: Magical, Scientific, and Religious Thinking in Children*, eds. Karl S. Rosengren et al. (New York: Cambridge University Press, 2000), 207. Note, "Minors' Free Exercise Rights," 2226.

31 Pascal Boyer and Sheila Walker, "Intuitive Ontology and Cultural Input in the Acquisition of Religious Concepts," in *Imagining the Impossible: Magical, Scientific, and Religious Thinking in Children*, eds. Karl S. Rosengren, et al. (New York: Cambridge University Press, 2000), 142.

32 Ibid., 149–50.

33 K.H. (Ina) ter Avest, "Dutch children and their 'God': Development of the 'God' concept among indigenous and immigrant children in the Netherlands," *British Journal of Religious Education* 31 (2008): 251–62, at 257.

34 See Kirk Johnson, "Far Flung Placement of Children in Texas Raid is Criticized," *New York Times*, May 20, 2008. See further the chapter by T. Jeremy Gunn herein on the Branch Davidians.

35 Mitchel Lasser, *Judicial Transformations: The Rights Revolution in the Courts of Europe* (Oxford: Oxford University Press 2009), 25–28.

36 See the chapters herein in by Carolyn Evans (on a Sikh schoolboy wearing his *kirpan* to school, the Islamic headscarf cases, and the *Folgerø* and *Lautsi* cases) by Jeremy Gunn (about the "permissible limitations" and hijab cases), by Johan van der Vyver (discussing Sunali Pinay, a Hindu girl in South Africa with a nose stud), and Madhavi Sunder (who discusses the French headscarf law and burqa ban).

37 *Lautsi v. Italy,* Application No. 30814/06 (EctHR, March 18, 2011) (Grand Chamber Judgment), overturning *Lautsi v. Italy*, 50 EHRR 42 (2010) (ECtHR, November 3, 2009) (Second Section Judgment).

38 *Lautsi v. Italy*, 50 EHRR 42 (2010) (ECtHR, November 3, 2009) (Second Section Judgment).

39 *Lautsi v. Italy* (2009) (Second Section Judgment).

40 As quoted in *Lautsi v. Italy* (2009) (Second Section Judgment)

41 Ibid., 10.

42 All quotes are translations by this author of statements from a newspaper article, "Accolta la richiesta di un'italiana di origine finlandese," *Corriere della Sera,* November 3, 2009.

43 *Lautsi v. Italy* (2011) (Grand Chamber Judgment)

44 Article 2 of Protocol No. 1 of the European Convention on Human Rights states: "No person shall be denied the right to education. In the exercise of any functions which it assumes in relation to education and to teaching, the State shall respect the right of parents to ensure such education and teaching in conformity with their own religious and philosophical convictions."

Protocol No. 1 to the European Convention for the Protection of Human Rights and Fundamental Freedoms, C.E.T.S. No. 9, E.T.S. No. 5, *adopted* in Paris, March 20, 1952, *entered into force* May 18, 1954, art. 2

RECOMMENDED READING

Brinig, Margaret F. "Children's Beliefs and Family Law." *Emory Law Journal* 58 (2008): 55–69

Fineman, Martha Albertson and Karen Worthington, eds. *What is Right for Children: The Competing Paradigms of Religion and Human Rights* (Surrey, UK: Ashgate Publishers, 2010)

Hodgkin, Rachel and Peter Newell. "[A?] Child's Right to Freedom of Thought, Conscience, and Religion," in *Implementation Handbook for the Convention on the Rights of the Child.* 3rd ed. (Geneva, Switzerland: United Nations Pubns, 2008), 185–194

ter Avest, K. H. (Ina) "Dutch children and their 'God': Development of the 'God' concept among indigenous and immigrant children in the Netherlands." *British Journal of Religious Education* 31 (2008): 251–262

Langlaude, Sylvie. *The Right of the Child to Religious Freedom in International Law* (Leiden, Netherlands: Martinus Nijhoff Publishers, 2007)

Marshall, Kathleen and Paul Parvis. *Honouring Children: The Human Rights of the Child in Christian Perspectives* (Edinburgh: Saint Andrew Press, 2004)

"Children as Believers: Minors' Free Exercise Rights and the Psychology of Religious Development." *Harvard Law Review* 115 (2002): 2205–2226

Rosengren, Karl S., Carl N. Johnson, and, Paul L. Harris. *Imagining the Impossible: Magical, Scientific, and Religious Thinking in Children* (New York: Cambridge University Press, 2000)

Todres, Jonathan, Mark E. Wojcik, and, Cris R. Revaz. *The UN Convention on the Rights of the Child: An Analysis of Treaty Provisions and Implication of U.S. Ratification* (Ardsley, NY: Transnational Publishers, 2006)

Woodhouse, Barbara Bennett. *Hidden in Plain Sight: The Tragedy of Children's Rights from Ben Franklin to Lionel Tate* (Princeton Princeton University Press, 2008)

_____. "A World Fit for Children is a World Fit for Everyone: Ecogenerism, Feminism and Vulnerability." *Houston Law Review* 46 (2009): 817–865

19 Religion and Economic, Social, and Cultural Rights

INGVILL THORSON PLESNER

There is an ambiguous relationship between religion and human rights. Religion can both challenge and support human rights, just as human rights can both challenge and support religion. This complex relationship emerges among various "freedom rights" enshrined in the 1966 International Covenant on Civil and Political Rights (ICCPR),[1] most obviously in the application of the right to freedom of religion or belief in Article 18. Complexities surrounding religion and religious freedom also emerge among various "welfare rights" enshrined in the 1966 International Covenant on Economic, Social and Cultural Rights (ICESCR).[2] These include the right to self-determination[3] and subsistence (Art. 1), to work (Art. 6), to "fair wages and equal remuneration," to a "decent living" and to "safe healthy working conditions" (Art. 7), to organize and join labor unions (Art. 8), to gain social security and social insurance (Art. 9), to marry and form a family (Art. 10),[4] to have an "adequate standard of living" including adequate food, shelter, and housing (Art. 11), to have adequate health care (Art. 12), to education (Art. 13), and to take part in cultural life and enjoy the benefits of scientific advances (Art. 14). These "welfare rights" elaborated in the ICESCR are supported by other international human rights treaties, including the UN Convention on the Rights of the Child (CRC) of 1989,[5] the UN Convention on the Elimination of All Forms of Discrimination Against Women (CEDAW) of 1979,[6] as well as regional instruments, such as in the 1950 European Convention on Human Rights (ECHR)[7] and in the European Social Charter of the Council of Europe.[8]

This chapter focuses on the complex relationships between religion and selected welfare rights, particularly the rights to education, health, and labor. Controversies in this field often involve the right to non-discrimination on the basis of religion, gender, and sexual orientation, and the right to freedom of religion or belief. Should churches and other faith communities have to comply with the gender equality statutes in labor law when they appoint religious leaders? Should hospitals run by churches be allowed to employ only their own members or those loyal to their beliefs or ethics? Should the State dictate what private religious schools teach about gender and sexual orientation? Should it intervene when parents reject medical treatments for their children due to their religious convictions? What compulsory religious education should be required and what restrictions on religious practice should be allowed in public schools without producing discrimination on the basis of religion or restrictions on the equal right to public education?

I take as my point of departure the most relevant articles regulating these issues in the ICESCR, since it has a global outreach and is a treaty that explicitly deals with the equal access to work, health, and education as human rights. But I also draw in the jurisprudence of the European Court and of various States Parties, and some of the theological reflections on these rights in the Western tradition.

■ THE INTERRELATION BETWEEN FREEDOM RIGHTS AND WELFARE RIGHTS

Controversies over the relationship between religion and the welfare rights to health, education, and labor are often part and product of broader controversies over the relationship between welfare rights and freedom rights altogether. Some human rights advocates claim that freedom rights are the most important human rights that states are duty-bound to respect, while welfare rights are mere aspirations that states may choose to fulfill to the degree and in the way they prefer. Some go further and say that welfare rights are not human rights at all, particularly in developing nations which often have few feasible means to achieve these rights and then make claims their people have the "right" to foreign aid and charity. Other human rights advocates, however, claim that welfare rights are the most important human rights, since many of these rights are necessary for human survival. Freedom rights, they argue, are useful only if first these basic welfare rights to food, shelter, health care, education, and security are adequately protected. The right to worship, speech, or the franchise means little to someone starving in the street or dying from a treatable disease.

Historically, the competition between freedom rights and welfare rights was a function of the competition between the East and the West during the Cold War, and it persisted through the fall of the Soviet empire in 1989. Since the Universal Declaration of Human Rights (UDHR) of 1948 focuses more on freedom rights, these became known as the "first generation of rights," while welfare rights are referred to as the "second generation of rights."[9] Some scholars also speak of "third generation" rights to peace, environmental protection, and orderly development, as articulated in the 1986 UN Declaration on the Right to Development and other documents.

This traditional juxtaposition of freedom rights and welfare rights, however, is now contested by the "interdependency approach" to human rights. This interdependency approach challenges the claim that there is a radical division between freedom rights and welfare rights. Instead it insists, as the 1993 Vienna Declaration on Human Rights put it, that human rights are "interrelated," "indivisible," and "interdependent."[10] The interdependency of freedom rights and welfare rights can be exemplified in various ways. For instance, freedom rights, like the freedom of expression or freedom to participate in political life, are essential for claiming welfare rights like the right to decent working conditions, to basic health care, or to food and shelter. Welfare rights to food, security, education, and basic health care, in turn, are essential for individuals to be capable of exercising their freedom rights.

The interdependency approach also emphasizes that many rights claims involve a whole web of rights. For example, the right to religious freedom involves not only freedom rights to religion, belief, expression, and association, but also various welfare rights and rights of self-determination. The simple act, say, of wearing a religious symbol or garb (a crucifix, yarmulke, or headscarf) in the workplace or at school involves not only freedoms of religion or belief [11] and expression,[12] but also equal rights to labor[13] and education[14] without religious discrimination, as well as the rights to religious and cultural self-determination.[15] While none of these rights claims is absolute, permissible limitations on each of them must meet rigorous standards of necessity and proportionality.[16]

Finally, the interdependency approach challenges the notion of separating out first, second, and third generations of rights. That terminology improperly implies that first generation freedom rights are more important than the others, or that first generation rights must be in place in a community before second or third generations of rights can be implemented. All three generations of rights can and must develop together, the interdependency approach insists. Not only freedom and welfare rights but also rights to self-determination, peace, environmental protection, and orderly development need to be part of an emerging human rights culture.

This focus on the interdependency of various human rights does not ignore possible tensions, even conflicts, between various human rights—both between and within the different groups of human rights. But it emphasizes the necessary complexity of human rights in general, and within that the complex relationships of religion and human rights. The next sections illustrate some of these complexities in the arenas of healthcare, education, and labor.

■ RELIGION AND THE RIGHT TO HEALTH CARE

The right to freedom of religion or belief in general,[17] and the right of parents to have the main responsibility for their child's upbringing in particular,[18] sometimes comes into conflict with the right of a child to health care. A good example is the rejection by Jehovah's Witnesses of blood transfusions for their children, even when such treatment is considered by doctors to be vital for the child's health or life. How do we resolve this conflict between the freedom rights of the parents with the welfare rights of the child? ICESCR Article 12.1 guarantees "the right of everyone to the enjoyment of the highest attainable standard of physical and mental health." It calls on States Parties "to achieve the full realization of this right" and especially to take all steps "necessary for the healthy development of the child." The 1989 UN Convention on the Rights of the Child further underscores the child's right to health and medical care.[19] ICCPR Article 18.4, however, includes specifically within the right to freedom of religion or belief, the right of parents to raise their child according to their own religious and moral convictions.[20] The 1981 UN Declaration on the Elimination of All Forms of Intolerance and Discrimination Based on Religion or Belief (Declaration on Religion) and the 1989 UN Convention on the Rights of the Child (CRC) underscore these parental rights of religious upbringing.

Under international human rights law, any restriction on an individual's expression or practice of religion must be "necessary" in order to achieve certain legitimate aims.[21] Most human rights scholars and tribunals consider the State's duty to protect the right to health and the life of a sick child as a legitimate and necessary ground to restrict the parents' rights to raise the child in accordance with their own religious and moral convictions. In this case, the child's basic right to life and health trumps the parents' rights to engage in the religious practice of refusing blood transfusions and other medical help for their children.

The same result holds true in conflicts between Muslim parents who insist on the right to have their young daughter circumcised, and the daughter's right to physical integrity per se and freedom from risks to her health from the side-effects of the surgery, especially when it takes place outside of usual health care settings. Here, too, the parents' general right to control their child's upbringing in accordance with their religious and moral convictions must give way to concerns for the child's health and physical integrity.

Such conflicts are more difficult when they concern the health of adults. What if a competent and fully informed adult Jehovah's Witness, on the basis of religious or moral convictions, refuses to accept a blood transfusion that is vital to his or her health or survival? That right to refusal needs to be respected. In these cases, the Witnesses' right to bodily integrity as well as religious conviction and self-determination will trump so long as the medical treatment has been offered and the medical consequences of refusal have been explained to the patient.

■ RELIGION AND THE RIGHT TO EDUCATION

Article 13 of the ICESCR provides for "the right of everyone to education." "Primary education shall be compulsory and available free to all." "Secondary education in its different forms, including technical and vocational secondary education, shall be made generally available and accessible to all by every appropriate means, and in particular by the progressive introduction of free education." "Higher education shall be made equally accessible to all." Read together with Article 2, this right to education, including the right to free primary education, applies equally to all regardless of their religious or non-religious affiliation.

Article 13 further guarantees the right of parents (or legal guardians) to ensure the "religious and moral education of their children in conformity with their own convictions," a provision that is elaborated in the 1989 United Nations Convention on the Rights of the Child (CRC) and in the European Charter of Human Rights (ECHR).[22] The CRC, however, emphasizes that the rights of parents in these matters should gradually give way to the child's own thoughts and beliefs, "with the evolving capacity of the child."[23] Article 13 also gives parents the right to establish or send their children to private schools as long as these schools comply with the "minimum educational standards as may be laid down or approved by the State."

Sometimes the child's welfare rights to education converge with the parent's freedom right to religion. A child's right to receive an education and a parent's right to educate their child in accordance with their convictions converge when parents choose to send their child to a religious private school that meets minimum educational standards and accords with the child's own wishes. But other times these rights collide. This can occur when a religious private school satisfies parental concerns for their children's education but does not meet the minimum standards for education required by the ICESCR and the CRC—say, when a private religious school does not teach students enough about other religious traditions or about the equal rights of men and women to prepare them for life in modern pluralistic societies.[24] Other conflicts arise in public schools when parents seek to exempt their children from classes that teach about sexuality, sexual orientation, or other topics that run afoul of the parents' religious or moral convictions.[25] Human rights advocates and tribunals are sharply divided on how to resolve these conflicts.

More tensions emerge when the rights of teachers to manifest or practice their religion conflict with the rights of students and their parents. Both international tribunals and national courts have made clear that public school teachers may not indoctrinate or influence the students to adopt a given religion or religious practice: Here the rights of students to be free from coerced participation in religion and the parent's right to raise the child in their own faith tradition trump the right of a teacher to practice or manifest his or her religion.[26] It's a harder case when public school teachers are forbidden to wear crucifixes, yarmulkes, headscarves, and other apparel in expression of their religious convictions. The European Court has allowed such restrictions on teacher's religious dress in one case.[27] The UN Human Rights Committee, however, seems to favor the teacher's rights to wear religious apparel and ornamentation.[28] The UN Committee on the Rights of the Child has further emphasized that a child's exposure to religious diversity among its teachers helps facilitate their education for religious tolerance, an important aspect of a proper education.[29]

The rights of children to manifest their own beliefs by wearing religious apparel or ornamentation raise even more complicated questions. Here, the right of the child to manifest his or her religious identity is supported by the child's equal right to attend free and public education and partly also by the rights of parents to decide in matters concerning their child's religious and moral upbringing. Nonetheless, some public schools ban religious apparel, particularly headscarves and *burqas* worn by Muslim students. State officials often base these prohibitions on the assumption that headscarves or *burqas* are signs of suppression of women and girls and hence justify these prohibitions as a means to combat gender discrimination. Officials also argue that it is the parents, not the girls themselves, who want these headscarves and thus justify these prohibitions as a way of defending the rights of the child against pressure from their parents. One consequence of banning students from headscarves and other "manifest religious symbols" in public schools, however, is that a number of girls, in particular Muslim girls, quit or are expelled from public school, sacrificing their right to free public education in so doing.

The possibility that such students can attend private schools does not excuse a state from allowing its public schools to undermine the equal right to attend such public education without discrimination on the basis of religion. This applies, in particular, to public primary education, which must be both available and free to all students according to ICESCR Article 13. Restrictions on religious expression by pupils in public schools, including prohibitions on headscarves, *burqas*, and other religious apparel, must meet strict criteria of necessity and proportionality when challenged as a violation of a child's rights of religion and belief and rights to education.[30] Any education on the history of religion or religious traditions must be conducted in a way that makes it possible for all students to attend without infringing on their freedom of religion or belief and of their parents' rights and responsibilities regarding their religious and moral upbringing.[31] And it may be wise to accommodate students who need *halal* or *kosher* food if the school offers meals to the students, and to accommodate the religious needs of minorities to certain days of rest following their religious calendar.

If the students attend home schools or private religious schools, the authorities do not and cannot monitor the quality of this education in an equally efficient way as they can in public schools. Furthermore, it is far from clear that this private education, at least the home-based education that many poorer students are forced to attend, is equally adequate for promoting the students' understanding of and experience with religious and cultural differences, as required by ICESCR, Article 13. For certain students, attending home education may deprive them of an important arena for meeting persons of other religious backgrounds and may foreclose connections with other parts of civil society in general.

■ RELIGION AND THE RIGHT TO LABOR

Other conflicts of rights occur in relation to the right to labor. For example, prohibitions against discrimination on the basis of gender, as enshrined in Article 3 of the ICESCR and Article 5 of CEDAW sometimes conflict with the right to self-determination of religious communities in religious matters, particularly when a faith community refuses to employ female clergy or to have women elected into other leading positions. Here, the collective dimension of the right to freedom of religion or belief must be weighed against state duties to combat gender-based discrimination.[32] These are controversial issues on which human rights scholars differ sharply. Some argue that the State has the burden of proof in justifying any limitation on the right of faith communities to decide its own internal affairs, particularly if the position in question is of vital importance to the religious doctrine or teaching of the faith community. This is the position of the UN Human Rights Committee in its General Comment No. 22 on Article 18 of the ICCPR as well as the European Court of Human Rights.[33] This approach gives priority to the rights of religious self-determination and freedom of religion and belief.

If prohibitions against gender discrimination are the point of departure, however, the State's burden of proof shifts. The state must now justify granting an exception to the general requirement of equal treatment of men and women. Both Articles 3 and 5 of CEDAW obligate states to take "all appropriate measures" to combat gender based discrimination,[34] both in public and in private settings, including within religious communities. The question then becomes, what are "appropriate measures" to promote gender equality and on what basis. Would it be appropriate for the State to require that the Catholic Church employ female bishops, or that Jewish congregations appoint female rabbis? Or would it be more appropriate to engage into a dialogue with those communities on how they may promote equal rights of men and women and combat gender stereotypes on the basis on their own doctrine and values? The latter approach seem more adequate if the rights in conflict are to be balanced, while the first would imply that freedom of religion or belief gave way for an active state intervention in order to promote gender equality.

A related controversy concerns the extent to which hospitals, schools, or other institutions run by faith communities may require that their employees be members of their faith community, or at least faithful to its teachings and practices. May a private religious college require that the school gardener be a member of their faith community? May a private religious school fire a physical education teacher because he entered into a relationship with another woman during his separation from his wife? May a Catholic hospital fire a doctor who states publicly that he is not against abortion, even if he remains loyal to the hospital's anti-abortion policy in his practice as a doctor? These are all delicate questions that turn, in part, on a judgment about how central the position or person is the teaching, doctrine, and identity of the religious institution. On this calculus, a school gardener who works on his own has more leeway than a physical education teacher who interacts regularly with students, let alone a Bible teacher who is in charge of the religious character of the religious school. European Community law and the labor laws of many nation-states deal with these questions in some detail,[35] and international human rights law give generous exemptions from general non-discrimination rules in labor law when the person or position is central to religious institution.[36]

■ EQUAL RIGHTS AND PROTECTION AGAINST RELIGIOUS DISCRIMINATION

We have illustrated some of the complexity of religion in relation to the rights to health, education, and labor. An integral part of all these rights and many other welfare rights is a general prohibition against discrimination. Articles 2, 3, 6, 12 and 13 of the ICESCR, read together, guarantee an equal right to labor, health, and education without any discrimination on the basis of religion, gender, race, color, sex, language, political or other opinion, national or social origin, property, birth, or other status. These prohibitions against discrimination match similar provisions in many other international human rights documents.[37]

In General Comment No. 20,[38] the United Nations Human Rights Committee provides that Article 2 of the ICESCR prohibits both formal or direct discrimination as well as de facto or indirect discrimination on the grounds of religion or other status.[39] Formal or direct discrimination on religious grounds occurs when an individual is treated less favorably than another person in a similar situation because of his or her religion. Explicit reference to a person's religious affiliation or practice as grounds for denying someone a job or admission to a school or hospital is a good example. De facto or indirect discrimination refers to laws, policies, or practices that are neutral on their face but in practice predictably affect only or mainly persons with a certain religious affiliation. For example, prohibiting all head covering in the work place or in a public school does not explicitly single out religions, but in practice it may affect mainly certain religious groups, including Sikhs wearing turbans, Jews wearing yarmulkes, or Muslim women wearing headscarves.

Some private forms of differential treatment on the basis of religion can be justified. Religious schools or employers may require a certain religious affiliation or loyalty when certain positions within a faith community are announced. Synagogues may restrict the rabbinate to Jews only without fear of being charged with religious discrimination. Private Christian schools may prohibit teachers from wearing headscarves or turbans as a legitimate way of protecting the freedom of religion or belief of the children and the parents who send their children to that school because of its religious orientation. It could also be a legitimate way of protecting the right of religious self-determination by the faith community that has established the school. Such internal restrictions and prohibitions on religious practice and identity by private religious institutions have long been upheld as legitimate.

While the State is prohibited from direct religious discrimination, it may indirectly restrict certain religious practices in order to protect life, health, and safety. For instance, the State can require all construction workers to wear helmets, even though this will mean a Sikh can't wear his turban, while a Jew can still wear his yarmulke. When the differential effect on the basis of religion is caused by policies or rules that have a legitimate aim and are a necessary means to reach that aim, it does not qualify as discrimination. Similarly, a state general prohibition on doctors and others to perform female circumcision would in practice mainly affect Muslims, but it could be justified as a necessary means to protect the health of women and girls and hence would qualify as a legitimate restriction on the right of parents to determine matters concerning their child's upbringing. It would hence be a legitimate, unequal, de facto treatment on the basis of religion that would not qualify as either direct or indirect discrimination.

■ RELIGIOUS AMBIGUITY IN RELATION TO WELFARE RIGHTS

As the foregoing sections have illustrated, religious communities sometimes contest certain human rights. In particular, many religions have not—to put it mildly—been in the forefront in developing and defending the equal rights of religious minorities, women, children, gays and lesbians, and others. Many of the strongest conflicts today and in the foreseeable future are between the rights of religious communities to religious freedom and self-determination and the rights of all individuals to enjoy all their freedom and welfare rights without discrimination. The delicate balancing of religious and other rights that we have illustrated in the arenas of education, labor, and health care will doubtless continue.

That said, many religious traditions today have made a general commitment to human rights on the basis of their belief in human dignity and mutual respect. In particular, most of the world's religions seem to agree that all persons deserve basic necessities for life—food, shelter, health care, and education—which are at the heart of the welfare rights enshrined in the ICESCR. Religious traditions differ mostly on whether such human goods or needs should be viewed as welfare rights or as social responsibilities, and whether these human rights or social duties should be vindicated by the State or by other social institutions, including the religious communities themselves.

The teachings of the Catholic Church are a good example. The general ideas of human dignity and human rights trace back to the classical natural law theories of the Catholic Church, expressed by thirteenth-century sage Thomas Aquinas, among many others. Still, for many centuries, the Catholic Church rejected the existence of "universal" human rights, both in theory and in practice. A turn in the Catholic Church' general approach came with the encyclical *Rerum Novarum* (1891) in which Pope Leo XIII, drawing on Thomas Aquinas' views, declared that "man precedes the state." In *Rerum Novarum,* Leo XIII found a religious basis for the commitment to develop decent social conditions for the poor, in general, and for workers, in particular. Responding to the social instability and labor conflict that had risen in the wake of industrialization, Leo XIII called for the development of certain welfare rights and for religious accommodation of such rights. He distinguished clearly between the role of the State and the role of the church in these matters. The state, he said, should promote social justice through the protection of rights, while the church should speak out on social issues in order to teach correct social principles and ensure social stability. Leo XIII restated the Church's long-standing teaching regarding the crucial importance of private property rights, but also underlined that the free operation of market forces must be tempered by moral considerations, as in the establishment of decent working conditions:

> Let the working man and the employer make free agreements, and in particular let them agree freely as to the wages; nevertheless, there underlies a dictate of natural justice more imperious and ancient than any bargain between man and man, namely, that wages ought not to be insufficient to support a frugal and well-behaved wage-earner. If through necessity or fear of a worse evil the workman accepts harder conditions because an employer or contractor will afford him no better, he is made the victim of force and injustice.[40]

In 1962–1965, the Second Vatican Council issued *Dignitatis Humanae Personae* (On the Dignity of the Human Person) that declared that religious freedom for all is fundamental to human dignity. Furthermore, it expressed the need for decent living conditions for all as matter of equal human dignity: "the right to religious freedom has its foundation in the very dignity of the human person, as this dignity is known through the revealed Word of God and by reason itself." Furthermore, because people cannot discharge their obligation to seek and do the truth without immunity from coercion, "the right to religious freedom has its foundation, not in the subjective disposition of the person, but in his very nature." The common welfare of the society requires the social conditions necessary for people to live out their sense of the truth. This welfare implies the protection of human rights in the manner proper to each.

While the Catholic Church and other religious traditions have, over the past century, come to support various welfare rights enshrined in the ICESCR, the rights to form a family, and more specifically, the right to marry set out in Article 10.1, is a new arena of contestation between religion and human rights. For thousands of years in the West, the basic foundation of a family was an enduring union between a man and a woman with fitness and capacity to marry each other. Marriage was a formalization of this union, involving a religious ceremony in which the couple got a religious blessing and also made a religious commitment to uphold their union.

With the evolving role of the modern state, marriage and family have become more secularized in many Western countries, and states have developed increasing concern for individual rights within marriage. Interfaith couples, same-sex couples, polygamous parties, and others have all sought the right to marry, even though religious communities have strongly objected, and have refused to host their weddings or recognize their unions for internal religious purposes.

Some scholars now claim that the conception of "family" and "marriage" in human rights conventions like the ICESCR Article 10 must be reinterpreted in light of these new developments in law in order to embrace a broader conception of non-discrimination, involving sexual orientation alongside gender, ethnicity, religion and other status. That move will introduce new controversies involving religion and human rights. Does the State's recognition of "the equal right to marry" imply that religious officials must marry interfaith or same-sex parties whose lifestyle contravenes their teaching? Or would such an imposition violate the right of faith communities to self-determination in doctrinal matters, which is an inherent part of the right to freedom of religion or belief? European case law[41] as well as statements made by the UN Human Rights Committee seems to support the latter.[42]

■ CONCLUSIONS

Human rights are interrelated and interdependent; they support each other and they also challenge and limit each other. This is true of the relation between freedom rights and welfare rights in general; it is also true of the relationship between rights to religion and belief and many other rights. The necessary interrelation, interdependency, and indivisibility of human rights implies that conflicts between rights should not be dealt with by arguing that one human right or one set of rights is by definition more important than the other. Instead it requires a balancing of different rights claims with an eye to maximizing the rights of all.

■ NOTES

1 International Covenant on Civil and Political Rights, G.A. res. 2200A (XXI), 21 U.N. GAOR Supp. (No. 16) at 52, U.N. Doc. A/6316 (1966), 999 U.N.T.S. 171, *entered into force* March 23, 1976 (hereinafter "ICCPR").

2 International Covenant on Economic, Social, and Cultural Rights, G.A. res. 2200A (XXI), 21 U.N. GAOR Supp. (No. 16) at 49, U.N. Doc. A/6316 (1966), 993 U.N.T.S. 3, *entered into force* January 3, 1976 (hereinafter "ICESCR").

3 See further the chapter by Johan Van der Vyver, herein.

4 See further the chapters of Barbara Woodhouse and Madhavi Sunder, herein.

5 Convention on the Rights of the Child. G.A. res. 44/25, annex, 44 U.N. GAOR Supp. (No. 49) at 167, U.N. Doc. A/44/49 (1989), *entered into force* September 2, 1990 (hereinafter "CRC").

6 Convention on the Elimination of All forms of Discrimination Against Women, G.A. res. 34/180, 34 U.N. GAOR Supp. (No. 46) at 193, U.N. Doc. A/34/46 (1979), *entered into force* September 3, 1981.

7 European Convention for the Protection of Human Rights and Fundamental Freedoms, (ETS No. 5), 213 U.N.T.S. 222, *adopted* in Rome, November 4, 1950, *entered into force* September 3, 1953 (hereinafter "ECHR")

8 European Social Charter (ETS No. 35) 529 U.N.T.S. 89, *entered into force* February 26, 1965. Th Social Charter was adopted in 1961 and revised in 1996 by the Council of Europe. The Revised Charter came into force in 1999 and is gradually replacing the initial 1961 treaty. The European Committee of Social Rights (ECSR) is the body responsible for monitoring compliance by States Parties. For further reading on the international legal framework of

welfare rights, see Scott Leckie and Anne Gallagher, eds., *Economic, Social and Cultural Rights: A Legal Resource Guide* (Philadelphia: University of Pennsylvania, 2006).

9 Henry J. Steiner, Philip Alston, and Ryan Goodman, *International Human Rights in Context: Law, Politics, Morals: Text and Materials* (Oxford: Oxford University Press, 2007).

10 "All human rights are universal, indivisible and interdependent and interrelated" (Art. 5), Vienna Declaration, World Conference on Human Rights, Vienna, June, 14–25, 1993, U.N. Doc. A/CONF.157/24 (Part I) at 20 (1993).

11 ICCPR, Art. 18; ECHR, Art. 9.

12 ICCPR, Art. 19; ECHR, Art. 10.

13 ICESCR, Art. 6.

14 ICESCR, Art. 13.

15 ICESCR, Art. 2.

16 See further the chapter by Jeremy Gunn, herein.

17 ICCPR, Art. 18.1–3.

18 ICCPR, Art. 18.4.

19 CRC, Art. 24.1.

20 ICCPR, Art 18.4.

21 ICCPR, Art. 18.3; ECHR, Art. 9, 2. Furthermore, these provisions in international human rights law require that any such restriction on the right to express or practice ones religion have a basis in national law.

22 "No person shall be denied the right to education. In the exercise of any functions which it assumes in relation to education and to teaching, the State shall respect the right of parents to ensure such education and teaching in conformity with their own religious and philosophical convictions." (Art. 2 of the additional protocol to the ECHR)

23 CRC, Art. 14.2.

24 CRC, Art. 29 states that education of the child should be directed to for instance: (d) "The preparation of the child for responsible life in a free society, in the spirit of understanding, peace, tolerance, equality of sexes, and friendship among all peoples, ethnic, national and religious groups and persons of indigenous origin."

25 Cf. *Kjeldsen, Busk Madsen, and Pedersen v. Denmark*, 1 EHRR 711 (1979-1980) (ECtHR 23, series A, December 7, 1976).

26 Cf. *Leirvåg et al. v. Norway* (Communication No. 1155/2003), U.N. Doc.CCPR/C/82/D/1155/2003 (2004).

27 Cf. *Dahlab v. Switzerland* (ECtHR 2001-V, 449, Feburary 15, 2001).

28 See, for instance, the decision of the UN Human Rights Committee in a case dealing with the right of a student at a state university in Uzbekistan to wear a hijab at work. United Nations Human Rights Committee, *Raihon Hudoyberganova v. Uzbekistan*, Communication No. 931/2000, U.N. Doc. CCPR/C/82/D/931/2000 (2004).

29 In its critique of the attempts of certain German states (*Bundesländer*) to prohibit Muslim public school teachers from wearing headscarves, the UN Committee on the Rights of the Child expressed this point in the following way: "The Committee . . . is concerned at laws currently under discussion in some *Länder* aiming at banning school teachers wearing headscarves in public schools because it does not contribute to the child's understanding of the right to freedom of religion and to the development of an attitude of tolerance, as promoted in the aims of education under Article 29 of the Convention." United Nations Committee on the Rights of the Child (CRC), *UN Committee on the Rights of the Child: Concluding Observations: Germany*, 26 February 2004, U.N. Doc. CRC/C/15/Add.226, 30.01. See also Ingvill Thorson Plesner, *Freedom of Religion or Belief: A Quest for State Neutrality?* (Oslo: UniPub, 2008).

30 Cf. *Şahin v Turkey*, 44 EHRR 5 (2007) (EctHR, 2005-XI, 175, November 10, 2005) (Grand Chamber Judgment), and see the chapter by Jeremy Gunn, herein.

31 Cf. *Leirvåg et al. v. Norway* (Communication No. 1155/2003), U. N. Doc. CCPR/C/82/D/1155/2003 (2004).

32 See further the chapter by Madhavi Sunder, herein.

33 *Metropolitan Church of Bessarabia v. Moldova* (ECtHR, 2001-XII, 860, December 13, 2001).

34 CEDAW, Art. 3: "States Parties shall take in all fields, in particular in the political, social, economic and cultural fields, all appropriate measures, including legislation, to ensure the full development and advancement of women, for the purpose of guaranteeing them the exercise and enjoyment of human rights and fundamental freedoms on a basis of equality with men." CEDAW, Art. 5.1: "States Parties shall take all appropriate measures: a) To modify the social and cultural patterns of conduct of men and women, with a view to achieving the elimination of prejudices and customary and all other practices which are based on the idea of the inferiority or the superiority of either of the sexes or on stereotyped roles for men and women."

35 Cf. Council of the European Union, Council Directive 2000/78/EC of 27 November 2000 establishing a general framework for equal treatment in employment and occupation Official Journal L 303 , 02/12/2000 P. 0016 - 0022 "Art. 1: "The purpose of this Directive is to lay down a general framework for combating discrimination on the grounds of religion or belief, disability, age or sexual orientation as regards employment and occupation, with a view to putting into effect in the Member States the principle of equal treatment." Art 2: "For the purposes of this Directive, the 'principle of equal treatment' shall mean that there shall be no direct or indirect discrimination whatsoever on any of the grounds referred to in article 1.' The right to exemption is dealt with in the Directive's Art. 4.1: 'Notwithstanding Article 2(1) and (2), Member States may provide that a difference of treatment which is based on a characteristic related to any of the grounds referred to in Article 1 shall not constitute discrimination where, by reason of the nature of the particular occupational activities concerned or of the context in which they are carried out, such a characteristic constitutes a genuine and determining occupational requirement, provided that the objective is legitimate and the requirement is proportionate. The Employment Equality Directive (2000/78/EC) also address the rights of churches and similar organizations in its Art. 4.2 and 4.3: (Art. 4.2) 'Member States may maintain national legislation in force at the date of adoption of this Directive or provide for future legislation incorporating national practices existing at the date of adoption of this Directive pursuant to which, in the case of occupational activities within churches and other public or private organizations the ethos of which is based on religion or belief, a difference of treatment based on a person's religion or belief shall not constitute discrimination where, by reason of the nature of these activities or of the context in which they are carried out, a person's religion or belief constitute a genuine, legitimate and justified occupational requirement, having regard to the organization's ethos. This difference of treatment shall be implemented taking account of Member States' constitutional provisions and principles, as well as the general principles of Community law, and should not justify discrimination on another ground.' (Art. 4.3) 'Provided that its provisions are otherwise complied with, this Directive shall thus not prejudice the right of churches and other public or private organizations, the ethos of which is based on religion or belief, acting in conformity with national constitutions and laws, to require individuals working for them to act in good faith and with loyalty to the organization's ethos.

36 See further the chapter by Natan Lerner, herein.

37 See the chapter by Nazila Ghanea, herein

38 See United Nations Committee on Economic, Social and Cultural Rights, "General Comment No. 20: Non-Discrimination in Economic, Social and Cultural Rights (art. 2, par. 2)," U.N. Doc. E/C.12/GC/20, June 10, 2009.

39 On the notions of direct and indirect discrimination in human rights law, see for instance Ronald Craig, *Systemic Discrimination and the Promotion of Ethnic Equality* (Leiden/Boston: Martinus Publishers, 2007) and Oddny Arnardottir, *Equality and Non-Discrimination Under the European Convention on Human Rights* (The Hague: Martinus Nijhoff Publishers, 2003).

40 Pope Leo XIII, *Rerum Novarum* (On the Rights and Duties of Capital and Labor) May 15, 1891.

41 See note 28 above.

42 United Nations Human Rights Committee, General Comment 22:Article 18 (Forty-eighth session, 1993), U.N. Doc. CCPR/C/21/Rev.1/Add.4 (1993), in particular par. 4: ". . . the practice and teaching of religion or belief includes acts integral to the conduct by religious groups of their basic affairs, such as the freedom to choose their religious leaders, priests and teachers, the freedom to establish seminaries or religious schools and the freedom to prepare and distribute religious texts or publications."

■ RECOMMENDED READING

Arnardottir, Oddny, *Equality and Non-Discrimination under the European Convention on Human Rights* (The Hague: Martinus Nijhoff Publishers, 2003)

Christoffersen, Lisbet, Kjell Å. Modeer, and, Svend Andersen, eds., *Law and Religion in the 21st Century–Nordic Perspectives* (Copenhagen: DJØF Publishing, 2010)

Leckie, Scott and Anne Gallagher, eds., *Economic, Social and Cultural Rights: A Legal Resource Guide* (Philadelphia: University of Pennsylvania, 2006)

Lerner, Natan. *Religion, Secular Beliefs and Human Rights: 25 Years After the 1981 Declaration* (Leiden: Martinus Nijhoff, 2006)

Lindholm, Tore, W. Cole Durham, Jr., and, Bahia G. Tahzib-Lie, eds. *Freedom of Religion or Belief: A Deskbook* (Leiden: Martinius Nijhoff Press, 2004)

Scharffs, Brett G. and W. Cole Durham, Jr., eds., *Law and Religion: National, International and Comparative Perspectives* (New York: Aspen Publishers, 2009)

Steiner, Henry J., Philip Alston, and, Ryan Goodman. *International Human Rights in Context: Law, Politics, Morals: Text and Materials* (Oxford: Oxford University Press, 2007)

Symposium. "The Permissible Scope of Legal Limitations on the Freedom of Religion or Belief." *Emory International Law Review* 19 (Summer 2005): 465–1320

United Nations Committee on Economic, Social and Cultural Rights, "General Comment No. 20: Non-Discrimination in Economic, Social and Cultural Rights (art. 2, par. 2)," E/C.12/GC/20, (2009)

20 Religion and Environmental Rights

WILLIS JENKINS

The controversial arena of environmental rights includes a range of different projects that develop rights-based responses to environmental problems. I organize them here into three kinds of argument: (1) those that specify an environmental condition of the human dignity protected in existing rights protections (e.g., a right to water); (2) those that expand the scope of human dignity to include rights to ecological memberships (e.g., a right of indigenous peoples to cultural biodiversity); and (3) those that recognize rights of other-than-human holders (e.g., rights of animals, species, or nature). Those three categories visibly move from anthropocentric to ecocentric foci. However, in each category there are projects that use rights to achieve environmental protection as well as projects that promote environmental protection for the sake of protecting human dignity.

This chapter can only sketch the related territory, but even an overview illuminates important thresholds in human rights theory and its intersections with religious thought. Because environmental rights strain the capacity of human rights frameworks to address emerging social problems, they pose important test cases for understanding the limits of human rights as moral discourse and as political instrument. Because religious communities and moral cosmologies sometimes impel these projects and sometimes resist them, environmental rights also present an important line of exploration into the shifting relation of religion and rights.

Religion attends environmental rights projects in multiple ways. Sometimes faith communities sponsor rights projects as part of their social mission. Sometimes religious beliefs about nature and humanity cause friction with new proposals. Sometimes the survival of a lived cosmology is the reason for a proposed right. Even when they have no explicit religious content, projects for environmental rights may exhibit a religious scope of inquiry as they renegotiate ideas of humanity and nature. It is important to recognize that rights-based approaches to environmental problems represent just one intersection of religious and ecological thought. The projects and questions described in this chapter have in common their use of rights as a guiding moral metaphor. Other approaches to the nexus of religion and ecology use different moral metaphors, sometimes because they consider rights insufficient for addressing environmental problems.

The Chipko movement of western India illustrates some of the intersections of religion, ecology, and rights—as well as the interpretive ambiguity involved in theorizing those intersections. The Chipko movement attracted worldwide attention for its central image of female peasants embracing trees slated for commercial logging. The protests incorporated Hinduism in various ways, including readings from the Bhagavad Gita, support from priests, and practices of fasting. Accounts of the movement variously present it as an environmental movement, as a religious movement, and as a political movement. Consider the various kinds of rights claims Chipko might illustrate. The practice of embracing trees seemed to communicate the sacredness of nature or a right of trees to exist, yet as a distinctly female movement it expressed demands for women's rights. As a peasant movement, it seemed to defend traditional rights to resource access, but it may have enacted rights of membership in an ecological community, or claimed political rights to participate in environmental decisions.[1] In order to understand the various rights in play and their role in cultural reform, we need to ask how agents deploy religious traditions to make political claims about ecological resources and relations.

■ THE POLITICAL ECOLOGY OF JUSTICE: RIGHTS TO NATURE

A first kind of argument describes how environmental degradations threaten the justice owed persons under the Universal Declaration of Human Rights (UDHR). The UDHR proceeds from "recognition of the inherent dignity and of the equal and inalienable rights of all members of the human family."[2] The UDHR does not specify any explicitly environmental rights, but proposals of this kind argue: (1) that existing rights implicitly include protections from environmental harms, or (2) that environmental harms constitute such a threat that they warrant recognition of a new human right. The initial question here: Can existing rights protect the ecological conditions necessary to human dignity, or must those rights be supplemented?

Answer (1) to that question argues that existing rights implicitly include protection from environmentally mediated harms.[3] Societies do not require a new environmental right on this view, although they may require new political action to guarantee rights amidst changing environmental conditions. Answer (2) argues that a new human right should be recognized with an explicit substantive and/or procedural declaration. This answer assumes that environmental destruction poses an emergent serial threat to human dignity, requiring a new guarantee of protection.

Proposals for a new human right began building after the 1972 Stockholm Environmental Conference declared: "Man has the fundamental right to freedom, equality and adequate conditions of life, *in an environment of a quality* that permits a life of dignity and well-being."[4] At the time, many developing nations were hesitant to endorse the proposal because they worried that it could conflict with rights to development. Their initial criticism points to two questions that any environmental rights project must address. First, does it conflict with other rights or compromise the indivisibility of human rights, thus fracturing the overall picture of human dignity that they support? Second, does it compromise the ability of the poorer populations to develop economic conditions that support realization of other rights? Those two questions are especially important for religious communities that have a cohesive account of moral personhood, a commitment to the common good, or a moral priority for the welfare of the poor.

Sensitive to the tensions at stake, in 1974 the World Council of Churches (WCC) started using the term "sustainability" to gesture toward a trajectory of social development that could integrate economic and environmental conditions of human dignity. As it became popular in the phrase "sustainable development," the term was challenged by those who saw sustainability become an excuse to subordinate both rights and conservation to the imperative of economic development. Henry Shue thus argues that to prevent sustainable development from allowing economic growth to function as de facto imperatives, the international community needs rights-based approaches to environmental problems.[5] A number of Christian theologians seem to agree, using the frame of "ecojustice" to reclaim a tight connection between human dignity and environmental protection. Ecojustice theologies typically generate environmental responsibilities with some account of the needs of the poor, and offer reasons to think rights protections and environmental conservation harmonize in a wider account of the common good.[6]

In the 1990s, the UN commissioned a series of reports, known as the Ksentini Reports after their lead researcher, to investigate whether ecological degradation warranted declaration of a new human right. Ksentini argued that there was strong reason for a new environmental right because of the emergence of environment-mediated threats to human dignity around the world and because other human rights could not be realized in the absence of a healthy environment.[7] On this view, a human environmental right is constitutive of the shared image of human dignity on which the UDHR depends.

Some religious leaders with a compatible view of human dignity, such as Pope John Paul II, supported the proposal.[8] However, Ksentini drew criticism for her attempt to claim religious support for a new human right by appealing to the environmental views of other religious traditions. For example, Ksentini found in Islam a duty to protect the environment, from which she adduced support for a human environmental right. Critics responded that while Islamic law certainly generates environmental duties, its support of modern human rights is less certain. Islamic jurisprudence exhibits a lively debate over how to reason from divinely given law, and specifically over whether theocentric principles can ground human rights, or whether rights are irremediably anthropocentric.[9] Some Christian thought has exhibited similar hesitancies about the grounds for human rights. Religious communities thus may hesitate over rights-based approaches to environmental protection not from ecological indifference but from concern about the metaethical implications of human rights. We will encounter this point again when we come to rights of nature: Traditions of religious ethics may generate robust environmental responsibilities while yet resisting rights-based approaches to environmental problems.

It was not for metaethical but trade reasons that the Ksentini recommendation failed in the UN, whose economic powers had come to fear that a new declaration could clog global commerce with disruptive rights claims. The failure was prefigured at the 1992 Rio "Earth Summit," which backed away from an explicit right, saying instead that humans "are entitled to a healthy and productive life in harmony with nature."[10] In global civil society, however, establishing a human right to the environment remains a live project of the Earth Charter. Developed through wide religious and cultural consultation, the Charter recognizes "the right of all . . . to a natural and social environment supportive of human dignity, bodily health, and spiritual well being, with special attention to the rights of indigenous peoples and minorities."[11]

The Earth Charter's mention of an environment conducive to spiritual well-being and its attention to minorities raises a question and points a way forward. Any proposal for a substantive human right to the environment faces the difficult task of specifying what the right protects. Must the human environment be safe, healthy, beautiful, diverse, wild, unpolluted, accessible, conducive to spirituality? Those evaluators correspond to a wide range of ecological management goals and seem to involve irresolvable controversies. Whose spirituality?

There are two alternative ways forward for this kind of argument. It can argue for new procedural rights that help citizens understand the environmental implications of existing legal protections, such as a right to information about environmental quality. Second, it can specify a substantive right to a particular environmental good. Both ways of arguing have informed the rights-based approaches pursued by environmental justice movements around the world. These movements characteristically begin from local disempowerment to develop a political ecology more supportive of equal human dignity. For that reason, they are sometimes called "liberation ecologies."[12]

In the United States, environmental justice movements represent one of the most effective and least noticed involvements of religion in addressing environmental problems. They are often overlooked as sources of a religious environmental ethic because they so thoroughly reconstruct environmental problems into human rights problems. While civic justice responses to environmental problems in the U.S. appeared earlier, a rights-based approach emerged in 1982, when African-American citizens in Warren County, North Carolina protested against a hazardous waste site. The key point was their mobilization of a civil rights framework that utilized religion and race to illustrate political injustice in the distribution of environmental risks.[13]

When a minister involved in the North Carolina protests reframed a toxic waste issue as "environmental racism," he clinched a hitherto undeveloped connection between human rights and environmental protection that quickly influenced regulatory governance.[14] The United Church of Christ's subsequent 1987 report,

Toxic Wastes and Race in the United States, presented groundbreaking statistical evidence of racist distribution of environmental hazards, depicting a landscape inscribed with injustice.[15] It also made environmental problems matter for religious commitments to civil rights. Liberation ecologies have inspired new dimensions in liberation theologies, although this remains an underdeveloped trajectory of Christian thought.[16]

Religious institutions, leaders, and ideas thus may help communities secure political rights to improve their habitats. That entails not only a right of non-discrimination in public decision-making, but rights to public information about health, environmental quality, and land use. It entails rights of political participation, including procedures for hearing and redressing grievances regarding environmental risks. Procedural rights relevant to one's living environment thus open possibilities for citizens to protect and reinterpret the ecology of human dignity. Dorceta Taylor has documented the prevalence of female leaders of color in environmental justice projects, and has argued that the projects do not conform to mainstream environmentalist ideas because they respond to race-based and gendered contexts of environmental oppression.[17]

"Environmental justice" may then refer not to a certain kind of environment, but to the rights needed by citizens in order to address new kinds of risks. However, the North Carolina protest failed to stop the toxic disposal in question because it could not defend a particular risk threshold as a violation of a particular right. That points to the need for substantive rights to specific environmental resources. Consider proposals for a substantive human right to water: As a specific good related to specific bodily needs of human persons, a minimum quantity can reasonably be set. Because many people are vulnerable to deprivation of that minimum by political decisions, a right to water seems reasonable.

Rights guaranteeing access to environmental goods allows citizens to contest the commodification of natural resources. In the case of water, rights-based approaches often counter initiatives to privatize water supply and delivery, on the view that economic production of scarcity that will affect the poorest and most vulnerable first. Because water is basic to human dignity, it is a non-compensable good. Other substantive rights must make a similar case that a specific quality of environment stands basic to human dignity.

Something more is happening in such proposals than the usual contest between theories of justice. Human rights to environmental needs (for safety from toxins, for supplies of water, etc.) begin to extend and open the minimally shared view of moral personhood implicit in existing human rights. They illustrate the ecological vulnerability of human dignity, showing how personhood is constituted and realized not only by social and political relations, but also by ecological relations. Just as there are political conditions of a decent justice, so there is a political ecology of human dignity.

This shift in underlying moral anthropology particularly matters for discussions of religion and rights. Those discussions often debate whether the moral anthropology of rights is supported by, derived from, or different than those in religious traditions. Here the minimal moral anthropology assumed by rights claims begins to expand, altering the usual set of tensions between accounts of the good and accounts of the right. If religious communities negotiate their stories of the good within pluralist societies organized by rights-based description of minimal needs, then proposals for human environmental rights make what was hitherto seen as a good (environmental goods) into a matter of basic justice.[18]

Shifts in views of humanity and of nature are evident in the first principle of environmental justice declared in a statement adopted by the National People of Color Environmental Leadership Summit, which "affirms the sacredness of Mother Earth, ecological unity, and the interdependence of all species, and the right to be free from ecological destruction."[19] Here a declaration of human rights to environmental goods locates itself in an ecological membership worthy of its own respect, and so begins to make a different kind of rights argument altogether.

■ EXPANDING PERSONHOOD: RIGHTS TO ECOLOGICAL MEMBERSHIP

Global ecological problems pose unique threats to two groups of potential victims: indigenous peoples and future generations. Members of these groups are uniquely vulnerable to environmental change because membership depends on extensive ecological relations. Protecting their human dignity may therefore require a group right to the environmental conditions of their shared identity. This set of rights claims supports a socially and ecologically expansive account of human dignity.

Many indigenous peoples sustain cultures intricately related to a particular bioregion, with narratives of human meaning deeply shaped by a long living in one place.[20] When that is so, members of indigenous groups can be more immediately and profoundly harmed by negative environmental change. Consider the plight of Arctic peoples living in a bioregion under accumulating stress from climate change. They have protested to the international community that warming already stresses their way of life and that trajectories of change may bring about their demise. For they will no longer be the same people in any imaginable way if their culture becomes environmentally impossible or if they are dislocated to a different bioregion. The injustice of the harm is stark: Powerful economic cultures more indifferent to environmental diminishment indirectly assault ecologically sensitive cultures, which have typically contributed very little to environmental destruction.

If an indigenous people understands itself in intimate relation with a jeopardized ecosystem, such that "their dependence on their habitat is so total that any interference with it would constitute an assault on their existence," as one scholar puts it, then destruction of their ecological surround may count as an act of genocide.[21] Genocide is the paradigm case in arguments for a human right held by a group, rather than by individuals, for it is violence directed against a specific group, or against individuals in virtue of their membership in that group. Whether groups can legitimately hold and exercise human rights shapes a lively debate in rights theory. By describing genocide by ecological diminishment, advocates make the outcome of that debate matter for environmental problems. What kind of human right can protect indigenous peoples from indirect, environmentally mediated harms with accumulating potential to destroy a people?[22]

Rights to religious freedom may be at stake. Where an indigenous people cultivates its sense of the meaning of life through particular ecological relations, by stories made with certain fellow creatures in a certain place, then a right to religion may extend to the environmental relations that support that meaning. A way of life, and its interpretation of cosmos and humanity, may be at stake. "Religion" can be a distortive category here; some indigenous representatives have argued that the very idea of a religious dimension of life separable from other dimensions may be inherent to the world from which they seek security. It may be that a group right to self-determination better describes the threat. However, appeals to a right to religion may illustrate to less ecologically sensitive cultures the depth of what is at stake for some indigenous peoples.

Appeals to a right of protection against genocide or of religious expression may also give dominant cultures reason to question the poverty of their own moral memberships and to protect alternatives. A group right for indigenous peoples protects accounts of human dignity that differ from the individualist ontologies of the self that are dominant in many other cultures. Group rights can protect more relational, environmental views of the self by protecting the social and environmental conditions of the societies that cultivate them.

Dominant cultures may come to think that they should share more with these accounts of human dignity. Perhaps a notion of human dignity that stands unaffected by environmental destruction until it becomes actually lethal to individuals is simply an impoverished view of human personhood. Perhaps the minimal moral anthropology secured by conventional human rights should be expanded to better account for humanity's social and ecological relations. Claims like that have been made in various ways by theorists of justice in previous decades, especially by religious and communitarian thinkers who argue that the self must be understood through its relation to interpretive communities collectively making sense of life. The plight of some indigenous groups before modern environmental problems suggests that claims for a relationally constituted self should include ecological relations.

Such claims reframe a key tension between religious thought and rights discourse. Religious thinkers have sometimes criticized the project of universal human rights, either for lacking foundations or for supporting individualist ontologies. Proposals for group environmental rights generate similar criticisms while yet remaining committed to a global human rights project. If the ecological vulnerability of indigenous culture and religion raises questions about the impoverishment of dominant views of the self, then all religious communities who have a stake in critiquing modern moral anthropology find here an invitation to do so in a way that does not undermine the social protections afforded by human rights.

The moral anthropology that began to thicken in proposals for a human right to a safe environment now opens to more extensive questions. Does human dignity include a right to biodiversity access? A right to relations with other animals? A right to open space, green space, or wilderness? A right to use and fructify land? A right to interact with the earth as sacred? Those questions wonder whether the minima of human dignity include rights to participate in ecological membership, and the answers effectively determine the ecological dimensions of human personhood.

Another dimension of personhood with its own ecological obligations arises in regard of a different group. Future generations stand in unique peril of environmental harms because of temporal asymmetry in some ecological problems. Greenhouse gas emissions in this generation, for example, have disproportionate impacts in the next. The incentive for those in the present generation to exploit a time lag in climate feedback from emissions, combined with the inability of future persons to make political protest or ask for redress, seems to justify a human right held by future generations. The temporal character of the harm warrants a temporally constituted right. Religious thinkers have sometimes supported such a right as an aspect of equal respect for all persons, regardless of location or time.[23]

Although an intuitive sense of obligation to the future often underlies public support for environmental conservation, justifying a human right held by future persons, even as a group, encounters conceptual difficulties. Critics object that a group of future persons cannot intelligibly hold a right since its members do not yet exist and so do not "present" real interests in policy decisions. The group would thus hold a right that could not be claimed against those in whom lies the possibility of their existence. Critics usually suggest that we have other forms of obligation to future generations, but not one based in rights.

But there is another way to think about rights and future generations. A group right held by a moral membership that exists across generations can protect the basic interests of its members to protect the integrity of that membership. Because the membership sustains a sense of human dignity precisely because it crosses generations, part of the dignity of present persons lies in their relationship not only to their predecessors but also their descendents. As descendents come into existence, the membership can expect that they will have basic interests similar to persons existing in the present because of the shared membership in a community that interprets and represents human dignity. On this ground, a group right may entail obligations to protect ecological integrity—especially places, species, and resources important to the membership—for the sake of future members of their group. These are not then rights *of* future generations, but rights held by a membership existing across time.[24]

A group right can therefore generate obligations to the future if it assumes a temporally expanded account of human personhood in need of protection from perils that uniquely face an intergenerational membership. Because the harms of climate change accumulate in the future, it likely poses a significant assault on intergenerational groups. While particular future individuals do not yet exist, because the potential risks accumulating in climate change will become real harms as coming generations arrive into agency, they presently constitute important harms for agents who understand their own dignity in relation to a moral membership across time.

Even if human rights can operate across time, the project still faces a second task in specifying the substance or content of these rights. What ecological conditions or relations must the present sustain in order to protect the possibility of a decent intergenerational membership? One way of answering looks to other human rights. If we recognize a human right to a safe environment, to clean water, to culture-supporting biodiversity, or to wilderness, then any group right of future generations must include the environmental rights recognized for present persons. Failure to do so would allow activities to undermine ecological conditions that we hold essential to the view of dignity that we hope to sustain over time and across generations.[25]

Respecting substantive rights across time can create conflicts with other rights if devoting resources to protect future generations makes present humans more vulnerable. In that case, an intergenerational community rights claim could imperil individual rights—just what the UDHR intends to prevent. Defenders of rights for future generations or intergenerational community must then provide some account of the investment of human dignity in the well-being of future persons that does not weaken other rights. Religious traditions may have imaginative resources for considering morally significant relations across time. Rachel Muers, for example, interprets Christian liturgy as an intergenerational exercise that disrupts overreaching attempts to control the future and reaffirms commitments to today's vulnerable.[26]

In any case, arguments for group rights begin to expand the entities that can receive direct protection from human rights. The question of future generations extends protection not only beyond human individuals to groups, but beyond the living present. In the next section we explore extensions of rights beyond the human world.

■ OBLIGATIONS BEYOND HUMANITY: RIGHTS OF NATURE

Thus far I have considered two kinds of environmental rights for humans; now a third kind proposes rights for others-than-human[27] Arguments for rights held by "nature" (a provisional term for the many rights holders here) challenge rights discourse by criticizing the anthropocentrism of existing human rights. The critical question here is whether rights of nature represent a consistent expansion of modern liberalism's sphere of moral concern, or whether they represent a critical flaw in the roots of the liberal tradition.[28] How religion matters for the rights of nature, then, will be shaped by various relations of religion and liberal justice.

This category includes multiple kinds of rights-holders, from individual animals to holisms like species, systems, or even the whole earth. While always held as a check on human action (not to regulate interaction among non-humans), the category includes a range of functions for rights, from legal institutions to soft norms. Justifications advanced for these rights also exhibit a range, from recognition of human-like vulnerabilities to respect for intrinsic value possessed without reference to humanity. Some warrant the right in virtue of a holder's special relationship to a human community (e.g., companion animals, totemic creatures), some in virtue of their difference from the human world (e.g., wild species), and some in virtue of an intrinsic value irrespective of categories of human and nonhuman (e.g., any creature that feels pain). The different warrants can create moral tensions between different rights proposals in this category. For an often-inflammatory example, an individual right of domesticated cats to protection from cruelty might conflict with a right to existence held by endangered bird species.

The diversity within this category merits more detailed analysis than I can offer here. However, the diverse proposals do share an important similarity: each uses the concept of rights to extend analogous protections to moral dignity found beyond human personhood. For religious traditions, these proposals test ideas of human uniqueness and moral values of creation, which—as we will see—can create new tensions between religion and rights.

The most important tension here, however, is that between rights protecting humans and those protecting nature for its own sake. Human rights advocates worry that extending rights to non-human holders jeopardizes the unique authority of rights claims. Can the idea of rights for humans survive expansion beyond the human world? Worry comes from the other side as well, as environmental and animal advocates wonder if rights that refer primarily to human protections can adequately respond to the threats faced by others. At the heart of the tension is the relation of rights to anthropocentrism, and a question about the implication of anthropocentrism in human violence against other creatures. If a major moral assumption on which the project of human rights depends also produces ecological destruction, then rights may not be the best devices to use for ecological protection. If, however, the humanist ethos of rights does not necessarily create moral indifference to the rest of the earth, then rights can more easily be extended to others-than-human.

First, consider proposals to extend human rights to animals who exhibit aspects of personhood. Animals like chimpanzees and dolphins might be eligible for rights in virtue of features that they share with human life, such as intelligence, self-recognition, or empathic capacities to interact with humans. The Great Ape Project, for example, declares that due to their genetic and actual similarity with humans, the great primates should be protected from similar grave threats; they are owed a right to life, a right to live in freedom from captivity, and a right to freedom from torture and experimentation. Many nations have more extensive protections for great primates than for other animals, and some nations are considering legal rights for primates.

Other proposals for animal rights cast a wider net of moral inclusion, beyond those few animals with human-like capacities to all animals vulnerable to violence at the hands of moral agents. This turns attention from eligibility for personhood to capacity to suffer, which is not a human trait shared by some animals, but a trait of all sentient animals including humans. Here, two uses of animal rights must be distinguished. Sometimes animal rights work in respect of the autonomous interests of the animal, much like duty-based explanations of human rights (with amendments made for the lack of reciprocal duty). Other times the rights language aims to illustrate the equal moral weight of equal suffering. Peter Singer, whose *Animal Liberation* remains a landmark work, makes this utilitarian argument, but Singer allows rights language as a shorthand for equality of interests and as a rhetorical strategy to bring other animals within the sphere of moral consideration.[29]

The project of animal rights in an important topic of debate in the academic intersection of "religion and animals," which investigates how religious ideas have shaped human relations with animals. The field also conducts more general research into the role of animals in religious traditions and practices, and the function of the category "animal" in moral cosmologies.[30]

As we investigate the legacies of anthropocentrism, the topic of religion and animals returns us to the central conflict of this third category of rights. Using rights to protect others-than-human begins to challenge moral ideas that have sustained the modern human rights project, but now stand under suspicion for permitting ecological destruction. Modern humanist thinkers drew a two-fold moral and epistemological boundary between humans and other creatures in order to protect the unique value of human individuals. Doing so, they combined a moral anthropocentrism that privileges human interests above others and an epistemic anthropocentrism that denies knowledge outside of human experience. Late into the twentieth century, serious thinkers debated whether animals feel pain and whether they have intelligence—a stunning achievement of ignorance. When reformers use rights language to question anthropocentric violence against others, they begin to render the human/nature boundary untrustworthy and so began to destabilize ideas foundational to the emergence of human rights.

Questioning the legacies of anthropocentrism has formed a major task for the field of religion and ecology. Work in the field often refers to historian Lynn White's 1967 thesis that religious cosmologies shape environmental behavior, and that Western Christianity's anthropocentrism provided license for the exploitative practices that led to modern ecological crises.[31] Scholars working in many religious traditions now examine how religion shapes environmental values and practices, and explore resources to recover or reconstruct an ethic of respect and responsibility for the natural world. Sometimes they, too, use rights ideas to summarize respect for nature.[32]

Extending rights beyond animal individuals to the rest of the earth cannot rely on empathy in the same way. So instead of arguing from embodied vulnerability shared with human persons, an argument for the rights of trees (for example) may call for respect of the different kind of moral value held by trees. Holmes Rolston argues that not only individual trees but species and ecosystems may defend intrinsic values, or may have rights-eligible value because they produce self-valuing organisms. Recognizing that sort of value, says Rolston, amounts to saying that nature is sacred.[33]

Calling nature sacred also works within some strategies of religious ethics. In just the Christian traditions, a great body of theological work has recovered resources for valuing creation as sacred. The earth may be holy in virtue of its relationship to a Creator, or because it is endowed with divine properties, or capable of mediating sacramental grace. Protestant theologian James Nash has done the most to develop creation's sacred value into support for "biotic rights."[34]

Nash suggests that Christianity may support a radical project of legal reform. In a famous legal brief, Christopher Stone argued in support of a Sierra Club petition to intercede on behalf of a forest threatened by logging by claiming that trees can be said to have rights. Stone observed that the law grants person-like rights to many odd entities, including corporations, ships, and trusts. A legal right just means that a threat or harm to the entity deserves judicial review when some action may be inconsistent with its interests. Stone proposed devices not unlike those used for trusts (e.g., proxies with legal standing) so that forests can institute legal action, allow courts to take injuries into account, and let relief run directly to their benefit. Stone's reasoning was rejected by the majority opinion, but has remained influential.[35] If Nash is right, Christian thought can not only overcome its association with anthropocentrism, but can support a project that directly counters it.

However, in other Christian traditions, especially in Protestant Evangelical thought, calling nature sacred and assigning it rights can undermine the central form of ethical reasoning. Moral reasoning in Evangelical theology usually centers in Jesus Christ's unmediated claim on the individual conscience. When nature appears as moral claimant, it can seem rival to that foundational relationship, and so threatens the logic of the whole tradition. Some Evangelical theologians have therefore sharply criticized projects for nature's rights, even while constructing a robust environmental ethic centered around the organizing metaphor of stewardship.[36] The example shows that there are many ways that religious traditions might generate environmental obligations, rights-based approaches just one approach among them.

Those differences shape how religious communities regard international proposals for a right for nature. A proposal for rights of nature was anticipated in the

World Charter for Nature adopted by the UN General Assembly in 1980. The Charter, recognizing that "every form of life is unique, warranting respect regardless of its worth to man," declared that "nature shall be respected and its essential processes shall not be impaired."[37] The Charter avoids the term "rights," but its declaration of respect for nature's worth prepared the way for more formal rights. Those appear most robustly in Ecuador's recent recognition of a constitutional right of nature (the constitution also includes human environmental rights). Ecuador's recognition is notable for its biocentric ground of justification, and its use of the indigenous term *Pachamama* ("Mother Earth"): "Nature, or Pachamama . . . has the right to exist, persist, maintain and regenerate its vital cycles." The constitution also recognizes nature's right to restoration from severe anthropogenic impacts.[38]

How rights of nature will develop in Ecuadoran jurisprudence may be less important than the shift in moral cosmology that they signal. Followers of Thomas Berry, the thinker of religious transition, might describe the shift as one from a collection of objects to "a communion of subjects."[39] Rights claims are usually made when political societies are failing to protect moral dignity from violence. Making claims for the rights of nature illustrates that political structures are failing to prevent environmental destruction. If the claims seem exotic to our sense of justice then that indicates that the cultural basis for our political structures needs to change as well. For those seeking cultural transformation, recognizing rights of nature is important less for the legal consequence than for facilitating a turn from exclusive humanism to a sacred ecological membership.

■ CONCLUSIONS

In the first two categories of rights, environmental protection is warranted as part of protecting human dignity. Doing so bears suggestions of nature's own value. Recall that the first principle of environmental justice included mention of sacred Mother Earth, and rights for indigenous peoples may include a right to ecological membership. Those suggestions are made explicit in the third category of rights. Nature is owed its own respect, and human dignity depends on respecting the dignity of others-than-human. In this third category, rights claims go beyond expanding human personhood to protesting against the sort of culture that needs to invent rights for nature.

That protest exhibits the central question raised by all three projects for environmental rights: Do environmental rights harmonize with the received conventions and cultures of human rights, or do they begin to shift, challenge, and reconstruct rights-oriented moral cultures? I would argue the latter: Environmental rights significantly challenge humanist cultures. Societies with strong cultures of human rights protection therefore have incentives to articulate environmental obligations that are not based in human rights. In other words, I predict the continuation of fragmented responses to socio-ecological problems that may well have common roots, and therefore, continued tension with religious commitments to integrated interpretations and comprehensive responses.

■ NOTES

1 See Ramachandra Guha, *The Unquiet Woods: Ecological Change and Peasant Resistance in the Himalaya* (Oxford: Oxford University Press, 1989).

2 Universal Declaration of Human Rights, G.A. res. 217A (III), U.N. Doc A/810 at 71 (1948), Preamble.

3 See Michael R. Anderson, "Human Rights Approaches to Environmental Protection: An Overview," in *Human Rights Approaches to Environmental Protection*, eds. Alan Boyle and Michael Anderson (Oxford: Clarendon Press, 1996), 1–24.

4 Declaration of the United Nations Conference on the Human Environment, U.N. Doc. A/CONF.48/14/Rev. 1 (1973), 11 I.L.M. 1416 (1972), Principle 1 (emphasis mine, masculine vocabulary theirs) (hereinafter "Stockholm Declaration")

5 Henry Shue, "Ethics, the Environment, and the Changing International Order," *International Affairs* 71(3) (1995): 453–61.

6 See Larry L. Rasmussen, *Earth Community, Earth Ethics* (Maryknoll, N.Y.: Orbis Books, 1996).

7 See Fatma Zohra Ksentini, Special Rapporteur on Human Rights and the Environment, "Human Rights and the Environment," U.N. Doc E/CN.4/Sub.2/1993/7 (1993) for the final report in the series.

8 Pope John Paul II, "Message of His Holiness for the Celebration of the World Day of Peace," January 1, 1990.

9 See Martin Lau, "Islam and Judicial Activism," in *Human Rights Approaches to Environmental Protection*, eds. Alan Boyle and Michael Anderson (Oxford: Clarendon Press, 1996), 285–301.

10 Declaration on Environment and Development, Principle 1, U.N. Doc. A/CONF. 151/26.

11 Earth Charter Commisssion, Earth Charter (launched June 29,2000), Principle 12, accessible at: http://www.earthcharterinaction.org/invent/images/uploads/echarter_english.pdf

12 Joan Martinez-Alier, *The Environmentalism of the Poor* (Northampton, MA: Edward Elgar, 2002).

13 Robert Bullard, Dumping in Dixie: Race, Class, and Environmental Quality (Boulder, CO: Westview Press, 2000).

14 Richard Lazarus, "Environmental Racism! That's What It Is." *University of Illinois Law Review* (2000): 255–74.

15 Commission for Racial Justice, "Toxic Wastes and Race in the United States: A National Report on the Racial and Socioeconomic Characteristics of Communities with Hazardous Waste Sites," (New York: United Church of Christ, 1987).

16 See Leonardo Boff, *Cry of the Earth, Cry of the Poor* (Maryknoll, N.Y.: Orbis Books, 1997).

17 Dorceta Taylor, "Women of Color, Environmental Justice, and Ecofeminism," in *Ecofeminism: Women, Nature, Culture*, ed. Karen Warren (Indianapolis: Indiana University Press, 1997), 38–81.

18 David Schlosberg, *Defining Environmental Justice: Theories, Movements, and Nature* (New York: Oxford University Press, 2007).

19 First National People of Color Environmental Leadership Summit, "Principles of Environmental Justice" (adopted 1991), Principle 1, accessible at: http://www.ejnet.org/ej/principles.html

20 See further the chapter by Ronald Niezen, herein.

21 R. S. Pathak, "The Human Rights System as a Conceptual Framework for Environmental Law," in *Environmental Change and International Law,* ed. Edith Brown Weiss (Tokyo: UN University Press, 1992), 233–4.

22 Patrick Thornberry, *Indigenous Peoples and Human Rights* (Manchester, UK: Manchester University Press, 2002).

23 See Emmanuel Agius and Lionel Chircop, *Caring for Future Generations: Jewish, Christian, and Islamic Perspectives* (Westport, CT: Praeger Press, 1998).

24 Edward Page, *Climate Change, Justice and Future Generations* (Northampton, MA: Edward Elgar Publishing, 2006).

25 See Richard Hiskes, *A Human Right to a Green Future: Environmental Rights and Intergenerational Justice* (New York: Cambridge Press, 2009).

26 Rachel Muers, Living for the Future: Theological Ethics for Coming Generations (New York: T&T Clark, 2008).

27 The awkward term "others-than-human" is often used by arguments in this category to avoid binary or derogatory implications of "non-human."

28 Roderick Nash, *The Rights of Nature: A History of Environmental Ethics* (Madison: University of Wisconsin Press, 1989).

29 For a quick introduction, see the essays by Tom Regan, Paola Cavalieri, and Peter Singer in *The Animal Ethics Reader*, 2nd ed., eds. Susan Armstrong and Richard G. Botzler (New York: Routledge, 2008).

30 See Paul Waldau and Kimberly Patton, eds., *A Communion of Subjects: Animals in Religion, Science, and Ethics* (New York: Columbia University Press, 2009).

31 Lynn White, "The Historic Roots of Our Ecologic Crisis," *Science* 155 (1967): 1203–7.

32 For an entry into the scholarship, see the recommended reading list.

33 Holmes Rolston III, "Caring for Nature: From Fact to Value, from Respect to Reverence," *Zygon* 39(2) (2004): 277–302.

34 James Nash, *Loving Nature: Ecological Integrity and Christian Responsibility* (Nashville, TN: Abingdon Press, 1991).

35 Christopher Stone, *Should Trees Have Standing? Toward Legal Rights for Natural Objects* (Los Altos, CA: William Kaufmann, 1974).

36 For further explanation of difference among Christian environmental theologies, see Willis Jenkins, *Ecologies of Grace: Environmental Ethics and Christian Theology* (New York: Oxford University Press, 2008).

37 United Nations General Assembly,"World Charter for Nature," U.N. Doc. A/RES/37/7 (1982).

38 Constituciones de 2008, Republica del Ecuador, Art. 71–72.

39 Sr. Patricia Siemen, "Earth Jurisprudence: Toward Law in Nature's Balance," *Barry Law Review* 11(1) (2008): 1–10.

▪ RECOMMENDED READING

Bauman, Whitney, Richard Bohannon, and, Kevin O'Brien. *Grounding Religion: A Field Guide to the Study of Religion and Ecology* (New York: Routledge, 2010)

Boyle, Michael and Alan Anderson, eds., *Human Rights Approaches to Environmental Protection* (Oxford: Clarendon Press, 1996)

Hill, Barry, Steve Wolfson, and, Nicholas Targ. "Human Rights and the Environment: A Synopsis and Some Predictions." *Georgetown International Law Review* 16 (2003): 359–402

Hiskes, Richard. *A Human Right to a Green Future: Environmental Rights and Intergenerational Justice* (New York: Cambridge Press, 2009)

Jenkins, Willis. *Ecologies of Grace: Environmental Ethics and Christian Theology* (New York: Oxford University Press, 2008)

Nash, Roderick. *The Rights of Nature: A History of Environmental Ethics* (Madison: University of Wisconsin Press, 1989)

Rasmussen, Larry L. *Earth Community, Earth Ethics* (Maryknoll, NY: Orbis, 1996)

Shrader-Frechette, Kristen. *Environmental Justice: Creating Equality, Reclaiming Democracy* (New York: Oxford University Press, 2002)

Stone, Christopher. *Should Trees Have Standing? Toward Legal Rights for Natural Objects* (Los Altos, CA: William Kaufmann, 1974)

Taylor, Prudence. "From Environmental to Ecological Human Rights: A New Dynamic in International Law." *Georgetown International Environmental Law Review* 10 (1997): 309–97

Tucker, Mary Evelyn and John Grim, eds. *Religions of the World and Ecology Series*, 9 vols. (Cambridge: Harvard University Press: 1997–2003)

Twiss, Sumner. "History, Human Rights, and Globalization." *Journal of Religious Ethics* 32.1 (2004): 39–70

21 Religion, Violence, and the Right to Peace

R. SCOTT APPLEBY

Most religions espouse some form of The Golden Rule: "None of you is a believer until he desires for his brother that which he desires for himself" (Islam). "What is hateful to you do not to your fellow man—that is the entire law, all the rest is commentary" (Judaism). "Blessed is he who preferreth his brother before himself" (Baha'i). "Do unto others as you would have done unto you" (Christianity). Moreover, they claim invariably to possess, preserve, and profess the wisdom that leads to peace.

Is there a *right* to peace, and do religions uphold it? While "rights-talk" as such is relatively new to religious traditions, in recent decades most have produced articulate proponents of human rights—even if these individuals are in the minority within their faith communities. Yet, strikingly, these religiously motivated rights champions have claimed a longstanding witness to "human rights" in ancient scriptures and ethical traditions, appropriated elements of the new rights talk, or hastened to formulate their own parallel discourses in which rights talk was challenged or complemented by the delineation of responsibilities to religion and society. Protestant, Roman Catholic, and Jewish leaders, for example, responded to the excesses of radical individualism in America by promoting a countervailing discourse of civic responsibility in service to the common good, and by reminding their fellow citizens of the longstanding contributions of religious communities to the cultivation of civic virtues and social accountability. Muslim scholars initiated a far-reaching debate over "Islamic democracy" and "Islamic human rights" in the Middle East, Africa, and South Asia.[1]

Nonetheless, modern religion retains its reputation as a major social and political obstacle to the full realization of human rights. Can this reputation be reversed? As one of the editors of this volume has argued, religion must be seen as a vital dimension of any legal regime of human rights. "Religions will not be easy allies to engage, but the struggle for human rights cannot be won without them."[2] Nowhere, perhaps, is this simultaneous caution and exhortation more relevant than in efforts to enlist religious actors and resources in support of a "right to peace."

THE RIGHT TO PEACE: A STATUS REPORT

Stephen P. Marks provides a succinct definition of the right to peace in the early years of its development:

> It is the right of every individual to contribute to efforts for peace, including refusal to participate in the military effort, and the collective right of every state to benefit from the full respect by other states of the principles of non-use of force, of non-aggression, of peaceful settlement of disputes, of the Geneva Conventions and Additional Protocols and similar standards, as well as from the implementation of policies aimed at general and complete disarmament under effective international control.[3]

The first articulation of the human right to peace came in 1979 from Karel Vasak, the former director of the International Institute of Human Rights, in his inaugural lecture to the Institute's tenth study session.[4] Vasak, and others following him, argued that a "right to peace" must be included in a third generation of human rights, one that builds upon first-generation civil, legal, and political rights as well as second-generation social, economic, and cultural rights—the latter comprising positive claims owed by the State, such as the right to work for a living wage, the right to safe housing and to healthcare, and the right to participate in the cultural life of the community.[5] To this schema of first- and second-generation rights, Vasak adds a third generation of collective rights, or "rights to solidarity." These rights include "the right to development, to environment, to the ownership of the common heritage of mankind (i.e., the ocean floor), the right to communication, and to peace."[6]

These rights belong neither to the negative freedoms of the first generation, nor the positive claims of the second. Instead, Vasak writes, third-generation rights "are new in that they may both be *invoked against* the State and *demanded* of it; but above all (and herein lies their essential characteristic) they can be realized only through the converted efforts of all the actors on the social scene: the individual, the State, public and private bodies, and the international community."[7] Third-generation rights can be claimed by these actors, but they can only be guaranteed by the mutual cooperation of such actors.[8] As Carl Wellman puts it, "Solidarity applies because these rights must be *group* rights and not reducible to the several rights of the individual members of these groups. This involves a radical rethinking of human rights because the first- and second-generation human rights have traditionally been taken to be only rights of individual human beings."[9] We can see this clearly in the right to peace, which concerns not only an individual's right to live in peace, but the greater right of societies to enjoy a common peace.

As much as it was part of the developing thinking on human rights in general, the right to peace was also a response to the nuclear proliferation of the 1970s and 1980s. The first international document on the right to peace, the United Nations General Assembly's Declaration on the Right of Peoples to Peace, approved in the General Assembly on November 12, 1984, invokes "the will and the aspirations of all peoples to eradicate war from the life of mankind and, above all, to avert a worldwide nuclear catastrophe."[10] Its preamble continues:

> Convinced that life without war serves as the primary international prerequisite for the material well-being, development and progress of countries, and for the full implementation of the rights and fundamental human freedoms proclaimed by the United Nations,
>
> Aware that in the nuclear age the establishment of a lasting peace on Earth represents the primary condition for the preservation of human civilization and the survival of mankind,
>
> Recognizing that the maintenance of a peaceful life for peoples is the sacred duty of each State. . . .[11]

In light of these preambles, the General Assembly:

1. Solemnly proclaims that the peoples of our planet have a sacred right to peace;
2. Solemnly declares that the preservation of the right of peoples to peace and the promotion of its implementation constitute a fundamental obligation of each State;
3. Emphasizes that ensuring the exercise of the right of peoples to peace demands that the policies of States be directed towards the elimination of the threat of war, particularly nuclear war, the renunciation of the use of force in international relations and the settlement of international disputes by peaceful means on the basis of the Charter of the United Nations;
4. Appeals to all States and international organizations to do their utmost to assist in implementing the right of peoples to peace through the adoption of appropriate measures at both the national and the international level.[12]

The Luarca Declaration on the Human Right to Peace, adopted in 2006 by an international commission of human rights experts, presents peace as a kind of ur-right. The constituent elements of the right, that is, are otherwise classified as separate rights themselves. These include, *inter alia,* the right to live in a safe and healthy environment, the right to civil disobedience, the right to the free exercise of expression and religion, and the right to development. According to this approach, the right to peace is not only the foundation for other human rights, but an umbrella under which previously distinct rights are grouped.[13] If the right to peace is prior to other rights, some scholars argue, it becomes an individual right and not a collective one; it lies before or at the first generation, not at the third.[14]

To date, the right to peace has not been formalized in any treaty or in the operative provisions of any hard human-rights instruments, except for the African Charter on Human and Peoples' Rights.[15] Furthermore, there is no clear consensus internationally on the nature of the right to peace, and, while references to the right to peace appeared in the preamble to the Universal Declaration of Human Rights, neither that declaration nor subsequent human-rights instruments properly express a right to peace.[16] However, many soft instruments have declared the right to peace to be a human rights, beginning with the Declaration on the Right of Peoples to Peace, and a number of human rights thinkers believe that the right should be further developed and codified in international documents.[17]

■ THE MIXED RECORD OF RELIGIONS

On April 30, 2002, Human Rights Watch (HRW) issued a report on the communal violence that engulfed the Western Indian state of Gujarat in February and March of that year. By that date, Indian government officials had already acknowledged that more than 850 people, most of them Muslims, had been killed in Gujarat beginning on February 27, after the Sabarmati Express train was forcibly stopped at Godhra City and burned by a Muslim mob, resulting in the fiery deaths of 59 Hindu passengers—mostly women, children, and seniors returning from the holy city of Ayodhya.[18] The attack prompted retaliatory massacres against Muslims on a large scale. In addition to the hundreds of people killed or reported missing, 523 places of worship were damaged or destroyed. Mosques and Muslim-owned businesses suffered the bulk of the damage. "The attacks on Muslims are part of a concerted campaign of Hindu nationalist organizations to promote and exploit communal tensions to further the BJP's political rule[19] —a movement that is supported at the local level by militant groups that operate with impunity and under the patronage of the state," the authors of the HRW report concluded. "State officials of Gujarat, India, were directly involved in the killings of hundreds of Muslims since February 27 and are now engineering a massive cover-up of the state's role in the violence."[20] Eventually, human rights activists, scholars, and independent observers alike concluded that Hindu nationalists had succeeded in using the infrastructure of one of the world's largest secular democracies, the Indian state, to commit atrocities against their Muslim compatriots.[21]

Sadly, the Gujarat "pogrom," as scholars termed it, is but one example of the capacity of modern extremist movements to manipulate both religions and states, enlisting both of these resource-rich institutional and social forces in violent and repressive campaigns to marginalize or eliminate the religious, ethnic, or political "other." Some of these extremist movements are manifestly religious in orientation and motivation, while others merely exploit the loyalties, fears, and aspirations of religious groups or populations, channeling their "militant" (i.e., self-sacrificial, evangelizing, world-transforming) energies to deadly purpose. I refer to the first type as "strong" religious movements (i.e., explicitly driven by religious ideas, doctrines, laws, etc., however these are interpreted), and the second as "weak" religious movements (i.e., driven primarily by ethnic, nationalist or other non-religious ideologies, identities and motivations, but recruiting religion in order to sacralize the cause).[22] Both types of religious actors, in addition to drawing on religious dynamics and resources, seek to harness the power and legitimacy of the modern nation-state. Building and maintaining a sustainable peace—in this usage, a social condition based on the protection and enforcement of first-, second-, and third-generation human rights—is not high on the agenda of extremist groups of this ilk. To the contrary, they seek to sow division, exploit and deepen social inequalities, and exclude some groups altogether from the protection of the law.[23]

In some settings, strong religious movements or coalitions of movements have seized control of the State, as did Shiite-led revolutionaries in Iran, or won control of the State at the ballot box, as did the Hindu nationalist BJP for a time in India. Systematic violations of human rights, often as a matter of state policy, followed in the wake of such triumphs. In 1979, in support of the Ayatollah Khomeini's bid to assume theocratic power over the Iranian state, the militant clerics in the Assembly of Experts rejected a draft of a republican constitution consistent with Shiite Islam, and replaced it with the Fundamental Law, a constitution that purported to be fundamentally Islamic and to incorporate specifically Shiite principles of government. The Fundamental Law of 1979 imposed severe restrictions on the rights of the individual, reserved freedom of association only for those parties and organizations that did not "violate the Islamic standards and the bases of the Islamic Republic," and explicitly established a theocracy by making sovereignty and legislation the exclusive possession of the One God. By way of these clauses, and by defining the Islamic republic as a political order based on belief in the five principle articles of faith in Shiite Islam, the Fundamental Law provided constitutional legitimacy for the ongoing persecution by the State not only of religious minorities such as the Baha'i but also of Shiites considered insufficiently unorthodox by the Supreme Jurist (Khomeini and his successors).[24]

In weak or failed states such as Afghanistan and Somalia, religiously motivated extremists have sought to fill the power vacuum; at this writing, the Taliban continues its insurgency in a bid to impose a harsh and intolerant regime of so-called Islamic law over all of Afghanistan, while the hardline Islamist groups Al-Shabaab and Hizbul Islam attempt the same feat in Somalia.

In a greater number of settings, however, a failed or failing state is not the prerequisite for the repression and persecution of religious, ethnic, or political minorities. Rather, the majority religion (or its extremist vanguard) and the State conspire to commit and to legitimate atrocities. Typically, the manipulation has been mutual: political leaders and state officials successfully played on the fears and prejudices of the religious population, while religious extremists effectively calculated the weaknesses of the State and leveraged the cultural power of the majority religion to prod the sometimes reluctant state to exceed the limits of what it considered prudent. Muslim extremists in the Pakistan military and intelligence services, religious Zionist Jews in Israel, and Buddhist nationalists in Sri Lanka, for example, have shrewdly exploited their rights and liberties in the service of co-opting state power to do their violent bidding.

From the time of the partition of India and creation of Pakistan in 1947, and even prior to the establishment of the Islamic Republic of Pakistan in 1956, religious minorities have seen their rights abolished or constricted. In 1974,

Ahmadi Muslims were declared "non-Muslims" by an act of Parliament and subjected to systematic discrimination and persecution for their religious views. The declaration was a victory for the Jamaat-i-Islami, a fundamentalist Muslim organization that had incited the anti-Ahmadiya riots of 1952 and positioned itself as a guardian of orthodoxy for the Islamic nation. One of the organization's critics, the expatriate Pakistani scholar Rafiuddin Ahmed, traces an evolution in Jamaat ideology and tactics following its failure to usher in a "theo-democracy" at the polls. Gradually, he writes, "the organization tailored itself to become a political pressure group that employs various tactics, including violence, to achieve a measure of influence with [a series of Pakistani] regimes that it has been unable to achieve with the general Muslim population of Pakistan."[25] More recently, the Pakistani Inter-Services Intelligence [ISI] has been accused of forming clandestine alliances with Lashkar-e-Taiba, the Pakistani Muslim extremist group accused of carrying out terrorist attacks in Mumbai, India in 2006 and 2008.[26]

The convergence and occasional conflation of ultra-religious and ultra-national perspectives, goals, and tactics in Israel is well known.[27] The radical messianic Jews who first settled the occupied territories following the Six Day War of 1967 (and with bolder forays after the 1973 War) acted illegally in so doing; but it soon became apparent that, in spearheading the settlement of "the whole Land of Israel" by encroaching upon Palestinian neighborhoods and intimidating Palestinian residents, the Jewish extremists were both forcing the hand of the State of Israel (what Israeli government, they reasoned, would dare move against Jews in favor of Palestinian Arabs?) and enacting its irredentist policies.[28]

Less well known is the role of nationalist *yeshivot* in cementing the tacit alliance between religious and secular nationalists. Based on the model of Mercaz Harav yeshiva, founded by Rav Avraham Yitzhak Kook (1865–1935), the country's first chief rabbi and progenitor of the Gush Emunim (Bloc of the Faithful) settler movement, these educational institutions were adapted to Zionist and expansionist imperatives even while retaining the traditional yeshiva's goal of immersing the student in the total world of Torah, Talmud, and *mitzvot* (religious duties). As successive Israeli governments provided public funding for these institutions of religious education, Religious Zionism grew to rival Orthodox and Haredi (ultra-Orthodox) expressions of Judaism as bearers of Israeli cultural and religious values.

Whereas the majority of rabbis and students associated with the nationalist *yeshivot* rejected the radical tactics of both the Jewish underground (which plotted attacks in the late 1970s and early 1980s against Islamic holy sites and attacked Arab mayors and Muslim college students) and the Kahane movement (which advocated expulsion of the Palestinian Arabs from Israel and the occupied territories), they did so not out of sympathy with Arabs and Arab holy places. To thecontrary, the leaders of the nationalist *yeshivot* movement identified with the State of Israel, notwithstanding its mistaken secularism, and sought to fuse nationalist extremism and religious extremism. In so doing, they shrewdly exploited the openings provided by Israel's democratic society, in order to build a core of militant Israeli citizens dedicated to reinforcing a political definition of "peace" based on the segregation of populations and the denial of the full range of human rights to the Palestinians. "Where freedom of expression is absent and political organizations are limited by the state, education cannot substitute for revolutionary activity," writes the Israeli political scientist Eliezer Don-Yehiya. "In a democratic state, however, it can."[29]

In Sri Lanka, Buddhist monks (*bhikkhus*) played a distinctive role in articulating the perceptions of Sinhalese extremists and thus in creating a political culture of war against the Tamil minority. Beginning in the mid-1950s, shortly after independence was achieved in 1948, following more than a century of successive Portuguese, Dutch, and British rule, a loosely organized Sinhalese Buddhist movement emerged, seeking to persuade the State to restore Buddhism to its rightful place at the cultural foundation and core of the nation. Concessions granted by the government in the 1960s did not prevent the movement from becoming more extreme. (Indeed, elite politicians such as S.W.R.D. Bandaranaike, the island's fourth prime minister, often sought to manipulate extremist sentiments to advance their own narrow political interests.) In 1977, 1981, and 1983, the Buddhist extremists helped to incite deadly anti-Tamil riots.[30]

The monks, who are virtually objects of worship in Sri Lanka, were able to play such a decisive and deadly role, James Manor argues, as a result of fragmentation and instability in the island's political institutions. Both its political parties and the formal institutions of the State, he writes, "have suffered from a national political elite which has long concentrated power in their own hands at the apex of the political system. The apex and the base have been poorly integrated because institutions at the intermediate and local levels have been given too little power to develop much substance."[31]

In certain cases of religion-state complicity, the host religion was, in my terminology, relatively "weak," that is, lacking in independence from the State. Accordingly, the specifically doctrinal-ethical core of the religion was readily subordinated, by the extremists, to ethno-religious, economic and political concerns. During the war in Bosnia of 1992–1995, for example, Slobodan Milosevic, the president of the Republic of Serbia, rallied Serbian Orthodox bishops and priests to endorse his genocidal campaign against Bosnian Serbs by playing on both the ethno-religious hatred and fears of some Serbian Orthodox clergy and laity. Despite protests from some Serbian priests and bishops, the most powerful leaders of the church entered into alliance with Milosevic, at least for a time. By providing ethical sanction for, and ritual celebration of the ultranationalist crusade, the Orthodox in effect sacralized the bloodshed, transforming a naked grab for territory and power into a type of holy war.[32]

In their attempts to sow discord and demonize the other, religious extremists, as these vignettes suggest, employ various strategies vis-à-vis the State, ranging from revolution to occupying a power vacuum to co-opting state power. In each case they present themselves as the designated or traditional custodian of social values and political culture. (Political scientist Ashutosh Varshney has argued that most if not all of the communal violence in contemporary India is not caused by spontaneous riots but rather is "produced by institutionalized riot systems"[33]—systems reinforced, if not created, by religious extremists who successfully project themselves as guardian of Hindu values or *Hindutva*.) The credibility of the extremists' claims to represent the religious majority rests on their ability to disguise their minority status within the host religion itself.

Challenging this distortion is one of the most important tasks of religious leaders who aspire to advance a regime of human rights and build a sustainable peace in their societies. They do so, increasingly, by emphasizing core teachings and precepts of the religious traditions—such as forgiveness, reconciliation, love of enemy, and solidarity with the poor and oppressed—that are generally not found in conventional political discourse but provide powerful warrant for the protection of human rights and, even more ambitiously, for the social foundations of a sustainable positive peace.[34] Not least among the consequences of this new push for peace within religious communities is increasing attention to the discipline of nonviolence as a privileged means of pursuing constructive social change, reinforced by the exhortation that it is the duty of every believer to contribute to efforts for peace. Among Christian groups, in particular, one observes the increasing prominence of efforts to provide official religious endorsement for the conscientious objector's refusal to participate in the military.[35]

Surprising convergences emerge between these retrieved and re-centered religious precepts and the philosophy underlying third-generation rights. One striking area of agreement is the felt need to recover the concept of individual duties that has been neglected in human rights thinking. Jason Morgan-Foster argues that, while all rights impose duties on individual human beings, third-generation rights move beyond the primary focus of the State guaranteeing rights to an individual and demand in a greater "element of individual duty." For example, individuals *should* have obligations placed upon them for the right to peace, inasmuch as they seek to enjoy that right themselves.[36]

Morgan-Foster, among others, sees links between collective rights and the Islamic conception of a just social order, which places great import on the individual's duty to the group. This is especially true, he notes, of the right to peace:

> The notion of peace is fundamental to Islamic law and religion. It is present in the salutation exchanged between Muslims at each meeting: *salaam alekom*, "peace be upon you." A peace greeting is repeated twice at the end of each of Muslims' five daily prayers. Indeed, the very word "Islam" shares its root with the word for "Peace" in Arabic, and peace is one of the ninety-nine attributes of *Allah*. There are over one hundred Quranic verses discussing the importance of peace. This ever-presence of Peace in Islam led Professor Mohammed Yessef to state: "The alpha and omega of Islam is peace."[37]

Indeed, Muslim scholars have developed an Islamic conception of the right to peace founded on three principles. The first of these is the obligation to seek mutual understanding—also articulated as coexistence or "international neighborliness with Islamic sources." Second is tolerance, the belief by Muslims that cultural differences are the will of Allah. Tolerance, like mutual understanding, emphasizes individual duties before rights are claimed. The third principle is the duty of individuals and states to honor obligations and keep vows—regardless of the weakness of enforcement mechanisms. In mutual understanding, tolerance, and the honoring of agreements, one finds not only grounds in Islamic law for the right to peace, but elements that can offer important lessons to international human rights law as a whole.[38]

Similar excavations of religious traditions for the purpose of prioritizing the imperative of peace as an active religious duty are ongoing in Christianity, Hinduism, Judaism, and Buddhism, among other religions.[39] These retrieved theological principles and ethical injunctions justify and inform a broad array of peacebuilding roles and activities being performed by religious actors operating in conflict settings at the local, national, and international level. David Steele groups these roles into four types of conflict transformation activities: *observation and witness* (e.g., fact-finding, monitoring of cease-fires, accompaniment of victims), *education and formation* (e.g., conflict resolution training, peace and justice education), *advocacy and empowerment* (e.g., mass protests, public policy reform efforts, programs linking peacebuilding and development), and *conciliation and mediation* (e.g., participation in truth and reconciliation commissions, facilitating peace processes, interfaith dialogues).[40]

Peacebuilding, which encompasses conflict prevention, conflict resolution, and post-violence social reconstruction, operates according to a long-term time horizon. Religions, accustomed to thinking and enacting mission in larger blocs of time, brings distinctive and essential resources to this sustained activity. Ritual and symbol, sacred music and art create spaces for healing and sustained cross-cultural dialogue, for example.[41] Prophecy—the withering critique of governmental and religious corruption, inequality, repression, and other moral failures—is a religious specialty that is particularly relevant to the task of opposing the hegemonic state and its violations of human rights. In other settings, where religious institutions are the strongest alternatives to states incapable or unwilling to secure order and provide basic social services, religious leaders are learning how to play the role of peacebuilder as well as prophet.[42]

■ CONCLUSIONS

The American philosopher Carl Wellman believes that attaining the goals of third-order rights would "require the creation of a new international order, a set of global institutions, that impose joint obligations upon all states." Moreover, he questions the usefulness of the category of "peoples," because of the difficulty of identifying who constitutes a people and what acts can be said to be acts of a people as a whole. (The same caveat might apply, regarding how to define "acts of a religion as a whole.") Even if it were possible, therefore, to add rights of peoples to international human rights law, peoples (and by the same token, I would add, religions) could not serve as a useful legal fiction, because states hold the power in international affairs. Thus Wellman cautions against imposing legal obligations on non-state actors for the attainment of these rights on the grounds that such obligations would be unfeasible.[43]

Here, the possible analogy with religion diminishes in usefulness, however, in that religions do, indeed, make it their business to impose obligations on their adherents. In assessing the odds that religions will succeed in building and maintaining a religious obligation to peacebuilding that would validate and enforce a right to peace, the question is: Which religious actors are to prevail in a given society? Encouragingly, there is evidence that increasing numbers of religious actors across a range of societies are clamoring and working for democracy and human rights, which they identify as the appropriate political and civil expressions of orthodox belief and practice.[44] To the degree that believers of this persuasion carry the day within their religious communities and within civil society, the advocates of a right to peace may not have to wait for the creation of a new international order.

■ NOTES

1 On Christian support for religious freedom, see the chapters herein by Nicholas Wolterstorff, Steven D. Smith, and Michael Perry. See also the chapter on human rights in Judaism, by David Novak, and the chapter on human rights in Islam, by Abdullahi An-Na'im.

2 John Witte, Jr., "Law, Religion, and Human Rights," *Columbia Human Rights Law Review* 28 (Fall 1996): 3.

3 Stephen P. Marks, "Emerging Human Rights: A New Generation for the 1980s?" *Rutgers Law Review* 33 (Winter 1981): 446.

4 Carl Wellman, "Solidarity, the Individual, and Human Rights," *Human Rights Quarterly* 22 (August, 2000): 639.

5 See further the chapter by Ingvill Plesner, herein.

6 James Avery Joyce, "Is There a Right to Peace?" *Christian Century* 99(6) (February 24, 1982): 202.

7 Vasak, as cited in Marks, "Emerging Human Rights," 441.

8 Carl Wellman writes that they are necessary precisely because they show the need for such mutual cooperation, because they stress the human need for social solidarity in order to flourish, and because they can help respond to worldwide threats to human rights that occur because of the new levels of global interdependence. Wellman, "Solidarity, the Individual, and Human Rights," 642.

9 Ibid., 644. See further the chapters by Ronald Niezen, Natan Lerner, and Willis Jenkins, herein.

10 United Nations General Assembly, Declaration on the Right of Peoples to Peace, G.A. res. 39/11, Annex, 39 U.N. GAOR Supp. (No. 51) at 22, U.N. Doc. A/39/51 (1984)

(hereinafter "Declaration on the Right of Peoples to Peace"). Jason Morgan-Foster, "Third Generation Rights: What Islamic Law Can Teach the International Human Rights Movement," *Yale Human Rights and Development Law Journal* 8 (2005): 87 cites the 1978 UN General Assembly Declaration on the Preparation of Societies for Life in Peace as the first codification of the right to peace as an individual and collective right. However, the phrasing of that codification is not as precise and firm as the 1984 Declaration on the Right of Peoples to Peace.

11 Declaration on the Right of Peoples to Peace.

12 Ibid.

13 Luarca Declaration on the Human Right to Peace, Asturias, Spain (October 30, 2006), 137 accessible at: http://www.nodo50.org/csca/agenda09/misc/ pdf/DerechoHumanoPazingles.pdf.

14 Office of the United Nations High Commissioner for Human Rights, "Report of the Office of the High Commissioner on the outcome of the expert workshop on the right of peoples to peace," U.N. Doc. A/HRC/14.38 (2010), 6, 15.

15 Ibid., 4–5.

16 Ibid., 11–12.

17 Mario Yutzis, former Chairperson of the Committee on the Elimination of Racial Discrimination, recently outlined some directions in which these developments could move. First, the right to peace is closely linked to and strengthens the right to life, both for peoples and individuals, and could therefore be argued to be a human right. Second, the right to peace entails the recognition of the oneness of humankind and works against any arguments that would divide groups of people or declare the superiority of one over the other. Third, the right to peace serves as a valuable resource in combating violence that impedes the free exercise of other human rights. Fourth, human rights instruments show the collective and individual dimensions of the right to peace, giving it greater credence. Fifth, this individual dimension was assessed through the Charter of the United Nations, the Universal Declaration of Human Rights (UDHR), the International Covenant on Economic, Social, and Cultural Rights (ICESCR), and the International Covenant on Civil and Political Rights (ICCPR). Carl Aage Nørgaard, a former member of the European Commission of Human Rights, adds that the right to peace—and other third-generation rights—should be recognized because doing so will strengthen and promote the first- and second-generation rights that depend on it. See Joyce, "Is There a Right to Peace?," 202.

Others view the right to peace less favorably. If, as Michael Ignatieff says, the purpose of rights language is to protect and enhance individual agency, critics of the right to peace and of third-generation rights in general fear that advocating and legislating such rights will only diminish first- and second-generation rights. Michael Ignatieff, *Human Rights as Politics and Idolatry* (Princeton: Princeton University Press, 2001), 18.

18 Paul Brass, *The Production of Hindu-Muslim Violence in Contemporary India* (Seattle: University of Washington Press, 2003), 387.

19 The BJP is the Bharatiya Janata Party (*Indian People's Party*), a major political party in India founded in 1980 and associated with Hindu nationalism and the notion of Hindutva ("Hindu-ness") by which all of India's religiously plural peoples are to be defined politically. The BJP, in alliance with several other parties, was in power from 1998 to 2004, with Atal Bihari Vajpayee as the Prime Minister and Lal Krishna Advani as his deputy. See further the chapter by Werner Menksi, herein.

20 Human Rights Watch, "*We Have No Orders To Save You*": *State Participation and Complicity in Communal Violence in Gujarat* (New York: Human Rights Watch Report, Vol. 14, No. 3(C), April 30, 2002), 4. The complicity of the State in the Gujarat violence was first claimed on April 3, 2002 in a preliminary report released by India's National Human Rights

Commission (NHRC) http://nhrc.nic.in/Gujarat.htm#no3/002E (accessed February 2005). For an example of critiques of the HRW Report, see Arvin Bahl, "Politics By Other Means: An Analysis of Human Rights Watch Report on Gujarat," in *Gujarat After Godhra: Real Violence, Selective Outrage*, eds. Ramesh N. Rao and Koenraad Elst (New Delhi: Har-Anand Publications Pvt Ltd, 2003), 172–200.

21 See A. Rashied Omar, "The Gujarat Massacre," unpublished paper, 2009. Omar notes that more than 60 national and international agencies that investigated the 2002 Gujarat violence concluded that officials of the Gujarat state were complicit. See, for example, Syeeda Hameeda, et al., *How has the Gujarat massacre Affected Minority? The Survivors Speak. Fact-finding by a Women's Panel* (Ahmedabad: Citizens Initiative, 2002); Kamal Mitri Shenoy, et al., *Gujarat Carnage*, 2002: An Independent Fact-Finding Mission: http://www.onlinevolunteers.org/Gujarat/reports/pudr/ (accessed February 2005). See also Brass, *The Production of Hindu-Muslim Violence in Contemporary India*, and Peter VanderVeer, "Tradition and Violence in South Asia," *Peace Colloquy* 4 (Fall 2003): 18–19. Investigative reports conclude that they confirm the charge that the BJP government of the state of Gujarat and its supporting Hindu religious network, the *Sang Parivar,* were complicit in the violence directed against Muslims in 2002. In January 2005, Amnesty International released their investigative report, which concluded that ". . . in relation to the violence in Gujarat in 2002, India has not fulfilled its obligations to protect fundamental rights guaranteed in its constitution and in international treaties to which it is a party. Reports received from human rights groups in India indicate that the Government of Gujarat may have been complicit in at least part of the abuses perpetrated in Gujarat in 2002. There is evidence of connivance of authorities in the preparation and execution of some of the attacks and also in the way the right to legal redress of women victims of sexual violence has been frustrated at every level. Furthermore, the Gujarat state has failed to meet their international obligations to bring to justice perpetrators of crimes against humanity." Amnesty International, "India Justice, the victim—Gujarat state fails to protect women from violence" (2005). http://web.amnesty.org/library/index/engasa200012005.

22 R. Scott Appleby, *The Ambivalence of the Sacred: Religion, Violence and Reconciliation* (Lanham, MD: Rowman & Littlefield, 2000), 69, 77–78.

23 Ibid., 81–91.

24 Said Amir Arjomand. "Shi'ite Jurisprudence and Constitution Making in Iran," in *Fundamentalisms and the State: Remaking Polities, Economies and Militance,* eds. Martin E. Marty and R. Scott Appleby (Chicago: University of Chicago Press, 1993), 90–95.

25 Rafiuddin Ahmed, "Redefining Muslim Identity in South Asia: The Transformation of the Jama'at-i-Islami," in *Accounting for Fundamentalisms: The Dynamic Character of Movements,* eds, Martin E. Marty and R. Scott Appleby (Chicago: University of Chicago Press, 1994), 670.

26 Emily Wax and Rama Lakshmi, "Indian Official Points to Pakistan," *The Washington Post*, December 6, 2008; "Pakistan role in Mumbai attacks," *BBC News*, September 30, 2006.

27 For an overview, see Gideon Aran, "Jewish Zionist Fundamentalism: The Bloc of the Faithful in Israel (Gush Emunim)" and Samuel C. Heilman and Menachem Friedman, "Religious Fundamentalism and Religious Jews: The Case of the Haredim," in *Fundamentalisms Observed,* ed. Martin E. Marty and R. Scott Appleby (Chicago: University of Chicago Press, 1991); .

28 See, *inter alia*, Ehud Sprinzak, *The Ascendance of Israel's Radical Right* (New York: Oxford University Press, 1991), David Landau, *Piety and Power: The World of Jewish Fundamentalism* (New York: Hill and Wang, 1993), and Gershom Gorenberg, *The End of Days: Fundamentalism and the Struggle for the Temple Mount* (New York : The Free Press, 2000).

29 Eliezer Don-Yehiya, "The Book and the Sword: The Nationalist Yeshivot and Political Radicalism in Israel," in *Accounting for Fundamentalisms*, 296.

30 James Manor, "Organizational Weakness and the Rise of Sinhalese Buddhist Extremism," in *Accounting for Fundamentalisms* , 771.

31 Ibid., 770.

32 See Michael A. Sells, *The Bridge Betrayed: Religion and Genocide in Bosnia* (Berkeley, CA: University of California, 1996).

33 Ashutosh Varshney, "Understanding Gujarat Violence in Contemporary Conflicts," http://conconflicts.ssrc.org/gujarat/varshney/ (accessed December 2004).

34 Gerard F. Powers, "Religion and Peacebuilding," in Daniel Philpott and Gerard F. Powers, eds., *Strategies of Peace: Transforming Conflict in a Violent World* (New York : Oxford University Press, 2010), 327. David Hollenbach, SJ, contends that religious grounding of human rights will strengthen endorsement of the concept of human rights in cultures around the world, particularly non-Western ones. See David Hollenbach, SJ, *The Global Face of Public Faith: Politics, Human Rights, and Christian Ethics* (Washington, D.C.: Georgetown University Press, 2003), 239.

35 See, *inter alia*, Daniel L. Buttry, *Christian Peacemaking: From Heritage to Hope* (Valley Forge, PA: Judson Press, 1994); Lisa Sowle Cahill, *Love Your Enemies: Discipleship, Pacifism, and Just War Theory* (Minneapolis: Fortress Press, 1994); Terry Nardin, ed., *The Ethics of War and Peace: Religious and Secular Perspectives* (Princeton: Princeton University Press, 1996); David R. Smock, *Religious Perspectives on War: Christian, Muslim, and Jewish Attitudes Toward Force,* rev. ed. (Washington, DC: United States Institute of Peace Press, 2002).

36 He writes: "The notion of individual duty in third-generation rights is incumbent not just on those in a position to help the right-holder realize the right, but also on the very individual that holds the right." For example, an individual's second-generation right to education is associated with a duty incumbent upon others in the society to become teachers. Compare this to the individual duty component of the third-generation right to a healthy environment. In that case, an individual's right to a healthy environment correlates to a state duty to protect the environment, the individual duty of others to protect the environment, and an individual duty *of the right-holder herself* to protect the environment. Morgan-Foster, 'Third Generation Rights,' 87–88.

37 Ibid., 95.

38 Ibid., 97–98. In this section, I have chosen not to address the thornier questions of *jihad*, which Morgan-Foster takes up, and *dhimmitude*, which he does not.

39 Consult the survey in Appleby, *The Ambivalence of the Sacred*, 245–80.

40 David Steele, "An Introductory Overview of Faith-Based Peacebuilding," in *Pursuing Just Peace: An Overview and Case Studies for Faith-Based Peacebuilders*, eds., Mark Rogers, Tom Bamat, and Julie Ideh (Baltimore: Catholic Relief Services, 2008), 22–32.

41 See Lisa Schirch, *Ritual and Symbol in Peacebuilding* (Bloomfield, CT: Kumarian Press, 2005).

42 The Catholic Peacebuilding Network, an alliance of Roman Catholic universities, Catholic Relief Services, Maryknoll, and other Catholic peace and justice agencies, has provided training in peacebuilding advocacy for Catholic bishops, priests, religious and laity in Africa, Asia, and Latin America. See Robert J. Schreiter, R. Scott Appleby and Gerard F. Powers, eds., *Peacebuilding: Catholic Theology, Ethics and Praxis* (Maryknoll, NY: Orbis Books, 2010).

43 Wellman, "Solidarity, the Individual, and Human Rights," 651–56.

44 See the essays in Thomas Banchoff, ed., *Religious Pluralism, Globalization and World Politics* (New York: Oxford University Press, 2008) and in *Democracy and the New Religious Pluralism*, ed. Thomas Banchoff (New York: Oxford University Press, 2007).

RECOMMENDED READING

Abu-Nimer, Mohammed. *Nonviolence and Peace Building in Islam: Theory and Practice* (Gainesville, FL: University Press of Florida, 2003)

Appleby, R. Scott. *The Ambivalence of the Sacred: Religion, Violence and Reconciliation* (Lanham, MD: Rowman & Littlefield, 2000)

Banchoff, Thomas, ed., *Religious Pluralism: Globalization, and World Politics* (New York: Oxford University Press, 2008)

______, ed., *Democracy and the New Religious Pluralism* (New York and Oxford: Oxford University Press, 2007)

Brass, Paul. *The Production of Hindu-Muslim Violence in Contemporary India* (Seattle: University of Washington Press, 2003)

Coward, Harold and Gordon S. Smith, eds. *Religion and Peacebuilding* (Albany: State University of New York Press, 2004)

Hollenbach, SJ, David. *The Global Face of Public Faith: Politics, Human Rights, and Christian Ethics* (Washington, DC: Georgetown University Press, 2003)

Little, David, ed., with the Tanenbaum Center for Interreligious Understanding. *Peacemakers in Action: Profiles of Religions in Conflict Resolution* (New York: Cambridge University Press, 2007)

Marty, Martin E. and R. Scott Appleby, eds., *Fundamentalisms and the State: Remaking Polities, Economies, and Militance* (Chicago: University of Chicago Press, 1993)

Nardin, Terry, ed., *The Ethics of War and Peace: Religious and Secular Perspectives* (Princeton: Princeton University Press, 1996)

Philpott, Daniel, ed., *The Politics of Past Evil: Religion, Reconciliation, and the Dilemmas of Transitional Justice.* Kroc Institute Series on Religion, Conflict and Peace Building. (Notre Dame, IN: University of Notre Dame Press, 2006)

Philpott, Daniel and Gerard F. Powers, eds., *Strategies of Peace: Transforming Conflict in a Violent World* (New York: Oxford University Press, 2010)

Rogers, Mark, Tom Bamat, and, Julie Ideh, eds., *Pursuing Just Peace: An Overview and Case Studies for Faith-Based Peacebuilders* (Baltimore: Catholic Relief Services, 2008)

Schreiter, Robert J., R. Scott Appleby, and, Gerard F. Powers, eds., *Peacebuilding: Catholic Theology, Ethics and Praxis* (Maryknoll, NY: Orbis, 2010)

Sells, Michael A. *The Bridge Betrayed: Religion and Genocide in Bosnia* (Berkeley, CA: University of California, 1996)

Smock, David R. *Religious Perspectives on War: Christian, Muslim, and Jewish Attitudes Toward Force.* rev. ed. (Washington, DC: United States Institute of Peace Press, 2002)

22 Patterns of Religion State Relations

W. COLE DURHAM, JR.

The configurations of religion-state relations across the world's legal systems are remarkably diverse, reflecting differences of history, philosophy, religious demography, culture, constitutional and political systems, and numerous other factors. Moreover, religion-state relations in every country are in constant flux. Sometimes these relationships change dramatically, as in the aftermath of the collapse of Soviet communism. More frequently, they undergo steady, minor adjustments as a result of legislation or case law affecting countless aspects of religious life. Yet broad patterns or types of relationships are discernible, and the nature of these relationships can have significant implications for more general human rights implementation.[1] This chapter draws on a typology developed in earlier work,[2] but seeks to expand and deepen comparative analysis of the religion-state relationships involved.

A COMPARATIVE FRAMEWORK FOR CONCEPTUALIZING

The nature of religion-state relations in a particular society may be assessed in terms of two continua: one involving the extent to which state action (or inaction) results in interference with religious belief and conduct (the religious freedom continuum), and another involving the extent to which governmental institutions are identified with (or separated from) religious institutions and beliefs (the identification continuum). The religious freedom continuum extends from zero to full religious freedom; the identification continuum extends from full identification of religion and state (positive identification), through various modes of separation, and continuing on to active persecution of religion (negative identification). All states oscillate within some range on each of the two continua).

Initially, there is a tendency to assume there is a straight line inverse correlation between the two continua. That is, as identification of religion and state goes up, religious liberty goes down. While this correlation appears to hold in some cases (e.g., United States and France), there are many cases where it clearly does not. Norway, Finland, and the United Kingdom have high identification with their established churches, and yet have high degrees of religious freedom, whereas countries such as Soviet Russia had low identification with religion matched with low degrees of religious freedom. The seeming lack of correlation is puzzling, because a primary aim of constitutional provisions in this sphere is to assure institutional arrangements that will optimize the place of religion in society. But if there is no apparent linkage between degree of identification and levels of religious freedom, it is difficult to know what optimal arrangements are likely to be. The answer to this seeming paradox lies in conceptualizing the identification continuum as a loop, with the ends of the continuum (strong positive and negative identification) correlating with low freedom of religion and the middle range of the continuum correlating with high religious freedom, as shown in the Figure 22.1:[3]

This rough schematization brings out several points. First, lack of religious freedom correlates with a high degree of *either* positive *or* negative identification of the state with religion. On reflection, this should come as no surprise. It is precisely when a state identifies strongly with a particular religious (or anti-religious) ideology that persecution of other (or all) religions is most likely. Less obvious is the fact that strong identification often reduces the freedom even of the predominant religion, since strong identification is likely to result in capture of that religion by the state. This was a major reason why the disestablishment of the Swedish state church in 2000 was supported by the state church itself.[4]

Another less obvious reality suggested by the diagram is that changes in political regimes where positive or negative identification is high may switch back and forth between extreme positions, skipping more moderate intermediate positions. For example, the history of church-state experience in Spain over the past two centuries reflects radical shifts back and forth from regimes strongly supportive of an established church to secularist, anti-clerical regimes.[5] Note that the loop opens up as states move from identification with particular religions or worldviews to more "open" societies. Finally, the schematization also shows that one cannot assume that the more rigorously one separates religion and state, the more religious liberty will be enhanced. At some point, moving toward greater separation (increasingly negative identification) switches back toward hostility and ultimately persecution.

Focusing now on the identification continuum, it is possible to identify a number of recurring types of religion-state relationships, as depicted by the diagram that follows and as more fully elaborated in the next section. Note that these are "ideal types" that are necessarily abstractions, and actual state systems are likely to differ. These types are framed with an eye to the nature of the relationship of the state to religious communities. Religious communities may have their own differing internal view of their actual and ideal relationship to the State.

The diagram in Figure 22.2 depicts two bands of pattern types. The outer band focuses on key structural features of the various types of religion-state relationships: theocratic states, established religions, religious status systems, and so forth. The inner band focuses on the posture or attitude of the state toward religion. The continuum as a whole marks out typical pathways of historical development, moving from positive identification of the state and religion to progressively more secular forms of the State.

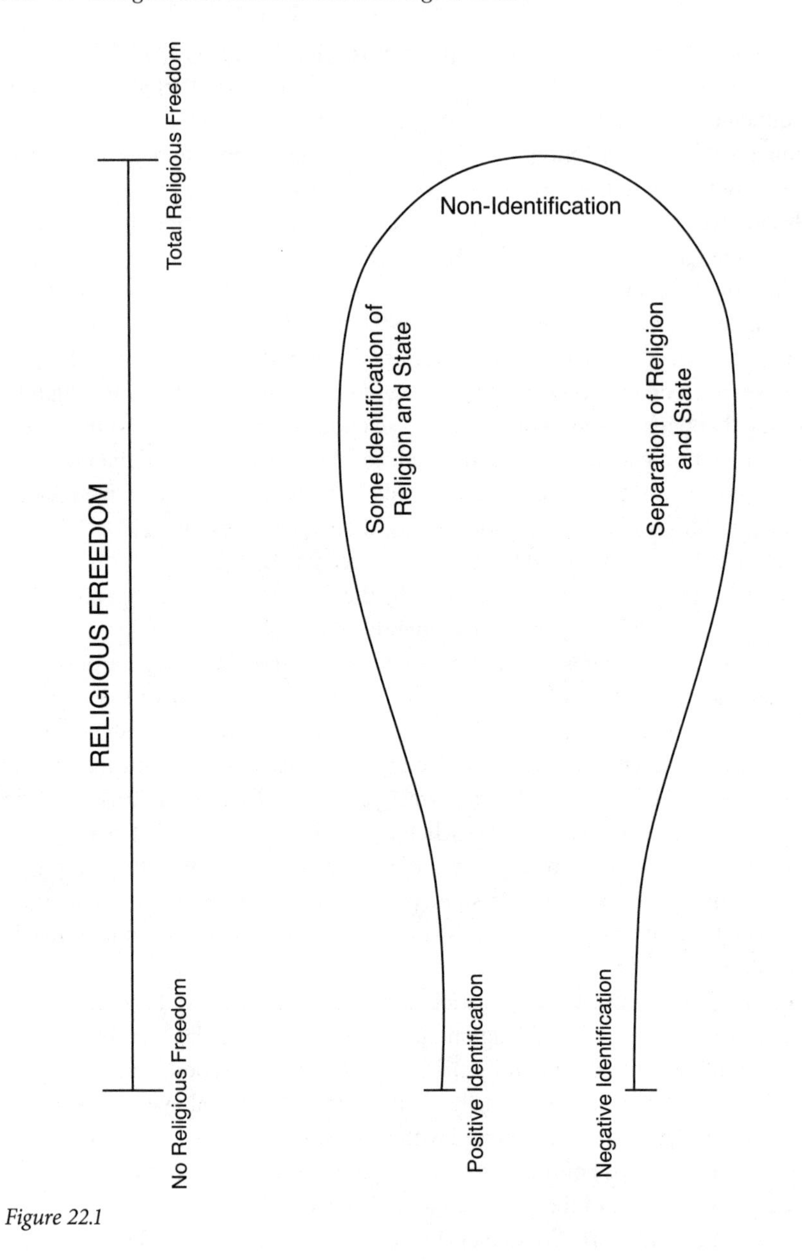
RELIGIOUS FREEDOM
Total Religious Freedom
No Religious Freedom
Non-Identification
Some Identification of Religion and State
Separation of Religion and State
Positive Identification
Negative Identification

Figure 22.1

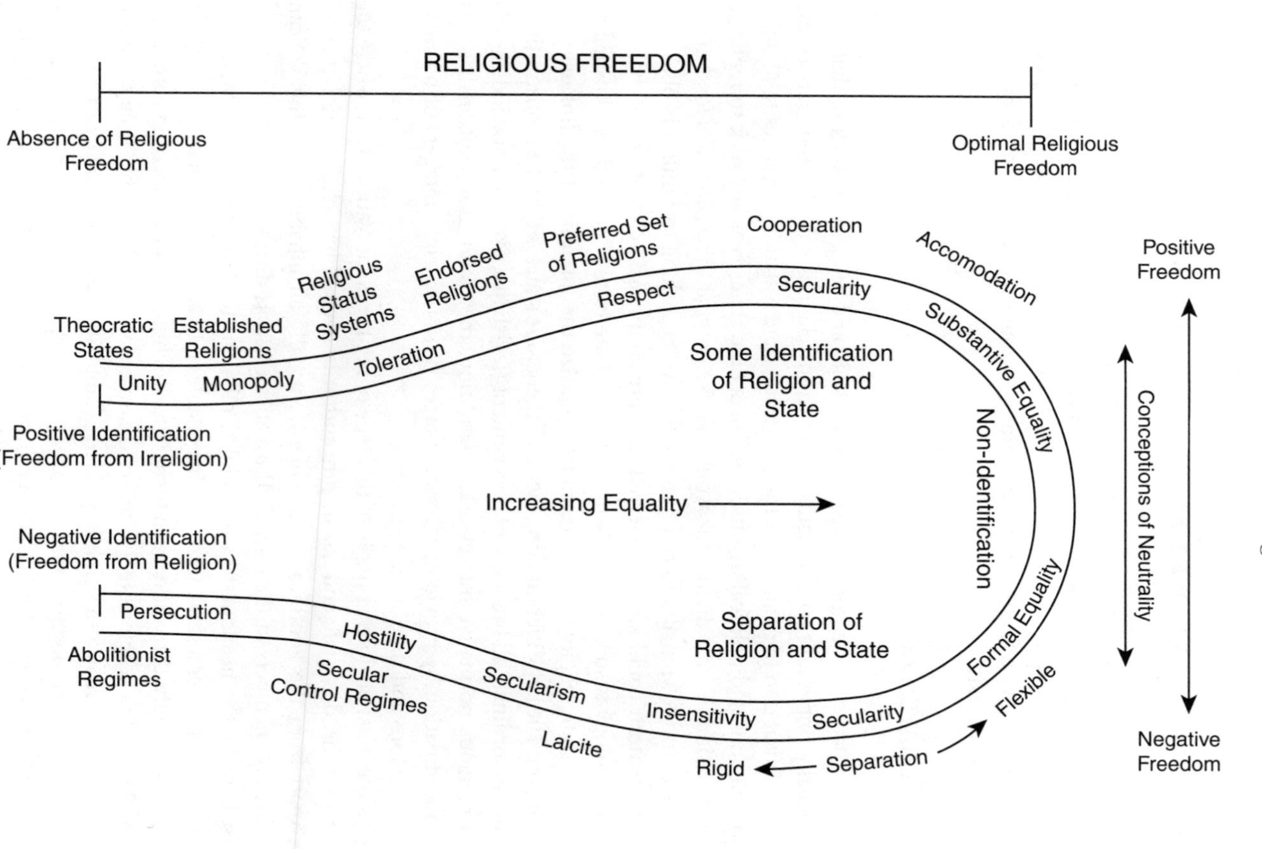
RELIGIOUS FREEDOM
Absence of Religious Freedom
Optimal Religious Freedom
Theocratic States
Established Religions
Religious Status Systems
Endorsed Religions
Preferred Set of Religions
Cooperation
Accomodation
Positive Freedom
Unity
Monopoly
Toleration
Respect
Secularity
Substantive Equality
Some Identification of Religion and State
Non-Identification
Conceptions of Neutrality
Positive Identification (Freedom from Irreligion)
Increasing Equality
Negative Identification (Freedom from Religion)
Persecution
Hostility
Secularism
Insensitivity
Secularity
Formal Equality
Separation of Religion and State
Abolitionist Regimes
Secular Control Regimes
Laicite
Rigid
Separation
Flexible
Negative Freedom

Figure 22.2

■ TYPES OF RELIGION-STATE STRUCTURES

With the foregoing analytic framework in mind, I now turn to a description of the various types of religion-state systems. Beginning at the positive end of the identification continuum, I describe the features of the key structural types. For each type, I give a few representative examples, but space constraints forbid going into much detail.[6]

Theocratic States

In this pattern type, the linkage between state and religion is so close that it is virtually impossible to distinguish state from religious rule. Indeed, part of the appeal (but also the danger) of the theocratic state is that it postulates total unity of religious and political institutions. Theocratic states typically seek to replicate their vision of what divine rule would be like or what this vision calls for, but are subject to the vicissitudes of human fallibility in seeking to fulfill this objective. This pattern could also be referred to more simply as "religious state," but that terminology is somewhat difficult to differentiate from states with established or official state religions, and does not emphasize the intensity of the linkage with religion. The key differentiating factor of theocratic states is that they constitutionally subordinate all branches of government (legislative, executive and judicial) to a religious normative framework. In addition, they tend to institutionalize this subordination by providing strong linkages (if not outright merger) of religious institutions and state bodies.

The most obvious example of this type of regime is the Vatican City, where the Pope is head of state and has *de jure* authority over all branches of state power.[7] Apart from the Pontifical Swiss Guard, virtually all inhabitants of the Vatican City are members of the clergy.[8] The Vatican City is distinctive, however, in that it is really the headquarters of a global religion that happens to be vested with sovereignty over a small territory that enables it to act as nation state.

Historically, there have been theocratic or religious states associated with many of the world's religions (e.g., the first Islamic state established by Mohammed in Medina, the first four "rightly guided" Caliphates (632–661), many of the later Caliphates (although in many of these, religion was often subordinate to state institutions), early Hindu and Buddhist empires, and possibly Aztec and Inca regimes).[9] Nepal and Bhutan remained Hindu and Buddhist states until 2006[10] and 2008,[11] respectively. Because Christianity emerged in the context of the Roman Empire, there has always been a sense that Christianity exists within the context of a separable if not separate state, and it is better to think of Christian states as established or state religions than as religious states.

The primary current examples of theocratic or religious states are found in the Muslim world. Countries that consider themselves to be Islamic states according to their constitutions or basic laws include Afghanistan, Bahrain, Brunei Darussalam, Iran, Maldives, Mauritania, Oman, Pakistan, Saudi Arabia, and Yemen.[12] In addition to constitutional affirmation of their status as Islamic states, these countries fit in the theocratic category because they affirm in various ways that the State is subordinate to Islamic law,[13] and because they also provide for an array of provisions giving religious leaders institutional supervision authority to assure compliance with Islamic law.[14] Some go further and entrench the religious character of the State by giving it constitutionally irrevocable status.[15] What is significant about this type of regime is that the State itself is subordinated to a particular religious system, and that this system is entitled to monopolize governance.

Established Religions

As indicated above, this category could be interpreted broadly (as the U.S. establishment clause does) to cover virtually the entire range of types that include positive identification. By "established religions" here, however, I mean systems in which there is an official state religion. As a general matter, theocratic states have an official state religion as well. The difference is that "established religions" remain in some sense distinct from and subordinate to the state, or stated differently, the State is not pervasively subordinated to the prevailing religion. In its ideal form, at least according to its Eastern Orthodox advocates, this type orchestrates a "symphony" of harmony between religion and the State. There is a broad range of possible "established religions," stretching from systems in which the state religion is granted a strictly enforced monopoly in religious affairs to much more tolerant regimes such as those one finds in contemporary England, Norway, and Finland. Roman Catholicism has in the past been the state religion of a number countries where it was predominant—most notably Spain and Italy and various Latin American countries. Evangelical Lutheranism remains the state church in Norway, Denmark, and Iceland,[16] and Sweden only recently disestablished its state Church (in 2000). Various branches of Eastern Orthodoxy constitute the established churches of Armenia and Greece.[17]

Typically, though not always, established religions are declared to be the state religion in their constitutions. In the Muslim world, this is the case with respect to Algeria, Bangladesh, Djibouti, Egypt, Iraq, Jordan, Kuwait, Libya, Malaysia, Maldives, Morocco, Qatar, Tunisia, and the United Arab Emirates.[18] For the most part, a religion or denomination is established for an entire country. But there are exceptions. Thus, in the United Kingdom, England and Scotland have established Anglicanism and Presbyterianism, respectively; in Switzerland, religion-state systems vary by canton, with some having established or prefer entially treated churches, while two (Geneva and Neuchatel) have opted for separation.[19]

Religious Status Systems

In a number of countries, often reflecting practice dating back to the millet system of the Ottoman Empire, the State recognizes the jurisdiction of a number of religious systems, typically in areas dealing with family law and inheritance. The legal system that applies typical depends on the religion of the individual. The European Court of Human Rights has held that such "plural legal systems" cannot be squared with the European Convention of Human Rights.[20] But such systems clearly exist, including those in Israel, India, Lebanon, and a number of Muslim countries.[21] One of the virtues of these systems is that they respect the autonomy of different religious communities and their right to administer their own religious law. This opens risks that such systems may be exercised in ways that limit exit rights of those who wish to leave the community, or to interpret its norms in distinctive ways. There is also a risk that dominant groups can exploit such autonomy to justify second-class status for minorities (e.g., *dhimmi*-tude[22]), and may use it to construct ghettos within the larger society.

In many countries where religious status systems persist, the "plural" or "parallel" legal system feature is overshadowed by other features of the system (e.g., the commitment to secularism in India[23]). But as a matter of theory and historical practice, they represent a distinct and notable advance in the direction of greater religious tolerance. While marking an advance in their day, however, such systems typically fail to provide full equality of treatment when assessed from the perspective of contemporary human rights law.

Endorsed Religions

This category includes systems that fall short of formally affirming that one particular religion is the official or state religion, but acknowledge that a particular religion has a special place in the country's history and traditions. This is now quite typical in countries with a Roman Catholic heritage, perhaps as a result of shifts linked to Vatican II. In a similar vein, Thailand, and Sri Lanka endorse Buddhism.[24] Characteristically, the religion in this type of regime is specially acknowledged, but there are also other provisions that protect the religious freedom rights of other religions. The endorsement or acknowledgement of a special historical and cultural role can take different forms ranging from financial to mere symbolic support. It may take the form of a general acknowledgement of religious heritage (e.g., Christian heritage in Poland[25] and Fiji[26]; Eastern Orthodoxy in Georgia[27] and Russia[28]); a recognition of the role of a particular religion in nation's formation (e.g., Timor-Leste[29] and Paraguay[30]); the recognition of a predominant religion[31]; or recognition of religious phenomena, such as the existence of God, specific characteristics of deity, creationism, God's omnipotence, omniscience and omnipresence, trinitarianism, monotheism, reference to religious founders, or other notions of sanctity.[32] Acknowledgement of religion can also appear in national mottos, on flags, and in other symbolic settings.[33] Sometimes endorsement is strictly limited to recognizing the important role a religion has played in a country's history and culture. In other cases, it operates as a thinly disguised method of preserving the prerogatives of establishment and channeling significant aid to the favored religions.

Preferred Sets of Religions

This can be a variation of other forms of positive identification, except that multiple religions are favored. Finland, for example, endorses both the Evangelical Lutheran Church of Finland and the Orthodox Church of Finland.[34] In an earlier day, one could have seen these as two established churches, but changes in recent years have changed the legal situation so these are more akin to two endorsed churches. There has been a tendency in a number of countries in recent years to favor "traditional religions" (e.g., Russia, Kazakhstan, Lithuania, and Romania).[35] Many European countries have multi-tier religion-state structures, the upper tier of which may in fact constitute a preferred set of religions.[36]

Cooperationist Regimes

The next category of regimes is distinguished by the fact that it takes a neutral but positive and "cooperative" stance toward religions in society. Germany is perhaps the prototypical example, but in fact most European systems at this point are cooperationist. Typical in such schemes is substantial cooperation in church finance, religious education, various humanitarian services, and so forth,[37] though at least in theory such aid is provided on a non-discriminatory basis (i.e., where differences in support are justified by objective differences among religions). Particularly where Roman Catholicism is strong, there tend to be agreements between major denominations and the State that among other things spell out the basis for such cooperation. A country's agreement with the Roman Catholic Church typically takes the form of a concordat with the Holy See, which is regarded as having the status of a treaty. Since other religious communities do not have a sovereign state to call their own, their agreements do not have the same status under international law. But states generally treat them as having the same characteristic of being amendable only with the consent of both parties. Despite the theory that cooperationist regimes remain neutral among religions, it is easy to slip from cooperation to patterns of state preference, with a tendency to favor the major religions in a country.

Accommodationist Regimes

Accommodationism might be thought of as cooperation without any direct financial subsidies. Accommodation can be seen both in allowing certain types of indirect financial and other support for different religions and in protecting the freedom to act in accordance with distinctive religious beliefs. With respect to support, accommodationist arrangements allow indirect support of religion in the form of tax exemption and tax deduction schemes. These allow support to be steered to religious organizations by voluntary choice, while minimizing state intrusion in religious affairs. Accommodationist regimes protect freedom by allowing exemptions from general state laws or policies under appropriate circumstances, or perhaps more accurately, by not allowing statutes to carve out exceptions to constitutional and human rights guarantees of freedom of religion or belief. Accommodation thus can take the form of respecting conscientious objection, whether to military service, to participation in abortion or other morally controversial medical procedures, or to particular educational policies that a religious group or individual may find to be objectionable. It can take symbolic forms, such as allowing moments of silence during a school day, which accommodates both the right to pray and not to pray. Standards of judicial review that call for strict scrutiny of state interference with manifestations of religious belief (e.g., compelling state interest/least restrictive alternative requirements in the United States or rigorous proportionality analysis in Europe)[38] promote accommodation of religion. In the United States, the Supreme Court has held that such rigorous review is not constitutionally mandated when neutral and general laws are under review, but half the States insist on strict scrutiny standards as a matter of state law and federal legislation governing many sectors subject to federal legislation also insists on strict scrutiny standards in broad areas of social life.[39] The extent to which European standards insist on comparable strict scrutiny standards in applying proportionality analysis is still evolving.[40]

Separation

Parallel to "establishment," the idea of separation can be used to cover a wide and diverse range of regimes that span the bottom half of the loop diagram. Depending on precisely how one counts, approximately one-third of the nations on earth have some type of separationist regime.[41] Some strands in the separationist tradition view separation primarily as a method for protecting religion from the State[42]; others see the "wall of separation" as a method of protecting the state and society from excessive religious power[43]; many, of course, see it as providing protections in both directions. At the "benign neutrality" end, separation differs relatively little from accommodation, except that in insists on a more rigorous separation of religious and state institutions, and is more categorical in disallowing state aid or support to religion. Similarly, it is more strict in disallowing public display of religious symbols that can be construed to endorse religion. Separationism may also call for stricter segregation of religious or secular roles, as for instance by not allowing clergy to hold public office or by proscribing religious political parties. Indeed, the mere reliance on religious premises in public argument may be deemed inconsistent with separationist principles.

Less benign forms of separationism make stronger attempts to cordon off religion from public life. Exemptions to accommodate religious difference are rejected as signs of inappropriate state favoritism of religion. In this regard, formal equality takes precedence over substantive equality; religious differences are not viewed as an appropriate justification for differential treatment. Inadvertent insensitivity to religious needs can easily result. Regulations initially formulated without religious animus can have the incidental effect of imposing unnecessary or disproportionately heavy burdens on religious groups. The functional result is that secularist outlooks may be privileged in a way that is the flip side of the subtle or not-so-subtle privileging of dominant groups in cooperationist regimes.

A major issue for separationist regimes is the extent to which religion is allowed a role in the public sphere. From an accommodationist perspective, compulsory exclusion of religion from public life constitutes a form of discrimination. From a more rigorously separationist perspective, in contrast, separation treats all religions equally by relegating them all to the private sphere. Of course, this overlooks the fact that secular outlooks are not constrained in the same way. One of the difficulties has to do with background shifts in the pervasiveness of the State. If religion is limited to the private sphere, and then the public sphere expands to fill a substantially larger share of total social space, the space available for religion can shrink substantially. One form this can take is a tightening of the State monopoly on charitable, educational, social, and welfare services. Separation in its most objectionable guise demands that religion retreat from any domain that the State desires to occupy, but is untroubled by intrusive state regulation and intervention in religious affairs.

Laïcité

Laïcité is the specifically French model of separation,[44] and has been retained in the legal systems of many of France's former colonies. Thirty-four constitutions characterize the relationship of religion and the state in their respective systems not by proscribing establishment or by calling explicitly for separation, but by affirming that they are secular states.[45] For the most part, these countries can trace this constitutional feature either to French influence or experience in the former Soviet empire. While there are a broad range of interpretations of the notion of *laïcité*, it tends in general to generate systems that are at the rigid separationist end of separationism.

Secular Control Regimes

Prior to the end of the Cold War, a number of communist states pursued a course of militant atheism which was actively hostile to religion and which brought about the existence of state structures designed to control and minimize the influence of religion. A small number of states such as China, Cuba, Vietnam, and North Korea continue to assert such policies.[46] Separationist/*laïcist* policies can shade into this type of regime. For example, Turkish secularism has tended to maintain very tight control over religions in Turkey, although there are some signs that this control may be loosening, in part as a result of efforts to make Turkey a more attractive potential entrant into the European Union.[47]

A control regime shares some surface similarities with established and historically favored religions, except that these regimes make a secular ideology the official worldview of the State, and seek to repress dissenters from that view (i.e., religious believers). As in regimes with established religions, the fear is that other belief systems may create alternative sources of legitimacy which could undermine the State and weaken those currently in control of state power. The practical consequence, however, is that those not following the official line are subject to powerful controls, and even those following the official line may be captured and controlled by the State.

Abolitionist States

At the negative end of the identification continuum lie regimes with the overt goal of eliminating religion as a social factor. During earlier periods, a number of secular control regimes have manifested this extreme characteristic. Albania during the Soviet era is perhaps the foremost example of this approach. The Holocaust is the most horrendous example.

■ ATTITUDINAL TYPES

The focus thus far has been on the structural types listed in the "outer band" of the identification continuum. The inner band can be addressed more quickly. Each of these types depicts an attitude or orientation which on the one hand resonates with the corresponding structural form, and at the same time contains the seeds of that structure's transformation in the direction of adjacent structural types. The "inner band" attitude can also open up the possibility of seeing that another structural form is possible, feasible, and perhaps more desirable. Thus, toleration can lead to respect for different religious legal systems (religious status systems) or for (some) different religions altogether (allowance of a place for other belief-systems within endorsement regimes, or preference for several religions). Respect can lead to further transformation toward views in which the State comes to provide a neutral framework (secularity) in a number of possible ways, from supporting religions in general in a more or less equal way (cooperation) to achieving equality by allowing no aid to any religious group. This in turn can sharpen the sense that the public sphere of the State should be totally secular, so that religion is relegated to the private sector. But this in turn can lead to insensitivity to specific religious differences, and then to religion more generally. The secular outlook can become its own source of legitimacy in the form of secularism as an ideology, but that perspective risks hostility to other (religious) bases for legitimacy, and can lead to secular control regimes, persecution of religion in general, and in the ultimate case, to regimes seeking to abolish religion in order to achieve full freedom from religion.

Note that the evolutionary pathways are not unidirectional. At any given point on the continuum, there will be political pressures from religious groups to afford greater legal protection against actual or perceived threats to their position in society, and this will provide energy (and arguments) for moving back toward systems with higher positive identification. This can also be seen as a movement in the direction of freedom from excessive division or pluralism toward greater unity, or alternatively as freedom from irreligion. Argumentative viewpoints (*topoi*) invoking freedom and liberation can thus be invoked to move in either direction along the continuum, depending on what one wants freedom *from*. Freedom and equality arguments come into better balance toward the middle of the continuum (the right end of the loop diagram).

It is also worth noting that positions on opposite sides of the loop are to a large extent religious or secular mirror images of each other. However, despite this formal similarity, shifts in regime type that "jump across" the loop structure typically result from high degrees of polarization and entail significant wrenching of basic normative structures in society. Shifts that skip across multiple types or flip from one type to its secular (or religious) opposite appear more revolutionary than evolutionary. Thus, the shifts from the (established) *ancient regime* to the *laïque* republic in France or from Czarist to Leninist Russia (established Church to a secular control or abolitionist regime) were revolutionary. But equally, the shift in the opposite direction from the regime of the Shah to the Islamic Republic in Iran was also revolutionary.

One contrast deserving particular attention is that between secularity understood as a neutral framework within which a broad range of religious communities can build a common life and secularism as a specific ideological orientation. In a recent study reviewing religion-state systems in forty-five countries, this contrast emerged as one of the key issues facing many legal systems in resolving a variety of concrete policy issues.[48] As a recent Canadian study described the contrast, there is on the one hand a strict or rigid form of secularism associated with areligiousness that places neutrality and a religion-free public sphere ahead of freedom of conscience and religion. What I am terming secularity, on the other hand, corresponds to a more flexible and open secular condition that relaxes neutrality and privatization of religion in the interest of promoting "respect for religious and moral equality and freedom of conscience."[49] The placement of secularity on both the upper and lower sides of the identification continuum in the loop diagram, spanning cooperationist to separationist systems, is intended to suggest that secularity is more likely than secularism to lead to optimal protection of religious freedom, and this is true across a variety of highly respectable legal systems.

The structural and attitudinal "bands" should be thought of as being both independent and elastic, so that (within limits) they can be thought to "slip around" the continuum. The slippage recognizes two things: (1) different types or patterns may be optimal for different societies, both as a general matter and in terms of optimizing religious freedom for the particular society; and (2) different attitudinal types may line up with different structural types. The discourse in different societies reacts to different remembered problems and different social realities, so that the equilibrium reached after balancing opposed political vectors in the society may settle on different structural types.

Significantly, the loops are not infinitely elastic. It is difficult to imagine that religious status systems could be "pulled" around the identification continuum to a point that correlates with optimal religious freedom. The closer a particular regime type is toward either end of the identification continuum, the more closed it is to other belief systems and the more likely it is to interfere with the freedom of religion and to discriminate against those other systems. This inevitably results in greater tension with the modern human rights requirements.

Part of the point of emphasizing elasticity of the bands is that there is no automatic correlation between a particular configuration and a particular degree of religious freedom. Thus, the established churches of England and Scandinavia of today afford substantially greater religious freedom than their historical antecedents. The positioning of types along the identification continuum is intended to show a progression from theocratic to progressively more secular regimes. Similarly, depending on how the notion of separation is implemented, it can protect religious freedom to a high degree or can validate state action that is quite hostile to religion. While as a historical matter there has tended to be a rough correlation between these types and the degree of religious freedom corresponding legal systems achieve, much depends on how the particular type of religion-state structure is interpreted and implemented.

Although the elasticity notion is helpful in some respects, it is misleading in others. It ignores the fact that the various types may overlap in significant ways, and that the traits of some of the regime types are included in other regime types. For example, accommodationist regimes include positive features of other attitudinal types. They are tolerant, respectful, protective of substantive equality among differing religious groups, and constitute a form of secularity.

It is also important to stress that there is not only a continuum of various pattern types, but within each type there is a range of interpretations, and these may overlap with similar scope of other rights. This is particularly evident, for example, with respect to *laïcité* and separation. Both of these types can be interpreted in a range of ways moving from flexible to rigid, and in ways that at least partially overlap. Indeed, *laïcité* can be thought of as a form of separation, with French and Turkish models of *laïcité* marking progressively stricter versions of secularism. Similarly, the concept of "established religion" can cover a broad range of legal arrangements. From the perspective of British history, establishment could in its more restrictive and early form mean a state monopoly for a single denomination, but it can also be squared with a much more tolerant system that protects religious freedom for minorities while maintaining the formal establishment of a state church.

■ OTHER INSIGHTS SUGGESTED BY THE ANALYTIC FRAMEWORK

Besides identifying and plotting a range of different types of religion-state regimes, the schematization suggested by the identification continuum loop is helpful in bringing out a number of other points about religion-state relations. First, it is important to remember that to the extent actual religion-state systems correspond to a particular type or pattern of regime, the resulting system is not static, but represents a temporary equilibrium point reached as a political response to a variety of competing religious, cultural and political pressures. We live in a highly interconnected world, and people living in one system are very aware of other organizational models, and the implications—both positive and negative—for their co-religionists and others living elsewhere. The identification continuum provides a kind of roadmap to the range of available options. One can also map the range of effective discourse in different societies. For example, the range of debate in U.S. society is essentially between accommodationists and separationists. The debate in a number of countries with established churches has been whether to disestablish. Sweden did so in 2000, and Norway is likely to do so in the near future. However, the shift is toward a cooperationist system, with substantial residual aid going to the dominant religions, not to a separationist regime. In some cases, commitment to a particular type of regime may frame debates in other ways. Thus, in separationist France, substantial aid in fact flows to major religions, both in subsidizing church structures and in financing religious education. However, this economic support is rationalized as secular support for historic monuments (only older churches receive the support) or as support for the secular side of education in religious schools. Reflection on the patterns suggests both the types of arguments that are likely to be effective in public discourse and the way that religion-state interactions may be conceptualized.

Second, while there are important differences between religious freedom and religious equality (e.g., one can imagine a society in which everyone is treated equally in that all are allowed no religious freedom), the general trend is that increasing equality and increasing freedom of religion go together. The actual ways that freedom and equality are balanced and optimized can be quite intricate. While the optimal balances are likely to vary across societies, however, they are likely as a general rule to be found toward the right end of the identification continuum loop.

Third, as suggested by the arrow at the far right of the diagram, differing types of free regimes may reflect differing conceptions of freedom. Cooperationist regimes reflect a positive conception of freedom, in that they assume that the State should help actualize the conditions of freedom, such as by providing funding or providing facilities for religious activities. Separationist regimes, in contrast, assume a negative conception of freedom according to which religious freedom is maximized by minimizing state involvement.

Fourth, different regime types among the cooperationists reflect differing assumptions about the neutrality of the State. One model of neutrality is State inaction. A second model is neutrality as the impartiality of an unbiased umpire. As applied to religious matters, this model requires that the State act in formally neutral and religion-blind ways. A third model views the State as the monitor of an open forum. The state in this model can impose time, place, and manner restrictions on the marketplace of ideas, and can impose certain constraints to avoid violence and fraud; but otherwise the State plays a minimalist role. The first three models support varying versions of separationism. A fourth model of neutrality calls for substantive equal treatment. That is, the basic principle is that similarly situated individuals should be treated equally, but substantive differences of position should be taken into account, and conscientious beliefs are relevant differences that should be accommodated. This model of neutrality correlates with the principles of an accommodationist regime. A fifth model is a "second generation rights" version of the fourth. That is, it views actualization of substantive rights as an affirmative or positive obligation of the State, and thus supports cooperationist regimes. Most credible religion-state regimes that are sensitive to human rights concerns inhabit a range somewhere in the neutralist zone, stretching from cooperation to separation and corresponding to at least one of the foregoing conceptions of neutrality.

■ CONCLUSIONS

Comparative study of the world's legal systems discloses a wide variety of types or patterns of religion-state systems over time and across cultures. These can best be conceptualized along a continuum stretching from positive to negative identification of the State with religion. A rough sense of alignment of these varied systems with the protection of religious liberty is suggested by the loop diagram, which suggests that extreme positive or negative identification of state and religion is most likely to lead to oppression, whereas the middle range of systems stretching from cooperationist through accommodationist to separationist regimes are most likely to optimize freedom of religion or belief. This range corresponds with the notion of secularity, understood as a framework for respecting and including adherents of a wide variety of belief systems. In contrast, secularism understood as an ideology seems less likely to have the same result. Historically, both notions have coexisted under the same label. The appeal of secularism as an ideology trades on the power of secularity as a neutral framework to make ordered life possible in a highly pluralized world. But secularism as ideology is just one more belief system that needs to be accommodated within the framework of the State. Too often, the common verbal label has masked the fact that secularism as ideology cannot do the work that we need secularity as neutral framework to perform.

■ NOTES

1 See Jeroen Temperman, *State-Religion Relationships and Human Rights Law: Towards a Right to Religiously Neutral Governance* (Leiden: Martinus Nijhoff Publishers, 2010).

2 W. Cole Durham, Jr., "Perspectives on Religious Liberty: A Comparative Framework," in *Religious Human Rights in Global Perspective,* eds. Johan D. van der Vyver and John Witte, Jr. (The Hague: Martinus Nijhof Publishers, 1996) 1–44; W. Cole Durham, Jr. and Brett G. Scharffs, *Law and Religion: National, International and Comparative Perspectives* (Austin, TX: Aspen Publishers, Wolters Kluwer Law & Business, 2010) 113–122.

3 I am indebted for this initial conceptualization of the identification loop to George R. Ryskamp, "The Spanish Experience in Church-State Relations: A Comparative Study of the Interrelationship Between Church-State Identification and Religious Liberty," *Brigham Young University Law Review* (1980) 616–653.

4 E. Kenneth Stegeby, "An Analysis of the Impending Disestablishment of the Church of Sweden," *Brigham Young University Law Review* (1999): 703–67.

5 Ryskamp, "The Spanish Experience," 620–34.

6 For a much more detailed effort to categorize the world's legal systems in accordance with a typology that resembles closely on that suggested here, see Temperman, 11–145.

7 New Fundamental Law of the State of the Vatican City (2000), Art. 1.

8 Temperman, *State-Religion Relationships and Human Rights Law,* 18.

9 Ibid., 19–21, 29–30, 39–41, 43.

10 Nepal House of Representatives Proclamation, sec. 5, par. 8 (18 May 2006) (declaring Nepal a secular state); Nepal Interim Constitution, Art. 4 (2007); see Temperman, *State-Religion Relationships and Human Rights Law,* 30.

11 Bhutan Constitution, Art. 3 (2008); see Temperman, *State-Religion Relationships and Human Rights Law,* 41.

12 Stahnke, Tad and Robert C. Blitt, "The Religion-State Relationship and the Right to Freedom of Religion or Belief: A Comparative Textual Analysis of the Constitutions of Predominantly Muslim Countries," *Georgetown Journal of International Law* 36 (2005) 955; Temperman, 21, 24.

13 See Temperman, *State-Religion Relationships and Human Rights Law,* 49–55 and Stahnke and Blitt, "The Religion-State Relationship and the Right to Freedom of Religion or Belief," 958–961.

14 Temperman, *State-Religion Relationships and Human Rights Law,* 55–61.

15 Ibid., 61–63.

16 Ibid. 45–46.

17 Ibid., 36–37; 46–47.

18 Ibid., 39; Stahnke and Blitt, "The Religion-State Relationship and the Right to Freedom of Religion or Belief," 955.

19 Ibid., 44, 47–48.

20 *Refah Partisi (The Welfare Party) v. Turkey* (Application Nos. 41340/98, 41342/98, 41343/93 and 41344/98, ECtHR, February 13, 2003), sec. 119.

21 See Temperman, *State-Religion Relationships and Human Rights Law,* 27, 193–94.

22 Ibid., 186–90; Abdullahi Ahmed An-Na'im, *Islam and the Secular State: Negotiating the Future of Sharia* (Cambridge: Harvard University Press, 2008) 32–33, 128–37.

23 See An-Na'im, *Islam and the Secular State* 145–47, 158–81; Tahir Mahmood, "Religion and the Secular State: Indian Perspective," in *Religion and the Secular State: National Reports*, Interim Edition issued for the Occasion of the XVIIIth International Congress of Comparative Law, eds. Javier Martinez-Torrón and W. Cole Durham, Jr. (Provo, UT: International Center for Law and Religion Studies, 2010) 387, 388.

24 Ibid., 66–67.

25 Constitution of Poland (1997), Preamble.

26 Constitution of the Republic of the Fiji Islands (1998), Preamble.

27 Constitution of Georgia (1995), Art. 9.

28 Russian Law on the Freedom of Conscience and Religious Associations, No. 125-FZ (1997), Preamble.

29 Constitution of the Democratic Republic of East Timor (2002), Art. 11.

30 Constitution of the Republic of Paraguay (1992), Arts. 24, 82.

31 See, e.g., Constitution of the Republic of Panama (1972), Art. 35 ("Catholic religion is practiced by the majority of Panamanians"); Law of Mongolia on the Relationship between the State and Religious Institutions of 11 November 1993, Art. 4 (the state "shall accept the predominant status of Buddhism in Mongolia in order to respect the historical traditions of harmony and civilization of the people of Mongolia").

32 Temperman, *State-Religion Relationships and Human Rights Law* 77–86.

33 Ibid., 87–88.

34 Matti Kotiranta, "Religion and the Secular State in Finland," in *Religion and the Secular State*, 273, 283–85.

35 The preamble to Russia's 1997 on Freedom of Conscience and Religious Associations, No. 125-FZ, gives special prominence to traditional Russian religions. Kazakhstan has sponsored a series of conferences in recent years focused on traditional religions. Regarding Lithuania, see Lithuanian Law on Religious Communities and Associations, No 89-1985, as amended by Law No. VIII-394 of July 2, 1997 and by Law No. VIII-1677 of May 11, 2000, which has special provisions for traditional religions in its Article 5 on "Traditional Religious Communities and Associations." Similarly, Romania recognizes 18 religious communities as denominations, and confers lower status on others. Law 489/2006 on the Freedom of Religion and the General Status of Denominations (2007).

36 W. Cole Durham, Jr., "Facilitating Freedom of Religion or Belief Through Religious Association Laws," in *Facilitating Freedom of Religion or Belief: A Deskbook*, eds. Tore Lindholm, W. Cole Durham, Jr. and Bahia Tahzib-Lie (Leiden: Martinus Nijhoff Publishers, 2004), 321, 329–30.

37 See generally Gerhard Robbers, "Germany", in *State and Church in the European Union*, 2nd ed., ed. Gerhard Robbers (Baden-Baden, Germany: Nomos Verlagsgesellschaft, 2005).

38 See Durham and Scharffs, *Law and Religion*, 205–06, 234.

39 See W. Cole Durham, Jr. and Robert T. Smith, "Religion and the State in the United States at the Turn of the Twenty-First Century," in *Law and Religion in the 21st Century: Relations Between States and Religious Communities*, eds. Silvio Ferrari and Rinaldo Cristofori, (Farnham, U.K.: Ashgate, 2010) 79–110; see William Bassett, W. Cole Durham, Jr. and Robert T. Smith, *Religious Organizations and the Law* (Eagan, Minnesota: Thomson West, 2009) sec. 2:58.

40 Durham and Scharffs, *Law and Religion*, 231–43, 383–89, 429–34. Relevant cases of the European Court of Human Rights are collected at www.strasbourgconsortium.org.

41 See Temperman, *State-Religion Relationships and Human Rights Law*, 121.

42 This is the view associated with Roger Williams. See generally, Mark DeWolfe Howe, *The Garden and the Wilderness: Religion and Government in American Constitutional History* (Chicago: University of Chicago Press, 1965).

43 This is the view associated with a number of early American figures, including John Adams and John Jay. See, e.g., John Witte, Jr., *Religion and the American Constitutional Experiment: Essential Rights and Liberties,* 2nd ed. (Boulder, CO: Westview Press, 2005), 54.

44 See, e.g., Jean Baubérot, ed., *La Laïcité: Evolution et Enjeux* (Paris: La Documentation Française, 1996); Jean Baubérot, *Histoire de la Laïcité Française* (Paris: PUF, 2000); T. Jeremy Gunn, "Under God but not the Scarf: The Founding Myths of Religious Freedom in the United States and *Laïcité* in France," *Journal of Church and State* 46 (2004) 7–24; Guy Haarscher, *La Laïcité* (Paris: PUF, 1996).

45 Temperman, *State-Religion Relationships and Human Rights Law,* 113–14.

46 Ibid., 139–145; Eric R. Carlson, "China's New Regulations on Religion: A Small Step, Not a Great Leap Forward," *Brigham Young University Law Review* (2005) 747, 749–57; Brett G. Scharffs and W. Cole Durham, Jr., "Foreword," in Kim-Kwong Chan and Eric R. Carlson, *Religious Freedom in China: Policy, Administration, and Regulation: A Research Handbook* (Santa Barbara: Institute for the Study of American Religion; Hong Kong: Hong Kong Institute for Culture, Commerce and Religion, 2005) viii–xi.

47 See, e.g., Ziya Meral, *Prospects for Turkey* (London: Legatum Institute, 2010).

48 See Javier Martinez-Torrón and W. Cole Durham, Jr., "General Report," in *Religion and the Secular State,* 3, 5–6, 12–14, 17–18, 29, 34–36, 45–49, 55–56.

49 José Woehrling and Rosalie Jukier, "Religion and the Secular State in Canada," in *Religion and the Secular State,* 183, 185, drawing on Gérard Bouchard and Charles Taylor, *Building the Future: A Time for Reconciliation* (Quebec City: Government of Quebec, 2008), 135, online: http://www.accommodements.qc.ca/documentation/rapports/rapport-final-integral-en.pdf.

■ RECOMMENDED READING

An-Na'im, Abdullahi Ahmed. *Islam and the Secular State: Negotiating the Future of Sharia* (Cambridge: Harvard University Press, 2008)

Durham, W. Cole, Jr. "Perspectives on Religious Liberty: A Comparative Framework," in *Religious Human Rights in Global Perspective,* eds. Johan D. van der Vyver and John Witte, Jr. (The Hague: Martinus Nijhof Publishers, 1996) 1–44

Durham, W. Cole, Jr. and Silvio Ferrari, eds., *Laws on Religion and the State in Post-Communist Europe* (Leuven: Peeters, 2004)

Durham, W. Cole, Jr. and Brett G. Scharffs, *Law and Religion: National, International and Comparative Perspectives* (Austin: Aspen Publishers, Wolters Kluwer Law & Business, 2010)

Ferrari, Silvio and W. Cole Durham, Jr., eds., *Law and Religion in Post-Communist Europe* (Leuven: Peeters, 2003)

Jackson, Vicki C. and Mark Tushnet. *Comparative Constitutional Law,* 2nd ed. (New York: Foundation Press, Thomson-West, 2006) 1364–1467

Lindholm, Tore, W. Cole Durham, Jr., and, Bahia Tahzib-Lie, eds., *Facilitating Freedom of Religion or Belief: A Deskbook* (Leiden: Martinus Nijhoff Publishers, 2004)

Martinez-Torrón, Javier and W. Cole Durham, Jr., eds., *Religion and the Secular State: National Reports,* Interim Edition issued for the Occasion of the XVIIIth International

Congress of Comparative Law (Provo, Utah: International Center for Law and Religion Studies, 2010), *available at* http://www.iclrs.org/index.php?blurb_id=975

Rivers, Julian. *The Law of Organized Religions: Between Establishment and Secularism* (Oxford: Oxford University Press, 2010)

Rehman, Javaid and Susan Carolyn Breau, eds., *Religion, Human Rights and International Law: A Critical Examination of Islamic State Practices* (2007)

Robbers, Gerhard ed. *State and Church in the European Union.* 2nd ed. (Baden-Baden, Germany: Nomos Verlagsgesellschaft, 2005)

Stahnke, Tad and Robert C. Blitt. "The Religion-State Relationship and the Right to Freedom of Religion or Belief: A Comparative Textual Analysis of the Constitutions of Predominantly Muslim Countries." *Georgetown Journal of International Law* 36 (2005) 947–1078

Temperman, Jeroen. *State-Religion Relationships and Human Rights Law: Towards a Right to Religiously Neutral Governance* (Leiden: Martinus Nijhoff Publishers, 2010)

INDEX

abolitionist states, 370
Abou el-Fadl, Khaled, 65, 69, 298
Abshar-Abdallah, Ulil, 65
absolute freedom of belief, 257–59
Abu-Nimer, Mohammed, 359
accommodationist regimes, 367–68
Act of Toleration (1689), 158
acultural beings, 90
adversariality, 114–16
Afghanistan, 3
Afkhami, Mahnaz, 298
agapism, 46–48
agent-dimension of moral order, 50
Ahdar, Rex, 23
Ahmadi Muslims, 351
Ahmed, Leila, 65, 69, 295, 298
Ahmed, Rafiuddin, 351
Ali, Kecia, 65
Ali, Shaheen Sardar, 65, 70
alimony, 284–85, 291–92
Alito, Samuel, 161
Alston, Philip, 329
Ambrose of Milan, 51–52
American Declaration on the Rights of
  Indigenous Peoples, 124
Ames, Roger, 90, 101
Amor, Abdelfattah, 187, 230
The Analects, 87–88
anatman, 109–10
Anaya, James, 133, 253
Andersen, Svend, 329
Anderson, Alan, 344
Angle, Stephen C., 102
animal rights, 32, 46, 110–11, 338–42
An-Na'im, Abdullahi, 23, 70, 136, 151,
  298, 377
anthropocentrism, 338–41
Anwar, Zainah, 289
Appleby, R. Scott, 23, 359
Aquinas, Thomas, 49, 155, 324
arbitrary force, 144–45, 146, 147
Arieh Hollis Waldman v. Canada, 181
Ariyaratne, A.T., 111
Arnardottir, Oddny, 315
Asad, Talal, 136, 147
"Asian values" debate, 101n28, 103,
  105–6, 114
asocial beings, 90
assimilation, of indigenous people, 120–25
association, freedom of
  autonomy of religious communities and,
    227–29
  conclusions on, 231
  international laws on, 220–22
  introduction to, 218–19
  reach and limits of, 222–25
  regulation of, 225–27
  for sects, cults, and new religions,
    230–31
atman Brahman, 83
Aung San Suu Kyi, 103, 105–6
Australia
  freedom of expression and, 192–93
  indigenous assimilation in, 121
autonomy
  Confucianism and, 90–93
  conscience and, 163–64
  of religious communities, 227–29
  right to, 50
ter Avest, K.H. (Inda), 314

Baderin, Mashood A., 70
Baer, Richard A., Jr., 187
Bamat, Tom, 359
Banchoff, Thomas, 359
Barnett, Barbara, 23, 151
basic rights, 139, 142, 146
Basil of Caesarea, 51–52
Bauer, Joanne R., 118
Bauer, Joseph, 23
Bauman, Whitney, 344
Baxi, Upendra, 72, 75, 76–77, 82, 85
Bayle, Pierre, 156
Beiner, Ronald, 164
Bell, Daniel A., 23, 101n28, 102, 118
benevolence, 94–95
Benhabib, Seyla, 298
Berman, N., 253

Bharatiya Janata Party (BJP), 349–50, 356n19
Bhargava, Rajeev, 85
Van Bijsterveld, Sophie, 211, 212, 217
biopiracy, 125
birth control, 286–87
Blair, Tony, 294
Blitt, Robert C., 377
bloc equality, 208, 210
Bonello, Judge, 311
Bosnia, 352
boundaries, land distribution and, 98–99
Bowen, John Richard, 298
Boyle, Michael, 344
Brahmins, 77, 79
Brass, Paul, 359
Breau, Susan Carolyn, 377
Brinig, Margaret F., 314
Brosius, Peter, 129–30, 133
Broyde, Michael J., 40
Bucar, Elizabeth M., 23, 151
Buddhism
 concerns over human rights in, 109–16
 conclusions on, 116
 introduction to, 103–6
 justification of human rights in, 106–9
 overview of human rights and, 16–17
 right to peace and, 352
Burma, 103, 105–6, 112
burqas, 190, 294, 321. *See also* headscarves

Cairo Declaration on Human Rights (Cairo Declaration) (1990), 13
Cambodia, 104–5, 115
Cambodian Institute of Human Rights, 104
Canada, 4, 247
Canadian Supreme Court, 270
Cane, Peter, 23, 85
Carfagna, Mara, 190
Carper, James C., 187
Casini, Pier, 309–10
Cassese, Antonio, 253
Cassin, René, 5, 143
caste system, 77, 79, 80
Catholic Church, 12, 274, 324–25
Cha'are Shalom ve Tsedek, 229
Chamarik, Saneh, 108–9, 118
Chan, Joseph C.W., 102
Chang, Peng-chun, 5
changing religions, right to, 171–72
Chen, Albert, 102
children's rights
 application of, 308–11
 education and, 180–81, 182, 183, 195–96, 319–20
 emergence of, 301–3
 introduction to, 299–301
 medical treatment and, 245, 318–19
 religious, 9, 303–5
 and religious development, 305–7
"chilling effect" of legislation, 193
China, 103–4, 114–15
Chipko movement, 330–31
choice, freedom of
 to change religion, 171–72
 conclusions on, 184–85
 discrimination and, 181–84
 distinctive features of, 170–71
 freedom from coercion and, 172–74
 introduction to, 170
 and manifestation of religion, 175–80
 of parents regarding children's education, 180–81
Christian Education, South Africa v. Minister of Education, 248–49
Christianity
 agapism and, 46–48
 Church Fathers and natural human rights, 50–52
 environmental rights and, 341
 introduction to, 42–43
 natural human rights in Scripture, 52–54
 natural rights and, 43–46
 possessive individualism and, 48–50
 similarities with Judaism and Islam, 16
Christoffersen, Lisbet, 329
Chrysostom, John, 51–52
Church Fathers, 50–52
Church of Jesus Christ of Latter-day Saints (Mormons), 257
civic reason, 67, 71
civil freedom, 101n29
civil law, 18, 37–38
civil rights, 91, 97–98, 99, 101n28
clothing
 freedom of choice and, 174
 freedom of expression and, 188–91, 197

limitations to religious manifestation and, 262, 264–65
self-determination and, 236–37
welfare rights and, 318, 320–21, 327n29
women's rights and, 292–96
Cobo, José Martinez, 132n4, 133
coercion in religious choice, freedom from, 172–74, 176–78
Cohen, Hermann, 40
Cohn, Haim H., 40
collective group right, 243
colonialism, 78–79, 251n21
commandments
given to humankind, 30–31, 32
given to Israel, 33
of neighbor-love, 34–36, 46–47
Commission on Human Rights, 5–6, 193
common law, 18–19
communities of religion, 213–15, 227–29. *See also* association, freedom of; sphere sovereignty
community-individual relations, 37–39
"compelling interest" test, 161, 162
Conaghan, Joanna, 85
Concluding Document of the Vienna Follow-Up Meeting of Representatives of the Participating States of the Conference on Security and Cooperation in Europe (Vienna Concluding Document) (1989), 7, 10–11, 221–22
"confessional state," 156
conflict resolution, 95–97
Confucianism
conclusions on, 99
incompatibility argument and, 89–93
introduction to, 87–89
overview of human rights and, 16–17
value and function of human rights in, 93–99
Confucius, 87–88, 95
conscience, freedom of
conclusions on, 166–67
dissolution of, 163–66
free exercise exemptions and, 159–62
introduction to, 155
as religious toleration, 156–59
"conscience laws," 286–87
conscientious objection, 159–62, 164, 165, 183, 353
consensus, overlapping, 138, 140
constitutional polities, 29
Constitution of the United States. *See also* First Amendment of U.S. Constitution
Free Exercise and Establishment Clauses in, 285, 301
free exercise exemptions and, 160–61
granting clause in, 255
limitations clause in, 257–58, 277–78n17
religious toleration and, 158–59
contraception, 286–87
control regimes, secular, 370
Convention on the Elimination of All Forms of Discrimination Against Women (CEDAW) (1979), 205, 281, 287–88, 290
Convention on the Rights of the Child (CRC) (1990), 9, 302–5, 318–19
Coomaraswamy, Radhika, 298
cooperationist regimes, 367, 373
Copenhagen Meeting of Representatives of the Participating States of the Conference on Security and Cooperation in Europe (Copenhagen Document) (1990), 9, 221, 222
Correlatives, Principle of, 43–44, 52
Council of Europe's Framework Convention for the Protection of National Minorities, 244
Covenant of the League of Nations (1920) (Article 22), 122
Coward, Harold, 359
cows, 81
criminal law, Jewish, 37–38
Criminal Procedure Code (India), 284–85
crucifixes, 197–98, 308–11
cults, 230–31
culture, women's rights and, 281–82
Cumper, Peter, 202

Dalacoura, Katerina, 70
Dalai Lama, 106, 111, 112–13, 114, 118
Danial Latifi v. Union of India, 291–92
Darrow, Clarence, 276n13
DeBary, William Theodore, 23
Declaration of the Rights of Man and Citizen (1789), 255

Declaration on the Elimination of All Forms of Intolerance and Discrimination Based on Religion or Belief (Declaration on Religion) (1981)
 autonomy of religious communities and, 229
 freedom of association and, 220–21
 freedom of religious choice and, 170, 171–72, 181–82
 non-discrimination and, 205
 rights enumerated under, 8–10
 self-determination and, 239, 243–44
"Declaration on Religious Liberty, 42
Declaration on the Right of Peoples to Peace (1984), 247–48
Declaration on the Rights of Indigenous Peoples (2007), 11–12, 124, 237, 246–47
defamation of religion, 193–95
democracy, xiii
dependency, human rights, 60
deprivation, of poor, 51
derogation, of religious rights, 171, 266n4
Dhamma, Ven. U. Rewata, 112
dharma, 82, 109
Dickson, B., 187
Dignitatis Humanae Personae, 12, 325
dignity, 94–95, 107, 155, 324–25. *See also* environmental rights
Dinstein, Yoram, 242–43, 253
discrimination. *See also* non-discrimination
 Cairo Declaration and, 13
 children's education and, 180–81
 Declaration on Religion and, 9–10
 defined, 205
 equal rights and protection against, 323–24
 freedom of expression and, 192
 freedom of religious choice and, 181–84
 right to labor and, 321–22
 self-determination and, 236–37
 women's rights and, 282–83
divine rights, 27–28, 30–39
divorce, 284–85, 291–92
Copenhagen Meeting of Representatives of the Participating States of the Conference on the Human Dimension of the Conference on Security and Co-operation in Europe. *See* Copenhagen Document.
domestic rights, 29
dominion, of humans, 31–32
Doniger, Wendy, 85
Donnelly, Jack, 112, 114
Don-Yehiya, Eliezer, 352
Dreisbach, Daniel, 169
Dreyer, Jaco S., 24
dual jurisdiction rationale, 157–58
Durham, W. Cole, Jr., 23, 226, 234, 329, 377
Dusche, Michael, 85
duties
 in relational spheres, 30–39
 rights and, 28–30, 43–44, 48, 82

Earth Charter, 333
ecclesiastical exception, 285–86
ecojustice, 332
economic rights, 97–98, 99
Edict of Nantes (1598), 158
education, 174, 180–83, 195–96, 319–21
Edwards, Paul, 276n13
E.E.O.C. v. Catholic University of America, 286
election, 35
Elon, Menachem, 40
Emerson, R., 253
Employment Division v. Smith, 127, 161
endorsed religions, 366
Engaged Buddhists, 103, 111
Engineer, Asghar Ali, 65, 70
Enlightenment, ix, 18, 42
enlightenmentability, 107, 109
environmental rights
 for animals and nature, 46, 338–42
 Buddhism and, 111
 conclusions on, 342–43
 environmental degradation and human dignity and, 331–35
 of future generations, 337–38
 of indigenous people, 335–37
 introduction to, 330–31
 Jewish perspective on, 32
equality
 Buddhism and, 108
 conclusions on, 215
 conscience and, 164–66
 freedom of religion and, 210–15
 Hinduism and, 79
 introduction to, 204

legal differentiations and, 245–46
McCrudden on, 208–10
non-discrimination and, 204–5, 207–8
women's rights and, 190–91, 206–7
Equality Without Reservations campaign, 290–91
Ertürk, Yakin, 289, 298
Esack, Farid, 65
established religions, 364–65
Establishment Clause, 285, 301
European Convention on Human Rights (ECHR) (1953), 258, 259–62
European Court of Human Rights, 147–48, 175–76, 191, 196–98
Evans, Carolyn, 23, 151, 202, 268
Evans, Malcolm, 23, 136–37, 147, 151, 202, 234, 268
expression, freedom of. *See also* clothing; manifestation of religion
and legislation, 193
clothing and symbols, 188–91
conclusions on, 198–99
hate speech and defamation of religion, 192–95
introduction to, 188
prayer and religious education, 195–96
symbols in public spaces, 196–98

Failinger, Marie, 164
family, 325–26
Family Law Code, 288–90
famines, 97–99
fascism, 143–45, 146, 147, 299, 309
Feinberg, Joel, 94, 102
Feldman, Noah, 165, 169
female genital mutilation, 289, 319, 324
Ferrari, Silvio, 223, 234, 377
Fineman, Martha Albertson, 314
Finland, 121
First Amendment of U.S. Constitution, 158–61, 241, 257, 285–86, 301
Five Lay Precepts, 107–8
Flowers, Ronald D., 234
force, arbitrary, 144–45, 146, 147
formal equality, 207
Framework Convention for the Protection of National Minorities (1995), 244
France, 229, 237, 292–93, 294, 373
Francis Hopu and Tepoaitu Bessert v. France, 126
Fredman, Sandra, 207, 208, 217
freedom rights, 6–7, 90–92, 108–9, 317–18
Free Exercise Clause, 285, 301
free exercise exemptions, 159–62, 164, 165, 183, 353
Friedlander, Robert, 253
Fundamental Law (1979), 350
fundamental questions, 270–71, 276nn7,9,10, 277n14
"fundamental" religious rights, 170–71
future generations, environmental rights of, 337–38

Gallagher, Anne, 329
Gambia, 289
Gandhi, Mahatma, 60–61
Garvey, John, 160, 253
Gelmini, Maria Stella, 198
gender equality, 190–91, 206–7, 321–22. *See also* women's rights
genocide, by ecological diminishment, 335–36
gentiles, Jewish relations with, 37
ger toshav, 36
Ghanea, Nazila, 23, 217
Glendon, Mary Ann, 143
globalization, 82
global warming, 335–36
God
children's concepts of, 306–7
conscience and, 164
God-human relations, 30–34
justification by, 53–54
rights of, 52
Goodman, Lenn E., 40
Goodman, Ryan, 329
government
interests, 272–74
responsibility of, 98–99
granting clauses, 254–55
Greco-Bulgarian Communities Case (1930), 242
Greenawalt, Kent, 169
Griffin, James, 97
Grim, John, 345
Grundgesetz (1949), 255
gui, 94–95

"Guidelines for the Review of Legislation Pertaining to Religion or Belief," 225
guilt, 44, 50
Gujarat riots, 73, 80, 349, 357n21
Gunn, T. Jeremy, 217, 268, 280
Gysi, Gregor, 279n27

Hackett, Rosalind I.J., 23
Hall, Kermit, 169
Hamburger, Philip, 160
Han Confucianism, 88
Hare, Ivan, 202
Harris, Paul L., 314
Hassan, Riffat, 65
hate speech, 192–95
headscarves
  freedom of choice and, 174
  freedom of expression and, 189–91
  limitations to religious manifestation and, 262, 264–65
  self-determination and, 236
  welfare rights and, 320–21, 327n29
  women's rights and, 292–95
health, public, 260
health care, 245, 318–19
Hebrew jurisprudence, 37–38
Henry IV, 158
Henry VIII, 156
Heschel, Abraham Joshua, 40
hijab. *See* headscarves
Hill, Barry, 345
Hillel the Elder, 35, 36
Hinduism
  conclusions on, 82–83
  and global human rights debates, 77–82
  introduction to, 71–72
  methodologies for pluralism and, 73–77
  overview of human rights and, 16–17
  as plurality of pluralities, 72–73
  right to peace and, 349
hindutva, 77
Hiskes, Richard, 345
Hitler, Adolf, 143–45, 146, 147
Hobbes, Thomas, 42, 49
Hodgkin, Rachel, 314
Hollenbach, David, 359
Holocaust, 143–45, 146, 147
Hoodfar, Homa, 203
Horwitz, Paul, 241, 253
House of Lords (Britain), 228
humanitarian efforts, 177–78
human relations, three spheres of, in Judaism, 30–39
human rights
  approaches to understanding, 93–94
  as concept, 59
  content of, 59
  context of, 59
  defined, 45–46, 58–59
  international framework for, 5–14
  introduction to, 3–5
  in religion, 17–21
  religion in, 14–17
Human Rights Committee, 147–48, 150n22, 162, 175, 182–83, 258
Human Rights Council, 193–94
human rights dependency, 60
human worth, 94–95
Humphrey, John Peters, 6
Hussain, Amir, 65
Husted, Wayne R., 118

Ideh, Julie, 359
identification continuum, 360–62, 372–73
idolatry, 33
Ihara, Craig, 102, 110
ijtihad, 65
Ilaiah, Kancha, 85
imago dei, 53
incompetence rationale, 156–57, 158
India
  colonial period in, 78–79
  Gujarat riots in, 73, 80, 349, 357n21
  Muslim alimony law in, 284–85, 291–92
  right to peace and, 349, 353
  secularism in, 76
Indigenous Knowledge (IK), 125
indigenous people
  assimilation and emergence of, 120–25
  defined, 132n4
  environmental rights of, 335–37
  right of, to self-determination, 11–12, 237, 246–47
Indigenous Religion
  assimilation and, 120–25
  common beliefs and contributions of, 128–30
  introduction to, 119–20

objectification and, 125–28
overview of human rights and, 16–17
public mediation and, 130–31
Indigenous Women's Caucus, 128–29
individualism, 48–50, 82, 92–93, 109–10, 248
individual(s), freedom of religion for, 212–13
institutional group right, 243
intellect, will and, 31–32
interdependency approach to human rights, 317–18
inter-human relations, 34–37
International Convention on the Elimination of All Forms of Racial Discrimination (CERD) (1969), 204–5
International Convention on the Protection of the Rights of All Migrant Workers and Their Families (1990), 205
International Covenant on Civil and Political Rights (ICCPR) (1966)
children's rights and, 302
freedom of association and, 219, 220
freedom of conscience and, 161
freedom of expression and, 191–92, 195
freedom of religious choice and, 170–74, 180
granting clause in, 254–55
incompatibility argument and, 90
indigenous rights and, 123
limitations clause in, 256, 258, 259–62
non-discrimination and, 204
rights enumerated under, 7–8
right to religious and moral freedom in, 269–70
self-determination and, 239
International Covenant on Economic, Social, and Cultural Rights (ICESCR), 90, 204, 302, 318–20
international human rights framework, 5–14
International Labour Organization Convention Concerning Indigenous and Tribal Peoples in Independent Countries (C169), 121, 123–24
International Labour Organization Convention No. 107, 122
Islam
alimony law under, 284–85, 291–92
conclusions on, 66–68
conversion from, 267n11
defamation of religion and, 193–94
discourse on human rights and, 62–66
environmental protection under, 332
freedom of expression and, 188–91
hate speech and, 192–93
Hinduism and, 77–78
human rights mediation and, 58–62
introduction to, 56–58
New Enlightenment and, 288–91
right to peace and, 349–50, 353–54
similarities with Judaism and Christianity, 16
statistics on, 68n1
Islamic Declaration. *See* Universal Islamic Declaration of Human Rights.
Islamists, 63–65
Israel
commandments given to, 33
election of, 35
right to peace and, 351
Italy, 197–98, 299–300, 308–11
ius civile, 18
ius gentium, 18–19
ius naturale, 18, 19
Ivanova v. Bulgaria, 174

Jack, H. A., 187
Jackson, Vicki C., 377
Jahangir, Asma, 226
Jamaat-i-Islami, 351
Jefferson, Thomas, 158
Jeffreys, Derek, 109–10
Jellinek, Georg, 15
Jenkins, Willis, 345
Jewish Central Consistory, 229
Jewish Free School, 228
John Paul II, 271, 277n14, 278n20
Johnson, Carl N., 314
Jones, Peter, 217
Joseph et al. *v. Sri Lanka*, 175
Judaism
rights and duties in, 28–30
rights-talk in, 27–28
right to peace and, 351–52
similarities with Christianity and Islam, 16
three spheres of human relations in, 30–39

Junger, Peter, 110
justice, 46–48, 92–93, 98–99
justification, 53–54, 105

Kalscheur, Gregory A., 280
Kambakhsh, Sayed Perwiz, 3
Kaplan, Benjamin J., 169
karma, 83
Karzai, Hamid, 3
Kedroff v. St. Nicholas Cathedral, 234n40, 241–42
Keown, Damien, 107–8, 118
Kierkegaard, Sören, 55
King, Sallie B., 118
kirpan, 190
Kokkinakis v. Greece, 176, 179
Konvitz, Milton R., 27, 40
Krishnaswami, Arcot, 151, 206, 214, 217
Ksentini Reports, 332–33

labor, right to, 321–22
laïcité, 223, 292, 293, 369, 372
land distribution, 98–99
Langer, Lorenz, 203
Langlaude, Sylvie, 203, 304, 305, 314
Larissis and Others v. Greece, 177
Lautsi v. Italy, 197–98, 308–11
Laycock, Douglas, 203
Leckie, Scott, 329
Lee Kuan Yew, 103
legal personality, 226–27
legal pluralism, 71–77
legal rights, versus moral rights, 29, 35
Leigh, Ian, 23
Lemkin, Raphael, 124
Lenin, V.I., 238
Leo XIII, Pope, 324
Lerner, Natan, 23, 151, 177, 187, 203, 234, 329
Levering, Matthew, 41
Levinas, Emmanuel, 41
limitations clauses
  absolute freedom of belief and, 257–59, 277–78n17
  analysis of, 259–62
  introduction to, 254
  meaning of, 255–57
  proportionality in, analysis, 262–66
Lindholm, Tore, 23, 152, 377
Lipner, Julius, 85
Liskofsky, Sidney, 187
litigation, 95–97
Little, David, 57, 152, 359
Locke, John, 42, 49, 146, 156–58, 160, 166, 273–74, 280
Luther, Martin, 156, 164

Machiavelli, Niccolo, 279n27
MacKinnon, Catherine A., 298
MacNaughton, Gillian, 208, 210, 217
Madison, James, 157, 160, 166
Maha Ghosananda, 104–5
Mahmoud, Saba, 298
Maimonides, 33
Malherbe, E.F.J., 240
Malik, Charles, 6, 140
"Manhattan Declaration," 162
manifestation of religion. *See also* clothing; expression, freedom of
  communities of religion and, 213–15
  discrimination and, 181–82
  limitations to, 257–62, 271–72, 277–78n17
  restriction of, 170
  and rights of others, 175–80
Manor, James, 352
Maritain, Jacques, xiii, 6
Marks, Stephen P., 347
marriage, 39n7, 287, 288, 325–26
Marshall, Kathleen, 314
Martens, Judge, 176, 179
Martin, J. Paul, 23, 152
Martin, Nancy M., 23
Martinez-Torrón, Javier, 268, 377
Marty, Martin E., 359
al-Mawdudi, Abu al-Ala, 63–65
Mayans, 129
Mayer, Ann Elizabeth, 70
McConnell, Michael, 160, 169
McCrudden, Christopher, 208–10, 217
McCullough, Michael E., 85
McDonough, Sister, 286
mediation, 59–61, 95–97
medical treatment, 245, 318–19
Mencius, 88, 91–95, 98–99, 102
Menski, Werner, 85
military service. *See* free exercise exemptions

Milosevic, Slobodan, 352
Minerath, Roland, 234
ministerial exception, 285–86
Minorities Declaration, 11
Mir-Hosseini, Ziba, 298
missionary work. *See* proselytism
Modeer, Kjell A., 329
Mohamad, Mahathir, 103
moral courage, 60–61
moral freedom. *See* religious and moral freedom, right to
morality, 115, 144–45
moral law, 36, 37, 38
moral order, 50
moral rights, 29, 35
More, Thomas, 156
Morgan-Foster, Jason, 353
Morocco, 288–90
Moudawana, 288–90
Mukherjee, Mithi, 85
murder, 52–54
Murphy, Andrew R., 169
Murray, John Courtney, 280
Musawah, 288–90
Muslim Women Protection of Rights Upon Divorce Act (MWPRDA), 285, 291–92
Mussolini, Benito, 274
Myanmar, 103, 105–6, 112

Nardin, Terry, 359
Nash, James, 341
Nash, Roderick, 345
National League for Democracy, 103
national security, 260, 267nn14,15
Native American Council of New York City, 128
natural law, 18, 19
Natural Right and History (Strauss), 49
natural rights
  agapism and, 46–47
  Christianity and, 42–43
  Church Fathers and, 50–52
  defined, 43–46
  in Jewish tradition, 27–28
  possessive individualism and, 48–50
  in relational spheres, 30–39
  in Scripture, 52–54
  secular rationale and, 146–47
Navajo Nation v. U.S. Forest Service, 127
negative equality, 208
neighbor-love, commandment of, 34–36, 46–47
Nelken, David, 86
neutrality, 57, 164–65, 373–74
Newell, Peter, 314
New Enlightenment, 282–83, 288–92
new religions, 230–31
New Sovereignty, 283, 284–88
Nichols, Joel A., 24
Niezen, Ronald, 23, 133
non-discrimination. *See also* discrimination
  conclusions on, 215
  equality and, 204–5, 207–10
  freedom of religion and, 210–15
  gender equality and, 206–7
  introduction to, 204
  legal differentiations and, 245–46
non-governmental organizations, 130, 147, 310
nonviolence, 108, 353
Noonan, John T., Jr., 5
normative politics, 75
Norway, 121, 126–27
nose stud, 236–37
Novak, David, 23, 41, 135–36
Novak, William J., 280
Nowak, Manfred, 234
Nussbaum, Martha, 282, 298
Nygren, Anders, 46–47, 55

objectification, of indigenous religious claims, 125–28
obligation, 271
Ockham, William of, 49
Oddie, Geoffrey, 78, 85
O'Donovan, Joan Lockwood, 55
O'Donovan, Katherine, 207
Oh, Irene, 70
Okin, Susan Moller, 281–82
Omvedt, Gail, 85
one-to-one equality, 210
order, public, 260
"original position," 150n26
Örücü, Esin, 86
overlapping consensus, 138, 140

parents
  and children's education, 319–20
  and children's health care, 245, 318–19
  children's religious rights and, 304–5
  religious rights of, 9, 180–81, 182, 183, 195–96
Partsch, Karl Josef, 172, 235
Parvis, Paul, 314
Paul VI, Pope, 280
Payutto, Phra, 109, 113, 115–16, 118
peace, right to
  conclusions on, 354–55
  introduction to, 346
  official declarations on, 347–49
  religion and, 349–54
Penan, 129–30
Penn, William, 156
peoplehood, 91–92, 242–43
People of the Book, 65
peremptory force, of rights, 44
Perera, L.P.N., 107, 118
Permanent Forum on Indigenous Issues, 128–29
Perry, Michael, 23, 135, 152, 280
personality, legal, 226–27
personhood, 91–92, 242–43
Pettiti, Judge, 176
peyote, in indigenous religious practice, 127, 161
Philpott, Daniel, 359
physical integrity, 245, 289, 319
Piaget, Jean, 305–6
Pienaar, Gerrit, 240
Pieterse, J.C., 24
Pillay, Sunali, 236
pluralism, legal, 71, 72–77
plurality of pluralities ("pops"), 71, 72, 74
"political constructivism," 138, 149n11
political independence, and right to self-determination, 246–48
political Islam, 63
political rights, 97–99, 101n28
politics, 73–76
polygamy, 257
positive equality, 208
possessive individualism, 48–50
Pottage, Alain, 134
Pöttering, Hans-Gert, 3
poverty, 51, 98–99
Powers, Gerard F., 359
prayer, in schools, 195–96
Prebish, Charles S., 118
preferred sets of religions, 366
prima facie rights, 44, 45–46
primordialism, 120
Principle of Correlatives, 43–44, 52
privacy, right to, 29
proportionality, in limitations clause analysis, 262–66
proselytism, 78–79, 162, 171, 175–80
public health, 260
public order, 260
public reason
  conclusions on, 145–48
  human rights language and, 138–44
  introduction to, 135–37
  Rawls' theory of, 137–38
public security, 190, 260
public spaces, religious symbols in, 196–98

Qazizada, Abdul Salam, 3
Quebec, 247
questions
  "religious or limit," 273–74
  ultimate, 270–71, 276nn7, 9, 10, 277n14

racism, 251n21, 333–34
Rai, Lal Deosa, 86
Raihon Hudoyberganova v. Uzbekistan, 174
Ramcharan, B.G., 187
Ramsey, Paul, 55
Rankin, Aidan, 86
Rasmussen, Larry L., 345
Rawls, John, 57, 137–42, 150n26, 152, 282
reason. *See* public reason
recipient-dimension of moral order, 50
Reed, Esther, 41
registration, of religious groups, 225–27
Rehman, Javaid, 377
Reid, Charles J., Jr., 42, 55
Reifeld, Helmut, 85
religion
  defining, ix
  in human rights, 14–17
  human rights in, 17–21
  and international human rights framework, 5–14

introduction to, 3–5
in politics, 73–75, 76
religion-state relations
additional insights on, 372–74
attitudinal types in, 370–72
conceptualizing, 360–62
conclusions on, 374
introduction to, 360
types of, structures, 362–70
religious and moral freedom, right to
conclusions on, 274–75
illegitimate government interests under, 272–74
introduction to, 269–72
Religious Corporation Law of New York, 242
religious freedom continuum, 360–62
Religious Freedom Restoration Act (1993), 127
religious institutions, 239–40, 242–43
religious leaders, 92, 181–82
"religious or limit" questions, 273–74
religious status systems, 365–66
religious toleration, 156–59
ren, 94–95
Republic of Serbia, 352
"resident sojourners," 36
responsibilities, versus rights, 111–13
Revaz, Cris R., 315
Richards, David, 164
righteousness, 94–95
rights. *See also* human rights; natural rights
asserting, claims, 94–97
basic, 139, 142, 146
common understanding of, 48–49
defining, ix
and duties, 28–30, 43–44, 48, 82
Jewish definition of, 27–28
versus responsibilities, 111–13
Rivers, Julian, 203, 377
Robbers, Gerhard, 377
Robinson, Zoé, 23
Rogers, Mark, 359
Rolston, Holmes, 341
Roosevelt, Eleanor, 5
Roosevelt, Franklin, 5
Rosemont, Henry, Jr., 89–90, 91, 102
Rosengren, Karl S., 314
Rosenzweig, Franz, 41
rule of law, vii
Runzo, Joseph, 23, 152
Russell, Bertrand, 270–71
Russian Association of Indigenous Peoples of the North (RAIPON), 123

Saamis, 121, 126–27
Sabbath, 33
Sachedina, Abdulaziz Abdulhussein, 70, 152
Sachs, Albie, 248–49
safety, public, 190, 260
"Saffron Revolution," 103
Safi, Omid, 65
Şahin, Leyla, 236–37, 262, 293
Şahin v. Turkey, 174, 264–65
Samdhong Rinpoche, 111
Sardar Ali, Shaheen, 65
Sarkozy, Nicolas, 294
SB v. Denbigh High, 188–89
Scharffs, Brent G., 23, 329, 377
Scheinin, Martin, 235
Schreiter, Robert J., 359
Scripture, natural human rights in, 52–54
Sears, J. T., 187
secession, and right to self-determination, 246–48
Second Vatican Council (1962-1965), 12, 42, 55
sects, 230–31
secular control regimes, 369
secularism, viii, 73–74, 76, 223, 292–93, 371, 374
secularity, 371, 374
security, public, 190, 260
self-defense, 147
self-determination, right to
conclusions on, 248–49
historical perspectives on, 238–39
of indigenous people, 121, 122, 123, 124
introduction to, 236–38
Islam and, 59–61
limitations of, 244–46
overview of, 11–12
right to labor and, 321–22
secession and, 246–48
sphere sovereignty and, 239–44
self-development, 109, 113

Sells, Michael A., 359
Sen, Amartya, 97–98
separationism, 368–69, 372, 373
Serbia, 352
Servetus, Michael, 156
sex equality. *See* gender equality; women's rights
Shah Bano, 284–85
Sharia, 58, 62–67, 287
Sharma, Arvind, 23, 73, 80–82, 86
Sherbert v. Verner (1963), 161, 162
Shrader-Frechette, Kristen, 345
Shun, Kwong-loi, 92, 102
Sidorsky, D., 41
Sikhs, 190
Sim, May, 102
Simpson, Edward, 78, 86
Singer, Peter, 340
Sinhalese Buddhism, 352
Siracusa Principles, 261, 272
skepticism, 74–75
Smith, Gordon S., 359
Smith, Steven D., 169
Smock, David R., 359
social justice, 98–99
social rights, 97–98, 99
social roles, in Confucianism, 91–92
solidarity, right to, 347
Song-Ming Confucianism, 88
Soroush, Abdolkarim, 65
South Africa, 240–41, 245–46, 248–49
speech, freedom of, 13, 192–95
sphere sovereignty, 239–44
Spinoza, Baruch, 156
Sri Lanka, 177–79, 352
stage theory of child development, 305–6
Stahnke, Tad, 23, 152, 377
Stalin, Joseph, 238
starvation, 97–99
state
  association regulation and, 225–27
  autonomy of religious communities and, 227–29
  freedom of religion or belief and, 210–15
  as guarantor of human rights, 16
status-based non-discrimination, 208
Steiner, Henry J., 329
Stephens, Alan, 23
Stone, Christopher, 341, 345
Strauss, Leo, 49, 55
Straw, Jack, 294
Suarez, Francisco, 147
substantive equality, 207, 208
Sulak Sivaraksa, 111–12, 118
Sullivan, D. J., 187
Sunder, Madhavi, 203, 298
sustainability, 332
Sweden, 121
symbols
  freedom of expression and, 188–91, 196–98
  self-determination and, 236–37
  welfare rights and, 318, 320–21
  women's rights and, 292–96
synthetic necessary truth, 43
Szyszczak, Erika, 207

Taha, Ustadh Mahmoud Mohamed, 65–66
Tahzib-Lie, Bahia G., 203, 377
Taylor, Charles, 108
Taylor, Paul M., 24, 152, 235, 268
Taylor, Prudence, 345
Temperman, Jeroen, 377
Ten Commandments, 52–53
ter Avest, K.H. (Inda), 314
Tesfagiorgis, G., 253
theocratic states, 363–64
third-generation rights, 347
Thornberry, Patrick, 134
Tibet, 103–4, 106, 114–15
Tierney, Brian, 42, 55, 169
Tirum, Nicolas Lucas, 129
Tiwald, Justin, 102
Todres, Jonathan, 315
tolerance, 81, 82, 354
toleration, religious, 156–59
Tomuschat, Christian, 224, 235
Torah rights, 27–28, 30–39
totalitarianism, 248
Touray, Dr. Isatou, 289
Traditional Indigenous Knowledge, 125
Traer, Robert, 152
trumping force, of rights, 44
truth claims, 211–12
Tuck, Richard, 42, 55
Tucker, Mary Evelyn, 345

Turkey, 293–94
Tushnet, Mark, 377
Twain, Mark, 155
Twiss, Sumner, 105, 345

ultima facie rights, 44
ultimate questions, 270–71, 276nn7, 9, 10, 277n14
United States. *See also* Constitution of the United States
  children's rights in, 301
  Convention on the Rights of the Child and, 303
  environmental rights and, 333–34
  freedom of conscience and, 162
  medical treatment in, 245
  sphere sovereignty of religious groups in, 241–42
  women's rights in, 285–87
Universal Declaration of Human Rights (UDHR) (1948)
  Confucianism and, 91
  environmental rights and, 331
  freedom of association and, 220, 222–23
  freedom of conscience and, 161
  freedom of religious choice and, 170, 171, 172
  granting clause in, 254
  and international human rights framework, 5–7
  Islam and, 57, 58
  Karel Vasak on, 17–18
  limitations clause in, 256
  non-discrimination and, 204
  right to religious and moral freedom in, 272
  secular rationale and drafters of, 139–46, 147, 150n22
Universal Islamic Declaration of Human Rights (Islamic Declaration) (1981), 12–13
universal responsibility, 112–13
universal rights, 46, 52–54, 59, 75, 76
Unno, Taitetsu, 114, 118
Urso, Maria, 299–300
usul al-fiqh, 62

Van Bijsterveld, Sophie, 211, 212, 217
van der Vyver, Johan D., 24, 253, 268
van Dyke, Vernon, 253
Van ver Ven, Johannes A., 24
Vasak, Karel, 17–18, 347
Vatican Council II, 12, 42, 55
veils. *See* headscarves
Vienna Concluding Document. *See* Concluding Document of the Vienna Follow-Up Meeting of Representatives of the Participating States of the Conference on Security and Cooperation in Europe.
Vietnam War draft, 165
Villey, Michel, 49
violence, 108. *See also* nonviolence; peace, right to
Vischer, Robert K., 169, 280
Viswanathan, Ed, 86
voluntariness/futility rationale, 157, 158, 160

Wadud, Amina, 65
Walden, Raphael, 23
Walkate, J. A., 187
water, 334
Weinstein, James, 202
welfare rights
  conclusions on, 326
  to education, 319–21
  freedom rights and, 317–18
  to health care, 318–19
  introduction to, 316–17
  overview of, 6–7
  protection against discrimination, 323–24
  religious ambiguity in relation to, 324–26
  right to labor, 321–22
"well-field system," 98–99
Wellman, Carl, 347, 354–55
Westen, Peter, 164
will, intellect and, 31–32
Williams, Elisha, 157
Williams, Roger, 146, 156
Willoughby, Brian L.B., 85
Wilson, Woodrow, 238
Witte, John, Jr., 24, 40, 42, 55, 157, 169, 235
Wojcik, Mark E., 315
Wolterstorff, Nicholas, 24, 55, 135, 152

women's rights. *See also* gender equality
conclusions on, 295–96
freedom of expression and, 190–91
introduction to, 281–83
manifestation of religion and, 292–95
New Enlightenment and, 288–92
New Sovereignty and, 284–88
non-discrimination and, 205
Wong, David B., 102
Woodhouse, Barbara Bennett, 315
Woolman, Stuart, 240
World Charter for Nature (1982), 342
worth, of human beings, 94–95, 106–7
Worthington, Karen, 314
wronged, being, 44–45, 50

Xunzi, 88, 92–93, 94, 102

Yamin, Alicia, Ely, 217
Yao, Xinzhong, 102
yeshivot, 351–52
yi, 94–95
Yutzis, Mario, 356n17